The Celtic Latin Tradition of Biblical Style

The
Celtic Latin Tradition
of Biblical Style

D.R. HOWLETT

FOUR COURTS PRESS

This book was set in
10.5 on 12 point Bembo
by Seton Music Graphics Ltd,
Gurtycloona, Bantry, Co. Cork, for
FOUR COURTS PRESS LTD
Kill Lane, Blackrock, Co. Dublin
and, in North America, for
FOUR COURTS PRESS LTD
c/o ISBS,
5804 NE Hassalo Street, Portland, OR 97213.

ISBN 1-85182-143-0

A catalogue record for this book
is available for the British Library.

Printed in Great Britain by Antony Rowe, Ltd., Chippenham, Wilts.

Abbati credenti
Ac comprehendenti
Ac Donato Scotto
Multa me docenti

CONTENTS

PROLOGUE

This book has grown out of an inquiry into the structure of works written in Latin and Old English at the court of King Alfred the Great in Wessex at the end of the ninth century. To account for features in them which seemed odd I examined other Old English verse composed before the end of the ninth century. After finding the same features I examined Anglo-Latin prose and verse from the seventh century onward, then Celtic Latin prose and verse from the fifth century onward, then the Bible in Latin, in Greek, and finally in Hebrew, with which I should have begun. As my knowledge of Celtic Latin texts increased the material would no longer fit as a second chapter of a book about the English tradition. But even with separate discussion the works of Saint Patrick would no longer fit in a second chapter of a book about the Celtic tradition. So three books now appear, in reverse order of discovery and composition, but in correct chronological order, as the *Liber Epistolarum Sancti Patricii Episcopi: The Book of Letters of Saint Patrick the Bishop, The Celtic Latin Tradition of Biblical Style*, and *British Books in Biblical Style*.

In trying to read and understand works of the Celtic Latin tradition I have learned much from colleagues and friends: Dr John Blundell, Dr Pierre Chaplais, the Revd Dr Bill East, Dr Anthony Harvey, Dr Leofranc Holford-Strevens, Dr Dáibhí Ó Cróinín, Dr Andy Orchard, Dr Jacques Paviot, Dr Richard Sharpe, Professor Patrick Sims-Williams, Dr Richard White, and Dr Neil Wright. To critics who have asked not to be named I owe thanks, as their skepticism has driven me to clearer thought, more focused perception, and more precise statement. For encouragement against disheartening hostility to the work I owe much to the Reverend Professor Abbott Conway and Professor Donnchadh Ó Corráin. Dedication of the book to these men is an inadequate token of the deepest affection and the highest respect.

BIBLICAL STYLE

INTRODUCTION

The subject of this book is Biblical style and its influence on Celtic Latin authors from the time of Roman Britain to the Norman Conquest and beyond. Initially the word 'style' is used as defined in the *Oxford English Dictionary* senses 14 and 15: 'those features of literary composition which belong to form and expression rather than to the substance of the thought or matter expressed' and 'a manner of discourse or tone of speaking'.[1] We shall learn first to recognize Biblical style and to see how various writers employ it in Hebrew texts of the Old Testament, then compare Greek and Latin versions to see whether translators recognized and reproduced particular features of the originals. We shall examine texts which consider the Creation, taken as the model for literary composition. We shall examine also some texts by Classical and Late Latin authors who discuss Creation, literary composition, rhythm, and mathematical and musical ratios. Though we shall concentrate at first on 'form and expression' we shall note later ways in which Biblical style influences profoundly 'the substance of the thought or matter expressed'.

THE RULES OF BIBLICAL STYLE

Biblical style is iterative; it consists in stating an idea and then restating it (as in this sentence). One finds Scriptural warrant for such an iterative style in Ecclesiasticus XLII 24:[2]

παντα δισσα εν κατεναντι του ενος
και ουκ εποιησεν ουδεν ελλειπον

rendered in the Vulgate at XLII 25:

---

1 I imply something more like the 'house style' of Oxford University Press as expressed in *Hart's Rules* than like a particular writer's idiosyncratic style.

2 Biblical quotations are taken in Hebrew from *Biblia Hebraica Stuttgartensia*, ed. K. Elliger et al. (Stuttgart 1969–76); in Greek from *Septuaginta*, ed. A. Rahlfs (Stuttgart 1935) and *The Greek New Testament*, ed. K. Aland et al., 3rd edn corr. (Stuttgart 1983); in Latin from *Biblia Sacra iuxta Vulgatam Versionem*, ed. B. Fischer et al. (Stuttgart 1969); and in English from the Revised Standard Version, 2nd edn, with occasional changes of word order to reflect the order of the original texts. Parallel indentations and superscript letters, as well as letters and numbers in the left margin, are intended to show what words and phrases are paired.

omnia duplicia unum contra unum
et non fecit quicquam deesse,

and in English:

all things are twofold, one opposite the other,
and He has made nothing incomplete.

There are three primary patterns of iteration. In the smallest unit of Biblical style, the structure of a single verse, the first and basic pattern is parallelism, a statement followed by a restatement in identical order, as Isaiah 1 10:

         e   d   c   b   a

שִׁמְעוּ דְבַר־יְהוָה קְצִינֵי סְדֹם

        e'   d'   c'   b'   a'

הַאֲזִינוּ תּוֹרַת אֱלֹהֵינוּ עַם עֲמֹרָה:

    a   b   c   d   e
ακουσατε λογον Κυριου αρχοντες Σοδομων.
    a'   b' c' d'   e'
προσεχετε νομον Θεου λαος Γομορρας.

    a   b   c   d   e
audite uerbum Domini principes Sodomorum
       a'   b' c'   d'   e'
percipite auribus legem Dei nostri populus Gomorrae.

    a   b   c   d   e
Hear the word of the Lord, you rulers of Sodom.
      a'   b'   c'   d'   e'
Give ear to the teaching of our God, you people of Gomorrah.

An example in English nursery rhyme is

To market, to market, to buy a fat pig,
  home again, home again, jiggety jig.
To market, to market, to buy a fat hog,
  home again, home again, jiggety jog.

The second but still basic pattern, which also appears in the structure of a single verse, is chiasmus, a statement followed by a restatement in reverse order, as Lamentations 1 1:

    ai   aii
εγενηθη ως χηρα
   bi   bii
πεπληθυμμενη εν εθνεσιν
  b'i   b'ii
αρχουσα εν χωραις
   a'i   a'ii
εγενηθη εις φορον

   aii   ai
הָיְתָה כְּאַלְמָנָה
  bii   bi
רַבָּתִי בַגּוֹיִם
  b'ii   b'i
שָׂרָתִי בַּמְּדִינוֹת
  a'ii   a'i
הָיְתָה לָמַס: ס

   a i   a ii
facta est quasi uidua   a   How like a widow she has become
    b i   b ii
domina gentium   b   she that was great among the nations;
    b'i   b'ii
princeps prouinciarum   b'   she that was a princess among the cities
   a'i   a'ii
facta est sub tributo   a'   has become a vassal.

An example in English nursery rhyme is

As I was going to Saint Ives
   I met a man with seven wives;
      each wife had seven sacks;
         each sack had seven cats;
           each cat had seven kits.
         Kits,
      cats,
    sacks,
  and wives,
how many were going to Saint Ives?

John Henry Newman's hymn is in the same form:

Praise to the Holiest
   in the height
   and in the depth
be praise,
   in all His words
      most wonderful,
     most sure
in all His ways.

Moving on to a larger unit, which extends to several verses, the third pattern combines parallelism and chiasmus, as Amos II 14–6:[3]

וְאָבַד מָנוֹס מִקָּל	aa
וְחָזָק לֹא־יְאַמֵּץ כֹּחוֹ	bb
וְגִבּוֹר לֹא־יְמַלֵּט נַפְשׁוֹ:	cc
וְתֹפֵשׂ הַקֶּשֶׁת לֹא יַעֲמֹד	dd
וְקַל בְּרַגְלָיו לֹא יְמַלֵּט	d' a'
וְרֹכֵב הַסּוּס לֹא־יְמַלֵּט נַפְשׁוֹ:	c' b'
וְאַמִּיץ לִבּוֹ בַּגִּבּוֹרִים	b' c'
עָרוֹם יָנוּס בַּיּוֹם־הַהוּא נְאֻם־יְהוָה: פ	a' d'

a *a*	"And flight shall perish from the swift
b *b*	and the strong shall not retain his strength
c *c*	and the mighty shall not save his life
d *d*	and he who handles the bow shall not stand
d' *a'*	and he who is swift of foot shall not save himself
c' *b'*	and he who rides the horse shall not save his life
b' *c'*	and he who is stout of heart among the mighty
a' *d'*	shall flee away naked in that day," says the Lord.

Note in a and a' the second words מָנוֹס 'flight' and יָנוּס 'he shall flee'; in b the penultimate word יְאַמֵּץ 'strengthen' and in b' the first word וְאַמִּיץ 'and the strong'; in c and c' the identical concluding phrase לֹא־יְמַלֵּט נַפְשׁוֹ 'shall not save his life'; in d and d' the similar concluding phrases לֹא יַעֲמֹד 'shall not stand' and לֹא יְמַלֵּט 'shall not save himself'. This makes a clear and consistent chiasmus. But there is also a parallelism. The last word of *a*, מִקָּל 'from the swift', is echoed by the first word of *a'* וְקַל 'and the swift'. The first word of *c*, וְגִבּוֹר 'and the mighty', is echoed by the last word of *c'*, בַּגִּבּוֹרִים 'among the mighty'.

Here is the Septuagint text of the same verses.

aa	και απολειται φυγη εκ δρομεως
bb	και ο κραταιος ου μη κρατησηι της ισχυος αυτου
cc	και ο μαχητης ου μη σωσηι την ψυχην αυτου
dd	και ο τοξοτης ου μη υποστηι
d' a'	και ο οξυς τοις ποσιν αυτου ου μη διασωθηι
c' b'	ουδε ο ιππευσος ου μη σωσηι την ψυχην αυτου
b' c'	και ευρησει την καρδιαν αυτου εν δυναστειαις
a' d'	ο γυμνος διωξεται εν εκεινηι τηι ημεραι λεγει Κυριος

---

3   Cf. N. W. Lund, *Chiasmus in the New Testament* (Chapel Hill, NC 1942), p. 86.

The chiasmus is partly reproduced. Note, for example, in c and c' the identical concluding phrase ου μη σωσηι την ψυχην αυτου and in d and d' the similar concluding phrases ου μη υποστηι and ου μη διασωθηι. Rahlfs rejected a variant reading of b', ο κραταιος ου μη ευρη, because there is no warrant in the Hebrew text for the negative. The reading does not reflect the original, but it is valuable evidence that some Greek-speaking editor or scribe recognized and tried to improve the chiasmus, making ο κραταιος ου μη ευρη or ευρησει a clearer parallel to ο κραταιος ου μη κρατησηι. The translator of this part of the Septuagint has rendered the chiasmus only imperfectly, and he has not reproduced the parallelism at all.

When we look at the Vulgate, however, we see that Jerome has reproduced both chiasmus and parallelism very well.

a *a* et peribit fuga *a ueloce*
b *b* *et fortis* non obtinebit uirtutem suam
c *c*   *et robustus* non saluabit animam suam
d *d*   et tenens arcum non stabit
d' *d'*   *et uelox* pedibus suis non saluabitur
c' *b'*   et ascensor equi non saluabit animam suam
b' *c'* *et robustus* corde *inter fortes*
a' *d'* nudus fugiet in die illa dicit Dominus.

He balances *fuga* in a with *fugiet* in a', uses the same concluding phrase at the ends of c and c', *non saluabit animam suam*, and similar concluding phrases at the ends of d and d', *non stabit* and *non saluabitur*. He even improves the chiasmus by making the last words of b', *inter fortes*, echo the first words of b, *et fortis*. But he also reproduces the parallelism, echoing the last words of *a*, *a ueloce*, with the first words of *a'*, *et uelox*, and repeating *et robustus* at the beginnings of *c* and *c'*. From these three paradigms and from those which follow we infer ten rules of Biblical style.

1. A statement may be followed by a restatement in identical order, parallelism, as Isaiah 1 10.
2. A statement may be followed by a restatement in reverse order, chiasmus, as Lamentations 1 1.
3. Parallelism and chiasmus may be combined, as ai aii bi bii, b'i b'ii a'i a'ii, or exhibited simultaneously, the same passage making both patterns abcd d'c'b'a' and *abcd a'b'c'd'*, as Amos 11 14–6.
4. The words of parallel members may be wholly or partly identical or synonymous, as Genesis 1 and John 1 below.[4]
5. The nouns of parallel phrases may belong to the same declension and the verbs to the same conjugation, or nouns, adjectives, adverbs, and

4 See pp. 33–47.

verbs in one may share the same roots as those in the other, as Genesis II
1–4 below.[5]

6 A key word in one member may appear in the same position as its pair
in the parallel, as Isaiah and Lamentations, or the first word of one
member may be echoed by the last word of its parallel, as Amos.

7 Parallel phrases or clauses may be syntactically similar, as all three
examples above.

8 Parallel members may be linked by puns or word play or by quotations
from or allusions to other texts, as Saint John's Gospel below.[6]

9 Parallel members may be linked by alliteration, assonance, or rhyme.

10 Ideas stated at the beginning and the end of the first part of a passage or
at the beginning and the centre of a passage may be restated together at
the end, as Saint John's Gospel below.[7]

These are ten fundamental rules of composition in Biblical style. There are
more, probably many more, but these may guide our inquiry for the present.
They are all verbal devices which order the statement and restatement of ideas.
But other sorts of device, which we may call adjuncts of Biblical style, govern
other aspects of composition and presentation of texts.

THE ADJUNCTS OF BIBLICAL STYLE

There are five other elements or adjuncts of Biblical style. The first, second,
and third, and the most pervasive, are cerebral, composition in mathematically
determined forms. The fourth is aural, composition in rhythmical formulae.
The fifth is visual, decoration of texts for the eye.

Concerning the first adjunct, arithmetical composition, Jews and Greeks
alike believed that Creation itself had been a mathematical act. Christian
authors could have learned this from four famous passages in the Old
Testament and another in the Apocrypha.

In Job XXXVIII 4–7, for example, God asks

Where were you when I laid the foundation of the earth?	אֵיפֹה הָיִיתָ בְּיָסְדִי־אָרֶץ
Tell me, if you have understanding. Who	הַגֵּד אִם־יָדַעְתָּ בִינָה׃ מִי־
determined	שָׂם
its measurements;	מְמַדֶּיהָ
surely you know!	כִּי תֵדָע
Or who	אוֹ מִי־
stretched	נָטָה
the line upon it?	עָלֶיהָ קָו׃

5   See pp. 35–6.   6   See pp. 45–9.   7   See p. 47.

On what were its bases
  sunk,
  or who
    laid
      its cornerstone,
when the morning stars sang together
and all the sons of God shouted for joy?

עַל־מָה אֲדָנֶיהָ
הָטְבָּעוּ
אוֹ מִי־
יָרָה
אֶבֶן פִּנָּתָהּ:
בְּרָן־יַחַד כּוֹכְבֵי בֹקֶר
וַיָּרִיעוּ כָּל־בְּנֵי אֱלֹהִים:

που ης εν τωι θεμελιουν με την γην
  απαγγειλον δε μοι, ει επιστηι συνεσιν.
    τις
      εθετο
        τα μετρα αυτης
  ει οιδας;
    η τις
      ο επαγαγων
        σπαρτιον επ' αυτης;
        επι τινος οι κρικοι αυτης
      πεπηγασιν;
    τις δε
      εστιν ο βαλων
        λιθον γωνιαιον επ' αυτης;
οτε εγενηθησαν αστρα,
ηινεσαν με φωνηι μεγαληι παντες αγγελοι μου.

ubi eras quando ponebam fundamenta terrae?
  indica mihi si habes intellegentiam
    quis
      posuit
        mensuras eius,
  si nosti,
    uel quis
      tetendit
        super eam lineam
        super quo bases illius
      solidatae sunt
    aut quis
      dimisit
        lapidem angularem eius
cum me laudarent simul astra matutina
et iubilarent omnes filii Dei.

Again in Isaiah XL 12 the prophet says that it is God

Who has measured
  in the hollow of His hand
    the waters
    and the heavens
  with a span
marked off
and enclosed
  in a measure
    the dust of the earth
and weighed
  in scales
    the mountains
    and the hills
  in a balance.

מִי־מָדַד
בְּשָׁעֳלוֹ
מַיִם
וְשָׁמַיִם
בַּזֶּרֶת
תִּכֵּן
וְכָל
בַּשָּׁלִשׁ
עֲפַר הָאָרֶץ
וְשָׁקַל
בַּפֶּלֶס
הָרִים
וּגְבָעוֹת
בְּמֹאזְנָיִם׃

τις εμετρησεν
  τηι χειρι
    το υδωρ
    και τον ουρανον
  σπιθαμηι
    και πασαν την γην
  δρακι;
τις εστησεν
  τα ορη
  σταθμωι
    και τας ναπας
  ζυγωι;

quis mensus est
  pugillo
    aquas
    et caelos
  palmo
ponderauit
quis adpendit
  tribus digitis
    molem terrae
et librauit
  in pondere
    montes
    et colles
  in statera.

Again in Proverbs VIII 22–31 Wisdom says

פ

22 יְהוָה קָנָנִי רֵאשִׁית דַּרְכּוֹ
קֶדֶם מִפְעָלָיו מֵאָז׃
23 מֵעוֹלָם נִסַּכְתִּי
מֵרֹאשׁ מִקַּדְמֵי־אָרֶץ
24 בְּאֵין־תְּהֹמוֹת חוֹלָלְתִּי
בְּאֵין מַעְיָנוֹת נִכְבַּדֵּי־מָיִם׃
25 בְּטֶרֶם הָרִים הָטְבָּעוּ
לִפְנֵי גְבָעוֹת חוֹלָלְתִּי׃
26 עַד־לֹא עָשָׂה אֶרֶץ וְחוּצוֹת

וְרֹאשׁ עַפְרוֹת תֵּבֵל:

27 בַּהֲכִינוֹ שָׁמַיִם שָׁם אָנִי
בְּחוּקוֹ חוּג עַל־פְּנֵי תְהוֹם

28 בְּאַמְּצוֹ שְׁחָקִים מִמָּעַל
בַּעֲזוֹז עִינוֹת תְּהוֹם:

29 בְּשׂוּמוֹ לַיָּם חֻקּוֹ
וּמַיִם לֹא יַעַבְרוּ־פִיו
בְּחוּקוֹ מוֹסְדֵי אָרֶץ:

30 וָאֶהְיֶה אֶצְלוֹ אָמוֹן
וָאֶהְיֶה שַׁעֲשֻׁעִים יוֹם יוֹם
מְשַׂחֶקֶת לְפָנָיו בְּכָל־עֵת:

31 מְשַׂחֶקֶת בְּתֵבֵל אַרְצוֹ
וְשַׁעֲשֻׁעַי אֶת־בְּנֵי אָדָם: פ

1a	22	The Lord created me at the beginning of His work [lit. 'way'],
b		the first of His acts of old.
2a	23	Ages ago I was set up,
b		at the first, before the beginning of the earth.
3a	24	When there were no depths I was brought forth,
b		when there were no springs abounding with water.
4a	25	Before the mountains had been shaped,
b		before the hills, I was brought forth,
5a	26	before He had made the earth with its fields,
b		or the first of the dust of the world.
6a	27	When He established the heavens I was there,
b		when He drew a circle on the face of the deep,
7a	28	when He made firm the skies above,
b		when He established the fountains of the deep,
8a	29	when He assigned to the sea its limit,
b		so that the waters might not transgress His command,
9a		when He marked out the foundations of the earth,
b	30	then I was beside Him like a master workman,
10a		and I was daily His delight,
b		rejoicing before Him always,
11a	31	rejoicing in His inhabited world,
b		and delighting in the sons of men.

The passage is a coherent unit, preceded and followed by the Masoretes'
letter ם for *petuchah*, marking a verse paragraph. The internal parallelism of the
verses here numbered 1–11 is so clear as to need no explication. Of these
eleven sections ten are linked by words at the beginnings and caesuras and

ends. Compare מַ at the end of 1a and the beginnings of 2a and 2b; בְּאֵין at the beginnings of 3a and 3b; בְּ at the beginnings of 3a, 3b, and 4a; בְ in 6a, 6b, 7a, 7b; בְּ, וַ, בְ, וְ in 8a, 8b, 9a, 9b; וּ, מְשַׂחֶקֶת, מְשַׂחֶקֶת, וּ in 10a, 10b, 11a, 11b. Adjacent lines are further linked by recurrences of words. Compare רֵאשִׁית 1a with מֵרֹאשׁ 2b; קֶדֶם 1b with מִקַּדְמֵי 2b; חוֹלָלְתִּי 3a and 4b; תְּהוֹם 6b and 7b; וָאֶהְיֶה 9b and 10a; שַׁעֲשֻׁעִים 10a with וּשַׁעֲשֻׁעַי 11b; מְשַׂחֶקֶת 10b and 11a.

The principal subjects of this passage are 'God' at the beginning of the first verse, 'I' Wisdom and 'with a compass' at the caesura of the central verse, and 'in the sons of men' at the end of the last verse.

Here is the Septuagint text of the same passage.

1a	22	Κυριος εκτισεν με αρχην οδων αυτου
b		εις εργα αυτου
2a	23	προ του αιωνος εθεμελιωσεν με εν αρχηι
b	24	προ του την γην ποιησαι
3a		και προ του τας αβυσσους ποιησαι
b		προ του προελθειν τας πηγας των υδατων
4a	25	προ του ορη εδρασθηναι
b		προ δε παντων βουνων γενναι με.
5a	26	Κυριος εποιησεν χωρας και αοικητους
b		και ακρα οικουμενα της υπ' ουρανον.
6a	27	ηνικα ητοιμαζεν τον ουρανον συμπαρημην αυτωι
b		και οτε αφωριζεν τον εαυτου θρονον επ' ανεμων.
7a	28	ηνικα ισχυρα εποιει τα ανω νεφη
b		και ως ασφαλεις ετιθει πηγας της υπ' ουρανον
8a	29	και ισχυρα εποιει τα θεμελια της γης
9b	30	ημην παρ' αυτωι αρμοζουσα
10a		εγω ημην ηι προσεχαιρεν.
b		καθ' ημεραν δε ευφραινομην εν προσωπωι αυτου εν παντι καιρωι
11a	31	οτε ευφραινετο την οικουμενην συντελεσας
b		και ενευφραινετο εν υιοις ανθρωπων.

Here is the Vulgate text of the same passage.

1a	22	Dominus possedit me initium uiarum suarum
b		antequam quicquam faceret a principio
2a	23	ab aeterno ordita sum et ex antiquis
b		antequam terra fieret
3a	24	necdum erant abyssi et ego iam concepta eram
b		necdum fontes aquarum eruperant

4a 25   necdum montes graui mole constiterant
  b   ante colles ego parturiebar
5a 26   adhuc terram non fecerat et flumina
  b   et cardines orbis terrae
6a 27   quando praeparabat caelos aderam
  b   quando certa lege et gyro uallabat abyssos
7a 28   quando aethera firmabat sursum
  b   et librabat fontes aquarum
8a 29   quando circumdabat mari terminum suum
  b   et legem ponebat aquis ne transirent fines suos
9a   quando adpendebat fundamenta terrae
  b 30   cum eo eram cuncta conponens
10a   et delectabar per singulos dies
  b   ludens coram eo omni tempore
11a31   ludens in orbe terrarum
  b   et deliciae meae esse cum filiis hominum.

As in the Hebrew text sections are linked by words at the beginnings and caesuras of verses, as *necdum* 3a, 3b, 4a; *quando* 6a, 6b, 7a; *quando, et, quando* 8a, 8b, 9a; *ludens* 10b and 11a. Adjacent lines are further linked by recurrences of words and phrases, as *cum eo* and *coram eo* 9b and 10b; *et delectabar* and *et deliciae meae* 10a and 11b.

As in the Hebrew text *Dominus* is the first word of the first verse; *quando certa lege et gyro uallabat abyssos* stands at the crux of the verses; and *filiis hominum* are the last words of the last verse. The first words of the central verse 6b are the central words of the passage, which is the source of well known representations of God creating the universe as a mathematical act with a compass.

Again in Wisdom XI 20 'Solomon' addressing the Creator, says, αλλα παντα μετρωι και αριθμωι και σταθμωι διεταξας, rendered at XI 21 in the Vulgate, *sed omnia mensura et numero et pondere disposuisti*, 'But Thou hast arranged all things by measure and number and weight'. Christian authors could have learned this also from Plato, who in a dialogue which continued to be read in the Latin West during the Middle Ages, makes Timaeus state:[8]

> Wherefore also God in the beginning of Creation made the body of the universe to consist of fire and earth. But two things cannot be rightly put together without a third; there must be some bond of union between them. And the fairest bond is that which makes the most complete fusion of itself and the things which it combines; and proportion is best adapted to effect such a union. For whenever in any three numbers, whether cube or square, there is a mean, which is to the last term what the first term is to it; and again, when the mean is to the first term as the last term is to the mean,

8   Plato, *Timaeus*, transl. Jowett §§ 31–2.

then the mean becoming first and last, and the first and last both becoming means, they will all of them of necessity come to be the same, and having become the same with one another will be all one. If the universal frame had been created a surface only and having no depth, a single mean would have sufficed to bind together itself and the other terms; but now, as the world must be solid, and solid bodies are always compacted not by one mean but by two, God placed water and air in the mean between fire and earth, and made them to have the same proportion so far as was possible (as fire is to air so is air to water, and as air is to water so is water to earth); and thus He bound and put together a visible and tangible heaven. And for these reasons, and out of such elements which are in number four, the body of the world was created, and it was harmonized by proportion, and therefore has the spirit of friendship; and having been reconciled to itself, it was indissoluble by the hand of any other than the framer.

In the Latin translation of Calcidius[9] this appears as

Et quia corpulentus uisibilisque et contiguus erat merito futurus, sine igni porro nihil uisibile sentitur nec uero tangi quicquam potest sine soliditate, soliditas porro nulla sine terra, ignem terramque corporis mundi fund-amenta iecit Deus. Quoniamque nulla duo sine adiunctione tertii firme et indissolubiliter cohaerent nexu enim medio extrema nectente opus est, nexus uero firmissimus ille certe est, qui et se ipsum et ea quae secum uinciuntur facit unum hoc porro modus et congrua mensura partium efficit. Cum enim ex tribus uel numeris uel molibus uel ulla alia potentia medietas imo perinde quadrat ut summitas medio, rursumque ut imum medio, sic medietas summo, tunc certe medietas a summo et item imo nihil differt rursumque extimis illis ad medietatis condicionem atque ad eiusdem parilitatem redactis cum medietas quoque extimorum uicem suscipit, fit, opinor, ut tota materia una et eadem ratione societur eoque pacto eadem sibi erunt uniuersa membra, quippe cum eorum sit una condicio; unis porro effectis membris unum erit atque idem totum. Quare, si corpus uniuersae rei longitudinem et latitudinem solam, crassitudinem uero nullam habere deberet essetque huius modi, qualis est corporum solidorum super-ficies, una medietas sufficeret ad semet ipsam uinciendam et extimas partes. Nunc quoniam soliditate opus erat mundano corpori, solida porro numquam una sed duabus medietatibus uinciuntur, idcirco mundi opifex inter ignem terramque aera et aquam inseruit libratis isdem elementis salubri modo, ut quae cognatio est inter ignem et aera eadem foret inter aera et aquam, rursum quae inter aera et aquam, haec eadem in aquae terraeque societate consisteret. Atque ita ex quattuor supra dictis materiis praeclaram

9   *Timaeus a Calcidio Translatus Commentarioque Instructus*, ed. J.H. Waszink in *Corpus Platonicum Medii Aevi*, ed. R. Klibansky (London & Leiden 1962), pp. 24–5.

istam machinam uisibilem contiguamque fabricatus est amica partium aequilibritatis ratione sociatam, quo immortalis indissolubilisque esset aduersum omnem casum excepta fabricatoris sui uoluntate.

Plato is undeniably stating that Creation was a mathematical act. More specifically, according to some, he is considering here the geometric mean, if not the golden mean or golden section, which was much discussed among ancient philosophers and mathematicians:[10]

we are told by Proclus that Eudoxus 'greatly added to the number of the theorems which Plato originated regarding *the section*, and employed in them the method of analysis'. It is obvious that *'the section'* was some particular section which by the time of Plato had assumed great importance; and the one section of which this can safely be said is that which was called the 'golden section', namely the division of a straight line in extreme and mean ratio.

Euclid dealt with the ratio in Book II proposition xi and Book VI proposition xxx of the *Elements*,[11] and later philosophers paid it considerable attention.[12]

That geometrical proportion was the proportion *par excellence* and primary, all other types of proportion being derivable from it, was stated by Adrastus, the Peripatetic (early second century A.D.), who wrote a commentary on the *Timaeus*, parts of which are preserved by Theon of Smyrna. The statement is repeated by Nicomachus (*Introd. Arith.* ii, 24 ...), by Iamblichus (*in Nicom. Ar. Introd.* ... as an opinion of the ancients, and ... citing our passage), by Pr[oclus] ii, 20 (referring to Nicomachus).

Most important for transmission to the early Middle Ages, Boethius discussed the ratio in *De Institutione Arithmetica* II LII:

quarta uero [medietas], quae in ordine decima est, consideratur in tribus terminis, cum tali proportione medius terminus ad paruissimum comparatur, quali extremorum differentia contra maiorum terminorum differentiam proportione coniungitur, ut sunt III. V. VIII.

---

10 *The Thirteen Books of Euclids Elements*, transl. T.L. Heath, 2nd edn (Cambridge 1956), vol. I p. 137.

11 *The First Latin Translation of Euclid's Elements' Commonly Ascribed to Adelard of Bath*, ed. H.L.L. Busard, Pontifical Institute of Mediaeval Studies, Studies and Texts LXIV (Toronto 1983), p. 20: 'There is a persistent belief that some rendering of Euclid's *Elements* existed in England before the celebrated versions of Adelard of Bath. If by this is meant some truncated Latin version such as that attributed to Boethius, or fragments such as those in the encyclopedic works of Macrobius, Martianus Capella, Cassiodorus, St. Isidore, and Bede, then the belief has some justification, since all of these works circulated in England.

12 F.M. Cornford, *Plato's Cosmology* (London 1937), p. 45.

In his most famous poem, '*O qui perpetua mundum ratione gubernas*', at the centre of *De Consolatione Philosophiae*, he compressed the teaching of the *Timaeus* about creation of the world, illustrating extreme and mean ratio in his text.[13]

There are other important ratios in Plato's account of Creation. In forming soul and body

> First of all, He took away one part of the whole [1], and then He separated a second part which was double the first [2], and then He took away a third part which was half as much again as the second and three times as much as the first [3], and then He took a fourth part which was twice as much as the second [4], and a fifth part which was three times the third [9], and a sixth part which was eight times the first [8], and a seventh part which was twenty-seven times the first [27]. After this He filled up the double intervals [i.e. between 1, 2, 4, 8] and the triple [i.e. between 1, 3, 9, 27], cutting off yet other portions from the mixture and placing them in the intervals, so that in each interval there were two kinds of means, the one exceeding and exceeded by equal parts of its extremes [as for example 1, 4/3, 2, in which the mean 4/3 is one-third of 1 more than 1, and one-third of 2 less than 2], the other being that kind of mean which exceeds and is exceeded by an equal number. Where there were intervals of 3/2 and of 4/3 and of 9/8, made by the connecting terms in the former intervals, He filled up all the intervals of 4/3 with the interval of 9/8, leaving a fraction over; and the interval which this fraction expressed was in the ratio of 256 to 243. And thus the whole mixture out of which He cut these portions was all exhausted by Him. This entire compound He divided lengthways into two parts, which He joined to one another at the centre like the letter X, and bent them into a circular form, connecting them with themselves and each other at the point opposite to their original meeting-point; and, comprehending them in a uniform revolution upon the same axis, He made the one the outer and the other the inner circle.

> unam sumpsit ex uniuerso primitus portionem, post quam duplicem eius quam sumpserat, tertiam uero sescuplam quidem secundae, triplam uero primitus sumptae, at uero quartam sumpsit duplicem secundae, quintam triplam tertiae, sexta fuit assumptio partibus septem quam prima propensior, septima sex et uiginti partibus quam prima maior. Quibus ita diuisis consequenter complebat interualla duplicis et triplicis quantitatis ex uniuersitate partes secans etiamnunc et ex his interuallorum spatia complens, quo singula interualla binis medietatibus fulcirentur. Medietatum porro altera quota parte limitis extimi praecellebat unum extimum limitem, tota praecellebatur ab alio extimo limite, altera pari summa et aequali ad numerum modo praecellebat et praecellebatur ab extimis.

13 See below pp. 49–53.

Natis itaque limitibus sescuplorum et item eorum quibus accedit pars sui tertia, quod genus a Graecis epitritum dicitur, item eorum quibus accedit pars sui octaua, qui numerus epogdous ab isdem uocatur, ex his nexibus illa prima spatia, id est epogdoi spatiis epitritorum omnium interualla complebat, ita ut ad perfectam cumulatamque completionem deesset aliquid epitrito, tantum scilicet quantum deest habita comparatione ducentis quadraginta tribus aduersus ducentos quinquaginta sex. Et iam omne fere commixtum illud genus essentiae consumptum erat huius modi sectionibus partium. Tunc hanc ipsam seriem in longum secuit et ex una serie duas fecit easque mediam mediae in speciem chi Graecae litterae coartauit curuauitque in orbes, quoad coirent inter se capita, orbemque orbi sic inseruit, ut alter eorum aduerso, alter obliquo circuitu rotarentur, et exterioris quidem circuli motum eundem, quod erat eiusdem naturae consanguineus, cognominauit, interioris autem diuersum.

Later Timaeus reports God as having said

'Gods, children of gods, who are my works and of whom I am the artificer and father, my creations are indissoluble, if so I will. All that is bound may be undone, but only an evil being would wish to undo that which is harmonious and happy. ... Three tribes of mortal beings remain to be created.' ... Thus He spake, and once more into the cup in which He had previously mingled the soul of the universe He poured the remains of the elements ... . And having made it He divided the whole mixture into souls equal in number to the stars, and assigned each soul to a star.

Dii deorum quorum opifex idem paterque ego, opera siquidem uos mea, dissolubilia natura, me tamen ita uolente indissolubilia, omne siquidem quod iunctum est natura dissolubile, at uero quod bona ratione iunctum atque modulatum est dissolui uelle non est Dei. ... Tria etiamnunc mortalia genera desunt uniuersitati quibus carens uniuersa res perfectione indigebit. ... Haec dixit et demum reliquias prioris concretionis, ex qua mundi animam commiscuerat, in eiusdem crateris sinum refundens eodem propemodum genere atque eadem ratione miscebat ... coagmentataque mox uniuersae rei machina delegit animas stellarum numero pares singulasque singulis comparuit easdemque uehiculis competentibus superimpositas uniuersae rei naturam spectare iussit.

In *De Institutione Musica* I X Boethius relates the myth of discovery of ratios by Pythagoras on hearing the blows of five smiths' hammers, four which produced musical ratios and one which produced dissonance:[14]

14 *Anicii Manlii Torquati Severini Boetii De Institutione Arithmetica Libri Duo, De Institutione Musica Libri Quinque*, ed. G. Friedlein (Leipzig 1868), transl. & ed. C.M. Bower & C.V. Palisca, *Fundamentals of Music* (New Haven & London 1989).

Primus Pythagoras hoc modo repperit qua proportione sibimet haec
sonorum concordia iungeretur. Et ut sit clarius quod dictum est sint
uerbi gratia malleorum quattuor pondera quae subter scriptis numeris
contineantur: XII. VIIII. VIII. VI. Hi igitur mallei qui XII et VI pon-
deribus uergebant, diapason in duplo concinentiam personabant. Malleus
uero XII ponderum ad malleum VIIII et malleus VIII ponderum ad
malleum VI ponderum secundum epitritam proportionem diatessaron
consonantia iungebatur, VIIII uero ponderum ad VI et XII ad VIII
diapente consonantiam permiscebant, VIIII uero ad VIII in sesquioctaua
proportione resonabant tonum.

Pythagoras was the first to ascertain through this means by what ratio the
concord of sounds was joined together. So that what has been said might
be clearer, for sake of illustration, let the weights of the four hammers be
contained in the numbers written below: 12 : 9 : 8 : 6. Thus the hammers
which bring together 12 with 6 pounds sounded the consonance of the
diapason in duple ratio. The hammer of 12 pounds with that of 9 (and the
hammer of 8 with that of 6) joined in the consonance of the diatessaron
according to the epitrita ratio. The one of 9 pounds with that of 6 (as well
as those of 12 and 8) commingled the consonance of the diapente. The one
of 9 with that of 8 sounded the tone according to the sesquioctave ratio.

Mediaeval readers, whose ideas were formed by reading the Bible, found
little in either Boethius or Plato discordant with a Christian understanding of
Creation.

One could hardly overestimate the importance of the idea, widespread in
Antiquity and restated in our time by Owen Barfield, J.R.R. Tolkien, and
C.S. Lewis,[15] that as Creation was a mathematical act of weighing, balancing,
measuring, and counting, an artist as 'sub-creator' should reflect in his work
what the Creator has done in the world. This is implicit in the etymology of
the English word 'poet', derived from Old French poete, which derives in turn
from Latin poeta, itself a borrowing from Greek ποιητης, 'a maker', related to
the verb ποιειν, 'to create, shape'. The same idea is expressed by Old English
scop 'poet', related to the divine title Scippend 'Creator', and to the verb scippan
'to create, shape, form'. Similarly Middle and Modern English 'maker(e)'
denotes both 'Creator' and 'poet' or 'author'. In Welsh prydydd 'poet' is
related to pryd 'shape, form' and in Irish creth 'poetry' to cruth 'form'.

A writer who believed that God had made omnia duplicia, unum contra unum,
might compose symmetrically, in which case he would make his work consist
of approximately, if not exactly, equal halves. This is easily done by writing

15   O. Barfield, Poetic Diction, A Study in Meaning, 3rd edn (Middletown, CT 1973); J.R.R. Tolkien
     'On Fairy Stories' in Essays presented to Charles Williams (London 1947), p. 82; H. Carpenter, The
     Inklings (London 1978), p. 138.

one unit freely and then making its parallel conform with the original. Any revision to either must thereafter entail comparable revision to the other.

A writer who believed that God had created by ratio might compose according to the golden section, in which case the minor part of his work (m) would relate to the major part (M) as the major part related to the whole (m+M), formulaically expressed as $m/M = M/(m+M) = (\sqrt{5}-1)/2$.[16]

One simple means of calculating the golden section is to multiply a number by 0.61803 to find the major part and by 0.38197 to find the minor part.

Another means of determining the golden section is to make a table of Fibonacci numbers, each of which is the sum of the two to its left.

I	I	2	3	5	8	13	21	34	55	89	144	233
I	2	3	5	8	13	21	34	55	89	144	233	377
I	3	4	7	11	18	29	47	76	123	199	322	521
I	4	5	9	14	23	37	60	97	157	254	411	665
I	5	6	11	17	28	45	73	118	191	309	500	809
I	6	7	13	20	33	53	86	139	225	364	599	963
I	7	8	15	23	38	61	99	160	259	419	678	1097
I	8	9	17	26	43	69	112	181	293	474	767	1241
I	9	10	19	29	48	77	125	202	327	529	856	1385
I	10	11	21	32	53	85	138	223	361	584	945	1529
I	11	12	23	35	58	93	151	244	395	639	1034	1673
I	12	13	25	38	63	101	164	265	429	694	1123	1817

An author who composes a passage containing thirty-four units knows by consulting such a table that the parallel passage should contain either twenty-one or fifty-five units.

Dr John Blundell suggests yet another way to calculate by dividing a number successively by 2 and 3.

$n =$	100			$n =$	196			$n =$	228		
÷ 2	50	+	50	÷ 2	98	+	98	÷ 2	114	+	114
÷ 2	25			÷ 2	49			÷ 2	57		
÷ 2	12½	+	12½	÷ 2	24½	+	24½	÷ 2	28½	+	28½
÷ 2	6¼			÷ 2	12¼			÷ 2	14¼		
÷ 3	$2^1\!/_{12}$			÷ 3	$^{49}\!/_{12}$			÷ 3	$5^7\!/_{12}$		
÷ 3	$^{25}\!/_{36}$	−	$^{25}\!/_{36}$	÷ 3	$^{49}\!/_{36}$	−	$1^{13}\!/_{36}$	÷ 3	$1^{21}\!/_{36}$	−	$1^{21}\!/_{36}$
	=		$61^{29}\!/_{36}$		=		$121^5\!/_{36}$		=		$140^{33}\!/_{36}$

This form of calculation is equivalent to multiplication by $^{89}\!/_{144}$.

---

16 R. Herz-Fischler, *A Mathematical History of Division in Extreme and Mean Ratio* (Waterloo, Ontario 1987). See also H. E. Huntley, *The Divine Proportion, A Study in Mathematical Beauty* (New York 1970), F. Lasserre, *The Birth of Mathematics in the Age of Plato* (Larchmont, NY 1964).

It is easy to find the golden section geometrically. One has only to follow
Euclid to learn how to divide a line by extreme and mean ratio. It is more
difficult to imagine how ancient and mediaeval writers who lived long before
Fibonacci calculated the golden section arithmetically, especially if they reckoned
in Greek or Hebrew letters or Roman numerals. Harder still to understand why
irrational numbers should be an important feature of literary composition which
can represent only integers. But there is much evidence, which we shall now
consider, that many writers did calculate with astonishing accuracy.

The units which writers might count include letters, syllables, words, metrical
feet, lines of verse, chapters, and entire books. The primary evidence for this will
be exhibited many times in this and the following chapters from the texts themselves, and from statements by the authors (sometimes straightforward and explicit,
sometimes veiled, ironic, or coy) about what they have done.[17] Secondary evidence will be shown from translations or imitations of mathematically composed
texts by writers who either reproduce or vary the patterns of their models.[18] It will
be shown also from texts by writers who demonstrate in revision of texts composed in this style that they understood the structure even if they did not reproduce
it. To establish that this is not universal we shall examine some translations which
imply ignorance of the style or a disinclination, if not complete failure, to reproduce it. A third form of evidence may be cited here to show that in Antiquity
scholars recognized these features of the texts they analysed. From the Hebrew
tradition one notes in the Talmud that in discussing the Book ספר sefer[19]

> the early [scholars] were called soferim because they used to count [safar] all the
> letters of the Torah. Thus, they said, the waw in gaḥon marks half the letters of
> the Torah; darosh darash, half the words; we-hithggalah, half the verses. *The boar
> out of the wood* [mi-ya'ar] *doth ravage it*: the 'ayin of ya'ar marks half of the
> Psalms. *But he, being full of compassion, forgiveth their iniquity*, half of the verses.
>
> R. Joseph propounded: Does the waw of gaḥon belong to the first half or
> the second? Said they [the scholars] to him, Let a Scroll of the Torah be
> brought and we will count them! Did not Rabbah b. Bar Hanah say, They
> did not stir from there until a Scroll of the Torah was brought and they
> counted them? They were thoroughly versed in the defective and full
> readings, but we are not.
>
> R. Joseph propounded: Does wehithgalaḥ belong to the first half or the
> second? Said Abaye to him, For the verses at least, we can bring [a Scroll]
> and count them! . . .
>
> Our Rabbis taught: There are 5888 verses in the Torah; the Psalms
> exceed this by eight; while Chronicles are less by eight.

17   See below p. 401.
18   See below pp. 273–333.
19   *Kiddushin* ch. I 30a–30b, transl. Rabbi Dr H. Freedman in *The Babylonian Talmud: Seder Nashim*,
     ed. Rabbi Dr I. Epstein (London 1936), vol. VIII, pp. 144–6.

Our Rabbis taught: *And thou shalt teach them diligently* [means] that the words of the Torah shall be clear-cut in your mouth, so that if anyone asks you something, you should not shew doubt and then answer him, but [be able to] answer him immediately . . . .

From this one infers unavoidably that the rabbis counted the verses, words, and letters of the text of the Hebrew Bible, probably because they believed that the writers of the text had done the same. With this passage of the Talmud in mind, if we return to the Hebrew texts considered above, we note that in Isaiah I 10 the first member contains five words and the second also five. The first half of Lamentations I I contains four words, two in each phrase, and the second also four, two in each phrase. In Job XXXVIII 4–7 the first phrase contains four words and the last two phrases four words each, the first half of the passage comprising eighteen words and the second seventeen words. In Isaiah XL 12 the phrases fall into patterns of four, three, four, three, and two words. There are twenty-five letters in the first part and thirty-nine in the second, sixty-four together. The golden section of 64 falls at 39.55 and 24.45. In Proverbs VIII 22–31 the mathematical structure is as clear as it could be.

22 יְהוָה קָנָנִי רֵאשִׁית דַּרְכּוֹ
קֶדֶם מִפְעָלָיו מֵאָז:
23 מֵעוֹלָם נִסַּכְתִּי
מֵרֹאשׁ מִקַּדְמֵי־אָרֶץ:
24 בְּאֵין־תְּהֹמוֹת חוֹלָלְתִּי
בְּאֵין מַעְיָנוֹת נִכְבַּדֵּי־מָיִם
25 בְּטֶרֶם הָרִים הָטְבָּעוּ
לִפְנֵי גְבָעוֹת חוֹלָלְתִּי:
26 עַד־לֹא עָשָׂה אֶרֶץ וְחוּצוֹת
וְרֹאשׁ עָפְרוֹת תֵּבֵל:
27 בַּהֲכִינוֹ שָׁמַיִם שָׁם אָנִי
בְּחוּקוֹ חוּג עַל־פְּנֵי תְהוֹם:
28 בְּאַמְּצוֹ שְׁחָקִים מִמָּעַל
בַּעֲזוֹז עִינוֹת תְּהוֹם:
29 בְּשׂוּמוֹ לַיָּם׀ חֻקּוֹ
וּמַיִם לֹא יַעַבְרוּ־פִיו
בְּחוּקוֹ מוֹסְדֵי אָרֶץ:
30 וָאֶהְיֶה אֶצְלוֹ אָמוֹן
וָאֶהְיֶה שַׁעֲשֻׁעִים יוֹם׀ יוֹם
מְשַׂחֶקֶת לְפָנָיו בְּכָל־עֵת:
31 מְשַׂחֶקֶת בְּתֵבֵל אַרְצוֹ
וְשַׁעֲשֻׁעַי אֶת־בְּנֵי אָדָם: פ

The seventy-six words divide by symmetry at 38 and 38. After תֵּבֵל 5b the thirty-eighth word is בְּתֵבֵל 11a. The central thirty-eighth word, which

stands at the caesura of the central verse, is בְּחֻקּוֹ 6b. 38 divides by symmetry at 19 and 19. From בְּחֻקּוֹ 6b to בְּחֻקּוֹ 9a inclusive there are nineteen
words. The seventy-six words divide by extreme and mean ratio at 47 and 29.
From רֵאשִׁית 1a to וְרֹאשׁ 5b inclusive there are twenty-nine words. 47
divides by extreme and mean ratio at 29 and 18, 29 at 18 and 11. There are
eleven words before אֶרֶץ 2b, and there are eighteen words after אֶרֶץ 9a. From
אֶרֶץ 2b to אֶרֶץ 9a inclusive there are forty-seven words. From אֶרֶץ 2b to
אֶרֶץ 5a inclusive there are eighteen words, after which אֶרֶץ 9a is the twenty-
ninth word. From תְּהֹמוֹת 3a to תְּהוֹם 6b inclusive there are twenty-nine
words.

The seventy-six words divide by duple ratio at 51 and 25. Between לֹא 5a
and לֹא 8b there are twenty-five words. The twenty-fifth word from the end
is וּמַיִם 8b. Between מַיִם 3b and וּמַיִם 8b there are thirty-two words, of
which the central are שָׁמַיִם שָׁם 6a.

In the translations of these texts we note that in Isaiah 1 10 the first member
of the Septuagint version contains five words and the second also five. The
first member of the Vulgate version contains five words and the second seven,
twelve together. The golden section of 12 falls at 7 and 5. In Lamentations 1 1
the first half of the Septuagint version contains six words, three in each phrase,
and the second half also six, three in each phrase. The first half of the Vulgate
version contains six words and the second half also six, arranged four, two,
two, and four; there are fourteen syllables in the first half and fourteen in the
second. In Job XXXVIII 4–7 the first half of the Septuagint text contains
twenty-eight words and 113 letters and the second twenty-five words and 121
letters, not a precise reflection of the Hebrew. The Vulgate does better,
twenty-three words and 125 letters in the first half and twenty-three words
and 123 letters in the second. The Septuagint version of Isaiah XL 12 ruins the
patterns of the Masoretic text, but the Vulgate reproduces them well. There
are nine words in the first part (five and four) and fifteen words in the second,
twenty-four together. The golden section of 24 falls at 15 and 9. There are
forty-nine letters in the first part (twenty-five and twenty-four) and seventy-
eight in the second, 127 together. The golden section of 127 falls at 78 and 49.

The second adjunct is, like the first, arithmetical. An author may place an
important word or several important words at intervals in a text. There are
three ways of reckoning this feature: first, counting from the first occurrence
of the word to the second occurrence inclusively; second, counting between
the occurrences of the word exclusively; third, including the first occurrence
and excluding the second or excluding the first and including the second.
There are conspicuous examples of all three ways of counting in passages from
the Books of Judges and Genesis and the *Rhetorica ad Herennium* and Cicero
De Oratore, which we shall consider soon.[20] We shall use specific locutions to
distinguish the different forms of reckoning.

20   See pp. 23–32.

The third adjunct is also arithmetical. In Hebrew, as in Greek, every letter of the alphabet has a numerical value, unlike Latin, in which only seven letters, MDCLXVI, normally represent numbers. In Hebrew, by gematria, גימטריא perhaps borrowed from γεωμετρια, a word or name may bear numerical value as well as semantic meaning.

The name Caleb, כָּלֵב, has a numerical value of 20+30+2 or 52. So in Greek the name Adam, ΑΔΑΜ, has a numerical value of 1+4+1+40 or 46 and the name Jesus, ΙΗΣΟΥΣ, 18+200+70+400+200 or 888, in Roman numerals DCCCLXXXVIII. In Latin *Diclux*, one of the names of Antichrist, who 'says' he is the 'light', exhibits this feature, the numerical value of the name being, like the number of the beast, 666 or DCLXVI.[21]

Numbers, like 7 and its multiples, and 46, 52, 666, 888, bear values other than strictly numerical. So do the numbers 10 as the triangular number 1+2+3+4; 144, symbolically important as the square of 12 and the twelfth number in the Fibonacci series, as well as the number of cubits in the wall of the heavenly Jerusalem, the inhabitants of which number 144,000 (Apocalypse XXI 17 and VII 4); 153 as the number of fishes in the net (John XXI 11) and the triangular number 1+2+3+4+5+6+7+8+9+10+11+12+13+14+15+16+17. But our principal concern here is the fact of numerical composition as distinct from the symbolical value of numbers.

The fourth adjunct of Biblical style is rhythm. It is not our purpose here to consider Hebrew rhythms, because during Late Antiquity and the early Middle Ages that language was not widely known among Celtic-speaking peoples. Among scholars some knowledge of names of letters of the Hebrew alphabet, and the meanings of some Hebrew words which had passed into Late Latin, and interpretations of some proper names from the Bible were current. There was a vogue among hisperic writers for coining Latin words from Hebrew or supposed Hebrew roots.[22] And there was an early form of the 'Theodulfian' corrections to Jerome's rendering of the Psalter *iuxta Hebraeos* at Canterbury, where it influenced the Old English poet who composed the *Kentish Psalm*.[23] But it would be hard to imagine a way in which the rhythms of Hebrew prose or verse, the analysis of which remains contentious among modern scholars, could have influenced early Celtic Latin writers.

As the primary purpose of Greek and Latin translators was to render the sense of the Bible one should not expect their translations necessarily to repro-

21 See, for example, the *quaestio* by a fourteenth-century Chancellor of the University of Oxford, Henry Harclay: '*Henricus de Herkeley: Utrum astrologi vel quicumque calculatores possint probare secundum adventum Christi*', ed. F. Pelster in *Archivio italiano per la storia della pietà* I (1951), pp. 53–82, esp. 80–1. Note in the number DCLXVI the descending numerical values of the letters and the relation to DCCCLXXXVIII.

22 M. Thiel, *Grundlagen und Gestalt der Hebräischkenntnisse des frühen Mittelalters* (Spoleto 1973). *The Hisperica Famina: II Related Poems*, ed. M.W. Herren, Pontifical Institute of Mediaeval Studies, Studies and Texts LXXXV (Toronto 1987), pp. 65–7.

23 S.L. Keefer & D.R. Burrows, 'Hebrew and the Hebraicum in late Anglo-Saxon England', *Anglo-Saxon England* XIX (1990), pp. 67–80.

duce the rhythms of their originals. But Greek writers from Thrasymachus in the fifth century B.C. and Classical Latin writers from the first century B.C. onward composed rhythmical prose. The tradition of composing clausulae, first in quantitative rhythms, then in mixed quantitative and stressed rhythms, and later in stressed rhythms only, evolved through the Late Latin period into the early Middle Ages.[24]

The subject of Latin prose rhythm is complicated and hotly debated, but few scholars would deny the validity of a scheme of four basic rhythms with two variant forms.

1	cretic + trochee or spondee	‒ ˘ ‒ ×	*fŏrmă uērbŏrŭm*
2	double cretic	‒ ˘ ‒ ˘ ×	*ārtĕ dētērmĭnăt*
3	cretic + double trochee or trochee + spondee	‒ ˘ ‒ ˘ ˘ ‒ ×	*nūptĭās cōnpărăbăt*
4	cretic + iambus	‒ ˘ ‒ ˘ ×	*āntĕ dīxĭmŭs*
5	resolved cretic + trochee or spondee	‒ ˘ ˘ ˘ ‒ ×	*ēssĕ pŭĕrĭlĕ*
6	resolved cretic + cretic	‒ ˘ ˘ ‒ ˘ ×	*ēssĕ pŭĕrĭlĭtĕr*

The fifth and sixth forms are simply variants of the first and second in which the last long syllable of the cretic is resolved into two short syllables. In all forms the first cretic may be strengthened to a molossus (‒ ‒ ‒). In all forms the last syllable is common. In the first two forms the first syllable of the cretic may be resolved. The third form appears sometimes only as a trochaic metron without the cretic.

The form of the cursus widely taught in the middle ages as part of the *ars dictaminis* required stressed rhythms which can be perceived as reflexes of these quantitative rhythms.

1	planus	/ × × / ×	*tráctibus trúdit*
2	tardus	/ × × / × ×	*fídens pernícibus*
3	uelox	/ × × \ × / ×	*agmínibus circumsaéptus*
4	medius	/ × / × ×	*exercére stúdeat*
5	trispondiacus	/ × × × / ×	*iaculórum catapúltas*
6	dispondeus dactylicus	/ × × × / × ×	*felíciter perfrúitur*

---

24   A.C. Clark, *The Cursus in Mediaeval and Vulgar Latin* (Oxford 1910). S.F. Bonner, 'Roman Oratory' in M. Platnauer, *Fifty Years of Classical Scholarship* (Oxford 1954), pp. 358–63; M. *Tulli Ciceronis in L. Calpurnium Pisonem Oratio*, ed. R.G.M. Nisbet (Oxford 1961), pp. xvii-xx; W.H. Shewring & K.J. Dover, 'Prose Rhythm' in N.G.L. Hammond & H.H. Scullard, *The Oxford Classical Dictionary*, 2nd edn (Oxford 1970), pp. 888–90; T. Janson, *Prose Rhythm in Medieval Latin from the 9th to the 13th Century* (Stockholm 1975); R. Nisbet, 'Cola and Clausulae in Cicero's Speeches' in E.M. Craik ed., *'Owls to Athens', Essays on Classical Subjects Presented to Sir Kenneth Dover* (Oxford 1990), pp. 349–59.

The fifth adjunct is visual. The textual divisions of a passage may be corroborated by illumination and decoration. Both textual divisions and rhythms may be marked by punctuation. We shall return to this subject later. For the present here is a Classical Latin text from the beginning of the first century B.C., which exhibits four of the five adjuncts, the *Rhetorica ad Herennium* IV XX 27–8:

A Conpar appellatur . quod habet in sē mēmbra ōrātiōnis .
de quibus āntĕ dīximŭs .
quae constent ex pari fere numero sȳllābārŭm .
Hoc non denumeratiōnĕ nōstrā fīĕt :
nam id quidem puerile est
sed tantum adferet usus et exercitatiō fācūltātis .
ut animī quōdām sēnsŭ .
par membrum superiori refērrĕ pōssimŭs
hōc mŏdō .

B   In proelio mortēm părēns ōppĕtēbăt .
domi filius nūptīās cōnpărăbăt .
haec omina grauis casus ādmĭnĭstrābănt .

B' Item .
Alii fortuna dedit felīcĭtātēm .
huic industria uĭrtūtēm cōnpărăuĭt .

A' In hoc genere saepe fĭērī pŏtĕst .
ut non plane par numerus sit sȳllăbārŭm .
et tamen ēssĕ uĭdĕatŭr .
si una aut etiam altera syllaba est āltĕrŭm brĕuĭŭs .
aut si cum in āltĕrō plūrēs sŭnt .
in altero longior aut lōngĭŏrēs .
plenior aut pleniores sȳllăbaē ĕrŭnt .
ut longitudo aut plenitūdō hārŭm .
multitudinem alterius adsequatur et exaequet .

A That is called isocolon which has within itself clauses of speech,
about which we have spoken before,
which should consist of an almost equal number of syllables.
This won't happen by our counting,
for that surely is childish,
but practice and habitual performance will produce such a faculty
that by a certain instinct of mind
we can bring as an echo a clause equal to the one preceding it
in this fashion:

B In battle the father was meeting his end;
at home the son was preparing for his wedding;
these omens were working out grievous misfortunes.

B' Similarly:
   To another man fortune gave good luck;
   to this man hard work supplied goodness.
A' In this form it can often happen
   that the number of syllables may not be absolutely equal
   and yet it may seem to be so
   if the second [clause] is shorter by one syllable or even by a second
   or if, though there are more [syllables] in one [clause],
   in the second [clause] a longer [syllable] or longer syllables,
   a fuller-sounding [syllable] or fuller-sounding syllables will occur,
   so that the length or fulness of sound of these [syllables]
   matches or equals the numerical quantity of the other [clause].

This paragraph falls naturally into three parts, introduction dealing with actual equality (A), exemplary clauses (B-B'), and conclusion dealing with apparent equality (A'), in five sentences, from *Conpar* to *syllabarum*, from *Hoc* to *hoc modo*, from *In proelio* to *administrabant*, from *Alii* to *conparauit* (introduced by *Item*), and from *In hoc genere* to *exaequet*.

Around the central exemplary clauses our author has disposed words chiastically.

1	est
2	et
3	ut . . . par
4	possimus
5	hoc modo
6	exemplary clauses
5'	in hoc genere
4'	potest
3'	ut non plane par
2'	et
1'	esse uideatur

In Paris, Bibliothèque nationale, MS latin 7696 folio 151va every sentence begins with a capital letter, and all but two clauses end with punctuation marks.[25] From this evidence one may arrange the text in blocks of nine, three, three, and nine lines.

The first sentence comprises three sections, of eight, four, and seven words, nineteen together. The second sentence comprises six sections, of five, five, seven, four, five, and two words, twenty-eight together. The nineteen words of the first sentence and the twenty-eight words of the second sentence comprise forty-seven words of introduction about actual equality. The golden

---

25 I owe thanks to Dr Jacques Paviot for collating this manuscript as well as Paris, Bibliothèque nationale, MS latin 7231 f. 39v. and MS latin 7714 f. 56; these exhibit similar but independent systems of punctuation, which imply the same division into phrases as arranged here.

section of 47 falls at 29 and 18. The third sentence comprises three exemplary clauses, of five, four, and five words, fourteen together. The golden section of 14 falls at 9 and 5. The fourth sentence comprises two exemplary clauses of four words each. The five exemplary clauses together comprise twenty-two words. The golden section of 22 falls at 14 and 8. The fifth sentence comprises nine sections totalling fifty-three words. The entire paragraph comprises 123 words, sixty-one before *Item* and sixty-one after it. The golden section of 123 falls at 76 and 47. The minor part is the forty-seven words of introduction about actual equality and the major part the seventy-six words of exemplary clauses and conclusion about apparent equality.

Our author is manifestly discussing the number of syllables, which, he tells us, it is childish to count. Whether achieved by counting or by a certain instinct of mind, his first sentence comprises forty-one syllables. The second sentence comprises sixty-six syllables. The first two sentences together comprise 107 syllables. The golden section of 107 falls at 66 and 41. The third sentence comprises three clauses, of twelve, twelve, and thirteen syllables, thirty-seven together, and the fourth two clauses, of thirteen and twelve syllables, twenty-five together. 37 + 25 = 62. The golden section of 62 falls at 38 and 24. The fifth sentence comprises 117 syllables. The entire paragraph comprises 288 syllables, 144 from *Conpar* to *administrabant* and 144 from *Item* to *exaequet*.

The first sentence comprises 101 letters. The second sentence comprises 152 letters. The three clauses of the third sentence comprise thirty, twenty-seven, and thirty-four letters, together ninety-one. The golden section of 91 falls at 56 and 35. The fourth sentence comprises thirty-one letters from *Item* to *felicitatem* and thirty-one from *huic* to *conparauit*. The fifth sentence comprises 275 letters. The entire paragraph contains 681 letters, 344 from *Conpar* to *administrabant* (without *conpar* 338) and 337 from *Item* to *exaequet*.

The subject of the passage is clear from the first and last words of the first line, *conpar* and *membra orationis*, echoed by the first words of the last line of the introduction, *par membrum*. Between *conpar* and *conparabat*, the last word of the central colon in the first group of examples, there are fifty-four words. The fifty-fourth word from the end of the paragraph is the last word of the second group of examples, *conparauit*. In the phrase *ex pari fere numero syllabarum* the adjective *pari* is central, the fourth word from the beginning of the clause and the fourth from the end. In the comparable phrase *non plane par numerus sit syllabarum* the adjective *par* is central, the fourth word from the beginning of the clause and the fourth from the end. In the clause *hoc non denumeratione nostra fiet*, the word *denumeratione* is central, third from the beginning and third from the end. The seventh word is *membra*. The thirty-fifth word after that (7×5) is *membrum*. Beginning at *conpar* the sixteenth word (8×2) is *pari*. Backward from *conparabat* the sixteenth word is *par*. There are twenty-four words (8×3) between *pari* and *par*. The *-ri* in *pari* is the thirty-second syllable (8×4). After *par* from *membrum* through *conparabat* there are forty syllables (8×5). The nineteenth word is *syllabarum*, of which the first syllable is the thirty-eighth (19 × 2). From the last occurrence of *syllabae* backward the nineteenth word is *syllaba*, *-ba* being the thirty-eighth syllable before *syllabae*. The twenty-first word from the beginning is *denumeratione*. The forty-second word from the end (21 × 2) brings one to *numerus*. The last syllable of *denumeratione* is fiftieth from the beginning. The first syllable of *numerus* is one hundredth from the end.

One could hardly divide this paragraph in any way different from that set out above. The ordering of the text is confirmed by grammar and syntax, by common sense, by symmetry and extreme and mean ratio reckoned by the number of words, syllables, and letters. Every clause but the fifth and the last ends with a clausula.[26]

The *Rhetorica ad Herennium* is by no means unique. Here, for another example, is Cicero *De Oratore* III 44. Boldface punctuation marks represent those of London, British Library, MS Harley 2736 folio 97ra-va, written by Lupus of Ferrières in the mid ninth century.[27]

A   hanc diligentiam subsequitur modus et fōrmă uērbŏrŭm
     quod iam uereor ne huic Catulo uideatur ēssĕ pŭērĭlē .

B   uersus enim ueteres illi in hac soluta oratiōnĕ prŏpēmŏdŭm
     hoc est numeros quosdam nobis esse adhibendōs pŭtăuērŭnt

C   interspirationis enim non defetigationis nostrae neque
     lībrārĭōrŭm nŏtĭs
     sed uerborum et sententiarum modo interpunctas clausulas in
     orationibus ēssĕ uŏlŭērŭnt

D   idque princeps Isocrates instituisse fertur ut inconditam
     antiquorum dicendi consuetudinem delectationis atque
     aūrĭŭm caūsă
     quem ad modum scribit discipulus eius Naucrates numerīs
     ādstrīngĕrĕt .

E   namque haec duo musici qui erant quondam eidem poetae
     machinati ād uŏlŭptātĕm sŭnt
     uersum ătquĕ cāntŭm
     ut et uerborum numero et uocum modo delectatione
     uincerent aurĭŭm sătĭĕtātĕm .

E'   haec igitur duo uocis dico moderationem et
     uerbŏrŭm cōnclūsĭōnĕm
     quoad orationis seueritas pătī pŏssĕt
     a poetica ad eloquentiam traducēndă dŭxĕrŭnt

---

26   The last could be made to exhibit a clausula by emending to *adsequatur atque exaequet*, but that
     would alter the number of letters.
27   *Lupus of Ferrieres as Scribe and Text Critic, A Study of his Autograph Copy of Cicero's De Oratore by
     Charles Henry Beeson With a Facsimile of the Manuscript*, The Mediaeval Academy of America
     Publication No. 4 (Cambridge, MA 1930); D.A. Russell & M. Winterbottom transl., *Ancient
     Literary Criticism* (Oxford 1972), pp. 262–3.

D' in quo illud est uel maximum quod uersus in oratione si
efficitur coniunctione uerborūm uitium est [MS .e.]
et tamen eam coniunctionem sicuti uersum numerose cadere
et quadrare et perfici uolumus [MS uolum:]

C' neque est ex multis res una quae magis oratorem ab imperito
dicendi ignaroque distinguat
quam quod ille rudis incondite fundit quantum potest et id quod
dicit spiritu non arte determinat .
orator autem sic inligat sententiam uerbis

B' ut eam numero quodam conplectatur et adstricto et soluto ;

A' nam cum uinxit forma et modis
relaxat et liberat inmutatione ordinis
ut uerba neque adligata sint quasi certa aliqua lege uersus neque ita
soluta ut uagentur .

A Following on this duty comes the shaping and balancing of words.
Catulus here, I fear, may find this puerile.

B The old writers thought that we should bring a certain rhythm,
almost amounting to verses, into our prose:

C and that speeches should have pauses dictated by the need to draw
breath rather than by complete exhaustion, and marked not by
scribes' punctuation but by the pattern of words and content.

D This is said to have been introduced first by Isocrates; as his pupil
Naucrates writes, his aim was to shackle with rhythm, for the sake
of the pleasure it gives our ears, the disorganized manner of speech
employed by the ancients.

E For these two things, verse and melody, were devised by musicians,
who at one time were identical with poets; their aim was pleasure:
they intended, employing word-rhythm and musical measure, to
defeat monotony by the delight afforded the ear.

E' They thus thought that these two factors, modulation of the voice
and rounding off of words, should, as far as the severity of prose
allowed, be transferred to eloquence from poetry.

D' The key point here is that if the sequence of words causes the
appearance of verse in prose, there is something wrong: yet at the
same time we want the sequence of words to end rhythmically,
just as a verse does, tidily and completely.

C' There is no one thing, out of so many, that more clearly marks off
the orator from the man who is ignorant and unskilled in speaking
than that the untutored pour out all they can shapelessly, letting
breath, not technique, dictate the pauses in what they say: while
the orator so binds his thought in words

B' that he imposes on it a rhythm at once disciplined and free.

A'   Having bound it with balance and rhythm, he relaxes and frees it
      by changes of order, ensuring that the words are neither subjected
      like verse to some particular rule nor so free as to wander at large.

Cicero arranged his words and thought chiastically. Compare *modus et forma
uerborum* in A with *forma et modis* and *uerba* in A', *numeros quosdam, adhibendos,* and
soluta in B with *numero quodam, adstricto,* and *soluto* in B', *interspirationis, uerborum et
sententiarum,* and *orationibus* in C with *spiritu, sententiam uerbis,* and *orator* twice in
C', *numeris adstringeret* in D with *numerose cadere* in D', *namque haec duo, poetae, et
uerborum,* and *uocum* in E with *haec igitur duo, poetica, et uerborum,* and *uocis* in E'.

He also composed mathematically. The seventeen words in A and the twenty-
six words in A' exhibit the sesquialter ratio (3:2). The thirty-six words of BC and
the fifty-five words of C'B' exhibit the same ratio. The fifty words in DE may be
compared with the forty-nine in E'D'.[28] Both clauses in A contain exactly twenty
syllables. A letter count reveals that the *h* of *haec* at the beginning of E' is the
649th letter from the beginning and the 649th from the end.

Note that in A *modus etiam et forma* begin at the fourth word, and in A' *forma et
modis* begin at the fourth word. In B *numeros quosdam* are the third and fourth
words of their clause, and in B' *numero quodam* are the third and fourth words of
their clause. Also in B *adhibendos* is the seventh word of its clause, and in B'
adstricto is the seventh word of its clause. In C the fourth word of the second
clause is *sententiarum*. In C' four words of the last clause bring one to *sententiam*. In
E the first three words are *namque haec duo*, and in E' the first three words are *haec
igitur duo*. Also in E the sixth word from the end of the last clause is *uocum*, and in
E' the sixth word from the end of the first clause is *uocis*. The eighth word of A is
the eight-lettered *uerborum*. In C eight words bring one to *uerborum*. In E eight
words from the end bring one to *uerborum*. In E' the eighth word is *uerborum*. In
D' the sixteenth word from the end (8 × 2) is *uerborum*. In C the ninth word of
the second clause is *orationibus*. In E' nine words from the end bring one to
orationis. In D' nine words from the beginning bring one to *oratione*.

Every clause ends with a clausula, eleven in the first half and twelve in the
second, eight of them marked by Lupus with punctuation.

The passages quoted above from Isaiah, Lamentations, and Amos have
shown us the basic patterns and rules of Biblical style in small units. The
passages from *Rhetorica ad Herennium* and Cicero *De Oratore* have shown us
most of the adjuncts, so precisely employed that we may be reasonably certain
of the exact placement of every word and its exact spelling. But the same
elements appear together in Biblical prose and verse in larger units such as
pericopes and chapters and groups of chapters. They extend even to entire
books. One finds them in many different types of Biblical text: creation myth,
law, historical narrative, major and minor prophets, psalms, proverbs, gospels,

---

28   If one followed some editors in deleting *delectatione* from E, then DE and E'D' would each contain
      forty-nine words. But deletion of the word would alter the letter count.

and epistles. The style is fully developed in the Masoretic text; it is occasionally reflected in the Septuagint; it is usually reproduced perfectly in the Vulgate.

After establishment of the Vulgate as the official Bible of Western Christendom the style was practised widely throughout the middle ages until, apparently, it fell into disfavour in the early modern period. But as long ago as the eighteenth century several English priests began to rediscover and expound elements of Biblical style. In a series of lectures delivered in the University of Oxford in 1753 the Revd Robert Lowth, later Bishop of London, drew attention to the importance of parallelism in Hebrew poetry.[29] The Revd John Jebb, later Bishop of Limerick, developed Lowth's theory by noting, among other things, the recurrence of chiasmus, which he called 'introverted parallelism'.[30] In 1824 the Revd Thomas Boys, Curate of St Dunstan's-in-the-West in London, acknowledged his debt to Lowth and Jebb and undertook 'to reduce whole Epistles to the form of single parallelisms'.[31] A generation later a Scot, the Revd John Forbes, applied Boys's technique in his book, *The Symmetrical Structure of Scripture*.[32] In the twentieth century some Biblical, Classical, and Old English scholars have pursued this line of inquiry, but few have devoted to it the rigorous systematic analysis it deserves.[33]

Ignorance of Biblical style has misled many scholars to infer that texts composed in it are corrupt or formless. By recognizing Biblical style we may acquire first a valuable textual critical tool for selecting correct readings among variants of corrupt texts, second a window into the minds of authors who have been misapprehended and misprized, and third new insights into an unrecognised tradition of composition which spans millennia.[34]

THE BOOK OF JUDGES

A clear example of composition in the unit of a paragraph occurs in the historical narrative prose of the Book of Judges III 7–11.[35] The paragraph is

---

29 R. Lowth, *De Sacra Poesi Hebraeorum* (Oxford 1753), transl. G. Gregory, *Lectures on the Sacred Poetry of the Hebrews* (London 1787).

30 J. Jebb, *Sacred Literature* (London 1820), p. 53.

31 T. Boys, *Tactica Sacra* (London 1824), p. 8.

32 J. Forbes, *The Symmetrical Structure of Scripture* (Edinburgh 1854).

33 A.C. Bartlett, *The Larger Rhetorical Patterns in Anglo-Saxon Poetry* (New York 1935); Lund, *Chiasmus*; J. Jeremias, 'Chiasmus in den Paulusbriefen', *Zeitschrift für die Neutestamentliche Wissenschaft* XLIX (1958), pp. 145–56. J.C. Fenton, *The Gospel of St Matthew*, Pelican Gospel Commentaries (Harmondsworth 1963); M.J.J. Menken, *Numerical Literary Techniques in John* (Leiden 1985); J. Smit Sibinga, '*Gedicht en getal*', *Nederlands Theologisch Tijdschrift* XLII (1988), pp. 185–207. J.W. Welch ed., *Chiasmus in Antiquity: Structures, Analyses, Exegesis* (Hildesheim 1981). Idem, *Chiasmus Bibliography* (Provo, UT 1987). Even these last two works, excellent as they are, address only one aspect of the problem.

34 The traditions of such composition are not exclusively Biblical, but in the Latin West during the early Middle Ages the matrix of literary culture was the Vulgate. Those who read Classical Latin literature had usually read the Bible, the Christian fathers, and the Christian poets before.

35 I owe thanks to Dr Richard White for drawing my attention to this passage as an example of Biblical style.

preceded and followed by the letter **ס**, marking the limits of the unit, which tells in five verses the story of the first of the Judges of Israel.

ס

Ia	וַיַּעֲשׂוּ בְנֵי־יִשְׂרָאֵל אֶת־הָרַע בְּעֵינֵי יְהֹוָה
a'	וַיִּשְׁכְּחוּ אֶת־יְהֹוָה אֱלֹהֵיהֶם
2a	וַיַּעַבְדוּ אֶת־הַבְּעָלִים וְאֶת־הָאֲשֵׁרוֹת׃
b	וַיִּחַר־אַף יְהֹוָה בְּיִשְׂרָאֵל
b'	וַיִּמְכְּרֵם בְּיַד כּוּשַׁן רִשְׁעָתַיִם מֶלֶךְ אֲרַם נַהֲרָיִם
a'	וַיַּעַבְדוּ בְנֵי־יִשְׂרָאֵל אֶת־כּוּשַׁן רִשְׁעָתַיִם שְׁמֹנֶה שָׁנִים׃
3a	וַיִּזְעֲקוּ בְנֵי־יִשְׂרָאֵל אֶל־יְהֹוָה
b	וַיָּקֶם יְהֹוָה מוֹשִׁיעַ לִבְנֵי יִשְׂרָאֵל
c	וַיּוֹשִׁיעֵם אֵת
4	עָתְנִיאֵל בֶּן־קְנַז
4'	אֲחִי כָלֵב הַקָּטֹן מִמֶּנּוּ׃
3'a	וַתְּהִי עָלָיו רוּחַ־יְהֹוָה
b	וַיִּשְׁפֹּט אֶת־יִשְׂרָאֵל
c	וַיֵּצֵא לַמִּלְחָמָה
2'b	וַיִּתֵּן יְהֹוָה בְּיָדוֹ אֶת־כּוּשַׁן רִשְׁעָתַיִם מֶלֶךְ אֲרָם
	וַתָּעָז יָדוֹ עַל כּוּשַׁן רִשְׁעָתָיִם׃
a	וַתִּשְׁקֹט הָאָרֶץ אַרְבָּעִים שָׁנָה
I'	וַיָּמָת עָתְנִיאֵל בֶּן־קְנַז׃ ס

Ia	And the people of Israel did what was evil in the sight of the Lord,
a'	forgetting the Lord their God,
2a	and serving the Baals and the Asheroth.
b	Therefore the anger of the Lord was kindled against Israel,
b'	and He sold them into the hand of Cushan-rishathaim king of Mesopotamia,
a'	and the people of Israel served Cushan-rishathaim eight years.
3a	But when the people of Israel cried to the Lord,
b	the Lord raised up a deliverer for the people of Israel,
c	who delivered them,
4	Othniel the son of Kenaz,
4'	Caleb's younger brother.
3'a	The Spirit of the Lord came upon him,
b	and he judged Israel;
c	he went out to war,
2'b	and the Lord gave Cushan-rishathaim king of Mesopotamia into his hand, and his hand prevailed over Cushan-rishathaim.
a	So the land had rest forty years.
I'	Then Othniel the son of Kenaz died.

1a	feceruntque malum in conspectu Domini
a'	et obliti sunt Dei sui
2a	seruientes Baalim et Astharoth
b	iratusque Dominus contra Israhel;
b'	tradidit eos in manus Chusanrasathaim regis Mesopotamiae
a'	seruieruntque ei octo annis;
3a	et clamauerunt ad Dominum,
b	qui suscitauit eis saluatorem
c	et liberauit eos
4	Othonihel uidelicet filium Cenez
4'	fratrem Chaleb minorem
3'a	fuitque in eo Spiritus Domini
b	et iudicauit Israhel
c	egressusque est ad pugnam
2'b	et tradidit Dominus in manu eius Chusanrasathaim regem Syriae et oppressit eum
a	quieuitque terra quadraginta annis
1'	et mortuus est Othonihel filius Cenez.

In the Masoretic text we see internal parallels in 1 in the double statement of the Israelites' evil and in the naming of the Lord twice; in 2 in the same verb וַיַּעַבְדוּ 'and they served', a and a', and the statement of the Lord's anger and its consequences in b and b'. Parallels that link parts 1–4 to parts 4'–1' include the naming of Cushan-rishathaim in 2 and 2', the word בְּיַד 'into the hand' in 2b' and בְּיָדוֹ 'into his hand' in 2'b, also שָׁנִים 'years' in 2a' and שָׁנָה 'year' in 2'a, and in 3 and 3' the references to the Lord in a, Israel in b, and deliverance and going out to war in c. In 4 and 4' Othniel is identified as both son of Kenaz and brother of Caleb. Both parts end identically with the name of the hero, 'Othniel the son of Kenaz' in 4 and 1'. Among the internal parallels in 1 there are seven words in a and four words in a', together eleven, which divide by sesquialter ratio (3:2) at 7 and 4; in 2 there are fifteen words in b'a' and nine words in ab, together twenty-four, which divide by sesquialter ratio at 14.4 and 9.6; in 3 there are seven words in bc and five words in a, together twelve, which divide by sesquialter ratio at 7 and 5; in 3' there are five words in bc and four words in a, together nine, which divide by sesquialter ratio at 5 and 4. Among parallels linking parts 1–4 to parts 4'–1' the twenty-four words of 2 and the seventeen words of 2' total forty-one, which divide by sesquialter ratio at 24.6 and 16.4. The twelve words of 3 and the nine words of 3' total twenty-one, which divide by sesquialter ratio at 12.6 and 8.4. The entire passage comprises eighty-four words, which divide by sesquialter ratio at 50 and 34. There are fifty words in parts 1–4 and thirty-four words in parts 4'–1'. The fifty-second word is כָּלֵב Caleb, the numerical value of which in Hebrew letters is 52. The word which follows that name, הַקָּטֹן 'younger', also means 'lesser, smaller', and it marks the minor part of the sesquialter ratio. The fifty-word major part divides by sesquialter ratio at 30 and 20, at the name of the oppressor אֶת־כּוּשַׁן רִשְׁעָתַיִם in 2a'. The central twenty-fifth word is the oppressor's title מֶלֶךְ אֲרַם נַהֲרָיִם in 2b'. The thirty-four-word minor part divides by sesquialter ratio at 20 and 14, at the oppressor's title מֶלֶךְ אֲרַם in 2'b. The central, seventeenth, word is the name of the oppressor אֶת־כּוּשַׁן רִשְׁעָתַיִם in 2'b. The story relates the dealings of God with Israel. God is named seven times, first in the seventh word of 1a. Between the second mention of God, in 1a', and the third, in 2b, there are seven words. From the third to the fourth inclusive, in 3a, there are twenty-one words (7 × 3). After one intervening word God is mentioned again in 3b; then there are fourteen words (7 × 2) until the next mention of the Spirit of God in 3'a. After that the seventh word is the seventh mention of God. The sons of Israel are mentioned first in 1a, after which the seventeenth word is 'against Israel'. From the third mention of 'the sons of Israel' in 2a' the seventh word begins 'the sons of Israel', and from that the seventh word ends 'for the sons of Israel'. Fourteen words after that (7 × 2) bring one to 'Israel', after which the seventeenth word is 'the land [i.e. of Israel]', which is the seventh word from the end of the paragraph. Six words before the naming of Othniel the son of Kenaz at the centre of the paragraph is the word 'Lord', and six words after the naming one comes to 'the Spirit of the Lord'.

The Vulgate reproduces the parallel and chiastic structure well. Among the internal parallels compare in 1 feceruntque and Domini in a with et obliti sunt and Dei in a', in 2 seruientes in a with seruieruntque in a', Gods anger and its consequences in b and b'. Among the parallels which link 1–4 with 4'–1' compare Dominus, tradidit, in manus Chusanrasathaim regis Mesopotamiae and annis in 2 with Dominus, tradidit, in manu, Chusanrasathaim regem Syriae, and annis in 2', Dominum, eis [i.e. Israhel], and et liberauit eos in 3 with Domini, Israhel, and egressusque est ad pugnam in 3'. Part 4 ends Othonihel uidelicet filium Cenez, and part 1' ends Othonihel filius Cenez. In the Vulgate text there are eighty-one words, of which the central, forty-first, word is the name of the hero, Othonihel. The eighty-one words divide by sesquialter ratio at 49 and 32 at in | eo, that is, Othonihel. The fifth word before Othonihel is eis in 3b, that is Israhel, and the fifth word after eo is Israhel in 3'b. The eighteenth word before eis is Israhel in 2b, which is the eighteenth word from the beginning; the eighteenth word after Israhel in 3'b is terra, that is Israhel, in 2'a, which is the ninth word from the end. The fifth word from the beginning is Domini in 1a. Ten words from that bring one to Dominus in 2b. From Dominus in 3a to Domini in 3'a inclusive there are twenty words. The tenth word after Domini is Dominus 2'b, which is the twentieth word from the end. In the forty-four words of parts 1–4 the central twenty-second words are in manus | Chusanrasathaim regis Mesopotamiae. In the thirty-seven words of parts 4'–1' the central nineteenth word is | in | manu eius Chusanrasathaim regem Syriae.

THE BOOK OF GENESIS

Let us see now what happens when a writer composes on a scale grander than
the paragraph, an entire chapter. Here is the story of the Creation from
Genesis I 1 – II 4.

Aı בְּרֵאשִׁית בָּרָא אֱלֹהִים אֵת הַשָּׁמַיִם וְאֵת הָאָרֶץ:

2a וְהָאָרֶץ הָיְתָה תֹהוּ וָבֹהוּ

b וְחֹשֶׁךְ עַל־פְּנֵי תְהוֹם

c וְרוּחַ אֱלֹהִים מְרַחֶפֶת עַל־פְּנֵי הַמָּיִם:

Bıa וַיֹּאמֶר אֱלֹהִים

bi יְהִי אוֹר וַיְהִי־אוֹר: וַיַּרְא אֱלֹהִים אֶת־הָאוֹר כִּי־טוֹב

ii וַיַּבְדֵּל אֱלֹהִים בֵּין הָאוֹר וּבֵין הַחֹשֶׁךְ:

i' וַיִּקְרָא אֱלֹהִים לָאוֹר יוֹם וְלַחֹשֶׁךְ קָרָא לָיְלָה

c וַיְהִי־עֶרֶב וַיְהִי־בֹקֶר יוֹם אֶחָד: פ

2a וַיֹּאמֶר אֱלֹהִים

bi יְהִי רָקִיעַ בְּתוֹךְ הַמָּיִם

ii וִיהִי מַבְדִּיל בֵּין מַיִם לָמָיִם:

iii וַיַּעַשׂ אֱלֹהִים אֶת־הָרָקִיעַ

ii' וַיַּבְדֵּל בֵּין הַמַּיִם אֲשֶׁר מִתַּחַת לָרָקִיעַ וּבֵין הַמַּיִם אֲשֶׁר מֵעַל לָרָקִיעַ

i' וַיְהִי־כֵן: וַיִּקְרָא אֱלֹהִים לָרָקִיעַ שָׁמָיִם

c וַיְהִי־עֶרֶב וַיְהִי־בֹקֶר יוֹם שֵׁנִי: פ

3a וַיֹּאמֶר אֱלֹהִים

bi יִקָּווּ הַמַּיִם מִתַּחַת הַשָּׁמַיִם אֶל־מָקוֹם אֶחָד

ii וְתֵרָאֶה הַיַּבָּשָׁה

iii וַיְהִי־כֵן:

ii' וַיִּקְרָא אֱלֹהִים לַיַּבָּשָׁה אֶרֶץ

i' וּלְמִקְוֵה הַמַּיִם קָרָא יַמִּים

ci וַיַּרְא אֱלֹהִים כִּי־טוֹב: וַיֹּאמֶר אֱלֹהִים

iia תַּדְשֵׁא הָאָרֶץ דֶּשֶׁא עֵשֶׂב מַזְרִיעַ זֶרַע

b עֵץ פְּרִי עֹשֶׂה פְּרִי לְמִינוֹ

c אֲשֶׁר זַרְעוֹ־בוֹ עַל־הָאָרֶץ

iii וַיְהִי־כֵן:

ii'a	וַתּוֹצֵא הָאָרֶץ דֶּשֶׁא עֵשֶׂב מַזְרִיעַ זֶרַע לְמִינֵהוּ
b	וְעֵץ עֹשֶׂה־פְּרִי
c	אֲשֶׁר זַרְעוֹ־בוֹ לְמִינֵהוּ
i'	וַיַּרְא אֱלֹהִים כִּי־טוֹב:
d	וַיְהִי־עֶרֶב וַיְהִי־בֹקֶר יוֹם שְׁלִישִׁי: פ
B'ia	וַיֹּאמֶר אֱלֹהִים
b	יְהִי מְאֹרֹת בִּרְקִיעַ הַשָּׁמַיִם
ci	לְהַבְדִּיל בֵּין הַיּוֹם וּבֵין הַלָּיְלָה
ii	וְהָיוּ לְאֹתֹת וּלְמוֹעֲדִים וּלְיָמִים וְשָׁנִים:
iiia	וְהָיוּ לִמְאוֹרֹת בִּרְקִיעַ הַשָּׁמַיִם
b	לְהָאִיר עַל־הָאָרֶץ
iv	וַיְהִי־כֵן: וַיַּעַשׂ אֱלֹהִים אֶת־שְׁנֵי הַמְּאֹרֹת הַגְּדֹלִים
iv'	אֶת־הַמָּאוֹר הַגָּדֹל לְמֶמְשֶׁלֶת הַיּוֹם וְאֶת־הַמָּאוֹר הַקָּטֹן
	לְמֶמְשֶׁלֶת הַלַּיְלָה וְאֵת הַכּוֹכָבִים:
iii'a	וַיִּתֵּן אֹתָם אֱלֹהִים בִּרְקִיעַ הַשָּׁמָיִם
b	לְהָאִיר עַל־הָאָרֶץ:
ii'	וְלִמְשֹׁל בַּיּוֹם וּבַלַּיְלָה
i'	וּלֲהַבְדִּיל בֵּין הָאוֹר וּבֵין הַחֹשֶׁךְ
d	וַיַּרְא אֱלֹהִים כִּי־טוֹב:
e	וַיְהִי־עֶרֶב וַיְהִי־בֹקֶר יוֹם רְבִיעִי: פ
2a	וַיֹּאמֶר אֱלֹהִים
bi a	יִשְׁרְצוּ הַמַּיִם שֶׁרֶץ נֶפֶשׁ חַיָּה
b	וְעוֹף יְעוֹפֵף עַל־הָאָרֶץ עַל־פְּנֵי רְקִיעַ הַשָּׁמָיִם:
ii	וַיִּבְרָא אֱלֹהִים
iiia	אֶת־הַתַּנִּינִם הַגְּדֹלִים וְאֵת כָּל־נֶפֶשׁ הַחַיָּה הָרֹמֶשֶׂת
b	אֲשֶׁר שָׁרְצוּ הַמַּיִם לְמִינֵהֶם
iii'a	וְאֵת כָּל־עוֹף
b	כָּנָף לְמִינֵהוּ
ii'	וַיַּרְא אֱלֹהִים כִּי־טוֹב: וַיְבָרֶךְ אֹתָם אֱלֹהִים לֵאמֹר
i' a	פְּרוּ וּרְבוּ וּמִלְאוּ אֶת־הַמַּיִם בַּיַּמִּים
b	וְהָעוֹף יִרֶב בָּאָרֶץ:
c	וַיְהִי־עֶרֶב וַיְהִי־בֹקֶר יוֹם חֲמִישִׁי: פ
3a	וַיֹּאמֶר אֱלֹהִים
bi	תּוֹצֵא הָאָרֶץ נֶפֶשׁ חַיָּה
ii	לְמִינָהּ

בְּהֵמָה וָרֶמֶשׂ	iii
וְחַיְתוֹ־אֶרֶץ לְמִינָהּ	iv
וַיְהִי־כֵן:	v
וַיַּעַשׂ אֱלֹהִים	v'
אֶת־חַיַּת הָאָרֶץ לְמִינָהּ	iv'
וְאֶת־הַבְּהֵמָה לְמִינָהּ וְאֵת כָּל־רֶמֶשׂ הָאֲדָמָה	iii'
לְמִינֵהוּ	ii'
וַיַּרְא אֱלֹהִים כִּי־טוֹב: וַיֹּאמֶר אֱלֹהִים	ci
נַעֲשֶׂה אָדָם בְּצַלְמֵנוּ כִּדְמוּתֵנוּ	iia
וְיִרְדּוּ בִדְגַת הַיָּם וּבְעוֹף הַשָּׁמַיִם	b 1
וּבַבְּהֵמָה וּבְכָל־הָאָרֶץ וּבְכָל־הָרֶמֶשׂ	2
הָרֹמֵשׂ עַל־הָאָרֶץ:	3
וַיִּבְרָא אֱלֹהִים אֶת־הָאָדָם	iiia
בְּצַלְמוֹ	b1
בְּצֶלֶם אֱלֹהִים	2
בָּרָא אֹתוֹ	a'
זָכָר	b'1
וּנְקֵבָה	2
בָּרָא אֹתָם:	a"
וַיְבָרֶךְ אֹתָם אֱלֹהִים וַיֹּאמֶר לָהֶם אֱלֹהִים	ii'a1
פְּרוּ וּרְבוּ	2
וּמִלְאוּ אֶת־הָאָרֶץ וְכִבְשֻׁהָ	3
וּרְדוּ בִדְגַת הַיָּם וּבְעוֹף הַשָּׁמַיִם	b 1
וּבְכָל־חַיָּה	2
הָרֹמֶשֶׂת עַל־הָאָרֶץ:	3
וַיֹּאמֶר אֱלֹהִים	a'1
הִנֵּה נָתַתִּי לָכֶם אֶת־כָּל־עֵשֶׂב זֹרֵעַ זֶרַע	2
אֲשֶׁר עַל־פְּנֵי כָל־הָאָרֶץ	
וְאֶת־כָּל־הָעֵץ אֲשֶׁר־בּוֹ פְרִי־עֵץ זֹרֵעַ זָרַע לָכֶם	
יִהְיֶה לְאָכְלָה:	3
וּ לְכָל־חַיַּת הָאָרֶץ וּלְכָל־עוֹף הַשָּׁמַיִם	b'1
וּלְכֹל רוֹמֵשׂ עַל־הָאָרֶץ אֲשֶׁר־בּוֹ נֶפֶשׁ חַיָּה	2
אֶת־כָּל־יֶרֶק עֵשֶׂב לְאָכְלָה	3
וַיְהִי־כֵן:	i'
וַיַּרְא אֱלֹהִים אֶת־כָּל־אֲשֶׁר עָשָׂה וְהִנֵּה־טוֹב מְאֹד	
וַיְהִי־עֶרֶב וַיְהִי־בֹקֶר יוֹם הַשִּׁשִּׁי: פ	d
וַיְכֻלּוּ הַשָּׁמַיִם וְהָאָרֶץ וְכָל־צְבָאָם:	A'ı
וַיְכַל אֱלֹהִים בַּיּוֹם הַשְּׁבִיעִי מְלַאכְתּוֹ אֲשֶׁר עָשָׂה	2a
וַיִּשְׁבֹּת בַּיּוֹם הַשְּׁבִיעִי מִכָּל־מְלַאכְתּוֹ אֲשֶׁר עָשָׂה:	b
וַיְבָרֶךְ אֱלֹהִים	3
אֶת־יוֹם הַשְּׁבִיעִי	4
וַיְקַדֵּשׁ אֹתוֹ	3'
כִּי בוֹ שָׁבַת מִכָּל־מְלַאכְתּוֹ	2'b

אֲשֶׁר־בָּרָא אֱלֹהִים לַעֲשׂוֹת: פ   a

אֵלֶּה תוֹלְדוֹת הַשָּׁמַיִם   I'a

וְהָאָרֶץ   b

בְּהִבָּרְאָם   c

בְּיוֹם עֲשׂוֹת יְהוָה אֱלֹהִים   c'

אֶרֶץ   b'

וְשָׁמָיִם: a'

A1		In the beginning God created the heavens and the earth.
2a		The earth was without form and void,
b		and darkness was upon the face of the deep,
c		and the Spirit of God was moving over the face of the waters.
B1a		And God said,
bi		"Let there be light" and there was light.
		And God saw that the light was good.
ii		And God separated the light from the darkness.
i'		God called the light day and the darkness He called night.
c		And there was evening and there was morning, one day.
2a		And God said,
bi		"Let there be a firmament in the midst of the waters
ii		and let it separate the waters from the waters."
iii		And God made the firmament
ii'		and separated the waters which were under the firmament from the waters which were above the firmament.
i'		And it was so. And God called the firmament heaven.
c		And there was evening and there was morning, a second day.
3a		And God said,
bi		"Let the waters under the heavens be gathered together into one place
ii		and let the dry land appear."
iii		And it was so.
ii'		God called the dry land earth
i'		and the waters that were gathered together He called seas.
ci		And God saw that it was good. And God said
ii	a	"Let the earth put forth vegetation, plants yielding seed,
	b	and fruit trees bearing fruit in which is their seed,
	c	each according to its kind, upon the earth."
iii		And it was so.
ii'	a	The earth brought forth vegetation, plants yielding seed according to their own kinds,
	b	and trees bearing fruit in which is their seed,
	c	each according to its kind.
i'		And God saw that it was good.

d   And there was evening and there was morning, a third day.

B'ıa   And God said,

b   "Let there be lights in the firmament of the heavens

ci   to separate the day from the night,

ii   and let them be for signs and for seasons and for days and years,

iii *a*   and let them be lights in the firmament of the heavens

  b   to give light upon the earth."

iv   And it was so. And God made the two great lights,

iv'   the greater light to rule the day and the lesser light to rule the night;

          He made the stars also.

iii'*a*   And God set them in the firmament of the heavens

  b   to give light upon the earth,

ii'   to rule over the day and over the night,

i'   and to separate the light from the darkness.

d   And God saw that it was good.

e   And there was evening and there was morning, a fourth day.

2a   And God said,

bi *a*   "Let the waters bring forth swarms of living creatures,

  b   and let birds fly above the earth across the firmament of the heavens."

ii   So God created

iii *a*   the great sea monsters and every living creature that moves

  b   with which the waters swarm, according to their kinds,

iii'*a*   and every winged bird,

  b   according to its kind.

ii'   And God saw that it was good. And God blessed them saying,

i' *a*   "Be fruitful and multiply and fill the waters in the seas,

  b   and let birds multiply on the earth."

c   And there was evening and there was morning, a fifth day.

3a   And God said,

bi   "Let the earth bring forth living creatures,

ii   according to their kinds:

iii   cattle and creeping things,

iv   and beasts of the earth according to their kinds."

v   And it was so.

v'   And God made

iv'   the beasts of the earth according to their kinds,

iii'   and the cattle according to their kinds and everything that creeps upon the ground,

ii'   according to its kind.

c i   And God saw that it was good. Then God said,
  ii *a*   "Let Us make man in Our image, after Our likeness,
    b 1   and let them have dominion over the fish of the sea
                 and over the birds of the air,
      2   and over the cattle and over all the earth."
      3   · and over every creeping thing that creeps
                 upon the earth."
  iii *a*   So God created man
    b 1   in His own image;
      2   in the image of God
    a'   He created him;
    b'1   male
      2   and female
    a''   He created them.
  ii' *a* 1   And God blessed them and said to them,
      2   "Be fruitful and multiply,
      3   and fill the earth and subdue it,
    b 1   and have dominion over the fish of the sea and
                 over the birds of the air,
      2   and over every living thing
      3   that moves upon the earth."
    a'1   And God said,
      2   "Behold, I have given you every plant yielding seed
                 which is upon the face of all the earth and every tree
                 with seed in its fruit.
      3   You shall have them for food.
    b'1   And to every beast of the earth and to every bird
                 of the air
      2   and to everything that creeps on the earth,
                 everything that has the breath of life,
      3   I have given every green plant for food."
  i'   And it was so. And God saw everything that He had
                 made, and behold, it was very good.
  d   And there was evening and there was
                 morning, a sixth day.
A'1   Thus the heavens and the earth were finished and all the host of them.
  2 a   And on the seventh day God finished His work which He had done,
    b   and He rested on the seventh day from all His work which He had
                 done.
  3   So God blessed
  4   the seventh day
  3'   and hallowed it,
  2'b   because on it God rested from all His work,

a	which He had done in Creation.
1'a	These are the generations of the heavens
b	and the earth
c	when they were created,
d'	in the day
c'	that the Lord God made
b'	the earth
a'	and the heavens.

The entire passage makes a great chiasmus, ABB'A'. The announcement of Creation and the description of the void in A are balanced by the perfection of Creation and Sabbath rest in A'. The sentence marked A'ı' at once concludes this passage and introduces the next Creation story of Genesis II, with its new divine title יְהוָה, 'Lord', distinct from the title אֱלֹהִים 'God' used throughout Genesis I. Within these bounds the six days make a parallelism in BB'. Each section is clearly introduced by 'And God said' and concluded by 'and there was evening and there was morning ...'. The creation of light and the distinction of light and day from darkness and night on the first day (BI) are balanced by the creation of lights to shine by day and night on the fourth day (B'I). The establishment of the firmament and the separation of the waters on the second day (B2) are balanced by the generation of creatures that fly beneath the firmament and live in the waters on the fifth day (B'2). The work of the third day (B3) is twofold: first the gathering of the seas and the emergence of dry land and then the appearance of grasses and trees with their seed. The work of the sixth day (B'3) is similarly twofold: first the production of beasts and creeping things on the dry land and then the creation of man with his dominion over creatures of sea, sky, and land, as well as grasses and trees with their seed.

This account of Creation follows the order of the seven-day week. Its first sentence comprises seven words and its second fourteen words, together twenty-one, of which the golden section falls at 13 and 8. There are two occurrences of the Name of God, between which there are thirteen words. From the beginning to the former occurrence inclusive there are three words, and from the latter occurrence inclusive to the end there are five words, together eight, of which the golden section falls at 5 and 3.

On the first day (BI) God created light. There are thirty-one words, of which the central, sixteenth, word is 'the light' in bii. The sixth word before that is 'light', and beginning with it the sixth word after is 'light'. The Name of God appears four times. From the first to the second inclusive there are seven words. From the second to the third inclusive there are seven words. From the third to the fourth inclusive there are seven words. From the first to the fourth inclusive there are nineteen words. Before the first there is one word and after the fourth there are eleven words, together twelve. The golden section of 31 falls at 19 and 12.

On the second day God created the firmament. There are thirty-eight words, of which the golden section falls at 23 and 15. The fifteenth word is 'the firma-

ment' in biii. The eleventh word before that is 'firmament' in bi, and the
eleventh word after it is 'firmament' in bii'. The fifth word before this is 'firmament', and the fifth word after it is 'firmament'. There are three occurrences of
the Name of God. From the first in B2a to the third in B2bi' inclusive there are
twenty-nine words, the golden section of which falls at 18 and 11. After the first
occurrence the eleventh word is the second occurrence of the Name of God at
the crux in B2biii. From the second occurrence to the third inclusive there are
eighteen words.

On the third day (B3) God created trees. There are sixty-nine words, of which
the golden section falls at 43 and 26. The forty-third word brings one to the end
of 'on the earth' just before the crux of the passage at ciii 'and it was so'. The
tenth word before the crux is 'trees' in ciib, and beginning at the crux the tenth
word after is 'and trees' in cii'b. The seventh word before the former 'trees' is the
Name of God, and seven words after the latter 'and trees' bring one again to the
Name of God. From the first occurrence of the Name of God in B3a to the
second in B3bii' inclusive there are fourteen words. Between the second and the
third in B3ci there are seven words. The fourth occurrence at the end of B3ci is
the forty-third word from the end of the passage. If we consider the internal
divisions of B3 we see that part b contains nineteen words, of which the central,
tenth, word is the beginning of the crux at 3biii. The golden section of 19 falls at
12 and 7. The seventh word from the end is the Name of God. Part c contains
forty-two words, of which the central, twenty-first from the beginning and
twenty-first from the end are 'on the earth', at the golden section of the entire
paragraph. The eighth word (4 × 2) from the beginning of part c is 'the earth'.
Between 'the earth' and 'trees' there are four words (4 × 1). Between 'trees' and
'the earth' there are eight words (4 × 2). The fourth word after 'the earth' (4 × 1)
is 'the earth', after which there are sixteen words (4 × 4) to the end of part c. The
number of words in the account of the first day, 31, added to the number in the
account of the second, 38, equals the number in the account of the third, 69.

On the fourth day (B'1) God created the sun, the moon, and the stars.
There are, as in the account of the third day, sixty-nine words. The forty-third
word, at the golden section at the end of the crux in iv', is 'stars'. The Name
of God occurs four times. From the first to the second inclusive there are
twenty-six words. Between the first and the third there are forty-three words.
Between the third and the fourth there are fourteen words.

On the fifth day (B'2) God created living creatures in the air and the water.
There are fifty-seven words, of which the golden section falls at 35 and 22.
The twenty-second word from the beginning and the thirty-fifth word from
the end are 'every creature' in iiia. Between the first and second occurrences
of the Name of God there are fourteen words.

On the sixth day, B'3a-b, in a passage of twenty-eight words, half as long as
the account of the preceding day, God made living creatures on the land. The
golden section of 28 falls at 11 and 17. The eleventh word is 'earth' in biv. The
seventh word before that is 'the earth', and the seventh word after it brings one

again to 'the earth'. The central word stands at the crux of the passage in v 'and it was *so*'. The Name of God occurs twice, once in B'3a and again in B'3bv'. The second is the fourteenth word after the first. From the beginning to the first inclusive there are two words, and after the second there are twelve words, together fourteen.

Next, in a passage of thirty-six words, ci-iii, God created man in His own image to have dominion over all the earth. The central, eighteenth, word from the beginning is 'the earth'. The golden section of 36 falls at 22 and 14. The twenty-second word is 'on the earth'. Then, in a passage of twenty-two words, cii'*a-b*, God commanded man to fill the earth. The central, eleventh, word is the earth. The eleventh word after that is also the earth. In a passage of fifty-seven words, cii'a'-i', equal in length to the account of the fifth day, God gave food to His creatures. The golden section of 57 falls at 35 and 22. The twenty-first and twenty-second words from the end of the passage are 'on the earth'. The seventh word before 'the earth' is 'the earth'. Fourteen words before that bring one to 'the earth'. Fourteen more words before that bring one to the beginning of the passage. The account of the sixth day ends with a sentence of six words in d. The triumph of the sixth day, from man's point of view, is that God created man in His own image. The account of the entire sixth day comprises 149 words, of which the golden section falls at 92 and 57. The fifty-seventh word from the beginning of the passage and the ninety-second word from the end of the passage are 'in the image of God'.

Finally the account of the seventh day comprises forty-six words, of which the central twenty-third words from the beginning and the end are יוֹם הַשְּׁבִיעִי 'the seventh day'. The golden section of 46 falls at 28 and 18. The eighteenth word from the end is שָׁבַת 'He rested'. There are 194 letters, of which the central, ninety-seventh, is the central ו of the central word יוֹם 'day'. The first occurrence of the Name of God is the seventh word of the paragraph in A'2a. The second occurrence of the Name of God is the fourteenth word after that in A'3. From the second occurrence to the third inclusive, in A'2'a, there are fourteen words. Before the first occurrence there are six words, and after the third there is one word to the end of verse 3, together seven. In verse 4, A'1', there are eleven words, of which the golden section falls at 7 and 4. Seven words bring one to the two Names of God, יְהֹוָה אֱלֹהִים, at the end of the crux in c'.

To recapitulate: the first sentence is half as long as the second (7+14). The number of words in the account of the first day (31) added to that of the second day (38) equals that of the third day (69), which is repeated in the account of the fourth day. The number of words in the account of the fifth day (57) is halved in the first part of the sixth (28), of which the second and third parts (36 and 22) are related by extreme and mean ratio; the fourth part repeats the number of words from the fifth day (57); and the account of the sixth day ends with a sentence of six words. The account of the seventh day (46) alludes to 'the seventh day' at the centre of its seven-part structure and states that 'He rested' at the golden section, with word-play on שְׁבִיעִי and שָׁבַת.

The account of Creation in Genesis I 1–II 4 comprises 480 words. The golden section of 480 falls at 296.65 and 183.35. Parts A and B' comprise 296 words. Parts B and A' comprise 184 words. The same account of Creation comprises 1877 letters. The golden section of 1877 falls at 1160 and 717. Parts A and B' comprise 1159 letters. Parts B and A' comprise 718 letters.

The Vulgate reproduces closely both the sense and the form of the Masoretic text.

AI	In principio creauit Deus caelum et terram
2a	terra autem erat inanis et uacua
b	et tenebrae super faciem abyssi
c	et Spiritus Dei ferebatur super aquas
BIa	dixitque Deus
bi	"Fiat lux" et facta est lux et uidit Deus lucem quod esset bona
ii	et diuisit lucem ac tenebras
i'	appellauitque lucem diem et tenebras noctem
c	factumque est uespere et mane dies unus
2a	dixit quoque Deus
bi	"Fiat firmamentum in medio aquarum
ii	et diuidat aquas ab aquis"
iii	et fecit Deus firmamentum
ii'	diuisitque aquas quae erant sub firmamento ab his quae erant super firmamentum
i'	et factum est ita uocauitque Deus firmamentum caelum
c	et factum est uespere et mane dies secundus
3a	dixit uero Deus
bi	"Congregentur aquae quae sub caelo sunt in locum unum
ii	et appareat arida"
iii	factumque est ita
ii'	et uocauit Deus aridam terram
i'	congregationesque aquarum appellauit maria
ci	et uidit Deus quod esset bonum et ait
iia	"Germinet terra herbam uirentem et facientem semen
b	et lignum pomiferum faciens fructum iuxta genus suum
c	cuius semen in semet ipso sit super terram"
iii	factumque est ita
ii' a	et protulit terra herbam uirentem et adferentem semen iuxta genus suum
b	lignumque faciens fructum
c	et habens unumquodque sementem secundum speciem suam
i'	et uidit Deus quod esset bonum
d	factumque est uespere et mane dies tertius
B'Ia	dixit autem Deus

b   "Fiant luminaria in firmamento caeli
ci   ut diuidant diem ac noctem
  ii   et sint in signa et tempora et dies et annos
  iii *a*   ut luceant in firmamento caeli
     b   et inluminent terram"
  iv   et factum est ita fecitque Deus duo magna luminaria
  iv'   luminare maius ut praeesset diei et luminare minus ut
                    praeesset nocti et stellas.
  iii'*a*   et posuit eas in firmamento caeli
     b   ut lucerent super terram
  ii'   et praeessent diei ac nocti
  i'   et diuiderent lucem ac tenebras
d   et uidit Deus quod esset bonum
e   et factum est uespere et mane dies quartus
2a   dixit etiam Deus
  bi *a*   "Producant aquae reptile animae uiuentis
     b   et uolatile super terram sub firmamento caeli"
  ii   creauitque Deus
  iii *a*   cete grandia et omnem animam uiuentem atque motabilem
     b   quam produxerant aquae in species suas
  iii'*a*   et omne uolatile
     b   secundum genus suum
  ii'   et uidit Deus quod esset bonum benedixitque eis dicens
  i' *a*   "Crescite et multiplicamini et replete aquas maris
     b   auesque multplicentur super terram"
c   et factum est uespere et mane dies quintus
3a   dixit quoque Deus
  bi   "Producat terra animam uiuentem
  ii   in genere suo
  iii   iumenta et reptilia
  iv   et bestias terrae secundum species suas"
  v   factumque est ita
  v'   et fecit Deus
  iv'   bestias terrae iuxta species suas
  iii'   iumenta et omne reptile terrae
  ii'   in genere suo
  ci   et uidit Deus quod esset bonum et ait
  ii *a*   "Faciamus hominem ad imaginem et similitudinem
                       nostram
     *b*1   et praesit piscibus maris et uolatilibus caeli
        2   et bestiis uniuersaeque terrae omnique reptili
        3   quod mouetur in terra
  iii *a*   et creauit Deus hominem
     *b*1   ad imaginem suam

2	ad imaginem Dei
a'	creauit illum
b'1	masculum
2	et feminam
a''	creauit eos
ii'a 1	benedixitque illis Deus et ait
2	"Crescite et multiplicamini
3	et replete terram et subicite eam
b 1	et dominamini piscibus maris et uolatilibus caeli
2	et uniuersis animantibus
3	quae mouentur super terram"
a'1	dixitque Deus
2	"Ecce dedi uobis omnem herbam adferentem semen super terram et uniuersa ligna quae habent in semet ipsis sementem generis sui
3	ut sint uobis in escam
b'1	et cunctis animantibus terrae omnique uolucri caeli
2	et uniuersis quae mouentur in terra et in quibus est anima uiuens
3	ut habeant ad uescendum"
i'	et factum est ita uiditque Deus cuncta quae fecit et erant ualde bona
d	et factum est uespere et mane dies sextus.
A'1	Igitur perfecti sunt caeli et terra et omnis ornatus eorum
2 a	conpleuitque Deus die septimo opus suum quod fecerat
b	et requieuit die septimo ab uniuerso opere quod patrarat
3	et benedixit
4	diei septimo
3'	et sanctificauit illum
2'b	quia in ipso cessauerat ab omni opere suo
a	quod creauit Deus ut faceret.
1'a	Istae generationes caeli
b	et terrae
c	quando creatae sunt
d	in die
c'	quo fecit Dominus Deus
a'	caelum
b'	et terram.[36]

36 The order of these words may reflect either the order of words in the Hebrew exemplar available
    to Jerome or his desire to make a parallel with the beginning of A'1. Or it may issue from an error
    in transmission of the Latin text.

As in the Masoretic text the first sentence of the Vulgate comprises seven words. The account of the first day (B1) comprises thirty-three words, of which the central are *et diuisit lucem*. The twelfth word from the beginning is *lucem*, and the twelfth word from the end is also *lucem*. The former stands three words before the beginning of the central phrase *et diuisit lucem* and the latter three words after the end of it. The account of the second day (B2) comprises forty-five words, of which the central, twenty-third, word is *firmamento*. The golden section of 45 falls at 28 and 17. The seventeenth word from the beginning is *firmamentum*, and the seventeenth word from the end is also *firmamentum*. Between the former and the central *firmamento* there are five words. Between the latter and the central *firmamento* there are also five words. The account of the third day (B3) comprises ninety-six words, of which the golden section falls at 59 and 37. The fifty-ninth word is the beginning of *et factum est ita* 'and it was so'. The fifteenth word before that is *lignum*, and the fifteenth word after it is *lignumque*. Note here that Jerome has rendered the Hebrew proclitic ㄱ 'and' not by *ac* or *atque* or *et* but by enclitic *-que*. The fifteenth word before the former *lignum* brings one to the end of the phrase *uidit Deus quod esset bonum*, and the fifteenth word after the latter *lignumque* brings one to the end of the phrase *uidit Deus quod esset bonum*. The account of the fourth day (B'1) comprises eighty-seven words. The golden section of 87 falls at 54 and 33. The fifty-fourth word stands after the end of the crux at the beginning of ciii'. The account of the fifth day (B'2) comprises sixty-five words. The account of the sixth day (B'3) comprises 186 words. The golden section of 186 falls at 115 and 71. The seventy-first word, at ciiia, brings one to the beginning of the creation of man, *et creauit Deus hominem*. The central, ninety-third, word stands at cii'a1, *crescite* 'be fruitful'. The account of the seventh day (A') comprises sixty-four words. The central, thirty-second, word is the first after the crux, *et* in 3'. There are 327 letters. The central, 164th, letter is the *o* in *diei septimo*. The entire account comprises exactly 600 words and 3100 letters. The golden section of 600 falls at 371 and 229. From the beginning of Creation in B1 the 371st word brings one to the beginning of the creation of man, to the beginning of *faciamus*. The golden section of 3100 falls at 1916 and 1184. Beginning at the same place the 1916th letter brings one to the end of *faciamus*.

THE GOSPEL ACCORDING TO SAINT JOHN

Saint John's Gospel begins with a chiastic and parallel Prologue (1 1–5):

A1	In the beginning	Εν αρχηι
2	was	ην
3	the Word,	ο λογος
4	and the Word	και ο λογος
5	was	ην

6	with God	προς τον θεον
7	and	και
6'	God	θεος
5'	was	ην
4'	the Word;	ο λογος,
3'	He	ουτος
2'	was	ην
1'	in the beginning with God.	εν αρχηι προς τον θεον.
B 1	All things	παντα
2	through Him were made	δια αυτου εγενετο
3	and	και
2'	without Him was made	χωρις αυτου εγενετο
1'	not one thing.	ουδε εν.
C 1	What was made in Him	ο γεγονεν εν αυτωι
2	life was	ζωη ην
3	and	και
2'	the life was	η ζωη ην
1'	the light of men.	το φως των ανθρωπων.
D 1	And the light in the darkness shines	και το φως εν τηι σκοτιαι φαινει
1'	and the darkness has not overcome it.	και η σκοτια αυτο ου κατελαβεν.

A 1	In principio
2	erat
3	Verbum
4	et Verbum
5	erat
6	apud Deum
7	et
6'	Deus
5'	erat
4'	Verbum;
3'	Hoc
2	erat
1'	in principio apud Deum.
B 1	Omnia
2	per ipsum facta sunt
3	et
2'	sine ipso factum est
1'	nihil.
C 1	Quod factum est in ipso
2	uita erat
3	et
2'	uita erat

ɪ' lux hominum.
Dɪ Et lux in tenebris lucet
ɪ' et tenebrae eam non comprehendérunt.

In A the author's ideas at the beginning of the first half, 'In the beginning', and at the end of the first half, 'with God', are restated together at the end of the second half, 'in the beginning with God'. Everything else is chiastically disposed. Compare 'was' in 2 with 'was' in 2', 'the Word' in 3 with 'He, the same' in 3', 'the Word' in 4 with 'the Word' in 4', 'was' in 5 with 'was' in 5', 'with God' in 6 with 'God' in 6', around the central 'and' 7.

Again the author writes chiastically in B, balancing 'all things' in 1 with 'not one thing' in 1' and 'through Him came into being' in 2 with 'without Him came into being' in 2' around the central 'and' in 3.

Yet again he writes chiastically in C, balancing 'what came into being through Him' in 1 with 'the light of men' in 1' and 'life was' in 2 with 'the life was' in 2' around the central 'and' in 3.

Finally he writes parallel in D, 'And the light in the shadows shines, and the shadows have not comprehended [or "grasped" or "overcome"] it'.

Observe the incremental unfolding of ideas. First the author defines his subject as one with God twice. Second he combines αυτου with εγενετο twice. Third he puts αυτωι and γεγονεν together with ζωη 'life' twice, which he describes as φως 'light'. Fourth he contrasts light with darkness twice. His thought runs 'in the beginning God', second 'He being or becoming or making', third 'He begetting life', 'life light', and fourth 'light shining triumphant'. Ten of the verbs are past, aorist, or perfect, but this one, φαινει, is present.

These chiastic and parallel structures, coinciding exactly with the statement and incremental restatement of ideas, are as clear as they could possibly be. There is not the slightest doubt about where they begin and where they end, nor about what they say. But there is more to them than this.

Counting the words in A one finds twenty-four, arranged twelve and twelve. In B there are ten, arranged five and five. In C there are fourteen, arranged seven and seven. In D there are thirteen, of which the seventh and central is the one present tense verb of the entire passage, φαινει.

There is more. Counting the syllables one finds in A thirty-three, arranged sixteen, one, sixteen. In B there are twenty-two syllables arranged eleven and eleven. In C there are twenty-one syllables, arranged eleven and ten. In D there are twenty-three syllables, eleven in the first clause and twelve in the second. These symmetries of word and syllable are apprehensible by ear. But there are more, apprehensible only by the eye.

Counting the letters one finds in A seventy-seven, arranged thirty-seven, three, and thirty-seven. In B there are forty-six letters arranged twenty-three and twenty-three. In C there are forty-five letters arranged twenty-three and twenty-two. In D there are twenty-six letters in the first clause and twenty-five in the second. But if we followed the variant reading αυτον, assuming that the antecedent was masculine λογος or ουτος or αυτος rather than neuter φως, there would be twenty-six letters in the first clause and twenty-six in the second.

All these symmetries are either perfect or within one of perfection. The author grabs and holds our attention with chiastic and parallel statement and incremental restatement, and whether we consider ideas or numbers of words or numbers of syllables or numbers of letters the centre is always in the same place. Symmetries for the ear and the eye. But there is more.

The number of words in the entire passage is sixty-one, which divides by extreme and mean ratio at 38 and 23. The thirty-eighth word from the beginning and the twenty-third word from the end are αυτωι ζωη, so the golden section falls at 'in Him life'. The number of syllables is ninety-nine, which divides by extreme and mean ratio at 61 and 38. (Note the sequence: 23 + 38 = 61; 38 + 61 = 99.) The sixty-first syllable from the beginning and the thirty-eighth syllable from the end are in αυτωι. The number of letters is 219, which divides by extreme and mean ratio at 135 and 84. The 135th letter from the beginning and the eighty-fourth letter from the end are the upsilon and tau of αυτωι.

This is only the Prologue to the Gospel. The very next sentence, chapter I verse 6, reads, 'There was a man sent from God whose name was John. He came for testimony, to bear witness to the light'. The chiastic pair to this is chapter XXI verse 24, 'This is the disciple who is bearing witness to these things and who has written these things, and we know that his testimony is true'. The former passage refers to Saint John the Baptist, and the latter alludes to Saint John the Evangelist, whose name is thus built into the fabric of the work without being explicitly mentioned.

When one has begun to appreciate the literary competence of a man who can write like this it is hard to accept the scholarly judgement of a critic who thinks that the Prologue 'remains intolerably clumsy and opaque' and that 'it is more consistent with the Johannine repetitive style, as well as with Johannine doctrine, to say nothing concerning the sense of the passage, to punctuate with a full stop after ὃ γέγονεν.'[37]

In Jerome's Vulgate translation of the Prologue, there are nineteen words in A, arranged, nine, one, nine; thirty-seven syllables, arranged eighteen, one, eighteen; eighty-three letters, arranged forty-one, two, forty. In B there are eleven words, arranged five, one, five; nineteen syllables, arranged nine, one, nine; forty-six letters, arranged twenty-two, two, twenty-two. In C there are twelve words arranged eight, four. There are twenty syllables, arranged twelve, eight. The golden section of 20 falls at 12 and 8. There are forty-seven letters, arranged twenty-nine, eighteen. The golden section of 47 falls at 29 and 18. In D there are five words in the first clause and five in the second. There are eight syllables in the first clause and twelve in the second, the golden section of 20 falling at 12 and 8. There are twenty letters in the first clause and thirty-one in the second, the golden section of 51 falling at 31.5 and 19.5.

37   Metzger, p. 196 and n. 2.

God is mentioned three times (3 × 1). The first example *Deum* is the ninth word (3 × 3). From the first *Deum* to the second *Deus* inclusive there are three words (3 × 1). From the second *Deus* to the third *Deum* inclusive there are nine words (3 × 3). After that there are thirty-three words (3 × 11) to the end of the Prologue. The verb *facere* appears three times, first as *facta*, the fourth word (4 × 1) of part B. Between the first *facta* and the second *factum* there are four words. After *factum* the fourth word is *factum*, after which there are twenty words (4 × 5) to the end of the Prologue. The fourth word after *factum* is *uita*. From *uita* to *uita* inclusive there are four words. From *lux* to *lux* inclusive there are four words. From *tenebris* to *tenebrae* inclusive there are four words, and *tenebrae* is the fourth word from the end of the Prologue.

Our author suggests in the first two words where he learned to compose like this. The only other text in the Bible which begins with those words is Genesis I 1. This unmistakeable allusion implies further that our author believes what he is telling us to be comparable in import with the Creation. If we bear in mind a passage from the beginning of Boethius *De Institutione Arithmetica* I II, *De substantia numeri*, '*Omnia quaecunque a primaeua rerum natura constructa sunt, numerorum uidentur ratione formata. Hoc enim fuit principale in animo Conditoris exemplar*', we might, as the Revd Professor Abbott Conway suggests, paraphrase John's Prologue 'In the beginning was proportion, and the proportion was with God, and God was the proportion; the same was in the beginning with God. All things through it came into being, and without it came into being not one thing. What came into being through it was life, and that life was the enlightenment of men. And the enlightenment in the darkness shines, and the darkness has not comprehended it.'

SOME CONCLUSIONS

These analyses of texts have shown us the same elements of Biblical style in short verses of Isaiah and Lamentations; in paragraphs of Amos and Judges; in entire chapters of Genesis and John. One could do this many times over with different texts in Hebrew and Greek and Latin. But the texts already cited show that one can learn quickly whether an author was trying to write like this and whether a translator was trying to reproduce form as well as meaning.

For those who already admire the work of Saint Jerome Biblical style affords a new cause for admiration. Of the texts cited above nearly all reproduce in Latin the exact lexical, structural, and mathematical features of the original Hebrew, and this with little that sounds stilted, barbarous, or deeply offensive to the ear of a Classical Latinist. This is due partly to Jerome's education, and partly to his own taste, which was, as we know from his famous dream, *Ciceronianus*.

Here is a final example, a poem from the centre of Boethius *De Consolatione Philosophiae* Book III metre IX.[38] Capital letters and punctuation marks in

---

38 I owe thanks to Dr Leofranc Holford-Strevens for drawing my attention to this text as an example of Biblical style.

boldface represent features of Oxford, Bodleian Library, MS Auct. F.I.15 folio 39v, Anglo-Saxon work of the tenth century. Those in square brackets represent features of Cambridge University Library, MS Kk.3.21 folios 49v–50r, from Abingdon about the year 1000.

O qui perpetua mundum ratione gubernas [.]
Terrarum caelique sator . qui tempus ab aeuo
Ire iubes . stabilisque manens das cuncta moueri ;
Quem non externae pepulerunt fingere causae
Materiae fluitantis opus . uerum insita summi   5
Forma boni liuore carens ; **T**u cuncta superno
Ducis ab exemplo . pulchrum pulcherrimus ipse
Mundum mente gerens . similique in imagine formans ;
Perfectasque iubens perfectum absoluere partes .
Tu numeris elementa ligas . ut frigora flammis ,   10
Arida conueniant liquidis . ne purior ignis
Euolet . **A**ut mersas deducant   pondera terras ;
Tú triplicis mediam naturae cuncta mouentem
Conectens animam per consona membra resoluis :
Quae cum secta duos motum glomerauit in orbes ,   15
In semet reditura meat : mentemque profundam
Circuit [.] et simili conuertit imagine caelum ;
Tu causis animas paribus uitasque minores
Prouehis . et leuibus sublimes curribus aptans
In caelum terramque seris . quas lege benigna   20
Ad te conuersas reduci facis igne reuerti ;
Da pater augustam menti conscendere sedem ;
Da fontem lustrare boni ; da luce reperta
In te conspicuos animi defigere uisus ;
Dissice terrenae nebulas et pondera molis [.]   25
Atque tuo splendore mica . **T**u namque serenum
Tu requies tranquilla piis . te cernere [.] finis
Principium . uector . dux . semita . terminus idem .

O You, Who with perpetual ratio govern the world, sower of the lands and of heaven, Who order time to proceed from eternity, and, remaining stable, grant all things to be moved, Whom external causes have not set in motion to create the work of flowing matter, but the implanted form of the highest good lacking malice; You lead all things by supernal example, most beautiful Yourself, bearing a beautiful world in Your mind and creating in like image, ordering perfect parts to complete a perfect [world]. You bind the elements by numbers so that frosts converge with flames, dry things with liquids, lest the purer fire should fly away or weights should press on sunken earth. You resolve the mean of threefold nature moving all things, connecting the soul through harmonious members which, when cut, has collected its movement into two orbs; bound to return to itself it proceeds and goes about the deep mind and rotates the heavens by a similar image. You with equal causes promote lesser souls and lives and fixing them in light chariots You beget noble [souls and lives] on heaven and earth, which You make to be led back to You, to be returned in fire. Grant, Father, to my mind to ascend the august throne, grant it to seek the fount of good, grant when the light has been found, to fix the cleared sights of my soul on You. Disperse the clouds and weights of the earthly lump and shine in Your splendour! For You are the cloudless sky, You the tranquil rest for the holy, to behold You is the end, beginning, transport, guide, path, and endmost point unchanged.

Boethius composed the prosimetron *De Consolatione Philosophiae* in five books: seven metres and six proses in I, eight metres and eight proses in II, twelve metres and twelve proses in III, seven metres and seven proses in IV, five metres and six proses in V. The seventy-eight metres and proses in the entire book divide by sesquialter ratio at 47 and 31. This text, Book III Metre IX, which stands at the symmetrical centre of the entire book, marks the sesquialter ratio at the forty-seventh section of the work. Its subject, an abridgement of the first part of Plato's *Timaeus*, is the structure of the universe and the place and function in it of men's minds and souls.

The metre contains twenty-eight lines of dactylic hexameter, of which the golden section falls at 17 and 11. The metre contains 179 words, of which the golden section falls at 111 and 68, that of 111 at 69 and 42, that of 68 at 42 and 26.

Boethius addresses God in a triple anaphora, *O qui, qui, quem*, and then addresses Him nine times, six times as *tu* and three times as *te*. There are nine second person singular indicative verbs addressed to God (*gubernas, iubes, das, ducis, ligas, resoluis, prouehis, seris*, and *facis*), and six participles (*manens, carens, gerens, iubens, conectens*, and *aptans*), and the imperative *da* three times.

Boethius arranged the 111 words and ideas from line 11 *purior ignis euolet* to the end chiastically.

a	12	deducant
b	12	pondera terras
ci	14	conectens animam
ii	14–15	resoluis … secta
di	16	reditura meat
ii	16	mentemque
iii	17	circuit
e	17	conuertit
f	17	caelum

g	18	Tu causis animas paribus uitasque minores prouehis
g'	19	et leuibus sublimes curribus aptans ... seris
f'	20	caelum
e'	21	conuersas
d'i	21	reduci facis igne reuerti
ii	22	menti
iii	22	conscendere
c'i	24	animi defigere
ii	25	dissice
b'	25	terrenae ... pondera molis
a'	28	dux

The forty-second word is *Tu* at the beginning of the crux in g.
Boethius also made another grand chiasmus.

A	2	terrarum caelique sator
B	3	ire
C	3	cuncta moueri
D	6–8	forma ... pulchrum pulcherrimus ipse mundum ... in imagine formans
D'	9	perfectasque iubens perfectum
C'	13	cuncta mouentem
B'	16	reditura
A'	20	in caelum terramque seris

In this passage between the outer markers *terrarum caelique sator* and *in caelum terramque seris* there are seventeen lines of verse and 111 words. As the forty-second word from the end is *mediam* 13, the golden mean of the passage falls at the word 'mean'.

There is a remarkable number of repeated words: *animam* 14, *animas* 18, *animi* 24; *boni* 6, 23; *caelique* 2, *caelum* 17, 20; *causae* 4, *causis* 18; *conuertit* 17, *conuersas* 21; *cuncta* 3, 6, 13; *ducis* 7, *deducant* 12, *reduci* 21, *dux* 28; *forma* 6, *formans* 8; *ignis* 11, *igne* 21; *imagine* 8, 17; *ire* 3, *reditura* 16; *mente* 8, *mentemque* 16, *menti* 22; *moueri* 3, *mouentem* 13; *mundum* 1, 8; *perfectasque* 9, *perfectum* 9; *pondera* 12, 25; *sator* 2, *insita* 5, *seris* 20; *terrarum* 2, *terras* 12, *terramque* 20, *terrenae* 25.

Note the words *animam* 14 and *animi* 24, which span eleven lines. There are eighty-three words before *animam* and twenty-eight words after *animi*, together 111. Between *animam* and *animi* is *animas* in the eleventh line from the end, the 111th word. Between *animam* and *animas* there are twenty-six words. From *animas* to *animi* inclusive there are forty-one words.

Before *boni* 6 there are thirty-three words, and after *boni* 23 there are thirty-five words, together sixty-eight. The second *boni* is in the seventeenth line after the first *boni*, and it is the 111th word after the first *boni*.

The words *cuncta* 3 and *cuncta* 13 span eleven lines. Between *cuncta* 6 and *cuncta* 13 there are forty-two words. The phrases *cuncta moueri* 3 and *cuncta mouentem* 13 illustrate duple ratio. Between them are sixty words. The 179 words of the poem divide by duple ratio at 119 and 60.

The words *forma* 6 and *formans* 8 mark one-ninth and eight-ninths of the work. From the first word to the second inclusive there are twenty words. The 179 words of the poem divide by one-ninth and eight-ninths at 20 and 159.

Menti 22 is in the fourteenth line after *mente* 8. Between them are ninety words, half the lines and half the words of the poem. The ninety intervening words divide by sesquialter ratio (3:2) at 54 and 36. There are thirty-six words between *mentem* 16 and *menti* 22.

Between *ne ... mersas deducant pondera terras* 12 and *dissice terrenae nebulas et pondera molis* there are seventy-seven words. The number 179 divides by sesquitertian ratio (4:3) at 102 and 77.

In Bodleian MS Auct. F.I.15 the first capital letter is green. The other letters at the beginnings of lines are red. Those in the text are in the same ink as the rest of the verses. Nearly half the caesuras are marked with punctuation points. Prosodically eleven verses exhibit a caesura at the third foot and seventeen a caesura at the fourth foot.

In Western Christendom the Vulgate has been from the moment of its appearance a primary model of general Latinity and particular Biblical style. Extant manuscripts and allusions and echoes prove that the *Rhetorica ad Herennium* and Cicero's works were often copied and widely read.[39] It is hardly necessary to debate the importance of Euclid or of Boethius *De Consolatione Philosophiae, De Institutione Arithmetica* and *De Institutione Musica*.[40]

In affirming that modern mathematics has little to do with modern literature one understates the case. But in Antiquity and the Middle Ages men perceived things differently. Any schoolboy might read in Proverbs IX 1 that *Sapientia aedificauit sibi domum excidit columnas septem* and infer that the seven pillars of Wisdom were the *triuium* 'the three ways' *grammatica, rhetorica, logica* and the *quadruuium* 'the four ways' *arithmetica, musica, geometria, astronomia*. The former three dealt with constructs in human language — grammar, rhetoric, and logic. The latter four dealt with constructs in the universe — arithmetic, music, geometry, and astronomy — all reflections of the Mind of God expressed in number: arithmetic as static number, music as moving number, geometry as measurement of the static earth, and astronomy as measurement of the moving heavens. The implication of this unified view of the pillars of Wisdom is that the

39 L.D. Reynolds et al. eds, *Texts and Transmission, Survey of the Latin Classics* (Oxford 1983 corr. rept 1990), pp. 98–100, 102–9.

40 From an immense literature see: H.R. Patch, *The Tradition of Boethius, A Study of His Importance in Medieval Culture* (Oxford 1935); P. Courcelle, *La Consolation de Philosophie dans la Tradition Littéraire, Antécédents et Postérité de Boèce* (Paris 1967); M. Gibson ed., *Boethius, His Life, Thought and Influence* (Oxford 1981); H. Chadwick, *Boethius, The Consolations of Music, Logic, Theology, and Philosophy* (Oxford 1981).

arts of the *quadruuium* are directly relevant to those of the *triuium*. One may expli-
cate the literary and linguistic arts by the rules of the numerical arts.[41] And not only
these, but the arts of draughtsman, painter, sculptor, and architect as well.[42]

How much of this is implicit in the arrangement of the *scholae* in the
seventeenth-century Schools Quadrangle of the Bodleian Library in Oxford?
There, entering through the great double doors from the east one sees the schools
of the *triuium* and the *quadruuium* mixed to the right and the left, and beyond
them, past the smaller arches on the north and south walls, the *Schola Moralis
Philosophiae* opposite the *Schola Naturalis Philosophiae*. On the western wall one
sees what were then as now graduate disciplines, the *Schola Veteris Iurisprudentiae*
and the *Schola Veteris Medicinae* flanking the central Queen of the Sciences, the
Schola Diuinitatis. At the western wall, turning to face east, one sees the Tower of
the Orders of Architecture, Tuscan, Doric, Ionic, Corinthian, and Composite,
each exhibiting its own proportions, rising from the schools of the *triuium* and
the *quadruuium*. How much of this was implicit long before construction of the
Bodleian Library in the four verses of Job XXXVIII 4–7?

The rules and adjuncts of Biblical style have been stated, exhibited, and attested
clearly. About the former there can be little doubt. The latter may still appear contentious. A claim, even a suggestion, that literary texts might have been composed
mathematically moves one into a field of debate, not to say a battlefield. There
hope that scholars might leave no stone unturned fades with experience of Mrs
Dolley's celebrated remark that they leave no stone unthrown. Here one can do
no better than to summarize some of the preceding texts. Job XXXVIII 4–7, Isaiah
XL 12, Proverbs VIII 22–31, and Wisdom XI 20 state that God created the world as a
mathematical act of weighing and balancing and measuring and counting. The
Timaeus states explicitly that God created the world mathematically. Euclid and
Boethius both discuss extreme and mean ratio. The Talmud speaks explicitly of
the counting of verses, words, and letters of the Hebrew text of the Bible. The
Rhetorica ad Herennium and Cicero *De Oratore* both discuss, and in discussing illustrate, principles of chiastic and parallel composition in both symmetry and extreme
and mean ratio. Boethius illustrates composition by extreme and mean ratio in his
finest poem, an abbreviation of the teaching of the *Timaeus* about the creation of
the world, at the very centre of *De Consolatione Philosophiae*. Every one of these
texts was known in Late Antiquity and in the Latin West during the Middle Ages.
It is time to turn to the works of writers who imitated these Ancient models.

---

41 C.A. Conway, 'Boethius, the Liberal Arts, and Early Medieval Political Theory' in *Literature and
    Ethics: Essays Presented to A. E. Malloch*, eds G. Wihl & D. Williams (Kingston & Montreal,
    Quebec 1988), pp. 96–110.

42 R.D. Stevick, 'The Design of Lindisfarne Gospels folio 138v', *Gesta* XXII (1983), pp. 3–12; Idem
    'The 4 x 3 Crosses in the Lindisfarne and Lichfield Gospels', Ibid. XXV (1986), pp. 171–84; Idem
    'The Shapes of the Book of Durrow Evangelist Symbol Pages', *Art Bulletin* LXVIII (1986), 182–94;
    Idem 'The Echternach Gospels' evangelist-symbol pages: forms from the "two true measures of
    geometry"', *Peritia* V (1986), pp. 284–309 and plates i–v; Idem 'A Geometer's Art: The Full-Page
    Illuminations in St Gallen Stiftsbibliothek Cod. Sang. 51, An Insular Gospels Book of the VIIIth
    Century', *Scriptorium* XLIV (1990), pp. 161–92 and plates 17–20.

II

THE BEGINNINGS
OF THE CELTIC LATIN TRADITION

INTRODUCTION

By the second century A.D. parts of the Bible had been translated into Latin, apparently to fulfil a general need rather than a specific bishop's or council's request. As translation and dissemination were apparently unsystematic, the texts of the *Vetus Latina* are not uniform. In 382 at the request of Pope Damasus Saint Jerome began to edit the Latin text, the *editio uulgata* or Vulgate, which became the authoritative version used by the Western Church. The oldest complete extant text of the Vulgate, now known as the *Codex Amiatinus*, was produced in Northumbria at Wearmouth or Jarrow between 690 and 700 for Abbot Ceolfrid.

Some form of the Old Latin Bible may have arrived in Britain as early as the end of the second century, for the oldest version of the *Passio Albani* ascribes the persecution of the first known British martyr, Saint Alban of Verulamium, to the reign of Septimius Severus (193–211).[1] The description of Saint Alban's judge as Caesar may refer to Geta Caesar, who served as governor of Britain while his father, Septimius Severus, and his brother, Caracalla, were campaigning against the Picts in 208–9.[2] About the same time the first great Christian Latin author, Tertullian, wrote of *Britannorum inaccessa Romanis loca Xpisto uero subdita*, implying perhaps that Christianity had spread even among the unromanized Picts.[3] A generation later, about 240, Origen asked *quando enim terra Britanniae ante aduentum Xpisti in unius Dei consensit religionem.*[4] Gildas dated the martyrdom of Aaron and Julius at Caerleon to the Diocletianic persecution, about 304.[5] The British bishops who attended the Council of Arles in 314 may have represented metropolitan churches:

---

1   W. Meyer ed., 'Die Legende des h. Albanus des Protomartyr Angliae in Texten vor Beda', *Abhandlungen der Königlichen Gesellschaft der Wissenschaften zu Göttingen, Philologisch-Historische Klasse, Neue Folge* VIII i (Berlin 1904), pp. 36–8.
2   J. Morris, 'The Date of Saint Alban', *Hertfordshire Archaeology* I (1968), pp. 3–4.
3   W.H.C. Frend, 'The Christianization of Roman Britain' in M.W. Barley & R.P.C. Hanson eds, *Christianity in Roman Britain, 300–700* (Leicester 1968), p. 38. A.W. Haddan & W. Stubbs eds, *Councils and Ecclesiastical Documents relating to Great Britain and Ireland* (Oxford 1869, rept 1964), vol. I, p. 3.
4   Ibid.
5   Ibid. pp. 5–6.

Eborius episcopus de ciuitate Eboracensi prouincia Britannia
Restitutus episcopus de ciuitate Londinensi prouincia suprascripta
Adelfius episcopus de ciuitate Colonia Londinensium [? l. Camulo-
    dunensium uel Lindunensium]
Exinde Sacerdos presbyter, Arminius diaconus.

Eborius may have represented the Church at York, Restitutus the Church at
London, and Adelfius (who was accompanied by the priest Sacerdos and the
deacon Arminius) perhaps the Church at Camulodunum (Colchester), the senior
Roman colony in Britain, or Lincoln.[6] Athanasius mentions Britain among the
provinces which accepted the canons of the Council of Nicaea in 325 and
supported him at the Council of Sardica in 343.[7] In 358 Hilary of Poitiers
addressed De Synodis to prouinciarum Britanniarum episcopis, among others.[8] At the
Council of Ariminum in 359 three British bishops accepted payment of their
expenses from the imperial treasury,[9] though one infers that others may have
been present who paid their own expenses. Early in the fifth century Palladius
and Theodoret mention pilgrimages by Britons to the Holy Land.[10] These
scattered literary references to the spread of Christianity in Roman Britain are
corroborated by an impressive and growing corpus of archaeological evidence.[11]

I. PELAGIUS

Commentary on the Pauline Epistles

The literary history of Britain and the history of Biblical style in British literature
begin in the fifth century. Between the years 404 and 409 the first known British
author, Pelagius, published in Rome a commentary on the Pauline Epistles. Here
are the first two paragraphs of the Argumentum omnium epistularum.[1] Capital letters
and punctuation marks in boldface represent features of Oxford, Merton College,
MS 26 folio 74ra.

Argumentum omnium epistularum
A I **PR**imum

6   Ibid. p. 7.
7   Ibid. pp. 7–9.
8   Ibid. p. 9.
9   Ibid. p. 10.
10   Ibid. p. 14.
11   J. Toynbee, 'Christianity in Roman Britain', Journal of the British Archaeological Association, 3rd
     series, XVI (1953), pp. 1–24; C. Thomas, The Early Christian Archaeology of North Britain (Oxford
     1971), pp. 229–45; Idem Christianity in Roman Britain to AD 500 (London 1981); B. Jones & D.
     Mattingly, An Atlas of Roman Britain (Oxford 1990), pp. 295–300.
1   BCLL 2. Pelagius' Expositions of Thirteen Epistles of St Paul, ed. A. Souter in Texts and Studies, ed. J.
     Armitage Robinson IX (Cambridge 1922–31 rept 1967), Part II Text and Apparatus Criticus, p. 3.

2 quaerĭtūr

3 quāre

B 1   post euangelia quae supplēmēntūm lēgĭs sŭnt .

1'   et in quibus nobis exempla et praecepta uiuendi pleníssime dīgēstă sŭnt :

1"   uoluerit apostolus has epistulas ad singulas ecclēsīās dēstĭnāre .

C 1   Ut initio nascentis ecclesiae nouis causis ēxsĭstēntĭbŭs :

1'   et praesentia atque orientia resecáret uítia .

    et post futuras exclŭdērēt quaēstĭŏnĕs

1"   exemplo prophetarum qui post édĭtām lēgēm Mŏ́ysī

D   in qua omnia Dei mandáta legebántur :

E   nihilo minus tamen doctrina sua rediuiua semper populi conpressēre pēccătă .

F   et propter exemplum libris ad nostram etiam memórĭām trănsmĭsērŭnt .

A'1 **D**einde

2 quaeritur

3 cur

B'1   non amplius quam decem epistulas ad ecclēsīās scrīpsĕrīt .

1'   **D**ecem sunt enim cum illa quae[2] dícitur ād Hēbraēŏs .

1"   **N**am reliquae quattuor ad discipulos speciáliter sŭnt pōrrēctaē .

C'1   Ut ostenderet nouum non discrepare a uétere tēstāmēntŏ :

1'   et se contra legem nōn făcĕre Mŏ́ysī .

D'   ad numerum primorum decalogi mandatorum suas epĭstŭlās ōrdĭnáuĭt .

E'1   et quot ille praeceptis a Pharaone instítuit lĭbĕrátŏs .

1'   totidem hic epistulis a diaboli et idololatriae seruitute édocet ādquīsītŏs .

F'   **N**am et duas tabulas lapideas duorum testamentorum figuram habuisse . uiri erudĭtīssĭmī trādĭdērŭnt .

A 1 First

2 it is asked,

3 for what reason

B 1 after the Gospels, which are the fulfilment of the Law,

1' and in which examples and precepts of living are most fully set out for us,

1" should the Apostle wish to send these letters to individual churches?

C 1 So that since new problems existed at the beginning of the nascent Church,

2 MS *enim sunt . cum que .*

1' he might both restrain present and emerging vices
    and afterwards prevent future questions,

1" on the model of the Prophets, who, after the Law of Moses had
    been issued,

D   in which all the commandments of God are read,

E   yet nonetheless by their renewed teaching always dealt with the
    people's sins,

F   and as a warning transmitted [it] in books to our recollection as well.

A'1 Then

2   it is asked

3   why

B'1 should he have written no more than ten letters to the churches

1' (for there are ten, including that which is called to the Hebrews,

1" for the remaining four are addressed specifically to disciples)?

C'1 So that he might show that the New does not differ from the Old
    Testament,

1' nor make itself contrary to the Law of Moses,

D' he ordered his own epistles to the number of the prime
    commandments of the Decalogue,

E'1 and with as many precepts as Moses instructed those freed from
    Pharaoh

1' with just so many epistles does Paul teach those rescued from the
    slavery of the devil and idolatry;

F' for the most erudite men have passed on the tradition that the two
    stone tablets represented a symbol of the two Testaments.

The parallelism of A and A' is clear. Compare the last clause of B, *has epistulas ad ecclesias destinare*, with the first clause of B', *decem epistulas ad ecclesias scripserit*, and *plenissime digesta sunt* of B with *specialiter sunt porrectae* of B'. With *ut ... nouis ... et ... legem Moysi* in C compare *ut ... nouum ... et ... legem ... Moysi* in C'. Compare the *mandata* of D with the *mandatorum* of D', the *doctrina* of E with the *praeceptis* of E', and the *et ... transmiserunt* of F with *et ... tradiderunt* of F'.

Note the internal symmetry of part C, comprising seven, eleven, and seven words, and of part B', comprising eight, nine, and eight words. Among the connections between the first and second paragraphs the four words in A and the three words in A' are the minor and major parts of the golden section of 7. There are twenty-five words in B and twenty-five in B', eight words each in the clauses containing parallel diction, B1" and B'1.

There are twenty-five words in C and fifteen in C', forty together. The golden section of 40 falls at 25 and 15. There are six words in D and eight in D', fourteen together. The golden section of 14 falls at 8.65 and 5.34. There are ten words in E and eighteen in E', twenty-eight together. The golden section of 28 falls at 17.3 and 10.6. There are nine words in F and twelve in F', twenty-one together. The golden section of 21 falls at 13 and 8. The title and paragraph A–F comprise eighty-two words, and paragraph A'–F' comprises eighty-one words. The former comprises 214 syllables and the latter 210. Paragraph A–F comprises 493 letters and paragraph A'–F' 494.

As most clauses end with both clausular and cursus rhythms, one infers that Pelagius strove to fulfil the requirements of both systems simultaneously.

Here is the Prologue to the first Epistle.[3] Capital letters and punctuation marks in boldface represent features of Oxford, Balliol College, MS 157 folio 2r-v.[4]

	Incipit prologus epístulae ād Rōmānōs.
A	**[R]OMANI** ex Iudaeis gentilibúsque crēdĭdḗrŭnt .
	Hii superba contentione volebant se alterutrō sŭpērpṓnĕrĕ .
B1	**N**am Iudaḗī dīcḗbănt :
2a	"Nos sumus populus Dei quos ab initio dilḗxĭt ēt fṓuĭt :
a'	nos circumcisi ex genere Abraham ex stirpe sā̆nctā dēscēndĭmŭs :
3	et 'notus' retro 'apud Iudaéam' tantum 'Déus' .
C	Nos de Aegypto signis Dei et uirtū̆tĭbūs lībērā́tī :
	mare sicco pertransī̆uĭmū s pĕ̄dĕ̆ :
	cum[5] inimicos nostros grauissimi flū́ctūs ĭnuṓluĕrē̆nt .
D1	Nobis mannam pluuit Dóminus īn dēsḗrtō :
	et quasi filiis suis caeleste pábulūm mĭnĭstrā́uĭt .
2	Nos die noctuque in columna nubis ígnīsquē praecḗssĭt :
	ut nobis in inuiō ĭtĕr ōstēndĕ̄rĕ̆t .
E1	**A**tque ut caetera eius circa nos inmensa benefī̆cĭā tăcĕā́mŭs :
2	nos soli digni fuimus Dei lḗgĕm ā̆ccī́pĕrĕ̄
3	et uocem Dei loquē̆ntĭs aūdī́rĕ̆ :
4	eiusque agnóscere uòluntátem
2'	in qua lege nobis promī̆ssū̆s ēst Xpī́stū̆s
3'	ad quos etiam ipse se uenisse testā́tūs ēst dī́cĕ̄ns :
4'a	Non ueni nisi ad oues quae perierū̄nt dŏmū̆s Īstrā̆hḗl :
a'	cum uos canes potius quam hominḗs ā̆ppḗllā̆uĕ̆rĭ̄t .
F1	**A**équumne érgo est : ut hodie ídola dēsĕrē̆ntĕ̄s
2	quibus ab initio deseruistis nobis cṓnpārḗmĭnī :
3	et non potius in proselytorum locum ex legis auctoritate et consuetudine dḗpŭtē̆mĭnī̆ .

---

3   Souter, *Expositions*, pp. 6–7.
4   The system of Oxford, Merton College, MS 26 f. 74rb-va is similar, but not identical.
5   MS *pede pertransiuimus: quom*.

G 1   Et hoc ipsum nŏn mĕrĕbămĭnĭ :

2   nisi quia larga Dei semper

                                clementia uoluit uos ad nostram

                                imitatiŏnẹm ādmĭttĕrĕ .

B' 1   Gentes etiam e contrárⁱō rēspōndēbăNT .

2a   Quanto maiora erga vos Dei beneficia nărrāuĕrĭtĭs :

a'   tanto maioris vos criminis reos ēssē mōnstrăbĭtĭs :

3   semper enim[6] his omnibus extĭtĭstĭs īngrătĭ .

C'   Nam ipsis pedibus quibus aridum máre transístis :

          ludebatis ante ídola quaē fĕcĭstĭs :

          et ipso ore quo paulo ante ob necem aduersarii Domino

          cántāuĕrătĭs:

          simulacra uobis fierī pŏpōscĭstĭs .

D' 2   Illis oculis quibus ueneranda Deum in nube uel igne

           conspícere sòlebátis :

           simulacra ĭntŭēbămĭnĭ .

1   Manna quoque uobis fastīdiō fŭĭt

           et semper in deserto contra Dóminum mŭrmŭrăstĭs :

           ad Aegyptum unde uos manu ualida eiecerāt uŏlēntēs

           redīrĕ .[7]

E' 1   Quid plura .

2   Ita patres uestri crebra prouocatione Dominum

             ĭnrītāuĕrŭnt :

3   ut omnes in héremo mòreréntuR :

4   nec plus ex senioribus eorum quam duo

                homines terram repromissiōnĭs ĭntrărĕnt .

1'   Sed quid antíqua replicámus : cum etiam si illa

           mínimē fĕcĭssētĭs

2'a   de hoc solo uos nemo dignos uénia iŭdĭcărĕt :

a'   quod Dominum Christum prophetarum

            semper uobis uócibus rèpromíssum

3'a   non solum suscípere nŏlŭĭstĭs :

a'   sed etiam morte péssimā pĕrēmĭstĭs :

4'a   Quem nos ut cognouimus státim credí-

             dimus :

a'   cum nobis de eo non fuerit āntĕ praedĭctŭm .

F' 1   Unde probamus[8] quod ídolĭs sēruĭuĭmŭs

2   non obstinationi mentis sed ignorăntiaē

            dēpŭtăndŭm .

---

6   MS .N.

7   MS *redire cupientes*.

8   MS *probatur:*

3 a	Quī ēnĭm[9] ăgnĭtŭm
b	ílico séquituR : [10]
b'	olim utĭquĕ sĕquĕrĕtŭr[11]
a'	sị ắntẹ ăgnōŭĭssĕt .[12]

G'1   Sic autem uos de generis
            nobilitātĕ iāctắtĭs :

2   quasi non morum imitatio
            magis quam carnalis
            natiuitas filios nos faciat ĕssĕ
            sānctŏrŭm .

3   Denique Ésau et
            Ísmahel : cum ex
            Ăbrăhaē stĭrpĕ sĭnt:
            minime tamen in filiis
            rèputántuR .

A'1a   His taliter áltercántibus : apostolus se médium ĭntērpŏnĕns
     b   ita partium dĭrĭmĭt quaĕstĭŏnĕs :
2a   ut neutrum eorum sua iustitia salutem merŭĭssĕ cōnfĭrmĕt :
   a'   ambos uero populos et scienter et gráuitēr dĕlĭquĭssĕ :
3a   Iudaeos quod per praeuaricationem legis Deum ĭnhŏnō -
         rắuĕrĭnt :
   a'   gentes uero quod cum cognitum de creatura Creatorem ut
         Deum debúerint uènerári :
         gloriam eius in manu facta mutáuerint sìmulácra .
2'a   Utrosque etiam similiter ueniam consecutos aēquālēs ĕssĕ:
         ueracissima ratĭŏnĕ dĕmŏnstrắt :
   a'   praesertim cum in eadem lége praēdīctūm sĭt : [13]
         et Iudaeos et gentes ad Christi fidem uocāndōs ōstĕndĭt .
1'a   Quam ob rem uicissim éos humílians
   b   ad pacem et ad concórdiām cōhōrtắtŭR .

Here begins the Prologue of the Epistle to the Romans.

A   The Romans believed because of [the witness of] Jews and Gentiles.
      Each wished in haughty contention to place themselves above the
      other.

B 1   For the Jews said,
  2a   "We are the people of God, whom from the beginning He chose
      and nurtured;
   a'   we, circumcised, have descended from the race of Abraham, from
      a holy stock,

---

9   MS .N.
11   MS *sequeremur.*
13   MS omits *sit.*

10   MS *sequimur:*
12   MS *antea cognouissemus.*

3   and 'God' has been 'known' for what He is from the beginning 'in Judaea'.

C   We, liberated from Egypt by the signs and powers of God, crossed the sea with dry feet, though the heaviest waves rolled over our enemies.

D1   For us God rained manna in the desert and served heavenly food as to His own sons.

2   Us He preceded by day and by night in a column of cloud and of fire, so that He might show us a way in the trackless waste.

E1   And, to say nothing of His other immense benefits to us,

2   we alone were worthy to receive the Law of God

3   and to hear the voice of God speaking

4   and to discern His will,

2'   in which law Christ was promised to us,

3'   to whom even Himself bore witness that He had come, saying,

4'a   'I have not come except to the sheep of the House of Israel which were perishing,'

a'   though He called you dogs rather than men.

F1   Is it fair therefore that you deserting today the idols

2   to which you have devoted yourselves from the beginning should be compared with us

3   and not rather be assigned by the authority of law and by custom to the place of proselytes?

G1   And you would not have deserved even this

2   except that the great mercy of God always wished to let you participate in the imitation of us."

B'1   The Gentiles also responded in opposition,

2a   "The more you relate the benefits of God to you

a'   the more you show yourselves to be guilty of a crime,

3   for you have been ungrateful for all these things.

C'   For with those very feet with which you crossed the dry sea you danced before the idols which you had made, and with the very mouth with which shortly before you had sung to the Lord because of the death of an adversary you asked for images to be made for you.

D'2   With those very eyes with which you were accustomed to behold the holy things of God in the cloud and in the fire you gazed on images.

1   Manna also was repugnant to you, and you always murmured against the Lord in the desert, wishing to return to Egypt, whence He had drawn you out with a strong hand.

E'1   What more?

2   Your fathers irritated the Lord with frequent provocation,

3	so that they all died in the desert
4	and not more than two of their elders entered the land of promise.
I'	But why should we go over the ancient [wrongs], since even if you had hardly done these things,
2'a	no man would judge you worthy of forgiveness on this alone,
a'	that the Lord Christ, always promised you by the voices of the prophets,
3'a	you not only did not wish to receive,
a'	but even killed with the very worst death,
4'a	Whom we believed in as soon as we knew,
a'	though concerning Him nothing had been previously foretold to us.
F'1	From which point we prove that our service to idols
2	should be attributed not to obstinacy of mind but to ignorance,
3a	for as He was recognized,
b	from that moment He was followed;
b'	He would have been followed long ago,
a'	if He had been recognized previously.
G'1	But you have boasted about the nobility of your race,
2	as if imitation of good morals rather than fleshly birth would not make you to be sons of holy men.
3	To sum up, Esau and Ishmael, though they are scarcely of the stock of Abraham, are reckoned among his sons."
A'1a	While they are wrangling thus the Apostle interposing himself as mediator
b	thus settles the questions of the factions,
2 a	so that he should prove that neither of them merited salvation by his own righteousness,
a'	for both peoples erred both knowingly and seriously,
3 a	the Jews because through transgression of the Law they dishonoured God,
a'	but the Gentiles because, although they should have worshipped God as Creator known through His creation, they changed His glory into images made by hand.
2' a	He demonstrates by the truest proof that both, having won forgiveness similarly, are equals,
a'	especially since he shows that in the same law it was foretold that both Jews and Gentiles would be called to the Faith of Christ.
1' a	On which account, humiliating them in turn,
b	he urges them to peace and to concord.

Pelagius introduces his subject in A, states the Jews' arguments in B–G and the Gentiles' arguments in B'–G', and resolves the issue in A'. Compare *Iudaei dicebant* in B1 with *Gentes respondebant* in B'1, *nos … nos* in B2 with *quanto maiora uos … narraueritis … tanto maioris uos … monstrabitis* in B'2, and note the recurrence of *Dei* in

B2a and B'2a. Compare *mare sicco pertransiuimus pede* and *inimicos* in C with *ipsis pedibus quibus aridum mare transistis* and *aduersarii* in C'; note further the internal parallelism of C' *ipsis pedibus quibus, ipso ore quo,* and *idola, simulacra.* Compare *mannam* and *in columna nubis ignisque* in D with *in nube uel igne* and *manna* in D'. Note the internal parallelism of E: *nos ... legem accipere* E2, and *in ... lege nobis promissus* E2'; *loquentis* E3 and *dicens* E3'; also the internal parallelism of E': *quid plura* E'1 and *quid replicamus* E'1'; *morerentur* E'3 and *morte ... peremistis* E'3'. Note further the parallelism between E and E': *caetera* E1, *plura* E'1; *nos soli digni* E2 and *solo uos ... dignos* E'2; *nobis promissus est Xpistus* E2' and *Xpistum ... uobis ... repromissum* E'2'a'. Compare *idola deserentes* in F1 with *idolis seruiuimus* in F'1 and *deputemini* in F3 with *deputandum* in F'2. Note further the little chiasmus in F'3: *agnitum* a, *agnouisset* a', *sequitur* b, *sequeretur* b'. Compare *imitationem* in G2 with *imitatio* in G'2, and note the *inclusio* of G'3, by which the end of the Gentiles' argument echoes the beginning of the Jews' in B: *ex Abrahae stirpe, Abraham ex stirpe.* These arguments are reconciled in A'.

In A'1 there are seven words in a and four in b, eleven together. The golden section of 11 falls at 7 and 4. In 1' there are six words in a and six in b. In part 2 there are eight words in each clause. In part 2' there are ten words in the first clause and sixteen in the second, twenty-six together. The golden section of 26 falls at 16 and 10. The sixteen words of part 2 and the twenty-six of part 2' comprise forty-two words together. The golden section of 42 falls at 26 and 16. At the crux in part 3 there are seven words in the first clause and nineteen in the second, twenty-six together, another golden section. The entire concluding paragraph comprises ninety-one words, thirty-four from 1a to 3a, the centre of the chiasmus, and fifty-seven from 3a' to the end. The golden section of 91 falls at 57 and 34.

There are five words in the first clause of A and seven in the second, twelve together. The golden section of 12 falls at 7 and 5. From the beginning of the text to the end of the Jews' arguments, in A and B-G, there are 189 words; from the beginning of the Gentiles' arguments to the end of the text, B'-G' and A', there are 307 words; 496 words together. The golden section of 496 falls at 307 and 189.

Pelagius uses clausulae consistently and precisely. Nearly every clause ends with both clausular and cursus rhythms. Seven exhibit only cursus rhythms (E4, one phrase of C', E'3, 2'a', and 4'a, F'3b, and G'3).

From evidence that did not include the works of Pelagius the philologist Kenneth Jackson inferred that the Latin of Romano-Britons 'must have seemed stilted and pedantic, or perhaps upper-class and "haw-haw"'.[14] The Latin lexicographer and Biblical textual critic Alexander Souter observed that Pelagius[15]

---

14   K. Jackson, *Language and History in Early Britain* (Edinburgh 1953 rept 1971), p. 108. For an opposing view see A.S. Gratwick, '*Latinitas Britannica*: Was British Latin Archaic?' in N. Brooks ed., *Latin and the Vernacular Languages in Early Medieval Britain* (Leicester 1982), pp. 1–79, reviewed by D. McManus, '*Linguarum Diversitas*: Latin and the Vernaculars in Early Medieval Britain', *Peritia* III (1984), pp. 151–88 and P. Russell, 'Recent Work in British Latin', *Cambridge Medieval Celtic Studies* IX (1985), pp. 19–29.

15   Souter, *Expositions*, pp. 79, 80, 82.

is a very correct writer. ... In the matter of word formation ... in him we find only the earlier stage [*e.g.* in the *Argumentum* the form *idololatriae* for *idolatriae* and in the *Prologus Istrahel* for *Israel*]. ... Pelagius is throughout very strict in regard to sequence of tenses. ... These facts at once place him in the better class of writers.

Pelagius reveals literary debts to the Christian Latin writers Ambrosiaster, Augustine, Rufinus (translating Origen), and Tertullian, as well as to the Classical Latin authors Caesar, Horace, Juvenal, Lucretius, Quintilian, Seneca, Statius, Tacitus, and Vergil.[16] His clear cultivated Latin may reflect his birth and education among Romano-British aristocrats. But even if Pelagius acquired his learning only among the Roman aristocrats to whom his work appealed, it was neither ignored nor unappreciated among his fellow provincials. Gennadius credits a British bishop named Fastidius with authorship of several Pelagian texts written about 420–30.[17] Britain became such a stronghold of Pelagianism that two Romano-Gaulish bishops, Saint Germanus of Auxerre and Saint Lupus of Troyes, conducted a mission in 428–9 to combat the heresy. During this mission they visited the tomb of Saint Alban at Verulamium, in which they deposited some relics and from which they removed some dust.

The Church has seldom countenanced the work of heresiarchs, but here is an important exception, for as Souter observes,[18]

> nearly every codex of the Pauline Epistles in the Vulgate text is provided with a prologue which is the work not of Jerome, but of Pelagius himself.

We have, then, in the work of the first British Latin author not only a commentary on the Bible, but prologues which have served since before the fall of Rome as perfect models of Biblical style.

II. SAINT PATRICK

Letter to the Soldiers of Coroticus and *Confession*

Although one would not ordinarily contemplate giving an account of the Celtic Latin tradition without mentioning the British Apostle of the Irish, publication of the *Liber Epistolarum Sancti Patricii Episcopi, the Book of Letters of Saint Patrick the Bishop* (Dublin 1994), removes the need to rehearse here Patrick's competence in Biblical style. One may observe, however, that if writers so utterly distinct as the highly polished Pelagius and the poorly

---

16 Ibid. p. 553; cf. part I, pp. 174–200.
17 Haddan & Stubbs, p. 16.
18 Souter, *Expositions*, p. 117.

educated Patrick both composed in Biblical style, it must have been inculcated at the earliest stages of education.

III. LICINIUS, MELANIUS, EUSTOCHIUS

Letter to Louocatus and Catihernus

The Biblical style in which Pelagius composed among highly literate Romans and Patrick composed among newly literate Irish was not forgotten among the Britons either at home in Britannia or across the Channel in Britannia Minor, to which many fled after displacement by Anglo-Saxons early in the fifth century. The oldest extant monument of Breton Latin literature is a letter from three Romano-Gaulish bishops, Licinius of Angers, Melanius of Rennes, and Eustochius of Tours, to two priests bearing Brittonic names, Louocatus and Catihernus, written sometime between 509 and 521.[1]

A   **DOMINIS BEATISSIMIS ET**[2] **IN XPISTO** fratribus
    Louocato et Catihērnō presbyteris
    Lecinius Melanius et Eustōchius ēpiscopi[3]

B1   Viri[4] uenerabilis Sparati[5] presbyteri relatiōne cōgnōuimus
 2   quod gestantes[6] quasdam tabulas per diuersorum ciuium
    uestrorum[7] capanas circumferre nōn dēsinātis .
 3   et missas ibidem adhibitis[8] mulieribus in sacrificiō diuīnō
 4   quas conhōspitas nōminātis
    fácere praēsūmātis .
    Sicut erogantibus uóbis eūcharistiās[9]
    illae[10] uobis positis calices[11] teneant et sanguinem Xpisti
    populo administrāre praēsūmant .
 5   **C**uius rei nouitas et inaudíta superstítio
 6   nos non[12] léuiter cōntristāuit

1   BCLL 823. 'Ein gallisches Bischofsschreiben des 6. Jahrhunderts als Zeuge für die Verfassung der Montanistenkirche', ed. A. Jülicher, Zeitschrift für Kirchengeschichte XVI (1896), pp. 664–71, hereafter J; A. Le Moyne de la Borderie ed., Histoire de Bretagne (Rennes & Paris 1898), vol. II, pp. 526–7, hereafter B. The text is here edited from Munich, Staatsbibliothek, MS Clm 5508 f. 102r–v, of which the capital letters and punctuation marks are represented in boldface. I owe thanks to Dr J. Blundell for collation.
2   JB omit.
3   MS eps.
4   MS uir.
5   J Sperati.
6   MS gestant ex.
7   J omits.
8   MS adhib&is, J abhibitis.
9   MS eucharistie, J eucharistias, B eucharistiam.
10   MS ille.
11   B calicem.
12   MS superstitionis non, JB superstitio nos non.

7 ut tam horrenda secta quae intra Gallias
numquam fuísse probátur .
Nostris temporibus uideátur mérgere[13]

8 quam patres orientales pepódianam[14] uócant .
pro eo quod Pepodius[15] auctor huius scísmatis
fúerit[16]

9 múlieres síbi

10 in sacrificio diuino socias[17] habére prae-
súmpsérit[18]

11 praecipientes ut quicumque huic errori
uolúerit ínhaérére

12 a communione ecclesiastica
reddátur[19] extráneús .

B' 1 Qua de re caritatem uestram in Xp[ist]i amore . pro ecclesiae
unitate et fidei catholicae [sócie]táte[20]
inprimis credídimus ádmónéndám .
obsecrantes[21] ut cum ad uos nostra[22] peruenerit[23] página[24] lítterárúm
repentina[25] de praedictis rebus emendátió súbsécútá[26]

2 id est de antedictis tabulis [27]quas a presbyteris non dubitamus ut
dícitis[28] cónsécrátás

3 et de muliéribus íllis

4 quas conhóspitás dícitis

5 quae nunccupatio non sine quodam tremore[29] dicitur
ánimí . uél audítúr

6 quod clérúm ínfámát .

7 et sancta[30] in religione tam detestandum nomen
pudorem íncutit ét hórrórém .

13 B *emergere.*
14 MS, B *pepondianam.*
15 B *Pepondius.*
16 J *.... Ich nehme hier eine Lücke an, mindestens etwas wie* si qui *(vgl. unten S. 666 Z. 8) muss ausgefallen sein.* B adds *et.*
17 MS *do socias,* B *consocias.*
18 MS, J *praesumpserint,* B *praesumpserit.*
19 MS *redatur.*
20 MS [.....]*tate,* J *integritate,* B *societate.*
21 J omits.
22 J omits.
23 MS, J *peruenerunt,* B .*pervenerit.*
24 J *paginae.*
25 MS *repentinam.* JB *repentina.*
26 B *subsequatur.*
27 MS *ut antedictas tabulas.* JB *de antedictis tabulis.*
28 J *decet.*
29 MS *primo.* JB *tremore.*
30 MS *sancte.*

8   **I**dcirco secundum statuta patrum caritati uéstrae
            praecípimus .³¹

9   **U**t non solum huiusmódi muliérculae .

10   sacramenta diuina pro inlicita
            administratiōnĕ nōn pōlluănt .

11   **S**ed etiam praeter matrem auiam .³²
                    sororem uel neptem intra tectum
                    cēllōlaē ³³ sŭaē̆ .

                    Si quis ad cohabitandum habére uolúerit .

12   canonum sententia a sacrosanctae³⁴
                    liminibus ecclésiae ārcēătŭr .

B"1   **C**onuenit itaque uobis³⁵ frātrēs kărīssĭmī̆
      ut³⁶ si ita est ut ad nos

2   de supradicto prouĕnīt³⁷ nēgōtĭŏ

3   emendationem celérrimam .³⁸ ēxhĭbĕrĕ̆ .

4   quia prō sălūtḝ ănĭmārŭm .
                et pro aedificatiōnĕ pōpŭlī̆ .

5   res ab ecclesiastico ordine tam turpiter deprauatas
                    uelociter éxpedit³⁹ ēmēndārĕ̆ .

6   **U**t nec uos pertinacitas huius obstinationis ad maiorem
                        confusiónem ēxhĭbĕăt .

                        Nec nobis necesse sit cum uirga ad uos uenire .
                        apostolica . si caritátem rēnuĕtĭs .⁴⁰

7   et tradere⁴¹ Satanae īn īntĕrĭtū ⁴² cărnĭs .
                            ut spiritus pōssĭt sāluărī̆ .

                            hoc est tradere Satanae⁴³ cum ecclesiastico grege prō
                            crīmĭnĕ sŭŏ

                            Quisquis⁴⁴ fuerit separatus . **N**on dubitet se a
                            daemonibus tamquam lupis rapácibus dēuōrāndŭm .

8   **S**imiliter et euangelicam commonemus
                        sententiam⁴⁵ ubi ait .

---

31 MS *praecipem*. BJ *praecipimus*.
32 MS *auia*.
33 B *cellulae*.
34 MS *.sacrosco*.
35 MS *nobis frr kmi*. J *vos fratres carissimi*. B *vobis fratres karissimi*.
36 J omits.
37 B *pervenit*.
38 MS *celeberrimam*. JB *celerrimam*.
39 MS *exp&it*.
40 MS *renu&is*. J *renuatis*. B *renuitis*.
41 MS *traderi*. JB *tradere*.
42 J *interitum*.
43 J *vielleicht später eingeschoben*.
44 B *quisque*.
45 MS *euangelicam commonemur sententiam*. JB *evangelica commonemur sententia*.

9	Si nos nostra scandalizauerint membra .[46]
10	quicumque[47] ecclesia catholica[48] haéresim intromíttit .
11	Ideo facilius[49] est ut unum membrum qui totam commaculat[50] ecclésiam abscidatur .
12	quam tota ecclesia in intéritu[51] deducatur .
A'	Sufficiant uobis haec pauca quae de multis praediximus

Date opera multa communiónem[52] caritátis .
et uiam regiam[53] qua paululum[54] deuiastis .
Auidissima intentione ingredi procuretis .
ut et uos fructum de oboediéntia càpiátis
et nos uos pro exoratione nostra congaudeamus esse saluandos

A   To the most blessed lords and brothers in Christ, Louocatus and Catihernus, priests, Licinius, Melanius, and Eustochius, bishops.

B   From the report of the man Speratus the venerable priest we have learned that bearing certain tables you do not cease to go about through the huts of your various citizens, and you presume to celebrate masses there with women present at the divine sacrifice, [women] whom you call 'fellow hostesses' so that for those requesting Eucharists from you those [women], placed by you, hold the chalices and presume to administer the blood of Christ to the people. The strangeness of this affair and the unheard of practice has saddened us not a little, that so horrendous a sect, which is proved never to have been within the Gauls, is seen to emerge in our times, [a sect] which the Eastern Fathers call 'pepodian' — for the reason that Pepodius was the founder of this schism; he presumed to have women as associates for himself in the divine sacrifice — [the Fathers] teaching that whoever would wish to adhere to this error should be judged as alien from ecclesiastical fellowship.

B' Concerning this affair we have come to believe that in the first place your charity should be appealed to in the love of Christ for the unity of the Church and the fellowship of the Catholic Faith, imploring that when the page of our letter will have come to you a speedy improvement from the foresaid conditions should follow, that is concerning the foresaid tables, which we suspect not to have been consecrated by priests, as you say, and

46 J adds <hoc est>.
47 B adds in.
48 J ecclesiae catholicae.
49 J utilius.
50 MS comaculat.
51 J interitum.
52 J operam multam communioni. B opera multa communione.
53 J adds a.
54 B paulum.

concerning those women whom you call 'fellow hostesses', a name which is not uttered or heard without a certain tremor of the mind, because it disgraces the clergy, and in holy religion so hateful a name inflicts shame and horror. Therefore according to the statutes of the Fathers we recommend to your charity not only that these foolish little women not pollute the divine sacraments because of their illegal ministering, but also that if anyone should wish to have for cohabiting under the roof of his humble dwelling any other than a mother, grandmother, sister, or female relative, by the sentence of the canons he should be kept away from the thresholds of Holy Church.

B" Therefore, dearest brothers, if what has come to our notice concerning the abovementioned business is true, it befits you to show the speediest improvement, because for the health of souls and for the edification of the people it is profitable to correct quickly the matters so foully perverted from ecclesiastical order, so that persistence of this obstinacy should not expose you to greater shame, nor should it be necessary for us to come to you with an apostolic rod, if you will refuse charity, and to hand you over to Satan for the death of the flesh so that the spirit might be saved, that is, to hand over to Satan with your ecclesiastical flock for its crime. Whoever would be separated should not doubt that he will be devoured by demons as by ravening wolves. Similarly we call to mind the Gospel sentence, where it says if our members should scandalize us, whoever in the Catholic Church introduces heresy, for so doing it is easier that one member who defiles the whole Church should be cut off than that the whole Church should be led away in destruction.

A These few things from the many which we have said before should suffice for you: give with much effort the communion of charity, and may you take care with the most ardent intent to enter into the royal way from which you have deviated a little, so that you may receive fruit from obedience and we may rejoice together that you because of our entreaty will be saved.

The bishops exercised great care in organizing this remarkable letter. They bound paragraph B to paragraph B' with the following parallels. Compare in parts 1 *cognouimus* with *credidimus*, in 2 *quasdam tabulas* with *de praedictis tabulis*, in 3 *et ... adhibitis mulieribus* with *et de mulieribus illis*, in 4 *quas conhospitas nominastis* with *quas conhospitas dicitis*, in 5 *inaudita* with *auditur*, in 6 *nos contristauit* with *clerum infamat*, in 7 *tam horrenda secta* with *sancta religione tam detestandum*, in 8 *patres* with *patrum*, in 9 *mulieres* with *mulierculae*, in 10 *in sacrificio diuino* with *sacramenta diuina*, in 11 *uoluerit* repeated exactly, in 12 *a communione ecclesiastica reddatur extraneus* with *a sacrosanctae liminibus ecclesiae arceatur*.

They also bound paragraphs B and B' to paragraph B" with the following parallels. Compare B"1 *uobis* with B2 *uestrorum* and B'1 *uestram*, B"1–2 *ad nos prouenit* with *cognouimus* and *credidimus*, and *de supradicto prouenit negotio* with *peruenerit* and *de praedictis rebus*, B"3 *emendationem* with B'1 *emendatio*, B"4 *populi* with B4 *populo*, B"5 *res ab ecclesiastico ordine ... deprauatas* with B5 *cuius rei nouitas* and *superstitio* and B'1 *de praedictis rebus*, B"6 *ad maiorem confusionem exhibeat* with B'6 *clerum infamat*, B"8 *similiter et euangelicam commonemus sententiam* with B'8 *idcirco secundum statuta patrum praecipimus* and B'12 *sententia*, B"11 *abscidatur* with B'12 *arceatur*, and B"12 *ecclesia* with B'12 *ecclesiae*.

Besides these parallels the bishops placed important words at fixed intervals throughout their text. The first nine words bring one to the title of the recipients, *presbyteris*. The source of the bishops' information is the report of *Sparati presbyteri*, whose title is the ninth word after that. In B'2 the bishops doubt whether Louocatus and Catihernus celebrate the Eucharist on tables duly consecrated by *presbyteris*. The word is 144th (9 × 16) from the beginning of B and eighty-first (9 × 9) from the end of B'.

The verb used for the action of heterodox persons is *praesumere*. The thirtieth word from the beginning of B brings one to the point at which Louocatus and Catihernus presume to celebrate masses in B4 *praesumatis*. Half that number of words (15) bring one to the action of the women who presume to administer chalices, *praesumant* at the end of B4. The forty-fifth word after that (30 + 15) marks the action of Pepodius, who *praesumpserit* in B11.

The verb used for the action of orthodox men is *praecipere*. In B'8, where our bishops tell what they are doing, *praecipimus* is the central, 202nd, word of this 404-word text. In B11 the bishops tell what the Eastern Fathers taught, *praecipientes*. From *praecipimus* to *praecipientes* inclusive there are ninety-six words. The ninety-sixth word before *praecipientes* is the first of our bishops' names. The ninety-sixth word after *praecipimus* occurs in the second clause of B"6, where the bishops tell what they will do if the priests should refuse their charity. The word is *caritatem* and it is the 107th word from the end of the letter. In B'1 the bishops appeal to the charity of Louocatus and Catihernus, where *caritatem* is the 107th word from the beginning of B. From *caritatem uestram* in B'1 to *caritati uestrae* in B'8 inclusive there are seventy-nine words. From *caritatem* in B"6 to *caritatis* in A' inclusive there are seventy-nine words.

In B' nine words (3 × 3) bring one to *ecclesiae* in B'1. Between that and the next occurrence of the word *ecclesiae* in B'12 there are 108 words (3 × 36). From *ecclesiae* in B'12 to *ecclesiae catholicae* in B"10 inclusive there are also 108 words. Between *ecclesiae* in B"10 and *ecclesiam* in B"11 exclusive there are twelve words (3 × 4). Between that and *ecclesia* in B"12 exclusive there are three words. After that there are three words to the end of the paragraph.

The last word of the phrase *cum ecclesiastico grege* in B"7 is fiftieth from the end of B". The first word of the phrase *communione ecclesiastica* in B12 is one hundredth from the beginning of B. The first word of the phrase *res ab ecclesiastico ordine* in B"5 is 150th from the end of *communione ecclesiastica*. From *res ab ecclesiastico ordine* to *cum ecclesiastico grege* inclusive there are fifty words.

After the word *catholicae* in B'1 there are 107 words to the end of paragraph B'. The 107th word of paragraph B" is *catholicae* in B"10. Before *catholicae* in B'1 there are thirteen words. In B"10 *catholicae* is the twentieth word from the end of the paragraph. The golden section of 33 falls at 20 and 13.

At the end of B3 one reads the phrase *sacrificio diuino*, which recurs at the beginning of B10. Paragraph B comprises 103 words. The golden section of 103 falls at 64 and 39. From the first *sacrificio* to the second *diuino* inclusive there are sixty-four words. Before the first there are twenty-five words and after the second there are fifteen, forty together. The golden section of 40 falls at 25 and 15.

The bishops doubt whether the priests' altars are duly consecrated in B'1, where from the beginning of the paragraph forty-two words bring one to *dubitamus*. They state what no one should doubt in B"7, where *dubitet* is the forty-second word from the end of the paragraph.

The clausular and cursus rhythms need little explication. There is only one problem: either the *o* in *Eustochius* is treated unetymologically as long or there is no clausula intended there. One may infer with some assurance that the text of this letter has come to us almost exactly as its authors penned it. Recovery of their structural style allows one to correct both the nineteenth-century editions and the manuscript itself. Parallelism confirms in B"1 the correctness of *uobis*, not *nobis* as in the manuscript or *vos* as in J, and the inclusion of *uestrorum* in B2, omitted by J. It strengthens the case for a singular verb *peruenerit* in B'1, to be compared with *conuenit* in B"1 and *prouenit* in B"2. The word counts show the incorrectness of both editors' deletions and additions of words, which ruin the patterns noted above without producing other more credible or attractive patterns. It might even be that misapprehended parallelism accounts for some of the manuscript errors. The false reading at B'2, *ut antedictas tabulas quas*, may issue from comparison with the accusative form in B2, *quasdam tabulas*. The ungrammatical first person plural passive or false deponent form *commonemur* in B"8 may have been influenced by the earlier erroneous form *pápem.* in B'8.

It would be rash to suppose that this analysis deals with all or even most of the bishops' epistolary artifice. There are, however, many indications in it that the bishops were well acquainted with Biblical style, which they expected their readers to notice and appreciate. The letter merits interest, not only as evidence for ecclesiastical historians, but as a monument to the literate culture of the sixth century.

IV. GILDAS

De Excidio Britanniae

About the middle of the sixth century a British cleric named Gildas composed an *Epistola de Excidio Britanniae*.[1] It is not what one usually reckons as epistolary, yet Gildas announces first what he intends to say *in hac epistola*,

1   BCLL 27. *Gildae Sapientis De Excidio et Conquestu Britanniae*, ed. T. Mommsen, *Monumenta Germaniae Historica, Auctorum Antiquissimorum Tomi XIII* (Berlin 1894), vol. III i pp. 1–85; *Gildae De Excidio Britanniae*, ed. & transl. H. Williams, Cymmrodorion Record Series III-IV (London 1899–1901). *Gildas: The Ruin of Britain and other works*, ed. & transl. M. Winterbottom, History from the Sources (London & Chichester 1978).

perhaps so called in imitation of Patrick's *Epistola*, which similarly chastises a British ruler. Like Patrick in his Apology in the *Confessio*, Gildas records his hesitation to write, and his invocation of God as witness, *ut mihi renum scrutator testis est Dominus*, may owe something to Patrick's phrases *testem Deum inuoco ... scrutatur corda et renes* (54, 57).[2] Like the Romano-British Pelagius and Patrick and the Romano-Gaulish bishops Gildas composed in Biblical style; like them he arranged his prose in chiastic and parallel patterns, especially in sevens. In the following analysis the traditional chapter numbers with Michael Winterbottom's subdivisions appear in arabic numerals in round brackets. The section numbers in roman numerals are mine and putatively the author's.

In a recent collection of essays Michael Lapidge and David Dumville have drawn attention to the three-book structure of *De Excidio*:[3]

Book I	(1–26)	Preface and *Historia*
Book II	(27–65)	Denunciation of British *tyranni*
Book III	(66–110)	Denunciation of British *sacerdotes*

Lapidge has argued that *De Excidio* is a seven-part forensic speech with the structure of a declamation pronounced by the prosecution against a vice-ridden country, a *uituperatio ... in patriam exosam*.[4]

Book I	(1–2)	*exordium*
	(3–26)	*narratio* of the sub-type *historia*
Book II	(27–36)	*propositio*
	(37–63)	*argumentatio*
Book III	(64–75)	*propositio*
	(76–105)	*argumentatio*
	(106–110)	*epilogus*

By comparing the work with the ancient rhetorical tradition which preceded *De Excidio* rather than with the medieval tradition which followed it Lapidge has thrown light upon a dark part of British literary history. His convincing analysis of correct, even punctilious, use of diction and rhetoric has rescued Gildas from misprision 'as an eccentric and idiosyncratic writer',[5] but his analysis of the structure is not persuasive.

The *epilogus*, for example, contains no backward reference to the tyrants, but follows without a break the exhortation to good priests which begins at (92.2). The *propositio* which Lapidge notes at (64–75) actually starts at (66), so that Book III, beginning *Sacerdotes habet Britannia*, stands parallel to Book II,

2   Both may derive from Psalm VII 10.
3   M. Lapidge & D. Dumville eds, *Gildas: New Approaches,* Studies in Celtic History IV (Woodbridge 1984), p. xii.
4   Ibid. pp. 43–4.
5   Ibid. p. 27.

beginning *Reges habet Britannia* at (27). The function of (64–5) is to ease the
transition from Book II to Book III, but Lapidge's analysis obscures this and
cuts across the manuscript division into books.

My analysis of *De Excidio* differs from Lapidge's.

Book I	Part I	(1)	*Praefatio* or *Exordium*
	II	(2–3)	*Praefatiuncula* and *Descriptio*
	III	(4–13)	History of Britain
	IV	(14–26)	Deliverance of the Britons
Book II	Part V	(27–63)	Address to the kings of Britain
	VI	(64–65)	Transition from secular rulers
			to spiritual leaders
Book III	Part VII	(66–110)	Address to the clergy of Britain

Part I begins with a Preface (1), the limits of which are marked by internal
chiasmus. Gildas states first that he will lament evil in *lacrimosis querelis* (1.1). He
states finally that soldiers of Christ will receive his message *cum lacrimis* (1.16).
Second he alludes to his long silence: *silui ... spatio bilustri temporis uel eo amplius
praetereuntis* (1.2). Penultimately he alludes to a long debate with himself about
whether to speak out: *per tot annorum spatia ... taceas; ... non paruo, ut dixi, tempore
cum legerim 'Tempus esse loquendi et tacendi'* (1.14–5). Third he lists Old Testament
passages, beginning *Legebam nihilominus* (1.3–4); then he considers their application to his day: *Videbam etiam nostro tempore* (1.5–6). Antepenultimately he lists
several New Testament passages, beginning *Legebam inquam* (1.8–10); then he
considers their application to his day in a parallelism:

> Sciebam misericordiam Domini, sed et iudicium timebam;
> laudabam gratiam, sed redditionem unicuique secundum opera sua
> uerebar (1.11–13).

At the crux of this seven-part Preface he states that after gazing at the Old
Testament as at a mirror of contemporary British life, he turned to the New
Testament, where things which had been dark were made more clear.

There are forty-four words in the first part and sixty-seven in the last, forty-
nine in the second and 207 in the penultimate. In the third part there are 115
words about the Old Testament passages and eighty-four about their application;
in the antepenultimate part there are 148 words about the New Testament
passages and 168 about their application. At the crux there are thirty-four words
describing Gildas's meditation first on the Old Testament and then on the New.
Exactly half-way through the passage he states that he turned *ad nouas [scripturas]*.
The Preface comprises 916 words. The golden section of 916 falls at 566 and 350.
The crux and the antepenultimate part, describing Gildas's meditation on the
New Testament and its application to his day, contain 350 words. The rest of the
Preface contains 566 words.

Part II (2–3) begins with a *Praefatiuncula*, in which Gildas announces the subjects he is about to treat, and a *Descriptio*, a short paragraph *De situ Britanniae*. Part II comprises 261 words.

In Part III (4–13) Gildas sketches chiastically the history of Roman and Christian Britain. He alludes first to the *uetustos immanium tyrannorum annos* (4.3–4), mentions the *nomen Romanae seruitutis*, and describes the island as *non Britannia sed Romania* (7). Finally he writes

> Item tandem tyrannorum uirgultis crescentibus et in immanem
> siluam iamiamque erumpentibus insula, nomen Romanum nec
> tamen morem legemque tenens ... (13.1).

Second in a paragraph comprising a single sentence he considers the advent of Christianity to Roman Britain (8). Winterbottom, after comparing this 'grand and elaborate sentence' with its source in Rufinus's translation of Eusebius's *Historia Ecclesiastica*, has rightly described it as 'wholly typical of its author', though not everyone will agree with him that its splendour is 'shapeless'.[6] The point of the sentence is that during the reign of Tiberius *absque ullo impedimento eius propagabatur religio*; the last word triumphantly identifies the subject, *Xpistus*. Penultimately in a paragraph comprising a single sentence Gildas considers the perversion of Christ's religion in Britain by Arianism: *mansit namque haec Xpisti capitis membrorumque consonantia suauis donec Arriana perfidia ...* (12.3). Third he alludes to the Diocletianic persecution and the destruction of churches (9.1). Antepenultimately he alludes to the end of that persecution and the restoration of churches (12.2). Fourth he considers *quantae diuersarum mortium poenae ... quantae gloriosorum martyrum coronae* (9.2). Fourth from the end he considers how some *diuersis cruciatibus torti sunt* and the *gloriosi ... martyrii sui trophaea* (11.2). The central part of this chapter is an account of the martyrdom of Saint Alban (10–11.1). The entire chapter contains 1202 words or, preferably, reading *iam iamque* in 11.1 and 13.1 as a single word,[7] an even 1200. The end of the crux brings one to *Ceteri* [*sc. martyres*] (11.2), the nine-hundredth word.

Part IV begins with a grand parallelism (14–8) in which Gildas relates two rescues of the Britons by the Romans. In the former part he describes first the departure of the legions from Britain (14), second the first attacks (*primum*) by the Scots and the Picts (14), third the first appeal to Rome (15.1), fourth the dispatch of a legion (15.2), fifth its success (15.2), sixth the order to construct the Antonine Wall (15.3), and seventh the failure of this turf wall because of its construction by an irrational mob (15.3). Then in the latter part he describes first the departure of the legion (16), second the reappearance of the same enemies (16), third the second appeal to Rome (17.1), fourth the dispatch of

---

6 Winterbottom, *Gildas*, p. 7.
7 Winterbottom prints this as two words at 11.1 and 13.1, but as a single word at 22.1. It should appear as one word throughout.

military and naval forces (17.2), fifth their success (17.2–3), sixth the order to construct Hadrian's Wall (18.1–2), and seventh the superiority of this wall to the other, *murum non ut alterum* (18.2–3). The former seven parts contain 153 words and the latter seven 354 words.

Part IV ends with an even grander parallelism (19–26). In it Gildas relates two occasions on which the Britons delivered themselves. In the former part he describes first the emergence of the old enemies (19.1), second their occupation of the northern part of the island (19.1), third the foolish reaction of the British army, *stupido sedili marcebat* (19.2), fourth the quick death which came to many, *immaturae mortis supplicium* (19.2), fifth waste by famine, *perexigui uictus breui sustentaculo* (19.4), sixth the appeal to the consul, *Agitio ter consuli* (20.1), seventh the failure of the aid sought from Rome (20.1), eighth a famine, *famis dira*, (20.2), ninth resistance *de ipsis montibus ac saltibus* (20.2), tenth the retreat of the enemies, *recesserunt hostes* (20.3), eleventh a marvellous prosperity (21.2), twelfth an ensuing decline in morality, *luxuria crescit ... non solum uero hoc uitium* (21.2–3), thirteenth a consequent hatred of the truth, *odium ueritatis* (21.3), and fourteenth the reception of Satan as an angel of light (21.3). Penultimately he denounces *filii sine lege* (21.5). Finally he denounces corrupt Churchmen (21.6). Then in the latter part he describes first the rumour of the reappearance of the old enemies (22.1), second their intention to dispossess the inhabitants and occupy the entire island (22.1), third the foolish reaction of the British, *comparati iumentis insipientibus strictis* (22.1), fourth the death for which many were destined, *per latam diuersorum uitiorum morti procliue ducentem ... uiam* (22.1), fifth waste by plague, *pestifera namque lues* (22.2), sixth the decision of the *consiliarii* (23.1), seventh the horrible consequences of the aid they sought from the Saxons (23.2–24.4), eighth a famine, *alii fame confecti* (25.1), ninth resistance from *montanis collibus ... et densissimis saltibus* (25.1), tenth the retreat of the enemies, *recesserunt domum crudelissimi praedones*, eleventh Ambrosius Aurelianus, under whose leadership the British recovered marvellously (25.2–3), twelfth an ensuing decline, (25.3), thirteenth the subversion of the truth, *cuncta ueritatis ac iustitiae moderamina concussa ac subuersa sunt* (26.3), and fourteenth the rush to hell (26.3). Penultimately he praises Mother Church's true sons, *solos ueros filios* (26.3). Finally he exempts from censure those who lead blameless lives (26.4) The former part of the parallelism contains 697 words and the latter part 1025 words.

Gildas has linked these parallelisms. He first refers to the Scots and the Picts by name (14) and then alludes to them as *illi priores inimici* (16). He states that the defending Romans *infigunt mucronum ungues* (17.2). Again he refers first to the Scots and the Picts by name (19.1) and then alludes to their arrival as the *aduentus ueterum* (22.1). He states that the defending Saxon force *infixit ungues* (23.4). The purpose of this is to link the former part of the first parallelism to the former part of the second, and the latter part of the first parallelism to the latter part of the second. Part IV comprises 2229 words. The golden section of 2229 falls at 1378 and 851. The former parts contain 850 words and the latter parts 1379 words.

Part V (27–63) is a seven-membered chiastic address to the kings of Britain. Gildas first indicts kings and judges (27): *Reges habet Britannia sed tyrannos, iudices habet sed impios.* Then he lists specific failings of five evil kings (28–36): Constantinus of Damnonia (28–29), Aurelius Caninus (30), Vortipor of the Demetae (31), Cuneglasus (32), and Maglocunus (33–36). Third he concludes his own attack upon these tyrants and denounces them with the words of God's Prophets (37):

> Hic ... concludenda erat uti ne amplius loqueretur os nostrum opera hominum ... . Respondeant itaque pro nobis sancti uates nunc ... .

Fourth at the crux of Part V he placed a catena of quotations from and allusions to Holy Scripture (38–61). Fifth he concludes the denunciations from the Prophets (62.1): *Haec de sanctorum prophetarum minis dixisse sufficiat.* Sixth he considers rules for the guidance of good kings (62.2–8). Seventh he addresses the kings and judges (63): *audite ... omnes reges et intellegite, discite, iudices finium terrae.*

A	(27)	General indictment of kings and judges
B	(28–36)	Specific sins of evil kings
C	(37)	Prologue to the words of God's Prophets
D	(38–61)	Quotations from Holy Scripture
C'	(62.1)	Epilogue to the words of God's Prophets
B'	(62.2–8)	Rules for the guidance of good kings
A'	(63)	Address to kings and judges

In Part VI Gildas turns his attention from secular rulers (64) to spiritual leaders (65).

Part VII (66–110) is a seven-membered chiastic address to the clergy of Britain. Gildas first indicts men in Holy Orders (66–68). Second he asks how British priests compare with their predecessors in Biblical and ecclesiastical history (69–75). Third he concludes his own attack upon his brother clerics and denounces them with the words of God's Prophets (76.1): *confugientes ... ad Domini misericordiam sanctorumque prophetarum eius uoces.* Fourth at the crux of Part VII he placed a catena of quotations from and allusions to Holy Scripture (76.2–91). Fifth he concludes the denunciations from the Prophets (92.1): *Sed sufficiant haec pauca de pluribus prophetarum testimonia.* Sixth he cites the *euangelica tuba* and the words of the services of ordination to call clergymen to their proper duties (92.2–109). Seventh he addresses clergymen and concludes with a prayer for better priests (110).

A	(66–68)	General indictment of clergymen
B	(69–75)	Examples of good priests from history (most clauses beginning *Quis* ... ?)

C	(76.1)	Prologue to the words of God's Prophets
D	(76.2–91)	Quotations from Holy Scripture
C'	(92.1)	Epilogue to the words of God's Prophets
B'	(92.2–109)	Exhortation to good priests (many clauses beginning *Quis* ... ?)
A'	(110)	Prayer for better priests

Gildas has bound the chiasmus of Part V to the chiasmus of Part VII in a grand parallelism. The first sentence of the former is echoed by the first sentence of the latter:

Reges habet Britannia sed tyrannos
   iudices habet sed impios
      saepe praedantes et concutientes sed innocentes
      uindicantes et patrocinantes sed reos et latrones
Sacerdotes habet Britannia sed insipientes
   quam plurimos ministros sed impudentes
   clericos sed raptores subdolos.

The specific address to the five tyrants is echoed by the specific address to the clergy. The prologue to the scriptural quotations in (37) is very similar to that in (76.1) Even the quotations follow a similar order, presumably the order of books in Gildas's Bible. The exhortation to kings in (62.2–8) may be compared with the exhortation to priests in (92.2–109), and the concluding address to kings and judges in (63) may be compared with that to clerics in (110).

Long ago Souter concluded 'that Gildas, about four generations after Pelagius, employed a text [of the Bible] substantially identical with his, and that of the *Book of Armagh*, ... the missing British form of the Old-Latin'.[8] Use of one form of the Bible does not entail uniformity of composition, as we see clearly from the literary idiosyncrasies of Pelagius and Patrick, which could hardly be more disparate. If their works nonetheless exhibit so many identical features of Biblical style, we must conclude that the style was widely cultivated among Romano-British Christians, and that it was inculcated during the earliest stages of education.[9] A century after the end of Roman dominion in Britain we see all the features of this style in Gildas *De Excidio Britanniae*. Gildas is a difficult writer. But, as we shall see from echoes in later Celtic Latin literature, he had readers who could not only comprehend his arguments but recognize, admire, and imitate his art.

In one important aspect of his art, the matter of prose rhythm, the ablest scholars who have considered the work of Gildas recently have come to varied conclusions. Winterbottom writes,[10]

8   Souter, *Expositions*, vol. I p. 146.
9   Patrick knew how to compose in this style although his education was interrupted by his kidnappers when he was a *puer inuerbis*, before being instructed by a rhetor.
10 Winterbottom, *Gildas,* p. 8.

Gildas knows nothing of this [sc. rhythm], or chooses to ignore it. He has cut himself off from something continental stylists had always prided themselves on. He has abandoned the practice of his own sources; he had certainly read the elegantly rhythmical Rufinus. And when he quotes the alleged words of the Letter to Aëtius, the old crisp declamatory manner contrasts weirdly with its baroque surroundings:

> Repellunt barbari ad mare, repellit mare ad barbaros;
> inter haec duo genera funerum aut iugulamur aut mergimur (20.1).

Neil Wright observes that[11]

these portions of hexameters embedded in Gildas's prose are important evidence that he understood Classical metrical quality.

Giovanni Orlandi is[12]

assured that Gildas sought certain types of metrical *clausulae* and was at the same time sensitive to the rhythm produced by the tonic accents.

François Kerlouégan concludes[13]

J'ai cru reconnaître l'existence chez Gildas d'un système métrique. Cela m'oblige à supposer qu'au moment où l'on passait, au moins dans la langue parlée, du système quantitatif au système accentuel — conséquence: la quantité va se regler sur l'accent et non plus l'accent sur la quantité.

Orlandi and Kerlouégan print tables of statistics, but as they do not exhibit their scansions these are unverifiable and completely useless. Here follow the first two sentences of *De Excidio*, then the ends of clauses marked by semicolons and full stops in the first twenty-six chapters, excluding texts quoted from other sources.

In hac epistola quicquid deflendo potius quam declamando, uili licet stilo, tamen benigno, fuero prosecutus, ne quis me, affectu cunctos spernentis omnibusue melioris, quippe qui commune bonorum dispendium malorumque cumulum lacrimosis querelis defleam, sed condolentis patriae incommoditatibus miseriisque eius ac remediis condelectantis edicturum putet, quia non tam fortissimorum militum enuntiare trucis belli pericula mihi statutum est quam desidiosorum. silui, fateor, cum inmenso cordis

---

11 N. Wright, 'Gildas's Prose Style and its Origins' in Lapidge & Dumville eds, *Gildas: New Approaches*, p. 113 n. 53.

12 G. Orlandi, '*Clausulae* in Gildas's *De Excidio Britanniae*' in ibid. p. 134.

13 F. Kerlouégan, *Le De Excidio Britanniae de Gildas* (Paris 1987), p. 466.

dŏlōrĕ, ut mihi renum scrutator testis est Dominus [Psalm VII 10], spatio bilustri temporis uel eo amplius praetereuntis imperitia sic ut et nunc, una cum uilibus me meritis ínhibéntibus, ne qualemcumque admonitiūnculām scrīberēm.

This is not the prose of a man who 'knows nothing of' rhythm. Gildas has composed his first two sentences in alternating clausular and cursus rhythms. Thereafter he writes consistently in good cursus rhythms.

1.3	non íntroiísse, éxitu pèriísse, spársim cecidísse
1.4	múltos strauísse, intulísse exítium, plangéntis alphabéto
1.7	ínlucescénte
1.10	sáperet èxcidéndum
1.11	iudícium timébam, súa uerébar, haeréseos nótam
1.12	timerétur incréuerat
1.13	aetátis factúrus est, íneluctábile
1.14	láteque protráctum, créditum et táceas, mánui fáre, spéculatóres, mutíre dísponis, cítra númerum, respirándi non hábent
1.15	condebitóres sensus méi, pórticu lùctabántur, caedénti demonstráuit
1.16	ínsipiéntibus, íllud excípient
2	dícere conámur
3.3	instrúctis decoráta
3.4	exundántibus irrígua
4.1	ingráta consúrgit, libidínibus régi
4.3	étiam adnécteret
3.4	pósitis mála, nón satis cláret
5.2	edíctis subiugáuit
6.1	trucidáuit dolósa
6.2	páce fidéles
7	Itáliam pétunt, Caesáris notarétur
8	praecépta Xpístus
9.1	apparéret permansére
9.2	festináret ecclésia
10.1	sé putant iústos
10.2	caritátis incúterent, pérstantes díco
11.1	fórtuis fáceret
11.2	trophaéa defígerent, animárum tutámina
12.1	caeléstis excípiunt
12.2	úsque destrúctas, pássim própalant, óreque confíciunt, ecclésiae confóti
12.3	optinénti infigébant
13.1	Máximum míttit

13.2   uíta pélleret, quodammódo deiécerat
14   gémitque ánnos
15.1   árceretur uóuens
15.2   captiuitáte liberáuit
15.3   ciuibúsque tutámini, cespítibus non prófuit
16   cálcant tránseunt
17.1   óbrosum uilésceret
17.2   gúrgite móles
17.3   éxaggerábant
18.2   fueránt directo líbrant, armórum relínquunt
18.3   nón reuersúri
19.1   ténus capéssunt
19.2   sedíli marcébat, állidebántur, éxitu dèuitábant
19.3   accelerántur crudèlióres, assimilarétur agréstium
19.4   latrocinándo temperábant, ártis solácio
20.1   módo loquéntes, paúca queréntes, adiutórii hábent
20.2   álios uèro núsquam, contínue rèbellábant
20.3   íllud Philónis, nostrórum malítia, súis sceléribus
21.1   ét mendácia, témporis rèuersúri, nonnúmquam faciéntes
21.2   tácitus pùllulánte, luxúria créscit, témpore dìcerétur
21.3   ángelo lúcis
21.4   trúcióribus
21.5   dísplicéntia
21.6   médico làrgirétur, in ínuio et nòn in uía
22.1   términum règiónem, díscurrebant uíam
22.2   uíui humáre, implerétur dicéntis
22.3   Amorrhaeórum compleréntur, decérni debéret
23.1   íntromitteréntur
23.2   amárius fáctum est, sénsus calíginem, méntis hebetúdinem, cúlmine ìnuitábant
23.4   ímpugnatúrus, manipuláribus spúriis, pampinísque púllulat
23.5   ánnonas dári, dícitur cànis faúcem, depópulatúros, efféctibus pròsequúntur
24.1   língua delámberet
24.2   déplorans áit
24.4   ángelis uèheréntur, racémus uel spíca
25.1   iúgulabántur, grátiae stàbat lóco, sínibus cantántes, trépidi perstábant
25.3   prouocántes ad proélium, ánnuente céssit
26.1   díligat èum án non, natíuitátis est
26.2   ínhabitántur, nón ciuílibus, téstes extitére, órdinem seruárunt
26.3   fílios hábet
26.4   quám defléuero, circúitu nàtiónes

III

LETTERS AND LEARNING

I. COLUMBAN OF BANGOR

First Letter to Gregory the Great

In the sixth and seventh centuries of the Christian era the Irish, with no common historical experience of the Christian Roman Empire, learned the Latin language with a zeal rarely paralleled even among native speakers. The results, surpassing what one might reasonably have expected from neophytes, were dazzling. But they are hard to see, partly because modern editors often darken their brilliance with a cloud of misprision, and more often ruin the jokes and miss the fun.

A good example is one of the oldest extant monuments of Irish Latin literature, a letter written A.D. 600 about the Paschal controversy from Columban of Bangor, Luxeuil, and Bobbio to Pope Gregory the Great. Here is the Salutation as represented in the most recent critical edition.[1]

> Domino Sancto et in Christo Patri, Romanae pulcherrimo Ecclesiae Decori, totius Europae flaccentis augustissimo quasi cuidam Flori, egregio Speculatori, Theoria utpote divinae Castalitatis perito, ego Bariona (vilis Columba), in Christo mitto Salutem.
>
> *tit.* epistola ad sanctum gregorium papam super quaestione paschae at aliis *praem.* M romano S divina S, Gundlach castulitatis S, causalitatis *coniec.* Gundlach perito Gundlach, potito M (*emend.* ex posito) and S Bariona *scripsi*, bargma M, bargoma S filius Columbae *coniec.* Gundlach
>
> To the Holy Lord and Father in Christ, the fairest Ornament of the Roman Church, as it were a most honoured Flower of all Europe in her decay, to the distinguished Bishop, who is skilled in the Meditation of divine Eloquence, I, Bar-Jonah (a poor Dove), send Greeting in Christ.

J.W. Smit has partially mended this by reading *divina ac actuali Statu potito*.[2] Might one mend it further, supposing that Columban may have written the Salutation like this?

1   BCLL 639. *Sancti Columbani Opera*, ed. & transl. G.S.M. Walker, *Scriptores Latini Hiberniae* II (Dublin 1970), pp. 2–13.
2   J.W. Smit, *Studies on the Language and Style of Columba the Younger (Columbanus)* (Amsterdam 1971), pp. 39–56.

		6	11	27
DOMINO SANCTO ET IN XPISTO PATRI		6	11	27
ROMANAE PULCHERRIMO ECCLESIAE DECORI		4	14	33
TOTIUS EUROPAE FLACCENTIS AUGUSTISSIMO QUASI				
CUIDAM FLORI		7	20	51
EGREGIO SPECULATORI		2	9	18
THEORIAE UTPOTE DIVINAE AC ACTUALIS STATUS POTITORI		7	21	45
EGO BAR IONA VILIS COLUMBA IN XPISTO MITTO SALUTEM.		9	1	84
		35	93	216

To the holy lord and father in Christ,
the most beautiful ornament of the Roman church,
as it were, a certain most august flower of all drooping Europe,
outstanding overseer,
as being master of divine contemplation and the active condition,
I, son of Jonah, vile Columba, send greeting in Christ.

Our author begins as he means to proceed, going straight to the top, flaunting his self-assurance and displaying his learning, arguing forcefully a question of the utmost importance to him, as he jokes with the highest authority in Christendom.

The Salutation is composed mathematically, by symmetry, by extreme and mean ratio, and by the musical ratios *duplus* 2:1, *sesquialter* 3:2, *sesquitertius* 4:3, and *sesquioctauus* 9:8.

The Salutation as arranged above comprises six lines, of which all but the last rhyme, on *patri, decori, flori, speculatori*, and *potitori*. The first two lines exhibit chiastic alliteration on *d, e, p, r, p, e, d*. The third line exhibits parallel alliteration on *au-, fl-, eu-, fl-*. This is a remarkable but unmistakeable example of alliterative rhyming prose.

There are thirty-five words, ninety-three syllables, and 216 letters. Words and ideas are stated and restated in chiastic order.

a i	domino
ii	in Xpisto
b	decori
c	augustissimo
d	quasi
e	flori
f	egregio
e'	speculatori
d'	utpote
c'	diuinae
b'	potitori
a'i	ego
ii	in Xpisto

The first word of the first line, ai *domino*, refers to the recipient of the letter, and the first word of the last line, a'i *ego*, refers to the author, both men connected in Christ. The fourth word from the beginning is the first of a'ii, the phrase *in Xpisto*, and the fourth word from the end is the beginning of a'ii, the phrase *in Xpisto*. The tenth word from the beginning is b, the noun *decori*, and the tenth word from the end is b', the noun *potitori*. These divide the Salutation by sesquitertian ratio, at 20 and 15. The fourteenth word from the beginning is c, the adjective *augustissimo*, and the fourteenth word from the end is c', the adjective *diuinae*. These divide the Salutation by sesquialter ratio, at 21 and 14. The fifteenth word from the beginning is d, *quasi* 'as it were', and the fifteenth word from the end is d', *utpote* 'as being'. These also divide the Salutation by sesquitertian ratio, at 20 and 15. The seventeenth word from the beginning is at part e, the noun *flori*, and the seventeenth word from the end is at part e', the noun *speculatori*. The central word, eighteenth from beginning and end, is the sixth part of the chiasmus of this six-lined Salutation. Here our author puns on the name and office of the recipient, *egregio* 'standing out from the flock' sharing the same etymology as *Gregorio* 'shepherd of the flock'. A *speculator* is not only a 'sentinel', a 'look-out man', but a Latin synonym of *episcopus*, from ἐπισκοπος, at once 'overseer' and 'bishop' and 'one who speculates' or 'theorizes'. In the next line Gregory is addressed with another pun, as *potitor*, both 'he who has imbibed' and 'he who is empowered with' and therefore both 'drunk, imbued with' and 'master of' both the active life, *actualis status*, and the contemplative life, *theoria diuina*. Our author refers to himself in the sixth line, containing nine words, which divide by one-ninth and eight-ninths, at 1 and 8, that is at *ego* and *mitto*, and by sesquioctave ratio (9:8) at 5 and 4, that is at *Columba*. This is also eight-ninths of the entire Salutation, as the thirty-first of thirty-five words is *Columba*. The eighty-third syllable of ninety-three is in the middle of *Columba*. The 192nd letter of 216 is in the middle of *Columba*. There is another epogdoic number of words, 4, in our author's explanation of his own name, which involves another pun: *Bar Iona uilis Columba*. Hebrew יונה *Jonah* means 'dove', for which *columba* is the appropriate Latin translation. Hebrew בר *Bar* means 'son', for which *filius* is the appropriate Latin translation. Our author has for *filius* 'son' written *uilis* 'vile' for two reasons. One is apparently to introduce the theme of humility in deference to the great lord to whom he is writing. The other is really to imply the opposite. He appropriates for himself the name *Bar Iona*, which is borne in Matthew XVI 17 by Saint Peter, Prince of the Apostles and first Bishop of Rome. Under this name 'vile Columba', a very bold man indeed, questions and criticizes and indicts the very successor of Peter who first appropriated for himself the title *seruus seruorum Dei*.

The chiastic pair to this chiastic Salutation, which we may label part A, is the chiastic Valediction, which we may label part A'.

    a   Et si ut audiui a sancto Candido tuo hoc respondere

		11	23	50
	uolueris			
b	temporis antiquitate roborata mutari non posse	6	18	41
c	manifeste antiquus error est	4	10	25
b'	sed semper antiquior est ueritas	5	11	28
a'	quae illum reprehendit.	3	7	20
		29	69	164

a   And if, as I have heard from your holy Candidus, you should wish
    to reply this,
b   that it is not possible for things confirmed by antiquity of time to
        be changed,
c   manifestly the error is ancient,
b'·   but ever more ancient is the truth
a' which reprehends it.

Columban anticipates an unwelcome response in a and reproves it in a', contrasts
the antiquity of error in b with the greater antiquity of truth in b', and admits
that error is ancient at the crux in c. The central word, fifteenth of twenty-nine,
is *mutari*, 'to be changed'. The twenty-nine words divide by extreme and mean
ratio at 18 and 11, at the eleventh word, *uolueris* at the end of part a, where
Columban anticipates Gregory's wrong will. The remaining eighteen words
divide by extreme and mean ratio at 11 and 7. The minor part of seven words
begins *temporis antiquitate*, and the major part of eleven words begins *antiquus*.
These eleven words divide by extreme and mean ratio at 7 and 4. Between
antiquus and *antiquior* there are four words. In the Valediction as in the Salutation
Columban refers to himself one-ninth and eight-ninths of the way through the
text, which falls at 3 and 26, at *audiui* 'I have heard'.

The last word *reprehendit* says much, implying that Columban feared from the
first word of the Salutation not to persuade the pope. If Columban failed the
whole Christian world in communion with the See of Rome would be ranged
against his tradition. Bearing such a thought in mind one reads again the third
line of the Salutation, addressed *totius Europae flaccentis augustissimo quasi cuidam
flori*, wondering whether to infer that Gregory is not a 'most august flower' but a
'most August flower' drooping with the rest of a hostile Europe.

The second paragraph of the letter, which one would ordinarily call the
captatio beneuolentiae, we may label part B.[3] It is dense with irony.

1   'Gratia tibi et pax a Deo Patre nostro et Domino nostro Iesu
        Xpisto.'
2a   Libet me o sancte papa — hyperbolicum tecum non sit —
            interrogandum de Pascha

---

3   For text and apparatus and translation see Walker, pp. 2–3. For discussion of emendations see
    Smit, pp. 56–69. The translation here is mine.

b   iuxta illud canticum
c   'Interroga patrem tuum et annuntiabit tibi
               maiores tuos et dicent tibi.'
a'   Licet enim mihi — nimirum micrologo —
b'   illud cuiusdam egregium sapientis elogium quod dixisse
               fertur quandam uidens comtu pictam
c'   'Non admiror artem
                   sed admiror frontem'
b"   ad te clarum a me uili scribendo potest inuri.
a"   Tamen tuae euangelicae humilitatis fiducia fretus
b'''   tibi scribere praesumo
               et mei doloris negotium iniungo
               uanitas namque scribendi nulla est
               ubi necessitas cogit quamuis maioribus scribi.

I   'Grace to you and peace from God our Father and from our Lord
           Jesus Christ.'
2a   It pleases me, O holy pope — let it not be extravagant in your
           sight — for Easter to be asked about
b   according to that canticle
c   'Ask your father and he will announce to you
                   your greater men and they will speak to you'.
a'   For it is fitting that on me — though of little remark —
b'   that outstanding remark of a certain wise man which he is
               said to have spoken seeing a certain woman with dyed hair
c'   'I do not admire the art
                   but I do admire the face'
b"   can be branded writing from vile me to bright you.
a"   Nonetheless relying upon the trust of your evangelical humility
b'''   I presume to write to you
               and enjoin the business of my grief
               for there is no vanity in writing
               where necessity compels that even greater men be written to.

The structure is clear. After the blessing in 1 Columban writes in 2a *libet me*, in
a' *licet mihi*, and in a" *tamen*. He writes in b *illud canticum*, in b' *illud elogium*, in
b" *scribendo*, and in b''' *scribere, scribendi, scribi*. He writes in c the text of the
canticum and in c' the text of the *elogium*.

Columban begins this paragraph with a quotation from Galatians 1 3, apparently innocuous until one recalls the context.[4] What preceeds the quotation is

Paulus apostolus non ab hominibus neque per hominem

4   For examples of this form of quotation see below, pp. 99–101, 130–1, 147, 149, 201, 204.

sed per Iesum Xpistum et Deum Patrem
qui suscitauit eum a mortuis
et qui mecum sunt omnes fratres.

What follows it is

qui dedit semet ipsum pro peccatis nostris
ut eriperet nos de praesenti saeculo nequam.

The context implies that our author, having appropriated to himself at the end of
the Salutation the name of the Apostle Peter, is here arrogating to himself the
authority of the Apostle Paul, and hinting that if Christ gave Himself *ut eriperet nos*
and that 'we' and *qui mecum sunt omnes fratres* are Columban and his party, then
Gregory, in opposing them, may be *de praesenti saeculo nequam*. Next he writes
not *licet me* or *oportet*, but *libet me* 'it pleases me', 'it delights me', and adds
parenthetically 'let it not be extravagant (or 'overstrained') in your sight', precisely
because the underlying etymology of ὑπερβολικός is 'overthrowing', 'hurling
over'; he knows that he is being provocative, even outrageous, and he is enjoying
it. He plays on the Classical senses of *interrogare*, not just the innocent 'to put a
question, ask', but the more aggressive 'to question judicially, examine, interrogate', and even the hostile 'to call to account, arraign, indict'. The next
quotation furthers Columban's purpose. He calls it a canticle because it comes
from the Song of Moses in Deuteronomy XXXII, which begins

Audite caeli quae loquor
audiat terra uerba oris mei
concrescat in pluuia doctrina mea
fluat ut ros eloquium meum … .

Columban arrogates to himself the authority of Moses, and though the quotation
says 'ask your father', the context implies that he is telling the Holy Father his
doctrine, which is exactly what his letter does. By the time one comes to his self-
description as *micrologus*, even the most serious reader must suspect that
Columbanus is playing, regardless of whether the word is used like Classical
Greek μικρολόγος to mean 'concerned with trifles' or with play on its etymological elements to mean 'little in understanding of the word', 'insignificant in
speech', 'defective in rhetoric'. Columban is none of these things; he knows he is
not; and he intends Gregory to know he is not. No one could fail to understand
what comes next. If *non admiror artem sed admiror frontem* was a remark famous
before Columban's time its use here shows clearly that our author was fluent
enough to appreciate the play of the Classical Latin senses of *admiror* as both 'I
feel admiration for' and 'I am astonished at', of *ars* as both 'craftsmanship, art' and
'craftiness, artificiality', of *frons* as both 'forehead, brow, face' (as in the *Oxford
English Dictionary* 'face' *sb*. sense I 'the front part of the head') and 'a person's

brow regarded as expressing modesty, shyness, or the lack of these' (as in the
Oxford English Dictionary 'face' *sb.* sense 7 'impudence, effrontery, cheek'). A good
reason for Walker's inability 'to trace the source or hero of this story'[5] may be
that Columban invented it, in which case he would be describing himself as
sapiens and his own *elogium* as *egregium*. This application to himself of the adjective
with which in the Salutation he described Gregory's status as *speculator* would be
consistent with his appropriation of the name of Gregory's most illustrious
predecessor and his arrogation of the authority of the Lawgiver Moses and the
Apostle Paul. Columban describes himself as 'vile' again, saving until the last
word of the clause the passive infinitive *inuri*, translated here as 'branded'. As the
indirect object of this word is *mihi micrologo*, who may be the 'wise man'
responsible for the remark about the woman with artificial hair, one recalls that
another Classical sense of *inurere* is 'to curl (hair) with hot tongs'. The central
words of the paragraph, forty-eighth and forty-ninth of ninety-six, are *sapientis
elogium*. The paragraph divides by extreme and mean ratio exactly at the centre of
that *elogium*: *non admiror artem* | *sed admiror frontem*. The paragraph ends with a
little writer's trick. Between the nine-lettered *scribendo* and *scribere* there are nine
words. After *scribere* the ninth word is *scribendi*. From *scribendi* to *scribi* inclusive
there are nine words.

The chiastic pair to this is the penultimate paragraph of the letter, which
we may label part B'.

1	Re̲scribere *te̲* persuade̲at ca̲ri̲tas.
	E̲xponere *te̲* non impe̲di̲at ca̲rtae aspe̲ri̲tas
2	quia i̲ra̲ in e̲rrorem fu̲ri̲t
	et honor de̲bitus co̲rdi est a me tibi da̲ri.
3	Me̲um fuit prouoca̲re interroga̲re roga̲re
	tuu̲m sit 'gratis accepta' non ne̲ga̲re
	foenerari 'p̲etenti' talentum et 'p̲anem' d̲octrinae Xpisto
	p̲raecipiente d̲a̲re.
4	P̲ax t̲ibi t̲uisque̲.
3'	Meae indulge quod sic audacter scripsi rogo procacitati,
	beate papa, et oro ut pro me uilissimo peccatore vel semel in
	tuis sanctis orationibus ad communem Dominum ores.
2'	Persuperfluum puto commendare tibi meos
	quos Saluator quasi in suo nomine ambulantes 'recipiendos'
	esse decernit.

1	Let charity persuade you to write back.
	Let the asperity of the letter not impede your responding,
2	because wrath rages into error
	and the honour owed, to be given to you from me, is in [my]

5   Walker, p. 3 n. 3.

heart.

3   It was mine to provoke, to interrogate, to ask; may it be
       yours not to deny things accepted freely, to give to one
       seeking to be lent to the talent and bread of doctrine, as
       Christ commands.

4   Peace to you and yours.

3'   Be indulgent, I ask, to my rashness because I have written so
       boldly, blessed pope, and I pray that for me, the vilest sinner,
       even once in your holy prayers you may pray to the
       common Lord.

2'   I think it more than superfluous to commend to you mine,
       whom the Saviour decrees to be received as if walking in His
       own name.

The first part of the paragraph is notable for rhyme, marked here by *italics*, and
alliteration, marked here by <u>underlinings</u>. The entire paragraph is notable for
echoes of diction from part B.

Second paragraph part B	Penultimate paragraph part B'
gratia	gratis
tibi et pax	pax tibi
Domino nostro	communem Dominum
Iesu Xpisto	Xpisto
o sancte papa	beate papa
interrogandum, interrogare	interrogare, rogare
a me uili	pro me uilissimo
scribendo	rescribere
scribere praesumo	audacter scripsi

The central word of the paragraph is the first word of the crux of the chiasmus,
pax. The themes of the paragraph are writing, asking, giving, and receiving. The
eighty-nine words of the paragraph divide by duple ratio at 59 and 30. The fifty-
ninth word is *oro*. From *oro* to *ores* inclusive there are sixteen words, which divide
by duple ratio at 11 and 5. From *orationibus* to *ores* inclusive there are five words.
From *dari* to *dare* inclusive there are twenty-one words, which divide by duple
ratio at 14 and 7. After *dari* the fourteenth word is *petenti*. From *rogare* to *rogo*
inclusive there are twenty-six words, which divide by duple ratio at 17 and 9.
From *rogare* to *petenti* inclusive there are nine words, after which *rogo* is the
seventeenth word. From *rescribere* to *scripsi* inclusive there are fifty-three words,
which divide by duple ratio at 35 and 18. Between *rescribere* and *petenti* there are
thirty-five words.

   The central part of the letter, which we may label part C, is divided into
four parts, of which the first is arranged chiastically.

1   Quid ergo dicis de Pascha

2 a   nimirum

  b   Anatolius

3   Hieronymus

4   collaudauit

5   Victorius

6   humilitati

7   sapientissimis

8 a   quia non mihi satisfacit post tantos quos legi auctores una istorum sententia episcoporum dicentium tantum,

  b   Cum Iudaeis facere Pascha non debemus.

9   Dixit hoc olim et Victor episcopus sed nemo orientalium suum recepit commentum sed haec soporans spina Dagonis hoc imbibit bubum erroris.

8'a   Qualis rogo haec tam friuola et tam impolita nullis scilicet diuinae scripturae fulta testimoniis sententia,

  b   Cum Iudaeis Pascha facere non debemus? Quid ad rem pertinet?

7'   sapientibus

6'a   Sed haec magis procaciter

  b   quam humiliter scribens

  c   scio euripum praesumptionis difficillimae me inuexisse enauigandum fore ignarus.

  d   Nec loci namque nec ordinis est ut magnae tuae auctoritati aliquid quasi discutiendo inrogetur

  e   et ridiculose te mei nimirum Petri cathedram apostoli et clauicularii legitime insidentem occidentales apices

  f   de Pascha sollicitent.

  e'   Sed tu non tam me uilem in hac re quam multos et defunctos et uiuentes haec eadem quae notaui firmantes magistros considerare debes

  d'   et quasi cum eis trahere colloquium te crede;

  c'   pie namque me scito

  b'   licet saltuatim

  a'   et hyperbolice chilosum os operire.

5'   Victorium

4'   laudaueris

3'   supradictum Hieronymum
2'a   nimirum
  b   Anatolium
1'   Sed haec de Pascha sufficiant.

This passage is arranged arithmetically in small units as in the whole. In part 6', for example, crux of the chiasmus is the sixth part. The central forty-fifth of eighty-nine words is the first of the crux. In the entire paragraph the crux appears at the ninth part of the chiasmus. The 926 words divide by sesquioctave ratio, 9:8, at 490 and 436, at the first word of part 8a. They divide by sesquialter ratio, 3:2, at 556 and 370, at the last word of 8'b.

The remaining topics follow in order.

> Ceterum de episcopis illis quid iudicas interrogo qui contra canones ordinantur, id est quaestu; simoniacos et Gildas auctor pestes scripsit eos.
> Tertio interrogationis loco responde adhuc ... Vennianus auctor Gildam de his interrogauit ... .
> Humilius et purius haec omnia et multo plura quae epistolaris breuitas non admittit ... .

There are one hundred words in the second paragraph beginning *Ceterum* and sixty-two words in the third paragraph beginning *Tertio*, together 162 words, which divide by extreme and mean ratio at 100 and 62.

The reference to Gildas places Columban firmly in the Insular tradition, illustrating both his deference to the authority of an earlier sixth-century British Latin *auctor* and one possible route for the transmission of Biblical style from late Antiquity to the early Middle Ages.

The most recent editor of this letter has concluded that 'some rather pedantic punning, and the employment of half-proverbial expressions, give a ponderous quality to the whole'.[6] It might be fairer to say that Columban is the first Irishman to have left extant written evidence of his ability to marshall a forceful argument in Latin prose, not only competent, but coruscating with wit, irony, and varied verbal punctilio. He is certainly not the last.

II. CUMMIAN

Letter to Ségéne and Béccán

The oldest extant Latin text of considerable length by an Irishman in Ireland is an *Epistola de Controuersia Paschali* from Cummian to Ségéne, fifth abbot of Iona, and Béccán, written in the year 633. Here is the beginning of the text, the former part of a chiastic envelope (ABC, 1, 2–5, 6–17) around the author's argument.[1]

6   Walker, p. xxxvi.
1   BCLL 289. *Cummian's Letter 'De Controversia Paschali' together with a related Irish Computistical Tract 'De Ratione Conputandi'*, ed. & transl. M. Walsh & D. Ó Cróinín, Pontifical Institute of Mediaeval

A **IN NOMINE DIVINO DEI SUMMI CONFIDO**

B **DOMINIS** sanctis et in Xpisto uenerandis Segieno abbati, Columbae sancti et caeterorum sanctorum successori, Beccanoque solitario, caro carne et spiritu fratri, cum suis sapientibus, Cummianus supplex peccator magnis minimus apologiticam in Xpisto salutem.

C Verba excusationis meae in faciem sanctitatis uestrae proferre pro-caciter [non] audeo. Sed excusatum me habere uos ut patres cupio, 'testem Deum inuocans in animam meam', quod non contemtus uestri gratia nec fastu moralis sapientiae, cum caeterorum despectu, sollempnitatem festi paschalis cum caeteris sapientibus suscepi. Ego enim primo anno quo cyclus quingentorum .XXX. duorum anno-rum a nostris celebrari orsus est non suscepi, sed silui. Nec laudare nec uituperare ausus utpote Aebreos, Gregos, Latinos. quas linguas, ut Ieronimus ait. in crucis suae titulo Xpistus consecrauit. superare minime in scientia me credens. Deinde apostolum interrogans dicen-tem. 'Omnia probate, quod bonum est tenete', antequam gustarem non fastidiui. Hinc per annum secretus sanctuarium Dei ingressus. hoc est scripturam sanctam, ut ualui inuolui. deinde historias. pos-tremo cyclos quos inuenire potui.

A I confide in the divine name of the most high God.

B To the holy and venerable lords in Christ, the Abbot Ségéne, successor of the holy Columba and of other holy men, and Béccán the hermit, beloved in body and a brother in spirit, along with their sages, Cummian, a suppliant sinner, the least to the great, sends a defence and greeting in Christ.

C I dare to offer the words of my excuse [not] boldly in the face of your holiness but I hope that you as fathers forgive me, 'calling upon God as witness on my soul' that it is not out of scorn for you nor puffed up with pride of moral wisdom and the contempt of others that I have undertaken, along with other sages, the solemnity of the Paschal feast. For in the first year in which the cycle of 532 years began to be celebrated by our party I did not accept it, but remained silent; I dared neither to praise nor to condemn it, since I believe that I by no means surpass in knowledge the Hebrews, Greeks, and Latins, whose languages, as Jerome says, Christ consecrated in the inscription of His cross. Therefore, asking the Apostle who says: 'Test everything, hold fast what is good', before I tried it, I did not disdain it. Hence, having cloistered myself for a year and having entered the

Studies, Studies and Texts LXXXVI (Toronto 1988), reviewed by R. Sharpe in *Journal of Theological Studies* New Series XLI (1990), pp. 271–4. I have collated London, British Library, MS Cotton Vitellius A XII ff. 79r–83r, which Walsh and Ó Cróinín have edited scrupulously, representing capital letters and punctuation marks in boldface, changing the editorial spelling to *Xpistus* and supplying *non* in the first sentence of C.

sanctuary of God (that is sacred Scripture) I studied as much as I was able, then I examined the histories, and finally the cycles which I could find.

Cummian's argument then begins *Et inueni primum in Exodo...* (18) and continues to *Loquacitatem nostram uestra fiducia prestat* (258), advancing under fifteen headings. Let us consider the diction with which he introduces his authorities.

I (18–31)

I	Et inueni primum in Exodo ... scriptum est enim
2	et in sequentibus
3	et inueni hoc Apostolum ... dicentem
4	item in Exodo
5	in Leuitico quoque
x	Hoc timui et inquisiui diligenter quid ... quod in sequentibus demonstrabo.

II (32–51)

I	Item in Exodo
2	et hoc in tractatibus diligenter inuestigaui quid sentirent.... eruditissimi uiri
3	quod Ieronimus pulcherrime explanat dicendo ...
4	item in Libro Questionum ... haec lxxxui questione
5	item xci
x	Hoc timui et me perculit.

III (52–8)

Item perscrutans inueni et Originem Calcenterum et uere Adamantinum dicentem

IV (59–85)

I	Deinde euangelio inueni Dominum meum Iesum Xpistum dicentem ...
2	quod Ieronimus explanat.

V (86–120)

I	Hac de re sinodis in unum congregatis ... ut legimus ... inueni scriptum ... statuta canonica quaternae sedis apostolicae, Romanae uidelicet, Ierosolimitanae, Antiochenae, Alexandrinae
2	Nicena etiam sinodus ... est adiuncta
3	item Arelatensi sinodo ... confirmante
4	ut Ieronimus ait
5ia	iuxta Psalterium
b	'in escam populis Ethiopibus'
c	et hoc uereor
d	sed uos considerate ... an Britonum Scottorumque particula ... hoc michi iudicate
ii	uos enim estis capita et oculi populi qui ...

  iii iuxta Ezechielem 'sanguine anime'
  ii' seniores uero nostri quos ...
  i'a iuxta Apostolum
  b omnia probate, quod bonum est tenete
  c sed uereor
  d iudicetis

VI (121–32)

  1 Quid plura? uenio ad Apostolum item dicentem ...
  2 quod Sanctus Agustinus pulchre explanat
  3 et hoc obsecro: ... si habetis ... si uero non habetis ...

VII (132–7)

  Scriptum est enim: Ve qui dicitis ...

VIII (137–49)

  1 Ieronimus item adest auxiliator dicens
  2 'angustiae michi undique'
  3 si ego hoc clamauero cum Ieronimo ... si non clamauero ...

IX (150–72)

  His perscrutatis uenio ad Cyprianum ... qui ait

X (173–80)

  His perterritus ad alia me conuerti et inueni Agustinum ... explanantem hunc ... Roma, Ierosolima, Alexandria, Antiochia, totus mundus soli Scotti et Britones

XI (180–5)

  Item Ieronimus

XII (185–9)

  Item tractans euangelium de illis inquit

XIII (190–6)

  Quid plura? Ad Gregorii ... uerba me conuerti

XIV (196–203)

  Unde et Paulus ait ...
  Et hoc timeo. Vos considerate compatienter fratres si merito est, an ignauia.

XV (204–58)

  Postremo ad cyclos computationum ... inueni
  Primum illum quem sanctus Patricius papa noster tulit et fecit ...
  Secundo
  Tertio
  Quarto
  Quinto
  Sexto
  Septimo
  Octauo
  Nono
  Decimo

Cummian has linked parts I and II with similar five-part structures concluded by *hoc timui* ... . Part V consists of five numbered headings, the fifth of which consists of five subdivisions, of which the first and fifth are further subdivided. It is preceded by part IV and followed by part VI, which exhibit similar formulas. Of the first fourteen parts the central, VII, contains the imprecation *Ve qui dicitis* ... . This is preceded by part VI and followed by part VIII, which both exhibit statements in the form *si ... si non*. Cummian linked parts IX and X with similar beginnings, *His perscrutatis* and *His perterritus*. He also linked parts XI and XII, which both begin *Item*.

Part V consists of fifteen parts. It refers to four patriarchal sees and to the Britons and the Irish. Part X also refers to four patriarchal sees and to the Irish and the Britons. Part XV lists ten computational cycles. These fifteen parts of Cummian's argument comprise 2567 words.

Cummian then proceeds to the latter part of his chiastic envelope, in parts C'B'A' (259–88, 289–302, 303–4).

C' **A**nno igitur, ut predixi, emenso, iuxta Deuteronomium, 'interrogaui patres meos' ut 'annuntiarent' michi. 'maiores' meos ut 'dicerent' michi. successores uidelicet nostrorum patrum priorum Ailbei episcopi, Querani Coloniensis. Brendini, Nessani, Lugidi quid sentirent de excomunicatione nostra, a supradictis sedibus apostolicis facta. At illi congregati in unum, alius per se, alius per legatum suum uice suo missum, in Campo Lene sancxerunt. et dixerunt: "**D**ecessores nostri mandauerunt per idoneos testes, alios uiuentes. alios in pace dormientes, ut meliora et potiora probata a fonte baptismi nostri et sapientiae et successoribus apostolorum Domini delata, sine scrupulo humiliter sumeremus." Post in commone surrexerunt, et super hoc, orationem, ut moris est nobis, celebrauerunt ut pascha cum uniuersali aecclesia in futuro anno celebrarent. **S**ed non post multum, surrexit quidam 'paries dealbatus, traditionem seniorum seruare' se simulans, qui utraque non fecit unum, sed diuisit et irritum ex parte fecit. quod promissum est. quem 'Dominus', ut spero, 'percutiet' quoquo modo uoluerit. **D**einde uisum est senioribus nostris iuxta mandatum, ut si diuersitas oborta fuerit 'inter causam et causam. et uariauerit iudicium inter lepram et non lepram'. irent 'ad locum quem elegit Dominus'; ut 'si causae fuerint maiores', iuxta decretum sinodicum. 'ad capud urbium sint referendae'. Inde misimus quos nouimus sapientes et humiles esse, uelut natos ad matrem, et 'prosperum iter in uoluntate Dei habentes'. et ad Romam urbem aliqui ex eis uenientes. tertio anno ad nos usque peruenerunt. Et sic omnia uiderunt sicut audierunt. sed et ualde certiora utpote uisa quam audita inuenerunt. Et in uno hospicio cum Greco et Hebreo. Scitha et Aegiptiaco in aecclesia sancti Petri simul in pascha, in quo mense integro disiuncti sumus, fuerunt. Et ante sancta sic testati sunt nostris, dicentes: "Per totum orbem terrarum hoc pascha, ut scimus, celebratur." Et nos in reliquiis sanctorum martyrum et scripturis quas attulerunt probauimus inesse uirtutem Dei. Vidimus oculis nostris puellam caecam omnino ad has reliquias oculos aperientem. et paraliticum ambulantem. et multa demonia eiecta.

B' Haec dixi non ut uos inpugnarem. sed ut me, ut 'necticuracem in domicilio' latitantem, defenderem. Sed si quid forte impolitum uel uitiosum per inmunda labia. dixi, bicipi labii uestri forcipe per igniferum Essaianum altaris Dei carbonem tangite, et preputium inculti logii bifaris ter quaternis cultris Ben-Nun, quinis-denis digitulis humatis cum pleuis precedite prioris preputiis. Nefas est enim errata tua non agnoscere et prolata certiora non approbare. Hereticorum est proprie sententiam suam non corrigere; maluere peruersam quam motare defensam. 'Scienti etenim bonum facere et non facienti, peccatum est illi.' 'Peccati uero stipendium mors est.' A qua nos diuina maiestas et simplex trinitas. et multiplex apex. subtus quem nichil est, intra quem nichil est, citra quem nichil, ultra quem nichil. supra quem nihil, 'sustinens' omnia 'sine labore. penetrans' omnia 'sine extenuatione, circumdans' omnia 'sine extensione, superans' omnia 'sine inquietudine', liberare dignetur. Amen. Amen.

A' 'GRANDIS LABOR EST' PRUDENTIAE. EXPLICIT EPISTOLA CUMMIANI DIRECTA SEGIENO ABBATI. DEO GRATIAS.

C' Therefore after a full year (as I said above), in accordance with Deuteronomy, I 'asked' my 'fathers' to 'make' known to me, my 'elders' (that is to say, the successors of our first fathers: of Bishop Ailbe, of Ciaran of Clonmacnois, of Brendan, of Nessan, and of Lugid) to 'tell' me what they thought about our excommunication by the aforementioned Apostolic Sees. Having gathered in Mag Léne, some in person, others through representatives sent in their place, they enacted and said: "Our predecessors enjoined, through capable witnesses (some living, some resting in peace), that we should adopt humbly without doubt better and more valid proofs proffered by the font of our baptism and our wisdom and by the successors of the Lord's Apostles." Then they arose in unison and after this, as is our custom, they performed a prayer, that they would celebrate Easter with the Universal Church the next year. But a short time afterwards a certain 'whited-wall' arose, pretending to 'preserve the tradition of our elders', who did not unite with either part but divided them and partly made void what was promised. I hope the 'Lord shall strike' him 'down' in whatever way He wills. Then it seemed proper to our elders, according to the command, that if disagreement arises 'between one side and another, and judgement vary between leper' and non-leper, they should go 'to the place which the Lord has chosen'; and that 'if the matters are major', according to the sinodical decree, 'they should be referred to the chief of cities'. Hence we sent those whom we knew to be wise and humble as children to their mother, and 'having had a prosperous journey through the will of God', some of them arrived at Rome, and returned to us in the third year. And they saw things just as they had heard about them, but they found them more certain inasmuch as they were seen rather than heard. And they were in one lodging in the church of St Peter with a Greek, a Hebrew, a Scythian and an Egyptian at the same time at Easter, in which we differed by a whole month. And so they testified to us before the holy relics, saying: "As far as we know, this Easter is celebrated throughout the whole world". And we have tested that the power of God is in the relics of the holy martyrs and in the writings which they brought back. We saw with our own eyes a totally blind girl opening her eyes at these relics, and a paralytic walking and many demons cast out.

B' I have said these things not to impugn you, but that I, 'a night owl', as it were, hiding 'in the home', might defend myself. But if perchance I have said anything rough or corrupt through impure lips, touch it with the two-edged tongs of your lips in the manner of the fiery Isaian coal from the altar of God, and cut off the foreskin of the unpolished word with the twelve double-edged swords of Ben Nun, the fifteen little fingers buried with the foreskins of the former people. For it is wicked that you do not recognise your errors, and that you do not acknowledge more certain proofs. It is proper to heretics not to correct their opinion; to prefer a perverse opinion rather than abandon one they had defended. 'One who knows what it is to do good, and who does it not, that is a sin for him.' 'For death is the reward of sin.' From this death may the Divine Majesty and undivided Trinity and Manifold Head (under Whom there is nothing, beyond Whom there is nothing, within Whom there is nothing, above Whom there is nothing, 'sustaining' all things 'without effort, entering' all things 'without diminution', surrounding all things 'without stretching, surmounting' all things 'without discomfort') deign to free us. Amen. Amen.

A' 'Great is the labour' of prudence. Here ends the Letter of Cummian directed to Abbot Ségéne. Thanks be to God.

Part A contains six words, three in each half; fourteen syllables, seven in each half; and twenty-nine letters. The central words are *diuino* and *Dei*. The central syllables are the last of *diuino* and the first of *Dei*. The central letter is the first of *Dei*. The six words divide by extreme and mean ratio at 4 and 2, after *Dei*. The fourteen syllables divide by extreme and mean ratio at 9 and 5, after *Dei*. The twenty-nine letters divide by extreme and mean ratio at 17.9 and 11.1; the seventeenth letter is the last of *Dei*.

Part A' contains twelve words, thirty-three syllables, and seventy-nine letters. The central words name the title and author, *Epistola Cummiani*. The central, seventeenth, syllable is the first of *Cummiani*. The twelve words divide by extreme and mean ratio at 7 and 5, after *Cummiani*. The seventy-nine letters divide by extreme and mean ratio at 49 and 30. The forty-ninth letter is the last of *Cummiani*.

Within this frame are a Salutation, which we may call part B (2–5) and a Valediction, which we may call part B' (289–302). The former contains thirty-three words and the latter 143. The beginning of the latter passage, which has puzzled earlier scholars, remains unexplained in Walsh and Ó Cróinín's edition, but it is explicable.[2]

> **H**aec dixi non ut uōs īnpūgnārēm .
> sed ut me ut necticuracem in domicilio latitāntēm dēfēndērēm .
> **S**ed si quid forte impolitum uel uitiosum per inmunda labia . dixi
> [? l. lábia díxi .]
> bicipi labii uestri forcipe per igniferum Essaianum altaris Dei cārbōnēm
> tāngītē
> et preputium
>   incúlti lógii
>   bifaris ter quaternīs cūltrīs
>   Bēnnūn
>   quinis denis digitulis
>   humatis cum pleuis precedite priōrīs
> prēpūtīīs .

> I have said these things not that I may impugn you,
> but that myself, like a night owl hiding in the house, I might defend.
> But if by chance I have said anything unpolished or vicious through
>   unclean lips,
> by the two-part forceps of your lips with the fire-bearing Isaiahan coal
>   from the altar of God touch
> and cut off the foreskin
> of the uncultivated word
> with the three-times-four double-edged knives
> of the son of Nun
> with the five [and] ten little fingers
> buried with the former people's [*i.e.* Israelites]
> foreskins.

---

2   Capital letters and punctuation marks in boldface represent features of the manuscript. I have marked clausular and cursus rhythms. The translation is mine.

Capital letters in British Library MS Cotton Vitellius A XII mark the beginnings of Cummian's sentences, and rhythms mark the ends of his clauses. There is a molossus-spondee in *uos inpugnarem*, a molossus-cretic in *latitantem defenderem*, a *cursus planus* in *lábia díxi*, a molossus-cretic in *carbonem tangite*, a *cursus medius* in *incúlti lógii*, a molossus-spondee in *quaternis cultris Bennun*, and a molossus-cretic in *prioris preputiis*. Cummian arranged the rhythms in a chiastic pattern, balancing the initial molossus-spondee and molossus-cretic with the concluding molossus-spondee and molossus-cretic, which surround the central *cursus planus* — molossus-cretic — *cursus medius*.[3]

A further clue to Cummian's meaning lies in the contexts of his three Biblical quotations and allusions. The first derives from the central Book of Psalms. The second derives from the first book of the four Major Prophets, which come after the Psalms. The third derives from the first book of the Former Prophets, which come before the Psalms.

Here is a passage of Psalm CI 5–10, from which Cummian quotes the crux:

a	quia oblitus sum comedere panem meum
b	a uoce gemitus mei
	adhesit os meum carni meae
c	similis factus sum pelicano solitudinis
d	factus sum sicut nycticorax in domicilio
c'	uigilaui et factus sum sicut passer solitarius in tecto
b'	tota die exprobrabant mihi inimici mei
	et qui laudabant me aduersus me iurabant
a'	quia cinerem tamquam panem manducaui.

With *quia*, *comedere*, and *panem* in a compare *quia*, *manducaui*, and *panem* in a'. With the parallelism *uoce gemitus mei* and *os meum* in b compare that in b', *exprobrabant mihi inimici mei* and *aduersus me iurabant*. With *similis*, *factus sum*, *pelicano*, and *solitudinis* in c compare *sicut*, *factus sum*, *passer*, and *solitarius* in c'.

Here is Isaiah VI 5–9, of which Cummian alludes to the crux:

a i	et dixi uae mihi quia tacui quia uir pollutus labiis ego sum
ii	et in medio populi polluta labia habentis ego habito
b	et Regem Dominum exercituum uidi oculis meis
c	et uolauit ad me unus de seraphin
	et in manu eius calculus quem forcipe tulerat de altari
d	et tetigit os meum et dixit
d'	ecce tetigit hoc labia tua
c'	et auferetur iniquitas tua
	et peccatum tuum mundabitur
b'	et audiui uocem Domini dicentis
	quem mittam et quis ibit nobis

3   The pattern remains if one should scan *inpugnarem* and *cultris Bennun* as double spondees.

> a'i   et dixi ecce ego sum mitte me
> ii   et dixit uade et dices populo huic ... .

With *et dixi, uae, ego sum* in ai compare *et dixi, ecce, ego sum* in a'i, and with *et*
and *populi* in aii compare *et* and *populo* in a'ii. With *Dominum* and *uidi* in b
compare *audiui uocem Domini* in b. Compare *tulerat* in c with *auferetur* in c' and
tetigit os in d with *tetigit labia* in d'.

In chapter IV of the Book of Joshua the Lord instructed Joshua to order one
man from each of the twelve tribes to take on his shoulder a stone from the
place where the priests' feet stood in the midst of the Jordan and lay it down
on the Canaanite side. Joshua also set up twelve stones in the Jordan where
the priests' feet stood. In chapter V the Lord instructed Joshua

> fac tibi cultros lapideos et circumcide secundo filios Israhel
> fecit quod iusserat Dominus et circumcidit filios Israhel in Colle
>   praeputiorum ...
> dixitque Dominus ad Iosue hodie abstuli obprobrium Aegypti a uobis
> uocatumque est nomen loci illius Galgala usque in praesentem diem
> manseruntque filii Israhel in Galgalis
> et fecerunt phase quartadecima die mensis ad uesperum in campestribus
>   Hiericho
> et comederunt de frugibus terrae die altero azymos panes et pulentam
>   eiusdem anni.

The source of Cummian's reference to burial is not the Vulgate but the
Septuagint text of Joshua XXIV 31a:

> εκει εθηκαν μετ' αυτου εις το μνημα, εις ο εθαψαν αυτον εκει,
> τας μαχαιρας τας πετρινας, εν αις περιετεμεν τους υιους Ισραηλ
> εν Γαλγαλοις.

> there they put with him into the tomb in which they buried him the knives
> of stone with which he circumcised the children of Israel in Galgala.

The point of Cummian's allusions is inferred, not from the words quoted, but
from their contexts. He describes himself as a night owl because the following
verses of Psalm CI refer to a solitary whose enemies attack him. Cummian's
verb *defenderem* strengthens the connection with the unquoted context. Then
Cummian invites Ségéne and Béccán to touch anything *impolitum uel uitiosum*
in his text, but he believes that he has written nothing unpolished or vicious.
Part ai of the passage from Isaiah reads *dixi uae mihi quia tacui*. Among his *uerba
excusacionis* Cummian wrote *Ego enim primo anno quo cyclus quingentorum .xxx.
duorum annorum a nostris celebrari orsus est non suscepi, sed silui* (11). His allusion
implies, moreover, that he can be silent no longer because he has seen the

Lord with his own eyes; his lips have already been cleansed; and he has heard the Lord directing him to correct his people. The point of the allusion to the twelve knives of Bennun[4] is that after Joshua had circumcised the Israelites at the Hill of the Foreskins 'the Lord said to Joshua, "This day I have rolled away the reproach of Egypt from you." And so the name of that place is called Gilgal [Hebrew גלגל from גלל 'to roll'] to this day.' This cleansed the Israelites, making them fit to celebrate פסח Pesach, Passover, at the correct time, appropriate for Cummian, who has written about the correct reckoning of *Pascha*, Easter. Cummian instructs his readers to cut off a *preputium inculti logii ... quinis denis digitulis humatis cum pleuis ... prioris preputiis* 'foreskin of the uncultivated word ... with the five [and] ten little fingers buried with the foreskins of the former people'. He believes, however, that he has written no *incultum logion*. The fifteen *digituli* are the articulations of his tract composed in fives and tens.

Within the frame of the Salutation and the Valediction are Cummian's *Excusatio*, which we may call part C (6–17), and its parallel, which we may call part C' (259–88). The order of words and ideas in the former is reversed in the latter.

C1a	festi paschalis	
b	celebrari	
2	Aebreos, Gregos, Latinos	
3	Ieronimus ait	
4	apostolum	
5	interrogans	
6a	per annum	
b	secretus sanctuarium Dei ingressus, hoc est scripturam sanctam	
C'6a	anno igitur, ut predixi, emenso	
b	iuxta Deuteronomium	
5	interrogaui	
4	apostolicis ... apostolorum	
3	for lines 274–7 cf. *Hieronymus In Aggaeum* II 11–5	
2	Greco et Hebreo, Scitha et Aegiptiaco	
1a	pascha	
b	celebratur	

Cummian wrote before reckoning from the Incarnation became common, but it is a notable coincidence that Walsh and Ó Cróinín date the text to the year

4 The word *cultris* is translated better 'knives' than 'swords' as in Walsh & Ó Cróinín p. 95. Their note 'Ben Nun] Not in the Vulgate' is incorrect. The name appears at the beginning and the end of the Book of Joshua, *Incipit liber Iosue Bennun id est Iesu Naue, Explicit liber Iosue Bennun id est Iesu Naue*, and it is explained in Joshua 1 1, *Iosue filium Nun*.

632/3, and the beginning and end of the text, parts ABC C'B'A' comprise exactly 633 words.[5]

Like Columban Cummian places himself in the Insular tradition. He quotes the first three words of A' from Pelagius's *Epistula ad Demetriadem*. He refers in lines 208–9 to the computational cycle *quem Sanctus Patricius papa noster tulit et fecit*. He may have learned the habit of alluding to the context of Biblical quotations from the works of Patrick or Columban.[6] The references to his long silence, *sed silui* in line 11, his fears, *hoc timui* in line 29 and *et hoc uereor* in line 107 and elsewhere, and his references to Scripture read like echoes of Gildas. He may have learned to arrange rhythmical patterns also from the works of Patrick and Gildas.[7] His Letter, lines 259–60 at the beginning of paragraph C', shares with the beginning of Columban's First Letter to Gregory the Great a quotation from the Song of Moses in Deuteronomy XXXII. As the quotation is pressed into service in a comparable manner of subtle aggressiveness one may infer that Cummian had read at home in Ireland a letter written by Columban in Bobbio.[8] As Columban shows that Irish Latin writers abroad had assimilated the British Latin tradition of composition in Biblical style before the end of the sixth century, so Cummian shows that Irish Latin writers at home had assimilated the same tradition by the second quarter of the seventh century.

III. COLMÁN

Letter to Feradach

Dr Richard Sharpe edited recently from Brussels, Bibliothèque royale, MS 5649–67 folios 186r–187v Colmán's Letter to Feradach,[1] of which the first paragraph follows.

> Dilectissimo et eruditissimo filio Feradacho[a] Colmanus.[b] Multa quidem ad nos a Romanis[c] scripta librorum exemplaria peruenerunt in quibus non-nulla quae[d] in nostris ante codicibus librariorum[e] neglegentia deprauata sunt emendatiora repperimus. Denique, ut de ceteris taceam, in libris Isidori quos ipse de aecclesiasticis scripsit officiis sub duobus tantum titulis tres ferme paginas a librariis in<ueni>mus praetermissas; multa praeterea in

---

5   As Dr Sharpe notes in his review p. 272, 'the word *non* should be retained in line 7; Ussher read it, there is space for it where the line is damaged, and the sense is better with it.' The number 633 is found by including the word *non* and by reading *Bennun* as a single word, as in many early manuscripts, and in the Stuttgart edition of the Vulgate, and in MS Cotton Vitellius A XII.

6   See above pp. 86–8 and Howlett, *Liber Epistolarum*, pp. 96–100, 120.

7   See above pp. 79–81 and Howlett, *Liber Epistolarum*, pp. 56, 96.

8   Compare p. 95 with p. 86.

1   BCLL 290. R. Sharpe, 'An Irish Textual Critic and the *Carmen paschale* of Sedulius: Colmán's Letter to Feradach', *The Journal of Medieval Latin* II (1992), pp. 44–54.

chronicis, multa in Sedulii paschali carmine corrupta, quod nunc apud nos[f] duplici legitur editione conscriptum. Quattuor siquidem quos ante uersibus condidit libellos, rursus eosdem imperante Macedonio, in theoricum sermonem stilo liberiore transtulit. Cuius operis primam partem in codicibus uestris habetis corruptam, secundam penitus ignoratis; ex quibus pauca tibi cognoscendi gratia quantum epistolaris angustia potuit transmittere curaui.

a MS *Feraclaclo* b MS *Calmanus* c MS *ad Romanis* d MS *qui* e MS *librorum* f MS *uos*

In the following arrangement of this text *per cola et commata* capital letters and punctuation marks in boldface represent features of the manuscript.[2] I have marked the cursus rhythms.

> **D**ilectissimo et eruditíssimo fílio . Féradacho . Cólmanus . [*or* Feradácho . Colmánus .]
>
> A **M**ulta quidem ad nos a **R**omanis scripta librorum exemplária pèruené-runt .
> B   in quibus nonnulla
> C   quae in nostris ante codicibus librariorum neglegentia déprauáta sunt
> D   emendatióra reppérimus .
> E   **D**énique . út de céteris táceam
> F 1   in líbris Isidóri
>   2   quos ipse de aecclesiasticis scrípsit officiis . sub duobus tántum títulis
> G   tres ferme paginas a librariis inuénimus praètermíssas .
> G'   **M**ulta praetérea in chrónicis .
> F'1   multa in **S**edulii **P**aschali **C**ármine corrúpta .
>   2   quod nunc apud nos duplici legitur editióne conscríptum .
> E'   **Q**uattuor siquidem quos ante uersibus cóndidit libéllos . **R**ursus eosdem imperante **M**ácedónio .
> D'   in theoricum sermonem stilo liberióre transtúlit.
> C'   cuius operis primam partem in codicibus uestris habétis corrúptam . secundam pénitus ignorátis .
> B'   ex quibus pauca
> A' tibi cognoscendi gratia quantum epistolaris angustia potuit trans-míttere curáui.

---

2   I owe thanks to Dr Sharpe for his transcript of the manuscript and for helpful criticism.

To the most beloved and most erudite son Feradach Colmán [sends greeting].

A   Many exemplars of books written by Romans have indeed come through to us,

B   among which some,

C   which in our codices were deformed by the negligence of scribes,

D   we have discovered more correct.

E   To sum up, as I shall be silent about the others,

F 1   in the books of Isidore,

   2   which himself wrote about ecclesiastical offices under at any rate two titles,

G   we have found almost three pages omitted by scribes.

G'   Many things besides in the chronicles,

F'1   many things corrupted in the Paschal Song of Sedulius,

   2   which now is read among us written out in a double edition,

E'   inasmuch as the four little books which he composed before in verses

                the same again at the command of Macedonius

D'   he translated in freer style into contemplative speech [*i.e.* prose]

C'   of which work you have the first part corrupt in your codices; the second part you are altogether ignorant of;

B'   from which few matters

A'   I have taken care to transmit to you for the sake of understanding as much as the narrow compass of a letter allowed.

Colmán shows at the very beginning of his letter that he knows how to write well, ending every clause with a correct cursus rhythm — *dispondeus dactylicus* twice: *Féradacho Cólmanus, praetérea in chrónicis*; *planus* three times: *editióne conscríptum, liberióre transtúlit, habétis corrúptam*; *uelox* three times: *exemplária pèruenérunt, inuénimus praètermíssas, pénitus ìgnorátis*; *medius* three times: *déprauáta sunt, tántum títulis, Mácedónio*; *tardus* four times: *eruditíssimo fílio, emendatióra reppérimus, céteris táceam, scrípsit offíciis*; and *trispondiacus* four times: *líbris Isidóri, cármine corrúpta, cóndidit libéllos, transmíttere curáui*.

He reveals his mastery of Biblical style, arranging his words and ideas by chiasmus and parallelism, as one observes by comparing *ad nos, scripta librorum exemplaria*, and *peruenerunt* in A with *tibi, epistolaris*, and *transmittere* in A', *in quibus nonnulla* in B with *in quibus pauca* in B', *quae, in nostris codicibus*, and *deprauata* in C with *cuius, in codicibus uestris*, and *corruptam* in C', the comparative *emendatiora* in D with the comparative *liberiore* in D', *denique* in E with *rursus* in E', *in libris Isidori* in F1 with *in Sedulii Paschali Carmine* in F'1, *quos, scripsit*, and *sub duobus titulis* in F2 with *quod, legitur conscriptum*, and *duplici editione* in F'2, *tres* and *praetermissas* in G with *multa* and *praeterea* in G'. The first clause begins with the word *multa*; the last phrase of the crux begins with the word *multa*; and the first clause after the crux begins with the word *multa*.

Colmán has guaranteed the authenticity and integrity of his text by disposing his repeated diction at mathematically determined intervals. After the Salutation there are 108 words in this paragraph, which divide by symmetry at 54 and 54. The first word is *multa*, and the fifty-fourth word is *multa*, so that both parts of the paragraph begin with the same word. Colmán uses the number 54 again less conspicuously: after *ante* the fifty-fourth word is *ante*; again after *duobus* the fifty-fourth word is *secundam*. Colmán links other words by symmetrical intervals: after *scripta* the thirtieth word is *scripsit*, after which the thirtieth word is *conscriptum*. The twenty-fourth word is *repperimus*, after which the twenty-fourth word is *inuenimus*. Similarly from *librorum* to *libris* inclusive there are twenty-four words, while from *librorum* to *librariorum* inclusive there are twelve words.

The 108 words divide by duple ratio at 72 and 36. Colmán links parallel words by intervals of seventy-two words: from *quae* to *cuius* inclusive there are seventy-two words; after *codicibus* the seventy-second word is *codicibus*.

The 108 words divide by extreme and mean ratio at 67 and 41; after *quidem* the sixty-seventh word is *siquidem*. Colmán links several other words in the same way. The forty-seventh word is *librariis*; 47 divides by extreme and mean ratio at 29 and 18; from *librariorum* to *librariis* inclusive there are twenty-nine words. Those twenty-nine words divide by extreme and mean ratio at 18 and 11; between *librariorum* and *libris* there are eleven words. From *libris* to *libellos* inclusive there are forty-four words; 44 divides by extreme and mean ratio at 27 and 17; from *libris* to *librariis* inclusive there are seventeen words. From *carmine* to *uersibus* inclusive there are fifteen words; 15 divides by extreme and mean ratio at 9 and 6; the sixth word after *carmine* is the beginning of the phrase *duplici legitur editione*, and the sixth word before *uersibus* is the end of the phrase *duplici legitur editione*. From *carmine* to *editione* inclusive there are nine words, and from *duplici* to *uersibus* inclusive there are nine words. Between *uersibus* and *partem* there are fifteen words, and the ninth word after *uersibus* is *sermonem*. The ninety-third word is *corruptam*; 93 divides by extreme and mean ratio at 57.5 and 35.5; from *corrupta* to *corruptam* inclusive there are thirty-five words. From *primam* inclusive to the end of the paragraph there are twenty-two words; 22 divides by extreme and mean ratio at 14 and 8; from *primam* to *secundam* inclusive there are eight words. The 103rd word is *quantum*; 103 divides by extreme and mean ratio at 63.66 and 39.34; from *tantum* to *quantum* inclusive there are sixty-three words. From *praetermissas* to *transmittere* inclusive there are fifty-nine words; 59 divides by extreme and mean ratio at 36 and 23; from *praetermissas* to *transtulit* inclusive there are thirty-six words.

In another form of numerical play Colmán has arranged his text so that after *duobus* the third word is *tres*, and after *duplici* the fourth word is *quattuor*.

Colmán's competence in this game needs no further demonstration. But his true subject is the serious business of textual criticism, the choosing of correct readings among variants transmitted in the available texts. The names Feradach and Colmán belong to an Irish milieu, in which *a Romanis scripta librorum exemplaria peruenerunt ... emendatiora*. By the time Cummian wrote his Letter in 633 delegates sent from an Irish synod to learn about Roman traditions of calculating Easter had returned from Rome to Ireland.[3] The need for Colmán to instruct Feradach in scansion of elegiac couplets may reflect the state of Irish knowledge about metres in the seventh century, or indeed the eighth, for though there are several original Latin compositions extant from Ireland in heptasyllabic, octosyllabic, decasyllabic, hendecasyllabic, dodecasyllabic, and pentadecasyllabic metres,[4] and Irish compositions in disyllabic, trisyllabic, tetrasyllabic, pentasyllabic, and hexasyllabic metres,[5] there is nothing in Classical quantitative metres. Some Anglo-Latin evidence involving elegiacs may help to fix Colmán's dates.

In his prodigious *Epistola ad Acircium* with its treatises *De Metris* and *De Pedum Regulis* surrounding one hundred verse *aenigmata* in quantitative metres,[6] the Anglo-Saxon Aldhelm addressed a subject which the Irish had not studied. He may have intended, as in his Letter to Heahfrith,[7] to exhibit the superiority of English learning represented by the school of Theodore and Hadrian at Canterbury for the benefit of those tempted to attend schools in Ireland. Such an exercise would have polemic value if the Irish were known to be preeminent practitioners of a wide range of syllabic poetic forms, but not of quantitative forms.

At the end of his Letter to Heahfrith, whom he dissuades from studying in Ireland, Aldhelm flaunts his own verse compositions in a form neither editor nor translator nor commentator has yet presented correctly. By dividing the initial line, *Digna fiat fante Glingio gurgo fugax fambulo*, which cannot be construed or scanned, and including a final elegiac couplet found in London, British Library, MS Royal 6 A VI and MS Cotton Domitian IX, one reads[8]

> ut uersidicus ait : **D**igna
> Fiat fante Glingio
> gurgo fugax fambulo .

3   See above p. 91–2. n.1.

4   'The Hymn of St Secundinus', ed. L. Bieler, *Proceedings of the Royal Irish Academy* LV C 6 (1953), 117–27. *The Hisperica Famina: II Related Poems*, ed. & transl. by M.W. Herren, Pontifical Institute of Mediaeval Studies, Studies and Texts LXXXV (Toronto 1987). M. Lapidge, 'A New Hiberno-Latin Hymn on St Martin', *Celtica* XXI (1990), pp. 240–51.

5   For syllabic analysis of Irish metres see G. Murphy, *Early Irish Metrics* (Dublin 1961), pp. 74–6.

6   *Aldhelmi Opera*, ed. R. Ehwald, *Monumenta Germaniae Historica, Auctorum Antiquissimorum Tomus XV* (Berlin 1919), pp. 59–204.

7   Ibid. pp. 486–94, transl. M. Herren, *Aldhelm: The Prose Works* (Cambridge 1979), pp. 160–4. D.R. Howlett, 'Aldhelm and Irish Learning', *Archivum Latinitatis Medii Aevi* LII (1994), pp. 37–75.

8   Ehwald, pp. 493–4, transl. M. Herren, pp. 163–4, 202 n. 37. See also M. Winterbottom, 'Aldhelm's prose style and its origins', *Anglo-Saxon England* VI (1977), pp. 39–76, esp. p. 47 n. 3, and Herren, 'Some New Light on the Life of Virgilius Maro Grammaticus', *Proceedings of the Royal Irish Academy* LXXIX C 2 (1979), pp. 27–71, esp. 43–5.

Neu timeat scriptor terrentis ludicra linguae .
Sic semper cupiunt scriptorum carpere cartas .
Ut caper hirsutus rodet cum dente racemos .
Nec tamen emendant titubantis gramma poetae .
Arbiter aeternus tibi iam miserescat in aeuum .
Fulgens diuitiis semper et ore claruS .

as the verse–utterer declares worthy things:
"Let," says Glingius,
"a fugitive chatterer become as a slave."
Let not the writer fear the sport of abusive tongues.
Thus they always hope to pluck the pages of poets,
As the hairy goat chews the grapes with his teeth.
Nonetheless they don't emend a letter of the reeling bard.
May the Eternal Judge now have mercy on you forever,
Shining in riches and always bright in speech.

Aldhelm begins his letter with a salutation of sixteen words (8 × 2). The first sentence contains eighty-eight words (8 × 11). The word *digna* is the 888th word of prose (8 × 111), followed by eight lines of verse (8 × 1) containing forty-four words (88 × .5), one hundred syllables, and 256 letters (8 × 32). Aldhelm's verse begins with a heptasyllabic couplet, as composed by the Irish, including rhyme on -*o* and alliteration on *f-f-g–g-f-f*. Aldhelm also parodies the most prolific and imaginative Irish grammarian, quoting the end of the first paragraph of *Epistola II De Pronomine* by Virgilius Maro Grammaticus:[9]

Verumtamen ne in illud Glengi incedam, quod cuidam conflictum fugienti dicere fidenter ausus est: gurgo inquit fugax fambulo dignus est, pauca tibi tui negotii necessaria de pronomine profabor.

This Joycean figure tells his readers how to split sounds and scramble words and sentences; he discusses bogus Hebrew and Greek words, quotes invented author - ities named Galbungus and Glengus, reports a debate among grammarians who for fourteen days and as many nights disputed the vocative of *ego*, and considers twelve Latinities. Aldhelm proceeds from two lines of parody of Virgilian nonsense to four dactylic hexameters, and he concludes with an elegiac couplet, presumably in the approved Canterbury style. In eight lines he contrasts the bogus learning represented by Ireland, Virgilius, and heptasyllables with the sound scholarship represented by England, Theodore and Hadrian, and Classical metres.

One might suppose tentatively that Colmán wrote to Feradach after establishment of contacts between Ireland and Rome in the second quarter of the seventh

9 *Virgilio Marone grammatico Epitomi ed Epistole,* ed. & transl. G. Polara & L. Caruso (Naples 1979), p. 206. See also Herren, 'Some New Light', and Ó Cróinín, 'The date, provenance, and earliest use of the works of Virgilius Maro Grammaticus', *Tradition und Wertigung* G. Bernt et al. eds. (Sigmaringen 1989), pp. 13–22.

century, perhaps during the following thirty or forty years, not distant from the time in which Aldhelm parodied a characteristic Irish verse form and addressed a subject not yet considered among Irish scholars.

IV. CELLÁN OF PÉRONNE

Letter to Aldhelm

In book V of his *Gesta Pontificum Anglorum* William of Malmesbury records a letter from an Irishman named Cellanus of Peronna Scottorum, Cellán of Péronne in Picardy, to Aldhelm as Abbot of Malmesbury asking for copies of his works.[1]

Hic quicquid litterarie artis elaborabat.
quod non adeo exile erat.
Aldelmi committebat arbitrio : ut perfecti ingenii lima .
eraderetur scabredo Scottica .
Ex ipso Francorum sinu . ad eum causa doctrine ueniebatur : ut hec epistola palam fatiet .

a i	DOMINO
ii	LECTRICIBUS DITÁTO STÚDIIS .
ii'	MELLIFLUISQUE ORNATO LUCUBRÁTIÚNCULIS .
i'	ALDHELMO . ÁRCHIMANDRÍTAE :
b	SAXONUM MIRIFICE REPERIÉNTI IN ÓRIS .
b'	QUOD NONNULLI CUM LABORIBUS ET SUDORIBUS IN ALIENO ÁERE VÌX LUCRÁNTUR :
a'i	CELLANUS
ii	IN HIBERNENSI ÍNSULA NÁTUS.
ii'	IN EXTREMO FRANCORUM LIMITIS LATENS ÁNGULO. ÉXUL
i'	FAMOSAE COLONIAE. XPISTI EXTREMUM ET VÍLE MANCÍPIUM.
c	IN TOTA ET TUTA TRINITÁTE SALÚTEM .

Et post pauca.

Quasi pennigero uolatu ad nostrae paupertátis accèssit aúres .	a
uestrae Latinitatis panagéricus rúmor :	x
quem agilium lectorum non horréscunt audítus .	b

1 BCLL 643. *Willelmi Malmesburiensis Monachi Gesta Pontificum Anglorum,* ed. N.E.S.A. Hamilton, Rolls Series (London 1870) V §191 337. *Aldhelmi Opera,* ed. R. Ehwald, pp. 498–9. Capital letters and punctuation marks in boldface represent features of William of Malmesbury's autograph, Oxford, Magdalen College, MS 172 f. 79v.

sine sanna aut amurcali impóstura nótus .   b
propter alburnum dictricis **R**omániae decórem .   c
Etsi te praesentem non merúimus audíre :   d
tuos tamen bona lance constructos légimus fástos .   b
diuersorum deliciis flórum depíctos .   b
Sed si peregrini triste refic[ere u]is córculum :   c
paucos transmitte sermunculos illius pulcherrimae lábiae túae .   d
de cuius fonte purissimo dulces diriuati riui . multorum possint
    reficere méntes :   a
ad locum ubi domnus **F**URSEUS in sancto et integro paúsat
    córpore .   d

Huic epistole quam liberaliter responderit . attestatur illa
cuius particula hic nuper apposita
dedit documentum Aldelmum
ex Saxonico genere ortum.

Here follows a recent translation of Cellán's letter into modern English prose.[2]

To the Lord Abbot Aldhelm, enriched by learned pursuits and adorned by
sweet lucubrations, admirably discovering on the shores of the Saxons what
some scarcely obtain, through labour and sweat, in a foreign clime,
Cellanus, born on the Isle of Ireland, an exile concealed in the farthermost
corner of the territory of the Franks, the lowest and (most) worthless servant of Christ in a famous settlement, (wishes) salvation in the whole and
wholesome Trinity.

The encomiastic report of your Latinity has reached the ears of our
Poverty as though by winged flight, nor does the hearing of able scholars
reject it: and it is noted, without twisting of nostrils or the pretence of
stink, for the brilliant beauty of its Roman eloquence. And although we
have not had the privilege of hearing you in the flesh, nonetheless we
have read your books, which are well constructed and balanced, and
adorned with the charms of various flowers; but if you would refresh the
sad little heart of the pilgrim, send us a few little sermons from those
most beautiful lips of yours from whose most pure source sweet rivulets,
when dispersed, may restore the minds of many to the place where
Master Furseus rests in holy and incorrupt body.

As William of Malmesbury's words *post pauca* imply that the text is an extract
of a longer work, both Ehwald and Herren have assumed that it is a fragment.[3]

---

2 M. Herren transl., *Aldhelm: The Prose Works* (Cambridge 1979), p. 167.
3 Ehwald printed the text of the letter preceded and followed by omission dots. Herren states
  explicitly in his introduction, p. 149, 'This fascinating correspondence is preserved only in the
  fragments quoted by William'.

But it makes complete sense, and there are indications that it is a complete text. Neither editor nor translator indicates that he has found anything amusing in this little lucubration, but Cellán did not hide his wit.

Let us translate the letter again *membratim et particulatim*.

> To the lord,
> enriched by studies appropriate to female readers
> and ornamented by honey-flowing little lucubrations,
> Aldhelm the archimandrite,
> wondrously discovering on the shores of the Saxons
> what some are scarcely acquiring with sweats and labour under a foreign
>   air,
> Cellán,
> born in the Hibernian island,
> an exile lying in an extreme corner of the border of the Franks,
> the most utter and vile servant of a famous colony of Christ,
> in the whole and safe Trinity [wishes] salvation.
>
> As if by feather-bearing flight there has approached to the ears of our
>   poverty [*i.e.* to poor me]
> a panegyric rumour of your Latinity,
> at which the hearings of agile lectors do not become horrified,
> noted without a sneer or oilily impure imposture
> on account of the whitely gleaming beauty of its eloquently wordy
>   Romanness [or 'of its Roman oratress'].
> And if we have not merited to hear you present,
> we have nonetheless read your books constructed with a good balance,
> adorned with the ornaments of diverse flowers [or 'painted up with the
>   fopperies of excerpts of diverse authors'];
> but if you wish to refresh the sad little heart of a pilgrim,
> send over a few little sermons of that most beautiful lip [or 'speech'] of
>   yours from the purest fountain, of which sweet streams led off [or
>   'artificial conduits diverted'] might refresh the minds of many
> at [or construed with *transmitte* 'to'] the place where the lord Fursey rests
>   in holy and complete body.

In the Salutation Cellán addresses Aldhelm by title and name in ai and i' and praises his study in aii and ii'. He contrasts wondrous discovery by Aldhelm on Saxon shores with the laborious need of others under a foreign sky in b and b'. He refers to himself by name and status in a'i and i', by place of birth and place of exile in b and b'. He names Aldhelm eight-ninths of the way through part a, the eighth word of nine. He names himself at the centre, the twenty-sixth word of fifty.

This Salutation may appear at first to be outrageously overblown, but it is the first part of a comprehensive joke. The fifty words of salutation relate to the eighty-two words of text of the letter by extreme and mean ratio, the golden section of 132 falling at 82 and 50.

In the letter proper the recurrence of words at fixed intervals suggests that the text is intact. Note *aures, auditus, audire*, of which the third is the thirty-fifth word. Of thirty-five words half is eighteen, and the central eighteenth word is *auditus*. Of the eighteen words half is nine, and between *aures* and *auditus* there are nine words. Note *Latinitatis* and *Romaniae*, of which the latter is the twenty-eighth word. The number 28 divides by extreme and mean ratio at 17 and 11. Between *Latinitatis* and *Romaniae* there are seventeen words. Note *lectorum* and *legimus*, of which the latter is the central word of the letter, forty-first of eighty-two. The number 41 divides by extreme and mean ratio at 25 and 16. Between *lectorum* and *legimus* there are twenty-five words. Note *fastos* and *sermunculos*. The former is forty-first from the end. The number 41 divides by duple ratio at 27 and 14. After *fastos* the fourteenth word is *sermunculos*, which is the twenty-seventh word from the end of the letter. Note *reficere* and *reficere*. They mark the golden section, as the eighty-two words of the letter divide by extreme and mean ratio at 51 and 31, and after the former there are thirty-one words to the end. The last thirty-one words of the letter divide by extreme and mean ratio at 19 and 12. After *reficere* the nineteenth word is *reficere*, after which there are twelve words to the end of the letter.

Cellán plays with Aldhelm's diction. In the Salutation only five words do not derive from the works of Aldhelm. One of those is the name *Cellanus*. Two others designate Aldhelm's activities, *lucubratiunculae*, and Aldhelm's title, *archiman-drita*. Of the remaining two, although Aldhelm does not use *angulus* and *colonia*, he does use *angulosus* and *colonus*. In the text of the letter only the words *sanna, alburnus, dictrix*, and *reficere* do not derive from the extant works of Aldhelm. Although Aldhelm does not use *amurcalis, Romania* or *Romanius, decor, corculum, transmittere*, or *sermunculus*, he does use *amurca, Romanus, decorare* and *decorosus, cor, mittere*, and *sermo*. Cellán's phrase *agilium lectorum non horrescunt auditus* plays on Aldhelm's *auditus nostri quatiuntur*, line 49 in the Letter to Heahfrith.[4] By mis-prision derived probably from a glossary Aldhelm uses the word *fasti*, which in Classical Latin designates lists of festivals or lists of consuls, to mean 'books'. Cellán's use of *fastos* in its Aldhelmian application may be pointed, a deliberate note of a word misunderstood by the recipient of this letter. But regardless of that Cellán's diction is perceptibly Aldhelmian. Parallels cited by Ehwald make it clear that Cellán quotes Gildas *De Excidio Britanniae* and Aldhelm's *Epistola ad Acircium, Epistola ad Heahfridum*, and the prose version of *De Virginitate*.

A reader who perceives irony in the letters of Patrick and Columban and Cummian and Virgilius Maro Grammaticus is unlikely to miss it here.[5] Let us assume not that Cellán had read every word of Celtic Latin ever composed, but that he knew Romano-Britons had been able to read and write urbane

---

4   Howlett, 'Aldhelm and Irish Learning', p. 39.
5   See above pp. 98–102.

Latin for at least 300 years and his fellow Irishmen for at least 250 years. Here
he is addressing the first Englishman, indeed the first man among all Germanic
nations, to become a Latin author. Is it likely that Cellán, whose grasp of
Latinity is firm enough to parody another man's style, would praise the
Romanness and Latinity of this English upstart without his tongue in his
cheek? Observe that in the Salutation he writes of Aldhelm as 'enriched by
studies appropriate to female readers'. The word for a masculine reader is *lector*,
which Cellán applies to himself in the text of the letter, and the adjectives
derived from it are *lectoralis* and *lectoreus*. The noun and adjective for a female
reader is *lectrix*. As the noun *studium* is neuter, Cellán either refers here to
Aldhelm's dedication of *De Virginitate* to women, or he implies that Aldhelm's
studies are appropriate to women rather than to men. He addresses Aldhelm as
reperienti, as if he were only just 'lighting upon', 'discovering the existence of',
or 'getting to know' Latin, 'which some are scarcely acquiring with sweats and
labour under a foreign air'. Cellán writes in the third person that *nonnulli ...
uix lucrantur*, not that he is one of them.[6] He implies clearly that he is one of
the *agilium lectorum*, as he would otherwise not know of their response to the
rumour of Aldhelm's Latinity. To write that these masculine 'agile lectors'
learned of Aldhelm's reputation *sine sanna aut amurcali impostura* is a form of
feint praise. Construing *dictrix* as an adjective and *Romania* as a noun equivalent to *Romanitas*, to extol 'the whitely gleaming beauty of eloquently
wordy Romanness' would be slightly odd. But construing *dictrix* as a noun and
Romania as an adjective the phrase would be offensive, implying that Aldhelm
writes in the effeminate style of a 'Roman oratress'. Cellán may well mean 'we
have nonetheless read your books constructed with a good balance', for even
someone who did not approve of their style would have to admire their
structure, implying the while that he was a competent judge, which Cellán
does. The phrase *diuersorum deliciis florum depictos* may mean 'adorned with the
ornaments of diverse flowers'. It may without the least wrenching or special
pleading mean also 'painted up with the fopperies of excerpts of diverse
authors'. Cellán's diminutives *corculum*, referring to his own little heart, and
sermunculos, referring to Aldhelm's desired works, little sermonettes, are probably playful and possibly ironic. His reference to 'that most beautiful lip [or
'speech'] of yours' is lippy, and his attraction of a normally neuter noun to the
feminine gender may be consistent with other implications that Aldhelm's
style is effeminate, issued *de cuius fonte purissimo*, as if the author were, in the
language of later parodists 'a particularly pure young man'. The words *dulces
diriuati riui* may mean 'sweet streams led off' or again without strain 'artificial
conduits diverted', implying that Cellán has read widely enough to recognise

6   Herren observes, p. 149, that 'the phrase could just as well mean "discovering on the shores of the
     Saxons *that* some scarcely benefit", etc. If taken that way, might not Cellanus's remark be a
     reference to the letter to Heahfrith, which might already have begun to be circulated with
     Aldhelm's compositions? If so, Cellanus's phrase could be taken as a gibe.'

Aldhelm's work as mannered and derivative. If Cellán had read only Aldhelm's *Epistola ad Acircium* and *De Virginitate* one might infer from this letter that he was, in simple prose in which each word bears only one obvious and superficial meaning, begging for more. But as the adjective *panagericus* implies that Cellán had read Aldhelm's most widely disseminated letter, the *Epistola ad Heahfridum*, with its aggressive claims for the soundness and superiority of English learning, and its parody, attacking the bogus nature of Irish learning, one infers that he responded with exactly the forms of wit, word-play, and irony practised by Irishmen writing Latin since at least the sixth century.

From Aldhelm's reply we may infer that he understood Cellán perfectly:[7]

> Quod autem **S**axonici generis fuerit .
> ipse in epistola quam Cellano cuidam misit .
> his edocet uerbis .
> **M**iror quod me tantillum homunculum
> de famoso et florigero Francorum rure
> uestrae frunitae fraternitatis industria interpellat .
> Saxonicae prolis prosapia genitum .
> et sub arctoo axe teneris infantiae confotum cunabulis .

> But that he was of Saxon race
> he himself in a letter which he sent to a certain Cellán
> he teaches in these words:
> I am amazed that me, such a very little manlet,
> from the famous and flower-bearing countryside of the Franks
> the industry of your learned brotherhood should solicit,
> born from the lineage of the Saxon breed
> and nurtured from the cradles of tender infancy under the northern pole.

Aldhelm's self-deprecating diminutives answer Cellán in kind. The innuendo implicit in a verb like *interpellere*, which means 'interrupt', 'obstruct', 'accost' (in the sexual sense), and even 'institute legal proceedings against', suggests that Aldhelm could give Cellán the same sort of lip he had received from him.

This correspondence may have been a perfectly ordinary epistolary exchange between members of a literate culture whose forms of play are not often or easily recognized by modern scholars. It might be useful for us to learn to recognize the forms, in order not to misread as dull pedantry what is actually the record of a witty needle-match.

---

7   *Gesta Pontificum*, V § 188 p. 333. *Aldhelmi Opera*, p. 499. Herren, p. 167.

V. ADOMNÁN OF IONA

De Locis Sanctis

The most famous writer of Columba's illustrious foundation was Adomnán Abbot of Iona 679–704, renowned for his *Vita Sancti Columbae* and for a work dictated by the visiting Bishop Arculf, *De Locis Sanctis*.[1] Here is the beginning.

IN NOMINE PATRIS ET FILII ET SPÍRITUS SÁNCTI CRAXARE LIBRUM DE LOCIS INCÍPIO SÁNCTIS

Arculf*us* sanct*us* epíscop*us* gènte Gállu*s*
diuersorum longe remotòrum peritu*s* locorum uerax index et sátis idóneu*s*
in Hierusolimitana ciuitate per menses nóuem hospitátu*s*
et loc*a* sancta cotidianis uisitationibus peragrans mihi Adomnano haéc uniuérsa
quae infr*a* craxand*a* súnt experiménta
diligéntius pèrcunctánti
et primo in tábulis dèscribénti
fideli et indubitabili narratióne dictáui
quae nunc in membranis breui téxtu scribúntur .

In the name of the Father and of the Son and of the Holy Ghost
I begin to write the book 'Concerning Holy Places'.

Arculf, a holy bishop, a Gaul by race,
learned about diverse remote places far away, an informant truthful and reliable enough,
having lodged in the city of Jerusalem for nine months
and traversing the holy places with daily visitations, to me, Adomnán, all these things
which were experienced, to be written out later,
[to me] very diligently interrogating
and writing down first on tablets
he dictated in faithful and undoubtable narration,
which are now written on membranes in a short text.

Both members of the incipit end with the the rhythm of the *cursus planus* and the word *sanctus*. The fourteen words of the incipit divide by extreme and mean ratio at 9 and 5, at Adomnán's reference to his writing of the book, *craxare | librum*. There are also five words between *sancti* and *sanctis*. The fourteen words divide by one-ninth and eight-ninths at Adomnán's reference to himself, *incipio*.

1   BCLL 304. *Adamnan's De Locis Sanctis,* ed. & transl. D. Meehan, *Scriptores Latini Hiberniae* III (Dublin 1958), pp. 36, 120. The translations here are mine.

The prose of the prologue exhibits rhymes and alliterations and cursus rhythms. It occupies fifty-six words, which divide by extreme and mean ratio at 35 and 21, at Adomnán's reference to writing his book, *craxanda* | *sunt*. There are also thirty-four words from the beginning to *sanctus* inclusive and from *sancta* inclusive to the end.

Together incipit and prologue comprise seventy words, which divide by extreme and mean ratio at 43 and 27, at Adomnán's reference to himself, *mihi* | *Adomnano*. They divide by one-ninth and eight-ninths at 8 and 62, at the reference to Arculf's dictation, *narratione* | *dictauit*. In these seventy words there are five references to dictating and writing, *craxare*, *craxanda*, *describenti*, *dictauit*, *scribuntur*. The seventy words divide by sesquitertian ratio at 40 and 30. After *craxare* the fortieth word is *craxanda*. From *describenti* to *scribuntur* inclusive there are thirteen words, which divide by sesquitertian ratio at 7 and 6. From *describenti* to *dictauit* inclusive there are six words, after which the seventh word is *scribuntur*.

Here is the end. Capital letters and punctuation points in boldface represent features of Paris, Bibliothèque nationale, MS latin 13048 folio 28r-v.

Obsecro ítaque *é*os
quicumque h*o*s breues **l**égerint **l**ib*é*llos
ut pro **e**odem . **sa**ncto . **sa**cerdóte **Á**rculf*o*
diuin*am* praecéntur cleménti*am*
Qui haec de sanct*is* expérimenta lóc*is*
eorum frequentator libentissime nóbis dictáui*t* .
Quae et égo quámlibe*t*
ínter labòriósa*s* et prope **í**nsustentábile*s*
tota die úndique cònglobáta*s*
ecclesiasticae sollicitudini*s* **oc**cupatiónes constitútu*s*
uil*i* quamuis sermone **de**scríbens **de**cláráu*i*
Hor*um* **e**rgo lectorem **a**mmoneo **e**xpériment*órum*
ut pro me miséllo pecc*atóre* eorúndem crax*atóre*
Xpist*um* iúdicem saèculór*um*
exoráre **n**on **n**églegat
LIBE**R** **TER**TIUS HÍC **TER**MINÁTUR

I beseech then those
who will have read these brief little books
that for the same holy priest Arculf
they may pray for divine clemency
who these experiences of holy places
the frequenter of them most willingly dictated to us,
which I also, assigned,
among however laborious and almost unsustainable
massed together all day on all sides
preoccupations of ecclesiastical anxieties,

have declared, writing [them] down albeit in vile style.
Therefore I admonish the reader of these experiences
that for me, a little wretched sinner, writer of the same,
he may not neglect
to pray to Christ the judge of the ages.
The third book is ended here.

The sixty-eight words of the epilogue divide by extreme and mean ratio at 42
and 26, at Adomnán's reference to himself, before *nobis*. The seventy-two
words of the epilogue and explicit divide by extreme and mean ratio at 44 and
28, at Adomnán's reference to Arculf and himself, *nobis dictauit | quae et ego ...
declaraui*. Reckoned another way, the twenty-eight words of the minor part
divide by symmetry at 14 and 14. The fourteenth word from the beginning is
Arculfo, that is the dictator of the book, and the fourteenth word from the end
is *misello*, that is the scribe of the book.

Half the words of the epilogue, thirty-four of sixty-eight, are in the passage
from *experimenta* to *experimentorum* inclusive. The other thirty-four divide by
extreme and mean ratio at 21 and 13. There are twenty-one words before
experimenta and thirteen words after *experimentorum*.

VI. JOSEPH SCOTTUS

Abbreviation of Jerome's Commentary on Isaiah

Of the career of Joseph Scottus, an Irishman at the court of Charlemagne, we
know a little from the correspondence of Alcuin. In a letter written to the Irish
magister, the *pio patri Colcu*, in A.D. 790 Alcuin mentions *Ioseph uernaculus tuus* as
being with him.[1] Writing to Joseph in the same year Alcuin mentions that *sanus
est magister uester Colcu*.[2] He concludes *te salutamus a longe et mandamus ut pascas bene
Ioseph cum sociis suis*.[3] Sometime between 790 and 793 Alcuin wrote again to *dilecto
filio Ioseppo* consoling him in ill health,[4] and sometime before 796 he asked Bishop
Remigius of Chur *iubeas obsecro orare pro anima Ioseppi discipuli mei*.[5] From Joseph's
hand we have some hexameter verses addressed to Saint Liudger,[6] four remarkable
carmina figurata addressed to Charlemagne,[7] and, undertaken at Alcuin's request,
an abbreviation of Jerome's Commentary on the Book of the Prophet Isaiah, of
which these are the Prologue and Epilogue.[8] Capital letters and punctuation

1   *Epistolae Karolini Aevi Tomus II*, ed. E. Duemmler (Berlin 1895), no. 7 p. 32.
2   Ibid. no. 8 p. 33.
3   Ibid. no. 14 p. 40.
4   Ibid. no. 14 p. 40.
5   Ibid. no. 77 p. 119.
6   *Poetae Latini Aevi Carolini*, ed. E. Duemmler, vol. I p. 150.
7   Ibid. pp. 152–9.
8   Ibid. p. 151. BCLL 648.

marks in boldface represent features of Paris, Bibliothèque nationale, MS latin 12154 folios 1 and 192r-v.

Isaiae breuibus lector mysteria uerbis		5	14	34
Pandere quis poterit tractans et cuncta uolutans ?		7	15	42
Hinc prius Hieronimus longis tractatibus usus .		6	15	40
Exposuit sapiens magnis ambagibus illum .		5	15	35
[C]uius ab inmensis temptabo excerpere libris .	5	6	15	38
Quae breuiter ualeant sensum nudare prophetae .		6	15	40
Sic placet Albino talem nos ferre laborem.		7	14	35
Hieronimus monuit postremi in fronte libelli ;		6	16	39
Ut cuicumque foret uerborum longior ipse		6	15	35
Textus . In Isaiam libros excerperet omnes ;		6	14	35
Et breuibus uastos uerbis constringere sensus ;		6	14	40
Sic idcirco tuis parens carissime iussis ;	5	6	14	35
Haec Albine tibi strictim collecta dicaui		6	14	36
Haec utinam nostri memorem te saepe rependaNT ;		7	15	39
Haec pater alme legens pro nobis sedulus ores ;		8	15	38
Saepius ac dicas Dominus conseruet Ioseph ;		6	15	36
Haec quoque uerba tibi toto de corde rependam ;	10	8	15	38
Care magister aue "Dominus te saluet ubique ;		7	16	36
Haec breui prout potui sermone in Isaiam de lacinioso Hierónimi tractátu		11		
sicut dilectissime magister Albine iussisti deuótus excérpsi ;		7		
Ita enim mihi praecipiébas ut in cúnctis		7		
pernecessarium tantum sensum et Hebraicae ueritatis trámitem séquens		8		
tam LXX . quam aliorum intérpretum èt tractórum	5	7		
incerta et confusa declinárem uestígia ;		5		
Duabus autem causis ut reor haec ita fieri uòluísti.		9		
ut uel fastidiosis tepidísque lectóribus		5		
tam longus libros legendi lábor leuarétur		6		
uel ingeniosis et ardentis ánimi homínibus	10	6		
promptior breuiorque quaerendae ueritatis uía redderétur ;		6		
Si quis autem haec quasi breuiora et ob id obscurióra dispíciat ;		11		
saepius enim breuitatem comitátur obscúritas		5		
ad fontem . Unde haec hausimus erecto céruice cúrrat .		8		
ET cui riuulus íste non súfficit	15	6		
de super ripis suis inundanti flúmine pótet ;		7		
Tu autem dilecte magister in nóstri labòris uícem		8		
tuae nobis benedictionis et orationis grátiam commúnices		7		
ut nostri Redemptoris cleméntiam pulsántes		5		

pro eius multa in multos mísericórdia   20   6
in nobis quoque opus manuum suarum respiciens nón
    dispíciat   9
sed superatis saeculi huius temptatiónum flúctibus   6
ruptisque nostrorum renium rétiáculis   4
nos ad inperturbatae uitae portum benigne perducat
    clemens dóminus Ihésus ;   24   10

Who, reader, could reveal [lit. 'spread out'], treating and scrolling, all the
mysteries of Isaiah in brief words? Earlier than this Jerome the wise, having
used long treatises, expounded him [*i.e.* Isaiah] in great maeanderings, from
whose [*i.e.* Jerome's] immense books I shall attempt to excerpt those things
which may be effective in laying bare briefly the sense of the prophet.

Jerome advised at the beginning of the book just finished that, should
there be for anyone a longer text of words, he should excerpt all the books
'On Isaiah' to compact even vast senses in brief words. So, dearest Alcuin,
obeying your orders on that condition I have devoted these compactly
collected readings to you. Would that they repay you, often mindful of us.
Reading these things, holy father, may you, attentive, pray for us, and may
you say quite often, "May the Lord preserve Joseph". I also shall repay
these words for you with a whole heart. Dear master, hail, may the Lord
keep you safe everywhere.

These things, as I could, in brief speech from Jerome's fringed treatise
on Isaiah, just as you have ordered, most beloved master Alcuin, I, devoted,
have excerpted. For so you kept instructing me that in all matters following
the great utterly essential sense and path of Hebraic truth [*i.e.* the Hebrew
text of the Old Testament] I should turn aside from the uncertain and
confused traces of both the Seventy [*i.e.* the Septuagint Greek text of the
Old Testament] and of other interpreters and translators. For two reasons,
moreover, as I suppose, you have wished these things to be done so, that
either so long a labour of reading books be lightened for fastidious and
unenthusiastic readers or that the way of truth to be sought be rendered
simpler and briefer for men ingenious and of zealous spirit. If anyone,
moreover, should look down on these things as if briefer and, because of
that, more obscure, for quite often obscurity accompanies brevity, let him
run with upright neck to the fountain whence we have drawn these things,
and for him to whom that rivulet does not suffice let him drink from the
river flowing above its own banks. May you, however, beloved master,
communicate in exchange for our labour the grace of your benediction and
prayer for us, so that importuning the clemency of our Redeemer for His
great mercy to great numbers, looking back also on us he may not look
down on the work of their hands, but with the waves of the temptations of
this age overcome and the little nets of our reins broken the clement Lord
Jesus may lead us kindlily to the port of unperturbed life.

In the verse Prologue lines 1, 2, 3, 5, and 7 exhibit internal rhyme; lines 2, 3, 4, and 5 exhibit internal alliteration; lines 1–2, 5–6, and 6–7 exhibit consecutive alliteration. Joseph has arranged his words and thoughts chiastically.

1	Isaiae	
2 a	breuibus	
b	mysteria	
c	pandere	
3	quis	
4 a	Hieronimus	
b	longis	
c	tractatibus	
5	exposuit sapiens magnis ambagibus illum	
4'a	cuius	
b	inmensis	
c	libris	
3'	quae	
2'a	breuiter	
b	sensum	
c	nudare	
1'	prophetae	

The poem contains seven lines, forty-two words, 103 or 104 syllables, depending upon whether *Isaiae* contains three syllables or four, and 264 letters. The central words *magnis* | *ambagibus* at the centre of the central line at the crux of the chiasmus refer to the great circuitous wanderings of Jerome's Commentary on Isaiah. The central syllable is the first of *magnis*, and the central letters are the first two of *magnis*.

Joseph refers to himself three times, at *quis*, *temptabo*, and *nos*. From *quis* to *nos* inclusive there are thirty-four words, which divide by extreme and mean ratio at 21 and 13. From *quis* to *temptabo* inclusive there are twenty-one words. The forty-two words of the entire poem divide by extreme and mean ratio at 26 and 16, at *inmensis* | *temptabo*. Joseph refers to Jerome three times, at *Hieronimus*, *sapiens*, and *cuius*. From *Hieronimus* to *cuius* inclusive there are ten words, which divide by extreme and mean ratio at 6 and 4; from *Hieronimus* to *sapiens* inclusive there are six words. Joseph refers to Isaiah three times, at *Isaiae*, *illum*, and *prophetae*. The forty-two words of the poem divide by sesquioctave ratio (9:8) at 22 and 20. The first word is *Isaiae*, and the twenty-second word after that, twentieth from the end, is *illum*. The major part of twenty-two words divides by sesquioctave ratio at 12 and 10. The twelfth word after *illum* is *prophetae*. At one-ninth and eight-ninths of the poem, 5 and 37, Joseph names Alcuin, *Albino*, who asked him to abbreviate Jerome's commentary on Isaiah.

To make a point about abbreviation Joseph employed duple ratio (2:1), which in his forty-two-word poem falls at 28 and 14. Between *breuibus* and *breuiter* there are twenty-eight words, of which the central fourteenth words are *longis | tractatibus*. After *longis* the fifth word is *magnis*, after which the fifth word is *inmensis*, after which the fifth word is *breuiter*. The twenty-ninth word is *libris*. The number 29 divides by extreme and mean ratio at 18 and 11. Between *libris* and *tractatibus* there are eleven words. *Tractatibus* is the seventeenth word; half of 17 is 9; the ninth word is *tractans*. The twelfth word is *uolutans*; half of 12 is 6; the sixth word is *pandere*.

Each of these three compositions is complete on its own, but they are linked. There are, for example, thirty-seven words before the name *Albino* in the verse Prologue. From *Albino* in the verse Prologue to *Albine* in the verse Epilogue inclusive there are thirty-seven words. From *Albine* to *care magister aue* inclusive there are thirty-seven words. In the verse Epilogue after *carissime* the thirty-seventh word is the first of *care magister aue*. The number 37 divides by symmetry at 19 and by extreme and mean ratio at 22.87 and 14.13. From *care magister aue* in the verse Epilogue to *dilectissime magister Albine* in the prose Epilogue inclusive there are twenty-two words; after *magister* the nineteenth word is *magister*.

The verse Prologue contains forty-two words and the verse Epilogue seventy-two, together 114 words; the prose Epilogue contains 169 words. Together the three compositions contain 283 words, which divide by sesquialter ratio (3:2) at 169.8 and 113.2.

VII. DUNGAL OF SAINT-DENIS AND PAVIA

Letter to an abbot

One of the more distinguished and prolific Irish *peregrini* on the Continent was Dungal of Saint-Denis and Pavia, whom Charlemagne consulted about the treatise *De Substantia Nihili et Tenebrarum* by the Anglo-Saxon Fridugisus, and who corresponded with Charlemagne's daughter Theodrada and other Carolingian abbots. Here is the sixth of his letters, written about 800–814.[1] Capital letters and punctuation marks in boldface represent features of London, British Library, MS Harley 208 folio 115r.

DÓM*IN*O IN XP*ÍST*O	aa
VENERABIL*I* . DILECTISSIMOQUE ABBÁT*I* ILLÚSTR*I* .	bbb
DUNGAL*US* EX*Í*G*UUS* FÁMUL*US*	ccc
PERPE*TEM* IN DOMINO SALVATÓRE SALÚ*TEM* .	dd

<u>V</u>estra ergo domine <u>c</u>arissime prosperitate <u>c</u>ógnita laet*áti*	a
et <u>uestrae</u> incolomitate <u>u</u>itae <u>com</u>pérta <u>c</u>onsol*áti*	a

---

1   BCLL 657. *Dungali Scotti Epistolae*, ed. E. Duemmler, *Epistolae Karolini Aevi Tomus II, Monumenta Germaniae Historica Epistolarum Tomus IV* (Berlin 1895), p. 581.

optamus uos semper in Domino uerae prosperitatis stabilitáte
    gaudére.   b
ut non in huius formidando saeculi pelago nauigantes
    Schylleae uos pulchritudinis fallácia decípiat   c
nec Serenarum loetiferi cántus obléctent   5   c
sed casto uelut ille prouidus Itachus aspectu obturatis aúribus
    inlaési   d
diuino agitante Spiraminis flatu ad supernae portum patriae deuicto
    hostilis Ílio múndi   d
superatisque uictores Frigibus pérueniátis .   e
Ubi bellicorum praesentis uitae successuum anxia incertaque
    trepidatióne excépti   a
ac de inprouisis periculosisque Caríbdibus liberáti   10   a
perpetua perfrui páce gaudeátis .   e
Haec ergo tibi domine dilectissime eueníre optámus   f
et assiduis in commemorationibus carissimorum nostrorum
    praécibus rogámus.   f

Núnc autem quod súperest .
Misi aliquid de argento . per illustrem uéstrum seruiéntem   15
et uolo rogare si uobis facilis est
ut iubeatis uni bono et perito de uestris fabricare illud
et facere inde ministerium calicem et patenam
et ut hoc diligenter a uobis sít commendátum
et iussum quasi ad uestrum proprium opus debuísset operári .   20
et ut hoc sciat ille faber quod hoc fabricatum
uobis ipsis debet iterum réddere et monstráre
ut iudicetis et probetis illud .
Sed sic hoc rogo
si uobis graue non est   25
sin autem non rogo .
Confidens ergo domine dilectissime de uestra pietate et
    benignitate
ausus sum uobis commemoráre et suggérere
de illo opere misericordiae et élemosynárum
quod olim ego praesens uos cum mira mentis alacritate et
    humilitate exercere uidi   30
ut non aliquando in uestro mónastério
et in reliquis uestrae potestatis locis tepéscat et rèfrigéscat
nec in illis occasiones quaedam inhumanitatis et inmisericordiae quas
    nón mandauit Déus
excogitentur contra pauperes et peregrinos súperueniéntes .
Dominus ergo meus et Deus meus Iésus Xpístus scit   35
quia pro uera animae et uitae dilectione haec dico .

ne uos neglegentiae aut culpae alterius reatum subeatis .
Scio enim quia si inde aliquid factum est uos ignoratis et nescitis .
Bene ualete semper in Domino domine reuerentissime atque
    dulcissime pater .   39

TO THE LORD IN CHRIST,
VENERABLE AND MOST BELOVED ILLUSTRIOUS ABBOT,
DUNGAL, FEEBLE LITTLE SERVANT,
[WISHES] PERPETUAL HEALTH IN THE LORD CHRIST THE
    SAVIOUR.

We, then, made happy by your known prosperity, dearest lord,
and consoled by the ascertained safety of your life,
wish you always to rejoice in the Lord with the stability of true prosperity,
so that, sailing on the to-be-feared sea of this age, the trickery of Scyllan
    beauty may not deceive you,
nor the death-bearing songs of the Sirens divert you,
but like that foresightful Ithacan with the chaste gaze of an uninjured
    man with ears plugged,
with the divine blast of the Spirit operating, to the port of the supernal
    fatherland with the Ilium of a hostile world conquered,
and with the Phrygians overcome you may come through as victors,
where taken away from the anxious and uncertain trepidation of the
    approaches of wars of the present life,
and liberated from the unforeseen and perilous Charybdes,
you may rejoice to enjoy thoroughly perpetual peace.
These things, then, for you, most beloved lord, we hope to come about
and ask with assiduous callings to mind in the prayers of our dearest ones.

But now, what remains.
I have sent something of silver through your illustrious servant,
and I wish to ask, if it is easy for you,
that you order one good and skilled from among your men to smith it
and to make from it a credence table, chalice, and paten,
and that this be diligently commended by you
and ordered as if he should work the work for your very own
and that that smith should know this, that this smithed work
he ought to give back again and show to yourself
that you may judge and approve it.
But I ask this
if it is not burdensome to you;
but if not, I do not ask.

Trusting, then, most beloved lord, in your piety and benignity
I have dared to call to mind and suggest to you

about that work of mercy and of alms

that formerly I, present, saw you exercise with wondrous alacrity and humility of mind;

so that in your monastery

and in the remaining places of your power, it should not at any time grow tepid and grow cold again,

nor should in them certain occasions of inhumanity and mercilessness, which God did not command,

be thought out against poor men and pilgrims coming upon them.

My Lord, then, and my God Jesus Christ knows

that I say these things for true love of soul and life,

lest you undergo the charge of negligence or any other guilt.

For I know that if anything has been done in consequence you are ignorant and do not know.

Be well always in the Lord, most reverent lord and sweetest father.

The Salutation begins *Domino in Xpisto*, and it ends *in Domino Saluatore salutem*. It contains fifteen words, of which the central eighth word is the author's eight-lettered name, *Dungalus*. The fifteen words divide by extreme and mean ratio at 9 and 6, at Dungal's reference to his recipient, *abbati | illustri*, and at the end of his reference to himself, *exiguus | famulus*.

There are three paragraphs, each thirteen lines long. The rhythm, alliteration, and rhyme are most systematically disposed in the first paragraph, which exhibits internal chiasmus.

a	uestra
b	ergo domine carissime ... optamus
c	uos semper in Domino uerae prosperitatis stabilitate gaudere
d	ut non in huius formidando saeculi pelago nauigantes Schylleae uos pulchritudinis fallacia decipiat
e	nec Serenarum loetiferi cantus oblectent
f	sed casto uelut ille prouidus Itachus aspectu obturatis auribus inlaesi
g	diuino agitante Spiraminis flatu ad supernae portum patriae
f'	deuicto hostilis Ilio mundi superatisque uictores Frigibus perueniatis
e'	ubi bellicorum praesentis uitae successuum anxia incertaque trepidatione excepti
d'	ac de inprouisis periculosisque Caribdibus liberati
c'	perpetua perfrui pace gaudeatis
b'	ergo tibi domine dilectissime ... optamus ... carissimorum
a'	nostrorum

There are exactly one hundred words, of which the fifty-first is the first word of the crux of the chiasmus in part g.

The second paragraph also exhibits internal chiasmus.

a	et uolo rogare
b	si uobis facilis est
c	ut iubeatis uni bono et perito de uestris fabricare illud
d	et facere inde ministerium calicem et patenam
e	et ut hoc diligenter a uobis sit commendatum
e'	et iussum quasi ad uestrum proprium opus debuisset operari
d'	et ut hoc sciat ille faber quod hoc fabricatum uobis ipsis debet iterum reddere et monstrare
c'	ut iudicetis et probetis illud
b'	si uobis graue non est
a'	non rogo

There are eighty-seven words, which divide by symmetry at 44, exactly at the crux of the chiasmus, at *commendatum*, the forty-fourth word, at the end of part e.

The third paragraph begins *Confidens ergo domine dilectissime* and ends with a little chiasmus that echoes the phrase:

a	domine
b	reuerentissime
c	atque
b'	dulcissime
a'	pater

The structure of three paragraphs exhibits duple ratio, symmetry, and extreme and mean ratio. The 302 words of the letter divide by duple ratio at 201 and 101, at the first word of the second paragraph, which introduces Dungal's request, *Nunc | autem quod superest*. The central words of the letter state Dungal's desire at the end of the crux of the chiasmus, *proprium opus debuisset operari*. The 302 words of the letter divide by extreme and mean ratio at 187 and 115, at the end of the second paragraph, *sin autem non rogo*.

VIII. DICUILL

Liber de Mensura Orbis Terrae

As we have seen above, the earliest extant letter by an Irishman abroad deals with the problem of the calculation of Easter. So does the earliest extant letter from an Irishman at home. Colmán's letter to Feradach deals with the technicalities of

scanning elegiac couplets and of textual criticism. Adomnán *De Locis Sanctis* deals
with matters of geographic, topographic, and exegetical interest. Joseph's
abbreviation of Jerome's Commentary on Isaiah also exhibits exegetical interest.
Here from a period slightly later than Joseph is a monument to the scientific
curiosity of an Irishman at the Carolingian court, *Dicuili Liber de Mensura Orbis
Terrae*, which ends with thirty-one hexameter verses.[1] Capital letters and
punctuation points in boldface represent features of Paris, Bibliothèque nationale,
MS latin 4806 folios 30v–31 and MS latin 9661 folio 50r-v.

DICUIL ACCIPIENS EGO TRACTA AUCTORIBUS ISTA .
Pauca loquar senis metro de montibus altis .
Summus Athos Athlas nubes transcendit Olympus .
Puluere ob hoc squalent terna alta cacumina quorum .
Montibus ambobus sed celsior instat Olympus .
Athlas inferior praedictis montibus altis .
Inde corona caput cingit sublime niualis .
Mons medius tendens excelsa cacumina caelo .
Undecies umbris obscurat milia septem .
Exta anno integro diuo custodit Olympus .
Inmaculata tenens oblata in uertice summo .
Non alios legimus montes excedere uentos .
Sublimem Athlantem torret sol feruidus Austri .
Iam binos alios Aquilonis frigus adurit .
Afri Athlanta tenent Adon Argi Grecus Olympum .
Arduus occiduas Athlas custodit harenas .
Grandis Alexandri tellus hos seruat auita .
Frigus in excelsis est feruor solis in imis .
Est medium spatium fouet aer omne serenus .
Athlantis triplicis fundentis flumina curua .
In partes Euri Zephyri Boreaeque uel Austri . .
Quinquaginta semel centum bis milia supra .
Mons Pelion tollens caput inter nubila condit ;
Quinque Alpes decies transfigunt milia sursum .
Solurius summo scandens sit uertice caelo .
Mensuram haud legi cuius quot milia complent .
Thessalus atque Italus Hispanus possidet ipsos ;
Post octingentos uiginti quinque peractos .
Summi annos Domini terrae aethrae carceris atri .
Semine triticeo sub ruris puluere tecto
NOCTE BOBUS REQUIES LARGITUR FINE LABORIS ·,·

1   BCLL 662. *Dicuili Liber de Mensura Orbis Terrae*, ed. & transl. J.J. Tierney with contributions by L.
    Bieler, *Scriptores Latini Hiberniae* VI (Dublin 1967), pp. 102–3.

I, Dicuil, having made my excerpts from these authorities, shall now write a few hexameters on the six high mountains. Lofty Athos, Atlas, and Olympus tower above the clouds, and so their three high summits are parched with dust. But Olympus is higher than the other two mountains, while Atlas is lower than the other two; that is why a wreath of snow surrounds its lofty head. The middle mountain holds its head aloft to heaven, and throws a shadow of seven miles eleven times. Olympus guards its offerings for the god for a whole year, keeping them unspotted on its highest peak. We do not read of other mountains being higher than the winds. The burning southern sun scorches high Atlas; it is the northern cold wind which burns the others. The Africans own Atlas, the Argives Athos, the Greeks Olympus. High Atlas guards the sands of the west, the ancestral land of Alexander the Great keeps the others. They are cold at the summit, burned by the sun at the base, a serene air bathes all the middle space, where Atlas with its triple range pours forth its winding rivers, to east and west, to north and south. Mount Pelion, raising its head a mile and a quarter, hides it among the clouds. The Alps pierce fifty miles aloft. Though Solurius rises to heaven with its topmost peak, I have not read how many miles make its measure. These mountains are respectively in Thessaly, Italy, and Spain. After eight hundred and twenty-five years finished of the high lord of earth, and heaven, and the dark prison, when the wheaten seed has been sown in the country earth, at night on ending their labours the oxen are granted rest.

Dicuill has arranged his words about six mountains in six chiastic patterns.

1a	Dicuil accipiens ego tracta auctoribus ista
	pauca loquor senis metro de montibus altis.
b	summus
c	Athos Athlas
d	nubes transcendit Olympus
e	Puluere ob hoc squalent terna alta cacumina quorum.
e'	Montibus ambobus
d'	sed celsior instat Olympus
c'	Athlas
b'	inferior
a'	praedictis montibus altis
2a	Inde corona caput cingit sublime niualis.
b	Mons medius
c	tendens excelsa cacumina caelo
d	Undecies umbris obscurat milia septem.
c'	Exta anno integro diuo custodit
b'	Olympus
a'	Inmaculata tenens oblata in uertice summo.
	Non alios legimus montes excedere uentos.	
3a	Sublimem Athlantem

b	torret
c	sol feruidus
d	Austri
e	Iam binos alios
d'	Aquilonis
c'	frigus
b'	adurit.
a'	Afri Athlanta tenent Adon Argi Grecus Olympum.
4	Arduus occiduas Athlas custodit harenas
	Grandis Alexandri tellus hos seruat auita.
	Frigus in excelsis est feruor solis in imis
	Est medium spatium fouet aer omne serenus
	Athlantis triplicis fundentis flumina curua
	In partes Euri Zephyri Boreaeque uel Austri.
5a	Quinquaginta semel centum bis milia supra
b	Mons Pelion tollens caput inter nubila condit.
c	Quinque Alpes decies transfigunt milia sursum.
b'	Solurius summo scandens sit uertice caelo
a'	Mensuram haud legi cuius quot milia complent.
6	Thesalus atque Italus Hispanus possidet ipsos.
	Post octingentos uiginti quinque peractos
	Summi annos Domini terrae aethrae carceris atri
	Semine triticeo sub ruris puluere tecto
	Nocte bobus requies largitur fine laboris.

In part 1 compare *montibus altis* in a with *praedictis montibus altis* in a', *summus* in b with *inferior* in b', *Athlas* in c and c', *nubes transcendit Olympus* in d with *celsior instat Olympus* in d', *terna* in e with *ambobus* in e'. In part 2 compare the snowy peaks in a and a', *corona caput cingit sublime niualis* and *inmaculata tenens oblata in uertice summo*, *mons medius* in b with *Olympus* in b', *excelsa cacumina* in c with *exta* in c', around the crux in d, *undecies umbris obscurat milia septem*. In part 3 compare *Athlantem* in a with *Athlanta* in a', *torret* in b with *adurit* in b', *feruidus* in c with *frigus* in c', *Austri* in d with *Aquilonis* in d', around the crux in e, *iam binos alios*. In part 5 compare *milia* in a and a', *mons Pelion tollens* in b with *Solurius scandens* in b', around the crux in c, *quinque Alpes decies transfigunt milia sursum*.

The central line of the poem, sixteenth of thirty-one, is the first of the central part 4. The central words are the last two words of that line, *custodit | harenas*. The thirty-one lines of the poem divide by extreme and mean ratio at 12 and 19, at the end of part 2. The 192 words divide by extreme and mean ratio at 119 and 73, at the end of part 2.

The poem is further integrated in a great chiasmus.

A	puluere
B1	caelo

2	anno			
C		uertice		
D		summo		
E		montes		
F 1			Athlantem	
2			Austri	
3			binos	
G1				frigus
2				adurit
3				Athlanta
H				custodit

I   Grandis Alexandri tellus custodit
                            harenas

H'				seruat
G'1			frigus	
2			fouet	
3			Athlantis	
F'1			Athlantis	
2			Austri	
3			bis	
E'		mons		
D'		summo		
C'		uertice		
B'1	caelo			
2	annos			
A'	puluere			

The symmetrical centre of the poem reckoned by both lines and words falls at the crux of the chiasmus, at I, *custodit* | *harenas*.

Within this chiasmus Dicuill has woven another.

A	caput		
B		medius	
C 1		excelsa	
2			sol feruidus
D			Argi
D'			Grecus
C'1		excelsis	
2			feruor solis
B'		medium	
A'	caput		

From *caput* to *caput* inclusive there are exactly one hundred words, of which the centre falls at the crux of the chiasmus, between *Argi* and *Grecus*.

Dicuill has further organized his words. Note lines 3, 5, 8, 10, 15: *Olympus, Olympus, mons medius, Olympus, Olympum*. He refers to Olympus as *mons medius* for several reasons. First, it is the third of six mountains named. In the first chiastic pattern, part 1, it is named *Olympus* first in the nineteenth of thirty-eight words. The last mention is *Olympum* at the end of part 3, the ninety-second word, and *medius* is exactly half of that, the forty-sixth word. Half of 92, 46, divides by extreme and mean ratio at 28 and 18. From the first mention of *Olympus* to *mons medius* inclusive there are twenty-eight words. From the second mention of *Olympus* to *mons medius* inclusive there are half of that, fourteen words. After the second mention of *Olympus* the third *Olympus* is the twenty-eighth word.

The 192 words of the poem divide by extreme and mean ratio at 119 and 73. The 119th word is *Athlantis* 20. The number 119 divides by extreme and mean ratio at 74 and 45. From *Athlantis* 20 to *Athlantis* 13 inclusive there are forty-five words. The number 45 divides by extreme and mean ratio at 28 and 19. From *Athlas* 3 to *Athlas* 6 inclusive there are nineteen words. Between *Athlantem* 13 and *Athlas* 16 there are nineteen words. The number 19 divides by extreme and mean ratio at 12 and 7. After *Athlantem* 13 *Athlanta* 15 is the twelfth word. Between *Athlanta* 15 and *Athlas* 16 there are seven words.

There are twelve words before *altis* 2. The twelfth word after *altis* 2 is *alta* 4. There are twelve words between *alta* 4 and *altis* 6.

Note *summus* 3, *summo* 11, *summo* 25. From the first occurrence of the word to the third inclusive there are 138 words, which divide by extreme and mean ratio at 85 and 53. After *summo* 3 *summo* 11 is the fifty-third word.

Note *milia* 22, 24, 26. From the first of these to the third inclusive there are twenty-seven words, of which the second is fourteenth after the first and fourteenth before the third.

Note the verbs *transcendit* 3 and *transfigunt* 24, which divide the poem by duple ratio, 128 and 64. From the beginning to *transcendit* inclusive and from *transfigunt* inclusive to the end there are sixty-four words. Between them are 128 words.

Our author names and refers to himself in the first three words of the first line, *Dicuil ... ego*. He states his subject and names his medium in the second line, *pauca loquor senis metro de montibus altis*. At one-ninth and eight-ninths of thirty-one lines, 3.4 and 27.6, and of 192 words, 21 and 171, he dates his verse to the year 825, *post octingentos uiginti | quinque peractos*. His last two words are, appropriately, *fine laboris*.

IX. SEDULIUS SCOTTUS

On Scholars of Clonard

In a recent survey of the role of the Irish as mediators of Antique culture on the Continent Dáibhí Ó Cróinín has attributed a little poem to that most accomplished and prolific of Irish Latin poets, Sedulius Scottus.[1] Part of the interest of these verses is their celebration of a tradition of Latin learning among scholars of the monastery at Clonard in County Meath. To note elements of the prosody double underlinings mark alliteration between halves of a line; single underlinings mark alliteration between adjacent lines; italics with dotted underline mark rhyme between the halves of a line; simple italics mark rhyme between the last word of one line and the first word of the next or between the last words of adjacent lines.

Aspice marmoreas superantes astra columnas	aa	5	16	38
Quas hic sanctigeri fulcit harena soli	bb	6	13	33
Felix famosus Heleranus Finnia Fergi	cc	5	14	32
Fulgida donifero lumina faeta Deo.	dd	5	14	29
O magnum Scotiae misit Pictonia diues		6	14	32
Munus relliquias quas uelit esse suas	aa	6	13	32
Unde uenit Tytan et nox ubi sidera condit		8	15	34
Quaque dies medius flagrantibus aestuat horis.		6	16	40
		47	115	270

Look on the marble columns surpassing the stars,
which the sand of the saint-bearing land supports here:
happy, famous Ailerán, Vinniau, Fergus,
shining lights made by gift-carrying God.
O He sent a great present of Scotland [i.e. Ireland], rich
relics which Pictonia [i.e. Poitiers] wishes to be its own,
whence comes Titan and where night establishes the stars
and where midday is hot with blazing hours
[i.e. the east and the west and the south].

The last two hexameters are quoted from Lucan Belli Ciuilis Liber I 15–6. The next two lines, which are not quoted, are

et qua bruma rigens ac nescia uere remitti
astringit Scythico glacialem frigore pontum.

If Pictonia is Pictauia, identified as Poitiers, these verses were composed in a region in which Ireland lay to the north. The poet could omit Lucan's verses 17–8 but rely upon his readers' knowledge of them to supply an association of northern Scotia with northern Scythia. The use of unquoted context to convey meanings is a habit ingrained in Celtic Latin authors, as we have seen already

1   D. Ó Cróinín, 'The Irish as Mediators of Antique Culture on the Continent' in P. L. Butzer & D. Lohrmann eds., Science in Western and Eastern Civilization in Carolingian Times (Basel 1993), pp. 41–52 at 49–50. Versus Scottorum, ed. K. Strecker, Poetae Latini Aevi Carolini IV ii-iii, Monumenta Germaniae Historica (Berlin 1923), p. 1124. For other works by Sedulius see BCLL 672–86.

in the works of Patrick, Columban, and Cummian,[2] and as we shall see in 'Saint Sechnall's Hymn' and the *Orationes Moucani*.[3]

The heroes celebrated are Finnia, Vinniau, a sixth-century British correspondent of Gildas mentioned by Columban,[4] venerated as founder of the monastery of Clonard; Aileran *Sapiens*, a seventh-century scholar of Clonard;[5] and Fergus, a ninth-century scholar of Clonard, to whom Sedulius addressed other poems.[6]

These eight verses divide by extreme and mean ratio at 5 and 3 in various ways. Five of the lines are hexameters, and three are pentameters. Five exhibit internal rhyme, and three do not. Five exhibit internal alliteration, marked here by double underlining, and three do not.

The forty-seven words divide by symmetry at the central twenty-fourth word from beginning and end, *Scotiae*, home of the celebrated luminaries and home of the poet. The forty-seven words divide by extreme and mean ratio at 29 and 18, at *donifero* | *lumina* and at *munus relliquias* | *quas*, alluding in both places to God's gift of learned Irishmen to the world. Note *astra* 1, *lumina* 4, and *sidera* 7. From *astra* to *sidera* inclusive there are thirty-seven words, which divide by extreme and mean ratio at 23 and 14. Between *astra* and *lumina* there are fourteen words. *Astra* is the fourth word from the beginning of the poem; after *sidera* there are seven words to the end of the poem; together eleven words, which divide by extreme and mean ratio at 7 and 4.

X. JOHANNES SCOTTUS ERIUGENA

Periphyseon

The most famous and influential Irishman of the Middle Ages and the greatest Western philosopher between Saint Augustine of Hippo and Saint Thomas Aquinas left his native land about 847, lived at the court of Charles the Bald, and published about 865 his masterpiece, the *Periphyseon*, a dialogue, of which the beginning follows.[1] Capital letters and punctuation marks in boldface represent features of Paris, Bibliothèque nationale, MS latin 12964 folio 1.

INCIPIT PRIMUS ΠΕΡΙΦΥϹΕΩΝ
[NUTRITOR]
SAEPE MÍHI COGITÁNTI

---

2 See above pp. 86–8, 99–101.
3 See below pp. 147, 149, 201, 204.
4 See above p. 91.
5 *BCLL* 299.
6 Ó Cróinín, 'The Irish as Mediators', p. 49.
1 *BCLL* 700. *Iohannis Scotti Eriugenae Periphyseon (De Diuisione Naturae)*, ed. & transl. I.P. Sheldon-Williams with L. Bieler, *Scriptores Latini Hiberniae* VII (Dublin 1968), vol. I, pp. 36–7, 36–7.

DILIGENTIUSQUE QUANTUM VIRES
SÚPPEtunt ìnquirénti
rerum omnium quae uel animo pércipi póssunt .
uel intentionem eíus súperant .
Primam summamque diuisionem . ésse . in èa quaé sunt   5
et in éa quae nón sunt
Horum omnium generale uocábulum óccurrit
quod Graece ΦΥCIC . Latine uero natúra uocitátur.
An tibi áliter uidétur .
     A[LUMNUS]
Ímmo conséntio .   10
nam et ego dum ratiocinandi uiam ingredior haec ita fieri
     repério.

NUTRITOR

As I frequently ponder and, so far as my talents allow, ever more carefully investigate the fact that the first and fundamental division of all things which either can be grasped by the mind or lie beyond its grasp is into those that are and those that are not, there comes to mind as a general term for them all what in Greek is called Φυσις and in Latin Natura. Or do you think otherwise?

ALUMNUS

No, I agree. For I too, when I enter upon the path of reasoning, find that this is so.

In Eriugena's rhythmical prose adjacent lines rhyme, and lines either alliterate within themselves or rhyme with succeeding lines or both. The first sentence occupies eight lines, which divide by extreme and mean ratio at 5 and 3, and forty-five words, which divide by extreme and mean ratio at 28 and 17, in the fifth line from the end at the word *intentionem*, the act of 'grasping' by the mind. The central word appears at the centre of the central line, *primam summamque diuisionem esse in ea quae sunt*, suggesting the title by which the book was generally known in the Middle Ages, *De Diuisione Naturae*. The sentence divides by one-ninth and eight-ninths at 40 and 5, at ΦΥCIC, suggesting the etymological basis for Eriugena's own title for his book, *Periphyseon*.

XI. RADBOD PRIOR OF DOL

Letter to King Æthelstan

In the *Gesta Pontificum Anglorum* William of Malmesbury recorded an inscription on a shrine which King Æthelstan had had made for the relics of

Saint Paternus or Padarn.[1] Into his own manuscript of this work, Oxford,
Magdalen College, MS 172, William inserted along the left and lower margins
of folio 93v the text of a letter written from Radbod Prior of Saint Samson's of
Dol to King Æthelstan, about the year 927.[2]

    ... quod has reliquias ex transmarinis partibus meruerit epistolam
    subitiam:

A	**S**umma*e* et indiuidua*e* Trinitátis honóre .
	omniumqu*e* sanctorum praecellentissima intercessióne .
	glorios*o* ac munific*o* régi Adelstáno :
	Samsonis summi pontificis ego Rádbodus praepósitus .
	istius saéculi glória*m* :
	et aeterni beátitúdine*m* .
B1	**B**enignitatis ac sullimitatis uéstrae pi*íssime* ,
	et in omnib*us* huius temporis régib*us* terrénis ,
	famosa laude praécellent*íssime* ,
	réx Adelstáne .
2	optime nóuerit píetas :
3	manente adhuc stabilitate nóstrae regiónis :
	quod pater uéster Edguárdus .
	per litteras se commendauit consortio fraternitatis ,
	Sancti Samsonis summi confessóris :
	ac Ioueniani archiepíscopi sènióris .
	ac consobrini mei ac clericorum eius .
C1a	**U**nde
b	usque hodie indeféssas regi Xpísto .
c	pro eius anima et pro salute uestra
2	fúndimus préces :
3	et die noctuque uidentes super nos magnam
	misericordiam apparere uestram :
4	in psálmis et míssis .
4'	oratiónibusque nóstris .
3'	quasi prouolutus ego et .XII. canónici méi
	genibus uéstris fuissémus :
2'	promittimus Deum clementem oráre
1'	pro uóbis .
D	Et módo relíquias ,
	quas omni terrena substantia uobis scimus ésse

---

1   For Ieuan ap Sulien's reference to Saint Padarn see below pp. 233–42. For a *Vita Sancti Paterni* see
     below pp. 342–6.

2   *BCLL* 830. *Willelmi Malmesburiensis Monachi Gesta Pontificum Anglorum,* ed. N.E.S.A. Hamilton,
     Rolls Series (London 1870) V § 249 pp. 399–400. Boldface capital letters and punctuation marks
     are from my transcription of Magdalen MS 172. I have marked the cursus rhythms.

carióres ,
tránsmitto uóbis :
id est ossa Sáncti Senatóris .
et Sáncti Patérni .
atque Sáncti Scubiliónis .
eiusdem Sancti Patérni magístri :
qui simíliter ùno díe, eademque hora cum
supradícto Patérno ,
migráuit ad Xpístum .
Isti certissíme dùo sáncti ,
cum Sáncto Patérno .
dextra leuaque iacuérunt in sepúlchro :
atque illórum sollèmnitátes sícut et Patérni
.IX. kalendas Octóbris celebrántur .

C'1abc   Igitur réx gloriós*e* .
sanctae exaltátor æcclésia*e* ,
gentilitatis húmiliàtor práua*e* .
regni túi spécu*lum* .
totius bonitátis exémp*lum* .
dissipátor hós*tium* .
páter cleric*órum* .
adiútor egén*tium* .
amator ómnium sanc*tórum* .
inuocátor angel*órum* :

2   deprecamur atque humíliter ìmplorámus .
B'3   qui in exulatu átque captìuitáte .
nostris meritis átque peccátis .
in Frántia còmmorámur :

2   ut non nostri óbliuiscátur
1   uestrae felicissimae largitatis magna mísericórdia .
A'   Et nunc amodo que mihi dignémini còmmendáre .
sine ulla mora potéstis imperáre :

Hec epistola inuenta est in scrinio apud Mideltunense cenobium . quod
idem rex a fundamento fecit . et ibi reliquias . Sancti Samsonis posuit .

... because he deserved these relics from overseas regions I shall insert
this letter.[3]

To King Athelstan, most glorious and munificent by the honouring
of the supreme and indivisible Trinity and by the excellent intercession
of all the saints, I Radbod, prior of the supreme bishop, Samson, wish
glory in this world and blessedness in the eternal world.

---

3   *English Historical Documents I c. 500–1042,* transl. D. Whitelock, 2nd edn (London 1979), pp. 228,
     892. I have added translations of Malmesbury's notes at the beginning and the end.

In your piety, benevolence and greatness, surpassing in renown and praise all earthly kings of this age, you, King Athelstan, will know well that, while our country was still at peace, your father King Edward commended himself by letters to the confraternity of St Samson, supreme confessor, and of Archbishop Jovenian my superior, and my cousin, and his clerics. Hence till now we pour out to Christ the King unwearied prayers for his soul and your welfare, and day and night, seeing your great compassion on us, we promise to pray to the merciful God on your behalf, in psalms and masses and prayers, as if I, with my twelve canons, were prostrate before you. And now I send to you relics, which we know to be dearer to you than all earthly substance, namely the bones of St Senator, and of St Paternus, and of St Scubillion, master of the same Paternus, who likewise departed to Christ on the same day and hour as the aforementioned Paternus. Most certainly these two saints lay with St Paternus in the sepulchre, on his right and left, and their solemnities like his are celebrated on 23 September. Therefore, most glorious king, exalter of Holy Church, subduer of wicked barbarism, mirror of your kingdom, example of all goodness, disperser of enemies, father of clerics, helper of the poor, lover of all the saints, invoker of the angels, we, who for our deserts and sins dwell in France in exile and captivity, pray and humbly implore that you with your blessed liberality and great compassion will not forget us. And now and henceforth you can command without delay whatever you will deign to entrust to me.

This letter was found in a shrine at Milton monastery, which the same king built from its foundation, and there he placed the relics of St Samson.

The letter begins with a Salutation from Radbod to King Æthelstan comprising twenty-six words. The central, thirteenth and fourteenth words, are *regi Adelstano*. In the second half the golden section of 13 falls at 8 and 5. The fifth word from the beginning and the eighth word from the end are *ego Radbodus*. Radbod's title occupies six words, and his concluding wishes for King Æthelstan occupy six words.

The letter ends with a Valediction comprising twelve words. The golden section of 12 falls at 7 and 5. The fifth word from the beginning of the Valediction is *mihi* [*i.e.* Radbod] and the sixth and seventh from the end are *dignemini commendare*, addressed to Æthelstan.

Between the Salutation in A and the Valediction in A' the text of the letter in B-C-C'-B' comprises five sentences of forty-nine, forty-seven, forty, twenty-two, and fifty-one words arranged in a chiasmus of nine parts.

1	Benignitatis ac sullimitatis uestrae piissime
2	nouerit
3	manente adhuc stabilitate nostrae regionis
4 a	pro eius [Edguardi regis] anima et pro salute uestra [rex Adelstane]

b	fundimus preces
b'	promittimus ... orare
a'	pro uobis
5	Et modo reliquias ... transmitto uobis
4'a	rex gloriose [Adelstane]
b	deprecamur atque humiliter imploramus
3'	in exulatu atque captiuitate ... in Frantia
2'	non obliuiscatur
1'	uestre felicissime largitatis magna misericordi

The central words of the entire letter are the first words of the crux of the chiasmus, *Et modo reliquias*. The opening words of the Salutation are *Summae et indiuiduae Trinitatis*. From the first word to the next mention of God, *Deum clementem*, there are 118 words. From the end of the letter, at *misericordia*, backward to the beginning of *Deum clementem* there are 118 words. From the beginning of the Salutation to *Xpisto* inclusive there are eighty-one words. From *Xpisto* to the next mention of Christ, *Xpistum*, there are eighty-one words. The body of the letter begins *Benignitatis ac sullimitatis uestrae piissime*, moves to an internal phrase *magnam misericordiam apparere uestram*, and ends *uestre felicissime largitatis magna misericordia*. From *et*, which follows *piissime*, to *nos*, which precedes *magnam*, there are sixty-five words. From *in*, which follows *uestram*, to *obliuiscatur*, which precedes *uestrae*, there are exactly twice as many, 130 words.

Radbod addresses Æthelstan ten times in second person pronouns: *tuus* once, *uos* three times, and *uester* six times. He refers to himself ten times in first person pronouns, *meus* twice, *ego* four times, and *noster* four times. He names the saints of his church ten times, Jovenianus, Senator, and Scubilio once each, Samson twice, and Paternus five times. From the first mention of *Paterni* five words bring one to *Paterni*, from which the tenth word is *Paterno*. The tenth word from that is *Paterno*. Ten words after that bring one again to *Paterno*, which is the fifth word from the end of the sentence. Radbod uses the word *sanctus* nine times. The seventh word (7×1) is *sanctorum*. The fifty-sixth word after that (7×8) is *sancti*, and the seventy-seventh word (7×11) after that is *sancti*. Following this third use of the word the third word is *sancti*, and the third word after that is *sancti*, and the third word after that is *sancti*. Reckoned another way the fortieth word from the end of the Valediction is *sanctorum*. Forty words before that bring one to *sancto*, and the twentieth word before that is *sancti*. The eighth word from the beginning of the letter is *praecellentissima*. Thirty-two words (8×4) bring one to *praecellentissime*.

Radbod has filled his letter with cursus rhythms. In only three places where they fail one might produce acceptable rhythms by reversing word order. In B3 for *clericorum eius* one might read *eíus clericórum*. In C1 for *salute uestra* one would produce both parallelism and rhythm by reading *pro eius anima et pro uéstra salúte*. In C3 reversal of *apparere uestram* as *uéstram apparére* would produce acceptable rhythm, but Radbod may have sacrificed it there in order to keep his word count between *nos magnam misericordiam apparere uestram* and *uestrae felicissime largitatis magna misericordia*, where *uestram* and *uestrae* are signals.

In the address to Æthelstan in C'1 two phrases may be out of order. By reversing *pater clericorum* and *adiutor egentium* one would produce a chiastic rhyme scheme, three rhymes in *-e*, two in *-lum*, two in *-tium*, and three in *-orum*. With these slight reservations we may trust the transcript of the usually reliable William of Malmesbury and infer that our text is very nearly as Radbod penned it.

IV

POEMS AND PRAYERS

I. 'SAINT SECHNALL'S HYMN'

Audite Omnes Amantes Deum

The composition of extant Latin prose began in Ireland with Patrick in the fifth century. The Irish annals attribute to one of Patrick's contemporaries the 'Hymn of Saint Secundinus' or 'Sechnall', whose death is recorded *s.a.* 447.[1] Even if one disbelieved both obituary and attribution, the presence of the text in the Antiphonary of Bangor on folios 13v–15v, suggests composition before the end of the seventh century, as one of the other poems in the manuscript addresses Crónán, Abbot of Bangor A.D. 680–91, in the present tense. But as quotation of this text by Muirchú and by other Irish Latin poets of the seventh century suggests composition not later than the early seventh century, it must be one of the oldest extant poems composed anywhere in the British Isles. The text presented here is that of the Antiphony of Bangor and the editions of Bieler and Orchard with only the following changes:

line	for	read
	Christus passim	*Xpistus* from MS spelling and analogy with line 81
1	*mereta*	*merita* from Classical Latin spelling, chiastic vowel rhyme within the line, and analogy with line 71
2	*Patrici episcupi*	*Patricii episcopi* from Classical Latin spelling and vowel rhyme with line 4
16	*etheream*	*aetheream*
19	*nauigi*	*nauigii*
19	*praetium*	*pretium*
39	*possedetur*	*possidetur* from Classical Latin spelling and analogy with corrected line 44
42	*candellabro*	*candelabro*
43	*possita*	*posita*

1 BCLL 573. 'The Hymn of St Secundinus', ed. L. Bieler, *Proceedings of the Royal Irish Academy* LV C 6 (1953), pp. 117–27. A. Orchard, '"Audite Omnes Amantes": A Hymn in Patricks Praise', ed. & transl. in D. N. Dumville et al., *Saint Patrick, A.D. 493–1993*, Studies in Celtic History XIII (Woodbridge 1993), pp. 153–73, at 166–73.

44	*Domnius possedet*	*Dominus possidet* from Classical Latin spelling and vowel rhyme with line 43
54	*quiscilia*	*quisquilia*
61	*meretis*	*meritis* from Classical Latin spelling and analogy with lines 1 and 71
67	*uassis*	*uasis*
68	*propinnansque*	*propinansque*
74	*condida*	*condita*
72, 92	*Israel*	*Israhel*
75	*humane*	*humanae*
75	*aessæque*	*essaeque*
76	*salleantur*	*salliantur*
81	*teris*	*terris*
85	*salmosque*	*psalmosque*
90	*intermisione*	*intermissione*

Capital letters and punctuation marks in boldface represent features of the manuscript. Underlinings suggest alliteration and *italics* rhyme. To the left numbers in the first column note stanzas; those in the second column note lines. To the right numbers in the first two columns note words in the octosyllabic and heptasyllabic parts of the line; those in the third and fourth note letters.

YMNUM SANCTI PATRICI MAGISTRI SCOTORUM .

1		**Au**dite omnes amantes Deum sancta merita	3	3	18	16
		uiri in Xpisto beati Patricii episcopi	4	2	17	16
		quomodo bonum ob actum similatur angelis	4	2	19	16
		perfectamque propter uitam aequatur apostolis ,	3	2	24	17
2	5	**Be**ata Xpisti custodit mandata in omnibus	3	3	19	16
		cuius opera refulgent clara inter homines	3	3	19	17
		sanctumque cuius sequuntur exemplum mirificum	3	2	24	17
		unde et in caelis Patrem magnificant Dominum :•	4	2	20	18
3		**Co**nstans in Dei timore et fide inmobilis	4	3	19	15
	10	super quem aedificatur ut Petrus aecclesia	3	3	20	17
		cuiusque apostolatum a Deo sortitus est	2	4	19	15
		in cuius portae aduersum inferni non praeualent	4	3	21	20
4		**Do**minus illum elegit ut doceret barbaras	3	3	18	17
		nationes et piscaret per doctrinae retia	3	3	18	17
	15	et de saeculo credentes traheret ad gratiam	4	3	20	17
		Dominum qui sequerentur sedem ad aetheream ,	3	3	21	16

5   **El**ecta Xpisti talenta   uendit euangelica   3   2   19   16
          quae Hibernas inter gentes   cum usuris exigit   4   3   23   15
          nauigii huius laboris   tum opere pretium   3   3   19   15
    20   cum Xpisto regni caelestis   possessurus gaudium   4   2   23   18

6   **Fi**delis Dei minister   insignisque nuntius   3   2   18   18
          apostolicum exemplum   formamque praebet bonis 2   3   19   21
          qui tam uerbis quam et factis   plebi praedicat Dei   6   3   24   17
          ut quem dictis non conuertit   actu prouocet bono   5   3   24   16

7   25   **Glo**riam habet cum Xpisto   honorem in saeculo   4   3   21   16
          qui ab omnibus ut Dei   ueneratur angelus   5   2   17   16
          quem Deus misit ut Paulum   ad gentes apostolum   5   3   21   17
          ut hominibus ducatum   praeberet regno Dei   3   3   18   17

8   **Hu**milis Dei ob metum   spiritu et corpore   4   3   17   16
    30   super quem bonum ob actum   requiescit Dominus 5   2   21   17
          cuiusque iusta in carne   Xpisti portat stigmata   4   3   20   20
          in cuius sola sustentans   gloriatur in cruce .,   4   3   21   16

9   **Im**piger credentes pascit   dapibus caelestibus   3   2   22   18
          ne qui uidentur cum Xpisto   in uia deficiant   5   3   22   14
    35   quibus erogat ut panes   uerba euangelica   4   2   19   15
          in cuius multiplicantur   ut manna in manibus   3   4   21   16

10   **K**astam qui custodit carnem   ob amorem *Domini*   4   3   23   14
          quam carnem templum parauit   Sanctoque Spiritui 4   2   24   17
          a quo constanter cum mundis   possidetur actibus   5   2   23   17
    40   quam et hostiam placentem   uiuam offert *Domino*   4   3   22   17

11   **L**umenque mundi accensum   ingens euangelicum   3   2   21   17
          in candelabro leuatum   toto fulgens saeculo   3   3   19   18
          ciuitas regis munita   supra montem *posita*   3   3   18   17
          copia in qua est multa   quam Dominus *possidet* .   5   3   18   19

12   45   **Max**imus namque in regno   caelorum uocabitur   4   2   20   17
          qui quod uerbis docet sacris   factis adimplet bonis   5   3   24   19
          bono praecedit exemplo   formamque fidelium   3   2   20   17
          mundoque in corde habet   ad Deum fiduciam ..,   4   3   20   14

13   **N**omen Domini audenter   adnuntiat gentibus   3   2   19   17
    50   quibus lauacri salutis   aeternam dat gratiam   3   3   20   18
          pro quorum orat delictis   ad Deum cotidie   4   3   21   13
          pro quibus ut Deo dignas   immolatque hostias .   5   2   20   17

14		**Om**nem pro diuina lege mundi spernit gloria	4	3	18	19
		qui cuncta ad cuius mensam aestimat quisquilia	5	2	22	18
	55	nec ingruenti mouetur mundi huius fulmine	3	3	19	17
		sed in aduersis laetatur cum pro Xpisto patitur .,	4	4	21	19
15		**Pa**stor bonus et fidelis gregis euangelici	4	2	20	16
		quem Deus Dei elegit custodire populum	4	2	17	16
		suamque pascere plebem diuinis dogmatibus	3	2	20	17
	60	pro qua a Xpisti exemplo suam tradit animam	5	3	20	16
16		**Qu**em pro meritis Saluator prouexit pontificem	4	2	22	18
		ut in caelesti moneret clericos militiae	4	2	19	16
		caelestem quibus annonam erogat cum uestibus	3	3	22	17
		quod in diuinis inpletur sacrisque affatibus ..,	4	2	21	18
17	65	**Re**gis nuntius inuitans credentes ad nuptias	3	3	20	18
		qui ornatur uestimento nuptiali indutus	3	2	20	15
		qui caeleste haurit uinum in uasis caelestibus	4	3	22	18
		propinansque Dei plebem spiritale poculum	3	2	21	16
18		**Sa**crum inuenit thesaurum sacro in uolumine	3	3	22	15
	70	Saluatorisque in carne deitatem peruidet	3	2	20	16
		quem thesaurum emit sanctis perfectisque meritis	4	2	24	19
		Israhel uocatur huius anima uidens Deum :,	3	3	19	15
19		**Te**stis Domini fidelis in lege catholica	3	3	19	15
		cuius uerba sunt diuinis condita oraculis	4	2	21	15
	75	ne humanae putent carnes essaeque a uermibus	4	3	21	17
		sed caelesti salliantur sapore ad uictimam :·	3	3	21	16
20		**Ve**rus cultor et insignis agri euangelici	4	2	21	14
		cuius semina uidentur Xpisti euangelia	3	2	19	15
		quae diuino serit ore in aures prudentium	4	3	18	17
	80	quorumque corda ac mentes Sancto arat Spiritu	4	3	22	17
21		**Xp**istus illum sibi elegit in terris uicarium	4	3	22	16
		qui de gemino captiuos liberat seruitio	4	2	19	15
		plerosque de seruitute quos redemit hominum	3	3	20	18
		innumeros de zaboli absoluit dominio .,	3	2	17	15
22	85	**Ym**nos cum Apocalipsi Psalmosque cantat Dei	3	3	18	19
		quosque ad aedificandum Dei tractat populum	3	3	21	17
		quam legem in Trinitate sacri credit nominis	4	3	20	18
		tribusque personis unam docetque substantiam	3	2	21	19

23		**Z**ona <u>D</u>omini praecinct*us* <u>d</u>iebus ac noctib*us*	3	3	21	16
	90	sine intermissione <u>D</u>eum orat <u>D</u>o*minum*	2	3	17	15
		<u>c</u>uius ingentis laboris <u>p</u>ercepturus prae*mium*	3	2	20	19
		<u>c</u>um <u>a</u>postolis regnabit sanctus super <u>I</u>srahel **..,**	3	3	20	19

The Hymn of Saint Patrick, teacher of the Irish

1   Listen, all who love God, to the holy qualities
       of Bishop Patrick, a sainted man in Christ
       how through good action he is likened to angels
       and by his perfect life he is matched with apostles.

2   5   He keeps Christ's blessed commands in all things,
       and his deeds shine bright amongst men;
       whose marvellous and holy example they follow
       by which they magnify the Lord their Father in heaven.

3   He is constant in the fear of God and firm in faith
   10 on whom, like Peter, the church is built,
       and whose apostolate he has from God,
       and against whom the gates of hell do not prevail.

4   The Lord chose him to teach the heathen nations,
       that he might fish with doctrine's nets
     15 that he might bring believers from worldly things to grace
       and they might follow the Lord to the seat of heaven.

5   He sells the choice talents of Christ's gospel
       and claims payment with interest from the heathen Irish;
       as his price for the toil of the labour of this voyage
   20 he will gain the joy of the heavenly kingdom with Christ.

6   He is a faithful servant of God, a splendid messenger
       who provides an apostolic example and model for the good,
       who preaches to God's people as much in words as deeds,
       that him whom he does not convert with words he incites by good action.

7 25   He has glory with Christ and honour in the world,
       and is adored by all as an angel of God,
       whom God sent, like Paul, as an apostle to the gentiles,
       to offer men guidance to the kingdom of God.

8   He is humble in mind and body through fear of God,
30   on whom because of his good deeds the Lord rests,
         and he carries the stigmata of Christ on his just flesh,
         he glories in the Cross, which alone sustains him.

9   Briskly he feeds the faithful with heaven's feast,
         lest those who are seen with Christ should falter on the way;
35   he offers the words of the gospel like loaves of bread,
         which are multiplied like manna in his hands.

10   He keeps his body chaste for love of the Lord,
         the flesh which he has prepared as a temple for the Holy Spirit,
         by which it is always possessed in pure actions,
40   the flesh which he offers as a living sacrifice, pleasing to the Lord.

11   Like a great evangelical light burning on the earth,
         raised high on a candelabrum, shining for the whole world;
         the fortified citadel of the King placed on a mountain-top,
         in which there is the great abundance which the Lord possesses.

12   45 For he will be called the greatest in the kingdom of heaven,
         who fulfils in good deeds what he teaches in sacred words,
         who provides a model in good example for the faithful
         and has confidence towards God in his pure heart.

13   Boldly he announces the Lord's name to the heathens,
50   to whom he grants eternal grace in the baths of salvation,
         for whose sins he prays daily to God,
         for whom he offers sacrifices worthy of God.

14   For God's law he despises all the glory of the world,
         at whose table he reckons all else worthless,
55   nor is he moved by the violent lightning of the world,
         but rejoices in adversity, since he suffers for Christ.

15   He is a good shepherd, faithful to the gospel flock,
         whom God has chosen to guard God's people,
         and to feed His people with sacred teaching,
60   for whom, after Christ's example, he lays down his life.

16   For his qualities the Saviour has made him a bishop,
         to advise the clerics in their heavenly service,
         to whom he dispenses food and clothing,
         which he supplements with holy and sacred sayings.

17 65   He is the King's messenger inviting the faithful to the wedding-feast,
          who is adorned and clothed in wedding garb,
          who drinks heavenly wine in heavenly vessels,
          and gives God's people a drink from the spiritual cup.

18   He finds a sacred treasure-store in the sacred volume,
    70   he sees the divinity of the Saviour in the flesh,
          a treasure-store he purchases with holy and perfect qualities.
          His soul is called Israel: 'seeing God'.

19   He is a faithful witness of the Lord in the catholic law,
          whose words are seasoned with the prophecies of heaven,
    75   that human flesh may not rot, eaten by worms,
          but be salted for sacrifice with the savour of heaven.

20   He is a true and splendid tiller of the gospel field,
          whose seeds seem to be Christ's gospels,
          which he sows with heavenly mouth in the ears of the wise,
    80   and ploughs their hearts and minds with the Holy Spirit.

21   Christ chose him to be His vicar on earth,
          who frees captives from a twin servitude:
          many he frees from bondage to men,
          and countless sets free from the Devil's domain.

22 85   He sings hymns and the psalms of God, together with the Apocalypse,
          which he recites to edify the people of God.
          He believes as a law in the name of the Trinity,
          and teaches one substance in three persons.

23   Girt with the girdle of the Lord, night and day,
    90   he prays to the Lord God without ceasing;
          he will receive his reward for that huge labour:
          holy, he will reign with the apostles over Israel.

This poem has endured harsh censure from historians and literary critics who
wish it were something other than what it is. Recently, however, Dr Andy
Orchard has published a text and translation with sources and analogues in an
appendix to a sensitive study of its literary features. He shows convincingly that
the author thoroughly understood the works of Patrick, having assimilated the
densely allusive manner in which they communicate meanings implied by the
unquoted context of their Biblical references. He shows also that the poem was
known and alluded to by several seventh–century Irish Latin authors.

Many of the most accomplished features of this poem have entirely escaped the notice of modern scholars. First the prosody. Editors, recognizing the abecedarian structure of the hymn, have arranged the text variously, in stanzas of eight lines with alternate verses of eight and seven syllables, or in stanzas of four lines of fifteen syllables with a caesura after the eighth. The latter is correct. There should be ninety-two lines of pentadecasyllabic verse in twenty-three four-lined stanzas, so arranged that the first letters of the stanzas follow the order of the roman alphabet from *A* to *Z*. The clearest Biblical model for abecedarian verses is the Book of Lamentations in four parts, in which Jeremiah made the first letters of the stanzas of parts I, II, and IIII follow the order of the Hebrew alphabet; in part III the first letters of triplets do the same. This was known to Insular Latin writers at least from the time of Gildas, who alluded in *De Excidio Britanniae* 1.4 to the voice of *Hieremiae ruinam ciuitatis suae quadruplici plangentis alphabeto*. Arrangement in four-lined stanzas is an essential element of the art of the poem, which is divided clearly into four parts, as we shall see below.

There is only one example of elision, in *sibi elegit* 81. There are two examples of synizesis, in *Patricii* 2 and *nauigii* 19. There are many examples of hiatus, as in *Patricii episcopi* 2, *mandata in* 5, *clara inter* 6. All these features recur frequently in Irish Latin syllabic verse.

In the octosyllabic parts of the verse the endings are invariable, all ninety-two lines exhibiting at the caesura paroxytone cadences, in which the penultimate syllable bears the stress. In the heptasyllabic parts of the verse the endings are variable, eighty-three lines exhibiting at the end proparoxytone cadences, in which the antepenultimate syllable bears the stress. The remaining nine lines exhibit neither carelessness nor licence. Four of them end /×/× (*praébet bónis* 22, *régno Déi* 28, *uídens Déum* 72, *cántat Déi* 85) and five of them end /××/× (*praédicat Déi* 23, *próuocet bóno* 24, *gloriátur in crúce* 32, *ádimplet bónis* 46, *nuptiáli indútus* 66). We shall consider below some structural reasons for this.

The poet uses alliteration, sometimes within the first part of the line, as *audite omnes amantes* 1a, sometimes within the last part, as *aequatur apostolis* 4b, sometimes within the whole line, as *actum ... angelis* 3a-b, sometimes in adjacent lines, as *angelis* 3b and *apostolis* 4b, sometimes in alternate lines, as *sancta* 1b and *similatur* 3b, sometimes chiastically, abba, as *constans in Dei timore et fide inmobilis* 9 and *in cuius portae aduersum inferni non praeualent* 12 around *super quem aedificatur ut Petrus aecclesia* and *cuiusque apostolatum a Deo sortitus est* 10–1. The poet uses rhymes of a single syllable and a single letter, as *beati* 2a and *episcopi* 2b or *apocalipsi* 85a and *Dei* 85b, or two letters, as *gratiam* 15b and *aetheream* 16b or *aedificandum* 86a and *populum* 86b, or two syllables and three letters, as *pretium* 19b and *gaudium* 20b, or four letters, as *caelestibus* 33b and *manibus* 36b, or five letters, as *dogmatibus* 63b and *affatibus* 64b. The rhymes connect sometimes the caesura and the end of a line, as *beati* and *episcopi* 2a-b or *Xpisto* and *saeculo* 25a-b, or the caesuras of adjacent lines, as *actum* 3a and *uitam* 4a or *custodit* 5a and *refulgent* 6a, or the ends of adjacent lines, as *angelis* 3b and *apostolis* 4b, or the caesura of one line with the end of the following line, as *carne* 31a and *cruce* 32b or *pascit* 33a and *deficiant* 34b, or the end of one line with the caesura of the following line, as *apostolum* 27b and *ducatum* 28a or *gloriam* 53b and *mensam* 54a. Sometimes there is vowel rhyme and consonant rhyme before the end of the line, as *omnibus* 5b and *homines* 6b or *mirificum* 7b and *Dominum* 8b, or chiastic vowel rhyme at the beginning and the end of a line, as *audite ... merita* 1a-b. Although these features recur throughout the poem they do not appear to be systematically or structurally disposed.

Each of the four parts of the hymn exhibits a chiastic structure.

Part I, stanzas 1–6, lines 1–24

1 a	1	Deum
b	3	bonum ob actum
2 a	3	angeli*s*
b	4	apostlis
3	5	beata Xpisti custodit mandat*a*
4	8	unde et in caelis Patrem magnificant Dominu*m*
5	11	a Deo sortitus es*t*
5'	13	Dominus illum elegi*t*
4'	16	Dominum qui sequerentur sedem ad aethere*am*
3'	17	electa Xpisti talenta uendit euangelic*a*
2'a	21	nuntiu*s*
b	22	apostolicum
1'a	23	Dei
b	24	actu bono

The etymological meaning of *angelus* 2a is the same as *nuntius* 2'a. One notes how often words and phrases which appear at the caesuras and the ends of lines exhibit the same terminal sound as their chiastic pairs (marked here by *italics*), even though they are separated by several intervening lines and stanzas.

Part II, stanzas 6–12, lines 21–48

1	21	fidelis
2	22	exemplum formamque
3	22	bonis
4	23	uerbis ... et *factis*
5	25	gloriam habet cum Xpisto honorem in saeculo
6a	29	spiritu
b	30	super quem
c	30	bonum ob actum
7	30	Dominus
8	31	in carne
9a	31	Xpisti portat stigmata
b	32	in cuius
9'a	34	cum Xpisto in uia deficiant

b	36	<u>in cuius</u>
8'	37	carnem
7'	37	Domini
6'a	38	Spiritui
b	39	a quo
c	39	cum mundis actibus
5'	45	maximus namque in regno caelorum uocabitur
4'	46	uerbis … *sacris* factis
3'	46	bono
2'	47	exemplo formamque
1'	47	fidelium

Part III, stanzas 12–18, lines 45–72

1a	46	sacris
b	48	mundoque in corde … Deum
2	49	nomen Domini audenter adnuntiat gentibus
3	52	pro quibus ut Deo dignas immolatque hostias
4	53	omnem pro diuina lege mundi spernit gloriam
5	56	pro Xpisto patitur
6	57	pastor
7	57	gregis euangelici
8	58	Deus
8'	58	Dei
7'	58	populum
6'	59	pascere
5'	60	pro qua a Xpisti exemplo suam tradit animam
4'	61	quem pro meritis Saluator prouexit pontificem
3'	63	caelestem quibus annonam erogat cum uestibus
2'	65	Regis nuntius inuitans credentes ad nuptias
1'a	69	sacrum
b	72	uidens Deum

Here we see an aspect of our poet's ability to manipulate texts from his sources into his own structures. He has connected parts 1b and 1'b by allusion to the text of Matthew V 8, *beati mundo corde quoniam ipsi Deo uidebunt.*[2]

Part IIII, stanzas 18–23, lines 69–92

1a	71	sanctis
b	72	Israhel
2	72	uidens

2   Orchard ed., p. 159.

3	72	Deum
4	73	Domini
5	73	lege
6	77	cultor
7	77	agri
8	78	Xpisti
9	79	quae diuino serit ore in aures prudentium
9'	80	quorumque corda ac mentes Sancto arat Spiritu
8'	81	Xpisto
7'	81	terris
6'	81	uicarium
5'	87	legem
4'	89	Domini
3'	90	Deum
2'	90	orat
1'a	92	sanctus
b	92	Israhel

Now let us see how our poet has connected parts I and II in a larger chiasmus.

1	1	Deum
2	3	bonum ob actum
3a	5	custodit
b	6	refulgent
c	8	Dominum
4	14	piscaret
5	15	credentes
6a	17	euangelica
b	18	quae
c	18	inter gentes
d	18	exigit
7a	20	cum Xpisto
b	20	regni caelestis
8	20	possessurus
9	20	gaudium
10	22	bonis
11	23	qui tam uerbis quam et factis plebi praedicat Dei
11'	24	ut quem dictis non conuertit actu prouocet

10'	24				bono	
9'	25				gloriam	
8'	25				habet	
7'a	25				cum Xpisto	
b	25					in saeculo
6'a	26			angelus		
b	27			quem		
c	27				ad gentes	
d	28					praeberet
5'	33			credentes		
4'	35–6			panes ... manna		
3'a	37		custodit			
b	42		fulgens			
c	44			Dominus		
2'	46		factis ... bonis			
1'	48	Deum				

Here again we see our poet's ability to coordinate texts from his sources. He has combined allusions to the texts of Matthew XIV 17, *Non habemus hic nisi quinque panes et duos pisces*, and Matthew XV 34, *'Quot panes habetis'* at illi dixerunt *'Septem et paucos pisciculos'*, and Matthew V 19 as quoted by Patrick in *Confessio* 40, *oportet quidem bene et diligenter piscare sicut Dominus praemonet et docet dicens 'Venite post me et faciam uos fieri piscatores hominum'*, in parts 4 and 4'.

Now let us see how our poet has connected parts III and IIII in a larger chiasmus.

1 a	48	Deum
b	49	Domini
a'	51	Deum
2	52	Deo dignas immolatque hostias
3 a	56	pro Xpisto
b	58	quem Deus Dei elegit custodire populum
4	63	caelestem ... annonam
5	64	quod in diuinis inpletur sacrisque affatibus
6	69	thesaurum
7	70	Saluatoris in carne deitatem peruidet
6'	71	thesaurum
5'	74	cuius uerba sunt diuinis condita oraculis
4'	76	caelesti ... sapore
3'a	81	Xpistus
b	81	illum sibi elegit in terris uicarium
2'	85	Ymnos cum Apocalipsi Psalmosque cantat Dei
1'a	89	Domini

b   90   Deum
a' 90   Dominum

Finally let us see how our poet has connected parts I and II to parts III and IIII in a grand chiasmus.

1 a	1	Deum
b	4	apostolis
2	10	aedificatur … aecclesia
3	12	in cuius portae aduersum inferni non praeualent
4	13	Dominus illum elegit
5	17	Xpisti
6	17	euangelica
7	21	nuntius
8 a	33	pascit
b	33	dapibus caelestibus
9	41	lumenque mundi accensum ingens euangelicum
10	45–8	maximus namque in regno caelorum uocabitur qui quod uerbis docet sacris factis adimplet bonis bono praecedit exemplo formamque fidelium mundoque in corde habet ad Deum fiduciam
9'	55	nec ingruenti mouetur mundi huius fulmine
8'a	59	pascere
b	63	caelestem … annonam
7'	65	nuntius
6'	77	euangelici
5'	78	Xpisti
4'	81	Xpistus illum sibi elegit
3'	84	innumeros de zaboli absoluit dominio
2'	86	ad aedificandum Dei … populum
1'a	90	Deum
b	92	apostolis

The poet's apparent metrical irregularities may now be seen as one feature among several which help to articulate his structure. Of the nine lines which do not end in proparoxytone cadences 46 is central among 92 lines, exactly at the crux of the grand chiasmus. Lines 22–4 are central among the first 46 lines, exactly at the crux of the large chiasmus of parts I and II. Line 66 stands at the centre of the sixth stanza from the centre, and line 72 stands at the end of the sixth stanza from the end. The first 46 lines divide by extreme and mean ratio at 28 and 18. Two of the remaining lines are 28 and 72, the former the 28th line from the beginning and the latter the 28th line from the beginning of the central stanza. Note how much of the diction from lines 45–8 is repeated or echoed at lines 21–4 and 69–72.

These apparently irregular lines recur at multiples of 7. There are no irregular cadences in the first twenty-one lines (7 × 3). Four occur in lines 22–8 (7 × 1). Between 24 and 32 there are seven lines. After 32 the fourteenth line (7 × 2) is 46. From 46 to 66 inclusive there are twenty-one lines (7 × 3). From 66 to 72 inclusive there are seven lines. From 72 to 85 inclusive there are seven lines, after which there are seven lines to the end of the poem.

One might suppose that a poet who arranged his stanzas in alphabetical order, articulated the structure of his verse with varied cadences, and arranged his words in three series of chiastic patterns — first in the four quarters of the poem, whose beginnings and endings he made to overlap, second in the two halves of the poem, and third in the complete work — had done enough to guarantee the authenticity and integrity of his composition. But our poet took further pains. He counted not only his stanzas and lines and syllables and varied cadences, but also his words. In the first chiastic pattern, stanzas 1–6, lines 1–24, there are 149 words, of which the central are *Dominus illum elegit* in a central line 13 of 24, exactly at the end of the crux of the chiasmus. In the second chiastic pattern, stanzas 6–12, lines 21–48, there are 187 words, of which the central are *cum Xpisto in uia deficiant* in a central line 34, fourteenth of twenty-eight, exactly at the crux of the chiasmus. In the third chiastic pattern, stanzas 12–18, lines 45–72, there are 174 words, of which the central are *Deus Dei* in a central line 58, fourteenth of twenty-eight, exactly at the crux of the chiasmus. In the fourth chiasmus, stanzas 18–23, lines 69–92, there are 143 words, of which the central are *Sancto arat Spiritu* in a central line 80, twelfth of twenty-four, exactly at the end of the crux of the chiasmus.

There is a further guarantee of the poet's original text, by which he allows us to recover with fair certainty his very orthography: he counted the letters of his poem. In the first chiastic pattern there are 888 letters, a number chosen because that is the value in Greek notation of the letters of the name ΙΗΣΟΥΣ, 10+8+200+70+400+200=888. The central letters, 444th from beginning and end, are in the first word of *Dominus illum elegit* at the crux of the chiasmus. In the second chiastic pattern there are 1050 letters, of which the 525th follows *cum Xpisto in uia deficiant*. In the third chiastic pattern there are 1045 letters, which divide by sesquioctave ratio (9:8) at 492 and 553. The 492nd letter is in the middle of *Deus* at the crux of the chiasmus. In the fourth chiastic pattern there are 880 letters, of which the 438th is the last of *Sancto arat Spiritu*.

As we have seen above, in the Salutation and *Captatio beneuolentiae* of his first letter to Gregory the Great Columban appropriated in his first sentence the name of the Apostle Peter, *ego Bar Iona*, then immediately in the second sentence arrogated the authority of the Apostle Paul by quoting from Galatians I 3 *Gratia tibi et pax a Deo Patre nostro et Domino nostro Iesu Xpisto*, and immediately in the third sentence adduced as his authority for interrogating the pope the Song of Moses in Deuteronomy XXXII, *iuxta illud canticum 'Interroga patrem tuum et annuntiabit tibi, maiores tuos et dicent tibi'.*[3] Here in reverse order to Columban's but in 'correct' chronological order our poet quotes first from the Old Testament the beginning of the Song of Moses in line 1 *Audite*, and names the New Testament authorities, the Apostle Peter in line 10, *super quem aedificatur ut Petrus aecclesia cuiusque apostolatum a Deo sortitus*, and the Apostle Paul in line 27, *quem Deus misit ut Paulum ad gentes apostolum.* The number of lines, 27, divides by extreme and mean ratio at 17 and 10, exactly the lines in which the apostles are named, the seventeenth and the tenth after that. The number of words from the beginning to *apostolum* is 171, which divides by extreme and mean ratio at 106 and 65. The sixty-fifth word is *sortitus*.

Let us suppose that our poet had noticed in and imitated from Christian hymns of late Antiquity alliteration and rhyme, both recurrent but neither used structurally or systematically. Let us suppose that his 'correct' chronological ordering of references to Moses, Peter, and Paul is the model, which Columban reversed for rhetorical effect, and that Columban's adaptation of that feature of this hymn fixes a *terminus ante quem* of A.D. 600. Might the 577 words of the hymn suggest the year of its composition, within a generation of the foundation of Bangor?[4]

II. *Respice In Me, Domine*

Another Irish Latin hymn from the Antiphonary of Bangor folio 13r–v is *Spiritus Diuinae Lucis Gloriae* or *Respice in me, Domine.*[1]

YMNUM AD MATUTINAM IN DOMINICA . ~~.

1		Spiritus diuinae lucis gloriae .	4	11	27
		Respice in me Domine ..,	4	8	17
2		Deus ueritatis	2	6	13
		Domine Deus Sabaoth .	3	8	17
	5	Deus . Israhel .	2	5	11
		Respice in me Domine ..,	4	8	17

3   *Sancti Columbani Opera*, ed. & transl. G. S. M. Walker, *Scriptores Latini Hiberniae* II (Dublin 1970) pp. 1–13. See above pp. 84–8.

4   For other examples of comparable forms of dating texts see D.R. Howlett, 'The Provenance, Date, and Structure of *De Abbatibus*', *Archaeologia Aeliana* 5th ser. III (1975), pp. 121–30, 'The Structure of the *Ecbasis Captivi*', *Studia Neophilologica* XLVII (1975), pp. 3–6. See below pp. 189 and 193.

1   BCLL 577.

3		Lumen de Lumine	3	6	13
		referemus Filium Patris	3	9	21
		Sanctumque Spiritum in una substantia . . .	5	13	33
	10	Respice in me Domine ..,	4	8	17
4		UNIgenitus et Primogenitus	3	11	24
		a te obtinemus	3	6	12
		redemptionem nostram .,	2	7	19
		Respice in me Domine ..,	4	8	17
5	15	Natus es Sancto Spiritu	4	8	20
		ex Maria Virgine	3	7	14
		in id ipsum in adoptionem	5	10	21
		filiorum qui tibi	3	7	15
		procreati ex fonte uiuunt .,	4	9	22
	20	Respice in me Domine ..,	4	8	17
6		Heredes et coheredes	3	8	18
		Xpisti tui in quo	4	6	14
		Et per quem cuncta creasti	5	8	22
		Quia in praedestinatione	3	10	22
	25	a saeculis nobis est	4	7	17
		Deus Ihesus qui nunc cepit	5	8	22
		Respice in me Domine ..,	4	8	17
7		UNIgenito ex mortuis .	3	9	18
		Deo obtinens corpus	3	7	17
	30	Claritatem Dei manens	3	8	19
		In saecula saeculorum	3	8	19
		Rex aeternorum :·	2	5	13
		Respice in me Domine ..,	4	8	17
8		Quia nunc cepit qui semper fuit	6	10	27
	35	Naturæ tuae Filius	3	8	17
		Diuinae lucis gloriæ tuae	4	10	23
		Qui est forma et plenitudo	5	9	22
		Diuinitatis tuae frequens .	3	9	23
		Respice in me Domine ..,	4	8	17
9	40	Persona Unigeniti	2	8	16
		Et Primogeniti	2	6	13
		Qui est totus a toto	5	7	16
		Diximus Lux de Lumine .,	4	8	18
		Respice in me Domine ..,	4	8	17
10	45	ET Deum uerum a Deo	5	8	15
		uero sese confitemur .	3	8	18
		tribus personis	2	5	14
		IN una substantia .,	3	7	15
	49	Respice in me Domine .	4	8	17

A Hymn for Matins on Sunday

1   Spirit of the light of divine glory,
           look round on me, Lord.

2   God of truth,
        Lord God of hosts,
    5   God of Israel,
           look round on me, Lord.

3   Radiance from radiance,
        we shall bring to mind the Son of the Father
        and Holy Spirit in one substance,
    10   look round on me, Lord.

4   Only-begotten and First-begotten,
        from You we obtain
        our redemption,
           look round on me, Lord.

5 15   You were born of the Holy Spirit
        from the Virgin Mary
        for the adoption for His very Self
        of sons who for You
        brought into being live from the font [of baptism],
    20   look round on me, Lord.

6   Heirs and fellow heirs
        of Your Christ, in Whom
        and through Whom You created all things,
        as in a predestination
    25   from the ages He is for us
        the God Jesus, Who has now begun,
           look round on me, Lord,

7 29   obtaining a body for God
    28   the Only-begotten from among the dead,
    30   remaining the brightness of God,
        for ages of eternal ages
        King,
           look round on me, Lord,

8   as He has now begun Who always was
    35   the Son of Your nature
        of the light of Your divine glory,
        Who is the form and constant fullness
        of Your divinity,
           look round on me, Lord,

9 40   the person of the Unbegotten
        and First-begotten,
        Who is whole from the whole,

> Light, we say, from Radiance,
>> look round on me, Lord,
10 45   and true God from true God
>> we confess Himself
>> in three persons
>> in one substance,
49   look round on me, Lord.

One notes first that the refrain *Respice in me Domine* divides this hymn into ten sections and that both the refrain and other words and phrases have been arranged chiastically.

A	Respice in me Domine
B	Deus ueritatis Domine Deus Sabaoth Deus Israhel
C	Respice in me Domine
D	Lumen de Lumine
E	referemus
F	Respice in me Domine. Unigenitus et Primogenitus
G	filiorum
H	Respice in me Domine
I	a saeculis
J	Deus Ihesus
K	Respice in me Domine. Unigenito ex mortuis
J'	Deo obtinens corpus claritatem Dei manens
I'	In saecula saeculorum
H'	Respice in me Domine
G'	Filius
F'	Respice in me Domine. Persona Unigeniti et Primogeniti
E'	diximus
D'	Lux de Lumine
C'	Respice in me Domine
B'	Et Deum uerum a Deo uero
A'	Respice in me Domine.

Words and phrases not included in this chiastic outline recur at mathematically fixed intervals. Leaving the refrain out of consideration for a moment, one notes that the first word of the hymn is *Spiritus* 1, the eighteenth and nineteenth words are *Sanctumque Spiritum*, and the thirty-third and thirty-fourth words are *Sancto Spiritu* 15. In the Fibonacci series 1–1–2–3–5–8–13–21–34 the number 34 divides by extreme and mean ratio at 21 and 13. Between *Sanctumque Spiritum* and *Sancto Spiritu* there are thirteen words. From *Spiritus diuinae lucis gloriae* 1 to *Diuinae lucis gloriae tuae* 35 inclusive there are exactly one hundred words, which divide by extreme and mean ratio at 62 and 38, at *Natus es Sancto Spiritu ex Maria Virgine in | id ipsum in adoptionem filiorum.*

The 134 words of the hymn divide by sesquioctave ratio (9:8) at 71 and 63, at *qui | nunc cepit 25.* The hymn divides by one-ninth and eight-ninths at 15 and 119. Between *nunc cepit 25* and *nunc cepit 33* there are fifteen words. The fifteenth word from the beginning is the first of line 8 *Referemus Filium Patris Sanctumque Spiritum in una substantia.* The chiastic pair to *referemus* is *diximus* 42, from which inclusive the fifteenth word is the first of *in una substantia 47.*

In the sections marked by the refrain the numbers of words are disposed mathematically. There are four words in the first section, seven in the second, eleven in the third, eight in the fourth, and nineteen in the fifth, together forty-nine, which divide by extreme and mean ratio at 30 and 19. The number of words in the first and second sections, 4+7, are the golden section of 11, the number of words in the third section, which, added to the number of words in the fourth section, equal 30, the golden section of the first forty-nine words. Note further that the fifth section ends at the nineteenth of forty-nine lines. The twenty-four words of the sixth section divide by symmetry within the section at 12 and 12. The thirteen words of the ninth section and the thirteen words of the tenth section divide by symmetry between adjacent sections. The fourteen words of the seventh section and the twenty-one words of the eighth section relate to each other by sesquialter ratio (3:2).

III. COLUMBAN OF BANGOR

Mundus Iste Transibit

In the second volume of the distinguished series *Scriptores Latini Hiberniae* Bieler and Walker ascribed to Columban of Bangor, Luxeuil, and Bobbio the *Carmen de Mundi Transitu, Versus Columbani ad Hunaldum, Versus Sancti Columbani ad Sethum, Carmen Navale,* and the adonic verses *Columbanus Fidolio Fratri Suo* with six concluding dactylic hexameters.[1] After critical consideration of the poems by other scholars[2] the standard bibliography of Latin literature by Celtic authors stripped all of them from the canon of Columban's writings.[3] But a case has been made for attributing the *Carmen De Mundi Transitu* to Columban again.[4]

1　　Sancti Columbani Opera, ed. & transl. G.S.M. Walker with indices by L. Bieler, *Scriptores Latini Hiberniae* II (Dublin 1970), pp. 182–97.

2　　J.W. Smit, *Studies on the Language and Style of Columba the Younger (Columbanus)* (Amsterdam 1971), pp. 209–53. M. Lapidge, 'The Authorship of the Adonic Verses "Ad Fidolium" Attributed to Columbanus', *Studi Medievali,* 3rd series, XVIII (1977), pp. 249–314.

3　　BCLL nos. 639–42 pp. 165–8, nos. 650–6 pp. 171–2, no. 819 p. 220.

4　　BCLL 819. D. Schaller, 'Die Siebensilberstrophen "de mundi transitu"—eine Dichtung Columbans?' in H. Löwe ed., *Die Iren und Europa im früheren Mittelalter I* (Stuttgart 1982), pp. 468–83, an attribution accepted by Lapidge, 'A New Hiberno-Latin Hymn on St Martin', *Celtica* XXI (1990), pp. 240–51, at 248.

The following text of *Mundus Iste Transibit* differs from Walker's in six places. For Walker's line 2 *cottidie decrescit* read *et cottidie transit*, with *et* supplied from the manuscript and *transit* (for the manuscript reading *crescit*) alliterating with *transibit* 1 and rhyming with *remansit* 4. For *Christo* 13 read *Xpisto*, and for *Christi* 57 read *Xpisti*. For *vagiat* 96 restore the manuscript reading, the correct Late Latin *uagitat* to rhyme with *habitat* 94. For the blank line 106 read *Melos decantata est*, *melos* sharing alliteration and consonant rhyme with *male* 107 and *decantata est* rhyming with *audita est* 108. For Walker's lines 111–2 *Quam nec mors nec meroris / Metus consumpturus est* consider the manuscript reading *quam nec mortis nec meroris metu consumptura est* and read *Quam mortis nec meroris / Meta consumptura est*,[5] deleting *metri causa* the first *nec*, and restoring the vowel rhyme, consonant rhyme, and end rhyme of *ueraque futura est* 110 with *meta consumptura est* 112 and alliteration of *meroris* 111 with *meta* 112. In the text underlinings mark alliteration and *italics* mark rhyme. To the left of the text the first column shows numbers of the stanzas, the second numbers of the lines, the third the rhyme schemes. To the right of the text the first column shows numbers of words, the second numbers of syllables, the third numbers of letters.

I		a	Mundus *iste* <u>tran</u>si*bit*	3	7	19
		b	*Et* cottidie <u>transit</u>	3	7	17
		a	<u>N</u>emo <u>uiu</u>ens *manebit*	3	7	17
		b	<u>N</u>ullus <u>uiuu</u>s rem*ansit*	3	7	19
2	5	x	To*tum* hum*anum* genus	3	7	17
		a	<u>O</u>rtu <u>u</u>titu*r* pari	3	7	14
		x	<u>E</u>t de sim*íli* ui*ta*	4	7	14
		a	Fine <u>c</u>adi*t* aequa*li*	3	7	16
3		x	Diff*erentibus* <u>u</u>itam	2	7	18
	10	a	<u>M</u>o*rs* incer*tà* <u>s</u>ub*ripit*	3	7	19
		x	Omne*s* <u>s</u>uper*bos* <u>u</u>agos	3	7	18
		a	<u>M</u>e*ror* <u>m</u>or*tis* cor*ripit*	3	7	19
4		a	<u>Q</u>uod *pro* <u>X</u>pisto largi*ri*	4	7	20
		a	Nol*unt* <u>o</u>mnes *auari*	3	7	16
	15	x	<u>I</u>nportune <u>a</u>mittunt	2	7	17
		a	Post *se* <u>c</u>olli*gunt* al*ii*	4	7	19
5		x	Paruum ipsi <u>u</u>í*uentes*	3	7	18
		a	<u>D</u>eo <u>d</u>are <u>u</u>í*x* au*dent*	4	7	16
		a	Mor*ti* cuncta relinquu*nt*	3	7	21
	20	a	Nih*íl* <u>de</u> ips*is* hab*ent*	4	7	18

5   Smit, p. 214, Schaller, p. 469 n. 8.

6		a	Cottidie decrescit	2	7	17
		b	Vita praesens quam amant	4	7	21
		a	Indeficiens manebit	2	7	18
		b	Sibi poena quam parant	4	7	19
7	25	x	Lubricum quod labitur	3	7	19
		a	Conantur colligere	2	7	17
		x	Et hoc quod se seducit	5	7	18
		a	Minus timent credere	3	7	18
8		x	Dilexerunt tenebras	2	7	18
	30	a	Tetras magis quam lucem	4	7	20
		x	Imitari contemnunt	2	7	17
		a	Vitae Dominum ducem	3	7	17
9		x	Velut in somnis regnant	4	7	20
		a	Una hora laetantur	3	7	16
	35	x	Sed aeterna tormenta	3	7	18
		a	Adhuc illis parantur	3	7	18
10		x	Caeci nequaquam uident	3	7	20
		a.	Quid post obitum restat	4	7	20
		x	Peccatoribus impiis	2	7	18
	40	a	Quod impietas praestat	3	7	20
11		x	Cogitare conuenit	2	7	16
		a	Te haec cuncta amice	4	7	17
		a	Absit tibi amare	3	7	14
		a	huius formulam uitae	3	7	18
12	45	x	Omnis en caro foenum	4	7	17
		a	Flagrans licet florida	3	7	20
		x	Sicque quasi flos foeni	4	7	20
		a	Omnis eius est gloria	4	7	18
13		a	Orto sole arescit	3	7	15
	50	a	Foenum et flos deperit	4	7	19
		x	Sic est omnis iuuentus	4	7	19
		a	Virtus cum defecerit	3	7	18
14		x	Pulchritudo hominum	2	7	18
		a	Senescens delabitur	2	7	18
	55	x	Omnis decor pristinus	3	7	19
		a	Cum dolore raditur	3	7	16

15		x	Vultus Xpisti radius	3	7	18
		a	Prae cunctis amabilis	3	7	19
		x	Magis diligendus est	3	7	18
	60	a	Quam flos carnis fragilis	4	7	22
16		x	Caueto filiole	2	7	13
		a	Feminarum species	2	7	16
		x	Per quas mors ingreditur	4	7	21
		a	Non parua pernicies	3	7	17
17	65	x	Plerique perpessi sunt	3	7	20
		a	Poenarum incendia	2	7	16
		x	Voluntatis lubricae	2	7	18
		a	Nolentes dispendia	2	7	17
18		a	Poculum impiissimae	2	7	18
	70	b	Noli umquam bibere	3	7	16
		a	Inde multos plerumque	3	7	19
		b	Vides laetos ridere	3	7	17
19		a	Nam quoscumque uideris	3	7	20
		b	Ridere inaniter	2	7	14
	75	a	Scito in nouissimis	3	7	17
		b	Quod flebunt amariter	3	7	19
20		x	Conspice carissime	2	7	17
		a	Sic esse libidinem	3	7	16
		x	Ut morsum mortiferum	3	7	18
	80	a	Quod uincit dulcedinem	3	7	20
21		a	Noli pronus pergere	3	7	17
		b	Per uiam mortalium	3	7	16
		a	Qua multis euenisse	3	7	17
		b	Conspicis naufragium	2	7	19
22	85	a	Perge inter laqueos	3	7	17
		b	Cum suspensis pedibus	3	7	19
		a	Per quos captos ceteros	4	7	20
		b	Incautos conperimus	2	7	18
23		x	De terrenis eleua	3	7	15
	90	a	Tui cordis oculos	3	7	15
		x	Ama amantissimos	2	7	15
		a	Angelorum populos	2	7	16

24		x	Beata familia	2	7	12
		a	Quae in altis habitat	4	7	18
	95	a	Ubi senex non gemat	4	7	16
		a	Neque infans uagitat	3	7	18
25		x	Ubi laudis Domini	3	7	15
		a	Nulla uox retinetur	3	7 . 17
		a	Ubi non esuritur	3	7	14
	100	a	Ubi numquam sititur	3	7	17
26		x	Ubi cibo superno	3	7	14
		a	Plebs caelestis pascitur	3	7	22
		a	Ubi nemo moritur	3	7	14
		a	Quia nemo nascitur	3	7	16
27	105	x	Ubi aula regia	3	7	12
		a	Melos decantata est	3	7	17
		x	In qua male resonans	4	7	17
		a	Nulla uox audita est	4	7	17
28		a	Ubi uita uiridis	3	7	14
	110	b	Veraque futura est	3	7	16
		a	Quam mortis nec meroris	4	7	20
		b	Meta consumptura est	3	7	18
29		x	Laeti leto transacto	3	7	18
		a	Laetum regem uidebunt	3	7	19
	115	a	Cum regnante regnabunt	3	7	20
		a	Cum gaudente gaudebunt	3	7	20
30		x	Tunc dolor tunc taedium	4	7	20
		a	Tunc labor delebitur	3	7	18
		x	Tunc rex regum rex mundus	5	7	21
	120	a	A mundis uidebitur	3	7	16

1

This world shall pass,
daily it declines [here 'and daily it is passing'];
none shall remain living,
no one has remained alive.

2   5

The whole human race
uses a like origin,
and after a common life
falls by an equal ending.

3
   10   For those who postpone life
death creeps on unsure;
all the proud wanderers
sorrow of death seizes.

4
          What to bestow for Christ
they will not, all misers
   15   lose out of season;
after them others gather.

5
          Living but little themselves,
they scarce venture to give to God;
to death they leave their all,
   20   they keep nothing of themselves.

6
          Daily declines
the present life they love;
unfailing remains
the penalty they prepare for themselves.

7   25   What slips and glides
they try to gather,
and because it beguiles them
too little do they fear to trust it.

8
   30   They have loved darkness
black rather than light;
they scorn to follow
the Lord and Leader of life.

9
          As in dreams they reign;
one hour do they rejoice;
   35   but eternal pains
are already prepared for them.

10
          Blind, they no wise see
what after death remains,
and for ungodly sinners
   40   what ungodliness affords.

11
          It is fitting that you think
of all these things, my friend;
far be it from you to love
the pattern of this life.

12   45   Lo, all flesh is grass,
          burning though green,
          and like as the flower of grass
          is all its glory.

13   At sunrise is scorched
     50   the grass, and the flower fades;
          so is all youth
          when manhood has failed.

14   The beauty of men
          shall vanish in old age;
     55   all former· comeliness
          is wiped away with grief.

15   The radiance of Christ's face,
          lovely before all things,
          is more to be desired
     60   than the frail flower of flesh.

16   Beware, my little son,
          the forms of women,
          through whom death enters,
          no light destruction.

17   65   Many have endured
          the fires of punishment;
          because of their volatile will
          they would not undergo the loss.

18   The cup of a most unrighteous will
     70   never drink at all;
          from it many often
          you see gladly smiling.

19   For all whom you have seen
          smiling idly,
     75   know that at the last
          they shall weep bitterly.

20   Observe, my dearest friend,
          that lust is so,
          even as a deadly bite
     80   which conquers pleasure.

21   Do not plunge headlong
          by the road of mortals,
          on which you see for many
          shipwreck has occurred.

22   85 Step between the nets
          with hesitant feet,
          for by those nets the rest
          we see were caught unawares.

23   From earthly things lift up
      90 your heart's eyes;
          love the most loving
          hosts of angels.

24   Blessed family
          which dwells on high,
      95 where the old does not groan
          nor the infant cry,

          Where of God's praise
25   no voice is restrained,
          where there is no hunger,
     100 where there is never thirst,

26   Where on celestial food
          the heavenly folk are fed,
          where none dies
          because none is born,

27   105 Where [in] the royal hall
          [a song is sung right through]
          in which resounding ill
          no voice is heard,

28   Where life green
     110 and true shall be,
          which neither death nor of sorrow
          the fear shall destroy

[here 'which the limit of death nor of sorrow is bound to consume'].

29		Joyful after crossing death
		they shall see their joyful king;
	115	with Him reigning they shall reign,
		with Him rejoicing they shall rejoice.

30		Then grief, then weariness,
		then toil shall be done away,
		then the King of kings, the pure King,
	120	shall be seen by the pure.

One notes first that the verse is consistently syllabic, all 120 lines being competent heptasyllables, with five examples of synizesis, in *alii* 16, *indeficiens* 23, *impiis* 39, *gloria* 48, *impiissimae* 69.

The poem is consistently stanzaic, all thirty stanzas containing four lines each.

The poem is stunningly alliterative. Sometimes lines alliterate internally, as *lubricum quod labitur* 25 — *conantur colligere* 26 — *et hoc quod se seducit* 27. Sometimes adjacent lines alliterate, as *nemo uiuens manebit* 3 — *nullus uiuus remansit* 4. Sometimes alternate lines alliterate, as *differentibus uitam* 9 — *omnes superbos uagos* 11, and *mors incerta subripit* 10 — *meror mortis corripit* 12, with alliteration also in the adjacent lines *subripit* 10 — *superbos* 11. Sometimes alliteration connects adjacent stanzas, as *raditur* 56 — *radius* 57. Sometimes alliteration complements linked rhyming patterns across an intervening stanza, as in lines 6–8 and 14–6, where one may compare *utitur* 6 — with *omnes* 14, *et* 7 — with *inportune* 15, *cadit* 8 with *colligunt* 16.

The poem exhibits rhyme, the rhymes extending variously from one letter to seven letters and from one syllable to three syllables, in *amice* 42 — *vitae* 44, *decrescit* 21 — *manebit* 23, *transibit* 1 — *manebit* 3, *delebitur* 54 — *raditur* 56, *subripit* 10 — *corripit* 12, *pascitur* 102 — *nascitur* 104, *futura est* 110 — *consumptura est* 112. In many places vowels rhyme in adjacent lines, as *totum humanum genus* 5 — and *ortu utitur pari* 6, and in alternate lines, as *uita praesens quam amant* 22 — *sibi poena quam parant* 24. This occurs even in stanzas which are not adjacent. Compare the first two and the last two syllables of *ortu utitur pari* 6 — and *nolunt omnes auari* 14, the penultimate syllables of *et de simili uita* 7 — and *inportune amittunt* 15, the second, fourth, sixth, and seventh syllables of *fine cadit aequali* 8 — and *post se colligunt alii* 16.[6] Half the stanzas, fifteen, rhyme in the pattern *xaxa* (2, 3, 7, 8, 9, 10, 12, 14, 15, 16, 17, 20, 23, 27, 30), seven in the pattern *abab* (1, 6, 18, 19, 21, 22, 28), six in the pattern *xaaa* (5, 11, 24, 25, 26, 29), and two in the pattern *aaxa* (4, 13).

---

6   If this observation is correct it entails revision of the analysis in G. Murphy, *Early Irish Metrics* (Dublin 1961), pp. 16–7: 'Columbanus († 615) was a younger contemporary of Colum Cille. In his syllabic poem (7^2 or 7^3) on the World's Impermanence, besides rimes in unstressed end-syllables, he has many stressed rimes, both perfect and imperfect. "Irish" rimes such as his **pari** : aequali may be compared with Augustine's **pace** : iudic**ate**.' Without denying the existence of 'Irish' rhyme one may affirm that Columban's rhymes here are pure, *pari* rhyming with *auari* and *aequali* with *alii*.

In the chiastic passages we shall consider below the first stanza and the sixth both exhibit the rhyme scheme *abab*. After reversal of the last two words of line 7 to *et de uita simili* the second stanza would exhibit, like the fifth, the pattern *xaaa*. That would alter correspondence of the sound *-it-* in *uita* 7 and *amittunt* 15, but it would produce rhyme in *pari* 6 — *simili* 7 — *aequali* 8 and correspondence of the sound *-i-* in *simili* 7 and *amittunt* 15. Either reading illustrates the poet's attention to rhyme schemes, vowel rhymes within lines, and alliterations that transcend an intervening stanza.

Rhyme schemes are chiastically disposed again in stanzas 22–28, *abab*, *xaxa*, *xaaa*, *xaaa*, *xaaa*, *xaxa*, *abab*, where the rhyme schemes complement the rhythms.[7] Stanzas 22–23–24 all exhibit proparoxytone cadences (4 × pp). The central stanza 25 exhibits one proparoxytone line and three paroxytone lines (pp p p p). Stanzas 26–27–28 exhibit paroxytone and proparoxytone cadences disposed chiastically by couplets (p pp pp pp, pp pp pp pp, pp pp p pp).

The last three stanzas exhibit three rhyme schemes *abab*, *xaaa*, *xaxa*, both adjacent and alternate rhyming lines, both internal and end rhymes, both internal and adjacent alliteration.

A notable feature of this poem is the chiastic disposition of diction. First in the first 22 lines.

I	a	mundus iste
I	b	transibit
2	c	cottidie
3	d	transit
3	ei	uiuens
4	ii	nullus
5	iii	totum
6–8	f	ortu utitur pari et de simili uita fine cadit aequali
10	g	mors incerta subripit
11	h	omnes superbos uagos
12	g'	meror mortis corripit
14–16	f'	nolunt omnes auari inportune amittunt post se colligunt alii
17	e'i	uiuentes
19	ii	cuncta
20	iii	nihil
20	d'	nihil de ipsis habent
21	c'	cottidie
21	b'	decrescit
22	a'	uita praesens quam amant.

7   Cf. M.J. McGann, 'The Distribution of Cadences in the *De Mundi Transitu* of St Columban', *Archivum Latinitatis Medii Aevi* XXXI (1961), pp. 147–9.

There is a second chiastic passage in lines 23–36.

23–24	a	indeficiens manebit sibi poena quam parant
29–30	b	dilexerunt tenebras tetras magis quam lucem
35–36	a'	sed aeterna tormenta adhuc illis parantur.

There is a third chiastic passage in lines 37–74.

37	a	uident
39	b	impiis
41	c	amice
45	di	caro
45	ii	flagrans
47	e	flos
49	f	arescit
50	g	deperit
51	h	sic est omnis iuuentus
52	g'	defecerit
54	f'	delabitur
60	e'	flos
60	d'i	carnis
60	ii	fragilis
61	c'	filiole
69	b'	impiissimae
72	a'i	uides
72	ii	ridere
73	i'	uideres
74	ii'	ridere.

At the beginning of the last part of the poem there is a parallelism in lines 77–88.

77	a	conspice
81	b	pergere
82	c	per
83	d	qua
83	e	multis
83	f	euenisse
84	a'	conspicis
85	b'	perge
87	c'	per
87	d'	quos
87	e'	captos ceteros incautos
88	f'	conperimus.

A great chiasmus extends from the first line of the poem to the last.

I	a	mundus			
I	b	transibit			
12	c	meror			
12	d	mortis			
22	e	uita			
32	f	Dominum			
43	g	amare			
61	h	filiole			
77	h'	carissime			
91	g'	ama amantissimos			
97	f'	Domini			
109	e'	uita			
111	d'	mors			
111	c'	meroris			
113	b'	transacto			
119–20	a'	mundus a mundis			

The poem is divided by symmetry and by extreme and mean ratio. The golden section of the thirty stanzas falls at 19 and 11. Columban addresses his friend the first time, *te amice*, in the eleventh stanza from the beginning. He addresses him the third time, *conspice carissime*, in stanza 20, the eleventh stanza from the end. He addresses him the second time, *caueto filiole*, at the beginning of a central, sixteenth, stanza.

In the first chiastic passage of twenty-two lines (1–22) the crux of the chiasmus falls at a central line, eleventh from the end. The central word of that line is the central word of the passage, thirty-fifth of sixty-nine, *mortis*, which also contains the central letters of the passage.

In the second chiastic passage of fourteen lines (23–36) the crux falls at a central line, seventh from the end. The first word of that line, *tetras*, is the central word of the passage, twenty-second of forty-three. There are 127 letters before *tetras* and 126 letters from *tetras* inclusive to the end of the passage.

In the third chiastic passage of forty lines (37–76) the golden section of lines falls at 15 and 25, in the fifteenth line, 51, at the crux of the chiasmus. Within this passage important words recur at arithmetically fixed intervals. From *florida* 46 to *flos* 47 inclusive there are four words (4 × 1). From *flos* 47 to *flos* 50 inclusive there are twelve words (4 × 3). Between *flos* 50 and *flos* 60 there are twenty-eight words (4 × 7). From *foenum* 45 to *foeni* 47 inclusive there are eight words (4 × 2). After *foeni* 47 *foenum* 50 is the eighth word (4 × 2). From *omnis* 45 to *omnis* 55 inclusive there are thirty-four words, which divide by extreme and mean ratio at 21 and 13. Between *omnis* 48 and *omnis* 55 there are twenty-one words. Those twenty-one words divide by extreme and mean ratio at 13 and 8. After *omnis* 47 the thirteenth word is *omnis* 51, between which and *omnis* 55 there are eight words.

From *cuncta* 42 to *omnis* 45 inclusive there are nine words, and between *omnis* 55 and *cunctis* 58 there are also nine words.

In the great chiasmus extending throughout the poem the crux falls between the second and third addresses to the poet's friend. As noted above, the latter of these stands at the golden section of stanzas, eleventh from the end, and the former stands at the symmetrical centre of the stanzas, lines, and syllables, the fifteenth stanza, sixtieth line, and 420th syllable from the end. The diction of the fifteenth stanza from the beginning echoes the diction of the crux of the second chiasmus:

> dilexerunt tenebras tetras magis quam lucem
> magis diligendus est quam flos carnis fragilis.

The central word of the entire poem, 183rd of 365 words, is the central word of line 59, *diligendus*. A central letter of the poem, 1055th of 2110, is the *s* of *diligendus*. Half of 59 is 30; half of 183 is 92; half of 1055 is 528. The first word before *diligendus* is *magis* in line 59, and the ninety-second word from *diligendus* inclusive is *magis* in line 30. The 528th letter from the *s* of *diligendus* inclusive is the *s* of *magis* in line 30, which is also the 528th letter from the beginning of the poem.

This work about the transitory world is calendrical. There are 365 words, for days in a year; 120 lines, for a decade of months; thirty stanzas, for days in a month; four lines per stanza, for weeks in a month; seven syllables per line, for days in a week. The Lord's praise is sung after the twenty-fourth stanza in the twenty-fourth line from the end, representing perhaps hours in a day. We shall observe below a matter of some interest after the twenty-fourth line from the beginning. Division of the thirty stanzas by extreme and mean ratio at 19 might represent the nineteen-year cycle through which solar and lunar calendars come into synchrony.

Schaller noted parallels in thought between the undoubted works of Columban and this poem. To these one may add that of the 365 words of this poem nearly two hundred recur in identical grammatical forms in identical spellings in Columbans undoubted works.[8] More than one 110 others recur as

---

8   a, absit, adhuc, aeterna, alii, amant, audent, caelestis, carissime, carnis, cibo, cordis, cottidie (*bis*), credere, cum (*prep.* × 4), cum (*conj.*), cuncta (*bis*), cunctis, dare, de (x 3), decrescit, Deo, dolor, Domini, Dominum, eius, en, esse, est (x 6), et (x 4), fine, foenum (*bis*), fragilis, gloria, habent, habitat, haec, hoc, hominum, hora, huius, illis, imitari, impietas, in (x 4), incerta, inde, infans, inter, ipsi, ipsis, iste, labor, laeti, licet, lucem, magis ... quam (*bis*), male, minus, mors (*bis*), mortis (*bis*), multis, multos, mundus ('*world*'), mundus ('*pure*'), nam, nascitur, naufragium, nec, nemo (x 3), nequaquam, neque, nihil, noli (*bis*), non (x 3), nulla (*bis*), nullus, numquam, oculos, omnes (*bis*), omnis (x 3), parua, per (x 3), post (*bis*), prae, praesens, pro, qua (*bis*), quae, quam (x 3), quas, quasi, quia, quid, quod (x 5), quos, regum, relinquunt, rex (*bis*), scito, se (*bis*), sed, sibi, sic (x 3), simili, sunt, te, tenebras, tibi, timent, totum, tui, tunc (x 4), ubi (x 8), uelut, uera, uiam, uideris, uides, uirtus, uita (x 3), uitae (x 2), uitam, uiuentes, uiuus, uix, una, uoluntatis, uox (*bis*), ut, Xpisti, Xpisto.

differently inflected forms of words found in his undoubted works.[9] Only fifty-seven do not recur among Columban's undoubted works,[10] of which thirty-four stand at the ends of lines,[11] where their uniqueness may be partly explained from requirements of end rhyme and vowel rhyme and alliteration.

Another feature may indicate composition by Columban. After the twenty-fourth line from the beginning of the poem the letters of the five words of the couplet

Lubricum quod labitur
Conantur colligere
'the elusive thing that slips away they try to fasten together'

may be rearranged to form the five words

COLUMBA LOQUITUR CLANCULO RIDET BENGUIRR
'Columba speaks secretly, Bangor smiles'.

This may be mere coincidence. If not, the anagram corroborates other forms of evidence that *Mundus iste transibit* issued from the pen of the first Irishman known to have become a Latin author, sometime perhaps between the foundation of Bangor in the 550s and Columban's departure to the Continent about 590.

IV. COLUMBAN OF BANGOR

Precamur Patrem

Here follows the text of a hymn considered by some the most extraordinary composition in the Antiphonary of Bangor, found on folios 4v–6v.

---

9   aequali, altis, ama, amantissimos, amare, amice, amittunt, angelorum, audita, beata, bibere, cadit, caeci, captos, caro, caueto, ceteros, cogitare, colligere, colligunt, conantur, conspice, conspicis, consumptura, contemnunt, conuenit, corripit, [decantata], decor, delebitur, differentibus, dilexerunt, diligendus, dolore, eleua, esuritur, euenisse, feminarum, flos (x 3), foeni, futura, gaudebunt, gaudente, gemat, genus, humanum, impiis, impiissimae, inaniter (cf. inanis), incendia, ingreditur, iuuentus, laetantur, laetos, laetum, laqueos, largiri, laudis (cf. laudabilis, laudare), manebit (*bis*), moritur, mortalium, morti, mortiferum (cf. morti), mundis, nolentes, nolunt, nouissimis, orto, ortu, parant, parantur, paruum, peccatoribus, pedibus, perge, plebs, populos, praestat, pronus, pulchritudo (cf. pulcherrimo, pulchrior, pulchriores), quoscumque, raditur, regem, regia, regnabunt, regnant, regnante, remansit, retinetur, ridere (bis), senescens (cf. senes), senex, sititur, somnis, species, superbos, suspensis, terrenis, transacto, uagos, uidebitur, uidebunt, uident, uincit, uiuens, utitur.

10 aula, familia, flagrans, flebunt, formulam, incautos, indeficiens, inportune, leto, lubricum, [melos], meror, [meta], morsum, obitum, plerique, poculum, poena, poenarum, sole, tetras, umquam, uultus.

11 amabilis, amariter, arescit, auari, conperimus, defecerit, delabitur, deperit, dispendia, dulcedinem, filiole, florida, labitur, libidinem, lubricae, meroris, pari, pascitur, pernicies, perpessi, plerumque, pristinus, radius, resonans, restat, seducit, subripit, superno, taedium, tormenta, transibit, [transit], uagitat, uiridis.

YMNUM APOSTOLORUM UT ALII DICUNT

Prologue		**Alleluia .**		1	8	1	1
		PRecamur Patrem Regem omnipotentem	aa	2	2	14	17
		et Ihesum Xpistum Sanctum quoque Spiritum	aa	3	3	15	21
2		**Deum in una** perfectum substantia	bb	3	2	9	19
		Trinum persona unum in essentia	bb	2	3	13	14
3	5	**UNI**uersorum fontis iubar luminum	aa	1	3	11	18
		aethereorum et orbi lucentium .	aa	1	3	11	15
Part I							
4		**Hi**c enim dies uelut Primogenitus	cc	3	2	11	17
		caeli ab arce mundi moli micuit .	de	3	3	11	15
5		**Si**c Verbum caro factum a principio	ff	3	3	13	16
	10	Lumen aeternum missum Patre saeculo .	af	2	3	13	18
6		**Ill**eque proto uires adimens chao	ff	2	3	12	16
		tum inprouiso noctem pepulit mundo .	ff	2	3	12	18
7		**It**a ueterno iste hoste subacto	ff	2	3	10	16
		polum nodoso soluit mortis uinculo .	ff	2	3	11	19
8	15	**Te**nebrae super ante erant abissum	ga	2	3	13	16
		quam radiaret primus dies dierum .	ea	2	3	12	16
9		**Ho**c quam prodiret uera lux mortalia	eb	3	3	15	15
		contexit alta corda ignorantia .	bb	2	2	12	15
10		**Eo**dem die rubrum ut aiunt mare	dd	2	4	8	17
	20	post tergum liquit liberatus Israhel .	eh	3	2	16	16
11		**Pe**r hoc docemur mundi acta spernere .	gd	3	3	13	17
		et in deserto uirtutum consistere .	fd	3	2	11	18
12		**Su**bmerso saeuo cincri canunt aemulo	ff	2	3	13	18
		certatim Deo laudes duci igneo .	ff	2	3	11	15
13	25	**Si**cque erepti nequam iubemur fretis	ic	2	3	12	19
		Laudare Deum explosis inimicis .	ac	2	2	11	16
14		**Et** sicut ille lucis fit initium	da	3	3	11	15
		Ita et iste salutis exordium .	da	3	2	9	15
15		**Lo**catur primus in tenore diei	ci	2	3	13	12
	30	secundus uero in calore fidei .	fi	2	3	12	13
Part II							
16		**IN** fine mundi post tanta misteria	ib	3	3	11	17
		adest Saluator cum grandi clementia .	gb	2	3	13	18
17		**Ta**mque aperte elementa praetendunt	de	2	2	12	19
		quam uatum ora lucide concelebrant .	be	3	2	12	18
18	35	**Na**tus ut homo mortali in tegmine .	fd	3	3	11	16
		Non deest caelo manens in Trinitate .	fd	3	3	13	17
19		**Va**git in pannis ueneratur a magis	cc	3	3	13	15
		fulget in stellis adoratur in caelis .	cc	3	3	15	16

20		Statura uili continetur praesepi	ii	2	2	11 18
	40	cuius pugillo potest orbis concludi .	fi	2	3	12 19
21		Primumque signum portendit discipulis	ac	2	2	15 19
		Aquae conuersae in sapore nectaris .	dc	2	3	14 16
22		Tum per prophetam completur ut dictum est	ae	3	4	15 20
		saliet claudus ut ceruus perniciter .	cg	2	3	13 18
23	45	Planaque fatur absoluto uinculo	gf	2	2	13 15
		lingua mutorum imperante Domino .	af	2	2	13 15
24		Surdi sanantur caeci atque leprosi	gi	2	3	13 17
		funere truso suscitantur mortui .	fi	2	2	11 17
25		Totidem panes quinque diuidit uirum	ca	2	3	12 19
	50	saturaturis procul dubio milibus .	cc	1	3	11 18
26		Post tantas moles diuinae clementiae .	cd	3	2	15 17
		exosus ille stimulo inuidiae .	dd	2	2	10 15
27		Qui inuidere et odire animam	da	2	3	11 13
		pro inimicis prorogans dat uictimam .	ca	2	3	11 20
28	55	ADuersus eum initur consilium	aa	2	2	11 15
		qui magni dictus consilii est nuntius .	cc	3	3	14 18
29		Accedunt ei ut latroni cum gladiis	ic	2	4	10 19
		furem aeternis tradituro aestibus .	cc	2	2	13 17
30		Tandem humano traditur iudicio	ff	2	2	12 15
	60	mortali rege damnatur perpetuus .	dc	2	2	11 17
31		CRuci confixus polum mire concutit	ce	2	3	13 17
		lumenque solis tribus obtendit horis .	cc	2	3	13 19
32		Saxa rumpuntur uelum scinditur templi	gi	2	3	13 20
		uiui consurgunt de sepulchris mortui .	ei	2	3	14 18
33	65	Conrosum nodis annis fere milibus	cc	2	3	13 16
		extricat saeuis inferi feralibus .	cc	2	2	14 15
34		Tunc protoplaustum lacrimosa suboli	ai	2	2	17 15
		abiecta mali morte saeua ultrice	id	2	3	11 17
35		Quemque antiquum paradiso incolam	aa	2	2	15 15
	70	Recursu suo clementer restituit .	fe	2	2	10 18
36		Exaltans caput uniuersi corporis	ec	2	2	13 16
		In Trinitate locauit aecclesiam .	da	2	2	11 17
37		IN hoc caelitus iubet portas principes	cc	3	3	13 20
		Regi cum sociis aeternales pandere	cd	3	2	13 17
38	75	ERrantem propriis euehens centesimam	ca	2	2	16 17
		supernis ouem humeris ouilibus .	ac	2	2	12 15
39		Quem expectamus adfuturum Iudicem	ca	2	2	14 16
		iustum cüique opus suum reddere .	dd	2	3	12 15

Epilogue

40		Rogo quam tantis talibusque donariis	cc	3	2	14 18
	80	uicem condigne possumus rependere .	dd	2	2	13 17

41	Quid tam mortales temptamus micrologi	ci	3	2	15	18
	narrare quiuit quae nullus edicere .:.,	ed	2	3	13	17
42	Solum oramus hoc idemque maximum	ca	2	3	11	17
84	nostri aeterne miserere Domine ..,	dd	2	2	13	14
	Alleluia .		1			8

Prologue   Alleluia.

We pray to the Father, omnipotent King,
and Jesus Christ, also the Holy Spirit,
God, perfect in one substance,
Triune in person, One in essence,
5   bright source of the fount of all illuminations
of the upper regions and of those lighting the orb of earth.

Part I

For this day, as Firstborn
He gleamed from the arc of heaven to the mass of the world,
the Word made flesh, from the origin,
10   eternal illumination sent from the Father to the age,
and He, removing powers from the primal chaos,
then repulsed night suddenly from the world.
Thus He, with the old adversary subdued,
loosed the pole from the knotty chain of death.
15   There were shadows above the abyss
before the first day of days radiated
this; before the true light went forth
deep ignorance covered over mortal hearts.
On the same day, as they relate,
20   liberated Israel left behind its back the Red Sea.
Through this we are taught to spurn the acts of the world
and to dwell together in the desert of virtues.
With the savage rival submerged [*i.e.* Pharaoh drowned] the
      unblemished sing
in competition praises to God, the fiery leader.
25   And so, snatched up from the evil waters we are ordered .
to praise God, with our enemies cast out.
And just as He is made the beginning of light
thus also is He the starting point of salvation.
He is placed first in the course of the day,
30   giving support in the true zeal of faith.
Part II

In the end of the world after so many mysteries
the Saviour is present with great clemency.
And the elements show forth as openly
as the mouths of seers lucidly make known

35 that a man is born in mortal covering.
He is not absent from heaven, remaining in the Trinity.
He cries in swaddling cloths; He is venerated by Magi;
He shines among the stars; He is adored in the heavens.
Bound to stand forever, He is held in a vile stall,
40 in Whose fist the orb of earth can be enclosed,
and He portends to disciples the first sign,
of water converted into the savour of nectar.
Then it is fulfilled as it was told through the prophet,
'The lame will leap as a stag nimbly
45 and with the chain loosed
the tongue of mute men speaks straightforward things with
    the Lord commanding.
Deaf, blind, and leprous men are healed;
with the funeral rite thrust away dead men are raised up.
He divides five loaves of bread for the same number of
    thousands of men
50 to be sated without doubt.'
After so many masses of divine clemency
He, hated because of the goad of envy,
gives a sacrificial victim, carrying over His soul for enemies
who envy and hate.
55 Counsel is plotted against Him
Who is called the Messenger of great counsel.
They approach as thieves with swords Him
Who is to be handed over as a robber to eternal blazes.
Finally He is handed over to human judgement,
60 the Perpetual [King] is condemned by a mortal king.
Fixed on a cross He shakes the pole wondrously,
and He veils the illumination of the sun for three hours.
Stones are broken; the veil of the Temple is split;
dead men rise together live from the tombs.
65 The man gnawed fiercely by knots for thousands of years [i.e.
    Adam]
He extricates from the savage fierce beasts of hell.
Then the primally fashioned man from the lacrimose race
degraded by savage death, the avenger of evil,
and the ancient dweller in paradise, whom
70 He restored clemently by His own return,
raising the head of every body
He placed the Church in the Trinity.
On this [day] from heaven He orders princes
to open eternal gates for the King with His comrades,

75   carrying the hundredth wandering
            sheep on His own shoulders to the supernal sheepfolds,
            Whom we hope for as the Judge to come
            to give to each man a just reward for his own work.
Epilogue

            What exchange, I ask, for so many and such gifts
80   can we repay worthily?
            Why do we mortals, obsessed with trifles [or 'with little
                understanding of the Word'], try
            to relate things which no man can know how to proclaim?
            Him alone and the Same, the Greatest, we pray for this,
            'Have mercy on us, eternal Lord'.

The hymn begins and ends with the word *Alleluia*. A Prologue of six lines (1–6) and twenty-eight words, is balanced by an Epilogue of six lines (79–84) and twenty-eight words. The hymn proper occupies seventy-two lines (7–78), divided into two parts, I of twenty-four lines (7–30) and II of forty-eight lines (31–78).

The prosody of this hymn is remarkable. Every line exhibits rhyme either within the line or between adjacent lines, if not both. Every line but 7 exhibits alliteration either within the line or between adjacent lines, if not both. The poet allows sixteen examples of hiatus, in lines 21b, 24b, 25a, 28a, 33a, 47b, 52b, 53a–b, 54a, 56b, 58b, 68b, 69a–b, 84a, avoids elision throughout, and allows synizesis of short unstressed *-i-* in *dubio* 50b, *consilii* 56b, *gladiis* 57b, *sociis* 74a, *propriis* 75a, and *donariis* 79b.

The unit of composition is the verse line of twelve syllables, five before the caesura and seven after the caesura, the number 12 dividing by extreme and mean ratio at 7 and 5. Throughout the poem in the pentasyllabic parts of the lines there are only two stress patterns, /xx/x as in *Déum in úna* 3 and *úniuersórum* 5, and x/x/x, as in *precámur Pátrem* 1 and *et Ihésum Xpístum* 2. In the first six lines of the Prologue, four exhibit the pattern /xx/x (3–6) and two exhibit the pattern x/x/x (1–2), the number 6 dividing by extreme and mean ratio at 4 and 2. In the next twenty-four lines of Part I, fifteen lines exhibit the pattern /xx/x (7–18, 25, 27–8) and nine exhibit the pattern x/x/x (19–24, 26, 29–30), the number 24 dividing by extreme and mean ratio at 15 and 9. In the next forty-eight lines of Part II, thirty exhibit the pattern /xx/x (32–3, 35–8, 40–50, 57–9, 61–6, 69–70, 74, 78) and eighteen exhibit the pattern x/x/x (31, 34, 39, 51–2, 53–4, 55–6, 60, 67–8, 71–3, 75–7), the number 48 dividing by extreme and mean ratio at 30 and 18. In the last six lines of the Epilogue, as in the first six, four exhibit the pattern /xx/x (79–80, 83–4) and two exhibit the pattern x/x/x (81–2), the number 6 dividing by extreme and mean ratio at 4 and 2. This perfectly controlled variety is not the work of a man insensitive to rhythm.

Words and ideas of Part I are arranged chiastically.

A	*Hic* enim *dies*
B	uelut *Primogenitus* caeli ab arce mundi moli micuit .
C	*Sic* Verbum caro factum *a principio*
D	*Lumen* aeternum missum Patre saeculo .
E	*Illeque*
F	proto uires adimens chao
G 1	tum inprouiso noctem pepulit mundo
2	Ita *ueterno* iste *hoste subacto*
	polum nodoso soluit mortis uinculo .
H	Tenebrae super *ante* erant abissum
I	quam radiaret *primus dies dierum* .
J	Hoc quam prodiret uera *lux* mortalia
	contexit alta corda ignorantia.
I'	*Eodem die* Rubrum ut aiunt Mare
H'	*post* tergum liquit liberatus Israhel .
G'1	Per hoc docemur mundi acta spernere .
	et in deserto uirtutum consistere .
2	*Submerso saeuo* cincri canunt *aemulo*
	certatim Deo laudes duci igneo .
F'	Sicque erepti nequam iubemur fretis
	Laudare Deum explosis inimicis .
E'	Et sicut *ille*
D'	*lucis* fit initium
C'	*Ita* et iste salutis *exordium* .
B'	Locatur *primus*
A'	in tenore *diei* secundus uero in calore fidei .

Part I contains twenty-four lines and 124 words, of which the central twelfth and thirteenth lines are 18–9, and the central words are *corda ignorantia* at the end of the crux of the chiasmus at the end of the twelfth line, and *eodem die* at the beginning of the thirteenth line. The 332nd letter from the beginning is the *a* of *corda*, and the 332nd letter from the end is the last *a* of *ignorantia*.

Words and ideas of Part II are also arranged chiastically.

A	In fine mundi *post tanta* misteria
B	*adest Saluator*
C 1	cum grandi *clementia*
2	ora
3	*manens in Trinitate*
4	*in caelis*
D 1	tum per *prophetam* completur ut *dictum est*
2	saliet claudus *ut* ceruus perniciter
3	absoluto uinculo
4	funere truso *suscitantur mortui*

E 5	procul dubio *milibus*
	Post tantas moles diuinae *clementiae*
	exosus ille stimulo *inuidiae*
	qui *inuidere* et odire animam
	pro inimicis prorogans dat uictimam
D'1	qui magni *dictus* consilii *est nuntius*
2	accedunt ei *ut* latroni cum gladiis
3	saxa rumpuntur uelum scinditur templi
4	uiui *consurgunt* de sepulchris *mortui*
5	fere *milibus*
C'1	recursu suo *clementer* restituit
2	caput
3	*in Trinitate locauit* aecclesiam
4	*in* hoc *caelitus*
B'	Quem expectamus *adfuturum Iudicem*
A'	iustum cuique opus suum reddere.

Part II contains forty-eight lines and 229 words, of which the central 115th word is *pro*, the first word of the central twenty-fourth line 54, the last line of the crux of the chiasmus. Part II contains 1424 letters, 712 from the beginning to the end of the crux of the chiasmus, lines 31–54, and 712 thence to the end, lines 55–78.

Part I is linked to Part II by parallel and chiastic arrangement of words and ideas.

A 1	caeli
2	a principio
B 1	lumen
2	nodoso
C 1	soluit
2	uinculo
3	mortalia
4	inimicis
5	initium
6	mortali
D	Primumque signum portendit discipulis
	aquae conuersae in sapore nectaris
C'1	absoluto
2	uinculo
3	mortui
4	inimicis
5	initur
6	mortali

B'1	lumenque
2	nodis
A'1	caelitus
2	principes

The central forty-second of eighty-four lines in the poem is *aquae conuersae in sapore nectaris*. The central 205th of 409 words is the last of *cuius pugillo potest orbis concludi* 40, immediately preceding the first words of the crux of the chiasmus, *Primumque signum*.

After stripping from the canon of Columban's works the poems now attributed to Columbanus of Saint-Trond, Lapidge wrote that Columban, 'the founder of Luxeuil and Bobbio, may finally take his leave from the annals of medieval Latin poetry'.[1] Later he changed his mind. Not only did he accept Schaller's attribution to Columban of *Mundus Iste Transibit*.[2] But because of the word *micrologi* in line 81, found elsewhere only in Columban's First Epistle and in Jonas's *Vita Columbani*, and because of the similarity of lines 35–6 to Columban's Fifth Epistle, *qui natus in carne nequaquam deerat caelo manens in Trinitate*,[3] he attributed this poem to Columban.[4] Our author takes no 'leave from the annals of medieval Latin poetry'. On the contrary, he may be credited with the first comprehensive disposition of varied rhythms, rhyme, and alliteration in verse, an achievement the importance of which in every subsequent European literature one could hardly overstate.

V. ANONYMI HYMNUS

Martine Deprecare

In *Analectica Hymnica* LI ii no. 247 p. 328 Blume presents the text of an Irish Latin hymn to Saint Martin.[1]

1. Martine, te de*precor*
       pro *me ro*gare patrem,
     Christum ac spiritum sanctum,
       habentem Mariam matrem.

2. Martinus, mirus *more*,
       ore laudavit Deum,

1   M. Lapidge, 'The Authorship of the Adonic Verses "ad Fidolium" Attributed to Columbanus', *Studi Medievali*, 3rd series, XVIII (1977), p. 311.
2   See above p. 156 n. 4.
3   Both these parallels had been previously noted.
4   M. Lapidge, 'Columbanus and "The Antiphonary of Bangor"', *Peritia* IV (1985), pp. 104–16.
1   BCLL 589.

                Puro corde *cantavit*
                atque *amavit* eum.

3.   Electus Dei *vivi*;
           signa *sibi* salutis
           Donavit Deus pacis
             magnae atque virtutis.

4.   Verbum Dei lo*cutus*,
           se*cutus* in mandatis,
           Virtutibus impletus
            mortuis suscitatis.

5.   Sanans homines lepra
           cura duplici mira:
           Magni*tudine* mala,
            aegri*tudine* dira.

6.   Deum, Dominum nostrum,
            passum pro nobis mire
           Volunt*arie* propter nos
            deprec*are*, Martine.

If this were the original text one would have to infer that our author was less than a proficient versifier. Let us, assuming that he was at least competent, use evidence from the undamaged parts of the composition to restore the damaged portions of his hymn. Let us suppose that he could count correctly and that he allowed elision,[2] as in *Xpistum ac*, and synizesis, as in *Mariam* and *uoluntarie*. Let us suppose that he sought varied rhymes: of a single syllable, of a single letter, as in *mire* and *Martine* 22–4, or of two letters, as in *lepra* and *cura* 17–8; of two syllables, of three letters, as in *more* and *ore* 5–6, or four letters, as in *cantauit* and *amauit* 7–8, or five letters, as in *Patrem* and *matrem* 2–4; of four syllables, of seven or eight letters, as in *laudauit Deum* and *amauit Eum* 6–8 or *magnitudine* and *aegritudine* 19–20; but that he always rhymed. In the following text boldface capital letters represent features of Dublin, Trinity College, MS 1441 page 86; *italics* mark rhymes and <u>underlinings</u> alliterations. To the right of the text the first column denotes the rhyme schemes, the second the number of words, the third the number of syllables, and the fourth the number of letters.

---

2   M. Lapidge, 'A New Hiberno-Latin Hymn on St Martin', *Celtica* XXI (1990), pp. 248–51, observing on p. 248 Irish Latin poets' usual avoidance of elision, suggests in n. 38 'that it would be simpler to delete *ac* and insert a comma after *Christum*'. But the chiastic structure of the hymn and counts of words and letters and disposition of words at arithmetically fixed intervals all show that the poet wrote and elided *ac*.

1		**M**artine _deprecare_	a	2	7	18
		pro me _rogare_ Patrem	ab	4	7	17
		Xpistum ac Spiritum Sanctum	c	4	7	24
		haben_tem_ Mariam matrem.	cb	3	7	20
						79
2	5	**M**artinus mirus more	d	3	7	17
		ore lau_dauit_ Deum	de	3	7	15
		Puro corde cantauit	f	3	7	17
		atque amauit Eum	fe	3	7	14
						63
3	10	**E**lectus Dei ui_ui_.	g	3	7	14
		Signa sibi salutis	gh	3	7	16
		Donauit Deus pacis	h	3	7	16
		magnae atque uirtutis.	gh	3	7	19
						65
4	15	**V**erbum Dei lo_cutus_,	i	3	7	16
		secutus in mandatis,	ij	3	7	17
		Virtutibus imple_tus_	i	2	7	18
		mortuis suscitatis	ij	2	7	17
						68
5	20	**S**anans homines lepra	k	3	7	18
		cura duplici mira	kl	3	7	15
		Magnitudine mala,	m	2	7	15
		aegritudine dira.	ml	2	7	15
						63
6		**D**eum Dominum nostrum	c	3	7	18
		passum pro nobis mire	cn	4	7	18
		.Voluntarie propter nos	a	3	7	20
		deprecare Martine.	an	2	7	16

Martin, pray for me, ask the Father, the Holy Spirit, and Christ, having Mary as mother.

Martin wondrous in conduct praised God with his mouth. With a pure heart he sang and loved Him,

the chosen one of the living God. To him the God of peace gave signs of salvation and of great virtue,

having spoken the word of God, having followed in His commandments, filled with virtues, with the dead raised,

healing men from leprosy, evil in its greatness, dire in its distress, with a
wondrous double cure.

Martin, pray to our Lord God [Who has] suffered wondrously for us,
    willingly on account of us.

All the lines end with paroxytone cadences except the penultimate, which
ends with an oxytone cadence.

There are six stanzas with fourteen rhymes in three paired rhyme schemes,
the first matching the second with three rhymes each, the third matching the
fourth with two rhymes each, the fifth matching the sixth with three rhymes
each. The rhyming of vowels and consonants extends throughout several of
the lines, and the alliteration is comparably rich. The poem begins and ends
with the same rhymes, a -*are* and c -*m*, the same alliteration, on *de* and *p*, and
the same words *Martine deprecare* and *deprecare Martine*.

The poet has disposed words and ideas chiastically.

1	Martine
2	deprecare
3	pro me
4a	Patrem Xpistum ac Spiritum Sanctum
b	mirus
5a	uiui
b	signa sibi salutis donauit
6	Deus
7	pacis magnae
7'	atque uirtutis
6'	Verbum Dei
5'a	mortuis suscitatis
b	sanans homines lepra cura duplici mira
4'a	Deum Dominum nostrum
b	mire
3'	propter nos
2'	deprecare
1'	Martine

The poem contains twenty-four lines and sixty-nine words, of which the
central, thirty-fifth from the beginning and end, is *magnae* in the central,
twelfth, line at crux of the chiasmus. The 410 letters divide by sesquioctave
ratio at 217 and 193. The 217th letter from the end is the *e* of *magnae*.

The poet has disposed words at arithmetically fixed intervals. There are five
words before *Patrem* 2 (5 × 1). There are five words in *Patrem Xpistum ac Spiritum
Sanctum* 2–3. From *Sanctum* 3 to *Deum* 6 inclusive there are ten words (5 × 2).
Between *Deum* 6 and *Eum* 8 there are five words. Between *Electus Dei* 9 and *Deus*
11 there are five words. Between *Deus* 11 and *Dei* 13 there are five words. From

Dei 13 to *Deum* 21 inclusive there are twenty words (5 × 4). After the next word *Dominum* 21 there are ten words (5 × 2) to the end of the hymn.

Martine is the first word and the last word of the hymn. Between *Martine* 1 and *Martinus* 5 there are twelve words. After *Martinus* 5 the twelfth word is the first of *Electus Dei* 9, that is *Martinus*. The poet names *Martinus* three times and refers to himself three times, observing a widespread convention of authorial self-reference at one-ninth and eighth-ninths of the way through a work. One-ninth and eight-ninths of 69 falls at 8 and 61. From the beginning to *pro me* 2 inclusive there are four words, and from *propter nos* 23 inclusive to the end there are four words, together eight. Between *pro me* and *propter nos* there are sixty-one words. The eighth word from the end is the first of *pro nobis* 22.

VI. ANONYMI HYMNUS

Deus Domine Meus

Recently Michael Lapidge published 'A New Hiberno-Latin Hymn on St Martin',[1] stripped of its disguise as a prose prayer and presented as a stanzaic hymn, probably from the seventh century, in heptasyllabic verse. The text is apparently sound but for five details. For Lapidge's *preclare* (for Heerwagen's *pure*) in line 19, one would expect by analogy with *tantae* 27, *comae* 35, *poenae* 36, 39, and *caelorum* 38, the Classically correct form *praeclare*. For Lapidge's *quaeso* 30 one would expect by analogy with the rhyme *presso* the Classically correct form *quaesso*, which recurs often in other seventh-century Irish Latin verse. In line 18 one would expect the spelling *Ihesu*, in line 13 *Xpiste*, in line 23 *Xpisti*. The analysis offered here may at once correct and corroborate the work of the editor and confirm the competence of the poet who honoured the saint.

In the text *italics* mark rhymes and <u>underlinings</u> mark alliterations. In the columns to the left of the text the first denotes the number of the stanzas and the second the number of the lines. In the columns to the right of the text the first denotes the rhyme scheme, the second the number of words, the third the number of syllables, and the fourth the number of letters.

1		<u>D</u>eus <u>D</u>omine *m*<u>e</u>us	a	3	7	14
		t*í*bi sum <u>m</u>ortis r*e*us:	a	4	7	17
		<u>e</u>sto <u>m</u>ihi *n*unc p<u>a</u>t*i*ens	b	4	7	19
	4	qu*í* <u>es</u> fortis <u>e</u>t p<u>o</u>t*ens*.	b	5	7	19
2		<u>A</u>di*u*ro Deum <u>u</u>er*um*	c	3	7	15
		<u>u</u>n*u*m semper *et t*rinum	c	4	7	18
		<u>u</u>t *n*unc <u>a</u>dire *t*antum	c	4	7	17
	8	possim <u>Sanctum Martinum</u>.	c	3	7	21

1   M. Lapidge, 'A New Hiberno-Latin Hymn on St Martin', *Celtica* XXI (1990), pp. 240-51.

3		Rogo nunc Regem regum	c	4	7	18
		qui est lumen diuinum	c	4	7	18
		ut ualeam nunc Sanctum	c	4	7	19
	12	uisitare Martinum.	c	2	7	16
4		Xpiste Deus deorum	c	3	7	16
		cuius est numen mirum	c	4	7	18
		fac me lugere sanum	c	4	7	16
	16	iuxta Sanctum Martinum.	c	3	7	20
5		Viam dirige plane	d	3	7	15
		O Ihesu Nazarene	d	3	7	14
		ut ualeam praeclare	d	3	7	17
	20	ibi peccata flere.	d	3	7	15
6		Mihi adiutorium	c	2	7	14
		erit per naufragium	c	3	7	17
		Xpisti militis miri	e	3	7	17
	24	suffragium Martini.	e	2	7	17
7		Volo te uisitare:	d	3	7	14
		fac me ad te uenire	d	5	7	15
		qui es uirtutis tantae	d	4	7	19
	28	O mi Sancte Martine.	d	4	7	16
8		O mi Sancte Martine	d	4	7	16
		nunc intercede quaesso	f	3	7	20
		pro me dolente male	d	4	7	16
	32	labe culparum presso.	f	3	7	18
9		O mi Sancte Martine	d	4	7	16
		pro me nunc intercede	d	4	7	18
		ne me contingant comae	d	4	7	19
	36	flammae perennis poenae.	d	3	7	21
10		O mi Sancte Martine	d	4	7	16
		turbae caelorum chare	d	3	7	19
		ne sim particeps poenae	d	4	7	20
	40	mihi auxiliare.	d	2	7	13
11		O mi Sancte Martine	d	4	7	16
		mihi auxiliare	d	2	7	13
		ut perfruar in fine	d	4	7	16
	44	uitae perenni pane.	d	3	7	16

| 12 | Gloria tibi *P*ater | g | 3 | 7 | 15 |
| 46 | qui es Frater et *M*ater. | g | 5 | 7 | 18 |

1   God, my Lord, I am the one responsible for Your death; be patient now with me, Who are strong and powerful.

2   I adjure the true God, always one and triune, that I may have power now to go to Saint Martin.

3   I ask now the King of Kings, Who is divine light, that I may be able now just to visit Saint Martin.

4   Christ, God of gods, Whose majesty is wondrous, make me to lament, healed, before Saint Martin.

5   Direct the way clearly, O Nazarene Jesu, so that I may be able excellently to bewail sins there.

6   For me an aid through shipwreck will be the support of Christ's soldier Martin.

7   I wish to visit you: make me to come to you, who are of such great virtue, O my Saint Martin.

8   O my Saint Martin, intercede now, I beg, for me, grieving ill, burdened by the disgrace of sins.

9   O my Saint Martin, for me now intercede, lest the wisps of flame of perennial punishment touch me.

10 O my Saint Martin, beloved of the throng of the heavens, lest I be a sharer of punishment help me.

11 O my Saint Martin, help me that I may enjoy at the end the perennial bread of life.

12 Glory to You, Father, Who are Brother and Mother.

Observing the use of hiatus, avoidance of elision, and synizesis of short unstressed *i* in *patiens* 3, Lapidge rightly associates this hymn with Irish Latin poems of the seventh century, but he errs in affirming that the poet's rhymes are 'sometimes … impure, and would more appropriately be described as assonance'.[2] As we have seen above, in the prosody of early Insular Latin poets rhymes of a single syllable and a single letter were deliberately sought and treated as pure, as legitimate an element of the verse as rhymes of two, three, and four syllables, and as many as eight letters. Lapidge errs further in stating[3]

> It is clear, however, that the poet was not concerned to achieve utter regularity in his stress-patterns, since in two lines (21–2), the natural stress falls on the antepenultimate or proparoxytone syllable (*adiutórium, naufrágium*).

2   Ibid. p. 248.
3   Ibid. p. 247.

This constitutes exactly the proof that the poet was concerned with regularity of stress. The only proparoxytone cadences in a poem otherwise of paroxytone cadences occur in lines 21–2, the centre of the forty-four lines of the hymn proper. One may compare the disposition of oxytone, paroxytone, and proparoxytone cadences in *Audite Omnes Amantes Deum, Mundus Iste Transibit*, and *Benchuir Bona Regula*[4] to confirm that this is another use of cadence to articulate poetic structure.

Even a casual reader will note in this poem the large amount of repeated diction. A careful reader may observe that the repetitions are deliberately ordered, first in a great chiasmus that extends from the first word to the last.

A	Deus Domine					
B		tibi				
C			mortis			
D			mihi			
E				nunc		
F 1					adire	
2						tantum
3							Sanctum Martinum
G						uisitare
H						Martinum
I 1						Xpiste
2							mirum
J							me
K							lugere
L								iuxta Sanctum Martinum
M								O Ihesu Nazarene
L'							ibi
K'							flere
J'							mihi
I' 1						Xpisti
2							miri
H'						Martini
G'						uisitare
F' 1					ad te uenire	
2						tantae
3							Sancte Martine
E'				nunc		
D'			mihi			
C'		in fine uitae				
B'		tibi				
A'	Pater ... Frater ... Mater.					

4   See above pp. 150–1, 165, and below pp. 192–3.

Woven into the last five parts of this large chiasmus is another series of chiastic patterns.

A	O mi Sancte Martine
B	nunc intercede
C	pro me
A'	O mi Sancte Martine
C'	pro me
B'	nunc intercede
D	ne me contingant comae flammae perennis poenae
A"	O mi Sancte Martine
D'	ne sim particeps poenae
E	mihi auxiliare
A'''	O mi Sancte Martine
E'	mihi auxiliare
D"	ut perfruar in fine uitae perenni pane.

The ordering of these repetitions should be obvious enough to convince the reader that every word is in its correct place. But the poet composed the hymn with further guarantees of its integrity.

The forty-six lines of the hymn divide by extreme and mean ratio at 28 and 18, reckoned from the beginning of the poem, at the end of line 18, *O Ihesu Nazarene*, the crux of the great chiasmus. The 159 words of the hymn divide by extreme and mean ratio at 98 and 61, at the beginning of line 18. The 322 syllables of the hymn divide by extreme and mean ratio at 199 and 123, exactly in the centre of line 18. The 777 letters of the hymn divide by extreme and mean ratio at 480 and 297, exactly at the O at the beginning of line 18.

Reckoned from the end of the poem the division of lines falls between the verse *O mi Sancte Martine*, stated first at line 28 and repeated at line 29, the eighteenth line from the end, the beginning of the series of smaller chiastic patterns.

The poet disposed words at arithmetically fixed intervals. *Deus*, for example, occurs four times. From the first to the fourth inclusive there are forty-seven words, which divide by extreme and mean ratio at 29 and 18. From the first *Deus* 1 to the second *Deum* 5 inclusive there are eighteen words. Thence to the end of *Deus deorum* 13 there are twenty-nine words. Among those twenty-nine words the central fifteenth word is the first of *Regem regum* 9.

From *Xpiste* 13 to *Xpisti* 23 inclusive there are thirty-two words, which divide by extreme and mean ratio at 20 and 12. From *Xpiste* 13 to *Ihesu Nazarene* 18 inclusive there are twenty words.

Before the first *Sanctum Martinum* 8 there are twenty-eight words (7 × 4). The second *Martinum* 12 is the fourteenth word (7 × 2) after the first. The third *Martinum* 16 is the fourteenth word after the second. Between *Martinum* 16 and *Martini* 24 there are twenty-one words (7 × 3). Between *Martini* 24 and *Sancte Martine* 28 there are fourteen words. Line 28 is repeated exactly as line

29. After *Martine* 29 *Martine* 33 is the fourteenth word. Between *Martine* 33 and *Martine* 37 there are fourteen words. From Martine 37 to Martine 41 inclusive there are fourteen words.

The poet refers to himself fourteen times, first as *meus* 1, the third word, second as *mihi* 3, the sixth word after that (3 × 2). From *mihi* 3 to *me* 15 inclusive there are forty-five words (3 × 15). After *me* 15 *mihi* 20 is the eighteenth word (3 × 6). From *mihi* 20 to *me* 26 inclusive there are fifteen words (3 × 5). After *me* 26 *mi* 28 is the ninth word (3 × 3). Between *mi* 28 and *mi* 29 there are three words. Between *mi* 29 and *me* 31 there are six words. Between *me* 31 and *mi* 33 there are six words. Between *mi* 33 and *me* 34 there are three words. From *me* 34 to *mi* 37 inclusive there are twelve words (3 × 4). Between *mi* 37 and *mihi* 40 there are nine words. *Mi* 41 is the third word after that, and *mihi* 42 is the third word after that.

The phrases *qui es* 4, 46, *qui est* 10, and *cuius est* 14 refer to God; *qui es* 27 refers to St Martin. Before *qui es* 4 there are eleven words. After *qui es* 4 the first of *qui est* 10 is the twenty-second word (11 × 2). Between *qui est* 10 and *cuius est* 14 there are eleven words. After *cuius est* 14 there are 110 words (11 × 10) to the end of the hymn. After *qui es* 27 the end of *qui es* 46 is the sixty-sixth word (11 × 6).

From *fac me* 15 to *fac me* 26 inclusive there are thirty-four words, which divide by extreme and mean ratio at 21 and 13. From *fac me* 15 to the end of the crux of the chiasmus *O Ihesu Nazarene* 18 there are thirteen words, whence to *fac me* 26 inclusive there are twenty-one words.

The poet asks Jesus to direct his way to the shrine of Saint Martin, 'there to weep for sins' *ibi peccata flere* 20. He asks Saint Martin to intercede for him now 'burdened by the disgrace of sins' *labe culparum presso* 32. The remedy lies in a direct appeal to the merit of Saint Martin, 'who are of such great virtue' *qui es uirtutis tantae* 27. From the first reference to sins to the second reference to sins, from line 20 to line 32 inclusive, there are thirteen lines and forty-three words. The thirteen lines divide by extreme and mean ratio at 8 and 5. The forty-three words divide by symmetry at 22. From the beginning of line 20 the twenty-second word is the first of the eighth line, *qui es uirtutis tantae* 27. The first two words are also part of the arithmetic arrangement of the phrase *qui es*, and the last is part of the great chiasmus F'2, a clear indication, like the interweaving of the greater and lesser chiastic passages, that the poet could coordinate multiple patterns.

The first five stanzas are addressed to God. The central sixth stanza describes the aid of Saint Martin against shipwreck on the journey between the poet's home, presumably in Ireland, and the shrine of Saint Martin, presumably at Tours. The last five stanzas are addressed to Saint Martin. The doxology is addressed to God. The most appropriate occasions for recitation of this hymn might be the two principal feasts of Saint Martin, 4 July and 11 November. For an Irishman whose year began on 1 January, as in the *Annals of Ulster*, that would be the fourth day of the seventh month and the eleventh day of the eleventh month.

There are two lines of doxology, four lines in each stanza, seven rhymes, seven syllables in each line, eleven stanzas. The eleven stanzas divide by extreme and mean ratio at 7 and 4. The seventh ends *O mi Sancte Martine*, and the last four all begin *O mi Sancte Martine*. The vocative form of the saint's name contains seven letters. The entire composition contains 777 letters, DCCLXXVII, an interesting stage on the way from the number of the beast, DCLXVI, to the numerical value of the Greek letters of the name IHΣOYΣ, DCCCLXXXVIII.

VII. *Sancta Sanctorum Opera*

The following text of *Sancta Sanctorum Opera*[1] differs from the manuscript of the Antiphonary of Bangor folio 36v in three places, reading etymologically correct· *Bennchorensi* for *Benchorensi* 3, *tempora* for *tempra* 6, and *dominum* for *domnum* 14.

MEMORIA ABBATUM NOSTRORUM

Prologue		Sancta sanctorum opera	3	8	20
		Patrum fratres fortissima	3	8	23
		Bennchorensi in optima	3	8	20
		Fundatorum aecclesia	2	8	19
	5	Abbatum eminentia	2	8	16
		Numerum tempora nomina	3	8	20
		Sine fine fulgentia	3	8	17
		Audite magna merita ;.	3	8	17
		Quos conuocauit Dominus .	3	8	21
	10	Caelorum regni sedibus :,	3	8	20
I		Amauit Xpistus Comgillum	3	8	22
		Bene et ipse dominum	4	8	17
		Carum habuit Beognoum	3	8	19
		Dominum ornauit Aedeum	3	8	20
	15	Elegit Sanctum Sinlanum	3	8	21
		Famosum mundi magistrum :,	3	8	21
		Quos conuocauit Dominus .	3	8	21
		Caelorum regni sedibus.	3	8	20
II		Gratum fecit Fintenanum	3	8	21
	20	Heredum almum inclitum	3	8	20
		Illustrauit Maclaisreum	2	8	22
		Kaput abbatum omnium	3	8	18
		Lampade sacrae Seganum	3	8	20
		Magnum scripturae medicum	3	8	23

1 *BCLL* 576.

25	Quos conuocauit Dominus	3	8	21
	Caelorum regni sedíbus.	3	8	20
III	Notus uir erat Berachus	4	8	20
	Ornatus et Cumenenus	3	8	18
	Pastor Columba congruus	3	8	21
30	Querela absque Aidanus	3	8	20
	Rector bonus Bäíthenus	3	8	20
	Summus antistes Critanus	3	8	22
	Quos conuocauit Dominus	3	8	21
	Caelorum regni sedíbus.	3	8	20
IIII 35	Tantis successit Colmanus	3	8	23
	Vir amabilis omnibus	3	8	18
	Xpisto nunc sedet supremus	4	8	23
	Ymnos canens. Quindecimus	3	8	22
	Zoen ut carpat Cronanus	4	8	20
40	Conseruet eum Dominus	3	8	19
	Quos conuocabit Dominus	3	8	21
	Caelorum regni sedíbus.	3	8	20
Epilogue	Horum sanctorum merita	3	8	20
	Abbatum fidelissima	2	8	18
45	Erga Comgillum congrua	3	8	20
	Inuocamus altissima	2	8	18
	Uti possimus omnia	3	8	16
	Nostra delere crimina	3	8	19
	Per Ihesum Xpistum aeterna	4	8	23
50	Regnaturum in saecula .	3	8	19

Prologue   Hear, brothers, the great merits, the most powerful holy works of holy fathers, founders in the best church of Bangor, the outstanding number, times, names of abbots, shining without end, whom the Lord has called together in seats of the realm of the heavens.

I   Christ loved Comgillus well, and He held Beognous dear; He adorned the lord Aedeus; He chose holy Sinlanus, famous master of the world, whom the Lord has called together in seats of the realm of the heavens.

II   He made Fintenanus gracious, celebrated nurturer of heirs; He illuminated Maclaisreus, head of all abbots, with the lamp of sacred scripture, Seganus the great doctor, whom the Lord has called together in seats of the realm of the heavens.

III   Berachus was a noted man and Cumenenus an adorned one, Columba a fit pastor, Aidanus without quarrel, Baithenus a good rector, Critanus the highest priest [or 'bishop', lit. 'he who stands before'], whom the Lord has called together in seats of the realm of the heavens.

IIII   To such men Colmanus succeeded, a man loveable by all. Now he sits supreme singing hymns to Christ. Fifteenth, that Cronanus may seize life may the Lord conserve him, whom the Lord will call together on seats of the realm of the heavens.

Epilogue   We invoke the loftiest most faithful merits of these holy abbots, fit [and interceding] with Comgillus, so that we can wipe out all our sins, through Jesus Christ, bound to reign for eternal ages.

The diction of the Prologue, *sanctorum, abbatum, tempora, sine fine, merita,* is echoed by that of the Epilogue, *sanctorum, abbatum, aeterna, in saecula, merita.* Both Prologue and Epilogue rhyme on -*a.* The refrain, which occurs five times, rhymes on -*us,* and the final couplet rhymes on -*a.* Note the chiastic vowel rhymes and alliteration in line 8, *a-i-e-m-a-a-m-e-i-a,* and the internal rhymes and alliteration of the refrain.

Prologue, Epilogue, and refrains surround four stanzas of six lines each. The initial letters of twenty-three of these twenty-four lines follow the order of the roman alphabet from *A* to *Z.*[2] Parts I and II rhyme on -*um,* and parts III and IIII rhyme on -*us.* Prologue, Epilogue, and refrains occupy twenty-four lines of verse and seventy-five words and and 192 syllables; the four parts of alphabetical verse occupy twenty-four lines of verse and seventy-five words and 192 syllables. Prologue, alphabetic stanzas, refrains, Epilogue, and final couplet together comprise 153 words, 153 being the number of fishes in the net in John XXI 11 and the triangular number 1–17. There are 153 letters in the Epilogue and final couplet, 152 in the Prologue. In the entire poem there are exactly 1000 letters, of which the 500th is the first letter of the central twenty-sixth line.

One reason for celebrating the succession of fifteen abbots may be that there were in the Book of Judges fifteen Israelite judges. The references to the most recent abbot Crónán in the present tense subjunctive mood and future tense indicative mood are usually assumed to indicate composition during the period of his regime, A.D. 680–91. The numbers of letters in the Prologue, the four alphabetic stanzas, and the refrain in the future tense about Crónán, 152 + 120 + 124 + 121 + 125 + 41, total 683, which may suggest the year of composition of this poem.

VIII.   *Benchuir Bona Regula*

Among the undoubtably Irish Latin compositions in the Antiphony of Bangor folio 30r-v is the following poem about the *familia* of the monastery of Bangor.[1]

---

2   See above p. 139–42, 145.
1   *BCLL* 574.

VERSICULI FAMILIAE BENCHUIR .

1	pp	**B**enchuir bona regula	a	3	7	18
	p	**R**ecta atque diuina	b	3	7	16
	pp	**S**tricta sancta sedula	a	3	7	19
	p	**S**umma iusta ac mira .	b	4	7	16
						69
2	5 p.	**M**unther **B**enchuir beata	c	3	7	20
	p	**F**ide fundata certa	d	3	7	16
	p	**S**pe salutis ornata	c	3	7	16
	p	**C**aritate perfecta :·	d	2	7	16
						68
3	p	**N**auis numquam turbata	c	3	7	19
	10 p	**Q**uamuis fluctibus tonsa	e	3	7	21
	p	**N**uptiis quoque parata	c	3	7	19
	p	**R**egi Domino sponsa ..,	e	3	7	16
						75
4	p	**D**omus deliciis plena	b	3	7	18
	p	**S**uper petram constructa	f	3	7	21
	15 p	**N**ecnon uinea uera	b	3	7	15
	p	**E**x **A**egipto transducta .	f	3	7	19
						73
5	p	**C**erte ciuitas firma	b	3	7	17
	p	**F**ortis atque munita	g	3	7	17
	p	**G**loriosa ac digna	b	3	7	15
	20 pp	**S**upra montem posita :.,	g	3	7	17
						66
6	p	**ARC**a **C**herubin tecta	d	3	7	17
	p	**O**mni parte aurata	c	3	7	15
	p	**S**acrosanctis reperta	d	2	7	19
	p	**V**iris quattuor portata	c	3	7	20
						71
7	25 p	**Xp**isto regina apta	d	3	7	16
	p	**S**olis luce amicta	h	3	7	15
	p	**S**implex simulque docta	d	3	7	20
	p	**U**ndecumque inuicta	h	2	7	17
						68
8	p	**V**ere regalis aula	i	3	7	15
	30 p	**V**ariis gemmis ornata	c	3	7	18
	p.	**G**regisque **X**pisti caula	i	3	7	20
	p	**P**atre **S**ummo seruata .	c	3	7	17
						70
9	p	**VIR**go ualde fecunda	j	3	7	17
	p	**H**aec et mater . intacta	k	4	7	18

35	p	Laeta ac tremebunda	j	3	7	17
	p	Verbo Dei subacta :·	k	3	7	15
						67
10	p	Cui uita beata	c	3	7	12
	p	Cum perfectis futura	l	3	7	18
	p	Deo Patre parata	c	3	7	14
40	p	Sine fine mansura :.,	l	3	7	15
						59
			119	280	686	

Benchuir bona regula :·

Bangor, good in its rule,
straight and divine,
strict, holy, sedulous,
highest, just, and wondrous.

Monastery of Bangor, blessed,
founded on a certain faith,
adorned with the hope of salvation,
perfect in charity.

Ship never turbulent,
though skimmed by waves,
also prepared for wedding festivities
as spouse for the Lord King.

House filled with delights,
constructed upon a rock,
also true vine,
led over out of Egypt.

City surely firm,
strong and fortified,
glorious and worthy,
placed atop the mount.

Arc covered by Cherubim,
gilded in every part,
devised for sacrosanct things,
borne by four men.

Queen fit for Christ,
clothed with the light of the sun,
simple and simultaneously learned,
everywhere unconquered.

Truly royal hall,
adorned with varied gems,
and fold of the flock of Christ,
protected by the Highest Father.

Virgin especially fecund,
this, and intact mother,
happy and trembling,
subdued by the Word of God,

To whom blessed life
to come, with the perfect,
prepared by God the Father,
bound to remain without end.

Bangor, good in its rule.

The poem is regularly stanzaic with forty lines in ten stanzas of four lines each. There are six examples of synizesis, in *Benchuir* 1 and 4, *quattuor* 24, *nuptiis* 11, *deliciis* 13, and *uariis* 30. The lines are thus all perfectly heptasyllabic. The cadences are regularly disposed, the first and third lines of the first stanza and the last line of the central stanza exhibiting proparoxytone cadences and all other lines paroxytone cadences.

There are twelve end rhymes, varying from one syllable and a single letter, in 2–4, 13–15, 17–19, or two letters, in 6–8, 21–23, 25–27, to two syllables and three letters, in 1–3, 5–7, 9–11, 14–16, 18–20, 22–24, 30–32, 37–39, 38–40, or four letters, in 10–12, 26–28, 29–31, 33–35, 34–36. The lines which end in rhymes of only one or two letters exhibit vowel rhyme of one other vowel before the end rhyme, in 2–4, 6–8, 13–15, 25–27, or two other vowels before the end rhyme, in 17–19, 21–23. The lines which end in rhymes of three or four letters exhibit vowel rhyme of one other vowel before the end rhyme, in 5–7, 18–20, 30–32, 38–40, or two other vowels before the end rhyme, in 1–3, 9–11, 10–12, 14–16, 21–23, 22–24, 26–28, or three other vowels before the end rhyme, in 29–31, 33–35. Some lines exhibit consonant rhyme as well as internal vowel rhyme, in 9–11, 13–15, 14–16, 30–32. Sometimes vowel rhymes at the end of one line are repeated at the beginning of the next, as 3–4, 6–7, 13–14.

All but two lines, 12 and 20, exhibit alliteration in one or more of four forms. In exactly half the verses there are at least two alliterating sounds within a line, in 1, 3, 5, 6, 7, 9, 13, 15, 16, 17, 18, 22, 23, 27, 28, 31, 32, 33, 34, 39. Words alliterate with those in the line immediately following in 1–2, 3–4, 9–10, 10–1, 13–4, 17–8, 18–9, 21–2, 25–6, 26–7, 29–30, 34–5, 37–8. Words alliterate with those in alternate rhyming lines in 6–8, 22–24, 26–28, 38–40, or between the first and last lines of a stanza in 33–36.

In the first half of the poem, stanzas 1–5, the first lines exhibit two alliterating words, *Benchuir bona* 1, *Benchuir beata* 5, *Nauis numquam* 9, *Domus deliciis* 13, *Certe ciuitas* 17. In the second half of the poem, stanzas 6–10, the sixth and seventh alliterate on *ch* in *Cherubin* 21 and *Xpisto* 25, the eighth and ninth alliterate on *u* and *r* in *Vere Variis* 29–30 and *Virgo ualde* 33. The tenth stanza, beginning *Cui uita beata* 37, echoes the alliteration of the beginning and the end of the first half on *B* and *C* and the alliteration of the second half on *C* and *V*.

The poet has disposed words at arithmetically fixed intervals according to ratios commended by Boethius in the account of Pythagoras and the smiths' hammers in *De Institutione Musica* I x. The poem celebrates God the Father and Christ the Lord, Whom the monastic *familia* of Bangor serve. By symmetry the forty lines divide at 20 and 20, the 119 words at 60, the 280 syllables at 140 and 140, the 686 letters at 343 and 343. The last word of line 20, the sixtieth word from beginning and end, the last syllable of which is 140th, is the proparoxytone *posita*, referring to the *ciuitas Benchuir supra montem posita*. The central letters of the poem stand in the middle of the central word of this line. The 119 words divide by sesquialter ratio, 3:2, at 71 and 48. The forty-eighth word from the end is *Xpisto*. Those forty-eight words divide by sesquialter ratio at 29 and 19. From *Xpisto* to *Xpisti* inclusive there are nineteen words. Of the first seventy-one words the central, thirty-sixth, is the last of *Regi Domino sponsa*, referring to God and Bangor. Of the twenty-nine words after *Xpisti* the central, fifteenth, is the first of *Verbo Dei subacta*, referring to God and Bangor. From *Dei* inclusive to the end of the hymn there are fourteen words, which divide by sesquialter ratio at 9 and 5. From *Dei* to *Deo* inclusive there are nine words. The 119 words divide by one-ninth and eight-ninths at 13 and 106. Between *Benchuir* 1 and *Benchuir* 5 there are thirteen words.

If the poet allowed one letter of his hymn for every year since the Incarnation one might date the composition to A.D. 686.[2] From *Audite Omnes Amantes Deum* line 43, *ciuitas Regis munita supra montem posita*, has been adapted to *certe ciuitas firma / fortis atque munita / … supra montem posita*. Regardless of the echo of the earlier work, the text of this hymn appears to have been transmitted very nearly in the form in which it issued from its author's pen.

IX. MOUCANI

Orationes

British Library MS Royal 2 A xx, a Mercian manuscript from the second half of the eighth century, contains lections from Gospels, prayers, hymns, canticles, and charms in Latin with later Old English and other glosses.[1] Among its contents one

---

2   See above pp. 159, 189.

1   *BCLL* 29. For description of the contents of the manuscript see the *Catalogue of Ancient Manuscripts in the British Museum* (London 1884), vol. II pp. 60 ff.; *An Ancient Manuscript of the Eighth or Ninth Century*, ed. W. de G. Birch, Hampshire Record Society II (London & Winchester 1889), app. A pp. 101–13, at 108; *The Antiphonary of Bangor*, ed. F. E. Warren, Henry Bradshaw Society X (London 1895), app. pp. 97–102, at 101; Sir George F. Warner & J.P. Gilson, *Catalogue of Western*

finds from folio 42r to folio 45r the *Ora' moucani*, edited once entire by Kuypers in an appendix to the *Book of Cerne*[2] and again in part by Meyer as *Oratio Moucani*.[3]

Who this Moucan might have been one can only guess. From a reference in the first chapter of Rhygyfarch's *Life of Saint David* to a *Maucanni monasterium quod nunc usque Depositi monasterium uocatur*,[4] from the invocation *Sancte Winuualoe, Sancte Maucanne, Sancte Gilda ora* in an eleventh-century Exeter litany,[5] from the references to *Maucanus* and *Moucanus* in the *Vita Sancti Cadoci* in British Library MS Cotton Vespasian A XIV (about 1200),[6] from the Pembrokeshire place-name Port Maugan, the Breckon place-name Llan-feugan, and the Anglesey place-name Capel Meugan, one infers that our author bore a Brittonic, and specifically an Old Welsh name. From the date of the manuscript one infers that he lived not later than the second half of the seventh century or the first half of the eighth.

The text has attracted hardly any attention,[7] partly because at first sight it appears to be merely a cento of Biblical quotations.

The title assigned to the work in the editions by Kuypers and Meyer implies that it is a single work, and both Hughes and Sims-Williams have assumed the same, though the latter two have recognized nine internal divisions. Because of the nature of his edition Kuypers did not divide the work. Meyer believed that the text 'zerfällt in 9 Abschnitte oder Gebete', but he printed only four. Warren believed that it had nine parts, but Birch described it as having eight and Warner and Gilson ten. There is no clear agreement about the existence or the number of internal divisions or the points at which they begin and end.

The text is introduced by a heading with a capital letter on folio 42r, *Ora' moucani*, the former word written in black ink and the latter in red. As a title in the middle of folio 42v reads *Item alia*, and the only possible antecedent is *Ora'*,

---

Manuscripts in the Old Royal and King's Collections (London 1921), vol. I pp. 33–6; J.F. Kenney, *The Sources for the Early History of Ireland: Ecclesiastical* (New York 1929 rept 1966), no. 576 pp. 719–20; N.R. Ker, *Catalogue of Manuscripts Containing Anglo-Saxon* (Oxford 1957 rept 1990), no. 248 pp. 317–8; E.A. Lowe, *Codices Latini Antiquiores*, 2nd edn., vol. II, (Oxford 1972), no. 215 pp. 28, 52–3 and refs. there cited; L. Webster & J. Backhouse, *The Making of England, Anglo-Saxon Art and Culture AD 600–900* (London 1991), no. 163 pp. 208–10.

2   *The Prayer Book of Aedeluald the Bishop, Commonly called the Book of Cerne*, ed. A. B. Kuypers, (Cambridge 1902), app. pp. 219–20.

3   Wilhelm Meyer, 'Poetische Nachlese aus dem sogenannten Book of Cerne in Cambridge *und aus dem Londoner Codex Regius* 2 A.XX', *Nachrichten von der Königlichen Gesellschaft der Wissenschaften zu Göttingen, Philologisch-historische Klasse* (1917), pp. 620–5.

4   *Rhigyfarch's Life of St David*, ed. & transl. J.W. James (Cardiff 1967), p. 1.

5   *The Leofric Collectar*, ed. E.S. Dewick, Henry Bradshaw Society XLV (London 1913), vol. I p. 440 f. 110b.

6   *Vitae Sanctorum Britanniae et Genealogiae*, ed. A.W. Wade-Evans, Board of Celtic Studies, University of Wales History and Law Series IX (Cardiff 1944) *Vita Sancti Cadoci*, § 45 p. 116 and § 67 p. 136. For an argument that the name *Moucan* > *Meugan* is specifically Welsh see P. Sims-Williams's review of *The Welsh Life of St David*, ed. D.S. Evans (Cardiff 1988) in the *Journal of Ecclesiastical History* XLIII (1992), pp. 468–70.

7   For recent consideration see Kathleen Hughes, 'Some Aspects of Irish Influence on Early English Private Prayer', O'Donnell Lecture in the University of Wales for 1969, *Studia Celtica* V (1970), pp. 48–61, at 57–9, and P. Sims-Williams, *Religion and Literature in Western England 600–800*, Cambridge Studies in Anglo-Saxon England III (Cambridge 1990), pp. 169, 280, 318, 320–2, 327.

one infers that there are at least two *orationes*; but various names of God appear to serve as a refrain or amen which implies that there are nine *orationes*. After the capital letter in the introduction all nine prayers begin with capital letters in the manuscript, and all nine prayers end with punctuation points before the various names of God. The first and the ninth conclude additionally with the Aramaic phrase *Eli Eli laba sabacthani*. Meyer believed that the prayers were 'in Reimprosa geschrieben. ... Hie und da finden sich Zeilen ohne Reim'. But the apparent lack of rhyme issues from failure to perceive the true structural principles and consequent inaccurate division. The lines correctly arranged all rhyme, variously from a single letter to six letters and from one syllable to three syllables.

In the following edition capital letters in large boldface represent letters in the manuscript marked with wash of various colours and surrounded by dots. Capital letters and rubrics in boldface represent features of the manuscript, as do the punctuation marks. Words and punctuation marks in square brackets I have supplied. *Italics* suggest possible rhyme and <u>underlinings</u> alliteration. I have marked the cursus rhythms, which conform to six widely practised types, all exhibited in the first prayer: *planus, Spíritum Sánctum* I 2; *tardus, píe iustíficat* I 10; *uelox, conpléctitur ùniuérsa* I 4; *medius, Déum Fílium* I 1; *trispondiacus, límphas ponderántem* I 7; and *dispondeus dactylicus, Sábaoth Ia Ádonai* I 14. To the right of the texts the first column notes the numbers of lines, the second the rhyme scheme, the third the number of words in each line, the fourth the number of syllables, and the fifth the number of letters.

Ora[tiones] moucani
[I]

<u>D</u>eum Patrem <u>Dé</u><u>um</u> Fílium		a	4	9	20
<u>Deum</u> <u>de</u>precor <u>S</u>pír<u>itum</u> <u>S</u>ánctum		a	4	10	27
c<u>ui</u>us magn<u>itú</u>do <u>in</u>mén<u>s</u>a		b	3	9	21
giro[8] <u>c</u>onpléctitur <u>ùni</u>uérsa.		b	3	10	24
<u>T</u>rínum[9] <u>in</u> persónis <u>a</u>tque[10] <u>ú</u>num	5	c	5	10	25
<u>in</u> natura. símplum *et* <u>trínum</u>[.]		c	5	9	23
terram <u>su</u>p*er* límpha<u>s</u> ponderántem.		d	4	10	29
*ae*thram *cum* á<u>s</u>tris <u>su</u>spendéntem.		d	4	9	28
m<u>í</u>hi <u>ut</u> <u>p</u>rop<u>í</u>tiu<u>s</u> <u>p</u>eccator<u>i</u> *fiat.* [? l. peccatori propítius *fiat.*]		e	5	13	28
qu<u>i</u> <u>omn</u>es <u>i</u>mp<u>i</u>os <u>p</u>íe iust<u>í</u>ficat	10	e	5	12	26
u<u>iu</u>it <u>u</u>i<u>u</u>ens contínue. *fiat*		e	4	10	23
Deus benedíctus in sæc<u>ula</u>		f	4	10	23
Ámen *fiat fiat:-*		e	3	6	12
<u>El</u>oe. <u>Sába</u>oth. Ia. Ádonai.		g	4	10	19
<u>E</u>li. <u>E</u>li. lába. <u>saba</u>cthání.	15	g	4	10	20

8   MS *y* added above *i*.
9   MS gloss in right margin *Trinitas*.
10 MS *et*.

I pray God the Father, God the Son, God the Holy Ghost,
Whose immeasurable greatness encompasses all things everywhere,
in persons three and one, in nature single and triune,
weighing out the earth above the waters, hanging the upper region with
    stars,
that He be propitious to me, a sinner, Who holily justifies all impious men,
Who lives, living continuously. Let
God be blessed for ages. Amen. Let it be so. Let it be so.
Eloe, Sabaoth, Ya, Adonai, Eli Eli lama sabacthani.

In this prayer there are only a few echoes of Biblical phrases. Lines 7 and 8 allude
to but do not quote Genesis I. The source of line 9, not noticed by Meyer, but
recognized by Sims-Williams,[11] is Luke XVIII 13, where the *publicanus a longe stans*
says *Deus propitius esto mihi peccatori*. That clearly establishes a penitential mood,
which makes nonsense of Meyer's suggestion that the source for the next line is
Proverbs XVII 15.[12] The verse *et qui iustificat impium et qui condemnat iustum
abominabilis est uterque apud Dominum* could hardly be more inapposite here. The
source is Romans IV 5, *ei uero qui non operatur credenti autem in eum qui iustificat
impium reputatur fides eius ad iustitiam*. The last line is quoted from Mark XV 34 or
Matthew XXVII 46. According to Kathleen Hughes, 'This is a kind of badge of
erudition, repeated over and over as a formula possessing in itself some virtue'.[13]
But even a layman might know this from the Passion narratives read in liturgies
for Holy Week. In fact Moucan does not repeat it over and over; he quotes it in
the last line of the first and last prayers, as the ultimate cry from the penitent's
heart. The spelling *laba* for *lama*, remarkable in an eighth-century Anglo-Saxon
manuscript, is consistent with the Old Welsh name of the author, suggesting that
he was a Welsh speaker accustomed to intervocalic lenition.[14]

    There is obvious parallelism in the lines of each couplet and a little
chiasmus with internal parallelism in lines 5 and 6:

a	trinum	
b i	in personis	
ii		unum
b'i	in natura	
ii		simplum
a'	trinum.	

There are fifteen lines with seven end rhymes in a scheme aabbccddeeefegg.
There are many more places in which vowels rhyme and consonants alliterate at

11 Sims-Williams, *Religion & Literature*, p. 318 n. 190.
12 Meyer, p. 622.
13 Hughes, p. 57; cf. Sims-Williams, *Religion & Literature*, p. 321 n. 201.
14 For another example see prayer IX line 28 n. 59 below. Note also the internal rhyme with the
    preceding line in *Sabaoth* and *laba*.

the same relative place within the lines, reckoned variously from beginning and end. In every couplet each of the pair of lines contains the same number of words: 4–4–3–3–5–5–4–4–5–5–4–4–3–4–4. Note the balance of threes and fours in the first and last lines, 4–4–3–3 and 4–4–3–4–4, around the symmetrically arranged central lines, 5–5–4–4–5–5. There is a remarkable regularity of syllables as well: 9–10–9–10–10–9–10–9–13–12–10–10–6–10–10. The first eight are parallel, 9–10–9–10, 10–9–10–9, and the last five symmetrical, 10–10–6–10–10. The golden section of the fifteen lines of the prayer falls at 9 and 6, that of the seven end rhymes of the prayer falls at 4 and 3. The division occurs by both criteria at line 9. The last two lines are symmetrical, comprising four words each and ten syllables each, the former nineteen letters and the latter twenty letters. With these symmetrically arranged divine names detached the prayer proper comprises thirteen lines, fifty-three words, and 127 syllables. The golden section of 13 falls at 8 and 5, that of 53 at 33 and 20, that of 127 at 78 and 49. Moucan speaks first and last of God, but at the golden section of lines, words, and syllables, he refers to himself. At the beginning of line 9, the thirty-third word is *mihi*. The seventy-eighth syllable is the last of *mihi*.

[II]

Da capiti[15] meo flébílem áquam		a	5	11	24
et oculis meis lácrimarum úndam.		a	5	11	27
quia obscurátum est aùrum témpli		b	5	11	28
quod in me [filio] praèparásti.		b	5	10	24
et sunt dispersi lapides sánctuárii[16]	5	b	5	13	31
pulcherrimi ólim et quadráti.		b	4	10	25
Caldaica motauit. flamma [? l. motauit Caldáica flámma]		c	3	9	21
duo chírubin.[17] dèauráta		c	3	9	19
candelabrum sciéntiae uélum		d	3	10	25
castitatis péne discíssum.[18]	10	d	3	9	23
et oleum unctiónis ad ménsam		a	5	11	24
Patri Xpisto Spirítui praèparátam.[19]		a	4	12	30
Duae colúmnae altàris bína		c	4	10	22
intus et foris ópera míra ;		c	5	10	21
mare aeneum lúteris múltæ	15	e	4	10	23
lebetes[20] ánimae súabte[21]		e	3	9	19
pelti fídei ámuli[22] scútri		f	4	10	21

15   MS *capite*.
16   MS *sanctuari*.
17   MS *e* altered from first *i*.
18   MS *s* added above last *s*.
19   MS *praeparata*. f. 42r ends here.
20   MS *labantes*, treated here as a feminine noun perhaps by analogy with Later Latin *lebeta*.
21   MS *p* added above *b*. For another example see prayer IX line 19 n. 57 below.
22   MS *scimuli*.

		f	5	12	25
uasa[23] innumera argénti et aúri.					
hec[24] in plateis ó[25] demólita		c	5	10	21
animae meæ átque conspérsa.[26]	20	c	4	10	24
heu in mihi meus quia incolátus		g	5	11	24
cum domíbus Cédar prolongátus.		g	4	10	26
multum incola fuit ánima méa.		c	5	12	24
patris cum adulteris consumsi bona:-		c	5	12	30
Éloe. Sábaoth.	25	h	2	6	11

Give to my head plaintive water [*i.e.* tears] and to my eyes a flow of tears,
because the gold of the temple is concealed, which You have prepared
    in me,
and the stones of the sanctuary are dispersed, once most beautiful and
    squared.
Chaldaean flame has shaken the two gilded cherubim,
the candelabrum of learning, the curtain of chastity almost rent,
and the oil of unction for the table prepared for the Father, for Christ,
    for the Spirit.
Two columns of the altar, double works wondrous within and without,
the brazen sea, many cauldrons with lavers, souls in their own fashion,
shields, stringed instruments, little buckets, shallow dishes, countless
    vessels of silver and gold,
these things of my soul, O, demolished and spread abroad in the streets.
Alas for me because my dwelling, Cedar with its houses, is far removed.
My soul was the inhabitant. I have consumed the goods of my father
    with adulterers.
Eloe. Sabaoth.

In this prayer Moucan echoes and alludes to many more Biblical texts than in
Oratio I.

Jeremiah IX 1	quis dabit capiti meo aquam et oculis meis fontem lacrimarum
Lamentations IV 1	quomodo obscuratum est aurum
Wisdom IX 8	similitudinem tabernaculi sancti tui quod praeparasti ab initio
Lamentations IV 1	dispersi sunt lapides sanctuarii
II Kings XXV 13	columnas autem aereas quae erant in templo
(=Jeremiah LII 17)	Domini et bases
	mare aeneum quod erat in domo Domini confregerunt Chaldei

23   MS *uassa* with the first *s* erased. For another example see prayer VIII line 10 n. 44 below.
24   MS *hoc*.
25   MS *ó aut*.
26   MS *conspisa*.

I Kings VI 23–8	fecit in oraculo duo cherubin ... texit quoque cherubin auro
I Kings VII 48–9	fecitque Salomon omnia uasa in domo Domini altare aureum et mensam ... et candelabra aurea
Mark XV 38	uelum templi scissum est in duo
Exodus XXIX 7	oleum unctionis fundes super caput eius [sc. Aaron]
I Kings VII 43–5	et bases decem et luteres decem super bases et mare unum et boues duodecim subter mare et lebetas et scutras et amulas omnia uasa quae fecit Hiram regi Salomoni in domo Domini de auricalcho erant
I Kings X 17	trecentas peltas ex auro probato
Lamentations II 10–1	consperserunt cinere capita sua accincti sunt ciliciis ... defecerunt prae lacrimis oculi mei conturbata sunt uiscera mea ... cum deficeret paruulus et lactans in plateis oppidi
Lamentations II 6	dissipauit quasi hortum tentorium suum demolitus est tabernaculum suum
Psalm CXIX 5–6	heu mihi quia peregrinatio mea prolongata est habitaui cum tabernaculis Cedar multum peregrinata est anima mea
Isaiah XLII 11	in domibus habitabit Cedar

The borrowings are unmistakeable. Moucan has collected from Old Testament and New Testament descriptions of the Tabernacle and the First and Second Temples. He has made the references to their destruction an allegory of damage to his own soul, housed in the temple of his body,[27] which is the true subject of the prayer.

He mentions himself at the very beginning, *Da capiti meo* 1, and references to *me*, *meus*, and *anima mea* recur throughout the prayer. Between *meo* 1 and *meis* 2 there are four words (4 × 1). Between *meis* and *in me* 4 there are eight words (4 × 2). After *in me* there are forty-eight words (4 × 12) to *animae suabte* 16. After *animae suabte* the sixteenth word (4 × 4) is the last of *animae meæ* 20. After *meæ* the fourth word (4 × 1) is *mihi* 21. From the next word *meus* 21 to *anima mea* 23 inclusive there are twelve words (4 × 3), and *mea* is the eighth word (4 × 2) from the end of the prayer.

The prayer proper comprises twenty-four lines, twelve in each half. The central words are *Duae columnae altaris* 13 at the beginning of the second half. There are 126 syllables in the first half and 126 syllables in the second half.

---

27 I Corinthians III 16–7.

Item alia

[III]

Nunc pænitúdinis uérba		a	3	8	21
sedula míhi sunt faténda.[28]		a	4	9	21
A quo stolam ínmortalitátis		b	4	10	24
spero et ánulam dìgnitátis.		b	4	10	23
qui meo aduéntui uítulum	5	c	4	10	21
de armentis iúgulat sàginátum.		c	4	11	26
Cuius cruore tótius múndi		d	4	10	22
machina repléta est spársi		d	4	9	23
cuius et ín figura ágni		d	5	9	19
sanguis et in límina pícti	10	d	5	9	22
per quem Didimi signatur manus [? l. mánus signátur]		e	5	10	26
Raab meretricis saluatur [29] domus. [? l. dómus saluátur.]	e	4	10	27
Eloe.		f	1	3	4

Now the painstaking words of penitence must be uttered for me.
He from Whom I hope for the stole of immortality and the ring of dignity,
Who for my arrival slays from the herd the fattened calf,
by Whose blood the structure of the whole world is restored,
and Whose blood in the figure of a lamb sprinkled and painted on
     threshholds,
by Whom the hand of the Twin [*i.e.* Thomas] is impressed [into Christ's
     wound],
[and] the house of Rahab the harlot is saved.
Eloe.

Luke XV 22–3	dixit autem pater ad seruos suos
	cito proferte stolam primam et induite illum
	et date anulum in manum eius et calciamenta in
	pedes et adducite uitulum saginatum et occidite
	et manducemus et epulemur quia hic filius meus
	mortuus erat et reuixit perierat et inuentus est
Exodus XII 21–2	uocauit autem Moses omnes seniores filiorum
	Israhel et dixit ad eos ite tollentes animal per
	familias uestras immolate phase fasciculumque
	hysopi tinguite sanguine qui est in limine et
	aspergite ex eo superliminare et utrumque postem
John XX 24–7	Thomas autem unus ex duodecim qui dicitur
	Didymus ... uenit Iesus ... deinde dicit Thomae
	... adfer manum tuam et mitte in latus meum

28   MS *fatenda sùnt.*
29   MS *saluatus.*

Joshua VI 25   Raab uero meretricem et domum patris eius
atque omnia quae habebat fecit Iosue uiuere et
habitauerunt in medio Israhel usque in
praesentem diem

Hughes has taxed Moucan with obscurity and error:[30]

> He finishes up by saying that the house of Rahab the Harlot was saved
> through the blood; either the author's own mistake or some error of
> transmission, for Rahab was in fact saved by the scarlet thread she tied to
> her window when the walls of Jericho fell down. These two sections
> [*i.e.* prayers II and III] move from allusion to allusion. They are couched
> in a most obscure form, as if the allusions had merit in themselves.
> Though the vocabulary is not hisperic, they are a kind of secret language
> for the learned, for only someone who knew the Scriptures well would
> be able to appreciate the references.

If the passage is translated correctly the references are in no way obscure. Moucan
alludes clearly to the killing of a beast to mark the salvation of the Prodigal Son
and the killing of a beast to mark the salvation of the Sons of Israel, one example
from the New Testament and one from the Old Testament. The scarlet thread
may be a red herring. Moucan says what he believed, that both Thomas and
Rahab were saved by Christ. After the Resurrection Thomas asked for a sign:
*nisi uidero in manibus eius figuram clauorum et mittam digitum meum in locum clauorum et
mittam manum meam in latus eius non credam* (John XX 25). Before him Rahab had
asked for a sign: *nunc ergo iurate mihi per Dominum ut ... detisque mihi signum uerum
et saluetis patrem meum et matrem, fratres et sorores meas* (Joshua II 12–3). Again
Moucan has presented one example from the New Testament and one from the
Old Testament.

The prayer comprises twelve lines, six in each half; fifty words, of which
the central occur in a central line, *Cuius cruore totius mundi* 7. There are fifty-
eight syllables in the first half and fifty-seven in the second, 136 letters in the
first half and 139 in the second.

[IV]

Pat*er* peccaui *in* cǽlum *et* córam t*e*	a	6	12	29
mis*ere*re méi *et* exaúdi m*e*.	a	5	11	21
i̯am non s*um* dignus uocari fílius túu*s*.	b	7	13	31
i̯n adiu*t*orium m*é*um intènde Déu*s*.[31]	b	5	13	27
Fac me sicut unum de mercennári*is*[32] túi*s*.	c	7	14	32

30   Hughes, p. 58; cf. Sims-Williams, *Religion & Literature*, pp. 321–2.
31   MS f. 42v ends here.
32   MS *mercinaris* corrected to *mercennariis*.

ignosce et párce peccàtis méis.		c	5	11	26
quia ualde ésurio tíbi.		d	4	10	19
dele impietátem peccáti méi.		d	4	12	24
Propitius esto mihi Dómine pèccatóri.		d	5	15	32
erue animam meam de mánu inférni.	10	d	6	14	27
memento mei Dominé in tuo régno		e	6	13	26
Eripe mé de peccáti lúto.		e	5	10	20
et Spiritum Sanctum tuum ne aúferas á me.		f	8	14	33
Neque in furore túo corrìpiás me.		f	6	13	27
ad te confugio Pátrem piíssimum[33]	15	g	5	12	27
non habens praeter té refúgium.		g	5	10	26
Solent et ad patres fúgere náti		h	6	11	26
licet post uulnera uel uerberati.		h	5	11	28
Pone me iuxta te Domine Déus uirtútum		i	7	14	31
quia cognosco [méum] peccátum.	20	i	4	10	24
Domine Deus uírtus salùtis méae		a	5	12	27
ne derelinquas mé usquequáque.		a	4	10	25
Eloe.		a	1	3	4

Father, I have sinned against heaven and in Your sight, have mercy upon
    me and hear me.
Now I am not worthy to be called Your son, attend to my help, God.
Make me like one of Your hirelings. Forgive and spare my sins.
Because I greatly hunger for You, wipe out the impiety of my sin.
Be propitious to me, Lord, a sinner; snatch my soul from the hand of hell.
Remember me, Lord, in Your kingdom; lift me up from the filth of sin,
and may You not take your Holy Spirit away from me, nor in Your
    wrath rebuke me.
To You I flee, a most holy father, not having a refuge except You,
and sons are accustomed to flee to their fathers, it is permitted after
    wounds or being beaten.
Place me next to You, Lord God of powers, because I acknowledge
    [my] sin.
Lord God, the power of my salvation, may You not abandon me utterly.
Eloe.

Luke XV 18b	pater peccaui in caelum et coram te
Psalm XXVI 7	miserere mei et exaudi me
Luke XV 19a	iam non sum dignus uocari filius tuus
Psalm LXIX 2	Deus in adiutorium meum intende
Luke XV 19b	fac me sicut unum de mercennariis tuis
Job XIV 16	parce peccatis meis

33   MS first *i* added above.

Psalm XXXI 5	remisisti impietatem peccati mei
Luke XVIII 13	propitius esto mihi peccatori
Psalm LXXXVIII 49	eruet animam suam de manu inferi
Luke XXIII 42	Domine memento mei cum ueneris in regnum tuum
Psalm LXVIII 15	eripe me de luto
Psalm L 13	et Spiritum Sanctum tuum ne auferas a me
Psalm VI 2 (= XXXVII 2)	ne in furore tuo arguas me neque in ira tua corripias me
Psalm CXLIV 9	Domine ad te confugi
II Samuel XIX 20	agnosco enim seruus tuus peccatum meum
Psalm L 5	quoniam iniquitatem meam ego cognosco
Psalm CXXXIX 8	Domine Domine uirtus salutis meae
Psalm CXVIII 8	non me derelinquas usquequaque

In this fourth prayer Moucan has combined cola principally from the story of the Prodigal Son and the Psalms, from Old Testament and New Testament alike. In the first eleven lines Moucan weaves quotations alternately from Luke and the Psalms. In the second eleven lines he borrows almost exclusively from the Psalms.

In the twenty-two lines of the prayer proper there are eleven lines, sixty-one words, and 294 letters in the first half and eleven lines, sixty words, and 294 letters in the second half.

[V]

Fortitudo mea Dómine diligám te		a	5	13	27
sub umbra alarum tuárum protége me.		a	6	13	29
Ihesu fili[34] Dauid míserere méi.		b	5	12	25
Vt aperias óculos còrdis méi.		b	5	12	24
Post te clamabo cum Canánica uídua	5	c	6	13	29
quia uulnerata est ánima méa		c	5	12	24
etiam cátuli cómedunt		d	3	8	19
micas quae de mensa Dómini cádunt.		d	6	11	28
Dic uerbo et sanabor sánitas múndi.[35]		e	6	12	29
Remitte impietátem peccáti méi.	10	e	4	13	27
Fimbrias túi si tetígero		f	4	10	21
saluus fiam á peccato méo.		f	5	10	21
Éloe Sábaoth.		g	2	6	11

My strength, Lord, I will love You; under the shadow of Your wings protect me.

---

34   MS *filii*.
35   MS f. 43r ends here.

Jesu, son of David, have mercy on me, that You may open the eyes of
my heart.
Afterwards I shall call to You with the Canaanite widow, because my
soul has been wounded,
'Even the pups eat the scraps which fall from the lord's table'
Speak with a word and I shall be healed, O health of the world.
Remit the impiety of my sin; if I shall touch the fringe of Your [garment]
I shall be saved from my sin.
Eloe. Sabaoth.

Psalm XVII 2	diligam te, Domine, fortitudo mea
Psalm XVI 8	sub umbra alarum tuarum proteges me
Mark X 47	fili David, Iesu, miserere mei
Isaiah XLII 7	ut aperires oculos caecorum
Matthew XV 22	mulier Chananea ... clamauit
Ecclesiasticus XXVII 22	effugit enim quasi caprea de laqueo quoniam uulnerata est
Matthew XV 27	nam et catelli edunt de micis quae cadunt de mensa dominorum
Luke VII 7	dic uerbo et sanabitur puer meus
Psalm XXXI 5	remisisti impietatem peccati mei
Matthew IX 20–1	fimbriam uestimenti eius ... si tetigero ... salua ero.

Moucan has rearranged the word order of the quotation from Psalm XVII to
produce rhyme with the quotation from Psalm XVI. The link between the New
Testament quotation in line 3 and the Old Testament allusion in line 4 is that the
first comes from the mouth of the beggar Bartimaeus, who was blind. The link
between Old Testament and New Testament allusions in lines 5–8 is animal
imagery, *caprea* and *catelli*. The Gentile Canaanite woman in Matthew asked that
her daughter be healed. The Gentile centurion in Luke asked that his servant be
healed. The Canaanite woman asked only for crumbs from the Lord's table. The
woman with the issue of blood asked only to touch the fringe of the Lord's
garment. Feeding and healing are variously sought from a powerful Lord Who
protects and forgives.

The prayer comprises twelve lines, sixty words, 139 syllables, and 303 letters.
The golden section of 12 falls at 7 and 5; that of 60 falls at 37 and 23; that of 139
falls at 86 and 53; that of 303 falls at 187 and 116. The word *Dominus* appears
twice, *Domine* 1 and *Domini* 8, occupying seven full lines of text. The second
example is the thirty-seventh word after the first. From *Domine* to *Domini*
inclusive there are eighty-six syllables. Before *Domine* and after *Domini* there are
fifty-three syllables. From *Domine* to *Domini* inclusive there are 187 letters. Before
Domine and after *Domini* there are 116 letters. Within the thirty-seven-word
section the golden section falls at 23 and 14. The twenty-third word after *Domine*
and the fourteenth word before *Domini* inclusive are *Cananica uidua*.

[VI]

Osanna réx Nazaréne		a	3	8 17
meo ex ore laúdem pérfice.		a	5	10 21
quia tacui inuéterauérunt		b	3	11 23
peccata mea et praéualuérunt.		b	4	11 25
alieni in me ínsurrexérunt	5	c	4	11 23
et portae mórtis conclusérunt.		c	4	9 26
Supergressi sunt caput meum méa delícta.³⁶		d	6	14 34
et anima méa est incurbáta[.]		d	5	11 22
contúrbauérunt me		e	2	6 16
dolores³⁷ mortis	10	f	2	5 13
et torréntes iniquitátis		f	3	9 22
súffocauérunt me.		e	2	6 15
Quare me déreliquísti		g	3	8 19
longe a salute mea Deus méus conuèrte míhi.		g	8	17 35
Éloe. Sábaoth.	15	h	2	6 11

Hosanna, Nazarene king! Perfect the praise from my mouth.

Because I have been silent my sins have become chronic, and they have prevailed.

Aliens have risen up against me, and the gates of death closed in.

My sins have gone over my head, and my soul is bowed down.

The griefs of death have disturbed me, and torrents of iniquity have stifled me.

Why have You abandoned me far from my salvation? My God, turn to me.

Eloe. Sabaoth.

John XII 13	Osanna benedictus qui uenit in nomine Domini rex Israhel
John XIX 19	Iesus Nazarenus rex Iudaeorum
Psalm VIII 3	ex ore infantium et lactantium perfecisti laudem
Psalm XXXI 3	quoniam tacui inueterauerunt ossa mea
Psalm LIII 5	alieni insurrexerunt aduersum me
Psalm XXXVII 5	quoniam iniquitates meae supergressae sunt caput meum
Psalm LVI 7	et incuruauerunt animam meam
Psalm XVII 5	circumdederunt me dolores mortis et torrentes iniquitatis conturbauerunt me dolores inferni circumdederunt me
Psalm XXI 2	quare me dereliquisti longe a salute mea

36 MS delicta mea.
37 MS e altered from i.

The entire prayer comprises fifty-six words, of which the central words, twenty-eighth from the beginning and twenty-eighth from the end, state Moucan's theme, *mea delicta* 7. This is also the syllabic centre of the poem, for the last of *mea* is the seventy-first syllable from the beginning, and the first of *delicta* is the seventy-first syllable from the end. The golden section of 28 falls at 17 and 11. Eleven words and sixty-one letters from the beginning bring one to Moucan's theme, *peccata mea* 4. Eleven words and sixty-two letters after the centre bring one again to Moucan's theme, *iniquitatis* 11. Half of the poem, twenty-eight words, lies between *peccata* 4 and *iniquitatis* 11. At the golden section of the half, the seventeenth of twenty-eight words after *peccata* is *delicta* 7.

[VII]

ERue a framea ánimam méam		a	5	12	21
et de manu cánis solue éam.		a	6	10	21
miserere mei Deus míserere míhi,		b	5	14	27
parce Omnipotens quía peccávi.		b	4	11	26
paenitentem ex córde súscipe.	5	c	4	10	25
pauperem de stércore érige.[38]		c	4	10	23
Si iniquitates[39] meas óbseruáberis.		d	4	13	29
sicut cera liquefiam a fácie ígnis.		d	6	14	29
plumbi póndere praègrauáta		e	3	9	24
uelut aréna[40] peccàta méa.[41]	10	e	4	10	20
Verbum Déi[42] mei sémen		f	4	8	17
suffocat in me spinarum nóxium grámen.		f	6	13	32
Éloe. Sábaoth.		g	2	6	11

Snatch my soul from the spear, and from the paw of the dog free it.
Have mercy on me, God, have mercy on me; spare [me], Omnipotent One, because I have sinned.
Receive one who is penitent from the heart; lift up the poor man from filth.
If You will observe my sins I shall liquify like wax from the face of the fire.
Weighed down by a weight of lead, my sins are like sand.
The noxious plant of thorns stifles in me the seed, the word of my God.
Eloe. Sabaoth.

38   MS *i* added above middle *e* of *erege*.
39   MS *e* added above last *i* of *iniquitatis*.
40   MS *h* added before first *a*. For a possible source see Sims-Williams, *Religion & Literature*, pp. 319–20.
41   MS f. 43v ends here.
42   MS *di*.

Psalm XXI 21	erue a framea animam meam et de manu canis unicam meam
Psalm LVI 2	miserere mei Deus miserere mei
Psalm CXII 7	de stercore erigens pauperem
Psalm CXXIX 3	si iniquitates obseruaberis
Psalm LXVII 3	sicut fluit cera a facie ignis
Matthew XIII 7	creuerunt spinae et suffocauerunt ea [semina]
Luke VIII 11	semen est uerbum Dei

Moucan's thought moves in three couplets marked by parallelism of thought and by rhyme in lines 1–6. The fourth unit is a chiastic quatrain in lines 7–10:

a	iniquitates meas
b	sicut cera
c	liquefiam
d	a facie ignis
d'	plumbi pondere
c'	praegrauata
b'	uelut arena
a'	peccata mea

Moucan ends the prayer with another couplet in lines 11 and 12 and two divine names in line 13.

The prayer proper comprises twelve lines, six in the first half and six in the second, fifty-five words, twenty-eight in the first half and twenty-seven in the second, 134 syllables, sixty-seven in the first half and sixty-seven in the second.

[VIII]

Ure renes méos et cor _méum_		a	6	10	21
ut non intres in iudício _mécum_		a	6	11	25
usque uiuens nátus de lúto.		b	5	9	22
Super animae meae náturália		c	4	12	24
sata seminauit inimicus hómo lólia.	5	c	5	15	30
Angustiae undique óccurrunt míhi.		d	4	12	29
Infelix ego homo tibi sóli peccáui		d	6	14	29
Quis me liberauit de córpore hùius mórtis		e	7	14	35
nisi gratia Dómini Sàluatóris.		e	4	12	26
Qui abstulit43 uása44 gigántis	10	f	4	9	23
de nobis tiránnidem45 uìndicántis.		f	4	11	28

43 MS *abstullit* with second *l* erased. For another example of double *l* see line 20 n. 47 below.

44 MS *uassa* with second *s* erased. For another example see prayer II line 18 n. 23 *supra*. Compare the puzzling usage *hec sunt in ualle gigantum*, glossed *i. in inferno*, in *The Writings of Bishop Patrick 1074–1084*, ed. & transl. A. Gwynn, *Scriptores Latini Hiberniae* I (Dublin 1955), p. 100.

45 MS *r* added above first *i*.

Deum meum laúdans inuocábo		b	4	10	23
Dominum et ab inimicis méis saluus éro.		b	7	15	32
Bonum míhi Dómine		g	3	7	15
quod humíliásti me	15	g	3	7	16
ut non extollar ín conspectu túo		b	6	11	27
Domine quia perimus exsúrge in naufrágio[46]		b	6	16	35
ístius mùndi nócte.		h	3	7	16
Da míhi Dómine		h	3	6	12
manum fragili[47] lintro péne demérso.	20	i	5	12	29
porréctam Petro claúso[48]		i	3	7	20
óre querèllam[49] Mósi.		d	3	7	16
meam suscipe út suscepísti		d	4	10	23
quia uulneratus sum in héremi[50] uía		j	6	13	28
et super iumentum túum me súbleua.	25	j	6	12	28
Dómine Déus :—[51]		k	2	5	10

Burn my reins and my heart
that You may not enter into judgement with me
until from the mud [I am] born living.
Over the natural elements of my soul
an inimical man has sown scattered tares.
Troubles block me everywhere.
I, unhappy man, against You only have I sinned.
Who will free me from the body of this death [by hypallage 'from this
    body of death']
except the grace of the Lord, the Saviour,
Who has taken away from us the vessels of the giant,
the tyranny of the vengeful man?
Praising my God I shall call upon
the Lord and I shall be safe from my enemies.
It is good for me, Lord, that You have humbled me,
so that I be not lifted up in Your sight.
Lord, since we are perishing, rise up in the shipwreck
of this world by night.
Give me, Lord, the hand, when the fragile
boat was almost sunk, stretched out to Peter.
Deal with my complaint from my closed mouth
as You dealt with Moses's.

46 MS nafragio.
47 MS fragilli. For another example of double l see line 10, n. 43 above.
48 MS claso.
49 MS quellam.
50 MS herimi.
51 MS f. 44r ends here.

Because I have been wounded on the way in the desert
lift me up even on to Your beast,
Lord God.

Psalm XXV 2	ure renes meos et cor meum
Psalm CXLII 2	et non intres in iudicio cum seruo tuo
Genesis II 7	formauit igitur Dominus Deus hominem de limo terrae ... et factus est homo in animam uiuentem
Matthew XIII 24	qui seminauit bonum semen in agro suo
Matthew XIII 27–8	unde ergo habet zizania ... inimicus homo hoc fecit
Daniel XIII 22	angustiae mihi undique
Romans VII 24	infelix ego homo
Psalm L 6	tibi soli peccaui
Romans VII 24	quis me liberabit de corpore mortis huius gratia Dei per Iesum Christum Dominum nostrum
Psalm XVII 4	laudans inuocabo Dominum et ab inimicis meis saluus ero
Psalm CXVIII 71	bonum mihi quia humiliasti me
Matthew VIII 24–5	et ecce motus magnus factus est in mari ita ut nauicula operiretur fluctibus ipse uero dormiebat et accesserunt et suscitauerunt eum dicentes Domine salua nos perimus
Matthew XIV 25	quarta autem uigilia noctis uenit ad eos ambulans supra mare
Matthew XIV 29–31	et descendens Petrus de nauicula ambulabat super aquam ut ueniret ad Iesum ... et cum coepisset mergi clamauit dicens Domine saluum me fac et continuo Iesus extendens manum adprehendit eum
Exodus IV 10	inpeditioris et tardioris linguae sum
Luke X 30–4	homo quidam descendebat ab Hierusalem in Hiericho et incidit in latrones qui etiam despoliauerunt eum et plagis inpositis abierunt semiuiuo relicto ... Samaritanus autem quidam ... alligauit uulnera eius ... et inponens illum in iumentum suum duxit in stabulum ... .

In this twenty-five-lined prayer there are five alliterating groups in the initial syllables of twelve of the first thirteen lines. Alliteration stops at the central, thirteenth, line. There are ten end rhymes. The central, sixtieth, word, of the entire 119-word prayer, is *Dominum* at the beginning of the thirteenth line.

[IX]

Erraui in móntibus Pàstor bóne		a	5	11	26
me in umeros túos ínpone.		a	5	10	20
Sicut ceruus desiderat fóntem aquae[52] uíuae.		b	6	14	36
ita anima mea tibi sitíat sáncteque		b	6	15	30
in medio maneas úberum meórum.	5	c	5	13	25
qui pascis et cubas ád meridiánum.		c	6	12	28
Custodi me ut pupillam óculi túi.		d	6	13	27
et introduc mé in domum uíni		d	6	10	23
fasciculis[53] guttae in uíneis Engáddi.		d	5	13	31
Patruelis meus míhi et ègo ílli.	10	d	6	13	26
Anima mea sicut térra sine áqua		e	6	13	26
Exarserunt uelut[54] igne uíscera méa.		e	5	13	29
Igne tui amoris et timoris cor méum ígneat.		f	8	17	35
tuus amor sanctusque timor qui cédere néscit.[55]		f	7	15	38
Da mihi Ihesu salientem aquam[56] in uítam aetérnam.	15	g	8	17	40
Animam meam unam petii a Dómino hànc requíram		g	8	18	38
ut in æternum sitiam numquam. Domine Ihésu súscipe		b	8	18	43
spiritum meum quia anima mea turbáta est uálde.		b	8	18	39
In manus tuas commendo spiritum méum súapte[57]		h	7	16	37
ne dormíam in mórte	20	h	4	7	16
ut non timeam a timóre noctúrno		i	6	12	26
neque a demonio meridiano.		i	4	12	22
Recipe me in réquiem Ábrahae		j	5	11	24
ubi patrum requiéscunt ánimae[58]		j	4	11	26
qui cum Patre uiuis dóminaris úna	25	e	6	12	28
cum Sancto Spiritu in sǽcula túta.		e	6	12	29
Eloe. Sábaoth. Ia. Ádonai		d	4	10	19
Eli Eli lábas[59] sabactháni.		d	4	10	20

I strayed in the mountains. Good Shepherd,
place me upon Your shoulders.
As the hart desires a spring of living water
so my soul thirsts for You,
and may You remain, Holy One, in the midst
of my breasts, Who feed and recline at midday.
Guard me as the pupil of Your eye

---

52   MS *aq3*. For another example see line 15 n. 56 below.
53   MS *ci* added above.
54   MS *uelud*.
55   MS *sanctusquequi nescit cedere timor*.
56   MS *aq3*. For another example see line 3 n. 52 above.
57   MS *p* written on erasure. For another example see prayer II line 16 n. 21 above.
58   MS f. 44v ends here.
59   MS *m* written above *b*. For another example see prayer I line 15 n. 14 above.

and bring me into the house of wine
with the bunches of grapes [lit. 'liquid'] in the vineyards of Engedi.
My uncle is for me and I for him.
My soul [is] like a land without water.
My bowels burned as with fire.
With the fire of Your love and fear may my heart burn,
Your love and holy fear which knows not how to yield.
Give me, Jesus, water welling up into eternal life.
My soul [is the] one thing have I sought from the Lord; this I require,
that in eternity I shall never thirst. Lord Jesus, receive
my spirit, because my soul is greatly disturbed.
Into Your hands I commend my spirit in its own fashion,
so that I may not I sleep in death,
so that I may not fear from the nighttime fear
nor from the midday demon.
Receive me into the rest of Abraham
where the souls of the fathers rest,
[You] Who with the Father live [and] reign together
with the Holy Spirit for secure ages.
Eloe. Sabaoth. Ia. Adonai.
Eli Eli lama sabacthani.

Song of Songs I 8	ecce iste uenit saliens in montibus
John X 11	ego sum pastor bonus
Luke XV 5	cum inuenerit eam [ouem] inponit in umeros suos gaudens
Psalm XLI 2–3	quemadmodum desiderat ceruus ad fontes aquarum ita desiderat anima mea ad te Deus sitiuit anima mea ad Deum fortem uiuum
Song of Songs I 12	fasciculus murrae dilectus meus mihi inter ubera mea commorabitur
Song of Songs I 6	ubi pascas ubi cubes in meridie
Psalm XVI 8	custodi me ut pupillam oculi
Song of Songs II 4	introduxit me in cellam uinariam
Song of Songs III 4	donec introducam illum in domum matris meae
Song of Songs I 13	botrus cypri dilectus meus mihi in uineis Engaddi
Song of Songs II 16	dilectus meus mihi et ego illi
Isaiah V 1	cantabo dilecto meo canticum patruelis mei uineae suae
Proverbs XXX 16	infernus et os uuluae et terra quae non satiatur aqua ignis vero numquam dicit sufficit
Jeremiah XXXI 20	idcirco conturbata sunt uiscera mea super eum
Lamentations II 11	conturbata sunt uiscera mea

John IV 14	sed aqua quam dabo ei fiet in eo fons aquae
	salientis in uitam aeternam
Psalm XXVI 4	unam petii a Domino hanc requiram
Acts VII 58	Domine Iesu suscipe spiritum meum
Psalm VI 4	et anima mea turbata est ualde
Luke XXIII 46	Pater in manus tuas commendo spiritum meum
Psalm XC 5–6	non timebis a timore nocturno … ab incursu
	et daemonio meridiano

This ninth prayer comprises twenty-eight lines, of which the golden section falls at 17 and 11, and 164 words, of which the golden section falls at 101 and 63. There are eleven lines, five before and six after lines containing the word *meridianus*, 6 and 22. From line 6 to line 22 inclusive there are seventeen lines. Before *meridianum* in line 6 there are thirty-two words and after *meridiano* in line 22 there are twenty-nine words, together sixty-three words. From *meridianum* to *meridiano* inclusive there are 101 words. The central words between them are *da mihi Ihesu* in line 15.

To read these nine prayers only as a single text is to misapprehend Moucan, each of whose prayers is distinct, though linked to the others. In the first of nine prayers Moucan mentions the triune God nine times: as *Deus Pater* 1, *Deus Filius* 1, *Deus Spiritus Sanctus* 2, *Deus* 12, *Eloe, Sabaoth, Ia, Adonai* 14, and *Eli* 15. Prayer I is linked to prayer IV by the recurrence of nine divine names and titles: *Pater* 1, *Deus* 4, *Domine* 9, 11, *Spiritum Sanctum* 13, *Patrem* 15, *Domine Deus* 19, 21, *Eloe* 23. The golden section of the fifteen lines of prayer I falls at 9 and 6, at line 9, *mihi ut propitius peccatori fiat*. The golden section of the twenty-three lines of prayer IV falls at 14 and 9, at line 9, *propitius esto mihi Domine peccatori*. Prayer I is linked also to prayer IX by the quotation *Eli Eli laba sabacthani*. Prayer II is linked to prayer IX by the phrases *animae suabte* 16 and *spiritum meum suapte* 19. The theme of the Prodigal Son links prayers III and IV. The phrase *miserere mei* links prayer IV 2 to prayer V 3 and prayer VII 3. Prayer IV 18 *licet post uulnera uel uerberati* is linked to prayer V 6 *quia uulnerata est anima mea* and prayer VIII 24 *quia uulneratus sum in heremi uia*. Prayer IV 12 *eripe me de peccati luto* is linked to prayer VIII 3 *usque uiuens natus de luto*. Prayer IV 10 *erue animam meam de manu inferni* is linked to prayer VII 1 *erue a framea animam meam*. Prayer V 12 *saluus fiam a peccato meo* is linked to prayer VIII 13 *ab inimicis meis saluus ero*.

Of these nine prayers the central is prayer V. The central word, 399th of 798, is the last of prayer V, *meo*. The central syllable, 929th of 1858, is in *meo*.

Throughout these prayers, but with wonderful variety especially in II, III, IV, and V, Moucan shows by the artful arrangement of quotations and allusions that he had assimilated, like Patrick and Columban and Cummian before him and many others after him, the Biblical technique of using not only quotations, but unquoted context to expand and deepen and enrich the meanings of borrowed words.[60] This is by no means a habit confined to learned men writing secret lan-

---

60   See above pp. 84–8, 99–102, and Howlett, *Liber Epistolarum*.

guage. It is a feature of the common culture of Celtic Latin, Anglo-Latin, Old and Middle English writers from the fifth century to the fifteenth.

X. JOSEPH SCOTTUS

Carmen Figuratum

Here follows one of four *carmina figurata* composed by Alcuin's disciple Joseph Scottus addressed to Charlemagne.[1]

IOSEPH ABBAS SCOTTUS GENERE HOS VERSUS QUI IN HAC PAGINA CONTINENTUR CONPOSSUIT

Primus auus uiuens en nos in morte redegit
Heu sic et mulier praebendo poma per ydrum
Fecit nos plagas iuste percurrere multas.
En nostrae mortis sementa fuisse uidemus.
Scorpio pulsando ualuit nam perfide fari: 5
Eua parata paret iusis heu ualde superbis.
Vincit te mulier pomi pulcherrima grandi
Vi species peris ammota tunc uirginitate.
Horruit auersus pariter seu coniuge tali   10
Ergo uir ex ligno mandens nos noxa peremit.
Inclyta uirgo fide sed raro uota sacrauit
Ista Maria nouam uitamue subire supernam
Et carnis prior ascultet sibi iura tenere
Ardua tunc toto cupiens castissima mundo.   15
Talis enim meruit regemque parire Deumue
Qui pie subuertit fregit et ferrea nostri
Iura mali. O uere feliciter hinc prior ibat
Lege sibi placita prauorum ferret ut iras.
Iam Deus ad lignum seruili nomine pendens   20
Porro sui miserum soluens ope solius Adam
Expirauit ita et celerat deferre serenam
De summis lucem. Sunt haec uexilla reuersa
Regni quae pridem clauserunt limina dein
Ipse uir et mulier arbor uitaeque relator   25
Procerum o serpens ultor uenatus ilidrum
Promunt hic uitam de ligni uecte redemtam.
Hic nam cum seruus dominum se paret haberi

---

1   BCLL 648. *Iosephi Scotti Carmina Poetae Latini Aevi Carolini*, ed. E. Duemmler, *Monumenta Germaniae Historica* (Berlin 1895), vol. I pp. 152–3.

Mortis eum iuste seu nos tunc ultio sumsit.
Sed uerus Dominus se serui uestit amictum   30
Et reparat mundum Rex optimus ille piorum.
Inlicitis ast Eua cibis os contulit audax
Sed mortem rapido contactu detulit orbis.
Inde Maria uiri ex te iura recidis habenda
Hinc genetrix uerae tu sumis semina uitae.   35

Joseph has arranged his words and ideas in three chiastic patterns, the first from
line 1 to line 10 inclusive, the second from line 11 to line 24 inclusive, and
the third from line 25 to line 35 inclusive.

```
1a      primus auus
 bi       mulier
  ii         poma
   c           scorpio pulsando ualuit nam perfide fari
    d             Eua
   c'          uincit te
 b'i      mulier
  ii         pomi
 a'     deprauatus auus
2ai     uir
  ii        uirgo
  iii          uitamue
 b             Deumue
  c               O uere feliciter hinc prior ibat
 b'            Deus
 a'i     uir
  ii        mulier
  iii          uitaeque
3a      uitam
 b        mortis
  c         Eua
 b'       morte
 a'     uitae.
```

Joseph connected all three parts of the poem with a chiastic pattern.

```
A 1    en nos in morte
  2      iuste
  1'   en nostrae mortis
B          ligno
C             regemque
D                O uere feliciter hinc prior ibat
```

C'   regine
B'   ligni
A'1   mortis
   2   iuste
   1'   mortem.

The central line of thirty-five is the eighteenth, at the crux of both chiastic
patterns 2c and D. The central word of 237 is the 119th, *ibat*, at the end of the
central line.

The word *uita* recurs at an arithmetically fixed interval. Before *nouam uitamue*
13 there are eighty-one words (9 × 9). Between *uitamue* 13 and *uitaeque* 25 there
are also eighty-one words. Between *uitaeque* 25 and *uitam* 27 there are nine words
(9 × 1). From *uitam* 27 to *uitae* 35 inclusive there are sixty-three words (9 × 7).

There are thirty-five lines in the poem, in which every line contains thirty-
five letters. By arranging the letters vertically one notes a further aspect of
Joseph's art. Embedded in this *carmen figuratum* are three words at the centre of
the poem in the shape of a cross which read

Lege feliciter Carle

and four further hexameter verses:

Ille pater priscus elidit edendo nepotes.
Mortis imago fuit mulier per poma suasrix.
Iessus item nobis ieiunans norma salutis.
Mors fugit uitae ueniens ex uirgine radix.

The first and third of these verses form a parallelogram descending from upper
left to lower right. The second and fourth of these verses form a parallelogram
descending from upper right to lower left.

The word *mulier*, referring to Eve, through whom the Fall from grace
came, recurs in identical position in lines 2 and 7. The word *Maria*, referring
to Mary, through whom restoration of grace came, recurs in identical position
in lines 13 and 34. The word *uita* occurs first as *uitamue*, symmetrically placed
in line 13 above the central words *lege feliciter Carle*. It occurs last as the last
word of the poem in line 35.

The 237 words of the thirty-five verses and the twenty-nine words of the
embedded verses together total 266, which divide by one-ninth and eight-ninths
at 29.56 and 236.44, at *uitae*, the last word of the thirty-fifth verse, having arrived
at which one begins to read the embedded verses. Of the twenty-nine words in
the embedded verses one-ninth and eight-ninths falls at 3 and 26, at the end of
the central verses addressed to Charlemagne, *lege feliciter Carle*.

P R I M V S A V V S I V E N S E N N O S I N M O R T E R E D E G I T
H E V S I C E T M V L I E R P R A E T E N D O P O M A P E R Y D R V M
F E C I T N O S P L A G A S I V S T E P E R C V R' R E R E M V L T A S
E N N O S T R A E M O R T I S S E M E N T A F V I S S E V I D E M V S
S C O R P I O P V L S A N D O V A L V I T N A M P E R F I D E F A R I
E V A P A R A T A P A T E T I V S I S H E V V A L D E S V P E R B I S
V I N C I T T E M V L I E R P O M I P V L C H E R R I M A G R A N D I
V I S P E C I E S P E R I S A M M O T A T V N C V I R G I N I T A T E
H O R R V I T A V E R S V S P A R I T E R S E V C O N I V G E T A L I
D E P R A V A T V S A V V S G V S T V S M I S E R A B I L I S A V S V
E R G O V I R E X L I G N O M A N D E N S N O S N O X A P E R E M I T
I N C L Y T A V I R G O F I D E S E D R A R O V O T A S A C R A V I T
I S T A M A R I A N O V A M V I T A M V E S V B I R E S V P E R N A M
E T C A R N I S P R I O R A S C V L T E T S I B I I V R A T E N E R E
A R D V A T V N C T O T O C V P I E N S C A S T I S S I M A M V N D O
T A L I S E N I M M E R V I T R E G E M Q V E P A R I R E D E V M V E
Q V I P I E S V B V E R T I T F R E G I T E T F E R R E A N O S T R I
I V R A M A L I O V E R E F E L I C I T E R H I N C P R I O R I B A T
L E G E S I B I P L A C I T A P R A V O R V M F E R R E T V T I R A S
I A M D E V S A D L I G N V M S E R V I L I N O M I N E P E N D E N S
P O R R O S V I M I S E R V M S O L V E N S O P E S O L I V S A D A M
E X P I R A V I T I T A E T C E L E R A T D E F E R R E S E R E N A M
D E S V M M I S L V C E M S V N T H A E C V E X I L L A R E V E R S A
R E G N I Q V A E P R I D E M C L A V S E R V N T L I M I N A D E I N
I P S E V I R E T M V L I E R A R B O R V I T A E Q V E R E L A T O R
P R O C E R V M O S E R P E N S V L T O R V E N A T V S I L I D R V M
P R O M V N T H I C V I T A M D E L I G N I V E C T E R E D E M T A M
H I C N A M D V M S E R V V S D O M I N V M S E P A R E T H A B E R I
M O R T I S E V M I V S T E S E V N O S T V N C V L T I O S V M S I T
S E D V E R V S D O M I N V S S E S E R V I V E S T I T A M I C T V M
E T R E P A R A T M V N D V M R E X O P T I M V S I L L E P I O R V M
I N L I C I T I S A S T E V A C I B I S O S C O N T V L I T A V D A X
S E D M O R T E M R A P I D O C O N T A C T V D E T V L I T O R B I S
I N D E M A R I A V I R I E X T E I V R A R E C I D I S H A B E N D A
H I N C G E N E T R I X V E R A E T V S V M I S P E M I N A V I T A E

XI. COLUMBANUS OF SAINT-TROND

Carmina

Until recently the myth of Ireland as a centre for study and transmission of Classical Latin literature in the sixth and seventh centuries depended upon attribution of several poems to Columban of Bangor, particularly those in varied Classical quantitative metres containing wide-ranging allusions to pagan myths and legends. But critical studies have given solid reasons for removing these poems from the canon of Columban's writings and attributing them to another Irishman, the Carolingian Columbanus (?) Abbot of Saint-Trond.[1] Two simple phenomena confirm the new attribution. One is that Columban of Bangor refers repeatedly to himself as *Columba* in *Epistolae* I, II, III, IV, and V and in the anagram in *Mundus Iste Transibit*,[2] though this poet names himself *Columbanus* in an acrostic *Columbanus Hunaldo* and in the second line of the *Versus Columbani ad Sethum*:[3]

> Suscipe Sethe libens et perlege mente serena
> Dicta Columbani fida te uoce monentis.

The other, an argument of some force, is that the undoubted signed works of Columban differ so markedly in diction, syntax, structure, style, irony, and wit from these poems that one wonders how anyone could ever imagine them to have issued from the same author.

Here are the acrostic *Versus Columbani ad Hunaldum.*

> Casibus innumeris decurrunt tempora uitae,
> Omnia praetereunt menses uoluuntur in annis;
> Labitur in senium momentis omnibus aetas.
> Ut tibi perpetuam liceat conpraendere uitam
> Molles inlecebras uitae nunc sperne caducae.   5
> Blanda luxuria uirtus superatur honesta.
> Ardet auaritia caecaque cupidine pectus.
> Nescit habere modum uanis mens dedita curis.
> Vilius argentum est auro uirtutibus aurum.
> Summa quies nil uelle super quam postulat usus.   10
> Hos ego uersiculos misi tibi saepe legendos;
> Ut mea dicta tuis admittas auribus oro.
> Ne te decipiat uana et peritura uoluptas.
> Aspice quam breuis est procerum regumque potestas.
> Lubrica mortalis cito transit gloria uitae.   15
> Da ueniam dictis fuimus fortasse loquaces.
> Omne quod est nimium semper uitare memento.

> With countless chances the seasons of life roll on,
> All things pass, the months revolve on years;
> At every moment age glides to senility.

1   *BCLL* 650–6. J.W. Smit, *Studies on the Language and Style of Columba the Younger (Columbanus)* (Amsterdam 1971), pp. 209–53. M. Lapidge, 'The Authorship of the Adonic Verses "Ad Fidolium" Attributed to Columbanus', *Studi Medievali* 3rd series. XVIII (1977), pp. 249–314.
2   *Sancti Columbani Opera*, ed. & transl. G.S.M. Walker, *Scriptores Latini Hiberniae* II (Dublin 1957), pp. 2, 12, 22, 26, 54. See above p. 169.
3   Ibid. pp. 184–7.

That you may lawfully apprehend the life eternal,
Now spurn the sweet deceits of transitory life.   5
By smooth luxury decent virtue is conquered.
The breast burns with avarice and blind greed.
A mind devoted to vain cares knows not how to keep measure.
Silver is cheaper than gold, gold than the virtues.
The highest peace is to wish for nothing beyond what need demands.

These little verses I have sent you to be read often;
I pray that you give my words entrance to your ears.
Let not a vain and perishing pleasure beguile you.
See how brief is the power of chiefs and kings.
The glory of mortal life slips quickly and is gone.   15
Pardon my words, we have perhaps been garrulous.
Ever remember to avoid all that is excess.

Here are the adonic *Versus Columbani Fidolio Fratri Suo* with their concluding hexameters.[4]

Accipe quaeso		Receive, I pray,	
Nunc bipedali		Now in two-foot	
Condita uersu		Verses measured,	
Carminulorum		Of little songs	
Munera parua	5	My tiny gifts;	
Tuque frequenter		And do you often	
Mutua nobis		To us in turn	
Obsequiorum		Of due service	
Debita redde.		Pay the duties.	
Nam uelut aestu	10	For as in heat	
Flantibus austris		When south winds blow	
Arida gaudent		The dry fields	
Imbribus arua		Rejoice in showers,	
Sic tua nostras		So your note	
Missa frequenter	15	Often sent	
Laetificabat		Made glad	
Pagina mentes.		Our minds.	
Non ego posco		I do not ask	
Nunc periturae		Now of perishing	
Munera gazae	20	Treasure the gifts,	
Non quid auarus		Not the gold	
Semper egendo		Which a miser ever in need	
Congregat aurum		Gathers together,	

4   Ibid. pp. 192–7.

Quod sapientum		Which blinds the eyes
Lumina caecat	25	Of wise men,
Et uelut ignis		And like a fire's
Flamma perurit		Flame burns up
Improba corda.		Wicked hearts.
Saepe nefanda		Often guilty
Crimina multis	30	Crimes to many
Suggerit auri		Dread lust
Dira cupido		For gold suggests,
E quibus ista		From those which
Nunc tibi pauca		Few deeds now
Tempore prisco	35	Of the old time
Gesta retexam.		I shall recount to you.
Extitit ingens		There arose as a great
Causa malorum		Cause of evils
Aurea pellis.		The golden fleece.
Corruit auri	40	There was corrupted
Munere paruo		By a small gift of gold
Cena deorum		The gods' banquet,
Et tribus illis		And for those three
Maxima lis est		Goddesses the greatest strife
Orta deabus;	45	Was born;
Hinc populauit		Hence were ravaged
Troiugenarum		The Trojans'
Ditia regna		Wealthy kingdoms
Dorica pubes.		By Greek youth.
Iuraque legum	50	And legal rights
Fasque fidesque		And justice and faith
Rumpitur auro.		Are broken by gold.
Impia quippe		As the unrighteous deeds
Pigmalionis		Of King Pygmalion
Regis ob aurum	55	For the sake of gold
Gesta leguntur.		Are read.
Sic Polidorum		Thus Polydorus
Hospes auarus		His greedy host
Incitus auro		Enticed by gold
Fraude necauit.	60	Slew with stealth.
Femina saepe		Often a woman
Perdit ob aurum		Loses for the sake of gold
Casta pudorem.		Her honour, though chaste.
Non Iouis auri		Jove did not
Fluxit in imbre;	65	Flow in a shower of gold;
Sed quod adulter		But because as an adulterer
Obtulit aurum		He offered gold,

Aureus ille		He is feigned to be	
Fingitur imber.		A golden shower.	
Amphiaraum	70	Amphiaraus	
Prodidit auro		Was betrayed for gold	
Perfida coniunx.		By his treacherous wife.	
Hectoris heros		Hector's body	
Vendidit auro		The hero Achilles	
Corpus Achillis.	75	Trafficked for gold.	
Hoc reserari		By this	
Munere certo		Sure gift	
Nigra feruntur'		The black portals of Hell	
Limina Ditis.		Are said to be opened.	
Nunc ego possem	80	Now I could	
Plura referre		Recount more,	
Ni breuitatis		Did not the cause	
Causa uetaret.		Of brevity forbid.	
Haec tibi, frater		As I send you,	
Inclite, parua	85	Famous brother,	
Litterularum		These small gifts	
Munera mittens		Of little letters,	
Suggero uanas		I counsel you	
Linquere curas;		To leave vain cares;	
Desine quaeso	90	Cease, I beg,	
Nunc animosos		Now to feed	
Pascere pingui		Your mettled steeds	
Farre caballos		On rich fodder,	
Lucraque lucris		And by piling	
Accumulando	95	Gains on gains	
Desine nummis		Cease to add	
Addere nummos.		Coins to coins.	
Ut quid iniquis		Why with the unjust	
Consociaris		Do you associate,	
Munera quorum	100	Whose gifts	
Crebra receptas?		You frequently receive?	
Odit iniqui		Christ hates	
Munera Xpistus.		The gifts of an unjust man.	
Haec sapienti		These to the wise	
Dispicienda	105	Are fit for scorning,	
Qui fugitiuae		Who ought to observe	
Atque caducae		That the times of life	
Cernere debet		Are the times of a fleeting	
Tempora uitae;		And transient thing;	
Sufficit autem	110	But it is enough	
Ista loquaci		That I have now sung	

Nunc cecinisse		These songs
Carmina uersu.		With wordy verse.
Nam noua forsan		For perhaps
Esse uidetur	115	It seems a novelty,
Ista legenti		This scheme of verse,
Formula uersus.		As you read it.
Sed tamen illa		But yet that
Graiugenarum		Famous poet
Inclyta uates	120	Of the Grecians,
Nomine Sapho		By name Sappho,
Versibus istis		In these verses
Dulce solebat		Used to write
Edere carmen.		A lovely song.
Si tibi cura	125	If perhaps
Forte uolenti		Your will is anxious
Carmina tali		To compose songs
Condere uersu		In such a verse,
Semper ut unus		Always let one
Ordine certus	130	Clear dactyl
Dactilus istic		Here in order
Incipiat pes;		Make the start;
Inde sequenti		Then in the following
Parte trocheus		Foot, a trochee
Proximus illi	135	Next to it
Rite locetur;		Be rightly placed;
Saepe duabus		Often with two
Claudere longis		Long syllables to close
Ultima uersus		The verse's end
Iure licebit.	140	Will be quite lawful.
Tu modo, frater		Only do you, my brother
Alme Fidoli,		Dear Fidolius,
Nectare si uis		If you will, sweeter
Dulcior omni		Than any nectar,
Floridiora	145	Leaving aside
Doctiloquorum		The more flowery
Carmina linquens		Songs of scholars,
Friuola nostra		Gladly accept
Suscipe laetus.		Our trifles.
Sic tibi Xpistus	150	Thus to you may Christ,
Arbiter orbis		Ruler of the world,
Omnipotentis		Of the Almighty
Unica proles		The sole Offspring,
Dulcia uitae		Grant sweet
Gaudia reddat	155	Joys of life,

Qui sine fine		Who without end		
Nomine Patris		In the Father's name		
Cuncta gubernans		All-controlling ·		
Regnat in aeuum.		Reigns forever.		

Haec tibi dictaram morbis oppressus acerbis	160	6	14	38
Corpore quos fragili patior tristique senecta;		6	16	40
Nam dum praecipiti labuntur tempora cursu		6	14	36
Nunc ad olympiadis ter senae uenimus annos.		7	15	36
Omnia praetereunt fugit inreparabile tempus;		5	17	39
Viue uale laetus tristisque memento senectae.	165	6	15	39

These things I had dictated for you when overwhelmed by the bitter ills
Which in my frail body and sad old age I bear;
For while the times glide with headlong course,
Now we have reached the years of our eighteenth Olympiad.
All things pass away, time flies without remeed;
God-speed, farewell and remember sad old age.

Columbanus begins these remarkable verses by telling Fidolius what they are: *Accipe quaeso nunc bipedali condita uersu carminulorum munera parua.* From line 114 he tells Fidolius the history of his verse form and relates for him the rules of composition of adonic verse. Within the text of the verses he announces at line 34, *Nunc tibi pauca tempore prisco gesta retexam*, and he concludes his mythological survey and moral admonition at line 113, *Sufficit autem ista loquaci nunc cecinisse carmina uersu.* The 159 verses divide by symmetry at 79.5. There are seventy-nine verses in lines 1–33 and 114–59, and there are eighty verses in lines 34–113. Exactly at the centre of the poem, between *gesta retexam* and *sufficit … cecinisse*, at line 80, he says *Nunc ego possem plura referre ni breuitatis causa uetaret.* Between the first sentence *Accipe quaeso nunc … debita redde* and the sentence *Desine quaeso nunc …*, there are eighty lines.

The 159 adonic verses divide by one-ninth and eight-ninths at 18 and 141 and the 330 words at 36.67 and 293.33, at *Tu modo, frater | Alme Fidoli.*

The concluding verses are composed on multiples of six. There are six lines of dactylic hexameter with twelve (6 × 2) words in each couplet, eighteen (6 × 3) words in each half, thirty-six (6 × 6) feet, as nearly one-ninth of the 318 feet in the preceding adonic verses as the poet could manage, and thirty-six words, as nearly one-ninth of the 330 words in the preceding adonic verses as the poet could manage. The numbers of syllables are chiastically arranged, 14–16–14 in the first half and 15–17–15 in the second half. There are 228 letters (6 × 38), 114 in the first half and 114 in the second half.

Words are arranged at arithmetically determined intervals. From *labuntur* to *praetereunt* inclusive there are twelve words. Between *tempora* and *tempus* there are twelve words. After *senecta*, the twelfth word, *senectae* is the twenty-fourth word. From *tristique* to *tristisque* inclusive there are twenty-four words.

The thirty-six words divide by both hemiolus and extreme and mean ratio at 22 and 14, at *ad olympiadis ter | senae uenimus annos*. According to the editor of these verses[5]

> Olympias in the Greek poets normally means a period of four years, but the Latins sometimes use it as equivalent to the five-year lustrum; the author's age is thus either 68–72, or 85–90.

Probably the author was at or approaching the age of seventy-two, twice thirty-six, or, as he has reckoned it here, 4 × 3 × 6.

XII. DUNGAL OF SAINT-DENIS AND PAVIA

Acrostic Poem to Hildoard

About the same time as or shortly later than Columbanus composed his acrostic verses to Hunaldus Dungal of Saint-Denis and Pavia composed his acrostic verses to Hildoardus,[1] the Preface to which explicitly mentions the alternate hexameters and pentameters and the acrostic.

> Hos uersus in honorem Hildoardi episcopi Dungalus peregrinus licet ille necglegens et incircumspectus conpossuit in quibus priores litterae singulorum uersuum unam porrectam sed in transuersum lineam efficientes nomen laudati et uersifici contexunt et demonstrant qui exametri pentametrique alternatim hoc modo rite discurrunt.

Hanc tibi uictrice*m* dux inclite sume corona*m*		7	15	38	
Intextam sert*is* floribus et uari*is*		5	12	30	
Luceat ut <u>u</u>estro fulgens in <u>u</u>ertice semper		7	14	36	
Diuina <u>e</u>xornans tempora <u>e</u>t <u>o</u>mne caput		6	14	32	
<u>O</u>ptatum <u>a</u>dducens Domini sublimis honorem	5	5	15	36	
<u>A</u>ltithroni Genitor qui [a]ethere sceptra tenet.		6	15	39 or 38	
<u>R</u>ex <u>r</u>egum et summus Princeps <u>Dominus</u> <u>domin</u>antium		7	15	42	
Dispositor sapi*ens* Conditor arc<h>itene*ns*		4	14	35 or 36	
Omnia qui <u>superat</u> replet <u>sus</u>tentat et ambi*t*		7	15	37	
Denique cuncta regi*t* praua sed ipse <u>domat</u>	10	7	14	35	

---

5   Ibid. p. 197 n. 2.
1   BCLL 659. *Versus Scottorum*, ed. K. Strecker, *Poetae Latini Aevi Karolini, Monumenta Germaniae Historica* (Berlin 1923), vol. IV pp. 411–2.

Unus ubique Deus Sancto Spiramine fulgens		6	15	36
Numine qui proprio cingere cuncta ualet		6	14	34
Gloria summa potens retinent quam s[a]eptaque nulla	7	16	43 or 42
Aera terra polus tartara nec pelagus		6	14	31
Laudibus inmensis quam milia sancta celebrant	15	6	15	40
Votiferae plebes et chorus angelicus		5	13	32
Sanctus amore pio sanctus super omnia sanctus		7	16	39
Trinus ubique Deus semper et unus adest.		7	14	33
Versibus his uestram obtamus uegitare salutem:		6	16	40
Exiguum et famulum commemorare tuum.	20	5	15	31
		122	306	719

HILDOARDO DUNGALUS TUE
	3	9	20
Exiguum et famulum commemorare tuum.	5	15	31
	130	330	770

These verses in honour of Hildoard the bishop Dungal the pilgrim, though he [is] negligent and uncircumspect, composed, in which the first letters of single verses making one straightened line, but a cross-verse, weave together and demonstrate the name of the man praised and of the verse-maker; which hexameters and pentameters run down alternately by rule in this fashion:

Renowned leader, take this victorious crown to you, inwoven with entwined and variegated flowers,
so that it may shed light, shining always on the top of your head, adorning [your] divine temples and whole head,
bringing to [it] the desired honour of the Sublime Lord, the Begetter of the Lofty-throned, Who holds the sceptres in the aether,
the King of Kings and Highest Prince, the Lord of those being lords, the Wise Disposer, the citadel-holding Founder,
Who rises above, refills, sustains, and surrounds all things, finally rules all things, but Himself subdues perverse things,
everywhere One God, shining in the Holy Spirit,
Who with His own power is able to bind all things,
the highest glory being powerful, which no enclosures hold back, air, land, the pole, the underworld, nor the sea,
which holy thousands celebrate with immense praises, vow-bearing peoples and angelic chorus:
"Holy, holy in pious love, holy above all things, everywhere, always, God is present Triune and One".
With these verses we desire to invigorate your health and recall to mind your feeble little servant.

Dungal to Hildoard: observe and recall to mind your feeble little servant.

In order to provide an object for the verb in the acrostic one may reread the twentieth line, which is introduced by the last letter in *tue*. In the text of the poem there are only three doubtful words, the orthography of which would affect a letter count. The initial *A* of *Aera* 14 is fixed by the acrostic, and that suggests that Dungal used the correct Classical spellings *aethere* 6 and *saeptaque* 13. His *Conditor arcitenens* may follow the usage of Aldhelm's *Aenigma* 100 line 19 *Pater arcitenens* or *De Virginitate* in verse line 1538 *Sator arcitenens* without an *h*.

The forty-two words of the Preface divide by symmetry at 21 and 21, by extreme and mean ratio at 26 and 16, at *in quibus | priores litterae singulorum uersuum unam | | porrectam sed in transuersum lineam | efficientes*. The forty-two words divide by one-ninth and eight-ninths at 5 and 37, at the name and title of the recipient, *Hildoardi | episcopi*. The forty-two words divide by duple ratio at 28 and 14; between *uersus* and *uersifici* there are twenty-eight words. They divide by sesquialter ratio at 25 and 17; between *uersus* and *uersuum* there are seventeen words. They divide by sesquioctave ratio at 22 and 20; between *uersus* and *transuersum* there are twenty-two words.

The verses occupy twenty lines and 122 words, ten lines and sixty-one words in each half. Dungal names God ten times, as *Dominus sublimis* 5, *Altithroni Genitor* 6, *Rex regum* 7, *summus Princeps* 7, *Dominus dominantium* 7, *Dispositor sapiens* 8, *Conditor arcitenens* 8, *unus Deus* 11, *Sanctum Spiramen* 11, *trinus Deus et unus* 18.

XIII. EUBEN

Carmina

Two *Carmina* are ascribed to a Welshman named Euben (Owain), perhaps from the middle of the eleventh century.[1] Capital letters and punctuation marks in boldface represent features of Cambridge, Corpus Christi College, MS 139 folio 167vb.

Adiu*tor* **b**e*nignus* ca*ris*		a
doctor *eff*ab*í*lis **f**on*ís*.		a
sit .i. Samueli		
Ga*udium* **h**onoris is*ti*		
katholica lege **magn***i* .		b
No*s* **o**mne*s* pre**c***amur*	5	c
qui **r**o*s* sit **t**utu*s* **u**t*atur* .		c

---

1   *BCLL* 35–6. D.N. Dumville, ed. & transl. in '"Nennius" and the *Historia Brittonum*', *Studia Celtica* X-XI (1975–6), pp. 78–95, at 83–6.

.i. Beulan

Xp[ist]e tribuisti patri		d
Samuelem leta Matre .		d
.i. Mater		
Ymnizat hec semper tibi		b
.i. Samuel		
Longeuus ben seruus tui .	10	b
Zona indue salutis		a
istum tis pluribus annis .		a

The gentle helper, doctor praiseworthy with dear voices:
(May there be) joy of great honour to him [Samuel] (in accordance
     with) universal law!
We all beseech (you), May he dwell safe who is a divine blessing!
O Christ, You granted Samuel to (his) father [Beulan], to the joy of his
     Mother;
She [Mother] hymns you forever. (May he [Samuel] be) a long-lived
     son, your servant;
Clothe him with the girdle of your salvation for many years!

There are twelve lines of alphabetic verse, six devoted to the letters *A-V* and
six to the letters *X-Y-Z*. Our author has imposed upon himself the difficulty of
making the first letter of each word in the first half of the poem follow
alphabetical order. In the second half the first word of each couplet completes
the alphabetical order.

There are forty-one words, twenty before *Xpiste* and twenty after *Xpiste*.
There are ninety-four syllables, the two central, forty-seventh and forty-eighth
syllables, occurring in *Xpiste*.[2] There are 224 letters, 112 in the first half and 112 in
the second half. The number of words per line is 3–3–3–3–3–5, and 3–3–4–
4–3–3. There is a chiastic rhyme scheme, the first and last couplets rhyming on
-is, the second and penultimate on *-i*, and the central on *-os -s -a- -ur* and *-ri- -ri-
-atri* and *-le- le- -atre*.

The golden section of 20 falls at 12 and 8. The twelfth word from the end
of the first half is *isti .i. Samueli*. In the second half the golden section of 21 falls
at 13 and 8. The thirteenth word from the beginning and the eighth word
from the end are *seruus tui*.

The other *carmen* names our poet.

>   **F**ornifer . qui digitis scripsit ex ordine trinis .
>   **I**ncolumis obtalmis sitque omnibus menbris .
>   **E**u uocatur ben notis litteris nominis quini[s] .

2   Dumville, p. 84 n. 6, observes that 'The first half of line 3 [here line 5] lacks two syllables. The
     continuity of the abecedarial form demonstrates that this is due to the poet's inadvertence, not to
     scribal error'. But the syllable count suggests deliberateness, not inadvertence. Euben wanted
     Xpiste to be the central syllables.

> May the bearer of gifts [*i.e.* a pupil who brings a gift of money or praise
> or a written text to his teacher], who according to custom has written
> with three fingers,
> be safe in eyes and all limbs!
> He is called Euben, the five letters of (his) name having been noted.

With his three fingers he wrote three lines (3 × 1) comprising eighteen words and eighteen feet (3 × 6), forty-four syllables, and 114 letters (3 × 38). The mid-point for lines, words, feet, syllables, and letters is the same place.

In the first one-ninth of the poem the poet refers to himself as *fornifer qui*. Eight-ninths of the way through the poem he mentions his name, *nominis*.

According to Dumville[3]

> Each line comprises two parts: 7 + 8 syllables with a caesura between.
> The end of the first part rhymes with that of the second (with one
> exception which may therefore be due to scribal error, *notis: quini<s?>*).
> These verses have a trochaic rhythm, the first half of each line being
> acatalectic. The second half of line two appears to lack one syllable. The
> verse-form does not seem to occur elsewhere.

The central line exhibits two heptasyllabic halves. In the first and third pentadecasyllabic lines the poet reverses the order of octosyllabic and heptasyllabic components exhibited in *Audite omnes amantes Deum sancta merita*.[4]

The letter count in multiples of 3 corroborates the evidence of the rhyme scheme that the last word should be *quinis*, not *quini*.

The signature in the last line of the second poem encourages one to return to the first for indications of the author's name. One may appear in the first line, which is an anagram of *gnarius do Iuben cartis*, 'with more discernment [that is, because hidden in an anagram] I present Iuben in literary works'. Another may appear in line 10, which is an anagram of *longus Euben seruus tui*, 'Euben your long-lasting servant'. Like the other verses both of these scan as octosyllables. They appear in positions in which authors frequently sign themselves. They match the metre of the verses in which they are embedded. And they make appropriate sense.

XIV. PATRICK BISHOP OF DUBLIN

Carmina

During the years 1074–1084 the diocese of Dublin was governed by Gille Padraig, Bishop Patrick, known as the author of five Latin works,[1] among

3 Dumville, p. 85 n. 4.
4 See above pp. 139–42.
1 *BCLL* 309–10. *The Writings of Bishop Patrick 1074–1084*, ed. & transl. A. Gwynn, *Scriptores Latini Hiberniae* I (Dublin 1955).

which we shall consider the last two, from a copy in British Library MS Cotton Titus D XXIV. The fourth poem, *Versus Allegorici*,[2] Patrick signed at the beginning with an invocation and two elegiac couplets giving his own name and the name of the recipient.

Inuocatio scriptoris huius libelli .i. Patricii episcopi.

Qui celum terramque regis pelagusque profundum;
Cuius ad arbitrium numina cunta tenes;
                    i. mundi.
Sis mihi nunc fautor cosmi rectissime tutor;
                i. Alduino.
Quo ualeam famulo scribere digna tuo;

An invocation by the writer of this book, Bishop Patrick.
Thou Who dost rule heaven, earth, and the deep ocean,
    Who dost hold all powers subject to Thy will:
Show me now Thy favour, O most just Guardian of the world,
    That I may be able to write verses worthy of thy servant Aldwin.

The verses then begin at line 5 *Mentis in excessu* and end with the same words at line 255. They are followed by five lines of hexameter verse, similarly signed with the name of the poet and the recipient.

Scabrida cum resonet mea lingua rubigine uerba;
                    s. Alduine.
Hec tibi transscripsi breuiter mi dulcis amice;
                    s. Patricium.
Quo mei commemorans redamas te semper amantem;
Protegat. edoceat. nutriat. regat. atque coronet;
Roboret. edificet. te Xpisti gratia seruet;

Whilst my tongue sounds forth these words that are rough with rust,
I have written them down briefly for thee, my dear friend,
    That being mindful of me thou mayest love one who ever loves thee.
May the grace of Christ guard thee, teach, nourish, guide and crown thee,
Strengthen thee, build thee up, keep thee ever safe!

The elegiac couplets contain twenty-five words, which divide by one-ninth and eight-ninths at 3 and 22. The recipient is referred to in the twenty-second word, above which his name is glossed. The hexameter verses contain thirty-three words, of which the central are *mei commemorans redamas*. The golden section of 33 falls at 20 and 13. Reckoned from the beginning it falls at *mi*

2   Ibid. pp. 84–101. London, British Library, MS Cotton Titus D XXIV ff. 64v, 74v.

dulcis | amice, s. Alduine, the recipient, and reckoned from the end it falls at *te semper | amantem, s. Patricium*, the author.

The fifth and most widely disseminated of Patrick's works is the *Liber de tribus habitaculis animae*.[3] Prefixed to this in two manuscripts are an invocation, two hexameters, and a prologue in adonics.

[Liber sancti Patricii episcopi]
Inuocatio sancti Patricii episcopi
i. secreta.
O Deus Omnipotens celorum dindima complens.
Remige[4] glaucicomos tithis alti comprime fluctus.

The Book of holy Patrick the bishop
The invocation of Bishop Patrick
Almighty God, Who dost fill the secret places of Heaven,
Hold back with Thy oar the grey-haired waves of the deep sea!

Incipit prologus libri sancti Patricii episcopi.

Here begins the prologue of the book of holy Patrick the bishop.

Perge carina		Onward, my barque,
Per mare longum		Through the long sea!
Xpistus in undis		Christ on the water
Sit tibi ductor		Be thy steersman,
Remige tuto	5	With sure oar
Sidere sudo.		And a clear sky!
Curre carina		Hasten, my barque,
Per mare cauum		Through the hollow sea,
Pallidulosque		And cleave the pale
Discute fluctus	10	And horrid waves
Roscida tetros		Foam-besprayed:
Nauta regente		Sailor-like, steered by
Flamine dextro.		A favouring breeze!
Perge libelle		Onward, my book,
Angelus assit	15	(Be an angel at thy side)
Per mare latum		Through the wide sea:
Visere sedem		To visit the dear home
.i. Wlstani.		
Presulis almam		Of Bishop Wulfstan!
Si valet ille		Is he well
Dignus honore	20	Who is worthy of honour

---

3   Ibid. pp. 102–25. London, British Library, MS Cotton Titus D XXIV f. 87r.
4   MS *regmine*.

Dulcis amore		Dear in love?	
Pelle merorem		Drive sadness from him	
Gaudia pange		Sing forth joy	
Nocte dieque		By day and night	
Voce canora	25	With sweet voice,	
Solis adusque		Even to the sun,	
Sidera summa.		To the topmost stars!	
Pagina perge		Hasten, my page,	
Per crucis alte		By the holy strength	
Robora sancta	30	Of the high cross!	
Vela tumescant		May thy sails swell	
Per freta pura		Through the clean waves!	
Disce marina		Learn, my barque,	
Tuta carina		To run in safety	
Currere campos	35	Through the fields of the sea!	
Assimilare		Learn to be like unto	
Dira marina		The dread monsters	
Monstra natatu		Of the sea, by swimming	
.i. amara.			
Aequora merra		Through the bitter waters!	
Perge libelle	40	Onward, my book!	
Letus in undis		Thou shalt go in joy	
Ibis et Austris		Through wind and wave.	
Squamea turba		The scale-clad throng	
Te comeabit		Shall keep thee company,	
Ac celeuma	45	And the helmsman's cry	
Carmine dulci		With sweet tone	
Equoris imo		Shall sound strongly	
Forte sonabit;		From the depths of the sea.	
Curre carina		Hasten, my barque,	
Leta per undas	50	In joy through the waters!	
Cornua ueli		May the tops of thy sail	
Sint tumefacta		Be swollen full	
Flatibus Euri;		By the eastern breeze!	
Te sine nube		Without a cloud	
Flabra ministrent	55	May the breezes serve thee,	
Obruat error		[Nor] may any error	
Anglica rura		O'erwhelm [thee]	
Tramite recto		Until thou art borne	
Usque feraris;		On a straight course	
Pagina perge	60	To the fields of England!	
Mente sequaci		Onward, my page!	
Te comitabor		In my thought following	
Ducor amore		I shall be thy companion.	

Pacis alumpnos		I am drawn by love	
Visere caros	65	To visit the dear	
Xpisticolisque		Fosterchildren of peace.	
.i. Wlstani.			
Presulis almi		To all Christ's faithful	
Omnibus eque		Of kind Bishop Wulfstan,	
Solue trigenas		To them all equally	
Rite salutes	70	Bring, as is fitting,	
Ordine pulcro;		Thrice ten greetings	
Perge libelle		In fair order!	
.i. uili.			
Carmine claudo		Onward, my book,	
s. episcopi.			
Patriciique		With halting verse:	
Mente fidelis	75	And from me, Patrick,	
.s. Alduino.		Loyal in memory,	
Rite sodali		Ask, as is fitting,	
Mille coronas		For my comrade Aldwin	
Posce salutis;		A thousand crowns of blessed life!	
[Explicit prologus.]		Here ends the prologue.	

Patrick has arranged his words and ideas in a great chiasmus.

```
1 a    Perge carina
  b       per mare longum
  a'   Curre carina
  b'      per mare cauum
  a"   Perge libelle
  b"      per mare latum
2 a          uisere sedem
  b             presulis almam
3                amore
4                  pagina perge
5                    uela tumescant
6                      carina
7                        currere
8                          aequora
9                            perge libelle
8'                         equoris
7'                       curre
6'                     carina
5'                   cornua ueli sint tumefacta
4'                 pagina perge
3'               amore
```

```
2'a          uisere caros
  b              presulis almi
1'a      perge libelle.
```

One might perhaps include among the parallels of part 1 the verbs *sit* 4 and *assit* 15. Overlapping with this chiasmus is another.

```
1      Xpistus
2          ductor
3              tuto
4                  sidere
5                      pelle
6                          merorem
6'                         gaudia
5'                     pange
4'                 sidera
3'             tuta
2'         ducor
1'     Xpisticolisque.
```

Within these two chiastic patterns he has included in the second half of the poem a parallelism.

```
1      Letus in undis
2          Austris
3              Te comeabit
4                  carmine
1'     Leta per undas
2'         flatibus Euri
3'             Te comitabor
4'                 carmine.
```

The poem occupies seventy-eight lines and contains 164 words. It divides symmetrically at the crux of the first chiasmus after the thirty-ninth of seventy-eight lines. It divides also by extreme and mean ratio, the golden section of 78 falling at 48 and 30, that of 164 at 101 and 63. From the beginning to the first reference to Bishop Wulfstan there are eighteen lines and forty words. From the second reference to Bishop Wulfstan to the end there are twelve lines and twenty-three words. The minor part of the poem occupies thirty lines (18+12) and sixty-three words (23+40). The minor part is itself divided by extreme and mean ratio, the golden section of 30 falling at 18 and 12, that of 63 at 39 and 24. Even these divisions are divided by extreme and mean ratio. In the first passage of eighteen lines, the parallelism *perge carina, curre carina, perge libelle*, recurs at lines 1,

7, and 14, falling into three sentences. The first occupies six lines and the second and third twelve lines, of seven and five lines respectively, the golden section of 12 falling at 7 and 5. The last twelve lines divide by extreme and mean ratio at 7 and 5, and the last twenty-three words divide by extreme and mean ratio at 14 and 9, at the reference to the poem and the poet, *carmine claudo* | *Patriciique*. Between the two references to Bishop Wulfstan lies the major part of forty-eight lines and 101 words.

The *presul almus* is Wulfstan II, Bishop of Worcester, elected on 26 August and consecrated on 8 September 1062, better known almost from the date of his death on 19 or 20 January 1095 as Saint Wulfstan.

XV. IEUAN AP SULIEN

Carmina

Rhygyfarch ap Sulien is best known for his prose *Life of Saint David*[1] with its stories of the national saints of Wales and Ireland, David and Patrick and Moucan, from the very beginnings of the Celtic Latin traditon. The *Planctus Ricemarch* or 'Rhygyfarch's Lament'[2] in one sense marks an end to a part of the Celtic Latin tradition with his verse complaint for the Norman Conquest of Wales. Our purpose here, however, is to consider from less unhappy circumstances the poetry of Rhygyfarch's younger brother Ieuan ap Sulien.[3] It survives in an autograph manuscript, Cambridge, Corpus Christi College, MS 199, from Llanbadarn Fawr from the end of the eleventh century. The first poem is found on folio 1v, an *Inuocatio Iohannis*.

> **IN** patris . natique simul . flatusque superni .
> **E**iusdem deitatis : opus hoc nomine tango .,
> **O**mnipotens clemensque deus . quem semper in altis .
> **S**iderei cœtus pariter solimeque phalanges .
> **N**omine mirifico uenerantur trinus . et unus .
> **A**d plenum scriptoris opus mis perfice tandem .
> **C**vuncti quem solito Iohannes famine fantur ..,

> In the name of the Father and the Son and the supernal Spirit together
> And His deity I undertake this work.
> Omnipotent and merciful God, Whom together in the heights

---

1 BCLL 32. *Rhigyfarch's Life of St David*, ed. & transl. J.W. James (Cardiff 1967).
2 BCLL 31. 'The Welsh-Latin Poetry of Sulien's Family', ed. & transl. M. Lapidge, *Studia Celtica* VIII-IX (1973–4) pp. 88–93.
3 BCLL 33. 'Welsh-Latin Poetry', pp. 78–89. I have collated the manuscript, marked the larger capital letters and the punctuation points in boldface and letters with wash in underlining, and corrected Lapidge's translation and notes in several places.

Sidereal throngs and Hierosolomitan troops equally
Worship Three and One in wondrous name,
Perfect me finally for the complete work of a writer,
Whom all call in customary language Ieuan.

The name *Iohannes* in the last line is washed with colour, as are all the underlined letters. The capital letters at the beginnings of the lines yield an anagram of the name *IOANNES* or, if we include all the initial leters, *IOCANNES.*

A longer and more remarkable poem is the

Carmen Iohannis de uita et familia Sulgeni
ARBiter altithrone nutu qui cuncta gubernas .
Ut nunquam ualeant modulum transire repostum.
Qui cursu propero sustentas iure potenter.
Stelliferi centri uergentia culmina circum.
Non cassura solo. cursum retinentibus astris.   5
Flammantemque globum Phoebi. lunamque bicornem.
Flexibus ambiguis reptantem more draconum.
Celatum lustrare polum. glebamque patentem.
Solem dans luci clarum. noctique sororem.
Sidera concedis necnon splendescere summa :   10
Quique manens semper iam summa sede coruscus.
Telluris molem circundans equore tanto.
Lymbo consimili. clari ceu tegminis oram.
Occianum prohibes minitantem murmure multo.
Undisono fremitu rumpat ne proxima terre.   15
Tu mihi poscenti sophiam concede supernam
Votiuas grates ualeam tibi reddere Xp[ist]e.
Qui me scriptorem libri uenerabilis asstans.
Nomine quem trino uocitant e iure fideles.

Optatum fessos fecisti carpere finem..,   20
Nam ceu cum nautæ iamiam minitante procella.
Contractis loris alnum mediante carina.
Consurgunt. uelis tenso sinuamine pansis.
Viribus arreptis temptant sua brachia remis.
Pupi iam celsa sidens auriga benignus.   25
Tramite directo librat trans æquora tanta.
At tunc turgescunt flabris rumpentibus euri.
Imbribus horrendis insultans peruenit aura.
Multiuago fremitu saltant ad sidera fluctus.
Atque patente sinu declarat tartara tellus.   30
At titubante genu frigescunt corda pauore.

Disperant nautæ uita. tunc ora precantum
Vocibus altisonis proclamant iure tonantem
Iam tandem miserente pio. uotisque fauente.
Optatum lassi portum libramine recto.   35
Tangunt. ymnidicis referentes cantica uotis.
Haut aliter scriptor tangens extrema libelli.
Bicipitis rostro gaudet concludere finem..,

Scriptoris nomen quisquis cognoscere curat. ·
Obtonsæ mentis torporem trudat inormem.   40
Scrutando minium nitens pertingere uerum.
Ingenio claro uersus iam perlegat istos.,

In primis nona texendi culmina cepit.
Ordine quartdecima considit rite secundo.
Has octaua manet post. tertia iure locanda.   45
Atque petit prima medium tunc ordine quarto.
Nulli tresdecima dubium sit quinta putetur.
Numine tresdecima repetendi sexta locatur.
Excipit et quintam formandi septimus ordo.
Sortibus octdecima pertingit ultima finis..,   50

ET gentem. patriamque simul. nomenque parentis.
Qui uelit. ut nota sint ordine noscere cuncta.
Intendat uersus post istos iure[4] sequentes..,

Atqui famosa natus sum gente Britonum.
Romanæ quondam classi cum uiribus obstat.   55
Iulus cum Cæssar refugus post terga recessit..,
Quod mihi Ceretica tellus sit patria certe.
Confiteor cunctis coram ditissima quondam.
Hostibus exossa. peregrinis atque benigna.
Hospitio cunctos excellens iure Britannos..,   60
Exprimit hec tabule formam iam quattuor oris.
Nam mons excelsus consurgit solis ad ortus,
Proficuus multis pecorum iam pastibus apte.
Inmensus fluuius dextrales irrigat oras.
Ac latus occiduum latum mare proluit inde.   65
At Boreæ partes flumen discriminat ingens.
Per mare sic. montemque simul. binosque per amnes.
Fertilis hæc regio discernitur undique uersus..,

---

4   Lapidge reports the MS reading as *lure* and emends to *iure*. Comparison of capital *I* in line 56 and lower case *ls* in *simul* 51 and *classi* 55 shows that Ieuan wrote *iure*.

Huius ad arctoas locus est metropolis altæ .
Antestes sanctus quo duxit iure Paternus.   70
Egregiam uitam septenos terque per annos.
Votiuus cælo quot mensis quotque diebus.,
Nam quiddam sæclo rationis nouit in isto.
Omnia quæ mundi sunt uana ac lubrica cernens.
Intendens animo cælestia numina toto.   75
Deuouit Christo totum seruire per æuum..,
Ac se iam sanctum mactans cruciamine corpus.
Semper inexhausto persistens ualde labore.
Orans. ieiunans. uigilans. lacrimansque gemensque.
Essuris alimenta simul. nexisque leuamen.   80
Hospitibus pandens aditum. sitientibus haustum.
Egrotis curam. nudis miseratus amictum.
Prudens quæque gerens. perfecit cuncta potenter..,
Ac sic lucifluum meruit conscendere regnum.
Cuncti quo sancti miro splendore beantur..,   85
Ortus hinc Sulgenus adest iam germine claro.
Nobilium semper sapientium iure parentum.,
Qui postquam primo nablam tener edidit infans.
Perlustrat scolas studio florente Britannas.,
At crescente simul ardore ac tempore multo.   90
Exemplo patrum commotus more legendi.
Iuit ad Hibernos sophia mirabili claros..,
Sed cum iam cimba uoluisset adire reuectus.
Famosam gentem scripturis atque magistris.
Appulit ad patriam uentorum flatibus actus.   95
Nomine quam noto perhibent Albania longe.,
Ac remoratus ibi certe tum quinque per annos.
Indefessus agit uotum. ceu fertile pratum.
Inueniens caltis candens. ardensque rosetis.
Dulciferoque thimo flagrans campestre per omne.   100
Cum sol flammiuomo Cancrum iam splendidus astro.
Transcurrit. scandens summi laquearia centri:
Taumate tum tanto siluas. camposque nitentes.
Conualles. montesque simul. maria altaque circum.
Comburens totum pariter. terramque polumque: 105
Ac clarus molli boreus cum sibelat aura.
Imbribus assiduis udus cum deficit Auster.
Iam subtilis apes degustat flore sapores.
Haut secus assiduo persistens nocte dieque.
Exsugit puro septeni gurgitis amne.   110
Pocula mellifluo flatu flagrantia longe..,
Nam simul inmenso discens scribensque labore.

Quicquid pernoctans scrutatur mente retenta.
Solem per clarum surgens scribebat acute..,
His ita degestis Scotorum uissitat arua.,   115
Ac mox scripturas multo meditamine sacras.
Legis diuinæ scrutatur sepe retractans..,
Ast ibi per denos tricens iam placidus annos.
Congregat inmensam pretioso pondere massam. .
Protinus arguta thesaurum mente recondens.,   120
Post hæc ad patriam. remeans iam dogmate clarus.
Venit. et inuentum multis iam diuidit aurum.
Proficiens cunctis discentibus undique circum.,
Reges, quem populi. cleri. cunctique coloni.
Omnes unanimes uenerantur mente serena.,   125
Quattuor ac proprio nutriuit sanguine natos.
Quos simul edocuit dulci libaminis amne.
Ingenio claros. iam sunt hæc nomina quorum.
Rycymarch sapiens. Arthgen. Danielque Iohannes.,
Qui quoque post tantam populorum famine famam.   130
Cunctorum precibus superatus. summus ut esset.
Vallis iam Rosinæ præsul deducitur ecce.
Vitam quo puram Dauid perfecit ouanter.
En igitur Sulgenus adest mihi iam pater almus.
Pontificis Dauid cathedram qui rexit amoenam.   135
Bis reuocatus ibi duodenos egerat annos.,
Soli nam Xr[ist]o secretam ducere uitam.
deuotus totum, pompossam liquerat illam.,
In senio cuius hæc tanta uolumina scripsi.
Iam complere uolens genitoris uota benigne.,   140
Ex cuius sophia nutritus qualiter haussi.,
Merces hæc mea semper erit benedictio cuius..,

Quid referam plura? uos deprecor ecce legentes.
Cura quibus sollers scrutandi sepe subinfert.
Præsulis excelsi clarum cognomine librum.   145
Augustinus. ouans clerus⁵ quem personat orbis.
Unanimes uotis letanter adeste precantes.
Pro mis commissis. uocitor quem rite Iohannes.
Hæc qui dictaui. scribendo quique peregi.
Ut genitor clemens solita pietate remittat.   150
Factis. aut dictis. quæ gessi corde nefando.
Proficuum dum tempus adest. certæque salutis.
Dum mihi uita manet. dum flendi flumina prosunt.

5   clerus as MS, not clerum as Lapidge.

Nam cum tartareis nullius cura subintrat.
Ac mihi post tandem finiti flaminis horam.   155
Pure perpetuam concedat scandere sedem.
Arbiter ex solio moderans iam secula summo.
Sanctorum coetus quo clamant cælitus omnes
Alleluia pio cantu sine fine per æuum..,
AmeN..,

Lofty-throned Judge, Who govern all things by Your command so that they may
never exceed their assigned positions, Who mightily sustain in its swift course the
turning zenith of the starry heaven at all points, [which] will never crash to earth
[so long as] the stars retain their course; and [sustain] the flaming globe of the sun,
and the two-horned moon in its ambiguous [i.e. two-way: waxing and waning]
movements after the manner of crawling dragons to illuminate the embossed
heavens and the receptive earth, [thus] giving the clear sun for light [in day-time]
and its sister [the moon] at night (9); You also grant that the highest stars are
resplendent; and Who, remaining always gleaming [on Your] supreme throne,
bounding the mass of earth with such [a body of] water, like a fine hem, just as
the margin of a coverspread [bounds it], You restrain the ocean threatening with
a great murmur so that it does not break in upon the near-by land with a flood-
tide roar (15). Grant heavenly wisdom to me who beseech [so that] I may be able
to return my promised thanks to You O Christ, You Who are assisting me the
writer of this reverend book, [You] Whom the faithful rightly call by threefold
name. You have made it so that the weary may achieve their longed-for goal for,
just as when sailors with a storm threatening, having drawn the guy-lines tight,
with the keel steadying the ship, they stand up together, the sails spread with a
tense furl, [and] taking possession of their strength they ply their arms to the oars
(24). At that point the kindly helmsman, sitting on the heights of the poop-deck,
maintains [the ship] in a direct path across such [troubled] waters. But just then
the east winds swell with shattering blasts; [another] wind arrives, bursting [upon
the ship] with horrendous rainfall. The swell with many-waved groan leaps to
the stars, and with its breast laid bare the earth reveals Tartarus. But on tottering
knees, the hearts of the sailors freeze with fear (31). The sailors despair of life. At
just that moment the mouths of those praying duly proclaim their Thunderer-
God with deep-sounding voices. At length, with the Holy One taking pity and
hearing their prayers, the tired [sailors] reach the desired port by correct guidance,
pouring out songs [in the form of] hymnful prayers. Not otherwise does the
author, reaching the end of his two-headed (?) book, rejoice to have reached its
conclusion with his prow (38).[6]

Whoever cares to know the name of the writer, let him expel the gross
torpor of his dull mind, [and] striving to attain to the truth by examining the
minium, let him read these verses with clear wit:

6   One might better construe this 'reaching the last parts of the book rejoice to conclude the end
     with the nib of his two-edged [pen]'.

First of all the ninth [letter of the alphabet: I] begins [by taking] the pre-eminent position of the construction; the fourteenth [O] duly sits in second place; after these the eighth [H] remains, filling out the third place; and the first letter [A] then seeks the middle [of the word], being in fourth place; let there be no doubt in one's mind that the thirteenth [N] be thought to be in fifth place; by virtue of repetition the thirteenth [N] is located in sixth place. And the seventh place acquires the fifth letter [E]. By chance the eighteenth letter [S] attains to the end of the end (50).

And whosoever wishes to know the race, the country, and the name of [my] father—so that they all be known—in turn, let him after these [above] verses direct his attention to these following lines (53):

For I am born of the famous race of Britons [which] once withstood the Roman army energetically, when Julius Caesar retreated, a fugitive (56). That the land of Ceredig [i.e. Cardiganshire] is certainly my homeland, I confess openly to all—once extremely rich, spiteful to enemies, kind to travellers, excelling all Britons in hospitality. This [land] exhibits the form of a table with four sides. For a lofty mountain [i.e. Plynlimon] rises at the source of the sun [i.e. in the east], advantageous [in providing] much pasture for flocks. An immense river [i.e. the Teifi] irrigates the right-hand side [of the country, i.e. the south]; and then the wide sea washes the western side. But a mighty river [i.e. the Dyfi] divides the region of the north (66). Thus by the sea, together with the mountain and the two rivers, this fertile region is discerned on all sides. At its northern part is the place of a high city [i.e. Llanbadarn Fawr], where the holy bishop Padarn led an outstanding life for twenty-one years, a devotee of heaven for as many months and as many days [as he was there]. For in this worldly life he knew something reasonable, recognizing that all things of the world are vain and transient (74); seeking after celestial divinity with all his soul, he devoted himself to serve Christ for ever, and sacrificing his holy body through deprivation, always persisting with inexhaustible effort praying, fasting, keeping vigil, weeping, lamenting, offering food to those hungering, consolation to those troubled, welcome to guests, drink to those in thirst, care to the sick and clothing to the naked on whom he took pity. Doing whatsoever [he did] prudently he accomplished all things fully and thus he deserved to ascend the light-flowing realm where all are blessed with a wondrous light (85).

Sulien was born here [i.e. at Llanbadarn Fawr] of a distinguished stock of noble [and] always wise parents, who, after he as a tender child had first produced a psalter, went through British schools, his studies flourishing. But, growing in ardour as time went on, and moved by the example of [Church] Fathers through his habit of reading, he set off for the Irish, distinguished by their remarkable learning (92). But although he wished to go, transported by his skiff, to the people famous for their writings and teachers, he landed in [that] country, moved by gusts of wind, which they call by the [well-]known name of Albania [i.e. Scotland]. And remaining there, to be sure, for five years, unwearied he pursues his desire just as a bee, finding a fertile meadow glowing with marigolds and

bright with rose bushes, fragrant with sweet thyme through the entire plain
(100),[7] when the radiant sun crosses Cancer with its fire-spewing star, climbing to
the vault of the highest heaven, then with such heat scorching the woods, the
shining fields, valleys, mountains at the same time, the deep seas on every side
[scorching] everything equally the earth and the heaven, and when the clear
north wind[8] whispers with a gentle breeze, when the moist south wind is lacking
its [usual] relentless showers that tiny bee sips off the savour from the flower
(108). Not otherwise [Sulien], persisting diligently [in his studies] by night and
day, extracted continuously from the pure stream of the sevenfold fountain [i.e.
trivium + quadrivium] cupfuls fragrant with mellifluous aroma. For, learning and
writing with immense effort, whatsoever he investigated during the night, having
been retained in his mind, arising at the clear light of day he wrote down
intelligently (114). Having done these things he visited the lands of the Irish, and
straightway he investigated the sacred scriptures of the divine law with much
meditation, often reflecting upon them. And staying there contentedly for ten
years he accumulated a store [of knowledge], immense in its precious weight.
Then, storing this treasure in his shrewd mind he thereafter came home,
returning [a man] distinguished in learning; he came and divided the gold he had
discovered among many, being of use to all disciples on every side, he whom
kings, the people, the clergy and all land-dwellers venerated unanimously with
serene mind (125). And he nurtured four sons of his own stock, intellectually
distinguished, whom he instructed with the sweet stream of [learning's] libation.
These are their names: Rhigyfarch the wise, Arthgen, Daniel, and Ieuan. After
Sulien [had attained] such repute in the mouths of the people, overcome by the
entreaties of all that he be the bishop of St David's, he was taken to where David
lived a pure life exultingly (133). Behold, therefore, Sulien, my genial father, who
ruled the beautiful bishopric of Bishop David: twice recalled, he spent twelve
years there. Then, resolving to lead a withdrawn life for Christ alone, he completely abandoned that stately [life]. During his old age I wrote these great
volumes, wishing kindly to fulfil the wishes of [him] my father, from whose
wisdom I was nourished as much as I wished to draw. My thanks shall always be
to his kindness (142).

   Why say more? I beseech you in whom all skilful care of learning is present,
who are here reading the distinguished work of the heavenly bishop—Augustine
by name—the cleric whose praises the rejoicing world sings—unanimous in your
prayers, now be present joyously praying for my undertakings, I who am
properly called Ieuan, who have composed this poetry and have completed it in

---

7   Lapidge states, n. 100, 'The adjective *campester* ... can be used as a substantive (as Ieuan has done
    here), but it has a meaning far remote from what Ieuan intended: it means the loin-cloth which
    athletes wore during exercise'. In Insular usage from Cogitosus and Aldhelm onward it means
    what Ieuan intends here, 'open country'. See below p. 243 and the *Dictionary of Medieval Latin
    from British Sources* s.v. *campestris* 1c.
8   Lapidge states, n. 106, that '*boreus* is not used elsewhere as a substantive', but it is so recorded in
    the eighth-century *Corpus Glossary* B 152.

writing, so that the merciful Creator may with His accustomed mercy forgive the deeds or sayings which I committed with sinful heart, while the time is appropriate for certain salvation, while I am still alive, while rivers of weeping still flow (153); for with the infernal regions no one's care is at hand [i.e. there's no one to care for you in Hell]. And, after the hour when my life's breath is spent, may the Judge moderating all ages from His heavenly throne grant that I may chastely ascend [to] the perpetual seat, where the entire assembly of saints sings celestially 'Alleluia' in devout song, without end for all time.

In his introductory paragraph Ieuan addresses God three times as *Arbiter*, *Xpiste*, and *nomine quem trino uocant*. In the first ten lines he applies three verbs to God's activities, *gubernas*, *sustentas*, and *concedis*; in the next five lines he applies three more, *manens*, *circundans*, and *prohibes*. He states in the first ten lines that God has ordered the heavens to keep their course and not to fall on to the earth; he states in the next five that God has ordered the ocean to keep its bounds and not to break on to the earth. Compare *altithrone, qui, gubernas ... sustentas* with *summa sede, quique, manens*; *stelliferi centri uergentia culmina circum* with *telluris molem circundans*; *non cassura* with *prohibes ... rumpat ne*; *solo* with *terre*; *concedis* with *concede*. He also repeats *iure* (3) at *e iure* (19).

Ieuan has marked the bounds of his second paragraph with *inclusio*, ending the first line *carpere finem* and the last *concludere finem*. Within the paragraph he considers disorder in winds from the heavens on the sea, comparing exhausted sailors who reach their desired port with a scribe who reaches the end of his book, in a parallelism: *optatum, fessos, naute, carina*; *optatum, lassi, haut aliter scriptor, rostro*.

He has further linked the first two paragraphs with parallel diction: *iure* (3, 33), *equore tanto* (12) *equora tanta* (26), *sidera* (10, 29), *uotiuas grates ... reddere* (17) *referentes cantica uotis* (36), *scriptorem libri* (18) *scriptor ... libelli* (37). Note that the last three of these are in the same relative lines of the paragraphs.

In the third paragraph Ieuan reveals his name after four lines of introduction in an acrostic of eight lines. The last word, *finis*, links this to the *inclusio* of the preceding paragraph.

In the fourth paragraph he says in three lines of introduction that he will name his race, his homeland, and his father in order, and so he does.

In the concluding paragraph he addresses his readers, refers to the book he has written, alludes to the poem he has composed, and hopes for heaven.

The first three paragraphs are linked by references to himself as *me scriptorem libri* (18), *scriptor libelli* (37), and *scriptoris nomen* (39). The last three paragraphs are linked by references to himself as *IOHANNES* (43–50), *Iohannes* (129), and *uocitor quem rite Iohannes* (148). The first three paragraphs comprise nineteen, nineteen, and twelve lines, fifty lines together. The golden section of 50 falls at 31 and 19. The minor part is the introductory prayer and the major part the comparison and signature. Within the major part the golden section of 31 falls at 19 and 12. The major part is the comparison and the minor part the signature. The fourth paragraph comprises ninety-two lines. The golden section of 92 falls at 57 and 35.

The major part relates the name and career of Sulien in fifty-seven lines, 86–142. The minor part is the thirty-five lines describing Ceredig, Llanbadarn Fawr, and Padarn, 51–85. Within the minor part the golden section of 35 falls at 21.6 and 13.4. At the twenty-first line, 71, Ieuan writes that Padarn lived his *egregiam uitam septenos terque per annos*. The last three paragraphs comprise twelve, ninety-two, and seventeen lines, 121 together. The golden section of 121 falls at 74.8 and 46.2. The forty-seventh line, 85, marks the end of the description of Padarn, and the seventy-fourth line from the end, 86, names Sulien. The entire poem comprises 159 lines. The golden section of 159 falls at 98.3 and 60.7, again at the end of the description of Padarn and the naming of Sulien.

From the beginning of Ieuan's name in line 43 to the first mention of Sulien's name in line 86 there are forty-four lines. From there to the second mention of Ieuan's name in line 129 there are forty-four lines.

Ieuan refers to himself one-ninth of the way through his poem, at line 18, *Qui me scriptorem libri uenerabilis asstans*.[9]

Lapidge has noted apparent borrowings in Ieuan's verse from the *Hisperica Famina* and from the first Anglo-Latin author, Aldhelm. As son of the Bishop of Saint David's Ieuan may have known the name and reputation of Asser, the biographer of King Alfred, whom we shall consider in chapter 5. His request in the *Inuocatio* was fulfilled; his place in the Celtic Latin tradition is secure and not inglorious.

---

9   For other examples of authorial self-reference one-ninth and eight-ninths of the way through a work see below p. 400.

V

HAGIOGRAPHERS AND HISTORIANS

I. COGITOSUS

Vita Sanctae Brigitae

The first Irish hagiographer whose name and work we know refers to himself in a concluding request to his readers: *Orate pro me Cogitoso nepote culpabili Aedo*. But he was not the first Irish hagiographer. His *Vita Sanctae Brigitae*[1] is a revision of the earlier *Vita I Sanctae Brigitae*, which may have depended, with the macaronic Old Irish and Latin *Bethu Brigte*, on an even earlier Life of Brigit.[2] Here is the text of his Preface as established in a critical edition not yet published but lent by Dr Richard Sharpe, to whom for this generosity and for helpful criticism I am grateful. The translation is mine.

Praefatio

Me cogitis, fratres, ut sanctae ac beatae memoriae Brigitae uirginis uirtutes et opera more doctorum memoriae litterisque tradere adgrediar, quod opus inpositum et delicatae materiae arduum paruitati et ignorantiae meae et ling-uae minime conuenit. Sed potens est Deus de minimis magna facere, ut de exiguo olei et farinae pugillo domum inpleuit pauperculae uiduae. Itaque iussionibus uestris coactus, satis habeo meam non defuisse oboed–ientiam, et ideo pauca de pluribus a maioribus ac peritissimis tradita sine ulla ambiguitatis caligine ne inoboedientiae crimen incurram patefacere censeo, ex quibus quanta qualisque uirgo uirtutum bonarum florida cunctorum oculis innotes-cat. Non quod memoria et mediocritas et rusticus sermo ingenioli mei tanti muneris officium explicare ualeret, sed fidei uestrae beatitudo et orationum uestrarum diurnitas meretur accipere quod non ualet ingenium ferre dictantis.

Haec ergo egregiis crescens uirtutibus et fama bonarum rerum ad eam de omnibus prouintiis totius Hiberniae innumerabiles populi de utraque sexu confluentes et uota sibi uouentes uoluntarie suum monasterium caput poene omnium Hybernensium ecclesiarum et culmen praecellens omnia monasteria Scothorum cuius parroechia per totam Hybernensem terram defusa a mari usque ad mare extensa est in campestribus campi Liffei supra fundamentum fidei firmum construxit et prudenti dispensatione de anima-

---

1 BCLL 302.
2 R. Sharpe, '*Vitae S Brigitae*: The Oldest Texts', *Peritia* I (1982), pp. 81–106. For a contrasting opinion see K. McCone, 'Brigit in the Seventh Century: A Saint with Three Lives?', Ibid. pp. 107–45.

bus suorum regulariter in omnibus procurans et de ecclesiis multarum
prouintiarum sibi adhaerentibus sollicitans et secum reuoluens, quod sine
summo sacerdote qui ecclesias consecraret et ecclesiasticos in eis gradus
subrogaret esse non posse, inlustrem uirum et solitarium Conlehet omnibus
moribus bonis ornatum, per quem Deus uirtutes operatus est plurimas,
conuocans eum de heremo et de sua uita solitaria et in ipsius obuiam
pergens ut ecclesiam in episcopali dignitate cum ea gubernaret atque ut
nihil de ordine sacerdotali in suis deesset ecclesiis accersiuit. Et sic postea
unctum caput et principale omnium episcoporum et beatissima puellarum
principalis, felici comitatu inter se et gubernaculis omnium uirtutum, suam
rexerunt principalem ecclesiam et amborum meritis sua cathedra episcopalis
et puellaris acsi uitis frugefera diffusa undique ramis crescentibus in tota
Hybernensi insula inoleuit, quam semper archiepiscopus Hybernensium
episcoporum [et] abbatissa quam omnes abbatissae Scothorum uenerantur
felici successione et ritu perpetuo dominantur.

Exinde ego ut supra dixi a fratribus coactus beatae huius Brigitae uirtutes
tam eas quas ante principatum quam alias quas in principatu gessit tanto
studio breuitatis licet praepostero ordine uirtutum conpendiose explicare
conabor.

You compel me, brothers, that I should undertake in the manner of
taught men to translate for memory and in letters the virtues and works of
the virgin Brigit of holy and blessed memory, which work imposed and
difficult in respect of the delicate subject is least suited both to the littleness
and to the ignorance of my tongue. But God is powerful to make great
things from the least, as from a little bit of oil and a fistful of flour He filled
the house of a poor little widow. And so, compelled by your commands, I
consider my obedience sufficient, not to have been deficient, and on that
count, lest I incur the crime of disobedience, I am deciding to lay open a
few things handed down from among very many by greater and the most
learned men without any obscurity of ambiguity, from which things how
great and what sort of virgin [she was], composed of the flowers of good
virtues, should become noted by the eyes of all men. Not that the memory
and meanness and rustic speech of my little intellect would be valid to
complete the function of so great a task, but that the blessedness of your
faith and the lengthiness of your prayers may deserve to receive what the
intellect of the man writing is not valid to bear.

This [saint] consequently growing in outstanding virtues and in the fame
of good things, to her from all provinces of the whole of Ireland innumerable people of either sex flowing together and voluntarily vowing vows to
her, her own monastery, the head of almost all the Irish churches and the
eminence excelling all the monasteries of the Scots, whose parish is extended, diffused through the whole Irish land from sea to sea, she constructed in
the fields of the plain of the Liffey on a firm foundation of faith and with

prudent dispensation taking care by rule in all things concerning the souls of her own men and encouraging those adhering to her from the churches of many provinces and reverting to her, because without the highest priest there could not be one who would consecrate churches and provide for the succession of ecclesiastical grades in them, the man illustrious and solitary, Conlehet, adorned with all good customs, through whom God has worked very many virtues, calling him from the desert and from his own solitary life and advancing as an obstacle to it she brought it about that he might govern the church with her in the dignity of a bishop and that nothing from priestly order would be deficient in her own churches. And thus afterwards the anointed and principal head among all bishops and the most blessed principal of girls, in happy comity between them and with the helms of all virtues they ruled the principal church, and by the merits of both of them their own cathedral of the bishop and of the girl, as if a fruitbearing vine diffused everywhere with growing branches, increased in the whole Irish island, which the archbishop of Irish bishops and the abbess whom all abbesses of the Scots venerate dominate forever in happy succession.

Thus I, as I said above, compelled by the brothers, will attempt to complete compendiously, with such great attention to brevity though in reverse order of virtues, the virtues of this blessed Brigit, as much those which she performed before her principate as those in her principate.

The text appears to me to be sound. Accepting Dr Sharpe's supply of *et* in the penultimate sentence, I would propose only two trifling changes: restoration of correct Classical spellings from *frugefera* to *frugifera* and from *defusa* to *diffusa*. The former word appears as *frugera* in MSS A★E★, *frugifera cett.*, *fructifera* lKg. The latter word occurs twice, spelled *defusa* in MSS A★EOQ *diffusa cett.* at its first occurrence and *diffusa* without variant at its second. As the chiastic arrangement of the prose shows that Cogitosus balanced the uses of this word, one infers from the unvaried orthographic correctness of the latter occurrence that the former occurrence was originally orthographically correct, as in the manuscripts other than A★EOQ.

Cogitosus composed his Preface consistently in Biblical style.

A1	Me cogitis	
2	fratres	
3a	ut sanctae ac beatae memoriae Brigitae	
b	uirginis	
c	uirtutes et opera	
d	more doctorum	
e	memoriae	
f	litterisque	
g	tradere	
h	adgrediar quod opus inpositum et delicatae	

materiae arduum paruitati et ignorantiae
meae et linguae minime conuenit.

4 a   Sed potens est Deus

   b   de minimis magna facere ut de exiguo
olei et farinae pugillo domum inpleuit
pauperculae uiduae.

   c   Itaque iussionibus uestris coactus satis
habeo meam non defuisse
oboedientiam

4'a   et ideo

   b   pauca de pluribus a maioribus ac
peritissimis tradita sine ulla ambiguitatis
caligine

   c   ne inoboedientiae crimen incurram
patefacere censeo

3'a   ex quibus quanta qualisque

   b   uirgo

   c   uirtutum bonarum florida

   d   cunctorum oculis innotescat.

   e   Non quod memoria et mediocritas

   f   et rusticus sermo ingenioli mei tanti muneris
officium

   g   explicare

   h   ualeret

2'   sed fidei uestrae beatitudo et orationum uestrarum diurnitas
meretur accipere quod non ualet ingenium ferre

1'   dictantis.

B1 a Haec ergo egregiis crescens uirtutibus et fama bonarum rerum

   b   ad eam de omnibus prouintiis totius Hiberniae innumerabiles
populi de utraque sexu confluentes et uota sibi uouentes uoluntarie

   c   suum monasterium caput poene omnium Hybernensium
ecclesiarum

   d   et culmen praecellens omnia monasteria Scothorum

2 a   cuius parroechia

   b   per totam Hybernensem terram diffusa a mari usque ad
mare extensa est in campestribus campi Liffei supra
fundamentum fidei firmum construxit

3   et prudenti dispensatione de animabus suorum
regulariter in omnibus procurans

4   et de ecclesiis multarum prouintiarum sibi
adhaerentibus sollicitans et secum reuoluens

5 a   quod sine summo sacerdote

   b   qui ecclesias

   c   consecraret

6	et ecclesiasticos in eis gradus subrogaret esse non posse
7	inlustrem uirum
8	et solitarium Conlehet omnibus moribus bonis ornatum
7'	per quem Deus uirtutes operatus est plurimas conuocans eum de heremo et de sua uita solitaria et in ipsius obuiam pergens
6'	ut ecclesiam in episcopali dignitate cum ea gubernaret
5'a	atque ut nihil de ordine sacerdotali
b	in suis deesset ecclesiis
c	accersiuit.
4'	Et sic postea unctum caput et principale omnium episcoporum et beatissima puellarum principalis, felici comitatu inter se et gubernaculis omnium uirtutum, suam rexerunt principalem ecclesiam
3'	et amborum meritis
2'a	sua cathedra episcopalis et puellaris
b	acsi uitis frugifera diffusa undique
1'a	ramis crescentibus
b	in tota Hybernensi insula inoleuit
c	quam semper archiepiscopus Hybernensium episcoporum
d	et abbatissa quam omnes abbatissae Scothorum uenerantur felici successione et ritu perpetuo dominantur.
A'1	Exinde ego ut supra dixi a fratribus coactus beatae huius Brigitae uirtutes tam eas quas ante principatum quam alias quas in principatu gessit tanto studio breuitatis licet praepostero ordine uirtutum conpendiose explicare conabor.

In part A Cogitosus refers to himself in 1 *me* and 1' *dictantis*, perhaps also in *cogitis*, implying play on possible meanings of his name as one who is both 'thoughtful' (from Classical Latin *cogitare* or *cogitatiuus* + -*osus*) and 'compelled' (from Classical Latin *cogere* or *coactiuus* + -*osus*) by his superiors to write. He refers to his ecclesiastical brothers in 2 *fratres* and 2' *uestrae* and *uestrarum*. Compare the pair of adjectives *sanctae ac beatae* in 3a with the pair of relatives *quanta qualisque* in 3'a, *uirginis* 3b with *uirgo* 3'b, *uirtutes* 3c with *uirtutum* 3'c, *more doctorum* 3d with *cunctorum oculis* 3'd, *memoriae* 3e with *memoria* 3'e, *litterisque* 3f with *rusticus sermo* 3'f, *tradere* 3g with *explicare* 3'g, *adgrediar* 3h with *ualeret* 3'h. Compare *sed* 4a with *et ideo* 4'a, *de minimis magna facere* 4b with *pauca de pluribus ... tradita* 4'b, *oboedientiam* 4c with *inoboedientiae* 4'c.

In part B compare 1a *crescens uirtutibus* with 1'a *ramis crescentibus*, 1b *de omnibus prouintiis totius Hiberniae* with 1'b *in tota Hybernensi insula*, 1c *monasterium caput* ...

Hybernensium ecclesiarum with 1'c *archiepiscopus Hybernensium episcoporum,* 1d *et ...
omnia monasteria Scothorum* with 1'd *et ... omnes abbatissae Scothorum,* 2a *cuius
parroechia* with 2'a *sua cathedra episcopalis et puellaris,* 2b *per totam Hybernensem terram
diffusa* with 2'b *diffusa undique,* 3 *et prudenti dispensatione* with 3' *et amborum meritis,* 4
de ecclesiis multarum prouintiarum sibi adhaerentibus with 4' *principalem ecclesiam,* 5a
sacerdote with 5'a *sacerdotali,* 5b *ecclesias* with 5'b *ecclesiis,* 5c *consecraret* with 5'c
accersiuit, 6 *ecclesiasticos in eis gradus subrogaret* with 6' *ecclesiam in episcopali dignitate
cum ea·gubernaret,* 7 *inlustrem uirum* with 7' *per quem,* around the crux in 8 *solitarium
Conlehet omnibus moribus bonis ornatum.* Compare *me, fratres, beatae, Brigitae, uirtutes,
coactus,* and *explicare* in A with *ego ut supra dixi, fratribus, beatae, Brigitae, uirtutes,
coactus,* and *explicare* in A'.

The mathematical structure confirms that the entire Preface is intact. In part
A of the 125 words the central sixty-third is *oboedientiam* at the crux of the
chiasmus in 4c, referring to the 'obedience' of Cogitosus 'compelled' to write
the Life of Brigit. In part B of the 212 words the central are *solitarium Conlehet
omnibus moribus bonis ornatum* at the crux of the chiasmus in 8, referring to
Conlaed, bishop of Brigit's community. The 370 words of the entire Preface
divide by extreme and mean ratio at 229 and 141, exactly at *solitarium |
Conlehet* and at those over whom he claimed jurisdiction *de omnibus prouintiis
totius Hiberniae |*. The 370 words divide by symmetry at 185 and 185, at *supra
fundamentum | fidei firmum construxit.*

Specific words recur at mathematically determined intervals. From *me cogitis*
to *coactus* inclusive there are fifty-seven words, which divide by extreme and
mean ratio at 35 and 22. The twenty-second word is *inpositum*. *Scothorum* is
the 330th word; 330 divides by symmetry at 165, at *Scothorum,* the 165th word.
The word *uirtus* recurs seven times. The words *ecclesia* and *ecclesiasticus* recur
seven times. The words *Hibernia, Hybernensis,* and *Scothus* recur seven times.
The word *Brigitae* is ninth from the beginning and twenty-third from the end,
together thirty-two words. In the headings *De Sanctae Brigitae uirtutibus* which
follow the *Praefatio* Cogitosus lists exactly thirty-two *uirtutes*.

The long and involved sentences belie the protestations of humble diffidence
by an author who exhibits clearly a sense of self-possessed competence.

Here is his conclusion.

[Subscriptio]

Veniam peto a fratribus ac lectoribus haec legentibus immo emendantibus
qui causa obedientiae coactus nulla praerogatiua scientia subfultus pelagus
inmensum uirtutum beatae Brigidae et uiris peritissimis formidandum his
paucis rustico sermone dictis uirtutibus de maximis et innumerabilibus
parua lintre cucurri. Orate pro me Cogitoso nepote culpabili Aedo et ut
audaciae meae indulgeatis atque orationum uestrarum clipeo Domino me
commendetis exoro, et Deus uos pacem euangelicam sectantes exaudiat.
Amen.

Explicit Vita Sanctae Brigidae uirginis

Afterword

I ask pardon from the brothers and readers reading, moreover emending, these things, [I] who, compelled for the sake of obedience, supported by no privileged learning, have run in a little light boat into the sea of virtues of blessed Brigit, immense and to be feared by the most learned men, with these few words in rustic speech about the greatest and innumerable virtues. Pray for me, Cogitosus, reprehensible nephew to Aed, and I entreat that you indulge my audacity and commend me to the Lord with the shield of your prayers, and may God hear you out searching for evangelical peace. Amen.

The Life of Saint Brigit the virgin ends.

Veniam peto a fratribus ác lectóribus	aa	6
haec legentibus immo émendántibus	aa	4
qui causa oboediéntiae coáctus	b	4
nulla praerogatiua sciéntia subfúltus	b	4
pelagus inménsum uirtútum 5	cd	3
Beátae Brígidae	ee	2
et uiris peritíssimis fòrmidándum	cd	4
his paucis rustico sérmone díctis	cc	5
uirtutibus de maximis et innúmerabílibus	aa	5
parua líntre cucúrri. 10	x	3
Orate pro mé Cogitóso	g	4
nepote culpábili Aédo	g	3
et ut audaciae méae indùlgeátis	h	5
atque orationum uestrárum clípeo	g	4
Domino me commendétis exóro 15	hg	4
et Deus uos pacem euangelicam sectántes exaúdiat.	x	7
Amen. Explicit Vita Sanctae Brígidae uírginis.	c	6

The alliteration and rhyme and rhythm are readily apparent. The only clauses which do not rhyme are the ends of the two sentences. The seventeen lines divide by sesquialter ratio (3:2) at 10 and 7, coinciding with the sentence structure. The seventy-three words divide by sesquialter ratio at 44 and 29, at the end of the seventh line from the end, at the name of the author, *Orate pro me Cogitoso | nepote culpabili Aedo*. The forty-four words of the major part divide symmetrically at *Beatae | Brigidae*. The twenty-nine words of the minor part divide symmetrically at *me | commendetis | exoro*.

II. MUIRCHÚ MOCCU MACTHÉNI

Vita Sancti Patricii

In sharp contrast to the polished prose of Cogitosus is the Prologue of Muirchú's Life of Patrick as represented in the most recent edition.[1]

<Prologus.> (1) Quoniam quidem, mi domine Aido, multi conati sunt ordinare narrationem utique istam secundum quod patres eorum et qui ministri ab initio fuerunt sermonis tradiderunt illis, sed propter difficillimum narrationis opus diuersasque opiniones et plurimorum plurimas suspiciones numquam ad unum certumque historiae tramitem peruenierunt: (2) ideo, ni fallor, iuxta hoc nostrorum prouerbium, ut deducuntur pueri in ambiteathrum in hoc periculossum et profundum narrationis sanctae pylagus turgentibus proterue gurgitum aggeribus inter acutissimos carubdes per ignota aequora insitos a nullis adhuc lintribus excepto tantum uno patris mei Coguitosi expertum atque occupatum ingenioli mei puerilem remi cymbam deduxi. (3) Sed ne magnum de paruo uidear finguere, pauca haec de multis sancti Patricii gestis parua peritia, incertis auctoribus, memoria labili, attrito sensu, uili sermone, sed affectu pîssimo caritatis sanctitatis tuae et auctoritatis imperio oboedens carptim +grauatimque explicare aggrediar.

<Preface>. (1) Considering, my Lord Áed, that many have attempted to write this story coherently according to the traditions of their fathers and of those who were ministers of the Word from the beginning, but that the great difficulties which the telling of the story presents, and the conflicting opinions and many doubts voiced by many a person have prevented them from ever arriving at one undisputed sequence of events, (2) I might well say that, like boys making their first appearance in the assembly (to quote a familiar saying of ours), I have taken my little talent—a boy's paddle-boat, as it were—out on this deep and perilous sea of sacred narrative, where waves boldly swell to towering heights among rocky reefs in unknown waters, (a sea) on which so far no boat has ventured except the one of my (spiritual) father Cogitosus. (3) However, far from giving the impression that I want to make something big out of something small, I shall (merely) attempt to set forth, bit by bit and step by step, these few of the numerous deeds of holy Patrick, with little knowledge '(of traditional lore)', on uncertain authority, from an unreliable memory, feebly and in poor style, but with the pious affection of holy love, in obedience to the command of your sanctity and authority.

---

1 BCLL 303. *The Patrician Texts in the Book of Armagh*, ed. & transl. L. Bieler, *Scriptores Latini Hiberniae* X (Dublin 1979), pp. 62–3.

If this fairly reproduced Muirchú's text, one would have to infer that by his day the standards of Latin composition had fallen sadly from the heights achieved earlier in the seventh century. That is a distinct possibility. If one recollects the beginning of the *Lorica* of Laidcenn MacBaith[2]

Suffragare Trinitatis Unitas	Help me, O Unity in Trinity,
Unitatis miserere Trinitas.	Take pity on me, O Trinity in Unity.
Suffragare quaesso mihi posito	Help me, I beseech, placed as it were
maris magni uelut in periculo	in the peril of a great sea,
ut non secum trahat me mortalitas	so that neither this year's plague
huius anni neque mundi uanitas	nor worldly vanity carry me away

and considers the implications of entries about the *mortalitas magna* in the *Annals of the Four Masters* and the *Annals of Ulster* for the years 663-666, one might infer that large numbers of learned Irishmen perished in recurrent plagues, leaving a reduced class of competent authors.

But perhaps by some accident *The Book of Armagh* does not faithfully reproduce Muirchú's text any more than it faithfully reproduces the text of Saint Patrick's *Confessio*. In order to imagine the form in which it issued from his pen let us consider his purpose and the literary models he may have imitated. First, a principal function of Muirchú's work was to advance the claims of the church at Armagh to metropolitan status over the whole of Ireland, in refutation and supersession of the claims made by Cogitosus for the church at Kildare. Muirchú begins by addressing the uncle of Cogitosus mentioned in the *Subscriptio* of the *Vita Sanctae Brigitae*. Muirchú may have appropriated words from the Prologue to the Gospel of Saint Luke in his first sentence because that is a more important text than I Kings XVII, to which Cogitosus alludes in the second sentence of his *Praefatio*. By appealing to a more authoritative Biblical text Muirchú may have intended to 'overswear' Cogitosus, as a litigant in an Irish court would override an opponent by citing the authority of a witness of higher social status. Reference to the work of *patris mei Coguitosi* suggests further that Muirchú had read the *Vita Sanctae Brigitae*. So does his choice of the words *tradiderunt, opus, plurimorum plurimas, ingenioli mei, magnum de paruo … finguere, pauca … de multis, sancti, gestis, memoria, oboedens, explicare,* and *aggrediar,* with which one may compare *tradere, opus, plurimas, ingenioli mei, de minimis magna facere, pauca de pluribus, sanctae, gessit, memoria, oboedientiam, explicare,* and *adgrediar* in the *Praefatio* by Cogitosus. So does his choice of the words *Aido, periculossum et profundum … pylagus, nullis lintribus, uili sermone,* with which one may compare *Aedo, pelagus inmensum … et … formidandum, parua lintre,* and *rustico sermone* in the *Subscriptio* by Cogitosus.

After comparison of the words *periculossum, pylagus, turgentibus, per ignota aequora, ingenioli, cymbam deduxi* with a short passage of a single letter, *inter*

2   *The Hisperica Famina: II Related Poems*, ed. & transl. M.W. Herren, Pontifical Institute of Mediaeval Studies, Studies and Texts LXXXV (Toronto 1987), pp. 77–8.

tempora periculosa, sed quia fragilis ingenii cymba non tam in altum iuxta uerbum Domini ducta est, and *licet hyperbolice pelagi uorticibus undique consurgentibus,* might one infer that Muirchú had read at least Columban's fifth epistle?[3]

What if Muirchú had learned from the Latin Bible and from his predecessors how to spell correct Late Latin, rather than some orthographically erratic dialect riddled with 'Hibernicisms'? What if he had learned from Patrick and Gildas and Cummian and Colmán and Cogitosus and perhaps Cellán how to write rhythmically?[4] What if he had learned from Columban and Cogitosus and Irish Latin hymn-writers how to rhyme and alliterate?[5] What if he had learned how to balance clauses, how to dispose diction at arithmetically fixed íntervals? What if, *in fine,* he wrote as all his illustrious predecessors in the Celtic Latin tradition had written? Might his Prologue have looked like this?[6]

Prologus.

'Quoniam quidem' mi dómine Aíde	I	a
'multi conati sunt ordinare narrationem' ístam utíque		a
secundum quod pátres eórum		b
et 'qui ministri ab initio fuerunt Sermonis' íllis 'tradidérunt'		c
sed propter difficillimum ópus narràtiónis	5	d
diuersasque opiniones et plurimorum plurimas súspiciónes		d
numquam ad unum certumque historiae trámitem pèruenérunt.		c
Ideo ni fallor iuxta hoc prouérbium nostrórum		b
ut deducuntur pueri in ámphitheátrum		b
in hoc periculosum et profundum narrationis sánctae pélagus	10	e
turgentibus proterue gúrgitum aggéribus		f
inter acutíssimos charúbdes		e
per ignota aequora insitos a nullis ádhuc líntribus		f
excepto tantum uno patris méi Cogitósi		g
expertum atque occupatum méi ingènióli	15	g
puerilem remi cýmbam dedúxi.		g

---

3 *Sancti Columbani Opera,* ed. & transl. G.S.M. Walker, *Scriptores Latini Hiberniae* II (Dublin 1970), *Epistula* V § 7 p. 42 l. 34, § 8 p. 44 ll. 22–3, § 11 p. 48 l. 22. M. Winterbottom, 'Variations on a nautical theme', *Hermathena* CXX (1976), p. 57 n. 12, suggests persuasively that the ultimate source is Cassian's *Collationes, CSEL* XIII, p. 4, 2: in quibus mihi nunc in portu silentii constituto inmensum *pelagus* aperitur, ut scilicet de instituto atque doctrina tantorum uirorum quaedam tradere audeam memoriae litterarum. Tanto enim *profundioris* nauigationis *periculis* fragilis *ingenii cumba* iactanda est quantum … .

4 See above pp. 78–81, 98–9, 103–4, 108–9, 249. For the suggestion that both Cogitosus and Muirchú quote Gildas, *De Excidio Britanniae* independently see Winterbottom, 'Variations', p. 57 n. 11.

5 See above pp. 83, 88, 138–93.

6 Letters in boldface represent features of the *Book of Armagh,* f. 20ra. See J. Gwynn, *Liber Ardmachanus, The Book of Armagh* (Dublin 1913), p. 39; E. Gwynn ed., *The Book of Armagh, The Patrician Documents,* Facsimiles in Collotype of Irish Manuscripts III, Irish Manuscripts Commission (Dublin 1937), p. 19.

Sed ne magnum de paruo uidéar fingere   a
pauca haec de multis Sancti Patrícii géstis   h
parua peritia incertis auctoribus memoria labili attrito sensu
    uíli sermóne   a
sed affectu piíssimo càritátis   20   h
sanctitatis tuae et auctoritatis império oboédiens   e
carptim grauatimque explicáre aggrédiar.   j

There are twenty-two lines and 131 words. The central word *gurgitum* falls in a central eleventh line. The twenty-two lines divide by extreme and mean ratio at 13.6 and 8.4, the 131 words at 81 and 50, at *excepto tantum uno* | *patris mei Cogitosi.* In the major part of 13.6 lines and eighty-one words the symmetrical centre falls at *certumque* | *historiae* | *tramitem.* In the minor part of 8.4 lines and fifty words the symmetrical centre falls at *pauca haec de multis Sancti Patricii* | *gestis.*

    One cannot be certain. But given the literary quality of the Latin written by Irishmen from the beginnings of the tradition to the end of the seventh century, and given Muirchú's manifest knowledge of some of it, the changes suggested in the text above seem more justified than an assumption of his ignorance or incompetence.

III. DONATUS SCOTTUS OF FIESOLE

Vita Metrica Sanctae Brigidae

The most recent editor of the *Vita Metrica Sanctae Brigidae* was uncertain whether the same man composed both the preliminaries and the text of the poem.[1] For our present purposes the uncertainty does not matter, as the preliminaries claim to have been written by an Irishman, usually identified as Donatus Bishop of Fiesole, who lived until A.D. 876, but who composed the work probably in the 830s.

He divided the preliminaries into four parts.

VITA SANCTAE BRIGIDAE
PROLOGUS
Has ego Donatus uirtutes sanguine Scottus
    Brigidae descripsi praesul et exiguus
Virginis; indocto carptim sermone repertas
    Pangere praesumpsi carmine dactilico.
Hoc opus incomptum tibi nunc transmittŏ magistro   5
    Rudibus et tarda uersibus atque manu.

---

1 *BCLL* 693. *Vita Metrica Sanctae Brigidae*, ed. D.N. Kissane, *Proceedings of the Royal Irish Academy* LXXVII C 3 (1977), pp. 57–192, esp. p. 62.

Hos tibi uersiculos indoctos, magne poeta,
    Tangat doctrinae aurea lima tuae.
Haec noua mētallis pretiosis uascula purget
    Aspera, propterea traximus igne modo.   10
Potus cum fuerit confectus pluribus herbis
    Est oculis uiridis, dulcis in ore tamen;
Si fore non poterit praesens mox potiŏ clara,
    Numquid, si fuerit turbida, non bibitur?
Aut si non praesens niuea similagine panis,   15
    Rusticus utiliter sumitur a pueris.
Perlege, sancte pater, nostrum, doctissime, librum,
    Scriptoris uitium corrige uelque meum.
Scripturae sacrae pelago tua grammata miscis,
    Scemata metrorum, tempora seu numerum.   20
Quae dixere prius prisci, qua digna, poetae,
    Teocritus Grecus, Ascrius Essiodus,
Aratus, radio designans caelitus astra,
    Grammata Prisciani, dogmata Virgilii:
Nulla latent libris Grecorum, nulla Latinis;   25
    De ueterum dictis omnia nuda tibi.
Propterea tibimet nostras nunc mittimus odas.
    Iudice te facto nostra fauetŏ, rogo.

ORATIO

Xpiste Dei uirtus, splendor, sapientia Patris
In Genitore manens, genitus sine tempore et ante   30
Saecula; qui nostram natus de uirgine formam
Sumpsit, nutritus, lactatus ab ubere matris;
Qui sancto nostras mundans baptismate culpas
Et noua progenies caelo perducitur alto;
Noxia qui uetiti dissoluit prandia pomi,   35
Vulnera et ipse suo curauit sanguine nostra;
Qui moriendŏ dedit uitam, nos morte redemit,
Cumque sepultus erat, mutauit iura sepulchri.
Surgens a morte et mortem damnauit acerbam;
Tartara qui quondam, qui nigri limina Ditis   40
Destruxit, scatebras superans Achirontis auari;
Qui hostem nigrum tortum detorsit in imo
Carceris inferni, Letheum trusit in amnem,
† Ascendit, duxit captiuam dextera Patris.†
Laudant uirtutes uictorem milia mille.   45
Tu quoque, qui tantas pro nobis sumere poenas
Dignatus miseris caelestia regna dedisti,
Da mihi precelsas Paradisi scandere scalas,

Fac bene pulsanti portas mihi pandere uitae.
Non mihi pes ueniat tumidus, non hostis auarus,   50
Necne externa manus me tangat, praemia tollat;
Sed me, Xpiste, tuum miserum nunc suscipe seruum,
Ut merear pauidus conuiuas uisere claros,
Quo tecum gaudent uideam conuiuia sancti,
Quo cum Patre manens regnas per saecula semper,   55
Spiritus et Sanctus pariter, Deus impare, gaudet.
          PRAEFATIO
Quisquis in hoc hominum fragili concluditur antro ...   57
Cernere post obitum mereamur pace futura.   124
          INCIPIT
Finibus occiduis describitur optima tellus   125
   Nomine et antiquis Scottia scripta libris.
Diues opum argenti gemmarum uestis et auri:
   Commoda corporibus aere putre solo.
Melle fluit pulchris et lacte Scottia campis
   Vestibus atque armis frugibus arte uiris.   130
Ursorum rabies nulla est ibi saeua leonum
   Semina nec umquam Scottica terra tulit.
Nulla uenena nocent nec serpens serpit in herba
   Nec conquaesta canit garrula rana lacu.
In qua Scottorum gentes habitare merentur   135
   Inclita gens hominum milite pace fide.
De qua nata fuit quondam sanctissima uirgo
   Brigida Scottorum gloria nomen honor.
Turris ad igniferi pertingens culmina caeli
   Lumen inexhaustum celsa corona Dei.   140
Fons benedictus ouans Scottorum corda reformans
   Recreat ipse ipsos curat alit uegetat.
Scala parata uiris pueris excelsa puellis
   Matribus et sanctis tendit ad astra poli.
Dubtagus eius erat genitor cognomine dictus   145
   Clarus homo meritis clarus et a proauis
Nobilis atque humilis mitis pietate repletus
   Nobilior propria coniuge prole pia.
Scripserunt multi uirtutes uirginis almae
   Ultanus doctor atque Elaranus ouans   150
Descripsit multos Animosus nomine libros
   De uita et studiis uirginis ac meritis.
Ordiar a minimis nec non maiora sequemur
   Sed prato pleno floribus apta legam.
Ordine si caeli fulgentia sydera cernens   155
   Altiuago cursu scire quot illa queat

Litore quis minimas numero discernit arenas
    Turgida quas terris sparserat unda maris.
Hic numerare potest uirtutes ritae puellae
    In qua perpetuus manserat ipse Deus.   160

In the *Prologus* Donatus has arranged his words and thoughts chiastically.

1	Has ego Donatus uirtutes sanguine Scottus Brigidae descripsi praesul et exiguus uirginis, indocto carptim sermone repertas pangere praesumpsi carmine dactilico
2	Hoc opus incomptum tibi nunc transmitto magistro rudibus et tarda uersibus atque manu
3	Hos tibi
4	uersiculos indoctos
5	magne poeta
6	tangat doctrinae aurea lima tuae. …
7	Perlege sancte pater nostrum doctissime librum
7'	Scriptoris uitium corrige uelque meum. …
6'	Quae dixere prius prisci qua digna
5'	poetae …
4'	De ueterum dictis
3'	omnia nuda tibi
2'	Propterea tibimet nostras nunc mittimus odas
1'	Iudice te facto nostra faueto rogo.

In the *Prologus* the twenty-eight lines of elegiac couplets divide by extreme and mean ratio at 17 and 11, and the 160 words divide by extreme and mean ratio at 99 and 61, at the crux of the chiasmus, at Donatus's reference to his *librum* at the end of the seventeenth line.

Similarly in the *Oratio* Donatus has arranged his words and ideas chiastically.

1	Xpiste Dei uirtus splendor sapientia Patris in Genitore manens genitus sine tempore et ante saecula
2 a	dedit
b	uitam
3 a	Surgens a morte
b	et mortem damnauit acerbam
4	Tartara qui quondam qui nigri limina Ditis destruxit scatebras superans Achirontis auari
5	Qui hostem nigrum tortum detorsit in imo Carceris inferni
4'	Letheum trusit in amnem
3' a	Ascendens duxit captiuam
b	laudant uirtutes uictorem milia mille

2'a   dedisti
 b   uitae
 1'   Xpiste ... Quo cum Patre manens regnas per saecula semper
         Spiritus et Sanctus pariter Deus impare gaudet.

The central lines, fourteenth from the beginning and fourteenth from the end
of twenty-eight, are 42 and 43 at the crux of the chiasmus. The central of 183
words are *imo carceris inferni*.

The fourth part of the preliminaries is the *Incipit*, thirty-six lines of elegiac
couplets and 218 words, of which the central are the last two words of the
eighteenth line 142. In the first half, lines 125–42, the ninth word from the
beginning is *Scottia* 126, and the ninth word from the end is *Scottorum* 141.
Between *Scottia* 126 and *Scottia* 129 there are nineteen words. From *Scottia* 129
to *Scottica* 132 inclusive there are nineteen words. After *Scottica* 132 *Scottorum*
135 is the nineteenth word. From *Scottorum* 138 to *Scottorum* 141 inclusive
there are nineteen words. The first of these is in the second line from the
beginning, and the last is in the second line from the end. The second is in the
fifth line from the beginning, and the penultimate is in the fifth line from the
end. The third is in the eighth line from the beginning, and the antepenultimate is in the eighth line from the end.

The thirty-six lines divide by extreme and mean ratio at 22 and 14; the 218
words divide by extreme and mean ratio at 135 and 83. The golden section of the
Incipit falls at the title and name of the heroine, *uirgo Brigida | Scottorum gloria*, the
eighty-third word in the fourteenth line 138. The 135 words from *Scottorum gloria*
to the end divide by extreme and mean ratio at 83 and 52. The fifty-second word
from the end is *uirginis* 152. The eighty-three words between *uirgo Brigida* and
uirginis divide by symmetry at another reference to her, *Dubtagus | eius | erat
genitor cognomine dictus*. They divide by extreme and mean ratio at 51 and 32, at a
reference to her father's ancestors, *clarus et | a proauis* 146.

The *Prologus* relates to the *Oratio* by symmetry, the former occupying
twenty-eight lines of elegiac couplets and the latter twenty-eight lines of
dactylic hexameters. The 160 words of the former relate to the 183 words of
the latter very nearly by sesquioctave ratio: 343 = 182 + 161. The *Oratio* of
twenty-eight lines and the *Praefatio* of sixty-eight lines are both in dactylic
hexameters. The *Prologus* and the *Incipit* are both in elegiac couplets, the
twenty-eight lines of the former and the thirty-six lines of the latter relating
very nearly by sesquitertian ratio (64 = 36.57 + 24.43), the 160 words of the
former and the 218 words of the latter by the same (378 = 216 + 162).

The most conspicuous features of the *Incipit* are praise of Ireland and the Irish,
of *Brigida* and *Dubtagus* and their ancestors, and of the earlier hagiographers
whom Donatus names. *Ultanus* is easily recognized as the common Irish Christian
name Ultán, *Elaranus* as the comparably common Ailerán, and *Animosus* as a
possible variant Latin rendering of the Irish name which underlies *Cogitosus*

'thoughtful'. The coincidence of these interests with the references to other
Celtic Latin works cited in Kissane's edition marks the *Vita Metrica Sanctae Brigidae*
as a self-conscious monument in a long tradition.

IV. CLEMENS OF LANDÉVENNEC

Hymn to Saint Winwaloe

The first of a closely related group of ninth-century Breton Latin writers is
Clemens of Landévennec, who composed a Hymn to Saint Winwaloe during
the years 857–884.[1]

INcipit prefatio ymni sancti Winvaloei a collegio Clemente compositi a
kalendis Nouembri usque in Pascha dominicis diebus post matutinum a
fratribus qui eius incolunt monasterium canendi ; a Pascha autem usque
ad prescriptas kalendas qualem uoluerint de rescriptis quos iam natali eius
coaptauimus ymnis canant . quia breuioribus succinctiores noctibus
constituendi sunt sermones **;;**

> **Pentametri** [v.l. Elegiaci] **uersus.**
> **E**cce tuo Clemens ymnum construxit honori,
>   **U**inualoee, decens attribuente Deo.
> **L**itterule quoties sunt aut iterantur in isto,
>   **T**u toties pro me fundito uerba Deo.
> **I**mpetres michi quo ueniam, non desine, sanctae;   5
>   **C**lementis famuli sed miserere tui,
> **D**eprecor, atque tui qui constant nempe sequaces,
>   **S**ic peragant fratres hoc in amore Dei.
> **H**unc quoque qui relegant una cum fratribus abbas
>   **C**ognoscant Aelam iusserit ut facerem,   10
> **T**empore quo Salomon Britones rite regebat,
>   **C**ornubie rector quoque fuit Riuelen.

Here begins the Preface of the hymn of Saint Winwaloe composed by the
colleague Clemens to be sung from the kalends of November until Easter on
Sundays after matins by the brothers who dwell in his monastery; but from
Easter until the forementioned kalends, if they prefer they should sing one of
the rewritten hymns which we have adapted for his birthday [or his day in the
kalendar], because briefer sermons are appointed for the shorter nights.

1   BCLL 824. 'Hymni Tres de S. Winwaloeo', ed. C. DeSmedt, *Analecta Bollandiana* VII (1888), pp.
    263–4. *Cartulaire de l'abbaye de Landevenec*, ed. A. LeMoyne de la Borderie (Rennes 1888), pp.
    124–8. *Analecta Hymnica* XXIII, no. 530 pp. 298–9. I owe thanks to Dr Jacques Paviot for collating
    the text of Paris, Bibliothèque nationale, MS latin 5601A ff. 77v–78v, from which capital letters
    and punctuation marks are represented in boldface.

Pentameter [*v.l.* Elegiac] verses.

Behold, Clemens has constructed a hymn fit for your honour, Winwaloe,
  as God assigned the task.

As many letters as are in it or as many times as they are repeated
  pour forth so many words for me to God.

May you entreat for me how I may come, do not cease, O holy one,
  but have mercy on Clemens your servant,

I pray, and your followers who are surely constant.

Thus do the brothers relate this in the love of God.

Those who reread this should know that I do as Abbot Aelam

ordered together with the brothers, in the time during which Salomon
  justly ruled the Bretons

and Riuelen was ruler of Cornouaille.

The prose Preface is a single sentence of fifty-one words, which divide at the central, twenty-sixth word, *canendi*.

The elegiac verses occupy twelve lines and seventy-four words. The golden section of 74 falls at 46 and 28. The subject of the verses is Saint Winwaloe, referred to in the second word, *tuo*. Twenty-eight words later one comes to the saint again at *sancte*. The saint is named in the seventh word, *Uinualoee*. Twenty-eight words later one comes to him again at *tui*. The third reference to the saint is *tu* at the beginning of line 4. Twenty-eight words later one comes to *hoc*, referring to the poem composed in Winwaloe's honour, and that is the twenty-eighth word from the end of the poem. The translation of Winwaloe is celebrated on 28 April.

The golden section of the twelve lines of verse falls at 7 and 5. The author names himself once in the first five lines, at *Clemens*, the third word. He names himself again in the seventh line from the end, *Clementis*. Between *Clemens* and *Clementis* there are twenty-eight words. Of the twelve verses six are hexameters and six pentameters. From *tuo* to *Uinualoee* inclusive there are six words. From *Uinualoee* to *tu* inclusive there are twelve words. From *sancte* to *tui* inclusive there are six words. From *tui* to *hoc* inclusive there are twelve words. From *fratres* to *fratribus* inclusive there are twelve words.

Clemens refers to God as *Deo* 2, the tenth word (5×2). From *Deo* 2 to *Deo* 4 inclusive there are fifteen words (5×3). Between *Deo* 4 and *Dei* 8 there are twenty-five words (5×5), and the latter is the twenty-fifth word from the end of the poem.

The number 74 divides by one-ninth and eight-ninths at 8 and 66. The sixty-sixth word from the beginning and the eighth word from the end are *Salomon Britones*.

Clemens refers to the recurrence of the letters of his hymn and the rereading of his poem, *litterule ... iterantur in isto* 3, *qui relegant* 9. Exactly half the words of the hymn lie between *iterantur* and *relegant*.

This Preface in prose and verse introduces an abecedarian hymn to Saint Winwaloe, which the Bollandist editor DeSmedt deformed, obscuring the alphabetic structure. After the first seven stanzas, which begin *Alme*, *Britigena*, *Caelicola*, *Dictis*, *Educatus*, *Felix*, and *Gliscebat*, DeSmedt printed *Nunc*, where *Hunc* is required, and after the ninth stanza, beginning *Instaurando*, *Catervasque*, where *Kateruasque* is required. Similarly in the antepenultimate stanza for *Christus Xpistus* is required and in the penultimate for *Hymnum Ymnum*.[2] As in the Preface, so in the first stanza of the Hymn the seventh word is *Uinualoe*.

This verse derives, with much else, from Biblical models through the Irish Latin tradition of alphabetic poetry, which was by the time of Clemens already three centuries old.[3]

V. BILI

Vita Sancti Machutis

The *Vita Sancti Machutis* of the Breton scholar Bili was written between the years 866 and 872.[1] The title and Salutation read

IN XP[IST]I NOMINE .
INCIPIT PROLOGUS VITAE SANCTI MACHUTIS
EPISCOPI ATQUE CONFESSORIS.
DOMINO:SANCTO:ET:MERITIS:VENERABILI:
TOTOQUE:PECTORIS: SINU:AMPLECTENDO[2]:
AC MEO MAGISTRO GREgorio
in Sancta Trinitate Ratuilio episcopo : inibi [*or* mihi] amantissimo Bili leuita humilis perpetuam salutem .

In the name of Christ here begins the Prologue of the Life of St Malo, bishop and confessor.

To the lord holy and venerable in his merits and to be embraced in the whole bosom of his breast, and my shepherdlike master in the Holy Trinity, Ratuili, the most loving bishop there [or 'to me'], Bili, a humble deacon, [wishes] perpetual salvation.

In the title there are eleven words, of which the golden section falls at 7 and 4. The seventh word from the beginning and the fourth word from the end are the title and name of the hero, *Sancti Machutis*. The Salutation comprises twenty-five words, of which the central, thirteenth, word is *gregorio*. One

2   Paris, Bibliothèque nationale MS latin 5601A ff. 77v–78v supplies the correct readings.
3   See above pp. 139–42, 187–8.
1   BCLL 825. *La Vie de Saint-Malo, Évêque d'Alet*, ed. & transl. G. LeDuc, *Le .Centre Régional Archéologique d'Alet*, ed. & transl. G. LeDuc, (1979), p. 2.
2   British Library MS Royal 13 A x f. 63r reads *amplectendo* correctly, not *amplectando* as in LeDuc's edition.

wonders whether Bili's use of this last word suggests knowledge of the play on *egregius* and *Gregorius* in Columban's Salutation to Pope Gregory the Great.[3] In the thirteen words from *gregorio* to the end the golden section falls at 8 and 5. The fifth word names the recipient, Bishop Ratuili. The fifth word from the end names the author, Bili. Title and Salutation together contain thirty-six words, which divide by one-ninth and eight-ninths at 4 and 32, at *Bili | leuita*.

At the end of the Salutation there are eleven hexameters.[4]

> Vitales qui cupis doctorum carpere fructus .
> Istius egregii calamum perquire libelli .
> Discite paginolas solers et mente sagaci .
> Sensibus elucet, lauto sermone nitescit .
> Inspirante Deo volui coniungere librum .
> Quae tenet in sacris monstret nudata figuris .
> Quae latuere diu ceco sub tegmine clausa .
> Qui rutilus nutu aspellat de monte latebras.
> Vincula disrumpat, cordis eluminet umbras.
> Inradietque sacro mentis spiramine fibras .
> Cordis opimus ager centenos reddere fructus .

You, who wish to pluck the life-giving fruits of teachers,
search out the pen [with play on the viticultural sense 'study the shoot']
    of this excellent little book.
Ingenious and with discerning mind learn its columns.
It shines out with ideas, gleams with splendid language.
With God inspiring me I have wished to put together a book.
The things it includes it should show exposed in sacred figures,
things which long lay hidden, enclosed under an impenetrable covering.
May it, glowing, dispel with its power the shades from the mountain,
break chains, illumine the shadows of the heart,
and irradiate with sacred breath [or 'by the Holy Spirit'] the recesses of
    the mind,
a choice field to yield hundredfold fruits of the heart.

Bili has linked these verses to what precedes and what follows. The number of verses recalls the eleven words of the title which precedes them, and the number of words, sixty-four, is the number of chapter headings, which begin immediately after.[5] Bili plays with the number 8. The golden section of 64 (8

---

3   See above p. 84.
4   MS ff. 64v–65r. LeDuc, p. 6. There is an apparent false quantity in the first verse in *qui*.
5   MS f. 65r. LeDuc, pp.7–10.

× 8) falls at 40 and 24. The twenty-fourth word (8 × 3), as in the verses of Clemens about Winwaloe, is *Deo*. After *libelli* in line 2 the sixteenth word (8 × 2) is *librum*. After *cordis* in line 9 the eighth word is *cordis*. After *sacris* in line 6 the twenty-fourth word is *sacro*. The sixteenth word from the beginning of the poem is *mente*. The fortieth word from that (8 × 5) is *mentis*, after which eight words bring one to the end of the poem. Between *elucet* in line 4 and *eluminet* in line 9 there are thirty-two words (8 × 4). After *nitescit* in line 4 the thirty-second word is *inradietque* in line 10. The first line ends with the words *carpere fructus* and the last line with *reddere fructus*. In both cases they are the fifth and sixth words of the verses.

After the sixty-four chapter headings,

INCIPIT YMNUS SANCTI MACHUTI
EPISCOPI ATQUE CONFESSORIS.[6]

The octosyllabic quatrains begin:

> Benedicite Dominum
> gubernatorem omnium
> qui suum dedit famulum
> Machutem ducem Brittonum.
>
> Sanctus Machu egregius
> in die Paschae est natus
> cum eo triginta tribus
> simulque natis penitus.

So it is fitting that the hymn should comprise thirty-four stanzas.

VI. A MONK OF REDON

Vita Conwoionis

Ratuili, to whom Bili dedicated his *Vita Sancti Machutis*, may have been a monk at Redon. Certainly he presided as Bishop of Alet at the funeral of Conwoion. The attribution by Lot of the *Vita Conwoionis* to Ratuili 'is widely accepted', but 'remains an unprovable hypothesis'.[1] One may consider the following text, without clear proof of authorship, as a third specimen of ninth-century Breton Latin composition. Here is the Prologue.[2]

---

6   MS f. 66v. LeDuc, pp. 11–20.
1   *BCLL* 826.
2   *The Monks of Redon 'Gesta Sanctorum Rotonensium' and Vita Conuuoionis*, ed. & transl. C. Brett, Studies in Celtic History X (Woodbridge 1989), pp. 226–7.

Prologus Auctoris.

1   Insignis catholicae fĭdēī pătrēs
         quorum 'conuersatio in caelis est'
         et 'uita abscondita cum Xpisto in Deo'

2a   qui uelut rutilantia firmamenti astra splendorem uirtutum
         mundō rēfŭndĕrĕ
         et ecclesiam Xpisti amore uernantem suo studuerunt illustrārẹ
         ēxēmplō

   b   attollere licet laudibus eorum in medium dēdŭcĕrĕ gēstă
         quos Xpistus in caelo cumulāŭit glōrĭā .

   c   Dignitatem quippe suae conditionis 'ad similitudinem Dei
           facti'

3   unde beatus gloriatur Iŏb cŭm dīxĭt
           'Manus tuae fecerunt me et plasmauerunt me'
           attendentes Conditori pro tanti muneris et priuilegii
           beneficio grātēs ēxsŏluĕrĕ
           et sui pectoris 'iuge sacrificium' 'in odorem suauitatis'
           immolare dēcrēuĕrŭnt
           tamquam hostias iuxta legem Domini sacrificio ŏffĕrēntēs.

2'a   Cum autem quique suarum ecclesiarum auctores immensis
         usque ad sidera efferānt praēcŏnĭīs
         'magno' enim iuxta poetam 'se iudice quisque tuetur'

   b   nos quoque eorum facta praeclara sānctōrŭm pāndĕrĕ
         per quos nostra meruit decorārī ēcclēsĭā

   c   minime arbitrāmŭr ĭndĭgnŭm
         et eis testimōnĭŭm pērhĭbĕrĕ

1'   quorum 'testis est conscius in excelsis' .

Prologue

1   The glorious fathers of the Catholic faith,
      whose 'communion is in the heavens'
      and whose 'life is hidden with Christ in God',

2   who, like shining stars of the firmament, have worked to shed the
      splendour of virtue on earth and to ennoble the Church, blossoming
      in the love of Christ, by their example, it is right to extol them with
      praise and to bring into the open the deeds of those whom Christ has
      crowned with glory in heaven.
      Inasmuch as they were aware of the dignity of their condition,
      'made in the image of God',

3   in which the blessed Job exulted when he said,
      'Your hands have made me and shaped me',
      they resolved to render thanks to the Maker for the benefit of such
      a great gift and privilege, and to offer 'the eternal sacrifice' of their
      hearts 'in the odour of sweetness', bringing them as victims for an
      offering in accordance with the law of the Lord.

2'   Now, as all exalt the founders of their churches to the skies with
       tremendous acclaim (for, as the poet says, 'Each supports himself
       with high authority'), we, too, think it not in the least improper to
       expound the excellent deeds of the saints by whom our church has
       deserved to be graced, and to bear witness on behalf of them,
1'   whose Witness in the heavens is aware of it.

The chiastic patterning is clear. Compare *quorum conuersatio in caelis est* in 1
with *quorum testis est conscius in excelsis* in 1', *astra ... attollere ... laudibus eorum in
medium deducere gesta ...* in 2a-b with *ad sidera efferant praeconiis ... eorum facta
praeclara ... pandere ...* in 2'a-b, *quos* in 2b with *per quos* in 2'b, and *dignitatem* in
2c with *indignum* in 2'c.

The editor has noted only quotations from Job X 8 in 3 and Lucan's
Pharsalia in 2'a, but the author also quotes Philippians III 20 and Colossians III 3
in 1 and Job XVI 20 in 1', as well as the commonplaces in 3 which might
derive from several texts in Exodus, Leviticus, Numbers, or Daniel.

There are two words in the title of the Prologue, sixteen words in 1, forty
words each in 2, 3, and 2', and six words in 1', together 144.[3]

The fourteenth word is *Xpisto* in 1. The fourteenth word after that is *Xpisti* in
2a. From *Xpisti* to *Dei* in 2c inclusive there are twenty-eight words (14 × 2).
From *Deo* in 1 the twenty-eighth word is *Xpistus* in 2b. From *Xpistus* in 2b to
Conditori in 3 inclusive there are twenty-eight words. The sixteenth word (8 × 2)
is *Deo* in 1. From *Dei* in 2c the sixteenth word is *Conditori* in 3. From *Conditori* in
3 to *Domini* in 3 inclusive there are twenty-four words (8 × 3). From *Domini* to
the end of the Prologue there are forty-eight words (8 × 6). From the beginning
of the Prologue the twenty-seventh and twenty-eighth words (14 × 2) are
ecclesiam Xpisti in 1. The fourteenth word from the end of the Prologue is *ecclesia*
in 2'b. The twenty-eighth word before that is *ecclesiarum* in 2'a.

Whoever wrote this may well have learned or taught in the same classroom as
Bili or written in the same scriptorium. A conspicuous feature of his prose is the
use of clausulae. Although we have noted above that Pelagius, Saint Patrick, the
Romano-Gaulish bishops, Gildas, and Cummian composed clausulae during the
fifth, sixth, and seventh centuries,[4] the ninth-century scholar Lupus of Ferrières
punctuated clausulae in his copy of Cicero *De Oratore*,[5] and the ninth-century
scribe Ferdomnach marked clausulae with capital letters and punctuation points in
his copy of Saint Patrick's Apology in the *Confessio*,[6] composition of new prose in
clausulae was not common among ninth-century writers. Yet excluding the
Biblical and Classical quotations every clause in this *Prologus Auctoris* ends with a
clausula.

3   See above p. 21.
4   See above pp. 56–7, 59–61, 66–9, 79–80, and Howlett, *Liber Epistolarum*, p. 56.
5   See above p. 26–7.
6   Howlett, *Liber Epistolarum*, p. 96.

VII. UURDISTEN ABBOT OF LANDÉVENNEC

Vita Sancti Winwaloei

The fourth in this group of ninth-century Breton authors and the third to sign his work clearly, is Uurdisten Abbot of Landévennec, who wrote about the year 880 a Life of Saint Winwaloe. Here is the Preface.[1]

Incipit Praefatio Vitae Sancti Uuinualoei Cornugillensis.

Vita breui studii contexitur ordine sacri
Eximii patris monachorum Uuinualoei,
Quam precibus relego fratrum communibus almam
Uurdestenus et albis conor scribere libris.

Quae quamuis nostro defloreat aucta labore,   5
Hanc quicumque uelit ueterum rescribere chartis,
Aut prohibere tamen aut uisus non aliquando
Radere compertam moneo; sed condita seruans,
Et nostrum relegat, sed et haec non neglegat, atque
Inter utramque uiam medius incessor utrimque,   10
Quaeque sibi placita an uetera nouaque eligat. Ergo
Non nostrum decarpat opus munimine patrum
Suffultum, modero, inuidiae neu ariete crebro
Conquatiat. Neque enim huic operi inuitum attraho quemquam,
Sed qui praeparui contentus muneris haustu,   15
Hunc nostrae ad modicae inuito conuiuia mensae;
Et qui clara sine ficto uult condere facta,
Explosis penitus naeuis et rusticitate,
Nostro degustet deuotus pectora musto,
Atque per egregiam praeductus munere portam   20
Inducens alios, doctus sit ductor habendus.
Haec fuerant denso ueterum uelamine tecta,
Lucidiora nitent sed nostro condita scripto.

Ergo rite suum Xpisto dicemus honorem,
Talia qui nobis haec munera tradidit, atque   25
Largius ipse mea dignetur soluere corda,
Reddere mirificae claras sibi munere linguae,
Summus in aetherea laudes qui presidet arce,
Arbiter excelsi perstans in uertice caeli,
Innumeris septus sanctorum pleniter aulis,   30
Rex qui mirificis perfulget splendidus astris.

1   *BCLL* 827. DeSmedt, p. 172.

Here begins the Preface of the Life of Saint Winwaloe of Cornouaille.

The Life of Winwaloe, the excellent father of monks, is composed in short order of sacred study, which holy [life] I, Uurdisten, retrace because of the common prayers of the brothers and try to write in clear books. Which Life, though it should flourish enhanced by our labour, I admonish whoever wishes to rewrite it against the documents of the ancients either to protect or never to erase what has been ascertained of its aspect, but keeping what has been composed let him both reread our [work] but also not neglect these things, and as a middle walker choose between either way on both sides whatever things are pleasing to him either old or new. Therefore, I ask, let him not detract our work supported by the foundations of the fathers, nor shake it repeatedly with a battering ram of envy. Nor do I draw anyone unwilling to this work, but he who is content with the draft of a very small gift; him I invite to the banquets of our modest table. And he who without feigning wishes to write of bright deeds, with blemishes and rusticity rejected utterly, let the devout man refresh his breast with our must and drawn forward by the gift through so excellent a gate leading others let the learned be considered a leader. These things of the ancients were covered by a dense veil, but they shine brighter written in our script. Therefore we shall duly say that his honour is from Christ Who has handed such gifts as these to us, and may He deign more generously to loosen my heart, to give back to Him bright praises with the gift of a wondrous tongue, He Who sits highest in the heavenly citadel, the Judge enduring in the height of lofty heaven, surrounded fully with innumerable halls of saints, the King Who shines splendid through wondrous stars.

The title of the Preface comprises six words. The first sentence of the Preface comprises four lines of verse and twenty-two words. The number 22 divides by extreme and mean ratio at 14 and 8. From the name of the subject of the Life, Winwaloe, to the name of the author of the Life, Uurdisten, inclusive, there are eight words. The last sentence of the Preface comprises eight lines of verse and forty-nine words, in which Uurdisten has stated some of his ideas twice.

Xpisto	Summus Rex
qui	qui
haec munera	munere
tradidit	reddere
mirificae	mirificis
in aetherea presidet arce	excelsi perstans in uertice caeli

The centre of the Preface is a chiasmus of nineteen lines containing 123 words. Compare line 5 with line 24, 6 with 23, 10 with 20–1, 15 with 19, and 16 with 17. The golden section of 19 falls at 12 and 7. The centre of the chiasmus lies between the twelfth line from the beginning and the seventh line from the end of the passage. The first four lines about Winwaloe and Uurdisten, and the last eight lines of praise to Christ, and the central nineteen lines together comprise thirty-one lines of verse. The number 31 divides by extreme and mean ratio at 19 and 12, the beginning and ending lines making the minor part of twelve verses and the central lines making the major part of nineteen verses, themselves divided again by extreme and mean ratio into twelve and seven verses. They are also divided symmetrically, for the central, tenth, of the nineteen lines (14), is prosodically distinct from the others, a dactylic hexameter with four elisions. The title, first four and last eight lines comprise six, twenty-two, and forty-nine words, together seventy-seven; the central verses 123 words; the entire Preface an even 200 words, which divide by extreme and mean ratio at 123.6 and 76.4. The number 200 divides by one-ninth and eight-ninths at 22 and 178. Twenty-two words from the beginning of the incipit bring one to the name of the author, *Uurdestenus*, the 178th word from the end.

Uurdisten is fond of word play, as one sees from *relegat* and *neglegat* in line 9, from *inuitum* in line 14 and *inuito* in line 16, and from *praeductus, inducens, doctus, ductor* in lines 20 and 21. He asks the hostile reader not to 'shake' his poem. Verse 14, which begins with the word *conquatiat*, is Uurdisten's most unshakeable verse, its words bound tightly with four elisions. It stands tenth from the beginning and tenth from the end of the block of central lines 5–23.

Uurdisten refers often to his own work. Twenty words (10 × 2) bring one to *conor scribere libris* in line 4. Ten more words bring one to *rescribere*, forty more (10 × 4) to *opus*, seventy more (10 × 7) to *scripto*, which is the fiftieth word (10 × 5) from the end. Another locution for Uurdisten's own work is *munus*. From *muneris* in line 15 thirty words bring one to *munere* in line 20, from which the thirtieth word is *munera* in line 25. Other words referring to his own work are *opus* and the past participle of *condere*. In line 12 *opus* occurs. From that to *operi* inclusive in line 14 there are fourteen words. The twenty-eighth word (14 × 2) before *opus* is *condita* in line 8, and the twenty-eighth word before *condita* is *Uurdestenus* in line 4. Fifty-six words (14 × 4) after *operi* bring one to *condita* in line 23. Twelve words from the beginning bring one to *relego* in line 3. Thirty-six words (12 × 3) bring one to *relegat* in line 9. Within the central nineteen-lined passage the first word of the central hexameter, *conquatiat*, refers to him who would try to shake the structure of Uurdisten's poem. That brings one to the central, sixty-second, word of the 123-word passage.

After a list of twenty-two chapter headings Uurdisten names the *auctores ... quibus nostram in istis libellulis suppleuimus sententiolam.*[2] Then *Incipit Vita Sancti Uuingualoei, quod est V Nonas Martias.* The first chapter reveals his borrowings from Gildas.[3]

---

2 Ibid. pp.173–4.
3 Ibid. pp.174–6.

'Britannia insula', de qua stirpis nostri origo olim ut uulgo refertur, processit, locorum amoenitate inclita, 'muris, turribus' magnisque quondam aedificiis 'decorata', haec magnam habuisse rerum copiam narratur .... Cui soli fecunditas suberat et 'Sabrina ac Tamensis fluuii' .... Et ne eius antiqua profundius repetam facinora, qui haec plenius scire uoluerit, legat sanctum Gildam, qui de eius situ et habitatione scribens .... Haec autem quondam patria Cyclopum, nunc uero 'nutrix, ut fertur, tyrannorum'.... .

The decision to write about Winwaloe implies his familiarity with the work of Clemens of Landévennec, and verse 22, *haec fuerant denso ueterum uelamine tecta*, reads like a restatement of Bili's verse 7, *quae latuere diu ceco sub tegmine clausa*. Uurdisten's place within the Breton Latin tradition, as within the wider Celtic Latin tradition, is clear.

VIII. UURMONOC

Vita Sancti Pauli Aureliani

The fifth of this group of ninth-century Breton authors and the fourth to name himself is Uurmonoc.[1]

Incipit prefacio uite S. Pauli Aureliani,
que [sic] colitur .iiij. idus marcjj.

1   **CUM IN PATRUM VENERABILIUM.** qui nos ad regna celestia precesserunt scriptis siue monimentis diuersarum magistros prouinciarum sanctorum certamina martyrum atque confessorum uitas librorum paginis inuenio commendasse: ut quasi ad eorum exemplum, qui post eos futuri essent pro lege sufficere possent: nec solum eos utpote uenerabiles sancte matris ecclesie patres. tali industria uideo floruisse: sed etiam quod dictu nefas est. gentilium sacrilege supersticionis fantasmata. mundane sapiencie fuco colorata quosdam poetas carminibus cecinisse: ac deinde talis materiei falsiloquam compositionem cartis repperio scriptitasse. ut quasi per hoc eorum superflue uanitati satisfacere uiderentur: cur non et ego eorumdem poetarum naufrago exemptus scyllaceo praedictorumque patrum uiuido roboratus iuuamine: aggrederer quasdam uitales alimonias salutarem infirmitati presentium medicinam allaturas in medium proferre. hoc est, inclita Sancti Pauli Aureliani facta in paginis describendo. omnium qui se saluari eius exemplis animati uelint saluti consulere?

2   Cuius gesta, 'quamuis nostro' 'lucidius' quam ut ante primitus ueteri constructione depicta sunt, 'aucta' uideantur floruisse 'labore': hec 'tamen'

---

1   BCLL 828. *Vita Sancti Pauli Episcopi Leonensis in Britannia Minori Auctore Wormonoco Analecta*, ed., F. Plaine, Bibliothèque nationale, MS latin 12942 ff. 113v and 129–30.

'quicumque ueterum cartis rescribere uelit'. 'prohibere' non uidebor. Sed hoc ab eo quisquis ille fuerit modis omnibus efflagito. ut non me in hoc reprehendendum existimet: utpote qui post 'uetera' noua cudere ausus sim. dum ille in potestate habet aut mea eligere. si sibi aliquid saporis habere uideantur: aut respuere si ea deliciosis repletus epulis. 'degustare' noluerit. Sciat enim quod hec a me non ingratis sed beniuolis: non superbis sed humilibus. non deliciosis sed pauperibus. comedenda offeruntur: pauper enim conuiua. conuiuas querit pauperes. Sub pauperis tectum: deliciosos intrare illicitum. est. Quicumque igitur tenui nostrae paupertatis refectione 'contentus'. ad communem intrare uoluerit 'mensam': nostro deuotus degustet edulio. Et postea cum pauperes saturati fuerint laudabunt Dominum. qui mihi dedit ut tale possem preparare conuiuium.

3   Pauperem ergo tui Pauli piissime pater Hinuuorete meae paruitatis conamine descriptam accipe uitam. sed a te inter festa episcopalis cathedrae conuiuia non neglegendam. Erit enim et ea non mediocre tui ingenii opibus supplementum. Gratias autem Deo. qui per me utcumque degestum tale opus ad finem perducere reddidit. Quod ut auderem. Uurdisteni mei preceptoris studium animauit. qui in Uuinuualoei sui sanctique mei describendis actibus. mirabile librorum construxit opus. Sub quo abbate ego presbyter et monachus nomine Uurmonocus. in eiusdem sancti regulari monasterio depinxi tale opus. Quorum simul protectus alis: exspecto me ab insanis inuidorum dentibus defendendum. qui mihi presenti blandientes. absenti tamen derogantes: de me falsa sermocinare non cessant: Sed illorum detractio. meorum erit peccaminum purgatio. Hoc autem opus. octingentesimo octogesimo quarto ab incarnatione Domini anno consummatum: Talem habeat prologum.

The Preface begins of the Life of Saint Paul Aurelian, who is remembered on the fourth of the ides of March. Since I find the masters of diverse provinces to have commended the struggles of holy martyrs in the writings or monuments of venerable fathers who have preceded us to the celestial realms and the lives of confessors in the pages of books, so that they could suffice as a law for an example for those who might come to be after them, I see not only those venerable fathers of holy mother church to have flourished by such industry, as is natural, but also, what is a horror in the telling, certain poets to have sung in songs coloured by the dye of mundane wisdom the phantasms of the sacrilegious superstition of the gentiles, and thence I discover to have written out the false-speaking composition of such material in manuscripts, so that through this they are seen to satisfy their overflowing vanity, why should not I also, lifted out of the Scyllan shipwreck of the same poets and strengthened by the lively help of the foresaid fathers, approach to bring forth into the open certain vital nourishments by writing about the renowned deeds of Saint Paul Aurelian in [my] pages, brought forward as salutary medicine for the infirmity of all present men who, endowed with spirit, may wish themselves to be saved by his examples, [and] saved, may wish to follow [them].

Whose accomplishments, though represented first in an old composition, are seen to have flourished more lucidly, improved by our labour, yet I will not be seen to prohibit whoever wishes to rewrite these things from the manuscripts of old writers. But this I demand from him in all respects, whoever he will be, that he judge me not to be reprehensible in this, who may have dared to beat out new things after the old, as is natural, while he has in his power, either to choose mine if they are seen to have anything of savour for him, or to spit them out if he may not wish to taste them, replete with luxurious delicacies. For he should know that these things are offered by me to be eaten not by the ungrateful but by the well-intentioned, not by the proud but by the humble, not by the luxurious but by the poor. For a poor common banqueter seeks poor common banqueters. It is forbidden for the luxurious to enter under the roof of a poor man. Therefore whoever would wish to enter to a common table content with the meagre refection of our poverty may, devout, taste our delicacy. And afterwards, when the poor men may have been sated they will praise the Lord Who granted to me that I should have power to prepare such a common banquet.

Receive therefore the poor Life of your Paul, most holy father Hinworet, written out through the effort of my insignificance, but not to be neglected by you among the festal common banquets of your episcopal cathedra. For there will be through it a not trivial addition to the resources of your intellect. But thanks to God, Who has appointed to bring to completion such a work set out as best one can by me. The enthusiasm of my teacher Uurdisten roused me to attempt that, Uurdisten who composed a wonderful work of books about deeds worthy of record of Winwaloe, his saint and mine. Under which abbot [Uurdisten] I, priest and monk, Uurmonoc by name, have written such a work in the regular monastery of the same saint [Winwaloe]. Covered by the wings of such men together, I hope myself to be defended from the insane teeth of envious men, who flattering in my presence but detracting in my absence, do not cease to preach false things about me. But the detraction of those men will be the purging of my sins. This work was completed in the year of the Incarnation of the Lord 884. One should regard this as a Prologue.

The Life follows in thirty-three chapters. Then

Explicit uita Sancti Pauli Aurelij Domnonensis, que colitur .iiij. idus Marcij. ·
Exametri uersus.
Vita sacrosancti descripta est ordine Pauli.
Hinuuorete tuis quam scripsi fidus alumpnis.
Cuius ad imperium qui constent nempe fideles;
Nunc tandem fratres uenerandi uota tenete.

& uestri propriis sancti gaudete tropheis.   5
Namque uiri uobis splendent exempla fidelis.
Moribus egregia. castis et florida factis.
Post hoc nullus eat praui per lubrica facti.
Nec pedibus pergat prauorum deuia morum.
Nec dextra laeuaque simul declinet oberrans.   10
Iusticiae potius sectator sed pius instet.
Tramitis, et recto lancem libramine penset.
Nunc ergo Dominum poscamus uoce fideli.
In commune simul. dignetur ut ipse paterna
Nos pietate suos semper defendere alumpnos: 15
Hostis ne ualeat nos uincere fraude malignus.
Ut postquam linquens terreni² corporis una
Spiritus hospicia discesserit: ad pia scandens
Culmina. sanctorum requies ubi fulgida fulget:
Cum Paulo uitam ualeamus habere perhennem;   20
DESUPER IN NOBIS XP[IST]I BENEDICTIO FIAT.;- - -

Here ends the Life of St Paul of Aurelian in Domnonée, which is
    remembered on the fourth of the ides of March.
                    Hexameter verses.
The life of St Paul is written down in order,
Which I, devoted, have written for your followers, O Hinworet,
To whose rule they certainly remain faithful.
Now then, venerable brothers, hold to your vows
And rejoice in the proper triumphs of your saint.
For the examples of that faithful man shine for you,
Outstanding in chaste morals and brilliant in his deeds.
After this no man should go through the slippery grounds of a depraved
    deed,
Nor with his feet proceed through the byways of depraved morals,
Nor wandering away depart from the right or the left alike.
But let the holy disciple rather set foot on the path of justice
And weight his scales on a proper balance.
Now therefore let us ask the Lord with a faithful voice
In common together that He may deign with fatherly holiness
To defend His followers always,
Lest the evil enemy be able to defeat us by deceit,
That after leaving the lodging of the earthly body the spirit at once departs,
Rising to the holy heights where the brilliant rest of the saints shines,
We may be worthy to have eternal life with Paul.
May the blessing of Christ be among us from above.

---

2   Plaine's reading *terram* is more difficult to construe, and it ruins the metre.

The second paragraph of the prose Prologue is filled with quotations from
Uurdisten's Preface. The third paragraph addresses Abbot Hinworet, named in
the seventh word, and refers to Winwaloe, named in the seventh word after
Uurdisteni. Uurmonoc names his teacher Uurdisten in the fifty-first word of the
paragraph. Backward from *consummatum* at the end of the Prologue, the fifty-first
word is the name *Uurmonocus.*[3] The Prologue comprises eleven words in the title,
135 in the first paragraph, 140 in the second, 130 in the third, together 416,
which divide by one-ninth and eight-ninths at 46 and 370. The 370th word is the
last of the sentence *Sub quo abbate ego presbyter et monachus nomine Uurmonocus in
eiusdem sancti regulari monasterio depinxi tale opus,* in which Uurmonoc has combined reference to his patron, himself, and his work.

In the concluding verses Uurmonoc has arranged his words chiastically.

1	uita	
2 a	sacrosancti	
b	Pauli	
3		tuis alumpnis
4		fideles
5		nunc tandem
6		moribus
7 a		factis
b		Post hoc nullus eat praui per lubrica
7'a		facti
b		Nec pedibus pergat prauorum deuia
6'		morum
5'		nunc ergo
4'		fideli
3'		suos alumpnos
2'a	sanctorum	
b	Paulo	
1'	uitam.	

There are twenty-one lines of verse containing 131 words. The golden section
of 131 falls at 81 and 50. The fiftieth word from the beginning of the verses is
lubrica, the end of the former part of the chiasmus, and the eighty-first word
from the end of the verses is *facti,* the beginning of the latter part of the
chiasmus. In the eighty-one-word major part, the forty-first word from the
end brings one to *pietate,* the fortieth word from the beginning. The twenty-
second word before *pietate* is *pius* in line 11. The twenty-second word after
pietate is *pia* in line 18. The golden section of 81 falls at 50 and 31. Between
Dominum in line 13 and *Xpisti* in line 21 there are fifty words. The thirty-first
word of the major part is *fideli* in line 13. In the fifty-word minor part of the
chiasmus the golden section of 50 falls at 31 and 19. The nineteenth word

3   The word count confirms the MS reading *consummatum:* against Plaine's supplied *est.*

from the beginning of the minor part is *fideles* in line 3, and from *fideles* the nineteenth word inclusive is *fidelis* in line 6. Uurmonoc cares about what happens to the *fideles*. The number of words in his verses, 131, added to the number of words in the heading, 13, is 144.

IX. ASSER

Life of King Alfred

The *Life of King Alfred* claims to have been written in the year 893 by Asser,[1] a Welsh cleric, whom Alfred summoned to his service in 886 and whom he later made Bishop of Sherborne. There are many and varied internal indications of authorship,[2] including Welsh spellings of English names, Welsh equivalents of English place-names, frequent use of the Welsh manner of giving directions, much detailed information about political conditions in South Wales, many geographical descriptions of English territory, presumably for the benefit of a Welsh audience, apparent mistranslations of an Old English source, and references to Englishmen as foreigners, to the English language as *lingua Saxonica*, and to Wessex as *Saxonia*. The cumulative weight of these indications is great, especially as Celtic philologists agree in ascribing the author's Welsh language to the ninth century.[3]

Only one copy of Asser's *Life of King Alfred* survived into the modern period, London, British Library, MS Cotton Otho A XII, and that was destroyed in the library fire of 23 October 1731. In 1721 Humphrey Wanley dated the script of the Cotton MS to 1000 or 1001 after comparing it with a dated charter.[4] A facsimile of the first folio of the Cotton MS, published in 1722, allows modern palaeographers to concur with Wanley's dating.[5]

Late in the tenth century or early in the eleventh Byrhtferth of Ramsey quoted extensively from Asser's Life in his historical miscellany.[6] Alistair Campbell believed that the author of the *Encomium Emmae Reginae*, written early in the 1040s, had read Asser's Life.[7] There is an apparent reference to the Life in a list of books, including, among other Alfredian titles, a *Liber Oserii*, presented to Exeter Cathedral by Bishop Leofric, who died in 1072.[8] Florence of Worcester, who died

1 BCLL 30.
2 *Asser's Life of King Alfred together with the Annals of Saint Neots erroneously ascribed to Asser*, ed. W.H. Stevenson (Oxford 1904), pp. lxxiv-lxxix.
3 Ibid. pp. lxxv-lxxvi.
4 Oxford, Bodleian Library, MS Ballard 13 f. 152r, cited by K. Sisam, 'MSS Bodley 340 and 342: Ælfric's *Catholic Homilies*', *Review of English Studies* VII (1931), p. 8 n. 4, rept *Studies in the History of Old English Literature* (Oxford 1953 corr. rept 1962), pp. 148-9 n. 3.
5 Stevenson, opp. p. xxxii. See also new impression, below n. 18, p. cxxxiii n. 1.
6 M. Lapidge, 'Byrhtferth of Ramsey and the early sections of the *Historia Regum* attributed to Symeon of Durham', *Anglo-Saxon England* X (1982), pp. 97-122.
7 *Encomium Emmae Reginae*, ed. & transl. A. Campbell, Camden Third Series (London 1949), pp. xxxv-xxxvii.
8 *The Exeter Book of Old English Poetry* (facsimile), With Introductory Chapters by R.W. Chambers, Max Förster, and Robin Flower (London 1933), pp. 28-9 fols. 1b-2a. See also Keynes & Lapidge, below n. 22, p. 220 n. 97.

in 1118, or John of Worcester, who *floruit* 1140, used the Cotton MS as a source for his compilation,[9] which shortly afterward became a source for Symeon of Durham. Symeon also incorporated Byrhtferth's historical miscellany into his work.[10] The anonymous compiler of the *Annals of Saint Neots* early in the twelfth century also used Asser's Life as a source.[11] He copied information which is not included in Florence's work, and several readings show that he used a better manuscript than Cotton Otho A XII. Unfortunately he also copied much information from a later hagiographic source. In 1574 Archbishop Matthew Parker published in Anglo-Saxon characters an edition of Asser's Life, based upon MS Cotton Otho A XII, but containing many interpolations from the *Annals of Saint Neots*, which he erroneously believed to represent a fuller version of Asser's text.[12] In 1602–3 William Camden reprinted in Roman characters Parker's edition with an additional interpolation designed to attest the existence of the University of Oxford before the ninth century.[13] Scholarly study of Asser's Life between the seventeenth century and the twentieth makes dreary reading and may be left to those interested in controversy.[14] During the twentieth century several scholars have advanced study of the Life. Charles Plummer rejected the interpolations from Camden and the *Annals of Saint Neots* and established on lexical and syntactical grounds the unity of Asser's genuine work.[15] W.H. Stevenson published a masterly edition of the Life, in which he distinguished the interpolations from the original text by smaller type. G.H. Wheeler proposed some textual emendations.[16] In an admirable essay Marie Schütt affirmed the 'underlying rational trend of thought' in Asser's work.[17] In 1959 Dorothy Whitelock surveyed recent work on Asser's Life of Alfred in a new impression of Stevenson's edition,[18] and in 1967 she defended the authenticity and integrity of the Life in the Stenton Lecture.[19] In both essays she replied persuasively to criticism of the Life by V.H. Galbraith, who had first implied doubts about its genuineness and then attempted to prove it a forgery by Bishop Leofric.[20] More recently David Dumville has suggested a solution to a

9   Stevenson, pp. lv-lvii.
10 Ibid. pp. lviii-lix. P. Hunter Blair, 'Some Observations on the "Historia Regum" attributed to Symeon of Durham' in K. Jackson *et al.*, *Celt and Saxon* (Cambridge 1963), p. 116.
11 Stevenson, pp. lvii-lviii., *The Annals of St Neots with Vita Prima Sancti Neoti,* ed D. Dumville & M. Lapidge, *The Anglo-Saxon Chronicle,* eds D. Dumville & S. Keynes, vol. XVII (Cambridge 1985).
12 Stevenson, pp. xiv-xxi.
13 Ibid. pp. xxi-xxviii.
14 Ibid. pp. xxviii-xxxii, xcv-cxxv.
15 C. Plummer, *The Life and Times of Alfred the Great,* Ford Lectures 1901 (Oxford 1902), pp. 5–68.
16 G.H. Wheeler, 'Textual Emendations to Asser's Life of Alfred', *English Historical Review* XLVII (1932), pp. 86–8.
17 M. Schütt, 'The Literary Form of Asser's "Vita Alfredi"', *English Historical Review* LXXII (1957), pp. 209–20.
18 Stevenson, new impression with article on recent work on Asser's Life of Alfred by Dorothy Whitelock (Oxford 1959), pp. cxxxii-clii.
19 D. Whitelock, *The Genuine Asser,* Stenton Lecture 1967 (University of Reading 1968).
20 V. H. Galbraith, *Historical Research in Medieval England,* Creighton Lecture in History 1949 (London 1951), *An Introduction to the Study of History* (London 1964), pp. 85–128.

textual problem,[21] and Simon Keynes and Michael Lapidge have published a translation with detailed introduction and commentary.[22]

There is no reason to doubt the authenticity or integrity of Asser's *Life of King Alfred*. Yet the work has puzzled and embarrassed even its ablest defenders. Plummer confessed himself[23]

> sometimes almost inclined to think that the compiler, while keeping his annals (as he could hardly help doing) in chronological order, cut up his biographical matter into strips, put the strips into a hat, and then took them out in any order which chance might dictate.

He identified as one of Asser's prominent characteristics a[24]

> trick of repeating a word or phrase, sometimes with a slight variation, at intervals, in some cases longer, in others very short ... . Occasionally he seems as if he could not get away from a phrase, but clings to it, as a drowning man clings to a plank; and I think that this feature is due ... to a poverty of expression like that which causes the repetitions of an unpractised speaker. These characteristics come out most strongly in the biographical sections, but they are not wholly absent from the others.

Stevenson agreed.[25]

> Confusion is also caused by the author's unmethodical habit of anticipating events and then returning suddenly without due notice, to the theme from which he has wandered away.

In order to defend Asser's 'unskilful transitions either by elaborate metaphors or by nothing at all' Schütt described Asser's text as 'only a draft'.[26] Whitelock concluded that 'the work as a whole does not leave on me the impression of a great intellect'.[27] Even Keynes and Lapidge, who are usually perceptive and sympathetic interpreters of the work, suggest that the Life transmitted to us 'is apparently an incomplete draft rather than a polished work in its finished state' and that 'Asser abandoned the work incomplete'.[28] Biblical style accounts for

21 D. Dumville, 'The "Six" Sons of Rhodri Mawr: A Problem in Asser's Life of King Alfred', *Cambridge Medieval Celtic Studies* IV (1982), pp. 5–18.
22 *Alfred the Great, Asser's Life of King Alfred and other contemporary sources,* transl. S. Keynes & M. Lapidge (Harmondsworth 1983).
23 Plummer, *Alfred*, p. 15.
24 Ibid. pp. 47–8.
25 Stevenson, p. xc.
26 Schütt, p. 210.
27 Whitelock, *Asser*, p.11.
28 Keynes & Lapidge, pp. 56, 58; also pp. 42, 57, 221 n. 110, 222 n. 118, 275 n. 260, 278.

nearly every apparent anomaly in Asser's work and removes the ground of nearly every criticism of his judgement and competence.

Asser implies much about his intentions in the dedication of the work:[29]

> Dómino méo uenerabili piissimoque omnium Brittanniae insulae Christianórum. rectóri. Ælfred. Anglorum Sáxonum régi. Asser. ómnium. seruórum Déi últimus. millemodam ad uota désideriórum. utriusque uítae. prospèritátem.

> To my esteemed and most holy lord, Alfred, ruler of all the Christians of the island of Britain, King of the Angles and Saxons, Asser, lowest of all the servants of God, wishes thousandfold prosperity in this life and in the next, according to the desires of his prayers.

There are twenty-five words, of which the golden section falls at 15 and 10. The central, thirteenth, word gives the recipient's title, *regi*, and the tenth word gives his name, *Ælfred*. The author may exhibit Biblical influence even in his name, which is not Welsh. It probably derives from Genesis XXX 13; it means 'happy'.[30] After dedicating his book to the living king of all the Christians in Britain, Asser introduces Alfred in chapter 1 (1) as a Christian king whose royalty is firmly established in Biblical genealogy.

Adam	Seth [recte Scef]	Fingodwulf	Creoda	Ingild
Seth	Beduuig	Frithuwulf	Cynric	Eoppa
Enos	Huala	Frealaf	Ceaulin	Eafa
Cainan	Hathra	Frithowald	Cuthwine	Ealhmund
Malaleel	Itermod	Uuoden	Cuda	Ecgberht
[Iared]	Heremod	Beldeag	Ceoluuald	Æthelwulf
Enoch	Sceldwea	Brond	Coenred	Ælfred
Mathusalem	Beauu	Geuuis		
Lamech	Tætuua	Elesa		
Noe	Geata	Cerdic		

The forms of Æthelwulf's genealogy are notoriously discrepant. In the *Anglo-Saxon Chronicle s.a.* 855 the Parker MS, containing forty-four names, does not inlude Creoda, but it does include Esla Giwising, Giwis Wiging, Wig Frea-wining, Freawine Friþogaring, Friþogar Bronding; it reckons Asser's Fingodwulf as two persons, Fin Godwulfing and Godwulf Geating; it does not include Huala, Beduuig, and Scef. MSS B and C, containing forty-six names, include Creoda,

---

29 Asser's text is cited from the 1959 impression of Stevenson's edition. Translations are from Keynes & Lapidge with occasional changes, mostly to reproduce the word order of Asser's Latin. Square brackets surround words which are not found in Keynes & Lapidge's English and words which are supplied to the received Latin text. Chapter numbers in arabic numerals in round brackets are those used by modern editors; those in roman numerals are mine and putatively Asser's.

30 Keynes & Lapidge suggest, p. 49, that this corresponds to the Old Welsh name *Guinn*, the modern Gwyn.

Esla, Wig, Freawine, Freoþogar, but not Friþuwald and Friþuwulf; they reckon Finn and Godulf as two persons; and they include Hwala, Bedwig, and Sceaf. The discrepancy between the Parker version and Asser's version may derive from conformity with different Biblical models. The Regnal Table makes Alfred's genealogy resemble that of Jesus in Matthew I 1–17.[31] Here Asser makes Alfred's genealogy resemble that of Solomon in I Chronicles I 1–III 5.

I Chron I 1	I 24	I 28–III 5	
Adam	Sem	Isaac	Naasson
Seth	Arfaxad	Israhel	Salma
Enos	Sale	Iuda	Boez
Cainan	Heber	Phares	Obed
Malelehel	Phaleg	Esrom	Isae
Iared	Raau	Ram	Dauid
Enoch	Serug	Aminadab	Salomon
Matusale	Nahor		
Lamech	Thare		
Noe	Abram/Abraham		

Asser's first ten generations are copied from the ten generations from Adam to Noah in I Chronicles I 1. His ten generations from Scef to Geata correspond to the ten generations from Sem to Abraham in I Chronicles I 24–7. The name Scef in Asser's list corresponds to Sem in the Chronicler's list. One does well to remember that Asser was a Welsh speaker, accustomed to lenition, by which operation the name Sem can be pronounced 'ʃev', for which the Old English spelling is Scef. This name links the English to the Biblical tradition, for according to the *Anglo-Saxon Chronicle* MSS B and C Scef was *filius Noe se wæs geboren on þære earce Noes*. According to Æthelweard[32]

> Ipse Scef cum uno dromone aduectus est in insula oceani que dicitur Scani, armis circundatus, eratque ualde recens puer, et ab incolis illius terrae ignotus. Attamen ab eis suscipitur, et ut familiarem diligenti animo eum custodierunt, et post in regem eligunt; de cuius prosapia ordinem trahit Aðulf rex.

> This Scef arrived with one light ship in the island of the ocean which is called Skaney, with arms all round him. He was a very young boy, and unknown to the people of that land, but he was received by them, and they guarded him with diligent attention as one who belonged to them, and elected him king. From his family King Æthelwulf derived his descent.

---

31 D.R. Howlett, *British Books in Biblical Style* (Dublin, forthcoming), ch. IV 'The Anglo-Saxon Chronicle and the Alfredian Laws'.

32 *The Chronicle of Æthelweard*, ed. & transl. A. Campbell, Nelson's Medieval Texts (London 1962), p. 33.

The same Scef is alluded to at the beginning of *Beowulf*. Beduuig, Itermod, and Tætuua are otherwise unknown, but Huala is compared with Alexander the Great and described as the best of kings in *Widsith* 14. Hathra may be identical with Saxo's Hother.[33] Heremod is mentioned in *Beowulf* 901 and 1709. Scyld is described as a descendant of Scef in *Beowulf* 4, and Beow(ulf) is described as *Scyldes eafera* in *Beowulf* 18–9. The last name in Asser's list is identical with the Geat mentioned in *Deor* 15. Like Abram/Abraham at the end of the Chronicler's list, Geat's name has two forms in Asser's text, Geta/Geata. Asser spells the name in the short form when he refers to benighted pagans who worshipped him as a god, *Getam iamdudum pagani pro deo uenerabantur*. A ten-line quotation from Sedulius's *Carmen Paschale* is included, not 'ineptly', as Sisam thought,[34] but to show that even foreign Christian poets knew of Geta; its last four lines draw attention back to the Christian tradition:

> Cur ego Dauiticis assuetus cantibus odas
> Chordarum resonare decem sanctoque uerenter
> Stare choro et placidis caelestia psallere uerbis
> Clara salutiferi taceam miracula Christi?

> Why should I, a poet accustomed to chanting the measures of the harp in the manner of David, and of taking my place in the holy chorus and hymning heavenly melodies in pleasing diction, be silent concerning the renowned miracles of Christ who brought us salvation?

Asser spells the name of Alfred's now honourable ancestor in the longer form Geata, comparable with the longer from Abraham. The ten generations from Fingodwulf to Cerdic, which have no counterparts in the Biblical chronology, represent the time between Abraham and the foundation of Wessex. The last fourteen generations correspond to the fourteen generations in I Chronicles 1 28–111 5. In the Biblical model there are ten generations from Creation to the Flood, ten from the Flood to the Covenant with the patriarch of twofold name, and fourteen from the Covenant to the third generation of the House of Jesse. In Asser's genealogy there are the same ten generations from Creation to the Flood, ten from the Flood to the hero of twofold name, ten more to the establishment of Wessex, and fourteen from the establishment of Wessex to the most glorious of its anointed kings, who belonged to the third generation of the House of Ecgbyrht.

Asser considers next Alfred's mother's ancestry in chapter II (2). Her name was Osburh, *filia Oslac famosi pincernae Æthelwulfi regis*. Some modern scholars have wondered why a noble should have performed so menial a task, but Asser doubtless knew and expected his readers to know that no less a man than the builder of

---

33 Howlett, *British Books*, ch. 111. iii 'Biblical Style in the Earliest English Texts: The Franks Casket.
34 Sisam, *Genealogies*, p. 313.

the walls of Jerusalem had been *pincerna regis* (Nehemiah I 11). Oslac was, according to Asser, a Goth, descended from Goths and Jutes, particularly from Stuf and Wihtgar, nephews to whom Cerdic had given the rule of the Isle of Wight.

Asser's first chapter derives from annal 855 of the *Anglo-Saxon Chronicle*. His second chapter contains information from annals 514 and 534. The last annal he used from the Chronicle is 887. All these borrowings have a bearing on alleged recensions of the Chronicle supposed by some to have ended at 855 and 887.[35] The genealogy at 855 stands, at the end of a chiastic passage which relates at its crux Alfred's anointing.[36] Asser's transfer of this genealogy to the beginning of the Life confirms the impression that its purpose is to strengthen Alfred's, not Æthelwulf's, title to rule Wessex. It does not suggest that a recension ended at 855. As annals 514 and 534 belong to the thematically, chronologically, and numerologically artificial arrangement at the beginning of the Chronicle, one infers that they received their present form in the recension of 891. Annal 887 reports the Danes' wintering at Chézy in 887–888 and along the Yonne in 888–889. It alludes to the death of Charles the Fat in January 888, to the accession of Berengar Margrave of Friuli, who was crowned at Pavia in January 888, to the Battle of Brescia at which Berengar defeated Guido Duke of Spolieto in the autumn of 888, and to the Battle of Trebbia at which Guido defeated Berengar in the spring of 889. Annal 887 cannot have been written in the form in which Asser and the Chronicle preserve it before the summer of 889. There is no reason to infer that the annal received this form before the Alfredian recension of 891. All the names in Asser's version of Alfred's genealogy can be found in manuscripts of the Chronicle, but not all of them can be found in any single copy. There are many other places in which Asser agrees with A against B and C, with B and C against A, and even with the late manuscripts D and E against A, B, and C.[37] As Asser preserves forms more archaic than those of any other version, such as *Sceapieg* at 851 and *Coenred* at 855, one infers that he used either the original of the Alfredian Chronicle of 891 or a copy of it closer to it than any of the extant copies.

Asser introduces chapter XIV (21.9–25.17) by echoing the language of Einhard's *Life of Charlemagne* and by developing the naval allusion of the preceding annal, *magna paganorum classis*, into a description of the Biblical style in which he relates the most famous story of Alfred's youth. Capital letters and punctuation marks in boldface represent features of Cambridge, Corpus Christi College, MS 100. I have marked the rhythms of the cursus.

A1   **S**ed ut more nauigántium
2   lóquar

35 *The Parker Chronicle 832–900*, ed. A.H. Smith (London 1951 ed. 3 rept 1968), p. 6 and refs. there given.
36 See above n. 31.
37 Stevenson, pp. lxxxv-lxxxviii.

 3 a   ne <u>diútius</u> nàuim úndis
   a'   et uelaméntis concedéntes,
 1'   et a terra longius <u>énauigántes</u>
 2'   longum círcumferámur
 3'a   <u>inter tántas</u> bellòrum cládes
   a'   et <u>annorum enúmeratiónes</u>
Bɪ   <u>ad id</u> quod nos maxime ad hoc ópus incitáuit:
 · 2   nobis <u>redeundum</u> ésse cénseo
Cɪ   scilicet <u>aliquantulum</u> *quantum meae* <u>cognitióni innótuit</u>:
 2   *de infantilibus et puerilibus dómini méi* <u>uenerabilis</u>
                     <u>Ǽlfredi</u>, <u>A</u>ngulsáxonum *régis moribus* hoc in loco
                     <u>breuiter</u> *inserendum* ésse *exístimo*,
Dɪ   Nam cum communi et ingenti patris sui et matris amore supra
      omnes fratres suos immo ab omnibus nimium díligerétur,
      et in regio semper curto inseparabíliter nùtrirétur:
      accrescénte infántili, et pueríli aetáte
      forma ceteris suis fratribus decéntior uìdebátur,
      uultuque et uerbis atque moribus grátiósior,
      Cui ab incunabulis ánte ómnia
 2   et cum omnibus praesentis uítae stúdiis
 3   sapientiae desiderium cum nobilitáte géneris,
         nobilis mentis ingénium suppléuit,
E   Sed <u>proh dolor</u>
F   indigna suorum parentum et nutritórum incúria.
             usque ad *duodecimum* aetatis *annum*, aut eo amplius
             illiterátus permánsit,
             Sed Saxónica poémata,
             die noctuque solers auditor relátu aliórum saepíssime
             aúdiens docibilis memóriter rètinébat,
             in omni <u>uenatoria</u> arte indústrius <u>uenátor</u>,
             incessabiliter láborat nòn in uánum.
             Nam incomparabilis omnibus peritia et felicitáte in illa
             árte, sicut et in céteris ómnibus Déi donis fúit.
G   sicut et nos saepíssime uídimus,
H   Cum ergo quodam die mater sua sibi et fratribus
                 suis quendam Saxonicum poemáticae àrtis líbrum,
                 quem in mánu habébat osténderet áit;
I   Quisquis uestrum discere citius istum *códicem* póssit;
                     dábo illi íllum,
J   Qua uoce immo diuina inspiratióne instínctus,
                         <Ǽlfredus>
K   et pulchritudine *principalis litterae* illius líbri
                             illéctus,

L 1	ita mátri respóndens
2	et fratres suos aetate quamuis non gratia senióres antícipans:
3	inquit, Verene dabis istum librum úni ex nóbis scilicet illi qui citissime intelligere et recitare eum ánte te póssit:
L' 1	Ad haec illa arrídens et gaúdens,
2	átque affirmans,
3	Dábo infit ílli;
K'	Tunc ille statim *tollens* líbrum de mànu súa, magistrum ádiit. et *légit,*
J'	Quo lecto mátri rétulit ét recitáuit,
I'	Post haec cursum diurnum id est celebratiónes horárum; ac deinde psalmos quosdam et orationes múltas [dídicit]
H'	quos in uno libro congregátos in sìnu súo, díe nóctuque
G'	sicut ípsi uídimus,
F'	secum inseparabiliter <u>oratiónis grátia</u>. inter omnia praesentis uítae currícula ubique círcumducébat,
E'	<u>Sed proh dolor</u>.
D' 1ai	quod maxime desiderabat,
ii	liberalem scilicet artem desidério súo
b	nón suppetébat:
2	eo quod ut loquebatur illo tempore lectores boni in toto regno Occidentalium Sáxonum non érant,
3	quod maximum inter omnia praesentis uitae suae impediménta et dispéndia crebris querelis et intimis cordis sui suspiriis fieri àffirmábat,
4 a	id est eo quod illo tempore quando
b	aetatem
c	et licentiam, atque suppetentiam discéndi habébat,
d	magístros non habúerat,
4' a	Quando uero
b	et aetate érat prouéctior
c	et incessabilius <u>die noctuque</u> immo omnibus istius. insulae <u>medicis,</u> <u>incognitis</u>, infirmitátibus, internisque atque externis regiae potestatis

sollícitudínibus nécnon et pàganórum, térra
maríque: infestatiónibus òccupátus,
immo étiam pèrturbátus

d   magistros et scriptores aliquantula ex párte
habébat legere ut non poterat,

3'   Sed tamen inter praesentis uítae impèdiménta

2'   ab infantia usque ad praesentem diem.

X   <et ut credo usque ad obitum uitae suae>

1'a   in eodem insaturabili désidério,

bi   sicut nec ánte destítuit,

i'   ita nec etiam adhuc inhiáre désinit,

A 1   But as in the manner of sailors

2   I shall speak,

3   lest for too long committing the ship to waves and sails

1'   and sailing quite far from the land
we be moved on a circular course for a long time

3'   among such terrible wars and in year-by-year reckoning,

B 1   to that which particularly inspired me to this work

2   I think I should return,

C 1   in other words, that some small account (as much as has come to
my knowledge)

2   of the infancy and boyhood of my esteemed lord Alfred, king of the
Anglo-Saxons, I consider should briefly be inserted at this point.

D 1   Now, he was greatly loved, more than all his brothers, by his
father and mother
indeed, by everybody with a universal and profound
love, and he was always brought up in the royal court and nowhere
else.
As he passed through infancy and boyhood
he was seen to be more comely in appearance than his other brothers,
and more pleasing in manner, speech and behaviour.
[For] from the cradle onwards, more than anything else,

2   in spite of all the demands of the present life,

3   the desire for wisdom, together with the nobility of his birth, has
characterized the nature of his noble mind;

E   but alas,

F   by the shameful negligence of his parents and tutors
he remained ignorant of letters until his twelfth year, or even longer.
But English poems
(by day and night an eager listener,
most frequently hearing them from the recitation of others)
he, apt at learning, retained in his memory.

	An enthusiastic huntsman, in all the art of hunting,
	he strives continually and not in vain.
	For incomparable above all others in skill and success in that art,
	he has been just as in all other gifts of God,
G	as I have so often seen for myself.
H	One day, therefore, when his mother was showing [to] him and his brothers a [certain] English
	book of poetic art
	which she held in her hand, she said,
I	'Whichever one of you can learn [this book] the fastest
	I shall give it to him.'
J	Spurred on by her voice, or rather by divine inspiration,
K	and attracted by the beauty of the initial letter in the book,
L 1	replying thus to his mother
2	and forestalling his brothers (ahead in years, though not in ability)
3	he said, 'Will you really give this book to the one of us [that is], to him who can understand it the soonest and recite it to you?
L' 1	Whereupon she, smiling and rejoicing,
2	and promising,
3	said, 'I shall give it to him'.
K'	He imediately took the book from her hand,
	went to his teacher and learnt it.
J'	When it was learnt, he took it back to his mother and recited it.
I'	After this the 'daily round', that is, the services of the hours,
	and then certain psalms and many prayers he learnt;
H'	these collected in a single book in his bosom, day and night,
G'	as I have seen for myself,
F'	amid all the affairs of the present life he took around with him everywhere for the sake of prayer, and was inseparable from it.
E'	But alas,
D'1ai	for what he desired the most,
i'	namely the liberal arts, to the extent of his desire,
b	he could not satisfy;
2	for, as he used to say, there were no good scholars in the entire kingdom of the West Saxons
	at that time.
3	He used to affirm, with repeated complaints and sighing from the depths of his heart,
	that among all the difficulties and burdens of his present life this had become the greatest,
4a	namely that at the time when
b	the right age
c	and the leisure and the capacity for learning he had,

d   he did not have the teachers.

a'   But when

b'   he was more advanced in age,

c'   and more incessantly preoccupied by day and night with or rather harassed by all kinds of illnesses unknown to the physicians of this island, as well as by the cares (both domestic and foreign) of the royal office, and also by the incursions of the Vikings by land and sea

d'   he had the teachers and scribes to some small extent, but he was unable to study.

3'   Nevertheless, among the difficulties of the present life,

2'   from infancy right up to the present day

X   <and will not, I dare say, to the end of his life>[38]

1'a   in the same insatiable desire

bi   just as he has not previously desisted

i'   so he does not even yet cease to yearn.

This extraordinary passage is tightly linked first internally. At the beginning in A compare *nauigantium* in 1 with *enauigantes* in 1' and *loquar* in 2 with *circumferamur* in 2'. The diction is appropriate: in composing chiastically Asser 'speaks' by 'moving on a circular course'. At the end in D' compare *desiderabat* and *desiderio* in 1ai and i' with *desiderio* in 1'a and the parallel clauses in 1'bi and i', *sicut nec antedestituit, ita nec etiam adhuc inhiare desinit*, with the phrase in 1b *non suppetebat*. Compare *illo tempore* in 2 with *ab infantia usque ad praesentem diem* in 2', the phrase *inter praesentis uitae impedimenta* in 3 with the same words in 3', *quando* in 4a with *quando* in 4'a, *aetatem* in 4b with *aetate* in 4'b, *magistros non habuerat* in 4d with *magistros habebat* in 4'd. Compare the identical phrases *sed proh dolor* in E and E', *sicut nos uidimus* in G with *sicut ipsi uidimus* in G', *die, quendam librum, in manu* in H with *uno libro, in sinu, die* in H', *discere* in I with the supplied *didicit* in I',[39] *qua* in J with *quo* in J', *libri illectus* in K with *tollens librum* in K', *matri respondens* in L1 with *illa arridens et gaudens* in L'1, *et anticipans* in L2 with *atque affirmans* in L'2, *inquit, dabis, illi* in L3 with *dabo infit illi* in L'3. Note further that the parallel verbs in L and L' all belong to the same conjugations, those in 1 to the second, those in 2 to the first, those in 3 to the third.

The passage is linked second to other literary sources. The words italicized in C derive from Einhard's *Vita Karoli Magni* Prologue and chapter IV. The words italicized in F recall Luke II 42–8, *cum factus esset annorum duodecim*, reminding readers of the age at which Jesus *suorum parentum incuria* showed his precocity *in templo in medio doctorum*. The words italicized in I, K, and K' derive from Saint Augustine's *Confessiones* Book VIII chapter XII, describing the moment of his conversion. Asser does not advertize any of these borrowings, but they are

---

38 This would be translated better 'And, as I believe, up to the end of his life'.

39 Supply of this verb is required first for sense, second as a parallel according to the fifth rule of Biblical style, third as yielding a *cursus medius* in a clause otherwise without rhythm, and fourth to fulfil the word count, as we shall see shortly.

unmistakeable. So are the implications that Asser is ennobling his already noble subject[40] by comparing his early longing for learning with that of Jesus, his resort to Holy Scripture with that of Saint Augustine, his Christian kingship with that of the Emperor Charlemagne. There may be a further, light-hearted, allusion. The art of remembering what is read from books is an unusual virtue to compare with success in the art of hunting, but the early ninth-century Irish poem *Pangur bán*, 'The Scholar and his Cat', combines them.[41]

> Messe ocus Pangur bán,
> echtar nathar fria saindán:
> bíth a menmasam fri seilgg,
> mu menma céin im saincheirdd.

I and white Pangur practise each of us his special art:
his mind is set on hunting, my mind on my special craft.

The passage is linked third to another part of Asser's *Life*. The words underlined throughout the passage recur in chapter XXVI, which we shall consider later.[42]

Although the story is set in the account of Alfred's eighteenth year it belongs to his *infantia*, to his sixth year at the latest, for it involves his *mater* Osburh, not his *nouerca* Judith. Asser mentions that Alfred remained illiterate until his *pueritia*, until at least his twelfth year, 860, the year marked by a resurgence of dynastic and national unity after a time of troubles. Asser makes Alfred's youthful desire for learning the thematic crux of the first part of the *Life*. He returns to this theme at the end of the first part, which is also the crux of the entire work, where he considers the education of children at Alfred's court.[43] But the story is not only the thematic crux; it is also the structural crux, for it is chapter XIV, and the first part of the *Life* extends to chapter XXVII. It is, moreover, the chronological crux, for it is set in the account of Alfred's eighteenth year, and the first part of the *Life* extends to annal 885, when Alfred was thirty-six.[44]

Introduced by a preface of three parts subdivided into twelve, the story proper from D through D' is divided into eighteen parts, of which the first (D) and the ninth (L) and the tenth (L') are further divided into three parts and the eighteenth (D') into eighteen parts. William of Malmesbury reported from Alfred's *Handboc* that Aldhelm had characteristically advanced from secular to sacred themes.[45] Here Asser reports that Alfred was interested first in vernacular poetry and later in prayers. In the same passages, F and F', he mentions Alfred's good fortune *inter omnia praesentis uitae curricula* and *in omnibus Dei donis*. He refers in H to the book of vernacular poems Alfred loved as a boy and in H' to the book of prayers he kept with him as a man.

40 An intention suggested by his words in D3.
41 *Early Irish Lyrics*, ed. & transl. G. Murphy (Oxford 1956 corr. rept 1970), pp. 2–3.
42 See below pp. 287–94.
43 See below pp. 295–6.
44 Stevenson (66–78). Keynes & Lapidge, pp. 86, 251 n. 123.
45 *Gesta Pontificum Anglorum* V § 188.

The infinitive *discere* in I and the rhythm of the *cursus medius* corroborate the supply of *didicit* in I'. The words *ad praesentem diem* in D'2' and *etiam adhuc* in D'1'bi' suggest that the clause X bracketed after D'2' is a clumsy interpolation. Insertion of that may have ruined the rhythm of the *cursus planus* in *diem praeséntem*. According to Keynes and Lapidge[46]

> Stevenson wanted to omit the passage in brackets, but this seems unnecessary: Asser is saying, admittedly in a somewhat muddled way, that Alfred did not desist from the desire from infancy up to the present day, that he still does not desist from it, and that he will not desist from it (in Asser's opinion) right up to the end of his life.

Their English translation connotes what the Latin does not denote, and it entails the inference that Asser was muddled. But nothing in the rest of the passage suggests muddle. As the clause has no chiastic pair, interrupts the train of thought, and ruins the word count, it should be deleted. The word *Ælfredus* at the end of J, bracketed in Stevenson's edition and inconsistent with Asser's usual nominative form *Ælfred*, should also be deleted. Including the supplied *didicit*, but excluding the two interpolations, Asser's text is almost, if not exactly, as he wrote it. The word *possit* at the end of L3 is the 204th word from the beginning of D and the 204th word from the end of D'. The introduction, ABC, comprises sixty-three words. The golden section of 63 falls at 39 and 24, between *censeo* at the end of B2 and *scilicet* at the beginning of C1, where Asser refers to himself and announces what he intends to tell us. The first part of the story proper, D, comprises, like the introduction, sixty-three words. The last part of the story proper, D', comprises sixty words in 1–4 and (without the bracketed clause) seventy words in 4'–1'. The entire passage A-D' comprises 470 words, of which the golden section falls at 290 and 180. The 290th word from the beginning is *legit* at the end of the crux at L'3. Keynes and Lapidge have wondered whether in '*et legit* the *et* is an error for *qui* (in which case the master "read" the book to Alfred)'.[47] It is likely that Asser wrote *et legit* and that he did not necessarily distinguish the senses 'read', 'recite', and 'learn of by reading', all possible in Classical Latin. He clearly means that whatever the action was Alfred did it, just as Saint Augustine himself followed the instruction *tolle, lege*. Keynes and Lapidge also suspect the last four lines of F and G:[48]

> This sentence, cast partly in the present tense, seems somewhat out of place here and may have been inserted by Asser at a later stage in the composition of the *Life*; it breaks the otherwise obvious connection between the previous sentence and the following chapter.

---

46 Keynes & Lapidge, p. 240 n. 52.
47 Ibid. p. 239 n. 48.
48 Ibid. p. 239 n. 47.

At what stage of composition the words were written I do not pretend to know, but it is clear that they belong where they now are, for the words in G are required to balance the words of G', and the reference to hunting in F here is balanced by the reference to hunting in part F of chapter XXVI.[49] Asser has taken some pains to associate Alfred's learning and success *in arte poetica* with that *in arte uenatoria*. Within the symmetrical story proper D-D' the first half of the 204-word first half falls at the 102nd word, *uenator*. Within the 290-word major part of the golden section the second half, of 145 words, begins *Sed Saxonica poemata*.

Asser's verb *circumferamur* is not simply figurative; it is a description of his chiastic composition in this passage, after which he begins again *circumferre*. His chapter XV (26) is the chiastic pair to chapter XIII. In the former, Alfred's eighteenth year, he reports the Danes' arrival in East Anglia; in the latter, Alfred's nineteenth year, he reports their departure from East Anglia.

In chapter XXVI (72) Asser begins with a notice of the actions of the Danes in East Anglia.

> Eodem quoque anno ille paganorum exercitus qui in Orientalibus Anglis habitauit pacem quam cum Ælfredo rege pepigerat opprobriose fregit.

> In that same year the Viking army, which had settled in East Anglia, broke in a most insolent manner the peace which they had established with King Alfred.

He also echoes again the language of Einhard's *Vita Karoli Magni* and returns to his naval imagery.

A 1   Igitur ut ad id unde digréssus sum rédeam,
   2   ne diuturna enauigatione portum *optatae quietis omíttere* cógar,
B   aliquantulum *quantum notitiae meae* innotuerit de *uíta et móribus,*
        et aequa *conuersatione atque ex parte non módica res géstas*
C   domini mei Ælfredi Angulsáxonum *régis,*
        postquam praefatam ac uenerabilem de Merciorum nobilium
        genere cóniugem dúxerit,
B'   *Déo annuénte* succinctim ac breuiter ne qua *prolixitate narrandi*
        noua quaeque fastidientium ánimos offéndam
A' 1   ut promisi
   2   expedíre procurábo,
D 1   Cum ergo nuptias honorabiliter in Mercia factas inter innumerabiles
      utriusque sexus populos sollémniter cèlebráret, post diuturna die
      noctúque conuíuia,
   2   subito et immenso atque omnibus medicis incognito confestim
      coram omni populo corréptus est dolóre, Incognitum enim erat

---

49 See below pp. 288, 293.

omnibus quí tunc áderant, et etiam hucusque cotídie
cernéntibus –

E 1   quod <u>proh dolor</u>

2   pessimum est,

3   tantam diuturnitatem a uigesimo aetátis suae ánno.
        usque quádragésimum, et eo ámplius ánnum

4   <u>per tanta annórum currícula</u>

5   incessánter,

6   protelásse –

D 3a   unde talis dolor óriebátur,

b   Multi namque pauore et fascinatione
                circumstantis populi hoc factum ésse autumábant,
                alii diaboli quadam inuidia, qui semper bonis
                ínuidus exístat,
                Alii inusitato quodam génere fébris, alii ficum
                exìstimábant, quod genus infestissimi doloris
                etiam ab infántia hábuit,

F 1 Sed quódam témpore

2   diuino nútu ántea

3   cum Cornubiam <u>uenandi</u> caúsa adíret,

4   et ad quandam ecclesiam orandi caúsa diuertísset, in qua
        Sanctus Guériir rèquiéscit
        <et nunc etiam Sanctus Niot ibidem pausat> súatim útens,
        Erat enim sedulus sanctorum locórum uisitátor,
        etiam ab infantia orandi et eleemosynam dándi <u>grátia</u>,

5   diu in oratione tácita prostrátus,

6   ita Domini misericordiam déprecabátur,

7   quatenus Omnípotens Déus

8   pro sua imménsa cleméntia

9   stimulos praesentis et infestantis infirmitatis
              aliqua qualicunque leuiori infirmitáte mutáret,

10   ea tamen condicione ut corporaliter
               exterius illa infirmitas nón apparéret:
               ne inutilis et despectus esset,
               Timebat enim lépram aut caècitátem,
               uel aliquem tálem dolórem,
               qui homines tam cito et inutiles et despectos
               suo aduéntu efficiunt,

11   Oratione autem finita coeptum íter arrípuit,

12   et non multo post tempore ut in
                oratione deprecátus fúerat,

13   se ab íllo dolóre

14   medicatum esse diuínitus sénsit,
                  ita ut funditus erádicarétur,

Quamuis et hunc dolorem in
primaeuo iuuentutis suae flore
deuóta oràtióne,
et frequenti Deo súpplicatióne.
pius supplex náctus fúerat
F'1 Nam ut de beneuola mentis suae deuotione Deo succínctim ac
bréuiter,
quamuis praeposterato órdine lóquar.
cum in primaeuo iuuentútis suae flóre,
2 antequam propriam cóniugem dúceret,
mentem suam propriam in Dei mandatis stabilire uellet,
et se a carnali desiderio abstinere non pósse cérneret,
offensam Dei incurrere si aliquid contrarium uoluntati illius
perágeret [métuens],
3 saepíssime gàlli cántu, et matutinis hóris clam consúrgens,
4 ecclesias, et reliquias sanctorum orandi caúsa uisitábat,
5 ibique diu prostrátus
6 orábat,
7 quo Déus Omnípotens
8 propter suam mísericórdiam
9 mentem illius amore suae seruitutis multo
robustius per aliquam infirmitatem quam
pósset sustinére,
10 non tamen quo eum indignum et inutilem
in mundanis rebus faceret ad se penitus
conuértens corròboráret:
11 Cumque hoc sepius magna mentis
deuotióne ágeret,
12 post aliquántulum ìnteruállum
13 praefatum fíci dolórem
14 Dei múnere incúrrit,
in quo diu et aegre per multos
ánnos láborans,
se etiam de uíta desperábat,
quousque oratione facta a se
penitus éum amóuit,
E' 1 Sed proh dolor,
2 eo amoto alius infestior in nuptiis ut diximus éum arrípuit,
3 qui a uigesimo aetátis suae ánno,
usque ad quadragésimum quíntum
4 eum díe noctúque
5 incessabíliter
6 fàtigáuit,

D'1   Sed si aliquando Dei misericordia unius diéi, aut nóctis. uel etiam
       unius horae interuallo illa infirmitas sepósita fúerat,

     2   timor tamen ac tremor illius execrabilis doloris unquam éum
          non déserit,
          sed quasi inútilem éum ut éi uidétur
          in diuinis et humanis rebus propemódum effécit,

A 1   Accordingly, in order that I may return to that point from which I
       digressed—

     2   and so that I shall not be compelled to sail past the haven of my
          desired rest as a result of my protracted voyage—

B   something, as far as my knowledge permits, about the life, behaviour,
       equitable character, and, without exaggeration,[50] the accomplishments

C   of my lord Alfred, king of the Anglo-Saxons,
       after the time when he married his excellent wife from the stock of
       noble Mercians,

B'   with God's guidance, so that I do not offend with my protracted nar-
       rative the minds of those who are scornful of information of any sort,

A'1   as I promised

     2   I shall undertake to say.

D 1   When, therefore, he had duly celebrated the wedding which took
       place ceremonially in Mercia in the presence of countless persons
       of both sexes, and after the feasting which lasted day and night,

     2   he was struck without warning in the presence of the entire gathering
          by a sudden severe pain that was quite unknown to all physicians.
          Certainly it was not known to any of those who were present on that
          occasion nor to those up to the present day who have inquired—

E 1   what, alas,

     2   is worst,

     3   that for so long a time, from the twentieth year of his age
          up to the fortieth year and beyond that

     4   through so many courses of years

     5   incessantly

     6   it has continued—

D 3a   how such an illness could arise.

     b   Many, to be sure, alleged that it had happened through the spells[51]
          and witchcraft of the people around him;
          others, through the ill-will of the devil, who is always envious of good

50 Asser may mean rather 'in no small measure'.
51 Keynes & Lapidge, p. 254 n. 140 state, 'The Cotton manuscript here read *fauore*, which gives the
    opposite sense to what is required by the context. It is not easy to conjecture what the (presumed)
    scribal error might conceal; perhaps *furore*, "inspired frenzy", and hence by extension "incantation" or
    "spell".' A simpler suggestion would be, as *f* and *p* are confusable in Insular script, *pauore*. Translate 'by
    the awe and witchcraft of people standing round'.

men; others, that it was the result of some unfamiliar kind of fever;
still others thought that it was due to the piles, because he had suffered
this particular kind of agonizing irritation even from his youth.

F 1   Now at a certain time,

2   by divine will, before,

3   he had gone to Cornwall to do some hunting,

4   and, in order to pray, had made a detour to a particular church in
which St Gueriir lies in peace
<and now St Neot lies there as well> (as is his [sc. Alfred's] wont),
for he was an enthusiastic visitor of holy shrines
even from his childhood for the sake of praying and giving alms;

5   he lay prostrate in silent prayer a long while

6   in order to beseech the Lord's mercy,

7   so that Almighty God

8   in His bountiful kindness

9   might substitute for the pangs of the present and agonizing infirmity some less severe illness,

10   on the understanding that the new illness would not be outwardly
visible on his body, whereby he would be rendered useless and
contemptible.
For he feared leprosy or blindness, or some other such disease,
which so quickly render men useless and contemptible by
their onslaught.

11   When he had finished praying he set out the way he had started,

12   and shortly thereafter—just as he had asked in his prayers—

13   himself from that malady

14   he felt divinely cured,
in such a way that it was going to be completely eliminated,
even though this malady in the first flowering of his youth by
devout prayer and continual supplication to God
the holy suppliant had contracted.

F' 1   For if of the kindly disposition of his mind towards God concisely
and briefly I shall speak, although I go back to the beginning,[52]
when in the first flowering of his youth,

2   before he had married his wife, he wished to confirm his own
mind in God's commandments, and when he realized that he was
unable to abstain from carnal desire,
[fearing] that he would incur God's disfavour if he did anything
contrary to His will,

3   he very often got up secretly in the early morning at cockcrow

4   and visited churches and relics of the saints in order to pray;

5   he lay there prostrate a long while,

52 Literally 'although in reversed order I shall speak'.

6   he prayed
7   that Almighty God,
8   through His mercy,
9   his mind in the love of His service much more staunchly by means
    of some illness which he would be able to tolerate—
10 not, however, that God would make him unworthy and useless in
    worldly affairs—turning himself totally to Him that He would
    strengthen.
11 When he had done this frequently with great mental devotion,
12 after some time
13 the [foresaid] disease of piles
14 through God's gift he contracted;
    struggling with this long and bitterly through many years,
    he would despair even of life,
    until that time when, having finished his prayers, He removed it from
    him completely.
E' 1 But, alas,
    2 when it had been removed, another more severe illness seized him
       at his wedding feast (as I have said)
    3 which from the twentieth year of his age until the forty-fifth
    4 him by day and night
    5 remorselessly
    6 plagued.
D' 1 And if at any time through God's mercy that illness abated for the
       space of a day or a night or even of an hour,
    2 his fear and horror of that accursed pain would never desert him, but
       rendered him virtually useless—as it seemed to him—for heavenly
       and worldly affairs.

This extraordinary passage is linked first internally. In the introduction
compare A1 *ut redeam* with A'1 *ut promisi* and in A2 *ne omittere cogar* with A'2
expedire procurabo, the reports of what Asser intends to relate in B and B', and the
name of his subject at the crux in C. Compare D1 *die noctuque* with D'1 *unius diei
aut noctis* and D2 *dolore* with D'2 *doloris*. In E and E' compare *proh dolor* in 1,
pessimum in E2 with *infestior* in E'2, *a uigesimo aetatis suae anno usque quadragesimum
et eo amplius annum* in E3 with *a uigesimo aetatis suae anno usque ad quadragesimum
quintum* in E'3, *incessanter* in E5 with *incessabiliter* in E'5, and *protelasse* in E6 with
fatigauit in E'6. Compare F2 *antea* with F'2 *antequam*, F4 *ecclesiam orandi causa
diuertisset* with F'4 *ecclesias ... sanctorum orandi causa uisitabat*, F5 *diu prostratus* with
the same phrase in F'5, *deprecabatur* in F6 with *orabat* in F'6, *quatenus Omnipotens
Deus* in F7 with *quo Deus Omnipotens* in F'7, *pro sua clementia* in F8 with *propter
suam misericordiam* in F'8, *aliqua qualicumque infirmitate* in F9 with *aliquam infirmitatem quam* in F'9, *tamen, inutilis, inutiles, efficiunt* in F10 with *tamen, inutilem, faceret* in

F'10, *oratione* in F11 with *deuotione* in F'11, *non multo post tempore* in F12 with *post aliquantulum interuallum* in F'12, *ab illo dolore* in F13 with *praefatum dolorem* in F'13, and *oratione, Deo* in F14 with *Dei, oratione* in F'14. There are further internal links between D and E'. Compare *nuptias* in the former with *in nuptiis ut diximus* in the latter, *correptus est* in the former with *arripuit* in the latter, and *die noctuque* in both paragraphs.

The passage is linked second to a literary source, Einhard's Preface to the *Vita Karoli Magni,* from which the words italicized in ABC and B' derive.

The passage is linked third to chapter XIV, to which the underlined words relate. One notes immediately how much of the diction and imagery of the introductory sentences in ABC is common to both passages. Equally remarkable is the repetition of phrases like *die noctuque* in XIV D' and XXVI D, *medicis incognitis* in XIV D' and *medicis incognito* in XXVI D, *proh dolor* in XIV E1 and E'1 and XXVI E and E', *uenatoria arte* and *uenator* in XIV F and *uenandi causa* in XXVI F, *orationis gratia* in XIV F' and *orandi gratia* in XXVI F.

The exactness of these structures helps one to correct slight disturbances in the text. The phrase bracketed in F4 is an anachronism which could not have been written in the year in which Asser states that he wrote the Life. At the end of F'2 sense and rhythm require the supply of some such participle as *metuens.*

Asser has fixed the text mathematically. As there are eighteen parts to the story of Alfred and the poetry manuscript related of his eighteenth year, so there are forty-five parts to this story related of his forty-fifth year. There are eight words in A1 and eight in A2, two words in A'1 and two in A'2, nineteen words in B and fourteen in B', and fifteen at the crux in C, together sixty-eight. In the story proper there are forty-five words in D1–2 and forty-four in D'1–2, twenty-four words in E and twenty-eight in E', 147 in F and 144 in F', that is, in D1–2, E, and F 216 words, and in F', E', and D'1–2 also 216 words. Including the introduction (72 and 73) and the anomalous D3 the entire passage comprises 559 words, of which the golden section falls at 345 and 214. The major part extends from the introduction to the end of F, 343 words, and the minor part extends from F' to the end, 216 words.

One notes here, as in chapters VI, VII, and VIII, the unusual ordering of narrative. Asser writes (first) that Alfred was stricken with a mysterious illness at his wedding and alludes (second) to the very end of the period under consideration, Alfred's fortieth year and beyond. Returning from the end of the period under consideration he states (third) that no one at the wedding knew the origin of this illness. Then he relates in a double regression (fourth) that Alfred had requested an earlier illness to be replaced by the one which struck him at his wedding and (fifth) even before that Alfred had requested the earlier illness. Asser ends by returning (sixth) to the present with his second statement of the date, Alfred's forty-fifth year, in which the Life was written.

Asser could hardly have given clearer indications of his chronology. He begins *cum nuptias factas post diuturna die noctuque conuiuia* and alludes second to Alfred's *quadragesimum et eo amplius annum.* He refers to the people standing round Alfred at his wedding and mentions the period before the wedding, *quodam tempore antea* and the reversed order *praeposterato ordine loquar* and Alfred's original request *in primaeuo iuuentutis flore*, returning to Alfred's *quadragesimum quintum annum.*

The text of F3 confirms what common sense implies: as Alfred was old enough to go hunting his *infantia* was past; he must have been at least in his *pueritia.* But the text of F'1–2 implies that he was even older, in his late teens, *in primaeuo iuuentutis flore*, shortly before his marriage in his twentieth year. It was then that Alfred sought some infirmity to help preserve his chastity. Almost immediately after making the request, *post aliquantulum interuallum*, he was stricken with the *ficus*, from which he had suffered in his *infantia.* As this was unbearable, he requested a *leuior infirmitas* at Saint Gueriir's tomb on his hunting trip. Almost immediately, *non multo post tempore*, he was healed of the *ficus*, but he was soon afflicted at his wedding with the mysterious disease which Asser describes as *infestior* and *pessimum.* The time between Alfred's prayer for the first illness and his wedding may have been very short, entirely within his twentieth year, as the long suffering from the *ficus* includes that from Alfred's *infantia.* Asser first mentions the illness at the end of chapter XIV, with its allusion to Alfred's past *infantia* and *pueritia.* In this chapter Asser refers repeatedly to the illness which persisted for the entire period of Alfred's *iuuentus*, from his twentieth to his fortieth year. Alfred's two efficacious prayers in F and F' may be compared with Solomon's two prayers at I Kings III 5–15 and IX 2–9. Stevenson described this passage as 'an instructive specimen of his [*sc.* Asser's] confused arrangement and puzzling phraseology'.[53] Keynes and Lapidge cite it as an example of 'confusing exposition'.[54] If we take Asser at his word, it is none of these things.

From mention of Alfred's wife in chapter XXVI Asser moves naturally to the last chapter of the first part of the Life, XXVII (75.1–15), in which he mentions Alfred's five surviving children: Æthelflæd, Eadweard, Æthelgeofu, Ælfthryth, and Æthelweard. This account of Alfred's descendants is the chiastic pair to chapter 1 with its account of his ancestors.

The chapters of the first part of the Life form a great chiasmus of three-six-nine-six-three chapters, I–III, IV–IX, X–XVIII, XIX–XXIV, XXV–XXVII. In this great chiasmus of five groups of chapters the first four groups have internal chiastic structures, and within these structures many units are chiastic compositions in which Asser counted and fixed mathematically every word. The text is a literary representation of Ezekiel's vision *quasi sit rota in medio rotae*, and this despite the predetermined order of much narrative from the Chronicle. In the second part of the Life Asser had a freer hand.

He begins the second part of the Life by considering the education of children at Alfred's court in chapter XXVIII (75.16–31).[55]

53 Stevenson, p. 294 n. 74.
54 Keynes & Lapidge, p. 221 n. 110.
55 Capital letters and punctuation marks in boldface represent features of Cambridge, Corpus Christi College, MS 100. I have marked the rhythms of the cursus.

A   **In** qua schola utriusque linguae libri
B 1   Latínae scílicet
  2   ét Saxónicae
  3   assídue
  4   lègebántur,
C 1   scriptioni quóque uacábant,
      ita ut antequam aptas humanis artibus uíres habérent,
  2   uenatoriae scilicet et céteris ártibus
  3   quae nobílibus conuéniunt.
  4   in liberalibus artibus studiosi et ingeniósi
  5   uideréntur,
D   Eádwerd et **Æ**lfthryth, semper in curto
      regio nutriti cum magna
      nutritorum et nutricum díligéntia.
      immo cum magno ómnium amóre,
      et ad omnes indigenas et alienigenas
      humilitate affabilitate et étiam lènitáte,
      et cum magna patris subiectione huc
      úsque perséuerant,
C' 1   nec etiam illi sine liberáli discíplina
  2   inter cetera praesentis uítae stúdia
  3   quae nobílibus conuéniunt
  4   otiose et íncurióse
  5   [uíuere][56] pèrmittúntur,
B' 1   **N**am et psalmos
  2   et Saxónicos líbros et maxime Saxónica cármina
  3   studióse
  4   didícere,
A'   et frequentissime libris [utriusque línguae][57] utúntur,

A   In this school books of either language,
B 1   that is to say, Latin
  2   and English,
  3   carefully
  4   were read;
C 1   they also devoted themselves to writing, to such an extent that,
      even before they had the requisite strength for manly skills,
  2   hunting, that is, and other skills
  3   appropriate to noblemen,
  4   devoted and intelligent students of the liberal arts
  5   they were seen to be.

56 Stevenson supplied *vivere*.
57 I supply *utriusque linguae*.

D   Edward and Ælfthryth were at all times fostered at the royal court
         under the solicitous care of tutors and nurses, and indeed with the
         great love of all; and to the present day they continue to behave with
         humility, friendliness and gentleness to all compatriots and foreigners,
         and with great obedience to their father.

C'1   Nor are they without liberal education,
   2   amid the other pursuits of this present life,
   3   which are appropriate to the nobility,
   4   idly and indifferently
   5   allowed [to live],
B'1   for both Psalms
   2   and English books and especially English poems
   3   attentively
   4   they have learned
A'   and they very frequently make use of books [of either language].

He ends the second part of the Life by considering the education of older men
in Alfred's service in chapter XLV (106.46–63).

Sed si aliquis litterálibus stúdiis aút pro sénio,
uel etiam pro nimia inusitati ingenii tarditate proficere nòn ualéret,
suum si habéret filium, aut etiam aliquem propinquum suum,
uel etiam si aliter non habeat suum proprium hóminem líberum,
uel seruum quem ad lectionem longe ánte promóuerat,
libros ante se die nocteque quandocunque unquam ullam haberet
     licentiam Saxonicos imperábat recitáre,
et suspirantes nimium intima ménte dolébant,
eo quod in iuuentute sua talibus studiis nón studúerant,
félices àrbitrántes, huius temporis iuuenes qui liberalibus artibus feliciter
     erudíri póterant,
Se uero infelices existimantes qui nec hoc in iuuentúte didícerant,
nec etiam in senectute, quamuis inhianter desiderarent póterant díscere,
Sed hanc senum iuuenumque in discendis literis solertiam ad praefati
     regis notitiam éxplicáuimus.,

But if one of them in learning to read—either because of his age
or because of the unresponsive nature of his unpractised intelligence—
     was unable to make progress,
the man's son (if he had one) or some relative of his
or even (if he had no one else) a man of his own, free
or slave whom he had caused to be taught to read long before,
the king commanded to read out books in English to him by day and
     night or whenever he had the opportunity.
[And] sighing greatly from the bottom of their hearts, these men regretted
that they had not applied themselves to such pursuits in their youth,

and considered the youth of the present day to be fortunate, who had
the luck to be instructed in the liberal arts,

but counted themselves unfortunate because they had not learned such
things in their youth

nor even in their old age, even though they ardently wished that they
had been able to do so.

But I have explained this concern for learning how to read among the
young and old in order to give some idea of the character of King Alfred.

This conclusion, often condemned as abrupt, is perfectly consistent with the
style of the rest of the Life. The first sentence begins with *Sed*, and so does the
last. The syntactic patterns are repeated, the first two lines reading *si ... aut ...
uel etiam*, and the next two lines also reading *si ... aut ... uel etiam*.[58] Only one
clause, the third, does not end with a correct cursus rhythm, and that could be
remedied by reversal of word order to *súum propínquum*. Reversal of word
order at the end of the sixth clause and the eleventh would yield cursus
rhythms, *recitáre imperábat* and *díscere póterant*, and rhymes *promouerat, imperabat,
didicerant, poterant*. Regardless of emendations there are signs of an attempt to
write rhythmical alliterative rhymed prose: *ualeret, promouerat, suum filium,
propinquum suum, suum proprium liberum*; *dolebant, studuerant, poterant, didicerant,
poterant*. There are many examples of internal and chiastic and consecutive
alliteration and rhymes elsewhere than the ends of lines. In chapter XXVIII
Asser wrote six words in A and six in A', six words in B and twelve in B',
thirty-eight words in ABC, thirty-eight in D, and thirty-seven in C'B'A', a
total of 113 words. In chapter XLV he wrote 116 words.

Asser divided the second part of the Life, bounded by these two chapters,
into two parts. The former extends from chapter XXIX (76.1–9) through
chapter XXXVII (91.1–28).

XXIX

A	Interea tamen rex	
B		inter bella et praesentis uitae frequentia impedimenta,
C		necnon paganorum infestationes et cotidianas corporis infirmitates,
D1		et regni gubernacula regere,
2		et omnem uenandi artem agere,
3		aurifices et artifices suos omnes et falconarios et accipitrarios canicularios quoque docere,
4		et aedificia supra omnem antecessorum suorum consuetudinem uenerabiliora et pretiosiora noua sua machinatione facere ... non desinebat.

58 It is not clear whether, to extend this pattern, one should emend the fourth and fifth lines to read *si
aliter non habeat suum proprium hominem [aut] liberum uel [etiam] seruum quem ad lectionem longe ante
promouerat.*

XXXVII

A	Erat itaque rex ille
B	multis tribulationum clauis confossus,
CI	quamuis in regia potestate constitutus,
2a	nam a uigesimo aetatis anno usque ad quadragesimum quintum annum, quem nunc agit,
b	grauissima incogniti doloris infestatione
3	incessanter fatigatur,
4	ita ut ne unius quidem horae securitatem habeat
4'	qua aut illam infirmitatem non sustineat,
1'	aut sub illius formidine lugubriter prope constitutus non desperet,
2b	praeterea assiduis exterarum gentium infestationibus,
a	quas sedulo terra marique sine ullius quieti temporis interuallo sustinebat,
3'	non sine materia, inquietabatur.
DI	Quid loquar de frequentibus contra paganos expeditionibus et bellis et incessabilibus regni gubernaculis?
2	De cotidiana [sollicitudine] nationum quae in Cyrreno mari usque ultimum Hiberniae finem habitant? Nam etiam de Hierosolyma ab El[ia] patriarcha epistolas et dona illi directas uidimus et legimus.
3	De ciuitatibus et urbibus renouandis et aliis ubi nunquam ante fuerant construendis?
4	[De] aedificiis aureis et argenteis incomparabiliter illo edocente fabricatis?
5	De aulis et cambris regalibus lapideis et ligneis suo iussu mirabiliter constructis?
6	De uillis regalibus lapideis antiqua positione motatis et in decentioribus locis regali imperio decentissime constructis?
7	Qui[d de] maxima, excepto illo dolore, perturbatione et controuersia suorum, qui nullum aut paruum uoluntarie pro communi regni necessitate uellent subire laborem?

XXIX

A	Meanwhile the king,
B	amidst the wars and the numerous interruptions of this present life,
C	not to mention the Viking attacks and his continual bodily infirmities,
DI	from directing the government of the kingdom,
2	pursuing all manner of hunting,
3	giving instruction to all his goldsmiths and craftsmen as well as to his falconers, hawk-trainers and dog-keepers,
4	making to his own design wonderful and precious new treasures which far surpassed any tradition of his predecessors … did not refrain.

XXXVII

A   King Alfred has been transfixed

B   by the nails of many tribulations,

C1   even though he is invested with royal authority;

  2 a from his twentieth year until his forty–fifth (which is now in course)

    b with the savage attacks of some unknown disease

  3   he has been plagued continually

  4   such that he does not have even a single hour of peace

  4' in which he does not either suffer from the disease itself

  1' or else, gloomily dreading it, is not driven almost to despair.

  2'b Moreover, by the relentless attacks of foreign peoples,

    a which he continually sustained from land and sea without any interval of peace,

  3' he was perturbed not without good reason.

D1   What shall I say of his frequent expeditions and battles against the Vikings and of the unceasing responsibilities of government?

  2   What of his daily [involvement] with the nations which lie from the Mediterranean to the farthest limit of Ireland? for I have even seen and read letters sent to him with gifts from Jerusalem by the patriarch Elias.

  3   And what of the cities and towns to be rebuilt and of others to be constructed where previously there were none?

  4   [And what of] the treasures incomparably fashioned in gold and silver at his instigation?

  5   And what of the royal halls and chambers marvellously constructed of stone and wood at his command?

  6   And what of the royal residences of masonry, moved from their old position and splendidly reconstructed at more appropriate places by his royal command?

  7   [And what of] the mighty disorder and confusion of his own people to say nothing of his own malady who would undertake of their own accord little or no work for the common needs of the kingdom?

The readings *Elia* in D2 and *De* in D4 are reproduced from Stevenson's text. The readings *sollicitudine* in D2 and *Quid de* in D7 are adopted from G.H. Wheeler. Wise's emendation of the manuscript form *Cyrreno* to *Tyrreno*, accepted by Stevenson, gives unacceptable sense if construed 'Tyrrhenian', especially as Asser mentions Patriarch Elias of Jerusalem in the next sentence. One might save the emendation by translating 'nations which dwell on [the shores of] the Tyrian Sea', but the manuscript reading makes good sense. In Old English Syrians are *Syrware*, 'dwellers in Syr'. Asser probably means *Cyrrenum mare*, 'Syrian Sea', the eastern Mediterranean.

The order of references to Alfred's wars against foreigners, supervision of craftsmen, and vast construction projects follows the order of II Chronicles I–II, in which Solomon *congregauit sibi currus et equites* (I 14), dealt with the *regibus*

Syriae (I 16) and especially with *Hiram rex Tyri* (II 3, 11), undertook *ut aedificem domum nomini Domini Dei* (II 4), and acquired for that purpose a *uirum eruditum qui nouerit operari in auro et argento, aere, ferro ... et qui sciat scalpere celata cum his artificibus quos mecum habeo* (II 7). Alfred's reconstruction of old cities and construction of new cities recalls Solomon's reconstruction and construction reported in II Chronicles VIII 2–6. Alfred's buildings of gold and silver and wood and stone remind one of Solomon's materials, described in II Chronicles IX. Asser's implication that Alfred received no ungrudging help from his subjects reflects the Biblical Chronicler's insistence at II Chronicles IV 22 that the Temple was Solomon's own work. The quality of Alfred's works, surpassing all of his predecessors', recalls the description of Solomon's work at II Chronicles IX 19: *non fuit tale solum in uniuersis regnis.*

Keynes and Lapidge have cited chapter XXIX (76.1–12) as one example of Asser's 'sprawling sentences'.[59] But by recognizing that Asser made the ideas in this sentence follow the same order as those in chapter XXXVII (91.1–28) and both of these to coincide with a Biblical model, one sees that it is not a shapeless sprawl, but a coherent composition which reads intelligibly, even in the un-English order set out above.

Chapter XXX (76.9–77.24) is one of the most important and remarkable in the Life. In it Asser tells us many more things than a first reading may imply.

A   Et Saxonicos libros recitare et maxime carmina Saxonica memoriter discere

B   aliis imperare et solus assidue pro uiribus studiosissime non desinebat.

C1a Diuina quoque misteria et missam scilicet cotidie audire,

  a' psalmos quosdam et orationes et horas diurnas et nocturnas celebrare,

  a" et ecclesias nocturno tempore, ut diximus, orandi causa clam a suis adire solebat et frequentabat.

  2   Eleemosynarum quoque studio et largitati

  3   indigenis et aduenis omnium gentium

  4   ac maxima et incomparabili contra omnes homines affabilitate atque iocunditate et ignotarum rerum inuestigationi

  5   solerter se iungebat.

  6   Franci autem multi, Frisones, Galli,

  7   pagani,

  6'   Britones et Scotti, Armorici

  5'   sponte se suo dominio subdiderant,

  4'   nobiles scilicet et ignobiles,

  3'   quos omnes sicut suam propriam gentem,

  2'   secundum suam dignitatem regebat, diligebat, honorabat pecunia et potestate ditabat.

59 Keynes & Lapidge, p. 221 n. 110.

1'a Diuinam quoque scripturam
  b   a recitantibus indigenis,
  c   aut etiam si casu quodam aliunde adueniret,
  b'   cum alienigenis pariter
  a' preces audire sedulus et sollicitus solebat.
      Episcopos quoque suos et omnem ecclesiasticum ordinem,
      comites ac nobiles suos,
      ministeriales etiam et omnes familiares admirabili amore diligebat.
      Filios quoque eorum qui in regali familia nutriebantur non
      minus propriis diligens, omnibus bonis moribus instituere et
      literis imbuere solus die noctuque inter cetera non desinebat.

D 1   Sed quasi nullam in his omnibus consolationem haberet,
  2   et nullam aliam intrinsecus et extrinsecus perturbationem
       pateretur,
  3   ita tamen cotidiana et nocturna anxius tristitia ad Dominum
       et ad omnes qui sibi familiari dilectione adsciti forent,
  4   querelaretur et assiduo gemebat suspirio,
  5   eo quod Deus Omnipotens eum expertem diuinae
         sapientiae et liberalium artium fecisset.

E 1   In hoc pium et opinatissimum atque opulentissimum Salomonem
      Hebraeorum regem aequiparans,
  2   qui primitus, despecta omni praesenti gloria et diuitiis
 • 3   sapientiam a Deo deposcit,
F   et etiam utramque inuenit, sapientiam scilicet et praesentem gloriam,
G 1 sicut scriptum est,
  2   'Quaerite ergo primum regnum Dei et iustitiam eius, et haec
      omnia praestabuntur uobis.'

H 1 Sed Deus, Qui est semper inspector
  2   internarum mentium meditationum,
  2'   et omnium bonarum uoluntatum
  1'   instigator,
I 1   necnon etiam,
  2   ut habeantur bona desiderata,
  3   largissimus administrator,
J   neque enim unquam aliquem bene uelle instigaret,
 I' 1 nisi et hoc,
  2   quod bene et iuste quisque habere desiderat,
  3   largiter administraret,
H'   instigauit mentem eius interius, non extrinsecus.
G' 1 sicut scriptum est,
  2   'Audiam quid loquatur in me Dominus Deus.'
F'   Coadiutores bonae meditationis suae, qui eum in desiderata sapientia
    adiuuare possent, quo ad concupita perueniret, quandocunque posset,
    acquireret;

E' 1   qui subinde, uelut apis prudentissima,

2   quae primo mane caris e cellulis consurgens aestiuo tempore, per incerta aeris itinera cursum ueloci uolatu dirigens, super multiplices ac diuersos herbarum, holerum, fruticum flosculos descendit,

3   probatque quid maxime placuerit atque domum reportat,

D' 1   mentis oculos longum dirigit,

2   quaerens extrinsecus quod intrinsecus non habebat, id est in proprio regno suo.

3   at tunc Deus quaedam solatia regiae beneuolentiae,

4   tam beneuolam et iustissimam querelam illius diutius non ferens,

5   ueluti quaedam luminaria, transmisit,

C' 1   Werfrithum scilicet, Wigernensis ecclesiae episcopum, in diuina scilicet scriptura bene eruditum, qui imperio regis libros Dialogorum Gregorii papae et Petri sui discipuli de Latinitate primus in Saxonicam linguam, aliquando sensum ex sensu ponens, elucabratim et elegantissime interpretatus est;

2   deinde Plegmundum,

3   Mercium genere,

4   Dorobernensis ecclesiae archiepiscopum,

5   uenerabilem scilicet uirum, sapientiae praeditum;

6   Æthelstan

7   quoque

7'   et

6'   Werwulfum,

5'   eruditos

4'   sacerdotes et capellanos,

3'   Mercios genere. Quos quatuor Ælfred rex de Mercia ad se aduocauerat, et multis honoribus et potestatibus extulit in regno Occidentalium Saxonum,

2'   exceptis his quae Plegmundus archiepiscopus

1'   et Werfrithus episcopus in Mercia habebant.

B'   Quorum omnium doctrina et sapientia regis indesinenter desiderium crescebat et implebatur.

A'   Nam die noctuque, quandocunque aliquam licentiam haberet, libros ante se recitare talibus imperabat.

A   reading aloud from books in English and above all learning English poems by heart;

B   issuing orders to his followers: all these things he did himself with great application to the best of his abilities.

C1a   He was also in the invariable habit of listening daily to divine services and Mass,

a' and of participating in certain psalms and prayers and in the day-
time and night-time offices,

a" and, at night-time, as I have said, of going (without his household
knowing) to various churches in order to pray.

2 To charity and distribution of alms

3 to the native population and to foreign visitors of all races,

4 showing immense and incomparable kindness and generosity to all
men, as well as to the investigation of things unknown

5 he similarly applied himself.

6 Wherefore many Franks, Frisians, Gauls,

7 Vikings,

6' Welshmen, Irishmen, and Bretons

5' subjected themselves willingly to his lordship,

4' nobles and commoners alike;

3' and, just as he did his own people, them all

2' as befitted his royal status, he ruled, loved, honoured, and
enriched with wealth and authority.

1'a Also to Holy Scripture

b being read out by his own countrymen,

c or even, if the situation should somehow arise,

b' in the company of foreigners,

a' he was in the habit of listening eagerly and attentively to these lessons.
With wonderful affection he cherished his bishops and the entire
clergy, his ealdormen and nobles, his officials as well as all his associates. Nor, in the midst of other affairs, did he cease from personally
giving, by day and night, instruction in all virtuous behaviour and
tutelage in literacy to their sons, who were being brought up in the
royal household and whom he loved no less than his own children.

D 1 But as if he derived no consolation from all these things,

2 and suffered no greater distress of any kind inwardly and outwardly

3 (and he did, to the extent that he would cry out in anguish by day
and night to the Lord and to all those who were known to him on
terms of intimacy),

4 he used to moan and sigh continually

5 because Almighty God had created him lacking in divine learning
and knowledge of the liberal arts.

E 1 In this respect he resembled the holy, highly esteemed and
exceedingly wealthy Solomon, king of the Hebrews,

2 who, once upon a time, having come to despise all renown and
wealth of this world,

3 sought wisdom from God,

F and thereby achieved both (namely, wisdom and renown in this
world),

G 1 as it is written,

2	'Seek ye therefore first the kingdom of God, and His justice, and all these things shall be given to you.'
H 1	But God, who is ever the observer
2	of our internal desires
2'	and of all our thoughts and good intentions
1'	the instigator,[60]
I 1	and also—
2	so that these good intentions may be fulfilled—
3	a most generous overseer
J	(for He never initiates any good intention,
I' 1	nor this
2	unless the person appropriately and rightly desires to be so,
3	does He bountifully bring it to fulfilment),
H'	stimulated King Alfred's intelligence from within, not from without,
G' 1	as it is written,
2	'I will hear what the Lord God speaks in me',
F'	so that he could acquire helpers in this good intention of his, who would be able to help him attain to the desired wisdom and enable him to fulfil his wishes whenever possible.
E' 1	Accordingly, just like the clever bee,
2	which at first light in summertime departs from its beloved honeycomb, finds its way with swift flight on its unpredictable journey through the air, lights upon the many and various flowers of grasses, plants and shrubs,
3	discovers what pleases it most and then carries it back home,
D' 1	King Alfred directed the eyes of his mind far afield
2	and sought without what he did not possess within, that is to say, within his own kingdom.
3	At that point God some comforts for this royal intention
4	(being unable to tolerate so well-intentioned and justifiable a complaint any longer)
5	certain luminaries, as it were, sent
C' 1	Werferth, the bishop of Worcester, a man thoroughly learned in holy writings who at the king's command translated for the first time the *Dialogues* between Pope Gregory and his disciple Peter from Latin into the English language, sometimes rendering sense for sense, translating intelligently and in a very polished style;
2	then Plegmund,
3	a Mercian by birth,
4	archbishop of Canterbury,
5	and an estimable man richly endowed with learning;

---

60 More precisely 'the inspector of the internal thoughts of our minds and of all good desires the instigator'.

6   Æthelstan

7   also

7'   and

6'   Werwulf,

5'   learned men,

4'   priests and chaplains,

3'   Mercians by birth. King Alfred summoned these four men to him from Mercia, and showered them with many honours and entitlements in the kingdom of the West Saxons

2'   (not counting those which Archbishop Plegmund

1'   and Bishop Werferth already possessed in Mercia).

B'   The king's desire for knowledge increased steadily and was satisfied by the learning and wisdom of all four men.

A'   By day or night, whenever he had any opportunity, he used to tell them to read aloud from books in his presence.

The text has been slightly disturbed in two places. In C1 the Cotton MS read *Diuina quoque ministeria*, but that destroys the doublet 'holy mysteries and mass', parallel to 'psalms and prayers' and 'diurnal and nocturnal hours'. Even the verbs are paired, *solebat et frequentabat*. Alfred heard 'mysteries' from the Liturgy and (in the chiastic member C'1'a and a') from Holy Scripture and prayers. Asser refers to texts, not to the 'ministers' who read them. The source of the corruption is the list in C1'a', in which Asser mentions in descending order 'bishops and the entire ecclesiastical order', 'ealdormen and nobles', 'even servants and all the members of Alfred's household', and finally the children of these last. Asser means that Alfred cared for the education even of his servants' children, not that the king attended to ecclesiastical servants as to mass. The reading *ministeria* in C1a may imply that a scribe misunderstood the outlines of the chiasmus.

In C'3' the Cotton MS read *Mercios genere eruditos*, but the order *Æthelstan quoque et Werwulfum eruditos sacerdotes* makes the description of these priests, *eruditos*, the chiastic pair to the description of Archbishop Plegmund, *praeditum*. It also yields a chiasmus in which the crux of C', as of C, is the seventh member.

In C Asser mentions Alfred's equal treatment of native and foreigner, as enjoined in Leviticus XXIV 16 and 22. At the crux he mentions seven types of foreigner who voluntarily submitted to Alfred: men from three Christian Continental nations in 6, men from three Christian Celtic nations in 6', and pagan Danes at the very centre. In C' Asser mentions four Mercians whom Alfred summoned to his service. Later he mentions Grimbald the Frank and John the Old Saxon and finally himself, the seventh of the king's scholars.

In the list of Christian nations Asser notes first those he considers central and most important, the Franks and the Welsh, second those to the 'left' or north, the Irish and the Frisians, and third those to the 'right' or south, the Gauls and the Bretons. This implies that Asser considered Grimbald and himself the principal scholars at Alfred's court. There are independent references to foreigners in Alfred's service to Plegmund the Mercian, Asser the Welshman, Grimbald the Frank, and John the Old Saxon in the Preface to King Alfred's Old English translation of *Pastoral Care*, to Frisians in annal 897 of the *Anglo-Saxon Chronicle*, to the Norseman Ohthere in the Alfredian translation of Orosius, to Welshmen in annal 893 of the Chronicle, and to Irishmen in annal 891. Until 893 the Chronicler records the deeds of the West Saxons, but at 893 he celebrates the victories of the Christians. Also in 893 Asser wrote the *Life of King Alfred*, partly to justify his own service to an English king and partly to encourage more widespread allegiance to the man described in his dedication as the legitimate ruler of all Christians in Britain.

The prominence Asser gives at this point to the presence of foreigners at Alfred's court reminds one that many foreigners came to hear Solomon's wisdom (I Kings IV 34) and that Solomon took a census of aliens (II Chronicles II 17). In E Asser explicitly compares Alfred with Solomon, and in E' he compares him with the prudent bee in a passage reminiscent of Aldhelm *De Virginitate* III. The quotation from the New Testament in G2 (Matthew VI 33) is balanced by a quotation from the Old Testament in G'2 (Psalm LXXXV 8).

Keynes and Lapidge have criticised parts H-D'2 (76.50–70) as another of Asser's 'sprawling sentences'.[61] But it is identical in structure and style with the rest of the chapter, in which the order of ideas is fixed chiastically and linked to the chiastic pair to chapter XXX, the equally remarkable chapter XXXVI (88.1–90.12).

> A1 a   Nam cum quodam die ambo in regia cambra resideremus,
>   undecunque sicut solito colloquia habentes,
>   ex quodam quoddam testimonium libro illi euenit ut recitarem.
>
>   b   Quod cum intentus utrisque auribus audisset
>   et intima mente sollicite perscrutaretur,
>   subito ostendens libellum,
>
>   2 a   quem in sinum suum sedulo portabat,
>   b   in quo diurnus cursus
>   b'   et psalmi quidam
>   b"   atque orationes quaedam,
>   a'   quas ille in iuuentute sua legerat, scripti habebantur,
>
> 1' a   imperauit quod illud testimonium
>   b   in eodem libello literis mandarem.
>
> 2' a   Quod ego audiens et ingeniosam beneuolentiam illius ex parte, atque etiam tam deuotam erga studium diuinae sapientiae uoluntatem eius cognoscens,
>
>   b   immensas Omnipotenti Deo grates, extensis ad aethera uolis, tacitus quamuis, persolui,
>
>   a'   Qui tantam erga studium sapientiae deuotionem in regio corde inseruerat.

---

61 Keynes & Lapidge, p. 221 n. 110.

1"b   Sed cum nullum locum uacuum in eodem libello reperirem,

  a   in quo tale testimonium scribere possem—erat enim omnino multis ex causis refertus —

aliquantisper distuli, et maxime quia tam elegans regis ingenium ad maiorem diuinorum testimoniorum scientiam prouocare studebam.

...

3 a   sicut scriptum est,

  b   'Super modicum fundamentum aedificat iustus et paulatim ad maiora defluit'

B   uelut apis fertilissima longe lateque gronnios interrogando discurrens, multimodos diuinae scripturae flosculos inhianter et incessabiliter congregauit quis praecordii sui cellulas densatim repleuit.

C   Nam primo illo testimonio scripto, confestim legere et in Saxonica lingua interpretari atque inde perplures instituere studuit,

B'   ac ueluti de illo felici latrone cautum est, Dominum Iesum Xpistum, Dominum suum, immoque omnium, iuxta se in uenerabili sanctae Crucis patibulo pendentem cognoscente ... submissa uoce clamaret, 'Memento mei cum ueneris in regnum tuum, Xpiste',

A'1   qui Xpistianae fidei rudimenta in gabulo primitus inchoauit discere; hic aut aliter, quamuis dissimili modo, in regia potestate sanctae rudimenta scripturae, diuinitus instinctus praesumpsit incipere in uenerabili Martini solemnitate.

2 a   Quos flosculos undecunque collectos a quibuslibet magistris discere et in corpore unius libelli, mixtim quamuis, sicut tunc suppetebat, redigere, usque adeo protelauit quousque propemodum ad magnitudinem unius psalterii perueniret.·

  b   Quem Enchiridion suum, id est Manualem Librum, nominari uoluit, eo quod ad manum illum die noctuque solertissime habebat, in quo non mediocre, sicut tunc aiebat, habebat solatium.

3 a   Sed sicut a quodam sapiente iamdudum scriptum est,

  b   'Inuigilant animi quibus est pia cura regendi' ...

A 1 a One day when we were sitting together in the royal chamber, discussing all sorts of topics (as we normally did), it happened that I was reading aloud some passage to him from a certain book.

  b   As he was listening intently to this with both ears, and was carefully mulling it over in the depths of his mind, he suddenly showed me a little book,

2 a which he constantly carried on his person,

  b and in which the day-time offices

  b' and some psalms

  b" and certain prayers

a'   which he had learned in his youth were written.

1'a   He told me the passage in question

· b   to copy into the little book.

2'a   When I heard his natural good-will on the one hand, and realized
as well his devout enthusiasm for the pursuit of divine wisdom,

b   I stretched out my palms to the heavens and gave mighty (albeit
silent) thanks to Almighty God,

a'   Who had sown such great enthusiasm for the pursuit of learning
in the king's heart.

1'b   But when I could find no empty space in the little book

a   in which I might copy the passage—for it was completely filled with
all manner of things—I hesitated slightly, mainly because I was eager
to draw the king's excellent intelligence to a fuller understanding of
passages of Holy Scripture. ...

3 a   just as it is written,

b   'The just man builds on a modest foundation and gradually proceeds
to greater things',

B   or like the busy bee, wandering far and wide over the marshes in
his quest, eagerly and relentlessly assembles many various flowers
of Holy Scripture, with which he crams full the cells of his heart.

C   Now as soon as that first passage had been copied, he was eager to
read it at once and to translate it into English, and thereupon to
instruct many others,

B'   just as we are admonished by the example of that fortunate thief—
who recognized the Lord Jesus Christ—his Lord and indeed Lord
of all things—hanging next to him on the venerable gallows of the
Holy Cross, and petitioned Him with earnest prayers. ... he called
out in a reverential voice, 'Christ, remember me when thou shalt
come into thy kingdom'.

A'1   This thief first began to learn the rudiments of Christian faith on the
gallows; the king likewise (even though in a different way, given his
royal station), prompted from heaven, took it upon himself to begin
on the rudiments of Holy Scripture on St Martin's Day

2 a   and to study these flowers collected here and there from various masters and to assemble them within the body of one little book (even
though they were all mixed up) as the occasion demanded. He
expanded it so much that it nearly approached the size of a psalter.

b   He wished it to be called his *enchiridion* (that is to say, 'hand-book'),
because he conscientiously kept it to hand by day and night. As he
then used to say, he derived no small comfort from it.

3a   But, just as it was written by a certain wise man a long time ago,

b   'The minds of those in whom there is conscious concern for
ruling are ever alert'.

Asser's use of the pluperfect tense in A2a' implies that on Saint Martin's Day, 11 November 887, Alfred's *iuuentus* was past. Reckoning strictly from the twentieth to the fortieth year, Alfred would still have been *in iuuentute* until the following year, 888. But Asser may have intended to relate Alfred's *infantia* in chapters I-III, his *pueritia* in chapters IV-XIV, and his *iuuentus* in chapters XV-XXVII. The second part of the Life, from chapter XXVIII, relates Alfred's *senectus*. His books reflect the changes of interest in these periods: a decorated and perhaps calligraphic manuscript of Old English poetry acquired during his *infantia*, a commonplace book of prayers and psalms kept from his *pueritia* and read throughout his *iuuentus*, and the *Enchiridion* or *Handboc* of extracts from his advanced readings with Asser during his *senectus*.

Near the centre of chapter XIV Asser wrote that by his mother's voice Alfred was *diuina inspiratione instinctus* to strive for his first book. The crux of chapter XXX relates how God *bene uelle instigaret* Alfred to summon scholars to his court. The crux of chapter XXXVI relates the issue of this in Alfred's learning to read and translate Latin into Old English. The two quotations of Biblical texts in the chapter XXX (G2 and G'2) are balanced by two quotations of proverbs in chapter XXXVI (A3b and A'3b). The four great comparisons in the two chapters make a chiasmus: Solomon—the most prudent bee—the most fertile bee—the Repentant Thief. Alfred resembles Solomon, who sought first the Kingdom of God, but he also resembles in his late learning of Latin the Repentant Thief, who in the last moments of his life said, 'Remember me when you come into your Kingdom.'

In chapter XXXI Asser states that Alfred could not read Latin (77.22–26).

> Non enim unquam sine aliquo eorum se esse pateretur—quapropter pene omnium librorum notitiam habebat, quamuis per se ipsum aliquid adhuc de libris intelligere non posset. Non enim adhuc aliquid legere inceperat.

> Indeed he could never tolerate being without one or other of them [the four Mercian scholars]—and accordingly, he acquired some acquaintance with almost all books, even though he could not at this point understand anything in the books by himself. For he had not yet begun to read anything.

In chapter XXXV (87) he states that Alfred began to read and translate Latin on one day.

> Eodem quoque anno saepe memoratus Ælfred Angulsaxonum rex diuino instinctu legere et interpretari simul uno eodemque die primitus inchoauit. Sed ut apertius ignorantibus pateat causam huius tardae inchoationis expedire curabo.

It was also in this year that Alfred, king of the Anglo-Saxons, first began
through divine inspiration to read [Latin] and to translate at the same
time, all on one and the same day. But in order that this process may be
understood more clearly by those who are uninformed, I shall take pains
to explain the reasons for this late start.

There are thirty-two words in the former passage and thirty in the latter.

In chapter XXXII (78) Asser relates Alfred's summoning of two Continental
scholars.

A	Sed cum adhuc nec in hoc quoque regalis auaritia, sed tamen laudabilis, grata esset,
B1	legatos ultra mare ad Galliam magistros acquirere direxit, indeque aduocauit Grimbaldum,
2	sacerdotem et monachum,
3	uenerabilem uidelicet uirum, cantatorem optimum,
4	et omni modo ecclesiasticis disciplinis et in diuina scriptura eruditissimum,
5	et omnibus bonis moribus ornatum;
B'1	Iohannem quoque,
2	aeque presbyterum et monachum,
3	acerrimi ingenii uirum,
4	et in omnibus disciplinis literatoriae artis eruditissimum,
5	et in multis aliis artibus artificiosum.
A'	Quorum doctrina regis ingenim multum dilatatum est, et eos magna potestate ditauit et honorauit.
A	However, since the royal 'greed' (which was entirely praise-worthy!) in this respect was not yet satisfied,
B1	he sent messengers across the sea to Gaul to seek instructors. From there he summoned Grimbald,
2	a priest and monk,
3	and a very venerable man, an excellent chanter,
4	extremely learned in every kind of ecclesiastical doctrine and in the Holy Scriptures,
5	as well as being distinguished by his virtuous behaviour.
B'1	Similarly, John,
2	also a priest and monk,
3	a man of most acute intelligence,
4	immensely learned in all fields of literary endeavour,
5	and extremely ingenious in many other skills.
A'	Through their teaching the king's outlook was very considerably broadened, and he enriched and honoured them with great authority.

There are fourteen words in A and fourteen in A'. There are fifty-six words in B and B', thirty-four in B and twenty-two in B'. The golden section of 56 falls at 34.6 and 21.4.

The chiastic pair to this summoning of two Continental scholars is chapter XXXIV (82–86), the last two annals which Asser derived from the Chronicle, 886 and 887, dealing mostly with Continental history. Grimbald may have supplied much of this information from correspondence with his friends who had remained on the Continent.

The fraud who composed the Oxford interpolation (83b), printed by Stevenson in small type, imitated Asser's style and interpolated the passage at the crux of the two annals 886 and 887.[62]

A 1   Eodem anno exorta est pessima ac teterrima Oxoniae discordia
   2   inter Grymboldum doctissimosque illos uiros ...
B   qui ... formulas ab eodem Grymboldo institutas omni ex parte amplecti recusabant.
C   Per tres annos haud magna fuerat inter eos dissensio ...
D 1   Quod ut sedaret rex ille inuictissimus Ælfredus ... Oxoniam se contulit ...
   2   causas et querelas utrinque illatas audiendo.
E   Caput autem huius contentionis in hoc erat positum ...
D'1   Rex ille inaudita humilitate
   2   utramque partem accuratissime exaudiuit ...
C'   ut mutuam inter se coniunctionem et concordiam tuerentur ...
B'   discessit rex quosque ... esse obtemperaturos et instituta sua amplexuros.
A'1 At Grymboldus ...
   2   tumbam ... transferri curauit ... quae erat facta subter cancellum ecclesiae Diui Petri
   3   in Oxonia.
   2'   Quam quidem ecclesiam idem
   1' Grymboldus exstruxerat ab ipso fundamento de saxo summa cura perpolito.

A 1   In the same year there arose at Oxford a most evil and shameful contention
   2 between Grimbald and those most learned men ...
B   who ... all refused to adopt the rules which had been established by the same Grimbald.
C   For three years there was no great dissension between them ...

62 Stevenson, p. 70. *Asser's Life of King Alfred*, transl. L.C. Jane (London 1926), pp. 65–7.

D 1   And that he might calm this, the unconquered King Alfred ...
      went to Oxford ...

2   hearing the arguments and complaints of each side.

E   Now the origin of this dispute consisted in this ...

D'1 The king with wonderful humility

2   and in detail heard each side ...

C'   urging them to preserve general harmony and concord with one
  ·   another ...

B'   So the king departed thinking that ... they would obey his counsel
      and keep his commands.

A'1 But Grimbald ...

2   took care to remove ... the tomb ... which had been made under
      the chancel of the church of Saint Peter

3   in Oxford.

2'   And, indeed, this church

1'   Grimbald had himself built, with great care and of polished stones,
      from the very foundations.

The interpolation is incredible. As Asser states in chapter XXIV (24.9–10) *ut [Ælfred]*
loquebatur illo tempore lectores boni in toto regno Occidentalium Saxonum non erant he
would hardly write here that the University of Oxford jealously guarded privileges
granted to it before the foundation of Wessex. The Church of Saint Peter in the
East has a documented history only from the Norman period. In early Mediaeval
Latin one wrote of Saint Peter as *Sanctus* or *Beatus* more frequently than as *Diuus*
Petrus. After such anachronisms the discrepant spellings *Grymboldus* and *Ælfredus*
may seem trifling niggles. Yet the interpolation offers valuable evidence that as late
as the seventeenth century someone could recognize and imitate Biblical style.

  At the crux of this part of the Life Asser refers to himself and his people in
an extended chiasmus in chapter XXXIII (79–81).

A 1   His temporibus ego quoque a rege aduocatus ... ad Saxoniam

2   adueni ...

B 1   in uilla regia quae dicitur Dene ...

2   cumque ... susceptus fuissem ...

3   me obnixe rogabat ut deuouerem me suo seruitio et
        familiaris ei essem

4   et omnia quae in sinistrali et occidentali Sabrinae parte
          habebam pro eo relinquerem,

5   quae etiam maiori mihi remuneratione reddere
            pollicebatur. Quod et faceret.

6ai   Respondi ego me talia incaute et temerarie
              promittere non posse;
              iniustum enim mihi uidebatur illa tam sancta
              loca in quibus nutritus et doctus ac coronatus
              fueram ... derelinquere ...

ii	Ad quod ille ait, '... ita ut per sex menses mecum fueris
iii	et tantundem in Britannia'.
b	Ad quod ego taliter respondi nec hoc suauiter et temerarie sine consilio meorum posse promittere.
c	At uero ... promisi
d	me iterum ad eum post sex menses
e	sospite uita
f	reuersurum
g	cum tali responso
h	quod mihi et meis utile
h'	ac sibi placabile esset.
g'	Cumque hoc sibi responsum uideretur probabile,
f'	dato reuertendi pignore statuto tempore ... ad patriam remeauimus.
e'	Sed ... febris infesta me arripuit in qua ... sine aliqua uitae spe laboraui.
d'	Cumque statuto tempore ad eum,
c'	sicut promiseram non peruenissem ...
b'	Discedente igitur infirmitate ex consilio et licentia nostrorum omnium,
a'i	pro utilitate illius sancti loci et omnium in eo habitantium ...
ii	ut per sex menses omni anno cum eo commanerem ...
iii	ut tribus mensibus in Britannia,
ii'	ut tribus in Saxonia commanerem,
i'	et illa adiuuaretur per rudimenta[63] Sancti Degui in omni causa tamen pro uiribus.
C	Sperabant enim nostri minores tribulationes et iniurias ex parte Hemeid regis sustinere ... si ego ad notitiam et amicitiam illius regis qualicunque pacto peruenirem.
D	Illo enim tempore et multo ante omnes regiones dexteralis Britanniae partis ad Ælfred regem pertinebat et adhuc pertinent ... .
C'	Nec in uanum illi omnes regis amicitiam acquisiuerunt ...
B'1a	Cum igitur ad eum aduenissem in uilla regia quae dicitur Leonaford ...
2	susceptus sum
3	et cum eo illa uice octo mensibus in curto mansi ...
4	cumque ab eo frequenter licentiam reuertendi quaererem ...

---

63 For Stevenson's *per* † *rudimenta* Pierre Chaplais suggests *parochia mea*.

5   tradidit mihi duas epistolas in quibus erat multiplex sup-
           putatio omnium rerum quae erant in duobus monasteriis
           ... Cungresbyri et Banuwille ...

A'1   et inde
2   ad propria reuertendi.

A 1   At about this time I too was summoned by the king ... to the
           Saxon land
2   I came ...
B 1   at the royal estate which is called Dean.
2   When I had been warmly welcomed ...
3   he asked me earnestly to commit myself to his service and to become
           a member of his household,
4   and to relinquish for his sake all that I had on the left-hand [northern]
           and western side of the Severn.
5   He promised to pay me greater compensation for it (which indeed
           he was to do).
6ai   I replied that I could not enter such an agreement incautiously and
           without due consideration.
           For it struck me as unfair to abandon those very holy places in which
           I had been brought up, trained, tonsured and eventually ordained ...
   ii   He replied to my remark ... 'whereby you would be with me for
           six months
   iii   and the same length of time in Wales'.
   b   To which I replied in the following terms: that even this I could
           not promise casually and rashly without being able to take the
           advice of my people.
   c   But when ... I promised that I to him
   d   in six months' time,
   e   health permitting
   f   would come back
   g   with an answer
   h   which acceptable to me and my people,
   h'   and agreeable to him would be.
   g'   Since this reply seemed acceptable to him,
   f'   I gave him my undertaking to return at the agreed time ... and
           rode off home.
   e'   However ... I was seized by a violent fever, in which I suffered ...
           without any hope of recovery.
   d'   So when at the agreed time to him
   c'   I had not returned as I had promised ...
   b'   Accordingly, when the illness finally abated, with the understanding
           and consent of all our people,

a'i   for the benefit of that holy place and everyone living there,

ii   on the condition that for six months of every year I would remain with him ...

iii   spending three months in Wales

ii'   and three months in the Saxon land;

i'   thus the latter would derive benefit in every respect from the learning of St David, to the best of my abilities at least.

C   For our people were hoping that, if I should come to Alfred's notice and obtain his friendship through some such arrangement, they might suffer less damaging afflictions and injuries at the hands of King Hyffaidd ...

D   At that time, and for a considerable time before then, all the districts of right-hand [southern] Wales belonged to King Alfred, and still do ...

C'   Nor did all these rulers gain the king's friendship in vain ...

B'1   Therefore, when I arrived in his presence at the royal estate known as Leonaford ...

2   I was honourably received by him,

3   and on that occasion I remained with him at court for eight months ...

4   When I repeatedly sought permission from him to return and was unable to obtain it by any means, and had finally decided to demand this permission no matter what ...

5   he presented me with two documents in which there was a lengthy list of everything which was in the two monasteries Congresbury and Banwell ...

A'1   and from there

2   to return home.

There are thirty-nine words in A, 346 in B, fifty-two in C, 151 in D, forty-three in C', 245 in B' and five in A', together 881. The account is divided nearly into equal halves. From the beginning to the crux, from A to C, there are 437 words, and from the crux to the end, from D to A', 444 words. Part B, in which Asser relates his first meeting with Alfred, divides at the thematic crux. The word *esset* at the end of B6h' is 174th from the beginning of B and 173rd from the end.

Asser implies in this passage that he was the latest scholar to be summoned to Alfred's service and the closest to the king. The model for Alfred's group of seven scholars is found in a list of high officials at I Kings IV 1–6, among whom seven would have been on a mediaeval reckoning in Holy Orders:

Azarias filius Sadoc sacerdos
Helioreph et Ahia filii Sesa scribae
Iosaphat filius Ahilud a commentariis ...

Sadoc autem et Abiathar sacerdotes ...
Zabud filius Nathan sacerdos amicus regis.

Asser may have intended to compare Plegmund with Azarias, Æthelstan and
Werwulf with Helioreph and Ahia, Werferth with Iosaphat, Grimbald and
John with Sadoc and Abiathar, and finally himself (the kinsman of Archbishop
Nobis) with Zabud son of Nathan, the priest and the king's intimate friend.
He may have intended to remind his clerical associates that Moses had blessed
his namesake above all others: *Aser quoque ait 'Benedictus in filiis Aser sit placens
fratribus suis'* (Deuteronomy XXXIII 24).
Chapter XXXVIII (91.28–35) is the crux of the second part of the Life.

> Sed tamen ille solus diuino fultus adminiculo susceptum semel regni
> gubernaculum, ueluti gubernator praecipuus, nauem suam multis opibus
> refertam ad desideratum ac tutum patriae suae portum, quamuis cunctis
> propemodum lassis suis nautis, perducere contendit, haud aliter titubare ac
> uacillare, quamuis inter fluctiuagos ac multimodos praesentis uitae turbines,
> non sinebat.

> Yet once he had taken over the helm of his kingdom, he alone, sustained
> by divine assistance, struggled like an excellent pilot to guide his ship laden
> with much wealth to the desired and safe haven of his homeland, even
> though all his sailors were virtually exhausted; similarly, he did not allow it
> to waver or wander from course, even though the course lay through the
> many seething whirlpools of the present life.

The naval imagery reminds us of that at the crux of the first part of the Life in
chapters XIII and XIV and at the crux of the entire Life in chapters XXVI and XXVII.
The passage in chapter XIV contains sixty-three words, that in chapter XXVI sixty-
eight words, and this passage forty-nine words, together 180, of which the golden
section falls at 111.2 and 68.8. The passages at the cruces of the first part and the
second part contain 112 words, and the passage at the crux of the entire work
contains sixty-eight words. This is hardly accidental; it affords an indication,
among many others, that the entire work is carefully composed and that it is
complete and mathematically fixed, very nearly as it left Asser's pen.

The last part of the Life extends from chapter XXXIX to chapter XLIV
(91.36106.46). It begins and ends with accounts of Alfred's dealings with his civil
servants.

XXXIX (91.36–72)

A1   Nam assidue suos episcopos et comites ac nobilissimos sibique
dilectissimos suos ministros necnon et praepositos

2   quibus post Dominum et regem omnis totius regni potestas,
sicut dignum, subdita uidetur

B   leniter docendo, adulando, hortando, imperando, ad ultimum
inoboedientes, post longam patientiam, acrius castigando,
uulgarem stultitiam et pertinaciam omni modo abominando

C1   ad suam uoluntatem et ad communem totius regni
utilitatem sapientissime usurpabat et annectebat.

2 a   At si inter haec regalia exhortamenta propter pigritiam
populi imperata non implentur, aut tarde incepta
tempore necessitatis ad utilitatem exercentium minus
finita non prouenirent,

b   ut de castellis ab eo imperatis adhuc non inceptis
loquar …

3   tunc contradictores imperialium diffinitionum

4   inani poenitentia pene exinaniti uerecundaban-
tur. Inanem enim poenitentiam scriptura teste
nomino, qua homines innumerabiles nimio
detrimento pluribus insidiis perpetratis saepe
perculsi dolent.

5   Sed quamuis per † hanc rem [? l. exem-
plum],[64] heu, proh dolor, eulogii
miserabiliter contristentur …

4'   Sera igitur poenitentia nimium attriti
poenitent

3'   et regalia [se] praecepta incuriose despexisse dolent
et regalem sapientiam totis uocibus collaudant,

2"a   et quod ante refutauerunt totis uiribus implere
promittunt,

b   id est de arcibus construendis

1'   et ceteris communibus communis regni utilitatibus.

A1   For he carefully and cleverly his bishops and ealdormen and nobles,
and his thegns most dear to him, and reeves as well

2   (in all of whom, after the Lord and the king, the authority of the
entire kingdom is seen to be invested, as is appropriate),

B   by gently instructing, cajoling, urging, commanding, and (in the end,
when his patience was exhausted) by sharply chastising those who
were disobedient and by despising popular stupidity and stubbornness
in every way,

---

64 Keynes & Lapidge, p. 271 n. 226.

C1   exploited and converted to his own will and to the general advan-
      tage of the whole realm.

2 a   But if, during the course of these royal admonitions, the commands
      were not fulfilled because of the people's laziness, or else (having
      been begun too late in a time of necessity) were not finished in time
      to be of use to those working on them

  b   (I am speaking here of fortifications commanded by the king
      which have not yet been begun) ...

3   then those who had opposed the royal commands

4   were humiliated in meaningless repentance by being reduced to vir-
      tual extinction. I say 'meaningles repentance' on the authority of
      Scripture, where numberless persons who had performed foul deeds
      were frequently struck down by a severe calamity and thus had cause
      for sorrow.

5   But even though (to follow up the example of the excellent authority)
      they are, alas, pitifully driven to despair ...

4'   Those who were severely afflicted, therefore, are contrite in untimely
      repentance,

3'   and are sorry that [they] had negligently scorned the royal com-
      mands; now they loudly applaud the king's foresight

2'a   and promise to make every effort to do what they had previously
      refused

  b   that is, with respect to constructing fortresses

1'   and to the other things of general advantage to the whole kingdom.

XLIV (105.10–106.46)

C   Nimirum quia etiam pene omnes illius regionis potentes et nobiles
      ad secularia magis quam ad diuina mentem declinauerunt negotia,
      magis enim unusquisque speciali etiam in secularibus negotiis quam
      communi [utilitate studebat]. Sedebat quoque in iudiciis etiam
      propter nobilium et ignobilium suorum utilitatem ... .

B   'Aut terrenarum potestatum ministeria quae habetis illico dimittatis,
      aut sapientiae studiis multo deuotius docere ut studeatis impero'.
      Quibus auditis uerbis, perterriti [ac] ueluti pro maxima uindicta
      correcti

A1   comites et praepositi ad aequitatis discendae studium totis uiribus se
      uertere nitebantur, ita ut mirum in modum illiterati ab infantia
      comites pene omnes, praepositi ac ministri literatoriae arti studerent,

2   malentes insuetam disciplinam quam laboriose discere quam
      potestatum ministeria dimittere.

C   Not surprisingly, since nearly all the magnates and nobles of that land
      had devoted their attention more to worldly than to divine affairs;

indeed, everyone was more concerned with his own particular well-being in worldly matters than with the common good. King Alfred used also to sit at judicial hearings for the benefit both of his nobles and of the common people ...

B   'I command you either to relinquish immediately the offices of worldly power that you possess, or else to apply yourselves much more attentively to the pursuit of wisdom.' Having heard these words, terrified [and] chastened as if by the greatest of punishments

A'1   the ealdormen and reeves strove with every effort to apply themselves to learning what is just. As a result nearly all the ealdormen and reeves and thegns (who were illiterate from childhood) applied themselves in an amazing way to learning how to read,

2   preferring rather to learn this unfamiliar discipline (no matter how laboriously) than to relinquish their offices of power.

The emendations in chapter XLIV part C, proposed by Wheeler, are corroborated by Asser's Biblical style. Alfred's dealings with his civil servants recall the account of Solomon's ministers at I Kings IV, and his reputation for sound legal judgement recalls Solomon's at I Kings III 28.

The long and complicated chapter XL (92–98), dealing principally with Alfred's monastic foundations, tells nearly everything that we know of John the Old Saxon.

A   De uoto quoque et proposito excellentissimae meditationis suae quam semper inter prospera et aduersa sua nullo modo praetermittere poterat, praetereundum esse hoc in loco utiliter non existimo.

B   Nam cum de necessitate animae suae solito cogitaret, inter cetera † diuturna [l. diurna] et nocturna bona, quibus assidue et maxime studebat, duo monasteria construi imperauit,

C1   unum monachorum in loco qui dicitur Æthelingaeg, quod permaxima gronna paludosissima et intransmeabili et aquis undique circumcingitur, ad quod nullo modo aliquis accedere potest nisi cauticis, aut etiam per unum pontem, qui inter duas [alias] arces operosa protelatione constructus est,

2   in cuius pontis occidentali limite arx munitissima praefati regis imperio pulcherrima operatione consita est,

3a   in quo monasterio diuersi generis monachos undique congregauit et in eodem loco collocauit.

b   Nam primitus

c   quia nullum de sua propria gente nobilem ac liberum hominem,

di   nisi infantes, qui nihil boni eligere nec mali respuere pro teneritudine inualidae aetatis adhuc possunt, qui

     monasticam uoluntarie uellet subire uitam, habebat;
     nimirum quia per multa retroacta annorum curricula
     monasticae uitae desiderium ab illa tota gente ...
     funditus desierat ... nescio quare,

ii   aut pro alienigenarum infestationibus, qui saepissime
       terra marique hostiliter irrumpunt,

ii'   aut etiam pro nimia illius gentis in omni genere
       diuitiarum abundantia,

i'   propter quam multo magis id genus despectae
      monasticae uitae fieri existimo.

a' Ideo diuersi generis monachos in eodem monasterio congregare
   studuit.

b'   Primitus Iohannem, presbyterum [et] monachum, scilicet
    Eald-Saxonum genere, abbatem constituit;

c'   deinde ultramarinos presbyteros quosdam et diaconos. Ex
     quibus cum nec adhuc tantum numerum quantum uellet
     haberet, comparauit etiam quamplurimos eiusdem gentis
     Gallicae

d'i   ex quibus quosdam infantes in eodem monasterio
      edoceri imperauit

ii   et subsequenti tempore ad monachicum habitum
       subleuari.

ii'   In quo etiam monasterio unum paganicae gentis
       edoctum in monachico habitu degentem,

i'   iuuenem admodum uidimus,[65] non ultimum scilicet
      eorum.

D1ai Facinus quoque in eodem monasterio quodam tempore perpetratum

  ii muti taciturnitate silentii obliuioni [non] traderem,

  i' quamuis indignum facinus est,

   ii' quia per totam scripturam impiorum turpia facta inter uenerabilia
    iustorum, sicut zizania et lolium in tritici segetibus interseminantur

 bi   bona scilicet

  ii   ut laudentur, sequantur, aequiparentur,

  iii   sectatores quoque eorum

  iv   omni honore uenerabili digni habeantur,

  i'   mala uero

  ii'   [ut] uituperentur, execrentur, et ut omnino effugiantur,

  iii'   imitatores quoque eorum

  iv'   omni odio et despectione ac uindicta corripiantur.

 2a Nam quodam tempore cum instinctu diabolico quidam sacerdos et
   diaconus Gallici genere ex praefatis monachis inuidia quadam

---

65 Stevenson, pp. 334–5 n. 94,9 suggested that this boy may have been Odo, who later became
 Archbishop of Canterbury.

[latenti][66] excitati contra suum abbatem praefatum Iohannem, nimium latenter in tantum amaricati sunt,

b   ut Iudaico more

c   dominum suum dolo circumuenirent et proderent.

3a   Nam duos eiusdem gentis Gallicae seruulos praemio conductos ita fradulenter docuerunt ut nocturno tempore cum omnes delectabili corporis quiete grauiter dormirent,

b   patefactam armati

c   intrarent ecclesiam; quam post se iterum solito more clauderent

d   et unicum abbatis aduentum in ea absconditi praestolarentur.

e   Cumque solus solito [more]

f   orandi causa

g   ecclesiam latenter intraret

h   et ante sanctum altare flexis ad terram genubus

i   se inclinaret

j   hostiliter irruentes in eum

k   tunc eum ibidem occiderent.

l   Cuius corpus exanime inde trahentes ante ostium cuiusdam meretricis, quasi illic occisus esset in meretricando iactarent. Quod etiam machinauerunt, crimen crimini addentes, sicut dictum est, Et erit nouissimus error peior priore.

4   Sed diuina misericordia, quae semper innocentibus solet subuenire, impiam impiorum meditationem maxima ex parte frustrata est, quo non per omnia euenirent, sicut proposuerant.

3'a   Omni itaque mala doctrina a malis doctoribus malis auditoribus elucubratim exposita et condicta, nocte adueniente atque suppetenti, et impunitate promissa, latrunculi duo

b   armati

c   in ecclesia [se] concluserunt

d   aduentum abbatis praestolantes.

e   Cumque media nocte Iohannes solito [more] furtim, nemine sciente,

f   orandi gratia

g   ecclesiam intrasset

h   et flexis genibus ante altare

i   incuruaret

j   tunc duo illi latrunculi ex improuiso dispoliatis gladiis

k   in eum irrumpunt

---

66 Stevenson, p. 82 n. 96,3 'latenti *om. S[ancti] N[eoti Annales] quod ex* latenter *versu sequenti errore inter scribendum profectum esse suspicatus, seclusi'.*

1   et crudelibus afficiunt uulneribus. Sed
ille ut solito ac semper acris ingenio et,
ut audiuimus de eo a quibusdam refe-
rentibus, bellicosa artis non expers, si in
meliori disciplina non studeret, statim ut
sonitus latronum audiuit, priusquam
uideret, insurgens acriter in eos, antequam uulneratur

2'a et uociferans quantum poterat reluctabatur, inclamitans daemones esse
et non homines; non enim aliter sciebat, quia nec hoc homines ausos
esse existimabat. Uulneratus est tamen antequam sui aduenirent. Sui
ergo hoc rumore expergefacti et etiam, audito daemonum nomine,
perterriti utrique et inexpertes, et etiam illi,

b Iudaico more

c   domini sui proditores, hinc inde ad ecclesiae ostia concurrunt,
sed antequam aduenirent latrunculi praecipiti cursu ad proxi-
mantia sibi gronnae latibula, semiuiuum abbatem relinquentes,
confugiunt.

i'ai Monachi uero seniorem suum semiuiuum colligentes cum gemitu
et moerore domum reportauerunt, sed nec etiam illi dolosi minus
lachrymabantur innocentibus.

ii Sed Dei misericordia tantum facinus

iii   impunitum fieri non permittente,

i' latrunculi qui hoc perpetrauerunt

ii' omnes tanti sceleris persuasores

iii'   capti ligatique per uaria tormenta morte turpissima periere.

b   His ita relatis ad incepta redeamus.

C'1 Aliud quoque monasterium iuxta orientalem portam Sceftesburg,
habitationi sanctimonialium habile,

2 idem praefatus rex aedificari imperauit,

3a in quo propriam filiam suam Æthelgeofu, deuotam Deo
uirginem, abbatissam constituit

b   cum qua etiam aliae multae nobiles moniales

c   in monastica uita Deo seruientes in eodem monasterio
habitant.

B' Quae duo monasteria terrarum possessionibus et omnibus diuitiis
locupletatim ditauit.

A' His ita diffinitis, solito suo more intra semetipsum cogitabat quid
adhuc addere potuisset, quod plus placeret ad piam meditationem;
non inaniter incepta, utiliter inuenta, utilius seruata est.

A At this point I do not think that I can profitably bypass the intention and resolve of his most excellent enterprise, which he never

allowed himself to overlook no matter whether things were going well or badly.

B   For when in his usual manner he had taken stock of what was most essential for his soul, amid his other good deeds performed by day and night (on which he concentrated attentively and fully), he ordered two monasteries to be constructed.

C1   One of these was for monks and was located at a place called Athelney, which is surrounded by swampy, impassable and extensive marshland and groundwater on every side. It cannot be reached in any way except by punts or by a causeway which has been built by protracted labour between two fortresses.

2   (A formidable fortress of elegant workmanship was set up by the command of the king at the western end of the causeway.)

3a   In this monastery he gathered monks of various nationalities from every quarter, and assembled them there.

b   The reason is, at first,

c   that no noble or free-born man of his own race

d i   who would of his own accord undertake the monastic life, except for children, who could not as yet choose good or reject evil because of the tenderness of their infant years—not surprisingly, since for many years past the desire for the monastic life had been totally lacking in that entire race ... I am not sure why:

ii   either it is because of the depredations of foreign enemies whose attacks by land and sea are very frequent and savage,

ii'   or else, because of the people's enormous abundance of riches of every kind,

i'   as a result of which (I suspect) this kind of monastic life came all the more into disrespect.

a'   In any case Alfred took pains to assemble monks of various nationalities in that monastery.

b'   In the first place, he appointed John, a priest [and] monk of Old Saxon origin, as abbot;

c'   and thereafter certain priests and deacons from across the sea. Among these (since he had not yet achieved the number he desired), he acquired a number of people of Gallic origin;

d'i   he ordered that certain of their children be educated in the monastery

ii   and at a later time be raised to the monastic order.

ii'   In that monastery too someone of Viking parentage who had been brought up there, living there in the monastic habit,

i'   I saw, quite a young man—and he was assuredly not the last of them to do so.

D1 a i   On one occasion a crime was perpetrated in that monastery

ii   which I would [not] commit to the oblivion of silence, mute in its taciturnity, i' (even though the crime itself is unworthy to be recorded),

   ii' since throughout scripture the foul deeds of the unrighteous are
       sown among the holy deeds of the righteous, like cockle and tares
       in the crop of wheat:

 bi the good deeds, that is,

  ii so they may be praised, followed, emulated,

 iii and their imitators

 iv may be esteemed worthy of every holy honour;

  i' the evil deeds, on the other hand,

 ii' [that] they may be disparaged, cursed and entirely shunned,

iii' and their imitators

iv' reproached with all hatred, contempt and punishment.

2a   On a particular occasion, then, a priest and a deacon of Gallic origin
      from among those monks mentioned above were aroused by envy at
      the devil's prompting against their abbot, the said John; they were
      secretly embittered to such a degree

 b   that, in the manner of the Jews [rather 'of Judas']

 c   they ambushed and betrayed their lord by treachery.

3a   In their treachery, they instructed two slaves of the same Gallic race
      (who became involved for a bribe) to the effect that, during the
      night when everyone was sleeping soundly in blissful bodily peace,

 b   armed, the unlocked

 c   church they would enter; and would close it again after them in
      the normal way

 d   and, hidden in the church, would await the approach of the abbot;

 e   and when alone, as he usually did,

 f   in order to pray,

 g   the abbot would quietly enter the church

 h   and on the ground in front of the holy altar on bended knees

 i   would lie down,

 j   they would attack him savagely

 k   and kill him on the spot;

 l   then they would drag his lifeless body away and dump it at the door
      of a certain whore, to make it seem as if he had been killed in the
      course of whoring. They devised this plan, adding crime to crime, as
      it is said: 'The last error shall be worse than the first'.

4   But divine mercy, which is always ready to help the innocent,
      frustrated to a large degree this evil plan of evil men, so that every-
      thing did not turn out as they had planned.

3'a When all the evil plan had been clearly expounded and outlined by
      the evil conspirators to their evil accomplices, when the night had
      arrived and was thought propitious, and a promise of impunity had
      been given, two villains

 b   armed

c shut [themselves] in the church
d to await the abbot's arrival.
e At midnight John secretly as usual (so that no one would know)
f in order to pray,
g entered the church,
h and on bended knees before the altar
i bowed down;
j then the two villains suddenly with drawn swords
k attacked him
l and wounded him severely. But he, being a man of customary sharp intelligence and (as I have heard about him from several sources) a man with some experience in the martial arts—had he not set his mind on a higher course—rose briskly to meet them as soon as he heard their commotion and before he saw them or was wounded by them.

2'a He called out and resisted them as best he could, shouting that they were devils and not men: he could not think otherwise, since he did not believe that men would attempt such a thing. However, he was wounded before his own men arrived: they had been awakened by the uproar but, having heard the word 'devils', were frightened and did not know what to do either. They
b (in the manner of the Jews [rather 'of Judas'])
c and the two betrayers of their lord all ran helter-skelter to the doors of the church; but before John's men got there, the villains had fled as quickly as possible to the depths of the nearby marsh, leaving the abbot half-dead.

I'ai The monks picked up their half-dead master and carried him home with lamentation and sadness. Nor did the deceitful conspirators shed fewer tears than the innocent.
ii For such a crime God's mercy
iii was unwilling to go unpunished:
i' the villains who had committed this deed,
ii' as well as all those who had instigated so great a crime,
iii' were captured and bound and underwent a terrible death through various tortures.
b Now that I have reported these events, allow me to return to my proper subject.

C'I The other monastery near the east gate of Shaftesbury as a residence suitable for nuns
2 King Alfred ordered to be built.
3a He appointed as its abbess his own daughter Æthelgifu, a virgin consecrated to God;
b and many other noble nuns with her
c live in the same monastery, serving God in the monastic life.

B'   Alfred abundantly endowed these two monasteries with estates of
land and every kind of wealth.

A'   When these affairs had been settled, he thought to himself in his
usual manner about what more he might add that would be more in
keeping with his holy resolve: and this resolve, initiated not without
profit and profitably conceived, was quite profitably sustained.

Asser writes of Alfred's *meditatio* in A and A', with twenty-seven words in each
passage. He mentions the two monasteries Alfred founded in B and B', considering one of them, at Athelney, and its abbot John the Old Saxon, in C, and
the other, at Shaftesbury, and its abbess Æthelgeofu, in C'. At the crux of this
seven-part chiasmus, in D, he discusses the *indignum facinus* in a seven-part
chiasmus. This narrative has been severely criticized,[67] but it exhibits the same
six-part structure as the narratives of chapters VI, VII, VIII, and XXVI. Asser writes
(first) in D1a that he is about to relate an *indignum facinus* and alludes (second) to
the perennial value of scriptural stories of good and evil. Returning to his own
story he states (third) in D2 the time and the circumstances. Then in a regression
he relates (fourth) the plot in the twelve parts of D3 and (fifth) the miscarriage of
the plot in the twelve parts of D'3. He concludes (sixth) with the issue of this
crime, *tantum facinus*, in D'1, to which he alludes also at the crux.

There are twenty-three words in B and ten in B', 251 in C and forty-two
in C', 206 in D1–3 and 223 in D3'–1', and twenty-three at the crux in D4,
together 778, of which the golden section falls at 480.8 and 297.2. From B to
D3, from the beginning to the crux, there are 480 words, and from D4 to B',
from the crux to the end, there are 298 words.

In chapter XLI (99.4–104.13) Asser considers Alfred as administrator.

A1   Nam iamdudum in lege scriptum audierat
2   Dominum decimam sibi multipliciter redditurum promisisse
atque fideliter seruasse decimamque sibi multipliciter redditurum fuisse.
3   Hoc exemplo instigatus et antecessorum morem uolens
transcendere
4   dimidiam seruitii sui partem
5   diurni scilicet et nocturni temporis ...
6   Deo deuote et fideliter toto cordis affectu pius
meditator se daturum spopondit ...
7   Sed ut solito suo more cautus euitaret quod in
alio diuinae scripturae loco cautum est, 'Si recte
offeras recte autem non diuidas peccas', quod
Deo libenter deuouerat quomodo recte diuidere
posset cogitauit,

67 Keynes & Lapidge, p. 221 n. 110.

8	et ut dixit Salomon, 'Cor regis in manu Domini' id est consilium; consilio diuinitus inuento
9	o mnium uniuscuiusque anni censuum successum bifarie primitus ministros suos diuidere aequali lance imperauit.
B	His ita diuisis
C I	partem primam secularibus negotiis pertinere addixit, quam etiam in tribus partibus sequestrari praecepit
2a	cuius primam diuisionis partem suis bellatoribus annualiter largiebatur ...
b	secundam autem operatoribus ...
c	tertiam autem eiusdem partem aduenis ex omni gente ad eum aduenientibus ...
D	sicut scriptum est, 'Hilarem datorem diligit Deus', hilariter impendebat.
C'I	Secundam uero partem omnium diuitiarum suarum ... in quatuor partibus aequis etiam curiose suos ministros illam diuidere imperauit, ea condicione
2a	ut prima pars illius diuisionis pauperibus uniuscuiusque gentis qui ad eum ueniebant discretissime erogaretur ...
b	secundam autem duobus monasteriis ...
c	tertiam scholae ...
d	quartum circum finitimis in omni Saxonia et Mercia monasteriis ... ecclesiis et seruis Dei inhabitantibus ...
B'	His ita ordinabiliter ab eodem rege dispositis
A'I	memor illius diuinae scripturae sententiae qua dicitur,
2	'Qui uult eleemosynam dare a semetipso debet incipere',
3	etiam quid a proprio corporis sui et mentis seruitio Deo offerret prudenter excogitauit ...
4	dimidiam partem seruitii mentis et corporis ...
5	diurno scilicet ac nocturno tempore
6	suapte totisque uiribus se redditurum Deo spopondit.

7　　　　　　Sed quia distantiam nocturnarum horarum omnino
propter tenebras et diurnarum propter densitatem saepissime pluuiarum et nubium aequaliter dignoscere
non poterat, excogitare coepit qua ratione fixa et sine
ulla haesitatione hunc promissum uoti sui tenorem leto
tenus incommutabiliter Dei fretus misericordia con-
seruare posset.

8　　　　　　　His aliquandiu excogitatis tandem inuento utili
et discreto consilio

9　　　　　　　　　suos capellanos ceram offerre sufficienter imperauit, quam adductam ad denarios pensari in
bilibri praecepit; cumque tanta cera mensurata
fuisset quae septuaginta duos denarios pensaret,
sex candelas, unamquamque aequa lance, inde
capellanos facere iussit … .

A 1　For he had once heard a passage in scripture
2　to the effect that the Lord had promised to repay His tithe many
times over, and had faithfully kept this promise.
3　Encouraged by this example and desiring to excel the practice of
his predecessors,
4　one half of his service
5　both by day and by night …
6　this man of holy resolve promised devoutly and faithfully with all
his heart to give to God …
7　But in order that, in his usual way, he might be able to avoid what
we are cautioned against in another passage of Holy Scripture—'If
thou offer aright, but dost not divide aright, thou sinnest'—he
considered how he might justly divide what he had generously
promised to God.
8　As Solomon says: 'The heart of the king' (that is, his wisdom) 'is in
the hand of the Lord'. Having received this wisdom from on high,
9　Alfred commanded his thegns to divide the revenue from all taxa-
tion in any one year into two equal parts in the first instance.
B　When the revenues had been divided in this way,
C 1　he decreed that the first part should be reserved for secular affairs.
He ordered this in turn to be divided into three portions.
2a　He paid out the first portion every year to his fighting men …
b　The second portion he gave to his craftsmen …
c　He paid out the third portion to foreigners of all races who came
to him …
D　As it is written, 'God loveth a cheerful giver'—with a cheerful
disposition he paid out.

C'1 The second part of all his riches ... he instructed his thegns to divide carefully into four equal portions, on the understanding

  2a that the first portion of the subdivision would be judiciously expended on the poor of every race who came to him. ...

    b The second portion he bestowed on the two monasteries ... .

    c The third portion was to be given to the school ... .

    d He gave the fourth portion to neighbouring monasteries throughout the Saxon land and Mercia; and ... to churches and the servants of God dwelling within them ... .

B' When the king had systematically arranged these matters in this way,

A'1 being mindful of the saying of Holy Scripture that

  2 'he who wishes to give alms ought to begin from himself',

  3 he reflected thoughtfully on what he might offer to God in the way of service of his own body and mind ...

  4 one half of his mental and bodily effort

  5 both by day and night

  6 he had promised to render to God, of his own accord and with all his strength.

  7 But because he could not in any way accurately estimate the duration of the night hours because of darkness, nor of the day-time hours because of the frequent density of rain and cloud, he began to reflect on how he might be able (sustained by God's mercy) to preserve the substance of his vow unfailingly until he died, by means of some enduring principle, without any kind of uncertainty.

  8 When he had thought about these things for some time, he at last hit upon a useful and intelligent solution.

  9 He instructed his chaplains to produce an ample quantity of wax, and when they had brought it, he told them to weigh it against the weight of pennies on a two-pound balance. When a sufficient amount of wax, equivalent in weight to seventy-two pennies, had been measured out, he told the chaplains to make ... .

In A2 he paraphrases Saint Ambrose and in A'2 his pupil Saint Augustine of Hippo. In both A7 and A'7 he considers correct division of offerings. There are fourteen subdivisions on either side of the crux.

Plummer 'wholly and entirely' distrusted Asser's account of Alfred's sevenfold division of revenues, affirming that 'at this point of his work Asser was attacked by an acute fit of imagination'.[68] But here, as elsewhere, Alfred adapted his policy and Asser his narrative to a Biblical model, as comparison with I Kings V 13–4 shows clearly.

legitque rex Salomon operas de omni Israhel et erat indictio triginta milia uirorum mittebatque eos in Libanum, decem milia per menses singulos

68 Plummer, *Alfred*, p. 130.

uicissim, ita ut duobus mensibus essent in domibus suis; in tribus namque
cohortibus praefati regis satellites prudentissime diuidebantur, ita ut prima
cohors uno mense in curto regio die noctuque administrans commoraretur
menseque finito et adueniente alia cohorte prima domum redibat et ibi
duobus propriis quiuis necessitatibus studens commorabatur mensibus.

In chapter XLII (104.13–36) Asser relates Alfred's invention of the horn lantern,
with which one may compare Solomon's construction of lamps and lampstands
in I Kings VII 49, and in chapter XLIII (105.1–10) Alfred's defence of the poor.
Chapter XLIV, the pair to chapter XXXIX, ends this part of the Life, and chapter
XLV, the chiastic pair to chapter XXVIII, ends the entire work.
Here is an outline of the whole Life.

Part I

3	A	I	(1)	Genealogy
	B	II	(2)	Mother's ancestry
	C	III	(3.1–10.9)	Chiastic annals 851–855, Alfred's royal anointing by the pope at the crux
6	D1	IV	(11.1–6)	Donation of Æthelwulf
	2	V	(11.6–10)	Alfred's journey to Rome
	3	VI	(11.10–13.8)	Æthelwulf's marriage to Judith and Æthelbald's usurpation
	3'	VII	(13.8–15.26)	Æthelwulf's policy toward Judith and Eadburh's scandal
	2'	VIII	(16.1–12)	Æthelwulf's will after returning from Rome
	1'	IX	(16.12–38)	Æthelwulf's benefaction
9	E	X	(17)	Æthelbald's uncanonical marriage to Judith
	F	XI	(18.1–19.5)	Æthelbald's and Æthelbryht's burials at Sherborne
	G	XII	(20)	The Danes in Kent (a chiasmus)
	H	XIII	(21.1–9)	The Danes' arrival in East Anglia
	I	XIV	(21.9–25.17)	Echo of Einhard, naval imagery, Alfred and the poetry manuscript
	H'	XV	(26)	The Danes' departure from East Anglia

	G'	XVI	(27)	The Danes in Northumbria (chiasmus and parallelism)
	F'	XVII	(28)	Ealhstan's burial at Sherborne
	E'	XVIII	(29.1–6)	Alfred's canonical marriage to Ealhswith
6	D'1	XIX	(29.6–12)	Alfred's mother-in-law Eadburh
	2	XX	(30.1–46.12)	Victory at Ashdown
	3	XXI	(46.12–51.4)	Naval victory of 875
	2'	XXII	(52.1–58.5)	Victory at Countisbury
	3'	XXIII	(59.1–68.9)	Naval victory of 882
	1'	XXIV	(68.9–70.11)	Alfred's stepmother Judith
3	C'	XXV	(71)	Alfred's relationship with the pope
	B'	XXVI	(72)	The Danes in East Anglia, echo of Einhard, naval imagery, Alfred's wife
	A'	XXVII	(75.1–15)	Alfred's descendants

Part II

	A	XXVIII	(75.16–31)	Education of children at the court school
9	B 1	XXIX	(76.1–9)	Alfred's construction amidst difficulties
	2	XXX	(76.9–77.24)	Love of wisdom, summoning of scholars to the court, translation into Old English, comparison of Alfred with Solomon and the most prudent bee
	3	XXXI	(77.22–26)	Alfred's inability to read Latin
	4	XXXII	(78)	Summoning of Continental scholars Grimbald and John
	5	XXXIII	(79–81)	Summoning of Asser
	4'	XXXIV	(82–86)	Continental history, annals 886–887
	3'	XXXV	(87)	Alfred's ability to read and translate Latin
	2'	XXXVI	(88.1–90.12)	Love of wisdom, learning with the king's scholar, translation into Old English, comparison of Alfred with the Repentant Thief and the most fertile bee
	1'	XXXVII	(91.1–28)	Alfred's construction amidst difficulties
	C	XXXVIII	(91.28–35)	Naval imagery
6	B' 1	XXXIX	(91.36–72)	Alfred's dealings with his civil servants
	2	XL	(92–98)	Alfred's monastic foundations
	3	XLI	(99.4–104.13)	Alfred as administrator

3'	XLII	(104.13–36)	Alfred as inventor
2'	XLIII	(105.1–10)	Alfred as defender of the poor
1'	XLIX	(105.10–106.46)	Alfred's dealings with his civil servants
A'	XLV	(106.46–63)	Education of older men in Alfred's service

This outline and the analyses which underlie it give solid grounds for revising earlier perceptions of the structure of the Life.[69] There is one chapter of Asser's Life for each year of Alfred's life at the time of presentation, forty-five in 893. The source of this figure, as of so much else, is the life of Solomon, who reigned for forty years (I Kings XI 42 and II Chronicles IX 30). Because of the anointing by Pope Leo in 853 Alfred had been by 893 a king for forty years. The golden section of 45 falls at 27.8 and 17.2. The first part of the Life comprises twenty-seven chapters, IX–XVII, and the second part eighteen chapters, XXVIII–XLV. The golden section of 18 falls at 11 and 7. The eleventh chapter of the second part of the Life is the crucial chapter XXXVIII, which is linked by its naval imagery and by the golden section to the crucial chapter of the first part of the Life and to the crux of the entire Life. There is not a single 'sprawling sentence' or 'confusing exposition' which lacks an intelligible structure. Nearly every alleged obscurity or infelicity can be clarified by comparing the passage in question with its parallel or chiastic pair. Allowing for difficulties that remain in a text transmitted to us by a single manuscript burned in 1731, we have in the Life of King Alfred not an incomplete draft, but a finished work, and not from the clumsy hand of a dim pretentious hack with an infirm grasp of Latin, but from the poised pen of a biographer capable of coherent thought and masterly organization on a grand scale.

Stevenson noted 'hints suggestive of any knowledge of the Continent'[70] found in the Life but not in the Anglo-Saxon Chronicle at the corresponding passages. He drew attention to the marked strain of Frankish Latinity in the Life and listed parallels with and borrowings from Einhard's Life of Charlemagne, Thegan's Life of Louis the Pious, and the anonymous astronomer's Life of the same emperor.[71] In his critical apparatus to chapter XV (26) he noted that Wise had reported of the phrase Anno Dominicae Incarnationis DCCCLXVII, natiuitatis Ælfredi praefati regis decimo nono, 'MS. Cott. habuit Karoli, sed deletur'.[72] All of these features, and their cumulative weight is considerable, imply that Asser worked closely with Grimbald the Frank before and after compilation of the Chronicle.

The prominence given in this Life to the Franks and the Welsh, and specifically to Grimbald and Asser, implies that the two men considered themselves central figures at the court. The greater influence may have been from Grimbald to Asser, but both men knew the Bible thoroughly; both based their work upon

---

69 Most recently that of Keynes & Lapidge, pp. 55–6.
70 Stevenson, p. lxxviii.
71 Ibid. pp. lxxx–lxxxii, xciii–xciv. These are mostly conjectural. Only the borrowings from Einhard are certain.
72 Ibid. p. 22.

Biblical models and used both explicit quotations and implicit allusions to good effect. By noting Asser's literal references to his own compositional techniques, by heeding his specific references and comparisons, by following his subtler hints and suggested leads, one can begin to appreciate the compactness and density and comprehensive unity of this text. Now, 1100 years after publication, Asser's work may begin to receive the understanding it so richly deserves.

X. 'NINNIUS'

Prologue to the Historia Brittonum

The *Historia Brittonum* is a ninth-century pseudo-historical compilation, which survives in eight recensions, among them an eleventh-century 'Nennian Recension',[1] which begins

> *Incipit eulogium breuissimum Brittannie insule quod Ninnius, Eluodugi discipulus, congregauit.* Ego Ninnius, Eluodugi discipulus, aliqua excerpta scribere curaui que hebitudo gentis Brittannie deiecerat, quia nullam peritiam habuerunt neque ullam commemorationem in libris posuerunt doctores illius insule Brittannie. Ego autem coaceruaui omne quod inueni tam de annalibus Romanorum quam de cronicis sanctorum patrum (id est Ieronimi Eusebii Isidori Prosperi) et de annalibus Scottorum Saxonumque, et ex traditione ueterum nostrorum quod multi doctores atque librarii scribere temptauerunt. Nescio quo pacto difficilius reliquerunt an propter mortalitates frequentissimas uel clades frequentissimas bellorum. Rogo ut omnis lector qui legerit hunc librum, det ueniam michi quia †cuius† sum post tantos hec tanta scribere quasi garrula auis uel quasi quidam inualidus arbiter. Cedo illi qui plus nouerit in ista peritia satis quam ego. *Explicit eulogium.*

[Here] begins a very short text [or 'most concise praise'] of the island of Britain, which Ninnius, a pupil of Elfoddw, gathered.

I, Ninnius, a pupil of Elfoddw, have taken care to write certain excerpts which the dullness of the British race let fall [or 'the stupidity of the British people threw away'], because the teachers of that island of Britain had no learning and they did not put any memory [or 'written record'] in books. But I have heaped together all that I have found, as much from the annals of the Romans as from the chronicles of the holy fathers (that is, of Jerome,

---

1   BCLL 130. *Historia Britonum cum additamentis Nennii*, ed. T. Mommsen, *Monumenta Germaniae Historica, Auctorum Antiquissimorum Tomi XIII Pars I* (Berlin 1894), pp. 111–222. *L'Historia Britonum*, ed. E. Faral, *La Légende Arthurienne, Études et Documents, Première Partie, Les Plus Anciens Textes* (Paris 1969), vol. III II pp. 1–62. *"Nennius": British History and the Welsh Annals*, ed. & transl. J. Morris, History from the Sources (London & Chichester 1980). The text is from D.N. Dumville, 'Nennius and the *Historia Brittonum*', *Studia Celtica* X–XI (1975–6), pp. 78–95, at 79–80. The translation is mine.

Eusebius, Isidore, Prosper), and from the annals of the Scots [*i.e.* Irish] and
the Saxons [*i.e.* English], and what many teachers and scribes have tried to
write from the tradition of our ancient ['men' or 'things']. By what
arrangement I do not know, whether because of very frequent plagues or
very frequent disasters of wars, they have left it rather intractable. I ask that
every reader who may read this book grant pardon to me because after
such great men I have ['dared' or 'attempted'] to write these, such great,
things, like a twittering bird or ineffectual onlooker. I yield to him who
may know rather more in this learning than I.
[Here] ends the text.

Dr Dumville has suggested that this *Eulogium* is the work of an eleventh-
century forger attributing the *Historia Brittonum* to Nemniuus, a learned pupil of
the scholarly eighth-century Welsh bishop Elfoddw, who was apparently responsible for the conformity of the Welsh churches in the dispute about calculation of
Easter. Let us read it as a monument in Biblical style, noting capital letters and
punctuation marks from Cambridge, Corpus Christi College, MS 139 folio 167va.

A	**Incipit eulogium breuissimum Brittánnie ínsule .**
	quod Ninnius Eluodugi discípulus còngregáuit.
B 1	Égo Nínnius Eluodúgi discípulus
2	aliqua excerpta scríbere curáui .
3	que hebitudo gentis Brittánnie deiécerat :
4	quia nullam perítiam hàbuérunt :
	neque ullam commemorationem in líbris posuérunt
5	doctores illius ínsule Brittánnie .
1'	Ego autem
2'	cóaceruáui
3'	ómne quod inuéni
4'	tam de annálibus Ròmanórum
	quam de cronicis sanctorum patrum .
	(id est Ieronimi . Eusebii . Isidori . Prosperi .)
	et de annalibus Scottórum . Saxonúmque .
	et ex traditione uéterum nostrórum .
5'	quod multi doctores atque librarii scríbere tèmptauérunt.
C	Nescio quo pacto difficílius rèliquérunt
D	an propter mortalitates fréquentíssimas :
D'	uel clades frequentíssimas bellórum .
C'	Rogo ut omnis lector qui légerit hunc líbrum .
B'1	det uéniam míchi .
2	quia † cuius† [? l. ausus uel conatus] sum post tantos hec tánta scríbere
3	quasi gárrula áuis .
3'	uel quasi quidam inuálidus árbiter ?

   2'   Cedo illi qui plus nouerit in ista perítia

   1'   sátis quam égo .

A' **Éxplicit eulógium .**

The Incipit in A is balanced by the Explicit in A'. The first word of B1 as of B'1 is *ego*, and the last word of B'1' is *ego*. The prose exhibits rhythm and alliteration and rhyme, parallel and chiastic composition, and mathematically determined disposition of diction. The 116 words of the *Eulogium* proper divide by extreme and mean ratio at 71.69 and 44.31. From *doctores* B5 to *post tantos* [*sc. doctores*] B'2 inclusive there are seventy-one words. Those seventy-one words divide by symmetry at 36. Between *doctores* B5 and *doctores* B'5 there are thirty-six words. From *scribere* B2 to *scribere* B'2 inclusive there are ninety-one words, which divide by extreme and mean ratio at 56 and 35. Between *scribere* B2 and *scribere* B5' there are fifty-six words. From *libris* B4 to *librum* C' inclusive there are sixty-six words, which divide by extreme and mean ratio at 40 and 25. Between *libris* B4 and *librariis* B5' there are forty words. The author of this paragraph was well aware of the tradition of composition in Biblical style.

XI. *Vita Prima Sancti Neoti*

The most recent editor of the *Vita Prima Sancti Neoti* has inferred from the author's reference to England as *Brittannia Anglica*, from his familiarity with the topography of Cornwall and his ignorance of the topography of East Anglia, from his use of Old English sources and his conformity with Cornish orthographic tradition that he was a mid-eleventh-century 'British-speaking native of Cornwall who had spent long enough in Anglo-Saxon schools to learn to read Old English and to adopt the Anglo-Saxon practice of writing Latin ostentatiously'.[1] Here is his Prologue,[2] in which capital letters and punctuation marks in boldface represent features of British Library, MS Additional 38130 folio 1r. <u>Underlinings</u> suggest alliterations and *italics* rhymes. I have marked the cursus rhythms.

INCIPIT PROLOGUS IN VITAM BEATISSÍMI NÉO*TI*

	a	6	17	37

ABBATIS GLORIOSI CÓNFESSORIS XPÍS*TI* . a 4 13 32

BEATI NEOTI C<u>O</u>NFESSORIS VITAM

   <u>c</u>ompendioso aggrediens obediéntiae tí*tulo* .   b 8 30 64

   <u>o</u>mnipotentis Dei misericordiarum fóntem ex<u>p</u>ós*tulo*   b 5 20 45

1   BCLL 117. *Vita Prima Sancti Neoti*, ed. M. Lapidge, *The Anglo-Saxon Chronicle*, eds D. Dumville & S. Keynes (Cambridge 1985), vol. XVII pp. cix-cxi.

2   Ibid. p. 111. I have followed Lapidge in restoring the etymologically correct second *b* in *abbatis*. For Lapidge's *e* I have represented the *e caudata* of the manuscript as *ae* in *caelesti* 5 and *iactantiae* 11 and normalized to *obedientiae* 3.

```
quatinus qui eundem sanctum caelesti adiunxit
      cóntubérnio :                                    5   c   7   20  51
michi huiusmodi opere indigno . ac merciarum
      sarcínis aggrauáto :                                 c   8   24  54
sua exuberanti dignetur pietate áttribúere                 d   5   19  38
de tam uenerabili uiro qué a fidélibus                     e   7   15  32
haud ambigua tradita súnt relatióne [? l. relatiónibus]    e   5   14  34
digne pro uíribus deprómere .                         10   d   4   10  24
et pompose iactantiae fómitem èuitáre .                    f   5   15  33
ac pariter hunc contra cuncta aduersantia
      suffragatórem habitáre.                              f   8   23  57
ÉXPLICIT PRÓLOGUS.                                         e   2    6  16
                                                      6  74  226 517
```

The Prologue begins On the Life of most blessed Neot
the glorious abbot, confessor of Christ.

Approaching the life of the blessed confessor Neot under
      the compendious title of obedience
I beseech the fountain of the mercies of omnipotent God
that He Who has joined the same saint to the celestial crew   5
may deem worthy in His own overflowing piety to assign   7
to me for a work of this kind, unworthy and weighed down by
      the burdens of duties,   6
to utter worthily according to [my] powers   10
those hardly doubtful things about so venerable a man which   8
have been handed down by faithful relatings   9
and to avoid the sin of ostentatious display   11
and to have him continually as a supporter in the same manner
      against all opposing things.   12
The Prologue ends.

The Prologue is composed in consistently rhyming rhythmical prose. The ten
words of the Incipit divide by symmetry at 5 and 5, by extreme and mean ratio at
6 and 4, by duple ratio at 7 and 3, at *beatissimi* | *Neoti* | *abbatis*. The ten lines of the
Prologue proper divide by symmetry at 5 and 5, by extreme and mean ratio at 6
and 4, by duple ratio at 7 and 3. The sixty-two words divide by symmetry at 31
and 31, by extreme and mean ratio at 38 and 24, by duple ratio at 41 and 21. The
central thirty-first word at the middle of the central line 5 is *dignetur*. The golden
section falls in the fourth line at the twenty-fourth word *indigno*, illustrating
extreme and mean ratio of both lines and words. Between that and *digne* in the
third line from the end there are twenty-one words, illustrating duple ratio of both
lines and words. Those twenty-one words divide by duple ratio at 14 and 7. The
seventh word after *indigno* is *dignetur*, between which and *digne* there are fourteen

words. The author refers to himself also at the duple ratio of lines and words, *michi* after the third line, in the seventh line from the end, the twenty-first word.

Although there is no point in denying Anglo-Saxon influence upon this author, it will be obvious from texts already considered that he composed in a tradition of Biblical style practised by writers from Celtic-speaking lands through seven centuries.

XII. *Vita Sanctae Wenefredae*

Here follows the Incipit and Prologue to a Life of a seventh-century Welsh virgin martyr Saint Gwenfrewi or Wenefred.[1] Capital letters and punctuation marks in boldface represent features of London, British Library, MS Cotton Claudius A v folio 138rb-va.

INCIPIT VITA SANCTE WENEFREDE[a]
VIRGINIS ET MARTYRIS.

Quanto *opere* regis archanum operíre salúbre *est* :
tanto *opere*[b] Dei magnalia non reuelare tórmentuósum *est* .
Quam ob rem[c] quicquid de beata **W**enefreda fauente Deo . nobis
traditione ueterum mánifestátum *est* :
ad laudem ipsius Dei et ad uirginis sue merita declaranda ut pote dígnum
est ìnchoándum .

a MS Wenfrede. b MS tantopere. c MS quamobrem.

HERE BEGINS THE LIFE OF SAINT WENEFRED
VIRGIN AND MARTYR

In as far as it is salutary to conceal the secret of a king
in so far is it painful not to disclose the mighty works of God.
Wherefore whatever is known to us by God's favour from the tradition
of our forefathers concerning the blessed Wenefred
is meet we should undertake to recount to the praise of God Himself in
declaring the merits of His virgin.

In the Incipit to the *Vita Sanctae Wenefredae* there are seven words, eighteen syllables, and forty-four letters. There are three words before and three words after the central word, the name of the saint. There are seven syllables before the name and seven syllables after it. The eighteenth letter from the beginning is the *W* of *Wenefrede*, and after the final *e* there are eighteen letters to the end of the

---

1   BCLL 115. *Vitae Sanctorum Britanniae et Genealogiae*, ed. & transl. A.W. Wade-Evans (Cardiff 1944), pp. 288–9.

Incipit. There is one letter of the Incipit for each word of the Prologue, which contains four lines, forty-four words, 106 syllables, and 241 letters. The central twenty-second word is the name *Wenefreda*; the central fifty-third syllable is the last of *Wenefreda*; the central 121st letter is the last of *Wenefreda*. The forty-four words divide by extreme and mean ratio at 27 and 17, at the author's reference to his source, *nobis traditione ueterum | manifestatum est*. From *Dei* to *Dei* inclusive there are twenty-four words, which divide by extreme and mean ratio at 15 and 9. From *Dei* to *Deo* inclusive there are fifteen words, whence to *Dei* inclusive there are nine words. The rhythm, rhyme, and alliteration are noteworthy, especially the nine consecutive vowel rhymes of the first two lines.

XIII. *Vita Sancti Paterni*

Sanctus Paternus or Saint Padarn was a fifth- or sixth-century Welsh monk and bishop, founder of Llanbadarn Fawr celebrated in Radbod's letter and in Ieuan ap Sulien's poem.[1] The editor of the *Vita Sancti Paterni* which follows believed that it issued from Llanbadarn Fawr and that

> it dates from about 1120, when it was being pretended that St Teilo had been diocesan bishop of Morgannwg, as St David of Rheinwg, and St Padarn of Seisyllwg. Whatever success had been expected to attend such inventions in favour of a diocesan bishop at Llanbadarn Fawr was shattered by the time this Life was composed.[2]

Capital letters and punctuation marks in boldface represent features of British Library, MS Cotton Vespasian A XIV folio 8ov.

INCIPIT VITA SANCTI PATERNI EPISCOPI .

§ 1	**X**pist*us*		a	1
	fili*us* Dè*i* uíu*i*		b	3
	terci*a* **T**rinitatis diuíne Persón*a*		c	4
	c̲oeternus et c̲onsubstancialis Patri et S̲píritui S̲áncto		d	7
	dedit hoc p̲receptum e̲cclesie . u̲t a̲ffectantius p̲rouocaret			
	hominum mentes ád religiónem :	5	e	11 (4+7)
	p̲ollicendo illis géminam mercéde*m* .		e	
	íd est hic centúplu*m* .		e	
	et uitam etérnam in futúr*o*.		d	
	Lucas uéro euàngelíst*a*		c	
	discipul*us* sanct*i* Paúl*i* apóstol*i* .	10	b	
	medicus córporis et ánime			

---

1   See above pp. 233–42.
2   *BCLL* 103. *Vitae Sanctorum Britanniae et Genealogiae*, ed. & transl. A.W. Wade-Evans (Cardiff 1944), pp. xii–xiii (introduction) and 252–3 (text).

hoc preceptum ob communem Xpistianórum salùtem scrípsit.
Talis autem est sensus ístius precépti.
Qui propter regnum Dei accipiendum omnes afféctus contémserit .
et omnes seculi diuicias luxúsque calcáuerit :   15
multo plura in presénti recípiet .
quam a fratribus atque consortibus propósiti súi .
qui ei spirituali glútino còlligántur.
Multo graciorem etiam in hac uita caritátem recípiet.
Hanc siquidem caritatem quam inter paréntes ac fílios 20
atque germanos . et cóniuges . èt propínquos .
siue societas copule . seu consanguinitatis necessitúdo coniúngit .
satis breuem constat ésse ac frágilem .
Qui igitur propter regnum Dei temporália spérnunt .
etiam in hac uita eiusdem regni gaudia certa fide degústant :
atque in expectatione pátrie celéstis .
omnium pariter electorum sincerissima dilectióne fruúntur.

§ 2   Ex quibus est sanctus Patérnus epíscopus .
qui terrenam hereditátem derelínquens
ac exilium uísitans súmmum   30
regni celestis fieri héredem .
atque cíuem concupíuit .
Qui gente quidem Armóricus fúit .
parentibus autem nobílibus órtus est .
Petrano scilicet patre . Mátre uero Guéan .   35
Qui uno conuéntu uténtes :
genuerunt sánctum Patérnum .
Postea uero se sempiterno Deo seruicio dédicauérunt .
Nam Petranus ilico Letáuiam déserens .
Hibérniam èxpetíuit .   40
Graciosa itaque apparuit natiuitas sáncti Patérni .
per quam pater eius sánctus efféctus est .
et mater eius famula Xpísti effécta .
religiosam uitam dúxit in etérnum.
Conuenienti igitur ordine a Déo preuísum est .   45
ut sicut Xpístus ex súmmo Pátre .
Déus de Déo .
Lumen de Lúmine órtus est .
ita Paternus sanctus ex sanctis paréntibus nàscerétur .
Ilico enim ut natus est ille : Xpistum séqui elégerunt .   50

Here begins the life of saint Padarn bishop.

Christ, the son of the living God, the third Person of the divine Trinity, coeternal and consubstantial with the Father and the Holy Spirit, gave this precept to the Church, that he might incite the minds of men with greater zeal to religion, promising them a double reward, that is, here a hundred-fold, and hereafter life eternal. And Luke the evangelist, the disciple of saint Paul the apostle, a physician of body and soul, wrote this precept for the common salvation of Christians. The purport of this precept is of such a kind. He who to obtain the kingdom of God shall despise all desires, and shall tread under foot all the riches of the world and luxuries, shall receive far more in the present time, as from the brethren and comrades of his prior, who are bound to him in a spiritual tie. A far more gracious love also shall he receive in this life, seeing that it is agreed that love which, whether the social bond or the necessity of blood relationship joins together as between parents and children and brethren and wives and neighbours, is sufficiently brief and fragile. Who, therefore, for the kingdom of God spurn temporal things, do even in this life by sure faith taste the joys of that same kingdom, and in the expectation of the heavenly country do enjoy the most sincere love equally with all the elect.

Of whom is saint Padarn, bishop, who abandoning an earthly inheritance and seeing complete exile, desired to become heir of the heavenly kingdom and citizen. Who by race was an Armorican, and was born of noble parents, to wit, from Petran, his father, and Guean, his mother. These availing themselves of one connexion begot saint Padarn. But afterwards they dedicated themselves in service to the eternal God. For Petran straightway leaving Letavia went to Ireland. Gracious, therefore, was the birth of saint Padarn, whereby his father was made a saint, and his mother made a handmaid of Christ, led a religious life for ever. Therefore it was foreseen by God in harmonious sequence that as Christ was sprung from the supreme Father, God of God, Light of Light, so saint Padarn was born of holy parents. For straightway that he was born, they elected to follow Christ.

Each of these first two paragraphs exhibits internal chiastic structure.

1	regnum Dei
2	etiam in hac uita
3	caritatem
3'	caritatem
2'	etiam in hac uita
1'	eiusdem regni

1	Sanctus Paternus ... gente ... Armoricus fuit parentibus autem nobilibus
2	ortus est
3	Petrano scilicet patre matre uero Guean

4	Sanctum Paternum
5	Nam Petranus ilico Letauiam deserens
5'	Hiberniam expetiuit
4'	Sancti Paterni
3'	pater eius sanctus effectus est et mater eius famula Xpisti effecta
2'	ortus est
1'	Paternus Sanctus ex sanctis parentibus nasceretur

The two paragraphs are linked by a larger chiasmus.

A	Xpistus filius Dei uiui ... coeternus ... Patri et Spiritui Sancto
B	ad religionem ... et uitam eternam
C	Sancti
D1	parentes
2	societas copule
3	coniungit
E	regnum Dei
F	temporalia spernunt
G	in expectatione patrie celestis omnium pariter electorum sincerissima dilectione fruuntur
F'	terrenam hereditatem derelinquens
E'	regni celestis
D'1	parentibus
2	uno conuentu
3	utentes
C'	Sancti
B'	religiosam uitam duxit in eternum
A'	Xpristus ex Summo Patre Deus de Deo Lumen de Lumine ortus est ... Xpistum

One notes that the first phrases of the first paragraph are composed on a Lucas series of 1–3–4–7–11 words and that the first word of the third phrase is *tercia*. One observes further the rhythm, alliteration, and rhyme, specifically the chiastic rhyme scheme of the first ten lines and the internal chiastic rhyme of line 35, *Petrano scilicet patre . Mâtre uero Guéan ., ean – o – atre – atre – o – ean*. One sees also that the prose exhibits sesquitertian ratio repeatedly. The 157 words of the first paragraph divide by sesquitertian ratio at 90 and 67. The smaller part of sixty-seven words extends from the beginning *Xpistus* to *regnum Dei*, the first part of the chiasmus. Within this passage note *hoc preceptum, hoc preceptum, istius precepti*, sixty-three words inclusive, which divide by sesquitertian ratio at 36 and 27. From *hoc preceptum* to *hoc preceptum* inclusive there are thirty-six words. Before the first *hoc preceptum* there are sixteen words, and after the second *hoc preceptum* there are eleven words, together twenty-seven, which divide by sesquitertian ratio at 15.43 and 11.57. The 119 words of the second paragraph divide by sesquitertian ratio at 68 and 51, at the beginning of the crux of the chiasmus, at *Nam Petranus ilico Letauiam deserens, Nam* being the sixty-eighth word from the end of the paragraph. The two paragraphs together occupy 276 words, which divide by sesquitertian ratio at 158 and 118, at the first word of the second paragraph, *Ex | quibus.*

The author's arrangement of *tercia* as the first word of the third clause draws attention not only as a structural phenomenon, but as a matter of some theological interest. A writer who describes Christ as 'Third Person of the divine Trinity' must imply that the Second Person is the Holy Spirit.[3] Such a statement suggests belief not only in the Holy Spirit as begetter of Jesus Christ in the Virgin Mary but in the Holy Spirit as proceeding from the Father. That implies, at the least, nonconformity with the teaching of double procession from the Father and the Son, as required by Theodore Archbishop of Canterbury at the Synod of Hatfield on 17 September 679,[4] and reluctance to affirm the *Filioque* clause, interpolated into the Creed of the Western Church at the time of Charlemagne.[5] It would be difficult to imagine public profession of this view by any prominent English churchman during or after the archiepiscopate of Theodore or by any prominent Welsh churchman during or after the archiepiscopate of Lanfranc. Affirmation of Christ as Third Person of the Trinity, like continued use of the *Vetus Latina*, is most easily explained as a habit of a Welsh churchman immersed in his own ancient traditions, isolated from centres in which such things were not encouraged or tolerated. Even in the remotest reaches of Wales that implies a date rather earlier than 1120.

XIV. *Vita Quarta Sancti Patricii*

Here follows the *Praefatio* to the *Vita Quarta Sancti Patricii*.[1] Capital letters and punctuation marks in boldface represent features of London, British Library, MS Additional 19890 folio 1r-v, a manuscript of the late eleventh or early twelfth century. Letters and numbers to the left of the text mark the outlines of parallel statement and restatement of words and ideas. To the right of the text numbers mark the lines and letters the rhymes. I have marked the cursus rhythms and supplied the translation.

> Incipit praefatio . de eo quod beatissimus Patricius
>   Hybernénsium apóstol*us* .   a
> in multis Moysi ducis populi Dei símilis *érat*.   b

---

3 In both Welsh and Irish there are idiomatic expressions which may be rendered with this sort of syntactic structure in Latin, but with a meaning more like 'one of three persons of the Trinity'. A description of the Son as one of the persons of the Trinity may be thought so obvious as hardly to be worth writing.

4 Bede, *Historia Ecclesiastica* IV XVII (XV): *Spiritum Sanctum procedentem ex Patre et Filio inenarrabiliter.*

5 A.E. Burn, *The Council of Nicaea* (London 1925), pp. 108–12. J.N.D. Kelly, *Early Christian Creeds*, 3rd edn. (London 1971), pp. 362–5. R.G. Heath, 'The Western Schism of the Franks and the *Filioque*', *Journal of Ecclesiastical History* XXIII (1972), pp. 102–8.

1 BCLL 366. *Vita Quarta Sancti Patricii, Four Latin Lives of St Patrick*, ed. L. Bieler, *Scriptores Latini Hiberniae* VIII (Dublin 1971), pp. 47–8.

A 1 Nam sicut Moyses antequam ad liberandum populum ad
    Aegýptum mitterétur .   c

  2 oues Iethro soceri sui cura pastoráli pascébat :   b

1'2' ita sanctus Patricius in pueritia curam óuium gerébat :   5 b

B 1 et sicut Moyses ab ángelo míssus . in Aegýptum ingréssus   a

2345a et populum de Aegyptia seruitute et de potestate
    Pharaonis post multa mirácula liberáuit .   d

  b et per mare rúbrum transdúxit .   e

  c atque per multa bella et praelia . septem Chananeorum
    regiónes aboléuit .   d

  d et populum cum uictoria ad terram repromissiónis
    perdúxit :   10 e

1'2'3 sic nimirum sanctus Patricius populum Hybernensium
    de tenebris ígnorántiae .   f

  4' et de iniqua spiritualis Pharaónis opprèssióne .   f
    destructis fanis idolorum .et delubris demonum ad
    níhilum redáctis .   gghghhg
    post multa praelia . et certamina contra diabolum et
    membra eius .   a
    contra regem scilicet paganissimum . et magos eius .   15 a

5' a et post . alia multa miracula . per uerbum praédicatiónis .   g
    quasi per uirgam Moysi . et per lauácrum baptísmatis   g

  b quasi per mare rubrum dúcens liberáuit .   d

  c et post . multa bella et praélia ut díctum est   i

  d ad ueram repromissionis patriam Domino gubernánte
    diréxit :   20 e

C 1 sicut apóstolus díxit .   e

  2 'Non est nobis colluctatio aduersus carnem et sanguinem .
    sed aduersus principatus et potestates :
    aduersus tenebrarum harum rectores :
    contra spiritualia nequitiae in caelestibus'.   25

  1' Et íterum díxit .   e

  2 'Nemo coronabitur . nisi qui legitime certauerit'.

D 1 2 Et sicut Moyses in monte Syna . xl . diebus et . xl . nóctibus
    ièiunáuit .   d

  1' ita **SANCTUS PATRICIUS** quando cateruas demonum
    contra se répugnántium   h
    uirtute ieiuniorum ét oratiónum   30 h
    in fúgam conuérterat .   b
    et de Hybérnia expúlerat .   b

  2' . xl . diebus et . xl . nóctibus ièiunáuit.   d

E 1 Et sicut angelus cum Moyse familiáriter lòquebátur .   c

  1 ita sanctus Patricius angelico collóquio ùtebátur.   35 c

Nam ex iuuentute sua cum angelo loqui familiáriter
   consuéu*erat* .   b
qui docebat eum ieiuniis . orationibus . et uigíliis insíster*e* .   f
in quibus omnipotenti Deo iúuenis plac*ébat.*   b

F i   Et sicut angelus de rubo locútus est ad Moýsen .
i'   sic ad sanctum Patricium de rúbo locút*us est* .   i
cum Dominus per angelum de obitu suo reuelauit
   ei [? l. éi reuel*áuit*] .   40   d
Nolens ut ad famosissimam ciuitatem suam quae
   Scottice Artmacta uocátur . reuèrter*étur* .   c
ubi sedes et cathedra eius ab omnibus Hyberniensibus
   populis cum ingenti honore et reueréntia hab*étur* .   c
dicens ei . "Non ibi benigna Dei prouidentia reliquias
   tuas requiéscere uól*uit*".   d
Prohibitus ergo ab angelo . ne ad praefatam urbem transiret .
ad campum Ínis reuérs*us est* .   i
Sed quae sequuntur . Deo adiuuante in loco suo
   diligéntius expédia*m.*   ·   45   h

G i   Et sicut Moyses centum uiginti annos in hác uita u*íxit* .   e
i'   ita sanctissimus Patricius in sancta conuersatione et inrepre-
hensibili uita .c.xx. annis omnipotenti Déo seru*íuit* .   d
quoniam ab infantia sua . gratia Spiritus Sancti plenus .
   Domino seruíre incaép*it* .   d
et usque ad .c.^mum xx.^mum annum inuiolabiliter in
sancta conuersatióne permáns*it.*   49   e

The Preface begins about the fact that most blessed Patrick, Apostle of
   the Irish,
was in many respects the like of Moses, leader of the people of God.
For just as Moses before he was sent to Egypt for freeing the people
herded sheep for Jethro, his own father-in-law, with pastoral care,
thus holy Patrick in boyhood bore the care of sheep,   5
and just as Moses, sent by an angel, having entered into Egypt,
freed the people both from Egyptian servitude and from the power
   of Pharaoh after many miracles and led [them] across the Red Sea
and through many wars and battles abolished seven regions of Canaanites
and led the people with victory through to the land of promise,   10
so doubtless holy Patrick leading freed the people of the Irish from
   the shadows of ignorance
and from the unjust oppression of a spiritual Pharaoh,
with fanes of idols destroyed and shrines of demons reduced to nothing,
after many battles and strifes against the devil and his members,
against, understand, the most pagan king and his wizards,   15
and after many other miracles through the word of preaching,

as if through the rod of Moses and through the bath of baptism,
as if through the Red Sea,
and after many wars and battles, as has been said,
directed [them] to the true fatherland of promise, with
    the Lord governing, 20
as the Apostle has said,
'For us the struggle is not against flesh and blood,
but against principates and powers,
against the rulers of these shadows,
against spiritual things of evil in heavenly places'. 25
And again he has said,
'No man will be crowned unless he will legitimately have striven'.
And just as Moses on Mount Sinai fasted for forty days and forty nights,
thus holy Patrick when throngs of demons fighting back against him
by the power of fasts and prayers 30
he had turned into flight
and had expelled from Ireland
fasted for forty days and forty nights.
And just as an angel habitually spoke familiarly with Moses,
thus holy Patrick habitually used angelic colloquy, 35
for from his own youth he had been accustomed to speak familiarly
    with an angel,
who used to teach him to persist in fasts, prayers, and vigils,
by which the youth used to please omnipotent God.
And just as an angel spoke from the bush to Moses so he spoke to
    holy Patrick from the bush
when the Lord through an angel revealed to him about his own
    death, 40
not wishing that he return to his own most famous city which
    in Scots [*i.e.* Irish] is called Armagh,
where his see and cathedra is held by all Irish peoples in
    immense honour and reverence,
saying to him, 'Not there has the benign providence of God
    wished your relics to rest'.
Prohibited therefore by an angel lest he go across to the foresaid
    city he returned to the Field of Inis.
But the things which follow, with God helping, I shall expound
    rather diligently in their own place. 45
And just as Moses lived one hundred twenty years in this life,
thus most holy Patrick in holy conversation and in irreprehensible
    life served omnipotent God 120 years,
since from his own infancy, filled by the grace of the Holy Spirit
    he began to serve the Lord

and until the one hundred twentieth year remained inviolably in
> holy conversation.   49

The author of this *Praefatio* clearly understood the manner in which Saint
Patrick had applied to himself the Biblical accounts of the lives and words of
Moses and Saint Paul.[2]
The seventh word from the beginning is *Patricius*, which recurs seven times.
The word *angelus* recurs seven times. There are seven parallels between Patrick
and Moses. The forty-nine lines of the *Praefatio* (7 × 7) divide by sesquioctave
ratio at 26 and 23, and the 406 words divide by sesquioctave ratio at 215 and
191, at the central fourth of seven occurrences of the name of the saint,
PATRICIUS in capital letters in line 26.

XV. CARADOG OF LLANCARFAN

Vita Sancti Gildae

The best known Welsh Latin hagiographer of the twelfth century is Caradog
of Llancarfan, with whose *Vita Sancti Gildae*[1] we may end the survey of this
genre. Capital letters and punctuation marks in boldface represent features of
London, British Library, MS Burney 310 folios 165vb–166ra.

NAu fuit <u>r</u>ex Scotie <u>n</u>obilissimus <u>r</u>egum áquilonáli*um*		a
<u>qu</u>i **.** XXIIII **.** filios habuit <u>u</u>ictóres bellicóso*s* **.**		b
<u>qu</u>orum <u>u</u>nus nóminabàtur **G**ílda*s* **.**		b
<u>qu</u>em parentes sui <u>c</u>ommiserunt <u>stúdio</u> litterár*um.*		a
Puer bone <u>indo</u>lis et <u>studio</u>sus flóruit <u>ing</u>éni*o* **.**	5	c
<u>qu</u>icquid <u>a</u>udiebat <u>a</u> ma<u>g</u>ístr*o* **.**		c
<u>c</u>ommemorabat diligentissime **.** nec ledébat oblíui*o.*		c
Studuit <u>studio</u>sus <u>a</u>ssidue inter <u>s</u>uates in <u>á</u>rtibus **.** <u>s</u>ép*tem* **.**		d
<u>d</u>onec peruénit ad <u>iùuen</u>tú*tem* **.**		d
<u>d</u>um <u>iuuen</u>is factus **:** cito deséruit règión*em.*	10	d
¶ Transfretauit máre **G**állic*um* **.**		a
in ciuitatibus <u>Galli</u>e remansit <u>s</u>tudens optime <u>s</u>patio **.** <u>s</u>ép*tem* **.**		
annór*um* **.**		a
Et in termino <u>s</u>ep*timi* <u>ann</u>i **:** cum <u>m</u>agna <u>m</u>ole diuersórum		
uolúmin*um*		a
remeauit ad <u>m</u>aiórem Británni*am.*		a

---

2 Howlett, *Liber Epistolarum*, pp. 95–103, 110, 120.
1 BCLL 37. *Vita Gildae Auctore Caradoco Lancarbanensi*, *Monumenta Germaniae Historica Auctorum
Antiquissimorum Tomi XIII*, ed. T. Mommsen (Berlin 1894), pp. 107–10. *Vita Gildae Auctore Caradoco
Lancarbanensi, Gildae De Excidio Britanniae, Fragmenta, Liber de Paenitentia accedit et Lorica Gildae*, ed. &
transl. H. Williams, Cymmrodorion Record Series III–IV (London 1899–1901), pp. 394–413.

¶ **A**udita fama famósíssimi áduen*e* :   15   e
confluxerunt ad eum scolares plúrimi úndiqu*e* .   e
Audierunt ab eo septem disciplinarum scientiam súbtilíssi*me* .   e
Unde ex discipulis magistri effecti sunt . sub magistráli honór*e*.   e
¶ **R**eligio sapientissimi doctoris magníficab*átur*   f
et conlaudabatur in tantum a Britannígenis óm*nibus*   20   g
quod nec par ei inuéni*ebátur* .   f
nec poterat inueniri pro suis meritis . éxcellént*ibus*.   g
Ieiunebat ut heremíta Antóni*us* .   h
orabat uir religiosissimus cilício indút*us*.   h
Quicquid dabatur ei : continuo impendébat paupér*ibus*.   25   f
Abstinebat se a lactea dulcédine èt a mélle .   e
caro fuit in odio . fontane herbe pótius in amór*e* .   e
panem ordeiceum comedebat commíxtum cíner*e*   e
fontanam aquam bibébat cotíd*ie*.   e
Balnea non intrabat . quod diligebatur a sua génte máxim*e*.   30   e
Macies apparebat in facie quasi quidam febricitans uidebátur
    grauíss*ime*.   e
Fluuialem aquam intrare solebat media noct*e* [?l. nócte médi*a*] .   e / i
ubi manebat stabilitus donec diceretur ab ipso ter orátio domíni*ca*.   i
His peractis repetebat suum óratóri*um*   a
ibi exorabat genuflectendo diuinam maiestatem úsque diem
    clár*um*.   35   a
Dormiebat modice . iacebat supra petram uestitus solummódo
    una ué*ste*.   e
Manducabat sine saturitate . satiatus tantum metando praémium
    cael*éste* .   e
caelestia praemia erant ei in désidér*io*.   . 38   c

Nau was the king of Scotia, the noblest of the northern kings,
who had twenty-four sons, warlike victors,
of whom one was named Gildas,
whom his parents committed to the study of letters.
The boy, of good natural disposition and studious, flourished in
    ingenuity;   5
whatever he used to hear from his master
he used to commit to memory most diligently and forgetfulness
    did not harm him.
He eagerly and diligently studied among his own people in the seven
    arts until he reached the age of youth;
when, on becoming a young man, he speedily left the country. 10
He crossed the Gallic Sea,
and remained studying well in the cities of Gaul for seven years;

and at the end of the seventh year, with a huge mass of volumes,
he returned to greater Britain.
Having heard the renown of the very illustrious stranger,   15
great numbers of scholars from all parts flocked to him.
They heard him explaining with the greatest acuteness the science
    of the seven rules of discipline,
according to which men, from being disciples, became masters,
    under the master's office.
The religion of the very wise teacher was magnified
and extolled to such a degree by the inhabitants of Britain,   20
in that his equal was neither found,
nor could be found, owing to superior merits.
He used to fast like the hermit Antony:
most thoroughly devoted to religion, he used to pray clad in
    goat's skin.
If anything was given him, he would forthwith expend it upon
    the poor.   25
He abstained from milk-foods and honey:
flesh was hateful to him: fresh-water herbs were rather a favourite
    dish with him:
he ate barley-bread mixed with ashes,
and drank spring water daily.
He used not to take a bath, a habit very much in favour by his
    nation.   30
Thinness appeared in his face, and he seemed like a man suffering
    under a very serious fever.
It was his habit to go into a river at midnight,
where he would remain unmoved until he had said the Lord's
    Prayer three times.
Having done this, he would repair to his oratory
and pray there on his knees unto the divine majesty until broad
    daylight.   35
He used to sleep moderately, and to lie upon a stone, clothed
    with only a single garment.
He used to eat without satisfying his wants, contented with his
    share of the heavenly reward;
the longing of his heart was after heavenly rewards.   38

It will be readily apparent that Caradog, though hardly one of the brighter
lights in the firmament, hoped for a place in the constellation of Celtic Latin
stars. His work is neither brilliant nor artless. The prose alliterates, rhymes, and
scans. There are seven clauses before the first *septem* and seven words before it
in the clause in which it first occurs. After it the twenty-first word (7 × 3) is
septem 12, and from *septem annorum* 12 to *septimi anni* 13 inclusive there are

seven words. The central words of the passage cited above are in line 21, there being an equal number of words before *nec* (121) and after *par* (121).

Caradog affords an instructive specimen of a hagiographer ignorant of facts, but informed by a tradition, every thread of which he wanted to tie into the fabric of his work. Having determined to write the Life of a saint about whom he knew little, if anything, Caradog provided a general backgound by comparing Gildas with Saint Anthony, the type of hermits, and inventing an encounter with a nameless pope, the type of bishops. All the other details take one on a grand tour of the Celtic realms. Gildas is represented as one of twenty-four sons of a king of Scotland. He is sent to school in Gaul, brought back to Britain, taken to Pepidiauc in South Wales, then to Armagh in Ireland, where he learns the issue of a council of war held in the Isle of Man, then back to Britain, to Nantcarfan, to Rome, back to Nantcarfan, then to the islands of Ronech and Echin in the Severn estuary, and finally to Glastonbury. The glaring exception from this itinerary is Brittany, perhaps to spare the sensibilities of monks of Glastonbury who wished to know nothing of Saint Gildas de Rhuys.[2]

Caradog took pains to connect his hero with great secular rulers of the Celtic tradition: Nau (perhaps correctly Cau) King of Scotland, King Trifinus of Pepidiauc, King Meluas of Devon and Cornwall, Guennuuar, and above all, King Arthur, slayer of Hueil, eldest brother of Gildas. Gildas is responsible for lifting the siege of Glastonbury, and for making peace between Arthur and Meluas, who had abducted Guennuuar.

Caradog connected Gildas also with great saints of the Celtic tradition. Although *praedicator erat clarissimus per tria regna Britannie* Gildas was prevented from preaching in Pepidiauc by the presence of Saint Nonnita, the expectant mother of Saint David. In order not to outshine the patron saint of Wales Gildas crossed the sea to bring innumerable converts to the Faith in Armagh, see of the patron saint of Ireland, whom Caradog does not name, and whom he implies that Gildas could outshine. Caradog subsequently reports the dealings of Gildas with Saint Cadog.

Observe how Caradog has woven the strands of his narrative after the intoduction quoted above.

§ 4   A   tria regna Britannie ... in Pepidiauc regione in tempore Trifini regis ... Nonnita pregnans Deuui sanctissimi pueri mater futura ... Gildas transiuit ad Hiberniam ... .

§ 5   B   Contemporaneus Gildas uir sanctissimus fuit Arturi regis totius maioris Britannie

      C   in insula Minau

      D   Gildas Britonum historiographus tunc remanens in Hibernia studium regens ...

§ 6   E 1   Interea sanctissimus Gildas uenerabilis historiographus uenit ad Britanniam

2   *BCLL* 914. ed. Mommsen, pp. 91–106, ed. Williams, pp. 322–88.

2		portans unam pulcherrimam et dulcissimam campanam
3		quam uouerat offerre apostolico Romane ecclesie
4		in presentationem.
5		Pernoctauit honorifice receptus a Cadoco uenerabili abbate in Carbana ualle, qui monstrauit illi laudabilem campanam, monstratam accepit, acceptam emere uoluit magno pretio, quam possessor uendere nolebat.
F		Audito aduentu Gildae sapientis ab Arthuro rege et primatibus totius Britannie episcopis et abbatibus, conuenerunt innumerabiles ex clero et populo ut Arthurum pacificarent ex supra dicto homicidio. At ille sicut primitus fecerat cognito rumore de obitu fratris indulsit inimico, ueniam postulanti osculum dedit et benignissimo animo benedixit osculanti. Hoc peracto rex Arthurus dolens et lacrimans accepit ab episcopis adstantibus penitentiam et emendauit in quantum potuit donec consummauit uitam.
§ 7 E'1		Inde egregius Gildas uir pacificus et catholicus adiuit Romam
2		et apostolico Romane ecclesie tribuit predictam campanam
3		que commota a manibus apostolici nullum sonitum emittebat.
4		Unde hoc ille uidens talia dicebat "O uir dilecte a Deo et ab homine, reuela mihi quod tibi contigit in itinere de hac presentatione".
5		At ille reuelauit Sanctissimum Cadocum Nancarbanensis ecclesie abbatem eam uoluisse emere sed quam uouerat Sancto Petro apostolo offerre nolebat uendere.
5'		Apostolicus his auditis dixit "Nosco Cadocum uenerabilem abbatem …"
1'		Gildas itaque
2'		benedictam campanam recepit et reuersus est et reportatam Sancto Cadoco gratis impendit.

	3'	Recepta a manibus abbatis intonuit illico pulsata ammirantibus cunctis.
	4'	Unde remansit omnibus portantibus per totam Gualiam pro refugio ...
§ 8	D'	Cadocus abbas Nancarbanensis ecclesie rogauit Gildam doctorem ut regeret studium scolarum per anni spatium ...
§ 9	C'	Cadocus et Gildas ... adierunt duas insulas scilicet Ronech et Echin ...
§10	B'	Glastonia ... obsessa est itaque ab Arturo tyranno cum innumerabili multitudine propter Guennuuar uxorem suam uiolatam et raptam a predicto iniquo rege [Meluas]
	A	Illico commouit exercitus totius Cornubie et Dibnenie ... .

Chapters 11–13 report the end of the saint's life as chapters 1–3 reported the beginning. Chapter 14 considers the etymology in Latin, Welsh, and English of the names of Glastonbury, then ends

Nancarbanensis dictamina sunt Caratoci:
qui legat emendet: placet illi compositori.

Caradoc of Nancarban's are the words;
Who reads, may he correct; so wills the author.

Caradog's thudding unimaginative dullness, his description of Arthur as *rex rebellis* in chapters 5 and 10 and *tyrannus* in 10, and the forgiveness of Arthur's *homicidium* at the crux of the chiasmus in chapter 6 earned from a fellow countryman a stinging rebuke, to which we shall come in the final chapter.[3]

---

3 See below pp. 373–5.

VI

PLAY AND PROPAGANDA

I. DUB INNSE BISHOP OF BANGOR

Alea Evangelii

Oxford, Corpus Christi College, MS 122, a Gospel book in an Irish hand of
the end of the eleventh century or the beginning of the twelfth, contains
Eusebian Canons and a summary scheme of the canons, followed by a table
ruled as a board for a game with the following title.[1]

> **IN**cipit Alea Euangelii quam Dubinsi Episcopus Bennchorensis detulit a
> rege Anglorum . id est a domu Adalstani regis Anglorum depicta a
> quodam Francone et a Romano sapiente . id est Israel .

> Here begins Dice of the Gospel, which Dub Innse Bishop of Bangor
> brought away from the King of the English, that is from the house of
> Æthelstan King of the English, devised [or 'set out' or 'written down']
> by a certain Franco [or 'Frenchman'] and by a Roman wise man [or
> 'Roman the Wise'], that is Israel.

The author of this title has composed in Biblical style even for a preface to a game
board. There are twenty-nine words, of which the central are *a domu Adalstani*.
The words divide by extreme and mean ratio at 18 and 11, at *id est a domu
Adalstani regis Anglorum*, of which the first word is eighteenth from the end and
the last is eighteenth from the beginning. The first eleven words divide by
extreme and mean ratio at 7 and 4, at *Dubinsi Episcopus Bennchorensis*, of which the
first word is seventh from the end of the phrase and the last is seventh from the
beginning. The last eleven words also divide by extreme and mean ratio at 7 and
4, at | *Francone et a Romano* |, of which the first word is fourth from the begin-
ning of the phrase and the last is seventh. The central words, which are also at the
golden section of the inscription, refer to the source of the game in England.
Reckoned from the beginning of the inscription the minor part of the minor part
of the golden section gives the name and title of the man who brought the game
to Ireland. Reckoned from the end of the inscription the minor part of the minor
part of the golden section names the men who devised the game.

---

1   BCLL 307. J. Armitage Robinson, *The Times of Saint Dunstan,* Ford Lectures (Oxford 1923 rept
    1969), p. 173 (text) and frontispiece (facsimile).

The *Anglo-Saxon Chronicle* records the death of Æthelstan under the year 940. The *Annals of the Four Masters* under the year 951 and the *Annals of Ulster* under the year 952 (*alias* 953) record the death of Dubinnsi Bishop of Bangor. In the title of this game we see clearly, as in quotations by Columban of Gildas and by Cummian of Pelagius and Patrick, in praise by Sedulius of Vinniau, in correspondence of Cellán with Aldhelm and of Radbod with Æthelstan, in dedication of work by Joseph to Alcuin, in patronage of Asser by Alfred, in address of poems from Patrick Bishop of Dublin to Aldwine and Wulfstan at Worcester, how British Latin, Irish Latin, and English Latin writers crossed each others' shadows and lived in each others' light, sharing Latinity, polity, and play over seven centuries.

II. CALVUS PERENNIS

A Note in the Book of Armagh

In the year 1004 or 1005 an Irish cleric, describing himself as *Caluus Perennis*, perhaps a translation of the Irish name *Mael Suthain*, advanced the metropolitan claims of the church of Armagh in a note added in a larger bolder hand than that of the preceding and following texts to folio 16v of the *Book of Armagh*.[1]

Sánctus Patrí[ci]*us*	aa	2	6	16
iens ad cael*um* mandáuit totum frúct*um*	bb	6	12	32
laboris súi <u>tam</u> babtísm*i*	cc	4	9	21
<u>tam</u> caus*arum* qu*am* <u>e</u>lemoisin*árum*	dd	4	11	28
deferendum <u>e</u>sse <u>a</u>postólicae <u>úr</u>bi		4	13	29
quae <u>Scot</u>ice nominátur <u>Ardd</u>mácha .		4	11	29
<u>Si</u>c reperi in bebliothíc[*i*]*s* <u>Scotórum</u> .	e	5	13	31
<u>Ego</u> <u>s</u>cripsi <u>i</u>d <u>e</u>st <u>C</u>áluus Perénnis		6	11	29
<u>i</u>n <u>c</u>onspectu Briain <u>i</u>mperatóri*s* <u>Scotórum</u>	e	5	14	36
et quod scrípsi finíui pro omnibus régibus Macériae .		8	18	44
		48	118	295

MS: 1 patrius. 7 bebliot^hics. 10 finituit *with both* ts *pointed for deletion.*

Saint Patrick
going to heaven commanded the entire fruit
of his labour, as of baptism,

1·   BCLL 616. *The Tripartite Life of Patrick, with Other Documents Relating to that Saint,* ed. W. Stokes, Rolls Series (London 1887), vol. II p. 336. *Liber Ardmachanus: The Book of Armagh,* ed. J. Gwynn (Dublin 1913), f. 16v, p. 32. There is a facsimile of this text as frontispiece. *Book of Armagh, The Patrician Documents,* ed. E. Gwynn, Facsimiles in Collotype of Irish Manuscripts III, Irish Manuscripts Commission (Dublin 1937).

as of legal cases so of alms,
to be brought to the apostolic city
which in Irish is named Armagh.
Thus have I discovered in the libraries [or 'Bibles'] of the Irish.
I, that is, 'Ever-Tonsured' [Mael-suthain], have written [this]
in the sight of Brian [Bóruma], emperor of the Irish,
and what I have written I have completed before all the kings of Cashel.

Here, in a note which may at first seem artless, are ten lines of prose, which divide by extreme and mean ratio at 6 and 4. In *The Book of Armagh* the first of the major six lines and the first of the minor four lines both begin with capital letters. All ten lines end with cursus rhythms. Among the first six lines there is one example of *cursus tardus*, three of *trispondiacus*, and two of *cursus planus*. Among the last four lines there are three examples of *cursus planus* and one *dispondeus dactylicus*. The first four lines exhibit internal rhyme, and the last six do not. There are twenty-four words in the six-lined major part and twenty-four words in the four-lined minor part. From the beginning to the central word *Arddmacha* exclusive there are fifty-nine syllables, and from *Arddmacha* inclusive to the end there are fifty-nine syllables. The central letter, 148th of 295, is in *Arddmacha*.

The golden section of the forty-eight words falls at 30 and 18, at *Ego*, the thirtieth word. In the eighteen-word minor part the golden section falls at 11 and 7, at the eleventh word from the end, *Briain*. Between *scripsi* 8 and *scripsi* 10 there are eleven words. After *Scotice* 6 *Scotorum* 9 is the eighteenth word. Before *Scotorum* 9 the eleventh word is *Scotorum* 7. The author refers to himself not only at the golden section, *Ego* in line 8, but also at eight-ninths of the forty-eight words, which falls at 5 and 43, at *scripsi | finiui* in line 10.

VII

WIDER HORIZONS

I. PETER ABAELARD

Historia Calamitatum

The greatest philosopher to emerge from the Celtic realms after Johannes Scottus Eriugena is Peter Abaelard, born at Le Pallet in eastern Brittany, from 1126 Abbot of Saint Gildas de Rhuys on the west coast of Brittany. This brilliant logician and brilliant stylist composed about 1131 or 1132 the most arresting autobiography of the Middle Ages.

Despite the gap between the date of composition and the dates of the earliest manuscripts the text of Abaelard's *Historia Calamitatum* is fairly secure.[1] By attending to some previously unnoticed structural features we may enhance that security, at once ascertaining the textual integrity of the work, acquiring new insights into the author's thought and art, and improving presentation of the text for future readers.

The following text of title, exordium or chapter I, and chapter II may be compared with the recent editions by Muckle and Monfrin. The title is my reconstruction.[2] Capital letters and punctuation marks in boldface represent features of Oxford, Bodleian Library, MS Add. C 271 folio 85vb. To the right of the text the first column notes the line number, the second the rhyme scheme, the third the number of words, the fourth the number of syllables, and the fifth the number of letters. In the subsequent analysis figures in round brackets refer to the line numbers of Monfrin's edition.

---

1 BCLL 874. 'Abelard's Letter of Consolation to a Friend (*Historia Calamitatum*)', ed. J.T. Muckle, *Mediaeval Studies* XII (1950), pp. 163–213. *Abélard: Historia Calamitatum*, ed. J. Monfrin, 3rd edn. (Paris 1967).

2 Consider the titles from the following manuscripts as reported by Muckle, p. 175 n. 2, and Monfrin, pp. 8, 60.

A ✓Paris Bibl. nat. MS lat. 2923	Abaelardi ad amicum suum consolatoria	
T Troyes Bibl. mun. MS 802	Abaelardi ad amicum suum consolatoria	
R Reims Bibl. mun. MS 872:	Epistola prima Petri Abelardi seu HistoriaCalamitatum (*s.m.*)	
B Paris Bibl. nat. MS lat. 2544:	Vita Magistri Petri Abaelardi (*s.m.*)	
D Douai Bibl. mun. MS 797:	Epistola magistri Petri Abaielardi ad amicam suam de temptationibus et calamitatibus in suis eventibus habitis et qualiter suam Heloysam sibi copulavit primitus in amorem et postmodum in uxorem (*p.m.*)	
F Paris Bibl. nat. MS n.acq.lat.13057	Epistola venerabilis magistri Petri Abaelardi (*s.m.*) CEY *om.*	

ABAELARDI AD AMICUM CONSOLATORIA EPISTOLA
DE CALAMITATUM MEARUM HISTORIA

A	Sepe humános afféctus	3	8	19
B	aut próuocant aut mítigant	4	8	23
C	amplius exémpla quam uérba .	4	9	23
D	Unde post nonnullam sermonis ad presentem habiti cónsolatiónem	8	21	55
E	de ipsis calamitatum meárum expèriméntis :	5	16	36
D'	consolatoriam ad absentem scríbere decréui .	5	17	38
C'	ut in comparatióne meárum	4	11	22
B'	tuas aut nullas aut modicas temptatiónes recognóscas	.7	18	46
A'	et tolerabílius féras . 9	3	9	19

Ego igitur oppido quódam oriúndus	a	5	14	29
quod in ingressu minoris Británnie constrúctum	b	6	15	41
ab urbe Namnetica uersus orientem octo credo miliáriis remótum	b	9	25	54
proprio uocabulo Palátium àppellátur .	c	4	15	33
sicut natura terre mee uel generis ánimo léuis . 5	a	8	18	39
ita et ingenio extiti et ad litteratoriam disciplínam fácilis .	a	9	25	53
Patrem aútem habébam	b	3	7	18
litteris aliquántulum imbútum	b	3	11	27
antequam militari cingulo ínsignirétur .	c	4	15	35
Unde postmodum tanto litteras amóre compléxus est : 10	d	7	17	43
ut quoscumque fílios habéret	e	4	10	25
litteris antequam armis ínstrui dispóneret .	e	5	15	38
Sicque profécto áctum est .	d	4	8	22
Me itaque primogenitum suum quanto cariórem habébat	f	7	20	45
tanto diligentius erudíri curáuit . 15	f	4	14	30
Ego uero quanto amplius et facilius in studio litterárum proféci .	g	10	10	55
tanto ardentius éis inhési .	g	4	11	23
et in tanto earum amóre illéctus sum :	b	7	14	30
ut militaris glórie pómpam	b	4	10	23
cum hereditate et prerogatiua prímogenitórum 20	b	5	18	40
meorum frátribus dèrelínquens :	a	3	10	27
Martis curie pénitus àbdicárem .	h	4	12	27
ut Minerue grémio èducárer .,	h	4	11	23
Et quoniam dialecticarum ratiónum armatúram	b	5	17	39
omnibus philosophie documéntis pretúli : 25	g	4	15	35
his armis ália còmmutáui	g	4	9	21

et tropheis bellorum conflictus pretuli dísputatiónum ·   b   6   19 48
Proinde diuersas disputando perámbulans prouíncias :   a   5   18 46
ubicunque huius artis uigere stúdium audíeram   b   6   18 40
peripateticorum emulátor fáctus su*m* ..   30   b   4   14 32

ABAELARD'S CONSOLATORY LETTER TO A FRIEND 'ON THE HISTORY OF MY CALAMITIES'

Often examples rather than words either provoke or mitigate human affections. Therefore after not-null consolation of speech had with you present about the experiences of my calamities I have decided to write a consolatory [letter] to you absent so that in comparison with mine you may recognize your trials as either null or little and bear [them] more tolerably.

I, then, born in a certain town
which, constructed at the entry of Lesser Britain,
removed from the city of Nantes toward the east by eight miles, I think,
is called by the proper name Le Pallet,
I, light in spirit as the nature of my land or race,
have been accordingly so in temperament and easily disposed to literary
    discipline.
For I had a father
imbued somewhat with letters
before he was honoured with a military girdle.
Therefore he afterwards embraced letters with such great love
    that however many sons he would have
he would dispose to be instructed in letters before arms.
And thus unquestionably it was done.
And accordingly in as much as he held me, his own firstborn son, dearer,
by so much he took care for me to be instructed more diligently.
But I, in as much as I made progress more amply and easily in the study
    of letters,
that much more ardently I clung to them
and so I was lured by such great love of them
that the pomp of military glory of the court of Mars
with the inheritance and prerogative of firstborn sons
leaving to my brothers
I resigned entirely
so that I might be educated in the bosom of Minerva.
And since the armature of dialectic reasonings
I preferred to all the teachings of philosophy,
I exchanged the others for these arms,
and I preferred the conflicts of disputations to the trophies of wars.

> Thence walking about through diverse provinces disputing
> everywhere I had heard the study of this art to flourish
> I was made an emulator of the peripatetics.

The reconstructed title prefigures the shape of the entire *Historia Calamitatum*, Abaelard's nine-lettered name being the first of the nine-word title, and the nine-part exordium being the first chapter of this nine-part work.

The structure is chiastic. In the exordium compare *aut ... aut* in B with *aut ... aut* in B', *amplius ... quam* in C with *in comparatione* in C', *sermonis ad presentem* and *consolationem* in D with *consolatoriam* and *ad absentem scribere* in D'. The central word, twenty-second of forty-three, states the subject of the work, *calamitatum*. The third word before it and the third word after it state the purpose of the work, *consolationem* and *consolatoriam*. The fifth word before it and the fifth word after it address the recipient of the work, *presentem* and *absentem*.

Divide the number of the central twenty-second word by half: $22 \div 2 = 11$. The first word after *calamitatum* is *mearum*; from *mearum* to *mearum* inclusive there are eleven words, and the latter is the eleventh word from the end of the exordium. From *presentem* to *absentem* inclusive there are eleven words. Divide the number 11 by symmetry, at 6. The sixth word from the beginning is the end of the first *aut ... aut*. After the second *aut ... aut* there are six words to the end of the exordium. From the beginning of the exordium the fourteenth word is *nonnullam*, between which and the central *calamitatum* there are seven words. After *calamitatum* the fourteenth word is *nullas*, after which there are seven words to the end of the exordium.

In parts A-C-E-C'-A' the words are arranged symmetrically 3–4–5–4–3. In parts B-D-D'-B' the words are arranged 4–8–5–7, twelve before the crux and twelve after the crux. The four words of B and the seven words of B' are the minor and major parts of the golden section of 11. The eight words of D and the five words of D' are the major and minor parts of the golden section of 13.

Parts A and A' contain not only three words each but nineteen letters each. Parts C and C' contain not only four words each; the former contains twenty-three letters and the latter twenty-two letters. Part B contains twenty-three letters, exactly half as many as part B', forty-six letters.

The rhythm of parts A and A' is identical, *humános afféctus* and *tolerabílius féras* each a *cursus planus*. The rhythm of parts B and B' is identical, *próuocant aut mítigant* and *temptatiónes recognóscas et* each a *dispondeus dactylicus*. The rhythm of C and C' is identical, *exémpla quam uérba* and *comparatióne meárum* each a *cursus planus*. The rhythm of D and D' is identical, *cónsolatiónem* and *scríbere decréui* each a *trispondiacus*, around *meárum experiméntis*, a *cursus uelox* at the crux in E.

The first letters of the nine lines of the exordium, *SAAUDCUTE*, are an anagram of *ECAUDATUS*, and the last letters, *STAMSIMSS*, are an anagram of *S[CITO] SIM MAS S[INE] T[ESTIBUS]*. Together they read *ECAUDATUS S[CITO] SIM MAS S[INE] T[ESTIBUS]* 'Know that I may be a de-tailed man without testicles'.[3] Unless this should be mere coincidence we see Abaelard referring to his calamities exactly at the centre of the exordium and at the beginning and the end of every one of its constituent phrases.

This exordium is balanced by the epilogue or valediction, the ninth chapter, which echoes much of its diction at the end of the text:

> Hec dilectissime fráter in Xpísto
> et ex diuina conuersatione familiaríssime cómes :
> de calamitatum meárum história
> in quibus quasi a cunabulis iúgiter láboro
> tue me desolationi atque iniurie illate scripsísse sufficiat .
> ut sicut in exordio prefátus sum epístole
> oppressiónem tuam in comparatióne meárum
> aut nullam aut modicam ésse iúdices .
> Et tanto eam patiéntius féras
> quanto minórem consíderas .
> Illud semper in consolatiónem ássumens
> quod membris suis de membris diaboli Dóminus predíxit .
> "Si me persecuti sunt et vos persequentur ..."

> These things, most beloved brother in Christ,
> and most familiar comrade in divine conversation
> about the history of my calamities
> in which I labour continually as if from the cradles
> it should suffice for me to have written for your desolation and reported
>   injury
> so that just as I foresaid in the beginning of this letter
> your oppression in comparison with mine
> you may judge to be either null or little.
> And by so much as you bear it more patiently
> by that much you consider it less,
> taking that always as consolation
> which the Lord foretold to His own members about the devil's
>   members,
> "If they have persecuted me they will also persecute you ...".

In the second chapter, directly after the exordium, Abaelard begins to write rhymed rhythmical prose, in which he makes patterns even of the most prosaic elements. Note the balance of *sicut* x *uel* y 5, *ita et* x *et* y 6, and *sicque* 13, *itaque* 14; *antequam* 9, *postmodum* 10, *antequam* 12;*tanto ... amore ... ut ...* and two subjunctive verbs, *haberet* and *disponeret* 10–12, balanced by *tanto ... amore ... ut abdicarem, ut educarer* 18–23; around *quanto ... tanto* 14–15 and *quanto ... tanto* 16–17.

---

3 The verb *scire* would ordinarily be followed by a verb in indicative mood. For *s.t.* as abbreviation for *sine testibus* see A. Cappelli, *Dizionario di Abbreviature Latine ed Italiane*, 6th edn (Milano 1967), p. 364.

Abaelard observes the widespread convention of authorial self-reference at the beginning, one-ninth and eight-ninths, and the sesquioctave part of the title and the second chapter. The nine words of the title divide by one-ninth and eight-ninths at 1 and 8. He names himself in the first word, the nine-lettered *Abaelardi*, and refers to himself in the eighth word, *mearum*. The 157 words of the second chapter divide by sesquioctave ratio at 83 and 74. The first word is *ego*, and the eighty-third word is *ego*. Divide 83 by symmetry, at 42. From *me itaque primogenitum* to *prerogatiua primogenitorum meorum* inclusive there are forty-two words.

At the beginning of the second chapter Abaelard refers to his birth in Brittany, *in ingressu minoris Britannie*, not far from Nantes, *ab urbe Namnetica*. At the beginning and the end of the eighth chapter, the chiastic pair to this, he refers again to Brittany, *in Britannia minore* (1235) and the Count of Nantes *Namneti ad comitem* (1511). These are the only places in the entire text in which the names of Brittany and Nantes occur.

In the second paragraph of the second chapter Abaelard refers to difficulties with his first master *Guilhelmus Campellensis* (31–44) in a parallelism of five parts, balanced by the account of difficulties with his second master *Anselmus Laudunensis* (161–221).

1	Perueni tandem Parisius ubi iam maxime disciplina hec florere consueuerat
2	ad Guilhelmum scilicet Campellensem preceptorem meum
3	in hoc tunc magisterio re et fama precipuum
4	cum quo aliquantulum moratus primo ei acceptus
5	postmodum grauissimus extiti cum nonnullas scilicet eius sententias refellere conarer
1'	In hac autem lectione
2'	magister eius Anselmus Laudunensis maximam ex antiquitate auctoritatem tunc tenebat
3'	accessi igitur ad hunc senem cui magis longeuus usus quam ingenium uel memoria nomen comparauerat
4'	ad quem si quis de aliqua questione pulsandum accederet incertus redibat incertior
5'	accidit autem quadam die ut post aliquas sententiarum collationes nos scholares inuicem iocaremur

Of the former he writes *hinc calamitatum mearum que nunc usque perseuerant ceperunt exordia* (41–2), which he attributes in the last word of the paragraph to *inuidia*.

In the third paragraph of the second chapter (45–80) he writes in a parallelism of twelve parts about his school at *Meliduni castrum* (48), his departure to Brittany *coactus sum repatriare* (67), and his absence from France *a Francia remotus* (68), balanced by the paragraph (117–61) in which he writes of his return to *Melidunum* (117), then removal to Paris *Meliduno Parisius redii* (127), departure to Brittany *mater mea Lucia repatriare me compulit* (155–6), and return to France *reuersus sum in Franciam* (158–9).

1	Meliduni castrum et sedem regiam
2	presensit hoc predictus magister meus et quo longius posset scholas nostras a se remouere conatus
3	priusquam a suis recederem scholis
4	habebat emulos
5	ad castrum Corbolii quod Parisiace urbi uicinius est quamtotius scholas nostras transferrem
6	assultus
7	non multo autem interiecto tempore
8	coactus sum repatriare
9	et per annos aliquot a Francia remotus
10	querebar ardentius ab his quos dialectica sollicitabat doctrina
11	preceptor meus ille Guilhelmus Parisiacensis archidiaconus ... ut quo religiosior crederetur
12	Catalaunensi episcopo facto
1'	Melidunum reuersus scholas ibi nostras sicut antea constitui
2'	cum ille intelligeret ... transtulit se et conuenticulum fratrum cum scholis suis ad uillam quandam ab urbe remotum
3'	statimque ego Meliduno Parisius redii
4'	ab emulo nostro
5'	extra ciuitatem in monte Sancte Genouefe scholarum nostrarum castra posui
6'	obsessurus
7'	dum uero hec agerentur
8'	mater mea Lucia repatriare me compulit
9'	reuersus sum in Franciam
10'	ut de diuinitate addiscerem
11'	sepefatus magister noster Guilhelmus
12'	in episcopatu Catalaunensi pollebat

These are the only places in the entire text in which he mentions the names of Melun and France and uses the verb *repatriare*.

The central part of this chapter (80–116) tells how Abaelard forced William to change his teaching about universals.

Abaelard refers in the first paragraph to literary studies five times, states that he went to William of Champeaux first for *dialectica doctrina* (69) and then for *rethoricam* (81), and to Anselm of Laon *de diuinitate* (159).

The chiastic pair to the second chapter exhibits an internal chiasmus of nine parts. Compare the first part (1229–303) with the ninth (1489–559), both referring to Brittany; the second (1304–28) with the eighth (1477–88), both

recounting Abaelard's dealings with the nuns who removed from Argenteuil
to the Paraclete; the third (1328–40) *quippe quo feminarum sexus est infirmior* with
the seventh (1459–76) *adeo namque sexus infirmior fortioris indiget auxilio*, the only
places in the entire text in which he uses the words *sexus infirmior*; the fourth
(1341–58) with the sixth (1445–59), both quoting Jerome; around the central
fifth paragraph (1358–444). The second chapter relates persecution of Abaelard
by his masters; the eighth relates persecution of Abaelard by his sons, that is the
monks who should have obeyed him.

The third chapter (222–48) relates his persecution by two rivals, *Albericus
Remensis et Lotulfus Lumbardus*. The chiastic pair to this, the seventh chapter
(1200–28), relates that his *priores emuli ... aduersum me nouos apostolos ... excitauerunt*.

The fourth chapter (248–69) recounts Abaelard's fame, as does the sixth
(1196–200).

The crux of the *Historia* is a triple account, first of Abaelard's relationship with
Heloise (280–622), second of the period from his entry into the monastery of
Saint-Denis and hers into the convent of Argenteuil to the burning of his book at
the Council of Soissons and his persecution by the abbot of Saint-Denis
(623–1016), and third of his arrival at the Paraclete (1017–195).

To establish the chiastic structure of the central narrative of the event which
inflicted on Abaelard his greatest grief compare the reference to *abbatia sancti
Dionysii* (628) with his return to it (936), his removal to the cell at Maisoncelle-
en-Brie (665) with his removal to the monastery of *sancti Medardi* (907), the
account of his *tractatum De Unitate et Trinitate Diuina* (692–3) with his enforced
recitation of the Athanasian Creed about the same subject (900 ff.), the references
to his *emuli* Alberic and Lotulf (702–25) with the charges *a falsis accusatoribus*
(880–90), *dicentes me tres deos predicare et scripsisse* (725) with *fides et teneat et profiteatur
tres omnipotentes esse* (876–7), the judging of his book by an incompetent legate
(726–35, 855–76), the Catholic Christian faith (736–49, 845–54), attacks by his
emuli (749–81, 838–45), deliberations of the council (782–9, 823–37), the advice
of *Gaudfridus Carnotensis episcopus* (789–97) compared with that of *beati Nichodemi*
(812–22), *si hunc preiudicio ... grauaueritis* (797–8) compared with *si autem canonice
agere in eum disponitis* (809), quotations from Jerome (801–4, 807–9), around the
crux (805–6):

> uidete ne plus ei nominis conferatis uiolenter agendo
> et plus nobis criminis ex inuidia quam ei ex iusticia conquiramus.

There are many more Biblical quotations than the editions have noted, most of
them purposeful and pointed. There is much more beauty in the prose than its
most ardent modern admirer has yet claimed. The structure is not simply or dis-
cretely chiastic. Elements from each section of the narrative are woven into other
sections, as if to illustrate the comprehensive and connected nature of the calamities, which Abaelard has commuted from paranoia and private grief into a public
work of art. Recognition of the structure allows one to correct misapprehensions

by earlier editors, to confirm the integrity of the text in minute particulars, and to clarify Abaelard's meanings by using the form of his narrative as an inbuilt commentary. Particular details of composition may offer new criteria that allow readers to distinguish Abaelard's style from Heloise's. But one may see clearly already new reasons to admire the coruscating brilliance of this remarkable writer.

II. GEOFFREY OF MONMOUTH

Historia Regum Britanniae and *Prophetiae Merlini*

Let us turn from a most acute thinker to consider a work of the most influential Celtic Latin writer of the entire Middle Ages. Most manuscripts of Geoffrey of Monmouth's *Historia Regum Britanniae*, published in the early 1130s, begin with a Preface of four paragraphs dedicated to Robert Earl of Gloucester.[1] In a few copies the writer addresses both Robert and in a fifth paragraph Waleran Count of Meulan. In one manuscript he addresses King Stephen and Robert. Though all three forms of the dedication are usually assumed to be Geoffrey's own work, there is no consensus about their order.

One line of argument begins with the text of the *Historia* itself, where Geoffrey writes at § 177

De hoc quidem, consul auguste, Galfridus Monumotensis tacebit, set ut in prefato Britannico sermone inuenit et a Walterio Oxenefordensi in multis historiis peritissimo uiro audiuit ... ,

clearly addressing a single patron. Neil Wright has alluded to 'the difficulty' that Geoffrey writes to Robert as *dux* in the Preface, but to the anonymous patron as *consul*,[2]

the term, that is, which is reserved for Waleran in the double dedication; however, earlier, fictional earls of Gloucester are called *consul* in *Historia Regum Britannie* §§ 105 (Eldol) and 156 (Moruid).

As the *Dictionary of Medieval Latin from British Sources* records six examples from the twelfth century and four from the thirteenth of *consul* in the sense 'earl' as recognized in post-Conquest England, this is not a difficulty. One infers therefore that the original dedication was to Robert Earl of Gloucester.

1   BCLL 39. *The Historia Regum Britanniae of Geoffrey of Monmouth with Contributions to the Study of its Place in Early British History*, eds. A. Griscom & R.E. Jones, (New York 1929). *Geoffroy de Monmouth Historia Regum Britanniae, La Légende Arthurienne, Études et Documents, Première Partie, Les Plus Anciens Textes*, ed. E. Faral, (Paris 1969), vol. III II pp. 63–303. *The Historia Regum Britannie of Geoffrey of Monmouth*, ed. N. Wright (Cambridge 1984). See also M.D. Reeve, 'The Transmission of the *Historia Regum Britanniae*', *The Journal of Medieval Latin* I (1991), pp. 73–117.
2   Wright, p. xiv and n. 20.

About the double dedications Wright agrees with Griscom that[3]

> the dedication to Stephen and Robert is manifestly a reworking of that to
> Robert and Waleran; the substitution of Stephen for Robert, and Robert
> for Waleran, has caused stylistic disruption, while the terms of the Robert
> — Waleran dedication are apposite to both men, but become far less apt
> when reapplied to Stephen and Robert. The dedication to Robert and
> Waleran therefore predates that to Stephen and Robert.

Analysis of the Preface as a composition in Biblical style affords an independent line of argument. Here is the text as preserved in Cambridge University
Library MS 1706.

I   Cum mecum multa et de multis sepius ánimo reuóluens
       in hystoriam regum Británnie incíderem .
       in mírum cóntuli
       quod infra mentionem quam de eis Gildas . et Beda luculento
         tractátu fécerant .
5   nichil de regibus qui ante incarnationem Xpisti ínhabitáuerant
       nichil etiam de Arturo ceterísque complúribus .
       qui post incarnationem successérunt repperíssem :
       cum et gesta eorum digna eternitate laúdis constárent
       et a multis populis quasi inscripta iocunde et memoriter
        prédicaréntur .
II   Talia mihi et de talibus multóciens cògitánti
       óptulit Wálterus
       Oxenefordensis árchidiáconus
       uir in oratória árte .
       atque in exoticis hystóriis èrudítus
15   quendam Britannici sermonis librum uétustíssimum .
       qui a Bruto primo rége Brítonum .
       usque ad Cadualadrum filium Caduallonis áctus ómnium
       continue et ex ordine perpulcris oratiónibus pròponébat .
III   Rogatu itaque íllius dúctus
20   tam et si infra aliénos órtulos .
       falerata uerba nón collégerim :
       agresti tamen stilo propriisque cálamis conténtus .
       codicem illum in Latinum sermonem transférre curáui .
       Nam si ampullosis dictionibus páginam illiníssem
25   tedium legéntibus ingérerem
       dum magis in éxponendis uérbis .
       quam in hystoria intelligenda ipsos commorári oportéret[4] .

---

3   Ibid. pp. xiv–xv.
4   MS oportet.

IV   **O**pusculo igitur meo Roberte dux Claudiocéstrie fáueas .
          ut sic te doctore te monitóre corrigátur .

30   quod non ex Galfridi Monemutensis fonticulo censeátur exórtum
          set sale minerue túe condítum
          illius dicátur edítio
          quem Henricus illustris rex Anglórum generáuit
          quem philosophia liberalibus ártibus èrudíuit

35   quem innata probitas in milicia milítibus prefécit
          unde Brittannia insula tibi nunc tempóribus nóstris
          ac si alterum Henricum adepta interno congratulátur afféctu .

V   **T**u quoque Galeranne cónsul Mellénti
          altera regni nóstri colúmpna

40   operam adhíbeas túam
          ut utriusque moderatióne commùnicáta :
          editio in medium producta púlchrius èlucéscat .
          Te etenim ex illius celeberimi regis Karoli stírpe progénitum
          mater phylosophia in gremio súo excépit

45   scientiarumque suarum subtilitátem edócuit .
          ac deinde ut in militaribus clareres éxercítiis
          ad castra régum diréxit :
          ubi commilitones tuos audácter supergréssus
          et terror hóstium exístere

50   et protectio tuorum esse paternis auspiciis áddidicísti .
          Fidelis itaque protectio tuórum exístens
          mé tuum uátem
          codicemque ad oblectamentum túi éditum
          sub tutela túa recípias

55   ut sub tegmine tam patulæ árboris récubans .
          calamum musæ tue coram inuidis átque ímprobis

57   tuto modulamine résonare quéam ;

I   When by myself going over in my mind quite often many things and about many men I would come upon the history of the kings of Britain, I would reckon it a wonder that after the mention of them which Gildas and Bede made in their excellent tract I would find nothing of the kings who lived before the Incarnation of Christ, nothing even of Arthur and very many others who succeeded after the Incarnation, though their deeds both are known worthy of an eternity of praise and are proclaimed with delight and good recollection by many people as if written down.

II   To me thinking very often such things and about such men Walter archdeacon of Oxford, a man learned in oratorical art and in exotic histories, offered a certain very ancient book in the British language, which from Brutus the first king of the Britons as far as

Cadwalader son of Cadwallon set out the deeds of them all continuously and in order in most beautiful narratives.

III   Led, then, by the request of that Walter, even though within others' gardens, I would not gather tinselled words, but content with uncultivated style and my own reed pens, I have taken care to translate that book into the Latin language. For if I daubed the page with bombastic words I would force disgust upon the readers, as it would be necessary for them to spend more time in explaining the words than in understanding the history.

IV   To my little work, therefore, may you show favour, Robert Earl of Gloucester, that with you as teacher, with you as adviser, it may be so corrected that it be supposed sprung not from the little fountain of Geoffrey of Monmouth, but seasoned with the salt of your intellect it may be called the publication of him whom Henry the illustrious King of the English begot, whom philosophy nourished in the liberal arts, whom innate excellence in war made preeminent among soldiers, so that the island of Britain now in our times, as if having secured another Henry, congratulates you with domestic affection.

V   You also, Waleran, Count of Meulan, the other pillar of our realm, may you provide your aid, so that with either's patronage shared the publication brought into the open may shine more beautifully. For you, begotten from the stock of that most renowned King Charles, mother philosophy has taken into her bosom and taught the subtlety of her sciences, and thence that you should shine in military exercises sent you to the camp of kings, where having boldly surpassed your fellow soldiers you learned under paternal auspices both to remain the terror of enemies and to be the protection of your own. Therefore remaining as the faithful protection of your own may you receive me your seer and the book published to your delight under your custody, that reclining under the cover of so spreading a tree I may be able to make the reed of your muse resound before envious and evil men with a secure harmony.

Geoffrey's thought moves smoothly in five little paragraphs. In the first, a single sentence of nine lines extending from *Cum mecum* to *predicarentur*, he expresses his surprise that Gildas and Bede made no mention of Arthur and many other kings. In the second, a single sentence of nine lines extending from *Talia mihi* to *proponebat*, he praises Walter archdeacon of Oxford, a man learned in exotic histories, who supplied him with a very ancient book which set forth the deeds of all the kings from Brutus to Cadwalader. In the third, two sentences of nine lines extending from *Rogatus* to *oporteret*, he describes his work as a translator, content with his own pens and eschewing bombastic diction. In the fourth, a single sentence of ten lines extending from *Opusculo igitur* to *affectu*, he addresses his prospective patron Robert, alluding to the salt of his wit and praising him in a triple anaphora. In the fifth, three sentences of twenty lines extending from *Tu quoque* to *queam*, he addresses his prospective patron Waleran. Each paragraph begins in the manuscript with a capital letter and ends with a punctuation point.

Geoffrey's prose moves in balanced doublets:

> multa et de multis;
> Gildas et Beda;
> nichil de regibus qui ante incarnationem ... inhabitauerant
> nichil etiam de ... compluribus qui post incarnationem successerunt;
> cum et ... constarent ... et ... predicarentur;
> talia et de talibus;
> in oratoria arte atque in exoticis hystoriis;
> qui a Bruto ... usque ad Cadualadrum;
> continue et ex ordine;
> magis in exponendis uerbis quam in hystoria intelligenda;
> te doctore te monitore;
> quod non ex Galfridi ... fonticulo ... exortum set sale minerue tue conditum.

He rises to a triple anaphora:

> quem Henricus ... generauit
> quem philosophia ... erudiuit
> quem ... probitas ... prefecit.

He links the beginning of the first paragraph to the beginning of the second, balancing *mecum* with *mihi*, *multa et de multis* with *talia et de talibus*, *sepius* with *multociens*, and *animo reuoluens* with *cogitanti*. He links the second, mentioning Walter, his *quendam librum*, and *Britannici sermonis*, to the third, mentioning *illius*, *codicem illum*, and *Latinum sermonem*. He also arranges his words in chiastic patterns:

a	uir		a	illius [i.e. Walteri]
b	in oratoria arte		b	ductus
c	atque		c	alienos ortulos
b'	in exoticis hystoriis		d	falerata uerba
a'	eruditus		e	non collegerim
			d'	agresti stilo
			c'	propriisque calamis
			b'	contentus
			a'	codicem illum [i.e. librum uetustissimum].

Reading this text aloud one can hardly fail to notice Geoffrey's consistent use of cursus rhythms.

planus	tardus	uelox
I laúdis constárent	I ínhabitáuerant	II multóciens cògitánti
prédicaréntur	ceterísque complúribus	hystóriis èrudítus
II oratória árte	II óptulit Wálterus	oratiónibus pròponébat
III illius dúctus	árchidiáconus	ártibus èrudíuit
transférre curáui	IV Claudiocéstrie fáueas	III páginam illiníssem
IV censeátur exórtum	dicátur edítio	
túe condítum		
tempóribus nóstris		
congratulátur afféctu		

medius	trispondiacus	dispondeus dactylicus
I mírum cóntuli	I ánimo reuóluens	I Británnie incíderem
tractátu fécerant	successérunt repperíssem	III legéntibus ingérerem
II uétustíssimum	III cálamis conténtus	
rége Brítonum	éxponendis uérbis	
áctus ómnium	IV monitóre corrigátur	
III aliénos órtulos	commorári oportéret	
nón collégerim	Anglórum generáuit	
	milítibus prefécit	

In ascending order of preference *dispondeus dactylicus, uelox, tardus, medius, trispondiacus, planus*, there are 2–5–6–7–8–9 rhythms. There are eighteen rhythms in the first half of the Preface and nineteen in the second.

Reckoning words, there are sixty-six in the first paragraph, forty-five in the second, forty-eight in the third, and sixty-three in the fourth, that is 111 words in the first half and 111 in the second.

The theme and structure are made clear by the symmetrical centre and the golden section of each of the paragraphs. In the first the central words stand at the centre of the central fourth of eight lines: *nichil de regibus qui | ante incarnationem Xpisti inhabitauerant*. The golden section is in the third and the fifth of eight lines: *infra mentionem quam de eis Gildas et | Beda luculento tractatu fecerant* and *nichil etiam de Arturo | ceterisque compluribus*. In the second the central word is in line 14: *quendam Britannici | sermonis | librum uetustissimum*. The golden section falls at *atque in | exoticis historiis eruditus* and *qui a Bruto | primo rege Britonum*. In the third the centre is in line 22: *codicem illum in Latinum | sermonem transferre curaui*. The golden section falls at *agresti tamen stilo propriisque | calamis contentus* and *nam si ampullosis | dictionibus paginam illinissem*. In the fourth the central word is in line 30: *quem | Henricus | illustris rex Anglorum generauit*. The golden section falls at *sed sale | minerue tue conditum* and *quem philosophia liberalibus | artibus erudiuit*.

One infers that in the original Prologue of four paragraphs Geoffrey strove for symmetry. In adding the fifth paragraph to Waleran he resorted to similar stylistic features of doublets:

> et terror hostium existere et protectio tuorum esse;
> me tuum uatem codicemque;
> sub tutela ... et sub tegmine;
> coram inuidis atque improbis;

and triplet:

> phylosophia ... excepit
> subtilitatem edocuit
> ac deinde ... direxit.

He also linked the fourth paragraph to the fifth.

Robertus dux Claudiocestrie	Galeranne consul Mellenti
faueas	adhibeas
ut	ut
editio	editio
Henricus illustris rex Anglorum	celeberimi regis Karoli stirpe
generauit	progenitum
philosophia	phylosophia
artibus	scientiarumque
erudiuit	excepit ... edocuit
in milicia militibus	in militaribus ... exercitiis
unde	ubi

Again he made use of cursus rhythms:

planus	tardus	uelox
cónsul Mellénti	stírpe progénitum	moderatióne commùnicáta
nóstri colúmpna	subtilitátem edócuit	púlchrius èlucéscat
adhíbeas túam	túa recípias	
súo excépit	árboris récubans	
régum diréxit		
áddidicísti		
tuórum exístens		
mé tuum uátem		

medius	trispondiacus	dispondeus dactylicus
éxercítiis	audácter supergréssus	hóstium exístere
túi éditum	résonare quéam	
átque ímprobis		

Though the ratios differ from those of the original Preface, he used in addressing Waleran twenty rhythms, exactly twice as many as he had used in addressing Robert. By using 103 words and 648 letters, he made the fifth paragraph relate to the fourth by extreme and mean ratio. Reckoning words, 63 + 103 = 166, of which the golden section falls at 103 and 63. Reckoning letters, 401[5] + 648 = 1049, of which the golden section falls at 648 and 401.

Here is Geoffrey's introduction to the *Prophetiae Merlini* at the beginning of Book VII.

5   Read *Britannia* with a single *t*, as in *Britannie* 2, *Britannici* 15, *Brito* and *Britonum* 16.

Nondum autem ad hunc locum historie perueneram cum de Merlino
    diuulgáto rumóre   a
compellebant me undique contemporanei mei prophetias ípsius édere   a
maxime autem Alexander Lincolniensis episcopus uir summe
    religiónis et prudéntie .   a
Non erat in clero siue in populo cui tot nobiles fámularéntur   b
quos mansueta pietas ipsius et benigna largitas in obsequium
    suum álliciébat .   5   c
Cui cum satisfacere preelegissem prophétias tránstuli   d
et eidem cum huiusmodi lítteris diréxi .   d
Coegit me Alexander Lincolniensis presul nobilitatis túe diléctio   e
prophetias Merlini de Britannico in Latínum transférre   a
antequam historiam perarassem quam de gestis regum
    Britannicorum inceperam .   10   f
Proposueram enim illam prius perficere istudque opus
    subsequenter explicare   a
ne dum uterque labor incumberet sensus meus ad singula minor
    fieret .   c
Attamen | quoniam securus eram uenie quam discretio
    subtilis ingenii tui donaret   c
agrestem calamum meum labellis apposui   d
et plebeia modulatione ignotum tibi interpretatus sum
    sermonem .   15   f
Admodum autem admiror quia id pauperi stilo dignatus eras
    committere   a
cum tot doctiores tot ditiores uirga potestatis tue coerceat   c
qui sublimioris carminis delectamento aures minerue tue
    mulcerent .   c
Et ut omnes philosophos totius Britannie insule preteream   f
tu solus es quod non erubesco fateri qui pre cunctis audaci
    lira caneres   20   g
nisi te culmen honoris ad cetera negotia uocaret .   c
Quoniam ergo placuit ut Gaufridus Monemutensis fistulam
    suam in hoc uaticinio sonaret   c
modulationibus suis fauere non diffugias et quicquid
    inordinate siue uitiose protulerit   c
ferula camenarum tuarum in rectum aduertas concentum .   24   f

But I had not yet come to this part of the History when, with a rumour
    about Merlin divulged,
my contemporaries on all sides compelled me to publish the Prophecies
    of the very man,
but especially Alexander Bishop of Lincoln, a man of the highest religion
    and prudence.

There was no one among the clergy or among the people whom so
    many nobles served,
whom his customary piety and benign generosity attracted to
    his service.   5
As I chose to satisfy him I translated and directed the Prophecies
to the same man with a letter of this form:
Alexander Bishop of Lincoln, the love of your nobility has compelled
    me
to translate the Prophecies of Merlin from British into Latin
before I have finished the History which I had begun about the
    deeds of the British kings.   10
For I had proposed to complete that before and subsequently to expound
    this work,
lest while either labour weighed on me my faculties might be inferior to
    both tasks.
Since, however, I was certain of the favour which the discernment of
    your subtle intelligence would give
I have placed my rustic reed to my little lips
and with plebeian measure I have interpreted unfamiliar speech
    for you.   15
But I wonder greatly that you had deigned to commit it to a poor pen,
since the rod of your power might coerce so many more learned and
    more splendid men,
who might soothe the ears of your intellect with a delight of more
    sublime song.
And though I should pass over all the philosophers of the entire island of
    Britain
you are the only man, I do not blush to state, who may sing it before all
    with a bold lyre,   20
except that the pinnacle of honour should call you to other occupations.
Since therefore it has been pleasing that Geoffrey of Monmouth should
    sound his own pipe in this prophesying,
may you not avoid favouring his measures, and whatever he may have
    brought forth inordinately or viciously
may you turn toward correct harmony with the little rule of
    your muses.   24

The 218 words of prose divide by symmetry at 109 and 109, by extreme and
mean ratio at 135 and 83, by one-ninth and eight-ninths at 24 and 194.
Reckoned from the beginning one-ninth falls at *Alexander Lincolniensis episcopus* |
uir summe religionis et prudentie. Reckoned from the end it falls at *Gaufridus
Monemutensis* | *fistulam suam*. From the beginning to *Alexander Lincolniensis
episcopus* to *Alexander Lincolniensis presul* inclusive there are sixty-nine words,
which divide by extreme and mean ratio at 43 and 26. Between *Alexander* and

Alexander there are forty-three words. From *Britannico* to *Britannie* inclusive there are ninety words, which divide by one-ninth and eight-ninths at 10 and 80. Between *Britannico* and *Britannicorum* there are ten words.

The exact chronology of publication of William of Malmesbury's *Gesta Regum Anglorum*,[6] the Henry of Huntingdon's *Historia Anglorum*,[7] and Geoffrey of Monmouth's *Historia Regum Britanniae* is obscure. All three authors spent much time in writing, and all three were diligent, not to say obsessive, revisers, who issued at least four, five, and three versions of their respective works. One should bear in mind three short passages, first from the *Gesta Regum Anglorum* book I § 8, vol. I pp. 11–2:

> Sed eo extincto Britonum robur emarcuit, spes imminutae retro fluxere; et jam tunc profecto pessum issent, nisi Ambrosius, solus Romanorum superstes, qui post Wortigernum monarcha regni fuit, intumescentes barbaros eximia bellicosi Arturis opera pressisset. Hic est Artur de quo Britonum nugae hodieque delirant; dignus plane quem non fallaces somniarent fabulae, sed veraces praedicarent historiae.

Second from book III § 287, vol. II p. 342:

> Sed Arturis sepulcrum nusquam visitur, unde antiquitas naeniarum adhuc eum venturum fabulatur.

Third from Henry of Huntingdon's Letter to Warin, as edited by Robert of Torigni.[8]

> Quaeris a me, Warine Brito, vir comis et facete, cur patriae nostrae gesta narrans, a temporibus Julii Caesaris inceperim, et florentissima regna, quae a Bruto usque ad Julium fuerunt, omiserim. Respondeo igitur tibi quod nec voce nec scripto horum temporum saepissime notitiam quaerens invenire potui. Tanta pernicies oblivionis mortalium gloriam successu diuturnitatis obumbrat et exstinguit! Hoc tamen anno, [qui est ab incarnatione Domini MCXXX. nonus,] cum Romam proficiscerer [cum Theobaldo Cantuariensi archiepiscopo], apud Becc[um, ubi idem archiepiscopus abbas fuerat], scripta rerum praedictarum stupens inveni. [Siquidem Robertum de Torinneio, ejusdem loci monachum, virum tam divinorum quam secularium librorum inquisitorem et coacervatorem studiosissimum, ibidem conveni. Qui cum de ordine historiae de regibus Anglorum a me editae

---

6 *Willelmi Malmesbiriensis Monachi De Gestis Regum Anglorum Libri Quinque, Historiae Novellae Libri Tres*, ed. W. Stubbs, Rolls Series 2 vols. (London 1887, 1889).

7 *Henrici Archidiaconi Huntendunensis Historia Anglorum, The History of the English, by Henry, Archdeacon of Huntingdon*, ed. T. Arnold, Rolls Series (London 1879).

8 *The Chronicle of Robert of Torigni, Chronicles of the Reigns of Stephen, Henry II., and Richard I.*, ed. R. Howlett, Rolls Series (London 1889), vol. IV pp. 65–6. Words in square brackets are Torigni's additions.

me interrogaret, et id quod a me quaerebat libens audisset, obtulit mihi librum ad legendum de regibus Britonum, qui ante Anglos nostram insulam tenuerunt]; quorum excerpta, ut in epistola decet, brevissime scilicet, tibi, dilectissime, mitto.

The first two passages imply that William, writing about 1125, considered what he had heard about Arthur to be merely *nugae, fallaces fabulae*, and *naeniae*. Henry of Huntingdon dedicated his *Historia Anglorum*, first published in 1129, to Alexander Bishop of Lincoln. The third passage explicitly records Henry's astonishment at his introduction to Geoffrey's book in 1139. Geoffrey dedicated the *Historia Regum Britanniae* to Robert Earl of Gloucester because William of Malmesbury had dedicated the *Gesta Regum Anglorum* to Robert Earl of Gloucester. Because William had placed his dedication at the centre of his work, at the end of the third of five books, Geoffrey placed the *Prophetiae Merlini* at the centre of his work, at the beginning of the seventh of twelve books, allegedly at the direction of Alexander Bishop of Lincoln, because Henry of Huntingdon had dedicated the *Historia Anglorum* to Alexander Bishop of Lincoln. In the game of literary oneupmanship Geoffrey awarded himself further points by writing in his envoi

Degenerati autem a Britannica nobilitáte Gualénses		a
numquam postea monarchiam insulae recúperauérunt		b
immo nunc sibi interdum Saxonibus íngrati cònsurgéntes		a
externas ac domesticas clades incessánter agébant.		b
Reges autem eorum qui illo tempore in Guáliis sùccessérunt	5	b
Karadoco Lancarbanensi contemporáneo méo		c
in materia scribéndi permítto		c
reges uero Saxonum Willelmo Málmesberiénsi		d
et Henrico Húntendonénsi		d
quos de regibus Britonum tacére iúbeo	10	c
cum non habebant librum istum Británnici sermónis		e
quem Gualterus Oxenefordensis archidiaconus ex Británnia aduéxit		f
quem de hystoria eorum ueráciter éditum		g
in honore predictórum príncipum		g
hoc modo in Latinum sermonem transférre curáui.	15	d

Both William and Henry enjoyed a rich array of Anglo-Latin primary sources — letters, charters, documents of various kinds, poems; and of secondary sources— works of chronology, chronicles, polished literary histories written in prose and verse by men of learning, judgement, and, in the case of Bede, genius. So extensive were the materials that William could disdain some of them, particularly those of whose style he disapproved, like Frithegod's *Breuiloquium Vitae Beati Uuilfredi* and Æthelweard's *Chronicon*. Both men also had direct access to vernacular Old English sources in addition to the *Anglo-Saxon Chronicle*. William was well informed about the works of Ælfric and about the works which had

issued earlier from the court of King Alfred, whose *Handboc* or *Liber Manualis* or
Encheiridion he had read. Henry even translated *The Battle of Brunanburh* into Latin
that reflected elements of Old English poetry.[9] Geoffrey by contrast had very
little, and of that even less was glorious. The oldest and finest Celtic Latin text
available was Gildas *De Excidio Britanniae*, which laments the degeneracy of
British kings, judges, and clergy. There is a twelfth-century *Vita Sancti Gildae* by
Caradog of Llancarfan, but, as we have seen above,[10] it is a tissue of hagiographic
commonplaces. Caradog describes Arthur twice as *rex rebellis* and once as *tyrannus*.
At the crux of his chiastic structure he makes Gildas forgive Arthur for the
homicidium of Hueil, one of the twenty-three brothers of the saint. Geoffrey may
have considered this intolerably unimaginative and utterly incompatible with his
vision of Arthur.

The eleventh-century *Eulogium* to the Nennian recension of the *Historia
Brittonum* laments the dullness and sloth of the Welsh and their consequent lack of
written sources, which drove the compiler to the annals of the Irish and the
English.[11] If the *Historia Brittonum* was the best that survived from the ninth
century, and the *hebitudo gentis Brittannie* forced an eleventh-century Welsh
scholar to gather what scraps he could find *de annalibus Romanorum, de cronicis
sanctorum patrum, de annalibus Scottorum Saxonumque*, but only *ex traditione ueterum
nostrorum quod multi doctores atque librarii scribere temptauerunt*, there cannot have
been much for a twelfth-century scholar to find. Remembering that Latin *inuenire*
means both 'to come upon, discover' and 'to devise, invent', we need not beg
any questions about what Geoffrey did to *inuenire* his sources. His *Historia Regum
Britanniae* provides for a people destitute of information about their past millennia
of history. It addresses the very patrons to whom William and Henry dedicated
their books. It rebukes William's disdain of stories about Geoffrey's greatest hero
and Henry's astonishment at his book. It plays with William's remarks at the end
of *Gesta Regum Anglorum*.[12] Finally it 'permits' Caradog and William and Henry
to write more, but 'commands them to be silent', denying them the ability to
write without access to Geoffrey's source. To Geoffrey the imaginative inventor
Caradog, who without any sources produced commonplaces, may have seemed
an intolerable hagiographic bore. To Geoffrey the patriotic Celtic historian
William and Henry may have seemed enviably supplied with an undeserved
richness of English historical sources. His response was to overwhelm the Welsh
dullard and surpass the ablest English historians. As they addressed their works
about recent English history to the most powerful and influential members of the
Anglo-Norman establishment, encouraging them to sink their roots into the

---

9 A.G. Rigg, 'Henry of Huntingdon's Metrical Experiments', *The Journal of Medieval Latin* I (1991),
   pp. 60–72.
10 See above pp. 346–51.
11 See above pp. 333–5.
12 Porro quoquo modo haec se habeant priuatim ipse mihi sub ope Xpisti gratulor quod continuam
   Anglorum historiam ordinauerim post Bedam uel solus uel primus : si quis ergo sicut iam susurrari
   audio post me scribendi de talibus munus attemptauerit mihi debeat collectionis gratiam sibi habeat
   electionis materiam.

English past, he addressed his work about the more glorious history of millennia to the same patrons, encouraging them to sink their roots into the pre-English, British, past. His literary, if not his professional, success was immediate, and it endured for centuries, generating more imaginative literature than any other text of the entire Middle Ages.

III. JOHN OF CORNWALL

Prophetia Merlini

John of Cornwall is 'the first secular master in theology in Oxford in the latter part of the twelfth century of whose writings we have record'.[1] He was born probably about 1125 or 1130, shortly before Abaelard composed the *Historia Calamitatum*. In 1155 at the command of Robert Warelwast Bishop of Exeter he translated from a British source and commented upon the *Prophetia Merlini*,[2] in the Prologue to which he acknowledges himself a pupil of Thierry of Chartres. In 1173 he witnessed a charter in London. In the summer of 1176 he was recommended, partly because of his competence in the Welsh language, to Henry II as a candidate for the vacant see of Saint David's. About 1179, when the Lateran Council was imminent, he composed the *Eulogium ad Alexandrum Papam Tertium*,[3] in which he quotes extensively from Abaelard. He acted as judge delegate at a case in Oxford in 1192 in the presence of at least nine other masters. He died in 1199.

Here follows his Prologue to the *Prophetia Merlini*.[4]

IOHANNIS CORNUBIENSIS PROPHETIA MERLINI

Venerabilis Roberte Presul Éxoniénsis		a
qui uirtutis et sapientie quadam prerogatiua súper modérnos		b
et in pósterum lúces		b
iussus ego Iohannes Córnubiénsis		ba
Prophetiam Merlini iuxta nostrum Británnicum expónere	5	cd
in uestri gratia affectui meo magis quam facultáti cónsulens		cb
breui admodum in scolari palestra íd eluctári		ee
puerili stílo conátus sum.		f
Qua in re utcúmque profécerim		g
non absque labore meo quícquam adéptus sum	10	f
cum pro uerbo uerbum lege interpretationis réddere studúerim.		g

1 E. Rathbone, 'John of Cornwall, A Brief Biography', *Recherches de Théologie Ancienne et Médiévale* XVII (1950), pp. 46–60, at 53, 59–60.
2 *BCLL* 41.
3 *BCLL* 42.
4 M.J. Curley, 'A New Edition of John of Cornwall's *Prophetia Merlini*', *Speculum* LVII ii (1982), pp. 217–49, at 231–2.

Pretermissa tamen ea que in hystória Anglór*um*		h
adusque principis Willélmi impéri*um*		h
de predecessoribus satis expedite contéxta repèriúntu*r*		g
ne ligna in siluam attulísse uidére*r*.	15	g
De his que secúntur Cónan*i*		h
lacrimabilem exitum ad présens superséd*i*		h
úsque dum agnósse*m*		i
quis esset istorum locus apud tante aúctoritàtis uíru*m*		i
in cuius locupletis armarióli sacrári*o*	20	j
scutum Minerue et gladium Mercurii non latet ésse repósit*a*.		k
Unde nisi uester fauor lóngius abstíter*it*		l
et de his et de illis alias et nuperrime supletum iri ánimaduérta*m*		i
qui si dexter áspiráuer*it*		l
aliorum morábor némine*m*.	25	i
Scio enim nonnúllo*s* insolénte*s*		d
utique nec degenere*s* fortúne fili*os*		d
presens opus clam detractionis spiculo óbstinatúr*os*		d
sed fórsitan iniúst*e*.		c
Obinde mouérer équi*dem*	30	i
nisi eórum et laú*dem*		i
et uituperium eque pensanda líquido còmperísse*m*		i
presertim cum non sint ipsi talis expériénti*e*		c
ut uel aliquod munimen litterali studio quéant excúlper*e*		c
et tante importunitatis ut maxima quelibet zelo nequítie		
inuádu*nt*	35	m
et contáminare uéli*nt*		m
quos magister meus Théodéricu*s*		d
tum uero nómine Phàraóne*s*		d
tum yronice fratres suos appelláre consuéu*it*.		l
Verum enim uero quatinus eiusdem philósophi móre*s*	40	d
aliquatenus referre uidéar ut dícitu*r*		g
"Astuta ingenium uulpes imitáta leóne*m*"		i
Qui meam citharam eneruáre uol*úerit*		l
aut nullas habeat aut sí hab*úerit*		l
det operam sue ne labéfiant týbi*e*.	45	c
His ita omissis iam mé reticént*e*		c
Merlini Vaticinium áccipiátu*r*.	47	g

Venerable Robert bishop of Exeter,
who by a certain prerogative of virtue and wisdom shine above modern
    men
and for posterity,
I, John of Cornwall, commanded,

have attempted to expound the Prophecy of Merlin according
    to our British language,   5
trusting in the grace of your intention more than in my ability
to strive toward that in a quite brief and scholarly exercise
with a childlike pen.
To whatever degree I will have succeeded in that attempt
I have not accomplished anything without my labour,   10
since I will have studied to give back a word for a word by the law of
    interpretation,
yet having left out those things in the history of the English which about
    predecessors
up to the rule of Prince William
are found covered rather quickly,
lest I be seen to have carried wood into the forest.   15
About those things which follow Conan's lamentable death
up to the present I have been silent [lit. 'sat upon']
until I should come to know
what would be their place with a man of such great authority,
in the sanctuary of whose rich armoury   20
it does not lie hidden that the shield of Minerva [*i.e.* wisdom] and the
    sword of Mercury [*i.e.* astuteness] are laid up.
Whence, unless your favour should be far removed
I shall observe that both on these matters and on those the deficiency
    will be supplied and very soon which [favour] if it be propitious and
    aid [lit. 'if propitious it have aided']
I shall direct my attention for the completed account to be gone over,
    both about the latter and about the former and subsequently most
    recently,
I who if the right hand should give aid
shall delay none of the others.   25
For I know some insolent men,
(if only they were not degenerate) sons of fortune,
about to set their minds on the present work secretly with the little spike
    of detraction,
but perhaps unjustly.
On which account I for my part would be moved   30
unless I could establish unequivocally that both their praise
and vituperation should be equally weighted,
especially since those men may not be of such experience
that they should be able to assault any fortification by literary study
and of such great importunity that they may set on certain very great
    matters with the zeal of evil,   35
and wish to contaminate,
men whom my master Thierry

was formerly accustomed to call sometimes by the true name 'pharaohs',
sometimes ironically 'his own brothers'.
For on the other hand up to a point I shall seem to refer to the mores of
    the same philosopher   40
up to a point, as it is said,
'The fox astute has imitated the ingenious lion'.
Who would wish to unstring my lyre
should either have no flutes or if he should have [them]
he should take care lest his own be dropped.   45
With these things thus left off, with me being silent,
let the Prophecy of Merlin be received.   47

One notes at the very beginning the alliteration and rhyme and rhythm of John's prose. In the first sentence of forty-seven words, which prefigures the Prologue of forty-seven lines, he addresses his patron in the first words, *Venerabilis Roberte Presul Exoniensis*, and refers to himself in the last words, *conatus sum*. He names his book and its source in the central words, *Prophetiam Merlini iuxta nostrum Britannicum exponere*. As 47 divides by extreme and mean ratio at 29 and 18, he refers to himself at the golden section reckoned from the beginning, *iussus ego | Iohannes Cornubiensis*; reckoned from the end he contrasts himself with his patron, *in uestri gratia | affectui meo magis quam facultati consulens*.

In the entire Prologue of 265 words he plays with other ratios. The 265 words divide by one-ninth and eight-ninths at 29 and 236, marked by two references to the title and subject. From the beginning to *Prophetiam Merlini iuxta nostrum Britannicum exponere* inclusive and *Merlini Vaticinium accipiatur* occupy twenty-nine words. The intervening text occupies 236 words. At the words *nisi eorum et laudem et uituperium | eque pensanda liquido comperissem* the text divides by duple ratio (2:1), one indication among many that John understood the rules of a game, in which he was not the least competent player.

IV. PETER OF CORNWALL

Pantheologus, Liber Revelationum, Liber Disputationum

The last mediaeval Celtic Latin writer we shall consider, Peter of Cornwall, came from a distinguished family.[1] The son of Jordan of Trecarrel (*floruit* 1120–70), nephew of Bernard the king's scribe, grandson of Ailsi (Old English *Æðelsige* 'noble victory'), great-grandson of Theodulf, was born about 1140 at Launceston in eastern Cornwall. After 1170 he entered the Augustinian priory of Holy Trinity, Aldgate, London, of which he became prior in 1197, and in which he was buried in 1221.

1 P. Hull & R. Sharpe, 'Peter of Cornwall and Launceston', *Cornish Studies* XIII (1986), pp. 5–53.

Between 1190 and 1197 he composed a vast work named the *Pantheologus*.[2] The entire Prologue to the first part is full of interest, but we may consider particularly the passage in which he discusses his style, learned from Gilbert Foliot Bishop of London 1163–88. Capital letters and punctuation marks in boldface represent features of London, British Library, MS Royal 7 E VIII folio 1rb.

Formam autem et módum hunc scribéndi :
ab illo ore aureo commúnis patris nóstri
uenerabilis Gilleberti Londoniensis epíscopi : mùtuáui .
Qui cum in sinodo iam nóuus canónicus
ad uenerabilis patris mei Stephani Sancte Trinitatis Londonie .
    príoris pédes :   5
humilis et attentus áuditor àssedíssem :
formam et modum sermonis eius quem fécit ad clérum .
ut audiui : admírans obmútui .
et laudans tacére non pótui .
Totus enim sermo ille quibusdam distinctiónibus uàriátus .   10
et flosculis uerborum et sententiárum depíctus .
et copiosa auctoritatum subiectióne roborátus :
a principio per tramites suos ad idem princípium dècurrébat .
ét recurrébat .
ut areolas agrorum multiplicibus riuulorum tractibus uniformi
    dissimilitúdine èxarátas :   15
et multiplici uernantis germinis fructu inter canalium[3] decursus
    fecundátas : cogitáres .
nec hominem sed superhominem esse : qui tanta auctoritátum cópia
per singulas sermonis distinctiones superhabundare potuísset : affirmáres.
Cum enim inter cetera Xpistum lápidem díceret :
protulit in medium illum lapidem angularem ab edificántibus
    rèprobátum.   20
protulit et in medium lapidem illum quem Iacob unxit oleo . et eréxit
in títulum .
protulit[4] in medium nichilominus lapidem illum in Daniele de monte
    sine mánibus abscísum.
Et cum circa hec et similia sermo eius in lóngum protràherétur
pulcherrima uerborum uarietáte distínctus
tanta uelocitate sine impedimenti inuidia quocunque uóluit decurrébat .
ut non iam excogitáta recitáre .
sed omnia ante oculos diligenti examinatione conscripta : légere putáres .
Tante igitur et tam preclare nouitatis dulcedine èxhilarátus :

---

2 *BCLL* 77. R.W. Hunt, 'English Learning in the Late Twelfth Century', *Transactions of the Royal Historical Society*, 4th series, XIX (1936), pp. 19–42.
3 Not *carnalium* as ed. Hunt.
4 Not *protulit et* as ed. Hunt.

tanteque et tam desiderande omnium utilitatis intentione ad presumendum
símília pròuocátus :
sepe et multum solus mecum tacitus ét sollícitus   30
cogitare cepi . quibusnam certe legis loris fugax memória tènerétur :
quo[5] certe artis fine rerum ac nominum incomprehensibilis infinitas
    comprehéndi ualéret .
Tandem uero post diuturnas lucubrationum[6] ignorantie nebulas : lumen
    pátuit querénti .
et scientie ianua apérta est pulsánti .
per quam inoffenso pede : ad interiora artis precépta percúrrerem .   35
et opus uotiuùm per methodum[7] artis inuentum[8] : ad finem diu
    desideratum úsque perdúcerem .
in quo lector studiosus omnia prout diximus sine mora que quérit
    inuéniet .
et in morem corolarii[9] se inuenisse que non sperabat optata : pro mercéde
    accípiet.   38

But the form, however, and this manner of writing
from that golden mouth of our common father,
venerable Gilbert Bishop of London, I have borrowed,
who, when in synod, then a new canon,
at the feet of my venerable father Stephen Prior of Holy Trinity of
    London   5
I would sit as a lowly and attentive hearer
the form and manner of his sermon which he made to the clergy
as I heard admiring I became dumb
and praising I could not be silent,
for that whole sermon varied with certain distinctions   10
and decorated with little flowers of words and sentences
and strengthened by the copious appending of authorities
from the beginning along its own paths to the same beginning kept
    running down
and running back
so that you would think of little seed beds of fields ploughed in uniform
    dissimilitude by multiplex drawings of rivulets   15
and made fecund with multiplex fruit of springing seed among the
    courses of channels
and you would affirm him not to be a man but a superman who with so
    great a supply of authorities

5   Not *et quo* as ed. Hunt.
6   MS corrected from *lugubrationum*.
7   Not *metodum* as ed. Hunt.
8   MS *inuentam*.
9   Not *corollarii* as ed. Hunt.

could superabound through particular distinctions of the sermon.

For when among other things he would call Christ a stone

he drew our attention to [lit. 'brought forth into the middle'] that corner stone rejected by the builders, 20

he brought forth also into the middle that stone which Jacob anointed with oil and erected as a monument,

he brought forth into the middle nonetheless that stone in Daniel cut away from the mountain without hands,

and when about these and similar things his sermon was drawn out in length,

distinguished by the most beautiful variety of words,

with such great speed, without the spite of an obstacle, wherever he wished, it ran down, 25

so that you would suppose he recited things not yet thought out,

yet he read all these things with diligent examination written out before the eyes.

Exhilarated therefore by the sweetness of such great and very radiant newness

and provoked to performing similar things by the intensity of such great and so desirable usefulness,

often alone with myself, silent and greatly anxious, 30

I began to think by what thongs of sure law, I ask you, might fleeting memory be held,

by what end of sure art the incomprehensible infinity of things and names might be able to be comprehended.

Finally, then, after long-lasting clouds of lucubrations of not knowing, the light shone to me seeking

and the door of understanding was opened to one knocking,

through which I might run with unoffensive foot to the interior precepts of art 35

and I might lead the work granted after prayer by the discovered method of art through to a long-desired end

in which the studious reader might, as we have said, find all things which he seeks without delay

and receive as a wished-for reward in the manner of a gratuity things which he did not hope he would find. 38

Peter's praise of Gilbert Foliot's sermon is unusually precise and detailed. His own rhetorical competence is readily apparent, hardly needing explication. This passage divides by symmetry at the triple anaphora. Of thirty-eight lines, the nineteenth from the end begins with the first *protulit in medium illum lapidem*. Of the 312 words the central 156th falls at the third *protulit in medium | nichilominus lapidem illum*. The 1243 words of the entire Prologue divide by extreme and mean ratio at 768 and 475, at the first *protulit in medium lapidem illum*. Not a mean feat.

During the years 1200 to 1206 Peter compiled a huge *Liber Reuelationum*,[10] which includes accounts of several visions that occurred to members of his own family. Here is the Prologue.

LIBER REVELATIONUM

INCIPIUNT VISIONES MULTIPLICES AILSI TAM DE HOC SECULO QUAM DE FUTURI SECULI PENIS ET GLORIA.

Tempore Henrici regis Anglie primi contigit uisio non dissimulanda cuidam uiro bono et sancto, auo scilicet Petri prioris ecclesie sancte Trinitatis Londonie quarti, qui hanc eiusdem uiri uisionem hic describit, prout post multorum curricula annorum potuit recolere a tempore quo pater suus Jordanus ei adhuc puero olim narrauerat. Hanc suam uisionem quondam narrauit predictus uir Ailsi nomine filio suo Jordano tunc iuueni qui eandem uisionem prout ipse potuit post multa tempora retinuisse filio suo predicto Petro adhuc puero qui iam nunc fere sexagenarius prout ipse ut diximus ad memoriam potuit reduxisse, eandem uisionem hic describit. Non autem omnia predicte uisionis menbra' sed uix modicam partem eiusdem uisionis tanquam in tercium uas iam infusam describere potuit, maxima uidelicet predicte uisionis parte iam a memoria sua elapsa.

The manifold visions of Ailsi both of this world and of the pains and glory of the next world.

In the days of Henry I, king of England, a vision not to be concealed came to a certain good and holy man, grandfather of Peter, fourth prior of Holy Trinity, London, who here describes this man's vision, in so far as he can remember it after a lapse of so many years gone by since his father Jordan used to relate it to him in his boyhood. This same vision was told in past years by Ailsi to his son Jordan who was then a youth; which same Jordan retold it, in so far as the passage of time had yet left it in his memory, to his said son Peter, then but a child but now approaching his sixtieth year. Jordan was not able to describe all elements of the vision but only a small part of it, as much, as it were, as could be poured into a third vessel, for the greater part had already slipped from his memory.

By noting the Biblical style in which Peter composed this passage one can both appreciate the craft of the Latin prose and correct the English translation. Capital letters and punctuation marks in boldface represent features of London, Lambeth Palace Library, MS 51 folio 23rb. I have marked the rhythms of the cursus.

---

10 *BCLL* 80. Hull & Sharpe, pp. 16–7.

INCIPIUNT VISIONES MULTÍPLICES AÍLSI .
TAM DE HOC SECULO QUAM DE FUTURI SECULI PÉNIS ET GLÓRIA .

A Tempore Henrici Regis **ANGlie** primi contigit uisio non dissimulanda cuidam uiro bóno et sáncto.

B 1 auo scilicet **Petri** prioris ecclesie **Sancte Trinitatis Londónie** quárti.

2 qui hanc eiusdem uiri uisiónem hic descríbit :

3a prout post multorum curricula annorum pótuit recólere

b a tempore quo pater suus Jordanus ei adhuc puero ólim narráuerat.

c Hanc suam uisionem quondam narrauit predictus uir **Aílsi** nómine

b' filio suo **Jordáno** tunc iúueni . qui eándem uisiónem

a' prout ipse potuit post multa tempora rétinuísse :

B'1 filio suo predicto **Pétro** adhuc púero .

2 qui iam nunc fere séxagenárius

3a prout ipse ut diximus ad memoriam pótuit rèduxísse :

b eandem uisiónem hic descríbit .

c Non autem omnia predicte uisionis menbra

b' sed uix modicam partem eíusdem uisiónis

a' tanquam in tercium uas iam infusam descríbere pótuit . maxima uidelicet predicte uisionis parte iam a memoria súa elápsa .

Here begin the multifold visions of Ailsi
both about this age and about the punishments and glory of the age to come.

A In the time of Henry I, King of England, a vision not to be concealed happened to a certain good and holy man,

B 1 that is, to the grandfather of Peter, fourth prior of the Church of the Holy Trinity of London,

2 who here describes the vision of that man,

3a just as he could, went over in his mind after the courses of many years,

b from the time in which his own father Jordan had narrated long ago to him, at that time a boy.

c This his own vision the foresaid man, Ailsi by name, once narrated

b' to his own son Jordan, then a youth,

a' who, just as he himself could, after much time retained the memory of the same vision

B'1 for his own son, the foresaid Peter, at that time a boy,

2 who now already almost a sixty-year-old,

3a just as he himself could, as we have said, recalled to memory

b here describes the same vision.

c Not, however, all parts of the foresaid vision,
b' but scarcely a little portion of the same vision
a' such as poured already into the third vessel he could describe,
    with the greatest portion of the foresaid vision, certainly, slipped
    out already from his own memory.

Compare *Petri* B1 with *predicto Petro* B'1, and B2 *qui* with B'2 *qui*. In B3 compare *prout post multorum curricula annorum potuit recolere* a with *prout ipse potuit post multa tempora retinuisse* a', *pater suus Jordanus adhuc puero* b with *filio suo Jordano tunc iuueni* b', around the crux in c, which refers to Ailsi's vision. In B'3 compare *prout ipse ut diximus ad memoriam potuit reduxisse* a with *tanquam describere potuit* and *a memoria sua elapsa* a', *eandem uisionem* b with *eiusdem uisionis* b', around the crux in c, which refers to Ailsi's vision. The subject of the third sentence is not Jordan but Peter, the third generation of the family to know the story and the third vessel into which memory of it had been poured.

From the beginning of the incipit to the end of the paragraph inclusive there are 140 words, which divide by symmetry at 70 and 70. The central words of the text, seventieth from the beginning and seventieth from the end, are *uir | Ailsi*, naming the man to whom the visions occurred. Peter considers the period from the visions during the time of Henry I to the transmission of them to himself. After *tempore [Henrici]* the seventieth word is *tempora [Petro]*.

The 140 words divide by by sesquialter ratio (3:2) at 84 and 56. From *Ailsi* to *Ailsi nomine* inclusive there are eighty-four words.

The 140 words divide by sesquitertian ratio (4:3) at 80 and 60. From *Petri* to *Petro* inclusive there are sixty words.

The 140 words divide by sesquioctave ratio (9:8) at 74 and 66 and by one-ninth and eight-ninths at 16 and 124. Between *Jordanus* and *Jordano* there are sixteen words. After *Jordano* the sixteenth word is *Petro*. After *tempore* the sixteenth word is *Petri*.

The 140 words divide by extreme and mean ratio at 87 and 53. From *hic describit prout ... potuit* to *describere potuit* inclusive there are eighty-seven words, which divide by extreme and mean ratio at 54 and 33. From the first *prout* to the third *prout* inclusive there are fifty-four words. After the first *potuit* the third *potuit* is the fifty-fourth word. From the first *potuit* to the second *potuit* inclusive there are thirty-three words. From *uir* to *uiro* inclusive there are forty-five words, which divide by extreme and mean ratio at 28 and 17. From *uir* to *uiri* inclusive there are seventeen words, after which *uiro* is the twenty-eighth word.

In the year 1208 Peter published an account of a dialogue he had conducted with a Jew,[11] of which the beginning of the Prologue, addressed to Stephen Langton, Archbishop of Canterbury, follows.

11 BCLL 79. R.W. Hunt, 'The Disputation of Peter of Cornwall against Simon the Jew' in R.W. Hunt, W.A. Pantin, & R.W. Southern eds, *Medieval Studies Presented to F. M. Powicke* (Oxford 1948), p. 153.

LIBER DISPUTATIONUM CONTRA SYMONEM IUDEUM

Dilectissimo dómino súo	a	3
et patri in Xpísto Stepháno	a	5
Dei gratia Cantuariensi árchiepíscopo	a	4
et totius Ánglie prímati	b	4
et sancte Romane ecclésie càrdináli 5	b	5
Petrus seruus eíus deuótus	c	4
et prior sancte Trinitatis Londónie díctus	c	6
cum salute corporis et anime sincéram dilèctiónem	d	7
et debitum subiectiónis famulátum.	d	4
Aures sanctitatis uestre in cuius sapienti eloquentia Gállia sápit 10	e	9
et in religióne quiéscit	e	4
et in utraque spem salutis Anglia firmiter concépit	e	8
flosculis uerborum Tulliane eloquéntie òneráre	f	5
uel multis sermonibus epistole prolixióris pulsáre	f	6
paruitatis scientie mée tímuit 15	e	4
erubuit indígnum iudicáuit.	e	3
Paucis igitur et uerbis simplicioribus sanctitátem uestram cúi	b	8
presentem librum disputationum contra Iudéos deuóui	b	6
exoro quatenus manus correctionis eméndet explánet	e	6
et feditates uerborum et errores sententiárum detérgat 20	e	7
et gratiam et auctoritatem quam in se libellus ílle non hábet	e	11
per uos plenissime recípere mèreátur	g	5
et qui nunc latet sub modio uel displicet per obscuritátem scriptóris	h	11
fulgeat super candelabrum per uitam et famam et doctrínam correctóris.	h	10
Valeat sanctitas uestra in euum páter ueneránde. 25	f	7

To his own most beloved lord
and father in Christ Stephen
by the grace of God archbishop of Canterbury
both primate of the whole of England
and cardinal of the holy Roman church   5
Peter his devoted slave
and called Prior of Holy Trinity of London
[sends] with salvation of body and soul sincere love
and owed service of subjection.
To burden the ears of your holiness, in whose wise eloquence Gaul
   grows wise   10
and becomes peaceful in religion
and in both of which England has firmly conceived the hope of salvation,
with little flowers of the words of Tullian eloquence

or to beat upon [your ears] with many speeches of a rather prolix epistle
the littleness of my understanding   15
has feared, blushed, judged unworthy.
Therefore with few and rather simple words I beseech your holiness, to
    whom
I have devoted the present book of disputations against the Jews,
that the hand of correction may emend, explain,
and wipe clean the foulnesses of words and errors of sentences   20
and both grace and authority which the little book does not have in itself
 · it may deserve most fully to receive through you,
and [the book] which now lies hidden under a bushel or displeases
    through the obscurity of the writer
may shine upon a candelabrum through the life and fame and teaching
    of the corrector.
May your holiness flourish for an age, venerable father.   25

The Salutation occupies forty-two words, which divide by symmetry at the
name of the author, *Petrus*, twenty-first word from the end, and by extreme
and mean ratio at 26 and 16. Reckoned from the beginning the golden section
falls at the central word of Langton's titles, *Cantuariensi archiepiscopo et totius
Anglie | primati | et sancte Romane ecclesie cardinali*. Reckoned from the end it
falls at the central word of Peter's title, *Petrus seruus eius deuotus et | prior |
sancte Trinitatis Londonie dictus*. At the centre of the entire Prologue Peter refers
to himself, *paruitatis scientie | mee timuit* 15. He also refers to himself at eight-
ninths of the Prologue *scriptoris* 23.

   As we began with an account of a dispute between Jew and Gentile by the
fifth-century Romano-Briton Pelagius we may conclude with another by a
thirteenth-century Cornishman, pausing to consider indications of both
continuity and development in the use of Latin by fifty astonishingly varied
Celtic Latin writers.

EPILOGUE

DONNCHADH Ó COBHTHAIGH

Dr Dáibhí Ó Cróinín, editing and translating one Latin and one Irish poem four centuries after their composition by Donnchadh Ó Cobhthaigh on Lough Derg in the year 1584, suggested that[1]

> The Latin hexameters are somewhat shaky but the composition is not devoid of merit for all that. The Irish verses by contrast represent a *tour de force* ... .

Affirming that Donnchadh's Latin metre is competent I offered a different translation.[2]

DONATI DUAE CARMINA

Lympha coacta gel*u* duris licet aemula sax*is*
 Desinit in tenue*m* lumine solis aqua*m.*
Soluit ita in lachrima*s* iusti commota dolor*is*
 Vis scelerum glacie*m* qua male corda rigen*t.*
Qua premor ergo Deu*s* uitiorum digere mole*m*
 Que cumulata graui*s* pondere dura mora es*t.*

Liquid, condensed by cold, though like hard rocks,
 Ends up in the sun's light as water thin.
So moved power of a just man's grief dissolves
 To tears the ice of crimes that freeze hearts ill.
Loosen therefore, O God, the mass of sins
 By which, heavy in weight, I am oppressed,
 Which, heaped up, is a hard impediment.

I did not recognize then but have noted since the ratios of harmony commended by Boethius in the myth of Pythagoras and the smiths' hammers, *De Institutione Musica* I X: *duplus* 2:1, *sesquialter* 3:2, *sesquitertius* 4:3, *sesquioctauus* 9:8.

 Donnchadh's *carmen* consists of three prosodic units, which coincide with three syntactic units: three elegiac couplets, three hexameters, three pentameters,

---

1 D.I. Ó Cróinín, 'A Poet in Penitential Mood', *Celtica* XVI (1984), pp. 169–74.
2 D.R. Howlett, 'Penance for an Editor', *Celtica* XVIII (1986), p. 150.

three sentences. There is a rhyme scheme of three sounds repeated at the well marked caesuras, *xababb*, and at the ends of lines, *babcac*.

Dividing the poem by symmetry one notes 107 letters in the first half and 107 letters in the second half. Of the ninety-one syllables the central, forty-sixth, is the last of the first half.[3] Of the forty-one words the central, twenty-first, is the first of the second half.[4] Dividing again by symmetry, half of 21 is 11. Between *lympha* 'fluid' and *aquam* 'water' there are eleven words. From *scelerum* 'crimes' to *uitiorum* 'sins' inclusive there are eleven words.

Dividing the poem by duple ratio (2:1) there are two couplets plus one couplet, four lines plus two lines, twenty-seven words plus fourteen words, sixty syllables plus thirty-one syllables, 143 letters plus seventy-one letters.

Dividing the poem by sesquialter ratio (3:2, 41=25+16) one sees that frozen hearts dissolve into tears, immediately before *lachrimas* 'tears', the twenty-fifth word from the end, and immediately before *corda* 'hearts', the sixteenth word from the end. Between the past participles *coacta* and *commota* there are sixteen words. Between the past participles *commota* and *cumulata* there are sixteen words.

Dividing the poem by sesquitertian ratio (4:3, 41=23+18), between the verb *desinit* 'ends' and the verb *rigent* 'freeze' there are eighteen words. Between the verb *soluit* 'dissolves' and the verb *digere* 'loosen' there are eighteen words.

Dividing the poem by sesquioctave ratio (9:8, 41=22+19), there are nineteen words between *gelu* 'frost' and *glaciem* 'ice', and *glaciem* is the nineteenth word from the end of the poem.

Dividing the poem by one-ninth and eight-ninths (41=5+36), the only repeated word recurs in the first and last lines. Before *duris* 'hard' there are three words and after *dura* 'hard' there are two words, together five. From *duris* to *dura* inclusive there are thirty-six words.

Donnchadh wrote nearly 1200 years after Pelagius. But the two of them and thousands of writers between them shared an understanding of and competence in a formal style of composition now so unfamiliar that many of our contemporaries deny vehemently that it ever existed. This little survey of fifty writers in a coherent Celtic Latin tradition may suggest various ways in which to enrich understanding of our inherited literary culture by beginning to recover the elements of this tradition.

CONCLUSIONS
AND SUGGESTIONS FOR FURTHER INQUIRY

We have surveyed compositions in prose and verse from nine centuries, from before the fall of the Western Roman Empire to the high Middle Ages, written by Romano-Britons, Romano-Gauls, Welshmen, Cornishmen, Bretons, Irishmen both at home and abroad, in a wide variety of registers, in many genres, about

---

3   According to the *Rhetorica ad Herennium* IV xx 27–28 a count of syllables admits an imbalance of
    one or two.

4   As one cannot count part of a word I have in all these calculations rounded to the nearest integer.

many subjects. The same rules are observed by writers from the beginning of the period to the end, and indeed beyond, but anyone who has read the preceding analyses is unlikely to confuse the idiolect of any of these authors with that of another. Recognition of the features of Biblical style allows the ordinary modern reader new ways to hear as utterly distinct voices which may previously have sounded similar. It provides inbuilt error-detection and error-correction programs that allow restoration to original integrity of voices that have become confused in transmission.

The titles of the last chapter and also of the book are at once appropriate and potentially misleading. Abaelard, Geoffrey, John, and Peter were born in Celtic lands which they left to pursue careers in a wider world. They are believed by some to represent the emergence of able men from a Celtic ghetto. Yet we may note that the wider horizons were there from the very beginning. Pelagius wrote not in his native Britain but in the Mediterranean world. Patrick wrote not in his native Britain but in Ireland. The Irish widened their own horizons from the moment of their conversion to Christianity; from the moment of their adoption of Latin as a literary language they widened others' horizons. Columban, trained at Bangor, wrote after long experience in Gaul to Gregory the Great from Bobbio. Cummian relied upon eyewitness testimony from a delegate sent to Rome, and Adomnán recorded the eyewitness testimony of a traveller to the Holy Land. Cellán, Joseph, Columbanus of Saint-Trond, Dungal, Dicuill, Sedulius Scottus, Donatus Scottus of Fiesole, Johannes Scottus Eriugena, and a host of other Irish *peregrini* lived and wrote on the Continent, where they worked in centres of power and privilege, addressing principal issues of their times.

Let us consider a few implications that emerge from the complex links among Celtic and Anglo-Saxon scholars throughout this period. Might exchanges like that of Columban with Gregory the Great be one cause of the latter's desire to evangelize the English? Is it possible that the pope hoped to spare himself further difficult and embarassing encounters with those drawn into the orbit of irregular, prickly, and witty Scots by sending his own missionaries to England?[5]

Colmán's Letter to Feradach about scansion of elegiac couplets may have been written soon after publication of the *Epistola ad Acircium* by Aldhelm, the first Anglo-Saxon to become a Latin author. Aldhelm's letter dissuading Heahfrith from study in Ireland praises the learning of Theodore and Hadrian's school at Canterbury and parodies Irish learning as represented by heptasyllabic verse and Virgilius Maro Grammaticus. Cellán may have conceived his Letter as a deliberately ambiguous response to Aldhelm's attack, a response to which Aldhelm replied in similar tone. Another response may well have been composition of the *Hisperica Famina* by Virgilius Maro himself, if not by members of his circle, to demonstrate the features of Latinity inculcated in Irish schools.[6]

5 By the time of Columban's correspondance with the pope Gregory's missionaries were already in England, but we needn't infer that this was the first exchange between an Irishman and a Roman.
6 For consideration of these and other texts see D.R. Howlett, 'Aldhelm and Irish Learning', *Archivum Latinitatis Medii Aevi* LII (1994), pp. 37–75.

Other evidence of communication among Celts and Anglo-Saxons includes the transmission of the *Orationes Moucani*, nine rhyming rhythmical prayers by a Welshman, perhaps of the seventh century, in an eighth-century Mercian manuscript, British Library MS Royal 2 A xx. These prayers offer a corrective to Bede's assertion that British Christians did not share their religion with Anglo-Saxons.

The dedication to Alcuin of Joseph's abbreviation of Jerome's Commentary on Isaiah, Dicuill's advice to Charlemagne about a treatise by the Anglo-Saxon Fridugisus, Asser's dealings with and biography of King Alfred, Radbod's Letter to King Æthelstan, Dub Innse's transport of a board game from Æthelstan's court to Bangor, the reliance of 'Ninnius' upon English annals, Bishop Patrick's address of verses from Dublin to Aldwine and Wulfstan at Worcester, and the English careers of Geoffrey of Monmouth, John of Cornwall, and Peter of Cornwall suggest the variety and complexity of links among Insular Latin authors throughout the period under consideration. Those dealt with in this survey comprise a mere fraction of the extant material.

The title of the book does not imply the existence of Celtic Latin as a separate entity. It should be clear from the texts presented in this study that from the very beginnings of the tradition our authors were writing standard literary Latin, not an erratic dialect of an off-shore island. Analyses of complex interlocked structures, consistent and almost universal observance of prose rhythm, rhymes, dispositions of words at arithmetically fixed intervals, and letter counts (above all in acrostics and anagrams and pattern poems which fix orthography) have provided many clear indications that writers at every position on the literary register, from Pelagius supposedly near the top to Saint Patrick allegedly at the bottom, were composing Biblical style in standard literary Late Latin. A century after the removal of Roman civil and military administration from Britain Gildas was still composing standard literary Late Latin, which compares favourably in matters of lexicon, grammar, and syntax with the prose of the Romano-Gaulish Gregory Archbishop of Tours. Half a century after Gildas Columban and a century after Gildas Cummian still composed Latin prose, which they had learned in Ireland, with hardly a trace of barbarism or soloecism. There is then no early evidence of 'Hiberno-Latin' as either a spoken or a literary dialect. The period of first exposure of the Irish to Latin literacy, perhaps the fourth century, certainly the fifth and sixth centuries, is characterized by correct standard Latinity, the orthographic system of which served as the model for Old Irish.[7] As Latin

---

7   J.M. Picard, 'The Schaffhausen Adomnán—A Unique Witness to Hiberno-Latin', *Peritia* I (1982), pp. 216–49. J. Stevenson, 'The Beginnings of Literacy in Ireland', *Proceedings of the Royal Irish Academy* LXXXIX C 6 (1989), pp. 127–65. A. Harvey, 'Early Literacy in Ireland: The Evidence from Ogam' *Cambridge Medieval Celtic Studies* XIV (1987), pp. 1–15. Idem 'Some Significant Points of Early Insular Celtic Orthography', *Sages, Saints and Storytellers, Celtic Studies in Honour of Professor James Carney*, ed., D. Ó Corráin et al., (Maynooth 1989), pp. 56–66. Idem 'Retrieving the Pronunciation of Early Insular Celtic Scribes: Towards a Methodology', *Celtica* XXI (1990), pp. 178–90. Idem 'Retrieving the Pronunciation of Early Insular Scribes: The Case of Dorbéne', Ibid. XXII (1991), pp. 48–63. Idem 'The Cambridge Juvencus Glosses—Evidence of Hiberno-Welsh Literary Interaction?', *Language Contact in the British Isles*, ed., P. Sture Ureland & G. Broderick (Tübingen 1991), pp. 181–98. P. Sims-Williams, 'The Additional Letters of the Ogam Alphabet', *Cambridge Medieval Celtic Studies* XXIII (1992), pp. 29–75.

conventions were not wholly suitable for representing sounds in Old Irish there were some modifications in spelling conventions for the vernacular language. These may in turn have affected the way speakers of Old Irish pronounced and spelled Latin, giving occasion for Continental Carolingian writers to joke about the Latin of certain Irishmen,[8] but that was a later development, of the eighth or ninth century, and despite it there remained throughout the period we have been considering many writers who composed standard Latin.

One may speak justifiably of a Celtic Latin tradition on two grounds: the geographical origins of the writers and the demonstrable chains of transmission in their works. The Romano-Britons Pelagius and Patrick were quoted by Cummian, the earliest extant named Irish Latin author writing an extensive treatise in Ireland in the year 633.[9] Patrick was quoted also in the oldest extant Latin poem composed in these islands, *Audite Omnes Amantes Deum*, in Muirchú's *Vita Sancti Patricii*, and in the *Vita Quarta Sancti Patricii*, and referred to in the note by Caluus Perennis.

Gildas was quoted as an authoritative and elegant writer by Columban, the earliest extant Irish Latin author writing abroad, in the year 600. Gildas was quoted independently by both Cogitosus and Muirchú and by the Venerable Bede in the *Historia Ecclesiastica Gentis Anglorum*, completed in the year 731. His providential view of British history was quoted by Alcuin in Latin letters written in 793 and 797 and echoed by Wulfstan the homilist, Bishop of Worcester and Archbishop of York, in his Old English *Sermo Lupi ad Anglos*. Gildas was also explicitly named and quoted by the ninth-century Breton Latin writers Uurdisten and Uurmonoc. Caradog of Llancarfan wrote his *Vita Sancti Gildae* early in the twelfth century. Abaelard was from 1126 to 1136 Abbot of Saint Gildas de Rhuys in Brittany. Geoffrey of Monmouth cited Gildas in the Preface to the *Historia Regum Britanniae*.

Vinniau, a correspondent of Gildas, was referred to by Columban and praised by Sedulius Scottus in a poem about scholars of Clonard.

The author of *Audite Omnes Amantes Deum* demonstrates clearly that he understood the structures as well as the meanings of Patrick's works, and his poem is quoted by later seventh-century Irish Latin poets, among them the author of *Benchuir Bona Regula*.

Cogitosus, the earliest named Irish hagiographer of Brigit, is explicitly named and quoted by Muirchú, the hagiographer of Patrick, and alluded to as Animosus by a later hagiographer of Brigit, Donatus Scottus of Fiesole.

Toward the end of the period under consideration the Welsh Latin hagiographers tried to draw together all the threads of their tradition with references to Saints Patrick, David, Moucan, Cadog, Illtyd, and Gildas. The most prominent of these hagiographers, Caradog of Llancarfan, is named by the most famous of all Celtic Latin writers, Geoffrey of Monmouth, in the envoi to the *Historia Regum Britanniae*.

8 K. Sidwell, 'Theodulf of Orléans, Cadac-Andreas and Old Irish Phonology', *The Journal of Medieval Latin* II (1992), pp. 55–62.
9 See also D. Dumville,'Late-Seventh- or Eighth-Century Evidence for the British Transmission of Pelagius', *Cambridge Medieval Celtic Studies* X (1985), pp. 39–52.

From the preceding pages it will be clear that every one of the texts analysed was composed with greater craftsmanship than the most ardent modern admirers have previously imagined. Yet in these pages there are few expressions of aesthetic judgement, because they would be premature. In the *Liber Epistolarum Sancti Patricii Episcopi* there is much evidence that the consensus of all modern scholars about the supposed literary incompetence of Saint Patrick depends upon grotesque misreading. Here there is more evidence that Walker's estimate of Columban, Bieler's of Muirchú, and Tierney's of the Carolingian poets want revision. If scholars with reputations as high as those of Dr Keynes and Professor Lapidge can misread Asser's architectonically brilliant *Vita Ælfredi Regis* as the unfinished draft of a confusing and incompetent writer there is something fundamentally wrong with the way modern men read. If a scholar as widely and deeply read as Dr Dumville can misprise deliberately sought artifice as 'inadvertence' there is something disordered about the way modern men perceive. And if misprision of the merely technical competence of Celtic Latin writers is so deepseated, there can be no secure basis for the exercise of aesthetic judgements. One needs to understand what an author was trying to do before telling others how well or badly he did it.

The first and most pressing need is to approach the Latin literature of these islands informed by the canons which its authors observed. Once we have shed some deforming preconceptions, freed ourselves from some illusions, and begun to learn to read, we may want to organize a programme of editing. Future editors would be well advised to pay closer attention than their predecessors have thought fit to literary structures, the layout of prose and verse, rhyme and rhythm in prose, numbers of lines, words, syllables, and letters, minute details of orthography, disposition of capital letters and punctuation marks in manuscripts, and the relation of the art of literary composition to the arts of music, manuscript illumination, sculpture, and architecture.

For those who will not do our authors the courtesy of reading them in Latin a programme of translating may be required. Not, however, in the manner that has passed as acceptable until now. Modern translators often pretend to tell readers what an author means, but they rarely tell readers even what an author says. To succeed in representing what an author says is difficult enough. But, in the light of the preceding analyses, to suggest in modern English the multiple meanings, the mathematically determined structural forms, the styles of quotation and allusion, the word play and wit and irony may prove more troublesome than many will think worthwhile. It might prove more efficient, as it would certainly prove more interesting and illuminating, to recover the Latinity.

In recovering the Latinity and the canons by which our authors composed it will become clear, if it is not already perfectly plain, that the features we have been considering are not mere decoration tacked on to nearly completed works. They are integral to the conception and execution of compositions, the meanings of which are utterly inseparable from their structures, and often not intelligible without understanding of the structures. There is both architecture and music in the texts we have been considering. The medium of such compositions is part of the message more often than it is merely the wrapping of the message.

Informed consideration of Celtic Latin texts will not, I think, confirm the old myth of Ireland as the home of pagan Classical Latin literature between the fourth century and the eighth. But it will reveal Celtic Latin authors as preservers and transmitters of Christian Latin literature, of the Bible and Biblical exegesis and Biblical style, of the tradition of rhythmic composition—clausulae in works of Pelagius, Patrick, the Romano-Gaulish bishops, Gildas, Cummian, even the ninth-century Monk of Redon. It will reveal nearly all these authors also as exponents of composition in cursus rhythms and rhymed prose.

We may abandon the widespread but erroneous notion that Irish Latin writers were insensitive to verse rhythms. The very indications formerly cited as evidence of insensitivity actually prove exquisite sensitivity. In the earliest of the Celtic Latin poems, *Audite Omnes Amantes Deum*, the shift from paroxytone to pro-paroxytone rhythms serves as structural articulation, in the twenty-third and the forty-sixth lines of the ninety-two-lined hymn. Similar disposition of rhythmic variety recurs in *Mundus Iste Transibit*, here ascribed to Columban before departure from Bangor. The seventh-century hymns *Martine Deprecare* and *Deus Domine Meus* and *Benchuir Bona Regula* also exhibit rhythmically varied lines as structural articulation. So does the solidly elided central line of verse which dissuades the reader from 'shaking' Uurdisten's poem. In Columban's hymn the four distinct sections, Prologue, Part I, Part II, and Epilogue of *Precamur Patrem*, all exhibit variations of rhythmic pattern in a single ratio.

The earliest of the hymns exhibits rhyme and alliteration and alphabetic structure used, as in the abecedarian hymn of the fifth-century author Caelius Sedulius, frequently but not with rigorous and comprehensive system. As that comprehensive deployment is found for the first time in *Mundus Iste Transibit*, one infers that systematic disposition of rhyme and alliteration in stanzaic structures occurred first among the Irish, perhaps at Bangor, during the fourth quarter of the sixth century.

There is in the texts cited here a great variety of syllabic metres (hepta-, octo-, deca-, hendeca-, dodeca-, and pentadecasyllabic verses, and the apparently unique form employed by Euben) and of quantitative metres (dactylic hexameters, elegiac couplets, and adonics).

The tradition of composing alphabetic verse runs through *Audite Omnes Amantes Deum*, *Sancta Sanctorum Opera*, Clemens of Landévennec's *Hymn to Saint Winwaloe*, and Euben's *Carmen*.

Acrostics recur in verses by Joseph Scottus, Columbanus of Saint-Trond, Dungal of Saint-Denis and Pavia, and Ieuan ap Sulien.

Anagrams recur in works of Columban, Euben, Ieuan, and Abaelard.

Calendrical features abound in Columban's *Mundus Iste Transibit*, composed before 590. In the seventh-century 777-lettered heptasyllabic hymn *Deus Domine Meus* recurring fours and sevens and elevens are appropriate to the festivals of Saint Martin on the fourth day of the seventh month and the eleventh day of the eleventh month. The twenty-eight-word intervals in Clemens of Landévennec's *Hymn to Saint Winwaloe* are appropriate to the translation of the saint on 28 April. Numbers of words or letters consistent with suggested years of composition recur in *Audite Omnes Amantes Deum* 577, Cummian's Letter 633, *Sancta Sanctorum Opera* 683, *Benchuir Bona Regula* 686, which we may now add tentatively to the explicit indications of age in the poetry of Columbanus of Saint-Trond and of dates in the works of Dicuill 825, Uurmonoc 884, and Asser 893.

Serial composition recurs in *Respice in me Domine*, the *Vita Sancti Paterni*, and Abaelard's *Historia Calamitatum*.

There are connections between numbers of elements in Prologues and numbers of elements in the texts they introduce in works by Cogitosus, Cellán, Bili, the *Vita Sanctae Wenefredae*, Abaelard, and John of Cornwall. There are connections between the numbers of elements and the sections in which they occur in Asser's *Vita Ælfredi Regis*.

There is play in the placement of appropriate diction and numerical and ordinal words in works by Columban, Cummian, Colmán, Dungal, Dicuill, Joseph, Bili, Ieuan, the *Vita Sancti Paterni*, and Peter of Cornwall, who makes the repeated phrase *protulit in medium* fall at both the symmetrical mean and the golden mean.

There are references at the centres of texts to titles and subjects and recipients in works of Cogitosus, Eriugena, Caluus Perennis, Euben, the *Vita Sanctae Wenefredae*, John of Cornwall, and Peter of Cornwall, to authors in works of Cummian, Cellán, Columbanus of Saint-Trond, and Dungal.

There are references at the golden sections of texts to subjects and recipients in works of Columban, *Anonymi Deus Domine Meus*, Dungal, Donatus Scottus, Clemens of Landévennec, Bili, Uurdisten, Dub Innse, Caluus Perennis, 'Ninnius', Patrick Bishop of Dublin, John of Cornwall, and Peter of Cornwall, to authors in works of Cogitosus, Muirchú, Adomnán, Joseph Scottus, Clemens of Landévennec, Uurdisten, Radbod, Dub Innse, Patrick Bishop of Dublin, Caluus Perennis, John of Cornwall, and Peter of Cornwall.

There are references at one-ninth and eight-ninths to titles and recipients in works of Joseph Scottus to both Alcuin and Charlemagne, Columbanus of Saint-Trond, Eriugena, Clemens of Landévennec, Uurmonoc, Caluus Perennis, Patrick Bishop of Dublin, and John of Cornwall, to authors in works of Adomnán, *Anonymi Martine Deprecare*, Uurdisten, Uurmonoc, Caluus Perennis, Euben, Geoffrey of Monmouth, and Peter of Cornwall, to the date in Dicuill's *Liber de Mensura Orbis Terrae*.

Biblical writers often made important points implicitly, by relying upon readers' knowledge of the unquoted context of their quotations and allusions. This habit, completely assimilated by Saint Patrick, recurs in the works of Columban, Cummian, Moucan, Cellán, Sedulius Scottus, Asser, Geoffrey of Monmouth, and many others. Recognition of it allows us to recover some of the irony and wit in the works of writers who have been misread previously as if they were solemn.

Our authors speak to us directly about techniques both mechanical and mental, with references to composition and writing out of texts by Adomnán, Uurdisten, Uurmonoc, Euben, Ieuan ap Sulien, and Peter of Cornwall. Cogitosus states explicitly that he will write *praepostero ordine*. Asser, departing from strict chronological order, writes *quamuis praeposterato ordine loquar*. Colmán tells Feradach how to scan elegiac couplets. Columbanus tells Fidolius how to compose adonic verses, in which art he is followed by Patrick Bishop of Dublin. In his abbreviation of the commentary on Isaiah Joseph plays with the words *breuibus, longis tractatibus, ab inmensis libris, breuiter, longior, breuibus uastos uerbis constringere sensus, breui sermone, promptior breuiorque, breuiora, breuitatem*, and the ratio 2:1. The Preface to Dungal's poem to Hildoard describes the acrostic and the alternating hexameters and pentameters of his elegiacs. Clemens of Landévennec refers to the number of letters in his poem. Peter of Cornwall describes in remarkable detail his exposure to the style of Gilbert Foliot.

This survey of the Celtic Latin tradition has included nearly every major figure and many minor ones from every one of the Celtic-speaking peoples, composing in every genre of prose and verse addressed in every century from the fifth to the thirteenth. It provides solid criteria for recovery not only of authors' *ipsissima uerba*, but even of their very orthography. The gains are great. We have new reasons for admiring old favourites and good reasons for learning to admire writers long misprised and despised but now revealed as coherent thinkers, competent craftsmen, even artists of a high order. Fifteen centuries after the beginning of the tradition we may approach this precious inheritance anew, devote to it the care it deserves, enjoy the delight and enrichment it can give us, and transmit it vigorously and sensitively to those who have yet to discover it.

in die Sancti Dauid
Anno Domini MCMXCIV
Oxoniae

INDEX

I. INDEX OF BIBLICAL TEXTS

II. INDEX OF MANUSCRIPTS

III. INDEX OF A BIBLIOGRAPHY OF CELTIC-LATIN LITERATURE
400–1200